THE GOSPEL

ACCORDING TO

SAINT LUKE

IN ANGLO-SAXON AND NORTHUMBRIAN VERSIONS
SYNOPTICALLY ARRANGED,
WITH COLLATIONS EXHIBITING ALL THE READINGS OF ALL THE MSS.

Edited for the Syndics of the University Press,

BY THE

REV. WALTER W. SKEAT, M.A.

LATE FELLOW OF CHRIST'S COLLEGE,
AND AUTHOR OF A MŒSO-GOTHIC GLOSSARY.

CAMBRIDGE:
AT THE UNIVERSITY PRESS.

LONDON: CAMBRIDGE WAREHOUSE, 17, PATERNOSTER ROW.
CAMBRIDGE: DEIGHTON, BELL, AND CO.
1874.

Cambridge:
PRINTED BY C. J. CLAY, M.A.
AT THE UNIVERSITY PRESS.

CONTENTS.

ERRATA.

Page 4, l. 4 from bottom. *Dele* full stop after 'prohibetur.'

" l. 2 from bottom. *Dele* full stop after 'edicitur.'

Page 40, col. 1, footnote to *v.* 19. *After* A. broðer, *alter the full stop to a semicolon.*

" " 2, footnote to *v.* 21. *Insert a semicolon after* ge-fullodum.

Page 43, *v.* 38. *In the* Rushworth MS., *the words* qui fuit dei *are glossed* seðe wæs goding. *This should have been inserted.*

PREFACE.

THE present volume forms the third portion of the exhaustive edition of the Anglo-Saxon Gospels, as planned by Mr Kemble. The first portion was published in 1858, with the title—"The Gospel according to St Matthew, in Anglo-Saxon and Northumbrian Versions, synoptically arranged: with collations of the best Manuscripts. Edited for the Syndics of the University Press. Cambridge: at the University Press. 1858." The second portion was published in 1871, with the title—"The Gospel according to St Mark, in Anglo-Saxon and Northumbrian Versions synoptically arranged, with collations exhibiting all the readings of all the MSS. Edited for the Syndics of the University Press, by the Rev. Walter W. Skeat, M.A. Cambridge: at the University Press, 1871."

Owing to the death of Mr Kemble before the first portion was completed, no Preface was written to that volume, beyond a short notice by Mr Hardwick explaining the circumstances under which he undertook to finish it. In the Preface to Saint Mark's Gospel, I endeavoured to give some account of the MSS., and of the principal points of interest concerning them. To this the reader is referred for further information, and it will only be necessary to repeat here the account of the mode of arrangement of the various texts and collations, and to make a few remarks upon some new points that have suggested themselves.

The arrangement of matter is the same in this volume as in the two volumes preceding it. The following is the scheme of the contents of any two opposite pages, after p. 13.

Left-hand Page.		*Right-hand Page.*
First Column.	*Second Column.*	
TEXT. MS. No. I. (Corpus).	TEXT. MS. V. (Hatton).	UPPER TEXT. MS. VII. (Lindisfarne); Latin, with Northumbrian gloss.
Various Readings; from MS. II. *or* A. (Cambridge); MS. III. *or* B. (Oxford); *and* MS. IV. *or* C. (Cotton, Otho C. 1).	*Various Readings; from* MS. VI. *or* Royal (Brit. Mus.).	LOWER TEXT. MS. VIII. (Rushworth); gloss only.

The numbers or names of these MSS. are:

I. (Corpus) MS. No. cxl (formerly S. 4) in the library of Corpus Christi College, Cambridge, described by Wanley in the second volume of Hickes's 'Thesaurus,' at p. 116.

II. (Cambridge *or* A.) MS. Ii. 2. 11 in the Cambridge University Library, described by Wanley, p. 152.

III. (Bodley *or* B.) MS. Bodley NE. F. 3. 15, now Bodley 441; described by Wanley, p. 64.

IV. (Cotton *or* C.) MS. Cotton, Otho C. 1, in the British Museum; described by Wanley, pp. 211, 212. *Imperfect*, and damaged by fire.

V. (Hatton) MS. Hatton 38, in the Bodleian library, Oxford; described by Wanley, p. 76.

VI. (Royal) MS. Bibl. Reg. 1. A. xiv (British Museum); described by Wanley, p. 181.

VII. (Lindisfarne) MS. Cotton, Nero D. 4 (British Museum); known also as the 'Lindisfarne MS.,' and as the 'Durham book[1].' Well known, and often described; see Wanley, p. 250.

VIII. (Rushworth) MS. Auct. D. ii. 19, in the Bodleian library, Oxford; commonly called the 'Rushworth MS.'

The rubrics in the left margin of the left-hand pages are from MS. A (*or* II). A few of them occur also in B. (Bodley), but they are mostly copied from A. (Cambridge) in a late hand, and are of no authority. In a few cases the rubrics in B. are in an older hand, and they are then duly noted.

The rubrics in the right margin of the right-hand pages are from the Hatton MS.; but they occur also in the Royal MS., without any variation.

The numbers in the right-hand margin of the right-hand pages are from the Lindisfarne MS., and refer to the "Ammonian sections," as well as to the sections into which the Gospel was divided for the purpose of being read at various times. They supply references to the parallel passages in the other Gospels.

The Latin text of the Rushworth MS. is omitted to save space; but its variations of reading are all recorded in the Appendix. It contains many clerical errors and corrupt forms of words.

The Northumbrian gloss in the Rushworth MS. is partly copied from that in the Lindisfarne MS., and sometimes answers to the Latin text of that MS. instead of to its *own* text; as already has been noted (Pref. to St Mark, p. xiii).

[1] See the publications of the Palæographical Society for good specimens of facsimiles from this celebrated MS.

At p. 1 of the present volume is a list, which was intended to shew the days on which certain portions of the Gospel were to be read. Unfortunately, the rubricator has omitted to insert the numbers of the sections at the side, so that the exact significance of it is left uncertain. The words at the top are—"Secundum lucan," glossed by "æft*er* luc*as*," i. e. according to St Luke; followed by the remark—"ðus mercong ælces gospel*les* ðe ontuoelm*ona*ð [*sic; for* on tuoelm*ona*ð] byres on lucases dæl," i. e. the marking of each gospel that, during the year, belongs to Luke's portion.

At p. 2, follows the life of St Luke commonly ascribed to St Jerome, though not found in the MSS. of his translation of the New Testament; as noted in Migne's edition of St Jerome's works, vol. x, col. 1049. It is found in several of the early printed editions of the Vulgate, and in some of the MSS., as e.g. in the Codex Amiatinus, edited by Tischendorf.

At p. 3, are the headings, or abstracts of the contents of each section into which the Gospel is divided.

The Critical Notes, in the Appendix, contain such observations, mostly of minor importance, as could not very well be printed with the text, for want of space. I may perhaps repeat here, that the Lindisfarne MS. not only employs the usual rune for "man" several times, but occasionally uses the very same character with its less usual signification of "day," as in Ch. xxi. 34; also in xxiii. 56 and xxiv. 1, where "sunna dæg" is written "sun̄," with the rune ·ᛞ· following. Another peculiarity is the occasional use of red ink, as noted at p. 23, where a word has been supplied by the glossator Aldred, who seems merely to have superintended the glossing of the first three gospels, but to have glossed the fourth gospel himself for the most part, as it is chiefly written in red ink, and has certain orthographical peculiarities. I may also note that, whereas it is commonly believed that the symbol þ does not occur in the Lindisfarne gloss at all, except when written with a cross stroke (ꝥ) as an abbreviation for "þæt," I have found just *two* instances of its occurrence, viz. in Ch. i. *v.* 59, where the MS. has þone for ðone, and in Ch. xxiv. *v.* 1, where the MS. really has þæm, not ðæm. The forms printed in those passages are not due to errors of the press.

Before concluding this Preface, however, it will be as well to place on record an account of a discovery, which enables us to trace the "pedigree" of the MSS., or their mutual relationship to each other, with considerable exactness. I have already shewn (Pref. to St Mark, p. x.) that the Hatton MS. was copied from the Royal MS.; and, accordingly, at the end of St Luke's Gospel, we find a few verses, omitted at the end of the Royal MS. as originally written, supplied in the very handwriting of the scribe of the Hatton MS., who has also written a few words on the opposite blank page preceding St John's Gospel. These words are—"Soðlice ge syn"—shewing that the scribe was merely trying his pen, and took a few words from a passage in Ch. xxiv. 48, which was just before his eyes; and he also added a memorandum to this effect—"Scē GREGORIES se mid grecum crissostomas (*sic*) ys haten;" i. e. St Gregory, who amongst the Greeks is surnamed Chrysostomus.

Not only, however, is the HATTON MS. (V) copied from the ROYAL MS. (VI), but the latter is itself a copy from the BODLEY MS. (III). This first appeared in the course of editing the 16th Chapter of this Gospel. On arriving at the words "Đas ðing" in *v.* 14, I found that the next leaf was *not in the same handwriting*, and it was at once obvious that a leaf had here been lost in the original MS., and the missing portion supplied in a recent hand[1], on newer vellum. This leaf must have been lost at a very early period; for, when the scribe of the ROYAL MS. came to it, he could not find it, and passed on at once (without any break beyond a slight space about a quarter of an inch long) to the next word which he *did* find, which of course was the first on the following leaf in the BODLEY MS., viz. the word "unmihtlic" in Ch. xvii. *v.* 1. The scribe of the HATTON MS. also missed the same passage, of course because it was not accessible to him. As soon as ever this clue was obtained, I was at once enabled to understand the whole matter: all the peculiarities of the ROYAL MS. are due to the BODLEY MS. which the scribe had before him. It was thence, for instance, that he copied the few rubrics which he has inserted, and it was thence that he derived certain peculiarities of spelling. At the same time, he made a few alterations at his own will, with the result that his MS. presents the text of the BODLEY MS. with a few later forms, just as the HATTON MS. represents the ROYAL MS., with more numerous alterations in the direction of later spelling. It is proper also to add, by way of making assurance doubly sure, that the few verses originally omitted at the end of the last Chapter in the ROYAL MS. were omitted for a precisely similar reason, viz. because another leaf was again lacking at that point in the BODLEY MS.; and the missing passage is again supplied on newer vellum by a later hand. After this, a careful re-examination of all the MSS. shewed that the COTTON MS. (IV) is (with the exception of a very few clerical errors) an absolute *duplicate*, word for word and letter for letter, of the BODLEY MS., whilst both of these, in their turn, agree so closely with the CORPUS MS. (I), also word for word, and *almost* letter for letter, that all three must be mere copies from one and the same original, not now forth-coming[2]. The CAMBRIDGE MS. (II), again, is exactly the very same text, word for word, but

[1] No doubt under the supervision of Archbishop Parker, who was much given to 'mending' MSS. He would have been better advised in letting them alone. As, however, it is owing to him that many MSS. have been preserved, criticism is out of place.

[2] I have said this before (Pref. to St Mark, p. vii). All I now do is to offer further proof, based on re-examination of the MSS.

with a few changes of spelling. This will appear more clearly from the analysis of a whole chapter, and I select for this purpose the 3rd chapter, as being conveniently short, and remarkable for the absence of the genealogy.

Taking the text as the standard, the sole variations of MSS. B. (III) and C. (IV) from it are these.

1. B. anwaldes (*for* anwealdes)[1]. C. forðan (*a mere clerical error for* feorðan, *which occurs twice, and the first time is spelt correctly*). 3. B. C. rice (*for* ricæ). 4. Clypiendes stefn (*for* Clypiende stefen, *and due to the fact that* Clypiende *is a clerical error in the* Corpus MS.). 7. B. C. hig (*for* hi; *the spellings* hi *and* hig *being convertible even in the same MS.*). B. C. cyn (*for* cynn). 8. C. gos (*a clerical error for* god). 9. B. C. wæstm (*for* wæsm; *due to the clerical error* wæsm *in the* Corpus MS.). 14. C. *repeats* ⁊ cwædon (*a clerical error*). 16. B. C. ⁊swarode (*for* ⁊swarude). 19. B. broður; C. broþur (*for* broðor). C. yfellu*m* (*for* yfelu*m*). 20. B. C. cwerterne (*for* cwearterne). 22. B. C. halga (*for* halega). C. aastah (*clerical error for* astah). B. C. stefn (*for* stefen). 23. C. þrittig (*for* þritig). B. C. men (*for* menn). 24. B. C. cneoresse (*once only, it being spelt* cneorysse *the first time, as in the text*).

Now what do these variations amount to? Putting aside absolute clerical errors, they merely give the following very slight alterations of spelling, viz.—anwealdes, anwaldes; ricæ, rice; stefn, stefen; hi, hig; cynn, cyn; ⁊swarude, ⁊swarode; broðor, broður; cwearterne, cwerterne; halega, halga; þritig, þrittig; menn, men; cneorysse, cneoresse. Here are twelve variations only, all of the slightest character, all of them merely such as are found within the compass of any one of the three MSS. taken individually, and solely due to the fact that the same words were not always spelt the same way by the same scribe. The three MSS. are practically, one and the same, representing the language of the same period, and all drawn from a common original, from which, for all that we can tell, they may have been copied nearly at the same time.

It is only thus that we can account for such close coincidences as are of frequent occurrence. One example may suffice to shew the nature of them. In Ch. xxii. *v.* 52, the word *to* is accidentally repeated in the CORPUS MS., and the same peculiarity occurs in the COTTON MS.; whilst in the BODLEY MS. the word was also repeated in the MS., in its original condition, though the second *to* has been carefully erased at a later period.

A similar investigation shews that the CAMBRIDGE MS. (II) is also from the same source; it differs somewhat in grammatical forms, and seems to be a little later in date than the rest.

[1] The variations of C. cannot always be ascertained, because the MS. is damaged; but the damage is, on the whole, very slight. Most of it can be read, at least throughout St Luke's gospel.

This enables us to make the following scheme of the pedigree of the MSS. containing the Wessex translation of the Gospels.

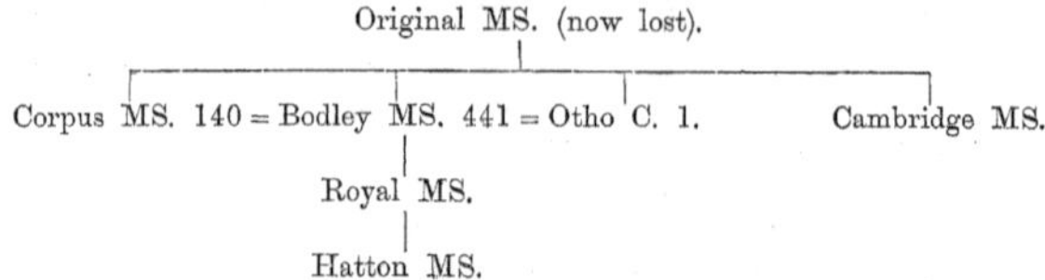

It seems worth while to repeat and insist upon the preceding facts, because they entirely dispose of some false ideas that have been put forward concerning this interesting Old English Version. Thus, when Mr Thorpe, in his preface to the A.-S. Gospels, talks of the Bodley MS. (III) as exhibiting "the tongue in its decline, and rapidly verging towards that state of barbarism into which it sank about the beginning of the twelfth century;" of Marshall's edition, which was really founded on the *same* MS., as exhibiting "an earlier (!) but not perhaps a purer text;" and of his own edition, which was a reprint of Marshall's edition with corrections from the other MSS., as "free from the objections above mentioned," it must be remembered that he is really describing, under three very different aspects, the same text all the while; which cannot but be puzzling to the uninitiated. When Sir F. Palgrave, in his History of the Anglo-Saxons, ed. 1867, p. 146, says, with reference to the Hatton MS. (V), that—"a colloquial language, approaching nearly to modern English, seems to have existed concurrently with the more cultivated language, which we call Anglo-Saxon, at a period before the conquest; and one of the versions of the New Testament[1] is in this language," we have to remember that the Hatton MS. is merely a modernised version (*later* than the conquest) of the Royal MS. (VI), which in its turn is copied from MS. Bodley (III). There is not a trace of any variation in the language, beyond the substitution of the word "lage" (law) in place of the then obsolescent "ǣ" with the same meaning, of the word "coc" for "hana" in ch. xxii. 60, and one or two other similar substitutions. What therefore Sir F. Palgrave calls "colloquial" is, in fact, merely "later."

A suggestion was made to me that, if the Royal MS. (VI) be earlier than the Hatton MS. (V), it should have occupied the *upper* part of the page, and the variations of the Hatton MS. should have come below it. But the fact is, that I have followed Kemble's plan of shewing the *latest* and *earliest* forms *side by side*, which is most convenient in practice, as shewing more directly what changes were introduced by mere lapse of time. It is very rarely indeed that this *can* be done; it is very seldom that copies of the same identical text can be found, differing

[1] He should have said—"of the Gospels." There is no trace of any translation of any other part of the New Testament.

from each other in no respect but date. If any student wishes to see how the older language was modified in the course of years, by examining the spellings of the same words in the same context at two different dates, the means for the investigation are here ready to his hand, unencumbered by actual changes in the phraseology. For philological purposes, this is no small matter. It should be remembered too, that I give *all* the variations in spelling of the Royal MS., so that it is practically printed *in extenso,* whilst the text in the left-hand column (the variations of B. noted and excepted) gives the text from which the Royal MS. was actually copied, so that the reader can see at once whence it came, and also into what form it passed.

Putting aside all preconceived fancies, the critical comparison of the MSS. points, in my opinion, to three results, which are, I suspect, rather different to those which have generally found acceptance. I imagine that many have supposed that there may have been several translations of the Gospels into Anglo-Saxon, that numerous copies were made of them, and that most of the copies have long since perished. Now, all these three things *may* have been true, and cannot be disproved; but the actual evidence is all the other way, and ought to receive its full share of recognition. When we consider these undoubted facts, that, out of the six MSS. now existing, it is absolutely certain that MSS. I., III., and IV. *scarcely differ in a single letter* (due allowances being made for variable spellings); that MS. V. is copied from MS. VI. and from nothing else, and that MS. VI. is copied from MS. III. and from nothing else, we are almost irresistibly led to conclude that perhaps *not* very many of the copies have perished, that they may *never* have been very numerous, and that there is at present not the faintest trace of any *other* version[1]. I feel the more bound to say this, because the results differ from what I expected to find, and those suppositions which we feel compelled to entertain are more likely to be true than those which we merely build upon conjecture.

It has also been a question hitherto, which of these copies of the Anglo-Saxon Gospels is the oldest. Putting aside the later HATTON and ROYAL MSS., and admitting that the CAMBRIDGE MS. (II) is probably the latest of the other four, we may be satisfied with noting that the remaining three—at whatever time written out, and I see no reason for making one much older than another—are practically the same text, and of one period, and may be referred, as they have usually been, to the last decade of the tenth century; the date of the translation itself may have been somewhat earlier. I have once before quoted the opinion of Sir F. Madden that "the Anglo-Saxon version of the Gospels may be safely attributed to the ninth century," with his further remark that "none of the

[1] The only hints of other versions are (1) the mention of a translation made by Beda (Smith's Bede, p. 753) and (2) the notion that a translation may have been made by order of king Ælfred (see my Preface to St Mark, p. ii).

MSS. appear to give the version in its original purity;" see Pref. to St Mark, p. iii.; but I now feel bound to say that the present evidence militates, to some extent, against both these suppositions. The close agreement of the MSS. seems to shew that the version is nearly as pure now as it ever was, and the language belongs rather to the tenth than to the ninth century. It seems, however, reasonable to suppose that this version of the Gospels is older than Ælfric's version of the Pentateuch, made probably after A.D. 990; for Ælfric would hardly have turned his attention to the books of Moses until he had ascertained that the Gospels had first been translated.

These remarks refer to the Anglo-Saxon or Wessex MSS. only. The Northumbrian glosses are altogether distinct from them and independent; but they are not independent of each other, since the gloss in the RUSHWORTH MS. (VIII) frequently depends upon that in the LINDISFARNE MS. (VII), and in many places must have been copied from it, as already shewn in my Preface to St Mark's Gospel, at p. xiii.

I again express my thanks to the Syndics of the Pitt Press, for undertaking the publication of this third volume of the series of the Anglo-Saxon and Northumbrian Gospels.

CAMBRIDGE, *June* 20, 1874.

[Cotton MS. Nero D. 4, Fol. 129, col. 2.]

æft*er* lucas ðus mercong ælces godspel*les* ðe ontuoelmo*na*ð byres on lucases dæl
SEcundum lucan

ieiunium s*an*c*t*i iohannis
  baptistae[1]
d*omi*nica . III . de aduentum (*sic*)
in nat*ale sancti* iohannis bap*tistæ*
in natale d*omi*ni
  admisa publica
in octabas d*omi*ni n*ost*ri ies*u* *christi*
post dominica IIII
  de epiphania
d*omi*nica prima
  de aduentum
  d*omi*ni n*ost*ri ies*u* *christi*
post . u . d*omi*nicas
  de aduentum
co[t]tidiana
in ieiunium apostolorum
co[t]tidiana
co[t]tidiana
per messes
post penticosten in ieiuni*um*
die sabbati
in apostolorum
in s*anct*orum

[Fol. 129 *b*, col. 1.]

post III d*omi*nicas
xlgisima feria . II .
co[t]tidiana
co[t]tidiana
in martiras
co[t]tidiana
co[t]tidiana
in s*anct*orum
cottidiana
in martyras
cottidiana
in ieiunium s*anct*orum
  iohannis et pauli
in unius confessores (*sic*)
cottidiana
post prima
  de aduentum
in ieiunium feria . IIII .
post prima d*omi*nica
  de aduentum
  feria . ui .
in natale episcopi
cottidiana
cottidiana

[col. 2]

in natale s*anct*i laurenti
in ieiunium s*anct*i laurenti
in unius martyris
cottidiana
cottidiana
cottidiana
in xlgisima paschae
cottidiana
post . III . d*omi*nicas
  xlgisima feria IIII[2]
feria . III . de ebdomada
  maiora[2]
cottidiana
item alia
feria . u . mane in cena
  d*omi*ni admissa
passio d*omi*ni n*ost*ri ies*u* *christi*
in apostolorum
die sabbati de albas
  pascæ
feria . III . de albas pascæ
feria . u . de albas pascæ
in ascensa d*omi*ni n*ost*ri ies*u* *christi*

[1] The word *baptistae* here occupies a line by itself; but it is 'set back' because I suppose it to belong to the line above. So also in other cases.

[2] These two lines are really 'set back' in the MS.

INCIPIT PRAEFATIO LUCAE

lucas ðe syrisca ðærræ burge ɫ ðærræ ceastra fostring mið cræfte lẽce discipul ɫ
[fol. 130.] Lucas Syrus anthiocensiae arte medicus disci-

larcneht ɫ fostring ðara postolra æft*er* ðon ðone paule ɫ ðæm paule gesohte ɫ gefylgde wið ondetnise
pulus apostolorum postea paulum secutus usq*ue* ad confessionem

his herde drihtne buta heh-synne *for*ðon ne ꝥ wif æfra hæfde ne suno
eius seruiens d*omi*no sine crimine nam neq*ue* uxorem umquam habens neq*ue* filios

hundseofontig wintra geliorade in bithiniã. in ðær byrig full of halig gast seðe miððy uut*edlice* ɫ gee
lxxiiii. annorum obiit in bithiniã plenus sp*iritu* s*ancto* qui cum iam

awrittinæ woeron ða godspella ðerh mathcu*m* æc soð*lice* on iudea ðerh marc*um* ðon*ne* on
scribata essent euangelia per mattheum quidem in iudeam per marcum autem in

Italia . i . ðeað (*sic*) halge instihtade ɫ dihtade gaste *in* ðær ðeade dalu*m* ðis aurat godspell
italia s*an*cto instigante sp*iritu* in achaiae partib*us* hoc scribsit euangelium

gemercade uut*edlice* he on *for*ueard ær oðero woere awritteno to huon ɫ to ðæm buta ða ðaðe
significans etiam ipse in principio ante alia esse describta cui extra ea quae

endebrednise ðæs godspellica gesetnisse tosceades ɫ ða maastu*m* nẽd-ðarf woerces ɫ ðæs wynnes wæs
ordo euangelicae dispositionis exposcit ea maxime necessitas laboris fuit

ꝥte ærest creciscum ðæm geleafulu*m* mið æghuoelcu*m* witgong tocymmendo in lichoma godes crist*es*
ut primum graecis fidelib*us* omni prophetatione uenturi in carnem dei *christi*

woerca ðio menniscniso ꝥte ne iudaiscu*m* sagum hia to behaldanne woere in an aes willo
manifesta humanitas ne iudaicis fabulis adtendi in solo legis desiderio

to-haldon ꝥte ne ɫ ɫ æc to-sliteru*m* sagum ⁊ unwislicu*m* gemnisu*m* besuicceno ɫ gemerredo
tenerentur né uel hereticis fabulis et stultis sollicitudinibus seducti

foerdon fro*m* soðfæstnise ꝥte miswunne æft*er* ðon ꝥte on fruma godspelles ioh*annes*
excederent a ueritate elaboraret dehinc ut in principio · euangelii iohannis

mið accennise *fo*r*e* ondfengca ɫ to hwæm godspell awrite ⁊ on ðæm se gecorene awrite ꝥte
natiuitate praesumta cui euangelium scriberet et in quo electus scriberet et

tahte. ge-cyðde ɫ getry*m*medo ⁊ in him gefylledo weron ðaðe weron fro*m* oðro*m* ongindo
indicaret contestans et in se completa esse quae essent ab aliis incoata

ðæm *for*ðon æft*er* fulwiht sunu godes fro*m* endung cneureses on crist gefylled
cui ideo post babtismum filii d*ei* á perfeccione generationis in *christo* impletæ

gesoht wero fro*m* fruma accennise ðæs mennisces ðio mæht ðerh-gelefed wæs ꝥte ðæm soecendu*m*
repetendae á principio natiuitatis humanae potestas permissa est ut requirentibus

ge-eaude in ðæm of-genom wæs sunu inn-gæ ðæs iornende in
demonstraret in quo ápræhendens [fol. 130 *b*] erat natham filium introire currentis in

god cneoreso to-sende ł to in godes bodade in monnes gecerræ in him ðerh
d*eum* generationis admisso indisparabilis d*ei* predicans in hominis redire in sé per

sunu dyde seðe ðerh dauið ðone fæder cymendu*m* getrahtade ł tosceada in crist ðæm
filium faceret qui per dauid patrem uenientib*us* interpretabat in *christo* cui

luc*e* ne is un-cynn gee ðæra writtra apostolica wundra mæht in ryne ł bið sald ꝥte
lucæ non inmerito etiam scribendorum apostolicorum actuum potestas in misterio datur ut

gode on god full ⁊ sune selenis gedrysned ł geendad gebed apostolu*m* gewordne mið hlod
d*eo* in d*eum* pleno et filio proditionis extincto oratione apostolis facta sorte

drihtnes gecorenes tal ⁊ sua paul*us* ðone endung mið apostolicu*m* wundru*m* ꝥte salde
d*omi*ni electionis numerus sicq*ue* paulus consummatione*m* apostolicis actib*us* daret

ðone long wið priclom eft-drægend drih*ten* gecease ꝥte redendu*m* ł eft-soecendum
quem diu contra stimulos recalcitrantem d*omi*n*us* elegisset quod legentib*us* aut requirentib*us*

god ⁊ gif ðerh suyndriga to areccganne fro*m* usig darflic woere wiste huoeðre ꝥte
d*eum* et si per singula expediari a nobis utile fuerat sciens tamen quod

ðæm wyrcende londbuend gerises of wæstmu*m* h*is* ꝥte getta we fo*r*gældon ł gesaegdon ł ꝥ bærlic
operante*m* agricolam oporteat de fructib*us* suis edere uitauimus publicam

feruitgiornis nere suiðor wilnendum god ꝥte we gesegen ðon
curiositatem né non tam uolentibus d*eum* uideremur quam fastidientib*us* prodissæ

onginnað ðe mercunga
INCIPIUNT CAPITULA

mið fora saga luc*as* ðeofi godspell saegeð ł becneð ðerh ende-brednise were gesceaden
I. PRAEFATIONE lucas theofilo euangelium indicat per ordinem describturu*m*

sacerdhad soðfæstes zacharie asægd bið ł is æc ða gesihðo in temple ofðon him
II. Sacerdotium iusti zacchariae refertur et uisio in templo qua ei

sunu ðe engel æd-eaude gehaten wæs ꝥte were accenned ðæs uut*edlice* ecnung ł accennise gemyndged is
filius angelo reuelante promittitur nasciturus cuius etia*m* conceptio memoratur

gesended wæs engel to maria ꝥte were accenned spreces ðone hæl*end* miððy sona acenned wæs
III. Missus angelus ad mariam nasciturum loquitur saluatorem quo mox concepto

gegroeted wæs fro*m* elizabeth gefeande in innað miððy ioh*anne* huona æf*ter*
salutatur ab helizabeth exultante in utero iohanne [fol. 131.] unde post

ðrĭm moneðu*m* eftgecerred wæs in hus hire miððy acenned wæs ioh*annes* mið stefne
tres menses reuersa est in domum suam IIII. Nato iohanne uox

gespreca ðæm dumbe gesald wæs ðæm feder sona witgende se cnæht *in* wæst*ern* is oðð on dæge
eloqui muto redditur patri ilico prophetanti puer in deserto est usq*ue* in diem

æd-eaudnise his to isr*ael* æc asægd is ꝥ bod ðæs caseras ⁊ accennise cristes
ostensionis suae ad israhel V. Refertur edictum caesaris et natiuitas *christi*

ðæm hiordu*m* fro*m* engel asægd bið ł wæs ofðon ł miððy ꝥ heofonlic cempo ða menigo
pastoribus ab angelo nuntiatur cum quo caelestis militiae multitudo

singeð wulder ł gefea sie in heonisu*m* gode englum of dune stigendu*m* ða hiordo færende
canit gloria in excelsis d*eo* VI. Angelis discendentib*us* pastores profecti

ðone hæl*end* in bi*nn*e gesetted gemoetdn god of*er* ðæm ðaðe gesegon efne-geheredon
saluatorem in praesepio positum repperer*unt* d*eu*m super his quae uidebant conlaudantes

ðe æhtaðe dæge ymbcorfnise his witgong onducardes semeones ðæs soðfæstes oððe
VII. Octauo die circumcisionis eius prophetiae praesentis simeonis iusti uel

annæs witg*an* ge-sægd is tuoelfwintro he eft-wunade fro*m* his fost*rum*(?) in temple
annae prophetissae narratur VIII. Duodennis ipse remansit á suis in templo

soecende moederes cuoeðende on ðæm ðaðe fadores mines sint gerises me ꝥte ic se
quaerenti matri dicens in his quæ patris mei sunt oportet me esse

ðio fifteiðo ger tiberes ðæs caseres ioh*annis* miððy aras bod acuoeden is of ðon
VIIII. Anno quinto decimo tiberii caesaris iohannis orta praedicatio dicitur qua

alle to hreownise getrymed bið ⁊ sceowum drih*tnes* hine geondetade unwyrðe
cunctos ad paenitentiam cohortatur et calciamentis d*omi*ni se fatetur indignum

herod*es* to caercherne seles ioh*annem* ⁊ ðrittig wintra mið ðio gefuulwad drih*tne*
X. Herodes carceri dat iohanne*m* et triginta annorum baptizato d*omi*no

ðrinise on fulwiht asægdnise ł tosceaded is cynno ⁊ hundseofontig seofon of criste
trinitatis in baptismo mysterium declaratur generationum septuaginta septem a *christo*

upp woende wið to god ende-bred*nis* gegeadred bið ł gewoefen feortig dagana
sursum uersus usq*ue* ad d*eu*m ordo contexitur XI. Quadraginta dierum

feast*ern* ⁊ ꝥ ðrifald costong diofles ꝥte of*er*suiðet wæs ædeaued is mersung eft-færende
ieiunium et trina temtatione diabolis superatus ostenditur XII. Fama regressi

in gal*ileam* geteled is ⁊ ꝥte esaias boc onfenge of him gefylede wæs cuoeð he ne
in galileam refertur et quod esaiae librum accipiens de se impletum dixerit nec

hæfde ðe witga âr in oeðel his eftasægd soðlic*e* ł æc ðio widua of
habere prophetam honorem in patria sua relata etiam uidua [fol. 131 *b*] de

serapta ł ðæs lic-ðroueres neman syri mið clænsunge ꝥte ðerh middu*m* hiora seðe hine
serapta uel leprosi neman siri mundatione quod per medium eorum qui eum

of more f*or*eglendra waldon of*er*-foerde asægd is ondetande in somnunge
de monte præcipitare uolebant transierit indicatur XIII. Confitentem in synagoga

ðone diowel f*or*draf of menn swer petres ⁊ monigra untrymmia ꝥ folc
daemonem pellit ex homine XIIII. Socrus petri et multorum infirmorum turba

gehældo ł gehæled wæs ⁊ ondetung diola f*or*boden is tuæm sciopu*m* feng
sanatur et confessio daemonum prohibetur. XV. Duob*us* nauiculis captura

fisca in word drihtnes feerlice wero gefylde ondo frohtendes petres foerano ðaðe his
piscium in uerbo d*omi*ni repente completis timor pauescentis petri sociorum quae eius

asægd is hreaf wæs geclænsed monigo mið mægne drih*tnes* gegemed woeron untrymigo
edicitur. XVI. Leproso mundato multi uirtute d*omi*ni curantur infirmi

ðone eorð-crypel miððy gehreafad wæs hus f*or*leten bef*or*e hi*m* ⁊ fro*m* synnu*m* ⁊ fro*m*
XVII. Paralyticum nudato tecto dimissum ante se et á peccatis et á

crypelnise gemeð ł gehæleð leui seðe ⁊ matheus of teloneo geced is hia lycedon
paralysi curat XVIII. Leui qui et mattheus de teloneo uocatur murmurantes

of bærsynnigra gebearscip ł of fæstern forbodeno ðæm bryd-gum æc woedes ⁊ wines
de publicanorum conuiuio uel de ieiunio athibita sponsi et uestimenti ac uini

niwes mið ceping becuoeð soecende of niming hera in sabatum
noui comparatione redarguit XVIIII. Quaerentes de uulsione spicarum in sabbatis

eftasægd dauid bisen forcuom on somnung hond drugi hælde gefylde woeron
relato dauid exemplo conuincit XX. IN synagoga manum aridam sanat repletis

in unwisdom æ-laruas ðerh-wæccende in gebed arlic tuoelfo apostolas
insipientia pharisaeis XXI. Pernoctans in oratione mane duodecim apostolos

nemneð ða hrinendo him gehæled biðon un-hale ðorfendo ðurstendo woependo oeht-
nominat tangentes eum sanantur aegroti XXII. Pauperes esurientes flentes perse-

nise ðolende ða eadgo ceigeð wæ ðæm wloncum ⁊ ðæm hlæhendum cuoeð æc ł gee ða flondas
cutionem patientes beatos uocat uáe diuitibus ác ridentibus dicens etiam inimicos

bebead to lufanne ⁊ slægendum ł ðæm nacode lytle to forstondanne of mote
praecepit diligendos et percutientes uel nudanti minime resistendum XXIII. De festuca

⁊ beame of tree æc goda ⁊ yfla ⁊ æc of ðæm hus getimberde geddunga setteð
et trabe arbore quoque bona et mala atque domo aedificanda parabola ponit

centuriones ðræl gemeð biddendum fore hine ældrum ⁊ megum sunu
XXIIII. Centurionis seruum curat rogantibus pro eo senioribus et amicis XXV. Filius

ancende widues moder dead gee to ceastre gebroht of beere aweht is ðæm færendum
unicus uiduae matris mortuus iam ciuitate elatus de feretro suscitatur XXVI. Regressis

iohannis erendwrecum monigo of his micelnise gespræc ⁊ cnæhtum sittendum in ðing-stowe
iohannis nuntiis multa de eius magnitudine loquitur et pueris sedentibus in foro

cneureso gemacade ł gemacað iudea hlingende drihtne foet ꝥ wif
generationem comparat iudaeorum XXVII. Discumbentis domini pedes mulier

mið tearuum aðoað ⁊ ælaruas smeung geddung tuoera geðread is scyldigra ðæm
lacrimis rigat et pharisaei cogitatio parabola duorum arguitur debitorum XXVIII. Euan-

bodande drihtne ⁊ ðegnum his wifo of hiora acuoeden is wælum embehtade
gelizanti domino et discipulis eius mulieres de suis dicuntur facultatibus ministrasse

geddung æc ðon ðæsauende (*sic*) ⁊ wæstm fore-sette ⁊ gesette ł sægde ꝥ leht-fæt
parabolam quoque seminantis fructuumque proponit atque exponit XXVIIII. Lucernam

under fæte ne to settanne ⁊ ða ꝥ moder ⁊ broðro ceigendo cuoeð ðaðe fadores doende
sub uase non ponendam et eos matrem fratresque uocandos ait qui patris fecerint

willo in scip slepende awæht wæs from frohtendum ⁊ un-woeder sæs
uoluntatem XXX. IN naui dormiens excitatur á periclitantibus et tempestatem maris

mið word gestiorde monno from diowla here agemde ðaðe in bergum
uerbo compescit. XXXI. Hominem á daemonum legione curauit quos in porcos

gegeonga gelefde foerde to dohter iares were awoeht ꝥ wif of iorning
ire. concessit XXXII. Pergens ad filiam iairi suscitandam mulierem á profluio

blodes hæled Aueccende ðæm mægdne gesald were bebead geeatta mið gebrochtu*m*
sanguinis saluat resuscitate puellae dari praecipit manducare XXXIII. Conlatis

mæhtu*m* sendeð tuoelfo*m* ꝥte bodande wero halwoendu*m* bodum inseteno mersunc
uirtutib*us* mittit duodecim praedicaturus praeceptis salutaribus institutos XXXIIII. Famam

his hero*des* geherde asægd is ⁊ apos*tolas* gecuoeden sint ðaðe dydon eft-brohte ł sægdon fif
eius herodis audisse refertur et apostoli dicuntur quae fecerant rettulisse XXXV. Quinq*ue*

hlafu*m* ⁊ tuæm fiscu*m* fif monno ðusendo gefylde gefrægnende
panib*us* et duob*us* piscib*us* quinq*ue* hominum milia saturat XXXVI. INterroganti

ða ðegnas ðone ł huoelcne hine cuoeden menn petr*us* geonduearde criste godes
discipulos quem eum dicerent homines petrus [fol. 132 *b*] respondit *christ*i dei

soð he fo*re*-sægde hine ðrouende læreð ꝥte hine ælc ł sua huelc fylgende hine woere
at ipse praenuntiat sé passurum XXXVII. Docet ut eum quisq*ue* secuturus

onsæca hine seolfne ⁊ sume ne gesego hia cuoeð deað wið ꝥ geseas ric godes sona
abneget semet ipsum et quosdam non uisuros ait morte*m* donec uideant regnum d*e*i mox

in is asægd of*er*-hiuade wæs on mor sumo sunu of diule ðreatað ł mið ðy
infertur transfiguratus in montem XXXVIII. Cuiusdam filium á daemonio incre-

wæs geðreatad cneoreses fro*m* ungeleafulnise gegemde eft*er* sona cuoeð hine ðrouande
pata generationis incredulitate curauit XXXVIIII. Iterum dicit sé passurum

were toweard ⁊ of aldordom smeaunga hiora gesettet wæs in middu*m* cnæht fo*r*bead eðmodnise
fore et de primato cogitationes eorum statuto in medio puero uetans humilitatem

læreð ⁊ ne to fo*r*beadane mæhto on his noma doende fyr of heofne of*er*
docet et non prohiberi uirtutes in ipsius nomine facientem XL. Ignem de cælo super

telendo ł hniðriendo gebida wilnando ðegnas ðreatað ⁊ ðæm cuoeðende ic fylgo ðec foxas holo
contemtores petere uolentes discipulos increpat et dicenti sequar te uulpes foueas

habbað getrymade esne fylgende fo*r*geafa ł fo*r*leta ða deado ⁊ ðone haldond sulh ne eft-locia
habere testat*ur* iuuenis sequenti dimittere mortuos et tenentem aratru*m* non respicere

on bæc of-gemærcade æc oð*rum* tuæm ⁊ unseofontigu*m* ðeadu*m* sileð bodo ðæm gerises
retro XLI. Designatis et aliis .lxx. duobus dat praecepta quib*us* debeant

bodage sona ða ungeleaffulloco geðreadas ł ða ceastro tuæm ⁊ unseofuntigu*m* eft-cerrendum ⁊
praedicare mox incredulas increpat ciuitates .lxx. duob*us* reuersis atque

ðæm gefeandu*m* bebead ne of under-drifen*ise* diowla ah of hiora in heofne noma
gaudentibus praecipit non de subiectione daemonum sed de suorum in caelo nominum

mið awrittne gefea ondetnise hernises in gefea asægd is to feder æft*er* ðon
scribtione gaudere XLII. Confessio laudis in gaudio refertur ad patrem postquam

i*n*sægeð ac ða fo*r*ðmesto soðfæste ðaðe geseað ða ðegnas ne gesego hia æs ðæm wise of
infert priores iustos quae uident discipuli non uidisse XLIII. Legis perito de

lif ece soecende ⁊ hua his were ðe neesta fraignende in-lædeð geddung ðæs wundes
uita aeterna quaerente et quis eius esset proximus sciscitante inducit parabolam uulnerati

ðæm gebroht fro*m* samaritanu*m* miltheortnise bebead gebisened
cui conlatam a samaritano misericordiam praecipit imitandam XLIIII. Quaerellam

ðæs embeht-monnes of suoester ne hia helpende gecoren hia ł ða ilco dæl
ministrantis marte de sorore non eam adiuuante optimam eam [fol. 133.] partem

gecease mið cuis stiorde ꝥ bisene gebedes fifo giunga were gebeden from
elegisse dicendo compescit XLV. Normam orationis quinque petitionum rogatus á

ðegnum gesalde frionde ðrio hlafas æd midder-næht ðæm biddende ꝥ getdung
discipulos (*sic*) tradit XLVI. Amici tres panes media nocte petiti parabolam

setto giwende soecende ⁊ cnylsende ðerh-gebiddes ðone dumba diulas mið
ponens petendum quaerendum pulsandumque persuadit XLVII. Mutum daemonia cum

ðy geboette gemeð ꝥ sprec ⁊ in diobla aldor ðuslico hine mæge cuoeðende from wepen-berend strongum
restituto curat eloquio et in belzebub talia eum posse dicentes de armato fortiore

forcummen ⁊ of gast unclæne seofofullice on menn eftfærende forcuoeð ðæm
deuicto et de spiritu immundo septem-pliciter in homine regresso redarguit XLVIII. Excla-

ceigende wife eadig were ꝥ innoð seðe hine gebere ⁊ geonduorde ꝥte were ðe eadig seðe
manti mulieri beatum esse uentrem qui eum portasset respondit esse eum beatum qui

gehealde word godes ⁊ of becon ionæs cuoeð ðio cuoen suð-dæles gemyndgade
seruauerit uerbum dei et de signo ionae dicens reginam austri commemorat

ꝥ leht-fæt cuoeðende ne were under mitte to gesettanne ꝥ ego læreð bliðe were
XLVIIII. Lucernam dicens non esse sub modio poni oculum docet simplicem esse

gerisnelic mið ælarua gehriordage gebeden wæs smeande ł ðencende from iudisca fulwihte
debere L. Apud pharisaeum prandere rogatus cogitantem de iudaico baptismate

becnade ł cydde ⁊ wæ scofa siða cuoeð monigo hiora yfla æc geðreade ðegnum
notans et uáe pharisaeis sexies dicens multa eorum mala coarguit LI. Discipulis

bebead ⁊ from dærstum esuicnise to behaldane ⁊ ða ðaðe lic-homa acuellas ne scyniga ne ꝥ
praecepit et á fermento hypocrisis cauere et eos qui corpus occidunt non metuere nec

in oehtnise huætd hia wero sprecendo ge-ðencæ ðæm wilnande sum ðing bituih him ⁊
in persecutione quid locuturi sint cogitare LII. Petenti quodam inter se et

broðer his were todæled erfe geddung gesette from welige ðæm gitsare sona ⁊ ðegnum
fratrem suum diuidi hereditatem parabolam ponit de diuite auaro mox et discipulis

gemnise mettes ⁊ woedes forgaes fuglas bebead to behaldanne lytlo edo
sollicitudinem cibi uestisque carent aues praecipit euitandum LIII. Pusillo gregi

ríc geheht to hæbbendo ł agnage fore ælmiso to bebscane ⁊ sido
regnum promittens possidenda uel possessa propter elemosynam uendi [fol. 133 *b*] lumbosque

ymbgyrdeno ⁊ leht-fato beornendo were gerisnelic hateð to wæccenne æc ðon ðræles godes ⁊ yfles
praecinctos et lucernas ardentes esse debere iubet uigilandum quoque serui boni malique

gemynd aworden ł awærð bebead esne wittende willa drihtnes monigom ðone uncyðig
mentione facta præcipiens seruum scientem uoluntatem domini multis igno-

ł unwittende æc huonum gemersia g[e]fæstnuið fyr innueard hine cuoeð ðærflicra
rantem uero paucis uapulare confirmat LIIII. IGnem internam se dicit necessitudinum

todælnise woere gesended ⁊ onsione heofnes cunnande reht-lice were tíd to oncnauanne eawunga ⁊ æc
diuissionem missurum et faciem caeli probantes debere tempus intellegere manifestum atque

geðiodsu*m*nise to ðæm fionde on woeg fo*r*e-sægeð weron gesægd sum oðero fro*m* pylat*e* ofslægeno
consentiendum aduersario in uia pronuntiat LV. Nuntiatis quib*us*dam a pilato occisis

cuoeð alle buta hreonise doað gelic ꝥte hia woero deado ꝉ sua ða tene ⁊ æhto
ait omnes nisi pænitentiam agant similiter perituros uel sicut illi dece*m* et octo

feallo torres fo*r*e-treden geddung æc ðon of unberendu*m* trēēs fic settende sægeð ꝉ tæcnað
ruina turris opp*r*essi parabolam quoque de sterili arbori fici ponens indicat

hreonis tosceadadon ⁊ ꝥ wif fro*m* wintru*m* tenu*m* ⁊ æhto gescryncan ahof of gemnise
paenitentiam differentes et mulierem ab annis dece*m* et octo curuatam erigens de cura

mið bisseno oxes to wætranne æfsægeð gefeande folc of his wundru*m*
sabbati murmurantes exemplo bouis adaquandi refellit gaudente populo de eius miraculis

wuldorlicu*m* ríc godes corn sinapis ge-efnade ⁊ to dærsto fro*m* naroneðe æc ðon
gloriosis LVI. Regnum d*e*i grano sinapis conparans et fermento de angusta quoq*ue*

lifes woeg lytla ꝉ lytelra sprecend woeron cuoeð ða forðmesto hlætmest ⁊ ða hlætmesto fo*r*ðmæsto
uitae uia paucorum loquens erunt inquit primi nouissimi et nouissimi primi

hero*dem* fox nemneð ⁊ hie*rusalem* geðreaðe oðru*m* his gescilde onsæccende
LVII. Herodem uulpem appellat et hierusalem increpat ális eius protegi respuentem

gegemde suelce of seaðe gefreod lycoedon
LVIII. Hydropicum sabbato curans uelut de umoris puteo liberatum murmurantes pharisaeos

asales ꝉ oxes on ðæm fælles of-trahtung gescende edmodnise æc ðon to fylgene lærde
asini uel bouis in eo cadentis extractatione confundit humilitatem quoq*ue* sectandam docens

on gebearscip ðæt fo*r*ma *h*ræst bebead ne sohte ꝉ nere to soecane ne weligo ah ða dorfendo ðaðe
in conuiuio primum accubit*um* praecipit non quaerendum nec diuites sed pauperes qui

ne eft-seleð were to foedanne seteð geddung of ðæm laðendu*m* seðe hine
non retribuant esse pascendos [fol. 134.] LVIIII. Ponit parabolam de inuitatis qui se

fo*r*cuoede gearuande ꝉ geteledon symbel ne woeron wyrðe laðum ða nedlicu*m* mið ðon
excusare studentes cena non fuerint digni LX. Odituris necessitudines insuper

⁊ sauel his ⁊ ondfenge rode gefylgendo woero ꝥ gelic ge-timbrendes torres ⁊ of gefeht
et animam suam et assumta cruce secuturi similitudinem aedificandæ turris et de bello

cyninga tuoege gesceadeð ⁊ ne sic hwæl[c] ꝉ ænig salt ah coro habbað to heranne
regum duorum exponit neué sit quis sál infatuatum sed aures habet audiendi

of synna gebearscip geddung scipes ⁊ cæsering setteð begetne
LXI. Murmurantib*us* de peccatoru*m* conuiuio parabolam ouis et dragmæ ponit inuentae

bebead ꝥ gefea fro*m* hreownisu*m* hælo tocymende geddung gesette fro*m*
commendans gaudium de paenitentum salute futuru*m* LXII. Parabolam ponens de

wæstmo ⁊ ðæm argæ sunum ꝥ eft-cerr behofe to feder hælo sægeð ðæra hreonise
frugi et luxurioso filiis reuersione*m* prodigi ad patrem salutem indicat paenitentum

fro*m* geroefa unreht-wisnise fro*m* ungelic*nise* seðe ꝥ scyld hlaferdes his hogascipē
LXIII. De uilico iniquitatis ex dissimilitudine qui debitum domini sui astu sollertiore

inn-eade ꝉ læde ne mæhte gode here ænig ⁊ gitsaras
minuerat introducit LXIIII. Non posse d*e*o seruire quemqua*m* et mamonae auaros

geðrað ða ælaruas ⁊ æ cuoeð ł witgo wið to ioh*annem* ⁊ ꝥte
increpat pharisaeos legemq*ue* dicens uel prophetas usq*ue* ad iohannem baptistam et quod

fo*r*leorte suahua wif gesyngade ðe unmiltheortne welige gehiuadne . i . mið felle ⁊
demittens quis uxorem moechatur LXV. INmisericordem diuitem purpuratum et

ðone ðorfe inlædde ædeaude hulco wero ðrouendo *h*reaferas sua geearnadon
pauperem lazarum introducens ostendit qualia sint passuri raptores sic maerentur

ꝥte hia were gepined scearplice wæ cuæ ðæm ondspyrnende ðeæm hræwende æc broðer
puniri tenaces LXVI. Uáe dicit scandalizanti paenitenti uero fratri

uut*edlice* undseofontig siða seofa siða heht ꝥte were fo*r*gefen ge-ēce him bedon ða apostolas
etia*m* septuagies septies præcipit remittendum LXVII. Augeri sibi petunt apostoli

⁊ geherdon of fo*r*esaga ł trees eðnise ⁊ geseteno mið bisene fro*m* esne herende
fide*m* et audiunt de translatione arboris facultatem positaq*ue* similitudine de seruo arante

ł foedende læreð ꝥ ða idlo hia gee gefyldon ðaðe beboden woeron geondetad sint
uel pascente docet ut inutiles sé etiam implentes quae praecepta sunt fateantur

tea ł teno hreafo geclænsade an nomaa ⁊ ðis uta-cund cynn to ðongunge
LXVIII. Decem leprosis mundatis [fol. 134 *b*] unus tantum et hoc alienigena ad gratias

gewoende ꝥte woero tosæccenne wæs frægnend fro*m* tīd rices godes geonduearde ne
reuertitur referendas LXVIIII. INterrogatus de tempore regni d*ei* respondit non

mið gehald tocymende ⁊ hine to ðuneri ge-efnade niomande ł hia cuoeð menn sua on
cum obseruatione uenturum eumque fulgori comparans occupandos eos dicit homines sicut in

dagu*m* noes ⁊ loth ⁊ of tuæm on hus on coern ⁊ on lond suindrio to onfoanne ⁊ ða syndrio
dieb*us* noe et loth et de binis in tecto in mola et in agro singulos asumendos et singulos

foresæggeð to fo*r*letenno to symble biddanne geddung fro*m* widua setteð wraco
pronuntiat relinquendos LXX. Ad semper orandum parabolam de uidua ponit ultionem

fro*m* wiðeruarde his fro*m* unrehtwis doeme giwigende of gebed ðæs ælaruas on temple
de aduersario suo ab iniquo iudice postulante LXXI. Oratione pharisaei in templo

⁊ bærsynnig fo*r*e-gesettet læreð ne to worpanne ða merdo ah to ondetende synno ða
et publicani proposita docet non iactanda merita sed confitenda peccata LXXII. Par-

lytlo fro*m* hi*m* hia adrifa fo*r*e-bead eðmodnise under hiora noma mercað to haldenne
uulos a sé uetari prohibens humilitatem sub eorum nomine significat optinendam

gefrægn ðone weligo fro*m* to byenna lif ēce ðiu æft*erra* onsuare unrōd gecearf
LXXIII. INterrogans diues de possidenda uita aeterna secunda responsione tristis abscidit

⁊ fo*r*letru*m* fo*r*e noma his lytlo drih*ten* ēce heht gesald
et relinquentib*us* propter nomen suum temporalia d*ominus* aeterna promittit LXXIIII. Tra-

he woere to hierusal*em* ⁊ woere geðrowende fo*r*e-cuoeð æt hie*richo* blinde ðorfende
dendum se hierosolimis passurumque praedicit LXXV. IUxta hiericho ceco mendicanti

leht on onduearde eft-sette ðerh-eode hie*richo* ðone aldormono
lumen in praesenti restituit LXXVI. Perambulans hiericho zaccheum publicanum

unband seðe cuom hal gedoe ꝥte losade bispell sette ðegna
absoluit qui uenit saluum facere quod perierat LXXVII. Parabolam ponit seruorum

from hlaferdo his of ꝥte hia gebohte from him ⁊ fiondas rices his
accipientium a domino suo decemnas ut negotiarentur ex eis et inimicos regni sui

fore-sægeð ðerh-gelicade ofer fola asales sætt allum cuoeðendum sibb on
pronuntiat perimendos LXXVIII. Super pullum asinae sedit cunctis dicentibus pax in

heofne ⁊ gefea on heanisum ⁊ of ðreatendum ðegnum his cuoeð gif ðas sægdon (*sic*) stanes
caelo et gloria in excelsis et de increpandis discipulis suis ait si hí tacuerint lapides

cliopadon gesæh ða ceastra gewæp ofer hia fore-sægde of-acerred
clamabunt LXXVIIII. Uidens ciuitatem fleuit [fol. 135.] super eam praenuntians euertendam

of temple bebyccendo fordraf uðuutum setendum of folce lustlice wæs gehered frægnende
de templo uendentes eicit scribis insidiantibus á populo libenter auditur LXXX. Sciscitantes

of mæhte his huoerflice of frægnende of iohannes fulwihte efne forcumen woeron
de potestate eius uicissim ab interrogante de iohannis baptismo conuincuntur

geddong cuoeð from buendum wingeardum seðe laferd his ⁊ esnes ⁊ sunu
LXXXI. Parabolam dicit de cultoribus uineae qui domini sui et seruos et filium

ofslogon costende of gæfel cæsares to forgeldanne penninges onwriting forcuom
occiderunt LXXXII. Temtantes de tributo cæsaris reddendo denarii inscribtione conuincit

from seofa broðero hlafe soecendum erist ⁊ ēc moises
LXXXIII. Sadducaeis de septem fratrum uxore quaerentibus resurrectionem etiam mosi

mið cyðnise ge-trymað soecað huu crist sunu sie dauið mið drihtno
testimonio confirmat LXXXIIII. Quaerit quomodo *christus* filius sit dauid cum domino

from him wære geceged in psalme hunteanteige nioða upp-hepbing æc ðon uuð-utana geðreade widua
ab eo uocaretur in psalmo centensimo nono elationem quoque scribarum arguit uidua

tuoge lyf sendende forðor allum were gefæstnad hergiendum
in gazophilacium duo aera mittentem plus omnibus misisse confirmat LXXXV. Laudantibus

getimbres tempel fore-cuoeð sona ðæs toslitnitnese ⁊ frægnendum of ende ge-onduærde yflo
aedificium templi praedicito cuius destruendum et interrogantibus de fine respondit mala

monigo fore-scyniga ne fore-smeande huæd gesald gesprecen weron ah in geðyld his
plurima praecessura nec praecogitandum quid traditi loquantur sed in patientia sua

hia agnagað sauela hiora ymb-sellenne from here hierusalem ⁊ wæ
possideant animas suas LXXXVI. Circumdandam ab exercitu hierusalem et uáe

ðæm berendum suord æc ðon ⁊ ꝥ ðeadom ⁊ tunglas heofnæs to-weardo ⁊hine to-cymende on wolcen
praegnantibus gladium quoque et captiuitatem signaque caeli futura seque uenturum in nube

mið mæhte micla ⁊ mið ðrym fore-cuoeð locas cuoeð ꝥte to-geneolecde
cum potestate magna et maiestate praedicit LXXXVII. Respicite inquit quia adpro-

ł to-geneolecað lesnise iuera from druncene æc ðon ⁊ gemnisum þisses lifes forbead
pinquat redemtio uestra ab ebrietate quoque et curis huius uitae prohibens

to wæccenne bead ⁊ to biddanne
uigilandum praecipit et orandum

ꝥte neh eostro is to redenne
[fol. 135 *b*] QUOD PROPE PASCHA LEGENDUM EST

iuðas sipbade mearde geruað ða ðegnas eostro geryno færma
LXXXVIII. IUDAS PACISCITUR pretium parant discipuli pascha mysterium caenæ

drihtnes ł drihtenlico gemersad aron ꝥ geflit ðegna hine seolfne ðæra
d*omi*nicae celebrantur LXXXVIIII. Contentionem discipulorum se ipsum illorum

embeht-monn gefælde genom ðæm ríc geheht cuoeð æft*er* oðera to petre getrym broðro
ministrum astruens tollit quib*us* regnum promittens ait post aliqua petro confirma fratres

ðino ðio redo mæge on sua huælc tíd cuoeða ðrounges deda asægd biðon ðer bituih
tuos quae lectio potest quolibet tempore dici XC. Passionis gesta narrantur ubi inter

oðero æc ðon ðio earliprece ðone ðæm cnæhte pet*rus* gecurfe ðio hond his miððy ge-
cetera etiam auric*u*la quam puero petrus absciderat ipsae (*sic*) manus suae tactu

sette ł eft-geboette ðæm hoendu*m* f*or*gefnise fro*m* feder of-gebæd æc an fro*m* ðæm sceaðum
restituit XCI. Crucifigentib*us* ueniam á patre deposcens etiam unum ex latronib*us*

hongende ł g (*sic*) ondedende unband arise hine ðarfo ðio engelica ædeaunise
crucifixum confitentem absoluit XCII. Resurrexisse eum mulieres angelica reuelatione

ongeton ⁊ pet*rus* to ðær byrgen*ne* gearn ⁊ ge-sæh ꝥte aworden wæs gewundrað
cognoscunt et petrus ad monumentu*m* currens ac uidens quod factum fuerat ammiratur

of tuæm ꝥ is ⁊ foera his ðæs noma geswigeð is ðæm geongen*dum* in ceastre
XCIII. A duob*us* id est cleopa et socio eius cuius nomen tacetur euntib*us* in castellum

ꝥte ða wæs geceiged æft*er* ꝥ efne-sprec longe on dælnise hlafes ongeten bið
quod tunc emmaus uocabatur post confabulationem prolixam in fractione panis agnoscitur

efne-sprecendu*m* ðegnu*m* astod on middum cuoe (*sic*) sibb iuh ⁊ ða get forhtende
XCIIII. Conloquentibus discipulis adstans in medio dicit pax uobis et adhuc pauentes

⁊ ꝥ gaast woendon æd-eaudnise ofer-fæst*o* hondo ⁊ fota gefæstnaðe (*sic*) gebræc fo*re*
sp*iritu*mque putantes ostensione transfixarum manuum pedumq*ue* confirmat edens coram

ðæm dæl fisces brededes ⁊ biobread wyniges læreð hia ꝥ hât fadores walde gesenda hine
ipsis partem pisces assi et fauum mellis instruit eos promissum patris missurum sé

cuoeð astag on heofne
dicens ascendit in caelum

ðios redo on ðære uica eostres miððy bið gereded geendad bið on stoue ðer
[fol. 136.] HAEC lectio in ebdomada paschae dum legitur finitur in loco ubi

cu*u*oeð ða huile we biðon gegearuud mið ðæm heigra mæht miððy uut*edlice* in astignise gereded bið
ait quoad usq*ue* induamini uirtutem ex alto Cum autem in ascensione legitur

oðero stoue onginneð ðer cuoeð ðegnu*m* ðas sint wordo ðaðe spreccend wæs iuh miððy
alio loco incoanda est quo dicit discipulis haec sunt uerba quae locutus sum uobis cum

get ic wæs mið iuh við ende godspelles
athuc essem uobiscum usq*ue* in finem euangeli

asægd aron ða merconga æft*er* lucas
EXPLICIUNT CAPITULA SECUNDUM LUCAM

THE GOSPEL

ACCORDING TO

ST. LUKE.

EUANGELIUM

SECUNDUM

LUCAM.

INCIPIT EUANGELIUM

SECUNDUM LUCAM.

Lucas boc ðæs halgan godspelleres. B. Her ongin . . lucas Boc Ðæs halgan godspelleres. C. Ðis god-spel ge-byrað on midde sumeres mæsse-æfen. Fuit in diebus herodis regis. A.

CHAPTER I.

1 Forþam ðe witodlice manega þohton
þara þinga race geende-byrdan þe
on ús gefyllede synt.
2 swa us betæhtun ða þe hyt of frymðe
gesáwon. ⁊ þære spræce þénas wǽron;
3 Me ge-þuhte geornlice eallum oð énde-
byrdnesse writan þe; þú se sélusta theó-
philus
4 ꝥ ðu oncnáwe þara worda soþfæstnesse
of ðam ðe þu gelǽred eart;
5 On herodes dagum iudéa cyninges.
wæs sum sacerd on naman zacharias of
abian túne. ⁊ his wíf wæs of áárones dohtrum. ⁊ hyre nama wæs elizabeth;
6 Soðlice hig wæron butu riht-wise be-
foran gode. gangende on eallum his bebod-
um ⁊ rihtwisnessum butan wrohte.
7 ⁊ hig næfdon nan bearn. forðam ðe.
elizabeth wæs unberende. ⁊ hy on heora
dagum butu forð-eodon;
8 Soðlice wæs geworden þa zacharias his
sacerdes hades breác on hys gewrixles
endebyrdnesse beforan gode.

Various Readings.

Text: MS. Corp. Chr. Coll. 140; *V.R. from* A (Camb. Univ. Lib. Ii. 2. 11); B (Bodley 441); and C (Cotton, Otho c. 1).

Title: A.B. Incipit—lucam.

Ch. i. v. 1. A. þæra. A. raca. A. synd. 2. A. betæhton. 3. A. eornlice. A. endebyrdnysse. A. þu ðe selesta. 4. A. þæra. A. soðfæstnysse. 5. B. C. cyninegos. 6. A. *om.* Soðlice. A. ryhtwysnyssum. 7. A. *om.* ðe. A. hig. B. C. hyra. B. C. forþ-eodun. 8. A. B. C. sacerd-hades. A. endebyrdnysse.

Nu we wille her eow are can lucas b þas halgen godspelleres

CHAPTER I.

1 for þan þe witodlice manega þohte
þare þinge race ge-ende-berden þe on us
ge-fylde synde;
2 swa us be-tahten þa þe hyt of fremðe
ge-sægen. ⁊ þare spræce þéenæs wæren.
3 Me ge-þuhte geornlice eallen oð ænde-
byrdnysse writen þe þu seleste theophi-
lus.
4 ꝥ þu oncnawe þare worde sodfæstnysse
of þam þe þu ge-lǣred ært.
5 On herode dagen iudea cyninges wæs
sum sacerd on namen zacharias of abian
tune. ⁊ his wif wæs of áárones dohtren. ⁊
hire name wæs elisabeth.
6 Soðlice hyo wæren ba twa rihtwise
be-foren gode. ⁊ gangenden on eallen hys
beboden ⁊ rihtwisnesse. ba twa wrohte.
7 ⁊ hyo nafden nan bearn. for-ðan elisabeth wæs un-berende ⁊ hyo on heore dag-
en baðe forð-eoden.
8 Soðlice wæs ge-worðen þa zacharias
hys sacerd-hades brea. on his ge-wrixles
endebyrdnysse be-fore gode.

Various Readings.

Title. willað; areccen; halgan.

Ch. i. v. 1. forðam; sint. 2. frimðe gesawon; þenas wæron. 3. eallum; ende-byrdnysse writan. 4. þara; eart. 5. dagan; naman; dohtrum; nama. 6. waron baðe; riht-wisse beforan; gangendum; allum; riht-wisnyssum. buton. 7. næfdon; R. *inserts* ðe *after* forðan; hyora dagan buto. 8. brea (*sic*); *as in* H.

LUCAS UITULUS

onginneð god-spell æfter lucas
INCIPIT EUANGELIUM SECUNDUM LUCAM

CAP. I.

forðon aec soð monigo cunnendo woeron ꝥte hia geendebrednadon ðæt gesaga ðaðe
1 *QUONIAM QUIDEM MULTI CONATI SUNT ORDINARE NARRATIONEM quae * I. lu. 1. x.

In usic gefylled aron ðingana suæ gesaldon us ðaðe from frumma ða gesegon ⁊
in nobis completae sunt rerum 2 sicut tradiderunt nobis qui ab initio ipsi uiderunt et

embehtmenn woeron wordes gesegen wæs æc me of-fylgde from fruma alle georne
ministri fuerunt sermonis 3 uisum est et mihi assecuto a principio omnia diligenter

mið ende-brednise ðe auritta ðu gecorene theofile ꝥte ðu ongette hiora worda of ðæm
ex ordine tibi scribere optime theophile 4 ut cognoscas eorum uerborum de quib*us*

gelæred arð on soðfæstnise wæs In dagum heroðes cyninges iudeæ sacerd sum
eruditus és ueritatem 5 *FUIT IN DIEBUS herodis regis iudaeae sacerdos quidam * II.

mið noma of lond abia ⁊ wif ðæm ł him of dohter*um* aaron ⁊ noma his elizabeth
nomine zacharias de uice abia et uxor illi de filiab*us* áron et nomen eius elisabet

woeron uut*edlice* soð-fæsto boego fo*re* gode færendo In allum bodum ⁊ soðfæstnissu*m*
6 erant autem iusti ambo ante d*eu*m incedentes in omnibus mandatis et iustificationib*us*

driht*nes* buta grornunge ⁊ ne wæs him ł ðæm sunu for*ð*on wæs elizab*eth* unberend ⁊ boege
d*omi*ni sine quaerella 7 et non erat illis filius eo quod esset elisabeth sterilis et ambo

gefeollon on dagu*m* hiora aworden wæs uut*edlice* miððy sæcerd-had gebrece in endebrednise
processissent in dieb*us* suis 8 factum est autem cum sacerdotio fungeretur in ordine

londes his fo*re* gode
uicis suæ ante d*eu*m

INCIPIT EUANGELIUM LUCAE¦

CAP. I. 1. forðon æc monige cymende werun ðæt gi-ende-bredadun ða gisagune ðingana ða in usih gifylled arun 2. swa gisaldun us ðaðe from fruma ða gisegun ⁊ embiht-menn werun wordes 3. gisegen wæs ⁊ me of-fyligde from fruma alra georne¦ mið endebrednisse ðe awrito ðu gicorne theon-phile 4. ðæt ðu ongete hiara worda of ðæm gilæred arð on soð-fæstnisse 5. wæs in dagum ... cyniges iudea sacerd sum mið noma zacharias of londe abia ⁊ wif ðæm of dohtrum arones ⁊ noma him elizab*eth* 6. werun wutudl*ice* soð-fæste boege fore drih*ten* færende in allum bibodum ⁊ soð-fæstnisse drih*tnes* buta grornunga 7. ⁊ ne wæs ðæm sunu hiæ forðon wæs elizabeth unberende ⁊ boege gifeollun in dagum hiora 8. giworden wæs wutudlice ðy sacerd-hade gibrece .. in ende-brednisse londes his fore gode

9 æfter gewunan ðæs sacerdhades hlotes. he eóde þæt he hys offrunga sette; Ða he on godes tempel eode

10 eall werod þæs folces wæs úte gebiddende on þære offrunga tíman;

11 Ðá ætywde him drihtnes engel standende on þæs weofodes swyðran healfe;

12 Ða wearð zacharias gedréfed ꝥ geseonde ⁊ him ege on-hreas;

13 Ða cwæð se engel him to. ne ondrǽd þu þe zacharias. forþa*m* þin bén ys gehyred ⁊ þin wíf elizabeth þe sunu cenð. ⁊ þu nemst hys naman Iohannes.

14 ⁊ he byð þe to geféan ⁊ to blisse. ⁊ manega on his acennednysse gefagniað;

15 Soðlice he byð mǽre beforan drihtne ⁊ he ne drincð wín. ne beór. ⁊ he byð gefylled on haligu*m* gaste. þonne gŷt of hys modor innoðe.

16 ⁊ manega israhela bearna he gecyrð to drihtne hyra gode.

17 ⁊ he gæð toforan him on gaste. ⁊ elías mihte. ꝥ he fædera heortan to heora bearnum gecyrre. ⁊ ungeleaffulle to rihtwisra gleawscype. drihtne full-fremed folc gegearwian;

18 Ða cwæð zacharias to þam engele. hwanun wât ic þis; Ic eom nu eald ⁊ mín wíf on hyre dagum forð-eóde;

19 Ða andswarode him se engel; Ic eom gabriel ic þe stande beforan gode. ⁊ ic eom asend wið þe sprecan. ⁊ þe ðis bodian;

Various Readings.

9. A. offrunge. 10. A. wered. A. byddende. A. offrunge. 13. A. forþa*m* ðe þyn. 14. B. C. acennednesse. A. gefahniað. 15. A. halgu*m*. 16. A. heora. 17. C. helias. B. C. hyra. A. B. C. fulfremed. 18. A. engle. A. hwanen. 19. A. se engel hym. A. gabrihel. A. *om.* þe *after* ic.

9 æfter ge-wunan. þara sacerdes hades hlotes he eode þæt he his offringe sette. Ða he on godes tempel eode

10 eall wered þas folkes wæs ute biddende on þare offrenge timen.

11 Ða atewede hym drihtenes ængel standende on þas weofedes swiðren healfe.

12 Þa warð zacharias ge-drefed þæt geseonde ⁊ hi*m* eige on-reas.

13 Ða cwæð se ængel hym to. ne ondred þu þe zacharias. for þan þin bene is ge-herd. ⁊ þin wif elisabeth þe sune kenð. ⁊ þu nemnest hys name Iohannes

14 ⁊ he byð þe to blisse. ⁊ manega on his akynnednysse ge-fageneð.

15 Soðlice he byð mære be-foren drihtene. ⁊ he ne drincð win ne beor. ⁊ he beoð ge-felleð mid halgen gaste; Þanne gyt of hys moder innoðe.

16 ⁊ manege israele bearne he ge-chyrd to drihtene heore gode

17 ⁊ he gæð to-foren him on gaste. ⁊ on helias ge-mihte. ⁊ he fǽderan heortan to heora bearnan ge-cyrre. ⁊ ungeleafulle. to rihtwise gleaw-scipe. drihtne fulfremed folc ge-gærewian.

18 Ða cwæð zacharias to þam engle. hwanan wat ich þis. Ic eom nu eald ⁊ min wif on heora dagen forð-eode.

19 Þa andswerede him se ængel. Ich eom gabriel se engel. ic þe stande be-foren gode. ⁊ ich eom asend wið þe sprecen. ⁊ þe þis bodien.

Various Readings.

9. offrunge. 10. þæs folces; offrunge. 11. ætywde; drihtnes engel; swiððran. 12. werð; cage. 13. engel; on-dræd; beane; nemst. 14. *After* þe R. *inserts* to fean ⁊; acennednysse ge-fagenigað. 15. beforan drihtne; byð ge-fylled on galgu*m* (*sic*); þonne. 16. mænega; gecyrð. 17. bernan; ungeleaffulle; rihtwisa; ge-garewian. 18. hire dagon. 19. Ic; ængel [*for* engel]; be-foran; ic; sprecan; bodian.

æft*er* gewuna sacerd-hades of *h*lodti eode ꝥte roecels gesette innfoerde on tempel
9 secundum consuetudinem sacerdoti sorte exiit ut incensum poneret ingressus in templum

drihtnes ⁊ alli ðio menigo wæs ðæs folces biddende uta æd tid lehtes æd-eauade
d*omi*ni 10 et omnis multitudo erat populi orans foris hora incensi 11 apparuit

uut*edlice* ðæm engel drihtnes stode to suiðru*m* wig-beddes beorning ⁊ gestyred
autem illi angelus d*omi*ni stans a dextris altaris incensi 12 et zacharias turbatus

wæs miððy gesæh ⁊ ondo gefeoll of*er* hine cuoeð uut*edlice* to ðæm ł to him se engel ne ondred ðu
est uidens et timor irruit super eum 13 ait autem ad illum angelus ne timeas

for*ð*on gehered wæs ł is gebeodo ðina ⁊ uif ðin elizabeth bereð ðe sunu ⁊
zacharia quoniam exaudita est depraecatio tua et uxor tua elisabet pariet tibi filium et

ðu ge-ceige noma his ioh*annes* ⁊ bið gefea ðe ⁊ glædnise ⁊ monigo in accennisse
uocabis nomen suum iohannem 14 et erit gaudium tibi et exultatio et multi in natiuitate

his biðon glæde bið for*ð*on micel bef*or*a drihtno ⁊ win ⁊ bear ne drinceð ⁊
eius gaudebunt 15 erit autem magnus coram d*omi*no et uinum et sicera non bibet et

gaaste halge gefylled bið ða gett wæs In inna moderes his ⁊ monigo suno isræle
spi*ri*tu s*an*c*t*o replebitur athuc ex utero matris suæ 16 et multos filiorum isra*e*l

gecerreð to drihtne gode hiora ł ðara ⁊ he f*or*egæð fore ðæm in gaast ⁊ of ł mið mæht
conuertet ad d*omi*n*um* d*eu*m ipsorum 17 et ipse praecedet ante illum in spi*ri*tu et uirtute

heliæs ꝥte ge-cerre hearta uutuna ł ældra In sunum ⁊ ða ungeleaffulo to hoga-scipe soð-fæstra
heliae ut conuertat corda patrum in filios et incredibiles ad prudentiam iustorum

gegearuiga drihtne folc wis-fæst ⁊ cuoeð zacharias to ðæm engel huona ðis witto
parare d*omi*no plebem perfectum 18 et dixit zacharias ad angelum unde hoc sciam

ic for*ð*on am ald ⁊ uif min gefeall in dagum his ⁊ ge-onduarde se engel cuoeð
ego enim sum senex et uxor mea processit in dieb*us* suis 19 *ET respondens angelus dixit * 2. v. mt. iii.

him ic am gabrihel seðe ic tostondo *fore* gode ⁊ sendet am ꝥ ic sprece to ðe ⁊ ðas ðe
ei ego sum gabrihel qui adsto ante d*eu*m et missus sum loqui ad te et haec tibi

gebodage
euangelizare

---

9. æfter giwuna sacer[d]-hades of hlote eode ðætte in recels gisete in-foerde on temple drih*tnes* 10. ⁊ allo ðio mengu wæs ðæs folches bidende ute æt tide lehtes 11. æt-eowde wutudlice ðæm engel drih*tnes* stod to swiðra wibedes biorning 12. ⁊ . . . gi-styred wæs miððy gisæh ⁊ ege gifeol ofer hine 13. cwæð wutudlice engel to ðæm ne ondred ðu . . . forðon gihered wæs ł is of gi-beodum ðinu*m* ⁊ wif ðin eliz*abeth* beres ðe suno ⁊ ðu giceg noma his ioh*annes* 14. ⁊ bið gifea ðe ⁊ glædnisse ⁊ monige in acennisse his glæde bioðun 15. bið forðon micel bifora drih*ten* ⁊ winn ⁊ bear ne drinceð ⁊ gaste halge gifylled bið ðæt gett wæs in ionna moeder his 16. ⁊ monige suno israeles gicerrað to drih*tne* gode hiora 17. ⁊ he fore-gæð fore ðæm of mæhte helies ꝥte gicerre heorta wutuna in sunum ⁊ ða ungileoffulle to hoga-scipe soð-fæstra gigeorwiga drihtne folc wis-fæst 18. ⁊ cwæð zach*arias* to ðæm engle hwona ðis ic wito ic forðon am ald ⁊ wif min gifeol in dagum his 19. ⁊ ond-worde þe engel cwæð him ic am . . . seðe ic to-stondo bifora gode ⁊ sended am ðæt ic sprece to ðe ⁊ ðas ðe gibodige

20 And nu þu byst suwiende. ⁊ þu sprecan ne miht. oð þone dǽg þe ðas ðing gewurðaþ. forþam þú mínum wordum ne gelyfdest. þa beoð on hyra tíman gefyllede;

21 And ꝥ folc wæs zachariam geanbidiende ⁊ wundrodon ꝥ he on þam temple læt wæs;

22 Ða he út-eóde ne mihte he him to sprecan. ⁊ hig on-cneowon ꝥ he on þam temple sume gesihtðe geseah. ⁊ he wæs bicniende him ⁊ dúm þurh-wunede;

23 Ða wæs geworden þa his þenunga dagas. gefyllede wæron. he ferde to his huse;

24 Soðlice æfter dagum elizabeth his wíf ge-eacnode ⁊ heo bediglude hig fíf monþas ⁊ cwæð;

25 Soðlice me drihten gedyde þus. on þam dagum þe he geseah minne hosp betux mannum afyrran.

Ðis sceal on wodnes dæg to þam ymbrene ær mydda wyntran. Missus est angelus gabrihel. A. Missus est gabriel angelus a deo in ciuitatem galileæ. B.

26 Soþlice on þam syxtan monðe wæs ásend gabriel se engel fram drihtne on galilea ceastre. þære nama wæs nazaréth.

27 to beweddudre fæmnan ánum were. þæs nama wæs iosep. of dauides húse. ⁊ þære fæmnan nama wæs maria.

28 Ða cwæþ se engel ingangende. hál wes ðú mid gyfe gefylled. drihten mid þe; Ðu eart gebletsud on wifum.

29 þa wearð heo on his spræce gedréfed. ⁊ þohte hwæt seo greting wǽre;

Various Readings.

20. A. swygende; B. C. suwigende. A. geweorþað. A. heora. 21. A. ge-anbidigende ⁊ wundrigende. 22. A. gesyhðe. A. hym bycnigende. C. dumb. A. þurh-wunode. 24. A. diglode. 25. A. betweox; B. C. betwux. 27. A. be-weddadre. 28. A. ge-bletsod.

20 End nu abydst swigende. ⁊ þu spræken ne miht oð þanne dayg þe þas þing gewurðad. for þan þu mine worden ne lyfdest þa byð on heora timan ge-fylde.

21 And þæt folc wæs zachariam ge-abydende. ⁊ wundredon. þæt he on þæt temple ge-læt wæs.

22 Ða he ut-eode ne mihte he heom to spræcen. ⁊ hyo on-cneowen þæt he on þam temple sume ge-sihte ge-seah. ⁊ he wæs beacniende heom ⁊ dumb þurh-wunede.

23 þa wæs ge-worðen þa his þenunga dages ge-fylde wæren. he ferde to his huse.

24 Soðlice æfter dagen elisabeth his wif ge-eacnode. ⁊ hy be-dyglede hyo fif monðas ⁊ cwæð.

25 Soðlice me drihten ge-dyde þus on þam dagen þe he ge-seah mine hosp betwux mannen afyrran.

26 Soðlice on þam syxten monðe wæs a-send gabriel se engel fram drihtene on galilée cestre þare name wæs nazareth.

Missus est angelus gabriel a deo in ciuitatem galilee..

27 to be-weddedre femnen anen were þas name wæs ioseph of dauiðes huse. ⁊ þare femne name wæs mariam.

28 Ða cwæð se ængel ingangende. Hal wæsse þu mid gyfe ge-fylled. drihten mid þe. þu ert ge-bletsed on wifen.

29 þa warð hyo on his spræce ge-drefed. ⁊ þohte hwæt syo gretunge wære.

Various Readings.

20. Ǽnd; þu byst swugende; sprecan; þone; gewurdað; minum wordum; tima ge-fyllede. 21. Ǽnd; wundrodon; ge-let. 22. ge-sihtðe; becniende. 23. þegnunga dagas gefylle (*sic*). 24. dagum; ge-eacnede; bedyglude. 25. dagum; minne; manum. Rubric; *so also in* R. 26. Sixtan; ængel; castre þa. 27. femnan anum; dauides; femnan nama. 28. wes; eart ge-bletsod; wifum. 29. wearð; gretyng.

⁊ heono ðu bist suigende ⁊ ne mæge ðu gesprece oðð on doege of ðæm ðas geworðes fore
20 *ET ecce eris tacens et non poteris loqui usq*ue* in diem quo haec fiant pro * 3. x.

ðon ꝥte ne gelefdest ðu wordum minum ða ðe gefylled biðon on tíd hiora ⁊ wæs
eo quod non credidisti uerbis meis quae inplebuntur in tempore suo 21 et erat

ꝥ folc bidende ⁊ awundradon ꝥte hlattade he in temple eode uut*edlice*
plebs expectans zachariam et mirabantur quod tardaret ipse in templo 22 egressus autem

ne mæhte spreca to him ⁊ on-geton ꝥ ꝥte gesihðo gesege in temple ⁊ he
non poterat loqui ad illos et cognouerunt quod uisionem uidisset in templo et ipse

wæs becnende ðæm ł him ⁊ ðerh-wunade dumb ⁊ aworden wæs ꝥte gefylde weron ða dagas
erat innuens illis et permansit mutus 23 et factum est ut impleti sunt dies

embihtes his eode In hus his æft*er* ðas uut*edlice* dagas acende [ł] gebær wif
officii eius abiit in domum suam. 24 post hos autem dies concepit elisabet uxor

his ⁊ gedegelde hia moneðum fifo cuoeð for*ð*on sua dyde me driht*en* on dagum
eius et occultabat sé mensib*us* quinq*ue* dicens 25 quia sic fecit mihi d*omi*n*us* in dieb*us*

ðæm eft-beheald to nummanne telnise min bituih monnu*m* on monaðe uut*edlice* ða seista
quib*us* respexit auferre opprobrium meum inter homines 26 *IN mense autem sexto * III.

gæsended wæs s[e] angel from gode in galilie ceastra to ðær noma to hehstalde
missus est angelus gabrihel á deo in ciuitatem galilaeae cui nomen nazareth 27 ad uirginem

gewoedded ł fæstnad heh-stald ðære noma wæs of hus dauið ⁊ noma ðære hehstaldes
desponsata*m* †uirgo cui nomen erat ioseph de domo dauid et nomen uirginis monno + viro (*in margin, in late hand*).

⁊ in-foerde se engel to hia ł hire cuoeð hal mið gefea full drihten ðec mið
maria*m* 28 et ingressus angelus ad eam dixit haue gratia plena d*omi*n*us* tecum

gebloedsad ðu in wifum ða ł ðiu miððy geherde gedroefad wæs in word his ⁊
benedicta tú in mulierib*us* 29 quae cum audisset turbata est in sermone eius et

geðohte hulig ł hu*u* wæs ł were ðios groeteng
cogitabat qualis esset ista salutatio

---

20 ⁊ heonu ðu bist swigende ⁊ ne mæge ðu gispreaca oððe on dæge of ðæm ðes worðes for-ðon ðætte ne gilefestu wordum minum ðaðe gi-fylled bioðun in tide hiora 21. ⁊ wæs ðæt folc biddende ⁊ wundradun ðæt he laðade he in temple 22. eode wutudlice ne mæhte spreoca to him ⁊ ongetun ðæt gisihðe ðe gi-sege in temple ⁊ he wæs becnende him ⁊ ðerh-wunade dumba 23. ⁊ giworden wæs ꝥte gifylled wærun dagas embihtes his eode in hus his 24. æfter ðas wutudl*ice* dagas gicende . . . wif his ⁊ degelde hiæ monoðas fife cwæð 25. forðon swa dyde me driht*en* in dagum ðæm eft biheold to niomanne telnisse mine bitwih monnum 26. on monoðe wutudl*ice* ðæs sesta sended wæs engel . . . fro*m* gode in cæstre . . . ðære noma wæs . . . 27. to fæfne giweddad ł gifæstnad were ðæs noma wæs . . . of huse dauiðes ⁊ noma ðare hehstalde maria 28. ⁊ infoerde engel to hir cwæð hal mið gifeo full driht*en* ðec mið gibletsad ðu bitwih wifum 29. ða miððy giherde gidroefed wæs in worde his ⁊ giðohte hulig ł hu were ðios groeting

30 Ða cwæð se engel. ne ondræd þu ðe maría; Soðlice þu gyfe mid gode gemettest;

31 Soðlice nú þu on innoðe ge-eacnast. ⁊ sunu censt ⁊ his naman hælend genemnest;

32 Se byð mǽre ⁊ þæs hehstan sunu genemned. ⁊ him sylþ drihten gód his fæder. dauides setl.

33 ⁊ he ricsað on ecnesse on Iacobes húse. ⁊ hys ríces énde ne byþ;

34 Ða cwæð maria to þam engle. hu gewyrð þis forðam ic were ne on-cnáwe;

35 Ða ⁊swarode hyre se engel; Se halga gast on þe becymþ ⁊ þæs heahstan miht þe ofer-sceadað. ⁊ forðam ꝥ hálige ðe of þe acenned byð byþ godes sunu genemned

36 ⁊ nú elizabeth þin mǽge sunu on hyre ýlde ge-eacnode. ⁊ þe monað ys hyre sixta. seo is únberende genemned.

37 forþam nis ælc wórd mid góde únmihtelic;

38 Ða cwæþ maría her is drihtnes þínen. gewurþe me æfter þínum wórde. ⁊ se engel hyre fram gewat.

Ðys gebyrað on frige dæg to þam ylcan fæstene. Exsurgens autem maria. A. Exurgens maria abiit in montana cum festinacione. B.

39 Soþlice on þam dagum arás maria ⁊ ferde on munt-land mid ofste. on iudeisce ceastre

40 ⁊ eode into zacharías húse ⁊ grete elizabeth;

41 Ða wæs geworden þa elizabeth gehyrde marían gretinge. þa gefagnude ꝥ cíld on hyre innoðe; And þa wearð elizabeth halegum gaste gefylled.

Various Readings.

30. A. ge-metst gife myd gode. 31. A. cennest. 33. A. ryxað. A. ecnysse. 34. A. *om.* ic. A. wer. 35. A. ⁊swerede. B. C. halie. 36. A. B. mage. A. þes monað. A. sixta monoð. 38. A. ge-weorðe. 39. A. iudeiscre. 40. A. grette. 41. A. fagnode. A. halgum.

30 Ða cwæð se ængel. ne on-dræd þu þe Maria. Soðlice þu gyfe mid gode gemettest

31 soðlice nu þu on innoðe ge-eacnest. ⁊ sune censt ænd hys name hælend ge-nemnest

32 ⁊ se byoð mære. ⁊ þas heagestes sune ge-nemned. ⁊ hym sylð drihten god his fæder dauides setll.

33 ⁊ he rixad on echnesse on Iacobes huse. ⁊ his riche ænde ne beoð.

34 Þa cwæð maria to þam ængle hu gewurð þis for þan ich were ne on-cnawe.

35 Ða andswerede hyre se ængel. Se halge gast on þe be-kymd ⁊ þas heagestan mihte þe ofer-scæde. ⁊ for þan ꝥ halig þe of þe akenned byð; byð godes sune ge-nemned.

36 Ænd nu elisabeth þin mage sune on hire elde ge-echnede. ⁊ þes moneð is hire syxto sye is unberende ge-nemned.

37 for-þy nis ælch word mid gode unmihte-lic.

38 Ða cwæð MARIA. Her is drihtenes þinen. ge-wurðe me æfter þinen worde. ⁊ se ængel hire fram ge-wat.

39 Soðlice on þam dagen aras MARIA ⁊ ferde on muntlande mid efste. on iudeisse ceastre.

Exurgens … RIA abiit … montana c… festination…

40 ⁊ eode in-to zacharias huse. ⁊ grette elisabeth.

41 Ða wæs ge-worðen. þa helisabeth ge-herde MARIE gretinge. þa ge-fagene þæt chyld on hire innoðe. ænd þa warð elisabeth halgen gaste ge-fylled.

Various Readings.

31. naman halend. 32. heastes; setl. 33. rixsað; ecnysse; rice ende; bið. 34. engle; forðam ic. 35. becymð; þæs heahstan; ofer-scadeð; ðam; acenned; sunu. 36. ge-ecnade; monað; sixte seo. 37. ælc. 38. þine. RUBRIC; *so also in* R. 39. dagum; iudeisce. 41. geworden; elizabeth; gefagenede; cyld; and; wearð; halgum.

⁊ cuoeð se angel him ne ondred ðu maria gemoetest ðu *for*ðon gefea mið gode
30 et ait angelus ei ne timeas maria inuenisti enim gratiam apud d*eum*

heono ge-ecnande in inna ⁊ ðu accennes sunu ⁊ ge-ceige ðu noma his hælend ðes bið
31 ecce concipiens in utero et paries filium et uocabis nomen eius i*esum* 32 hic erit

micel ⁊ sunu ðæs heiste ge-ceiged bið ⁊ seleð him se driht*en* sedle dauiðes fadores his ⁊
magnus et filius altissimi uocabitur et dabit illi d*ominus* sedem dauid patris eius 33 et

he ricsað In hus iacobes in ecnisse ⁊ rices his ne bið ende cuoeð uut*edlice*
regnabit in domo iacob in aeternum et regni eius non erit finis 34 dixit autem maria

to ðæm engel huu worðes ðis *for*ðon wer ne conn ic ⁊ geonduearde se angel
ad angelum quomodo fiet istud quoniam uirum non cognosco 35 et respondens angelus

cuoeð him gaast halig of*er*-cymeð on ðeh ⁊ mæht ðæs heisto of*er*-wrigað ðe ⁊ for*ðon* ⁊
dixit ei sp*iritus* s*anctus* superueniet in te et uirtus altissimi abumbrabit tibi ideoquae et

ꝥte accenned bið halig bið geceid sunu godes ⁊ heono foereld ðin ⁊ ða acende
quod nascetur s*anctum* uocabitur filius d*ei* 36 et ecce elisabeth cognata tua et ipsa concepit

sunu on hældo hire ⁊ ðis moneð is ðe seista ðær ðiu ge-ceiged is un-bere[n]d ꝥte ł *for*ðon
filium in senecta sua et hic mensis est sextus illi quae uocatur sterilis 37 quia

ne bið un-mæhticlic mið god all ł eghuoelc word cuoeð ðon*ne* ' heono ðiwa
non erit inpossibile apud d*eum* omne uerbu*m* 38 dixit autem maria ecce ancilla

drihtnes sie me æft*er* word ðinu*m* ⁊ fearrade fro*m* hia se angel aras uut*edlice*
d*omi*ni fiat mihi secundum uerbu*m* tuum et discessit ab illa angelus 39 exurgens autem

on dagum ðæm foerde on morum mið oefeste on ceastre ⁊ in-foerde
maria in dieb*us* illis abiit in montana cum festinatione in ciuitatem iuda 40 et intrauit

in hus zachariæ ⁊ ge-groette ⁊ aworden wæs ꝥte he geherde groeting mariæs
in domum zachariae et salutauit elisabeth 41 et factum est ut audiuit salutationem mariae

gefeade se cild In inna hire ⁊ gefylled wæs halge gaste
elisabeth exultauit infans in utero eius et repleta est sp*iritu* s*ancto* elisabeth

---

30. ⁊ cwæð ðe engel him ne ondred ðu ðe ... ginimestu forðon gifea mið gode 31. heono giecnade in ionnaðe ⁊ ðu cennes suno ⁊ giceg ðu noma his hælend 32. ðes bið micel ⁊ suno ðæs hesta giceged bið ⁊ seleð him driht*en* god seðel dauiðes fædres his 33. ⁊ he rixað in huse iacobes in ecnisse ⁊ rices his ne bið ende 34. cwæð wutudl*ice* to ðæm engle huu worðes ðis forðon wer ne con ic 35. ⁊ ond-sworade ðe engel cwæð him gast halig ofer-cymeð on ðec ⁊ mæht ðæs hesta ofer-wrið ðec forðon ðætte acenned bið halig giceg bið sunu godes 36. ⁊ heonu ... ⁊ færeld ðin ⁊ ðio acende sunu on hælo hire ⁊ ðis monoð is ðe sesta ðer ðio giceged bið un-berend 37. ꝥte forðon ne bið unmæhtiglic mið gode eghwelc word 38. cwæð wutudl*ice* ... ðiowa driht*nes* sie mec æfter worde ðinum ⁊ feorrade fro*m* hir ðe engel 39. aras wutudl*ice* ... on dagum ðæm eode on moras mið oefiste on cæstre iudea 40. ⁊ infoerde in hus zacharies ⁊ gigroette ... 41. ⁊ aworden wæs ꝥte giherde groetinge maria ... gifeado ðæt cild in ionna hir ⁊ gifylled wæs gaste halgu*m*.

42 ⁊ heo clypode micelre stéfne. ⁊ cwæþ; Ðu eart betwux wífum gebletsod. ⁊ gebletsud ys þínes innoðes wæstm.

43 ⁊ hwanun is me ðis ꝥ mines drihtnes modor to me cume;

44 Sona swa þinre gretinge stefn on minum earum gewórden wæs. þa fahnude mín cild. on minum innoþe;

45 And eadíg þu eart ðu þe gelyfdest ꝥ fulfremede sýnd. þa ðing þe ðe fram drihtne geséde synd;

46 Ða cwæð maria min sawl mærsaþ drihten;

47 And min gast geblissude on gode minum hælende;

48 Forðam þe he geseah hys þinene eadmodnesse; Soþlice heonun-forð mé eadige secgað ealle cneoressa.

49 forðam þe me micele þing dyde se ðe mihtig is. ⁊ hys nama ys hálig

50 ⁊ hys mild-heortnes of cneoresse on cneoresse hyne ondrædendum.

51 He worhte [mægne] on hys earme. he to-dælde þa ófer-módan. On móde hyra heórtan;

52 He awearp þa rícan of setle. ⁊ ða eaðmodan up ahóf;

53 Hingriende he mid gódum gefylde. ⁊ ofer-móde idele for-lét;

54 He afeng israhel hys cniht. ⁊ gemunde hys mildheortnesse;

55 Swa he spræc to úrum fæderum abrahame ⁊ hys sæde on á woruld;

42 ænd hyo cleopede hludere stefne. ⁊ cwæð. Ðu ært be-twux wifen ge-bledsed. ⁊ ge-bletsed ys þines innoðes wæstme.

43 ⁊ hwanen is me þis þæt mines drihtenes moder scolde to me cume.

44 Sone swa þinre gretinge stefne on minan earen ge-worðan wæs. þa fagenede min chyld on minen innoðe.

45 Ænd eadig þu ert þu þe ge-lyfdest þæt fulfremede sinde þa þing. þe þe fram drihtene ge-saigde synde.

46 Ða cwæð maria min saule mersed drihten.

47 and min gast ge-blissode on gode minen hælende.

48 For þam þe he ge-seah his þinene eadmodnysse. Soðlice henen-forð me eadige seggeð ealle cneornesse.

49 for þam þe me mychele þing dyde se þe mihtyg ys. ⁊ his name is halig

50 ⁊ hys mildheortnysse of cneornisse. on cneornesse hine on-drædende.

51 He worhte mægne on hys earme. he to-dælde þa ofermode. on moda heora heortan.

52 He warp þa rice of setlle. ⁊ þa eadmode he up an-hof.

53 Hyngriende he mid gode ge-felde. ⁊ þa ofor-mode ydele for-let.

54 He afeng israel his cniht ⁊ ge-mynde hys mildheortnysse.

55 Swa he spræc to ure fæderen abrahame. ⁊ his sæde on a weorlde.

Various Readings.

42. A. betweox. A. gebletsod (*twice*); B. C. gebletsud (*twice*). 43. A. hwanen. A. moder ys to me cumen. 44. A. fægnode. 45. B. C. synt [*for* 1*st* synd]. 46. A. sawel. 47. A. ge-blyssode. 48. A. eadmodnysse. A. heonen-forð. A. segcað. A. cneoryssa. 50. A. myldheortnys. A. cneorysse (*twice*). 51. mægne *supplied from* Hatton MS.; *text and* A. B. C. *omit*. A. heora. 52. A. eadmodan. 53. A. Hyngrigende. A. fylde. 54. A. myldheortnysse. 55. A. fæder habrahame. A. weorold.

Various Readings.

42. cleopode; myclere [*for* hludere]; eart; wifum gebletsod; ge-bletsod; wæstm. 43. hwanan; drihtnes modor; *om.* scolde; come. 44. stefen; minu*m* earu*m* ge-worden; cyld; minu*m*. 45. eart; sint; drihtne gesægede siud. 46. sawul mærseð. 47. Ænd; minu*m* halendu*m*. 48. henon-; secgað; cneoresse. 49. mycele; nama. 50. myldheortnes of cneornesse. 51. ofermod; heorte. 52. wearp; rican; setle; eadmoden; ahof. 53. godu*m* ge-fylde; ofer-mode. 55. uru*m* fæderu*m*; aweorulde.

⁊ ge-ceigede stefn mið micla ⁊ cuoeð gebloedsad ðu bituih wifum ⁊ gebloedsad wæstm
42 et exclamauit uoce magna et dixit benedicta tú inter mulieres et benedictus fructus

Innaðes ðines ⁊ huona ðis me ꝥte cyme moder drihtnes mines to me heono *forðon*
uentris tui 43 et unde hoc mihi ut ueniat mater d*omi*ni mei ad me 44 ecce enim

aworden wæs stefn groetenges ðines In ear*um* minum gefeade In glædnisse se cild ł* In innað minu*m*
facta est uox salutationis tuæ in aurib*us* meis exultauit in gaudio infans in utero meo

⁊ eadigo ða ðio gelefde *forðon* ðerh-geendad biðon ða ðaðe ge-cuoeden sint him fro*m* drihtne
45 et beata quae credidit quoniam perficientur ea quae dicta sunt ei á d*omi*no

⁊ cueð wundriað ł *miclað** sauel min ðone driht*ne* ⁊ gefeade ł† gaast min in
46 et ait maria Magnificat anima mea d*ominu*m 47 et exultauit sp*iritu*s meus in

gode halwoende mine *forðon* eft-locade eðmodnise ðiuæs his heono *forðon* of ðisu*m* eadigo
deo salutari meo 48 quia respexit humilitatem ancillæ suae ecce enim ex hoc beatam

mec cuoeðað alle cneoreso *forðon* dyde me micło seðe mæhtig is ⁊ halig
me dicent omnes generationes 49 quia fecit mihi magna qui potens est et s*anctu*m

noma his ⁊ milt-heortnise his in soð cneoreso ⁊ cneoreso ondredendum hine dyde
nomen eius 50 et misericordia eius in progenies et progenies timentib*us* eum 51 fecit

mæht on arme his to-straegd ða of*er*hygdego mið ðoht heortes his to-sceaf ða mæhtigo of
potentiam in brachio suo dispersit superbos mente cordis sui 52 deposuit potentes de

sedle ⁊ ahof ða eðmodo ða hyngerendo gefylde mið godu*m* ⁊ ða weligo *for*leort ða idlo
sede et exaltauit humiles 53 esurientes inpleuit bonis et diuites dimisit inanes

ondfeng isr*ae*l cnæht his ꝥte were gemyndgad milt-heortnise his suæ gesprecen wæs
54 suscepit israhel puerum suum memorari misericordiæ suæ 55 sicut locutus est

to fadores usra ⁊ sēde his In worulde
ad patres nostros abraha*m* et semini eius in sæcula

* ł is added in red ink.
* ł miclað is added in red ink.
† ł is added in red ink.

---

42. ⁊ gicegde stefne micler ⁊ cwæð gibletsad ðu bitwih wifum ⁊ gi-bletsad wæstem ionnoðes ðines 43. ⁊ hwona ðis mec ꝥte cyme moder drihtnes mines to me 44. heonu forðon ꝥte aworden wæs stefn groetinge ðines in earum minum ⁊ giworðe glædnisse in ionnoðe minu*m* ðæt cild in gifea 45. ⁊ eadige ðaðe hia gilefde forðon ðerh-giendad bioðon ða ðaðe gicweden sint him fro*m* drih*tne* 46. ⁊ cwæð .... wundrað ł miclað sawel min drih*ten* 47. ⁊ gi-feade gast min in gode hal-wendo mine 48. forðon eft-locade eðmodnisse ðiowe his heonu forðon of ðissu*m* eodge mec cweoðas alle cneoreswo 49. forðon dyde mec micelo forðon mæhtig is ⁊ halig noma his 50. ⁊ mild-heortnisse his in soðe cneoreswo ⁊ cneoreswe ondreordun hine 51. dyde mæhte on eorme his tostrægd ofer-hygd mið ðohte heorte his 52. to-sceof ða mæhtgu of sedle ⁊ ahof ða eðmodu 53. ða hycrende gifylde mið godu*m* ⁊ ða welge forleort ða idlo 54. onfeng israhelum cnæhte his ꝥte were gimyndgad mild-heortnisse his 55. swa sprecende wæs to feder userne abrahamo ⁊ sede his oð to weorlde

Ðys gebyrað on myd-sumeres mæsse-dæg. Elizabeth autem impletum *est* tempus pariendi. A.

56 Soþlice maria wunude mid hyre swylce þrý monþas. ⁊ gewende þa to hyre huse;

57 Ða wæs gefylled elizabethe cenning-tíd. ⁊ heo sunu cende.

58 ⁊ hyre nehcheburas ⁊ hyre cuðan ꝥ gehyrdon ꝥ drihten hys mild-heort-nesse mid hyre mærsude. ⁊ hig mid hyre blissodon;

59 Ða on þa*m* ehteoþan dæge hig comon ꝥ cild ymsniþan. ⁊ nemdon hyne hys fæder naman zachariam.

60 Ða andswarode his modor nese soþes. ac he byð iohannes genemned;

61 Ða cwǽdon hig to hyre. nis nán on þínre mægðe þyson naman genemned;

62 Ða bicnodon hi to hys fæder hwæt he wolde hine genemnedne béon.

63 þa wrát he gebedenu*m* wex-brede; Iohannes is hys nama; Ða wundrodon hig ealle;

64 Ða wearð sona hys muð ⁊ hys tunge geopenod ⁊ he spræc drihten bletsiende;

65 Ða wearð ege geworden ofer ealle hyra nehcheburas. ⁊ ofer ealle iudéa munt-lánd. wæron þas wórd gewid-mærsode.

66 ⁊ ealle þa ðe hit gehyrdon on heora heortan settun ⁊ cwǽdon; Wenstu hwæt byð þes cnapa. witodlice drihtenes hand wæs mid him;

67 And zacharias his fæder wæs mid halegu*m* gaste afylled. ⁊ he witegode ⁊ cwæþ;

56 Soðlice Marie wunede mid hire swylce þreo monðes; ⁊ ge-wende þa to hire huse.

57 Ða wæs afelled elisabethe kenning-tyd. ⁊ hyo sune kende.

58 ænd hire nehcheburas ⁊ hyre cuðan þæt ge-herden þæt drihten hys mildheort-nysse mid hire mærsede. ⁊ hyo mid hire blisseden.

59 þa on þam ehtode daige hyo comon þæt chyld to embscniðen. ⁊ nemden hine his fæder name zachariam.

60 þa andswerede his moder nese soðes. ac he beoð Iohan ge-nemned.

61 Ða cwæðen hyo to hire. nis nan on þinre mægðe þisse name ge-nemned.

62 Ða cwæðen hyo to his fæder. hwæt he wolde hine ge-nemned beon.

63 þa wrat he ge-beðenen wexbrede Io-hannes ys hys name. Ða wundredon hyo ealle.

64 Ða warð sona hys muð ⁊ hys tunge ge-opened ⁊ he spræc drihten bletsiende.

65 Ða warð eige ge-worden ofer ealle heora nehchegeburas ⁊ ofer ealle iudea munt-land wæren þas worð wið-mærsede.

66 ⁊ ealle þa þe hyt ge-hyrdon on heore heorten setten ⁊ cwæðen. Wenst þu hwæt beoð þes cnapa; witoðlice drihtnes hand wæs mid hym.

67 Ænd zacharias hys fæder wæs mid halgen gaste ge-fylled. ⁊ he wito-gode. ⁊ cwæð.

Various Readings.

56. A. wunede. A. þreo. 57. A. cenninge-tyd. 58. A. nehhe-buras. A. myldheortnysse. A. mærsode. A. hy. 59. A. ehtoðan. A. ymb-snyðan. 60. A. C. moder. 61. C. hi. A. þyssu*m*. 62. A. hig. A. *om.* to. B. woldo (!). 63. A. wundredon. 64. A. bletsigende. 65. A. eall heora nehhe-buras. 66. A. setton. A. wenst ðu. A. dryhtnes. 67. A. halgu*m*. A. B. C. gefylled.

Various Readings.

56. þry. 57. afylled; heo. 58. ge-hyrdan; blissodon. 59. ehtoþan; cyld; ymsniðan; nendon (*sic*); fader naman. 60. modor; byð. 61. cwæden; naman. 62. becnedon [*for* cwæðen]; *om.* to; fader. 63. ge-bedenu*m* wexe-brede; wundrodon hie. 64. wearð. 65. wearð ege; hyora nehheburas; waron; wid-mærsede. 66. heora. 67. And; fader; halgu*m* galgu*m* gastum (*sic*).

ge-wunade uut*edlice* mið hia suælce monaðum ðriim ⁊ eft-cerde ł awoended wæs In
56 mansit autem maria cum illa quasi mensib*us* trib*us* et reuersa est in

hus his ðon*ne* gefylled wæs ðio tid acennise ⁊ acende sunu ⁊
domum suam 57 *Elisabeth autem impletum est tempus pariendi et peperit filium 58 et * IIII.

geherdon ða neheburas ⁊ ða cuðamen hire *for*ðon suiðe gemiclade se drih*ten* miltheortni*sse* his
audierunt uicini et cognati eius quia magnificauit d*ominus* misericordiam suam

mið hia ł ðær ⁊ efne-geðoncadon hir ⁊ aworden wæs on dæge ða æhtaðe cuomon to ymb-
cum illa et congratulabantur ei 59 et factum est in die octauo uenerunt circum-

cearfanne þone cnæht ⁊ ge-ceigde hine noma fadores his ⁊ geonduearde moder
cidere puerum et uocant eum nomine patris eius zacharia*m* 60 et respondens mater

his cuoeð ænigo*m* ðing ah ge-ceiged bið ioh*annes* ⁊ cuoedon to ðær ilca ꝥte ne ænig is
eius dixit nequaquam sed uocabitur iohannes 61 et dixerunt ad illam quia nemo est

in cyððo ðin seðe ge-ceiged ðisu*m* noma gebecnadon ðon*ne* feder his huoelcne wælde
in cognatione tua qui uocetur hoc nomine 62 innuebant autem patri eius quem uellet

ge-ceiga hine ⁊ ge-giuade wæx-bred arat cuoeð ioh*annes* is noma his ⁊ gewundradon
uocari eum 63 et postulans pugilarem scribsit dicens iohannes est nomen eius et mirati sunt

alle untyned wæs ðon*ne* sōna muð his ⁊ tunga his ⁊ spræcend wæs gebloedsade
uniuersi 64 apertum est autem ilico ós eius et lingua eius et loquebatur benedicens

god ⁊ aworden wæs ondo of*er* alle neheburas hiora ⁊ of*er* alle mor-londa iudæes
d*eum* 65 et factus est timor super omnes uicinos eorum et super omnia montana iudaeae

weron gemersad alle worda ðas ⁊ geseton alle ðaðe geherdon in heorta hiora
diuulgabantur omnia uerba hæc 66 et posuerunt omnes qui audierant in corde suo

cuoeðendo huæd woenes ðu cnæht ðes bið ⁊ bið hond driht*nes* wæs fo*ra* hine ⁊
dicentes quid putas puer iste erit et erit manus d*omini* erat coram illo 67 et zacharias

fader his gefylled wæs halge gaaste ⁊ gewitgade cuoðende ł cuoeð
pater eius impletus est sp*iritu* *sancto* et prophetauit dicens

---

56. giwunade wutudl*ice* .... mið hia swelce monoðas ðria ⁊ æfter giwendad wæs in hus his 57. .... ðonne gifylled wæs ðio tid acennisse ⁊ acende suno 58. ⁊ giherdun ða nehgiburas ⁊ ða cuðemen hire forðon swiðe miclade drih*ten* mildheortnisse his mið hia ⁊ efne-giðoncadun hir 59. ⁊ giworden wæs on dæge ðy æhtoða ꝥte comon ⁊ to ymbceorfanne ðone cnæht ⁊ cegdun hine noma fædres his .... 60. ⁊ giond-worde ðio moder his cwæð nænig ðing ah giceged bið .... 61. ⁊ cwedun to ðær ilca ne ænig is in cyððo ðinre seðe giceged ðissu*m* noma 62. ⁊ gibecnadun ðon*ne* fæder his hwelcne walde gicegan hine 63. ⁊ gigiowade onfeng wex-bredes ⁊ wrat cwæð iohannes is noma his ⁊ giwundrade werun alle 64. ontyned wæs ðonne sona muð his ⁊ tunga his sprecende wæs gi-bletsade god 65. ⁊ giworden wæs ondu ofer alle nehgiburas hiora ⁊ ofer alle morlond iudea ⁊ werun gimersad all word ðas 66. ⁊ setun alle ðaðe giherdun in heorte hiora cweðende hwæt woenestu cnæht ðes bið ⁊ forðon hond drih*tnes* mið hine 67. ⁊ .. fæder his gifylled wæs gaste halgu*m* ⁊ giwitgade cweðende

68 Gebletsud sí drihten israhela god. forþam þe he geneosode. ⁊ his folces alysednesse dyde;

69 ⁊ he ús hǽle horn arærde. on dauides huse hys cnihtes;

70 Swa he spræc þurh hys halegra witegena muð. þa he of worldes frymðe sprǽceon.

71 ⁊ he alysde us of urum feondum. ⁊ of ealra þara handa þe ús hatedon;

72 Mildheortnesse to wyrcænne mid úrum fæderum. ⁊ gemunan his halegan cyþnesse;

73 Hyne us to syllenne þone að. þe he úrum fæder abrahame swór.

74 ꝥ we butan ege of úre feonda handa alýsede him þeowian.

75 On halignesse beforan him. eallum urum dagum;

76 And þu cnapa byst þæs hehstan witega genemned. þu gæst beforan drihtnes ansyne. his wegas gearwian;

77 To syllenne his folce hys hǽle gewit on hyra synna. forgyfnesse;

78 Þurh innoþas úres godes mildheortnesse. on þam he ús geneosode of eastdǽle up-springende;

79 Onlihtan þam þe on ðystrum ⁊ on déaþes sceade sittað. ure fét to gereccenne on sybbe weg;

80 Soþlice se cnapa weóx. ⁊ wæs on gáste gestrangod. ⁊ wæs on westenum oþ þone dǽg hys æt-iwednessum ON ISRAHEL;

Various Readings.

68. A. Gebletsod. B. C. ge-neosude. A. alysednysse. 70. A. haligra. A. wuldres. 71. A. þæra. 72. A. myldheortnysse. A. wyrcanne; B. C. wyrcenne. A. halgan cyð-nysse. 73. A. syllanne. 75. A. halignysse. 76. A. wytegan. A. gegearwian. 77. A. syllanne. A. heora. A. for-gyfenysse. 78. A. myld-heortnysse. B. C. geneosude. 79. A. ge-reccanne. 80. A. æt-ywednyssum.

68 Ge-bletseð syo drihten israele god; for þan þe he ge-neosede. ⁊ hys folces alysendnysse dyde.

69 Ænd he us hæle horn arærde on dauides huse. hys cnihtes.

70 Swa he spræc þurh hys halgene witegene muð. Ða þe of weorldes fremðe spræken.

71 ⁊ he alesde us of uren feonden. ⁊ of ealre þare handen þe us hateden.

72 Mildheortnysse to werchen mid ure fæderen. ⁊ ge-munen hys halgen kyðnesse.

73 hyne us to sellene þanne að þe he uren fader abrahame swor.

74 þæt we buton eyge of ure feondon handen alesde hym þeowian.

75 on halignesse be-foran hym eallen ure dagen.

76 ⁊ þu cnapa gæst ⁊ beost þas heageste witega ge-nemned. Ðu gæst be-foran drihtnes ansiene hys wegas gearewian.

77 To syllene hys folce his halge ge-wit on hira synna for-gefenyssa.

78 Ðurh innoðes ures godes mildheortnyssa. on þam he us neosede. of eastdæle up-springende.

79 on-lihtan þam þe on þeostrum ⁊ on deaðes scade sitteð. ure fet to ge-reccenne on sibbe weig.

80 Soðlice se cnape weox. ⁊ wæs on gaste ge-stræncþed. ⁊ wæs on westene oð þanne dayg his atewednysse on israel.

Various Readings.

68. Ge-bletsed sy; þam; alysednysse. 69. End; cnihtas. 70. witegane; spræcen. 71. alysde; urum feondum; ealra þara handan; hatedon. 72. wyrcenne; urum faderum; halgan cyðnysse. 73. sillenne þonne. 74. butan ege; handan. 75. halignisse; eallum urum dagum. 76. best; heagasta; before; ansyne; wigas garwian. 77. syllenne; hale; forgyfenesse. 78. milheortnysse (*sic*). 79. ðystrum; sceade sittað. 80. cnapa; ge-strangod; westenum; þonne; ætywednysse.

se gebloedsad driht*en* god isr*ae*la fo*r*ðon gesohte ⁊ dyde lesnise ł lesing folces his
68 Benedictus d*ominus* d*eus* israhel quia uisitauit et fecit redemtionem plebi suae

⁊ ahof horn ł hælo us In hus dauiðes cnæhtes his suæ sprecend wæs ðerh
69 et erexit cornum salutis nobis in domo dauid pueri sui 70 sicut locutus est per

muðe haligwara ðaðe fro*m* worulde woeron ł sint witgena his hælo fro*m* fiondu*m* usu*m*
ós s*anct*orum qui a sæculo sunt prophetarum ei*us* 71 salutem ex inimicis nostris

⁊ fro*m* hond allra ðaðe laeðdon usic to doenne milt-heortnise mið fadorum
et de manu omnium qui oderunt nos 72 ad faciendam misericordiam cum patrib*us* nostris

⁊ gemyndga cyðnise his halges âð ꝥ gesuoren ꝥte gesuor to ab*raham* feder
et memorari testamenti sui s*anc*ti 73 ius-iurandum quod iurauit ad abraham patrem

usum walde gesealla hine hus ꝥte buta ondo of hond fionda usra gefreo*u*ad we se
nostrum daturum se nobis 74 ut sine timore de manu inimicorum nostroru*m* liberati

here we him on halignise ⁊ soðfæstnise bef*or*e hine allum dagum usum ⁊ ðu
seruiamus illi 75 in s*anct*itate et iustitia coram ipso omnib*us* dieb*us* nostris 76 et tu

cnæht witga ðæs heista geceiged bist ðu bef*or*e fæeres fo*r*ðon fo*r*e onsione drihtnes gearuiga wegas his
puer propheta altissimi uocaberis praeibis enim ante faciem d*omi*ni parare uias eius

to selenne wisdom hæles folce his In fo*r*gefnise synna hiora ðerh
77 ad dandam scientiam salutis plebi eius in remisionem peccatorum eorum 78 per

ðoht miltheortnise godes uses in ðæm gesohte usariseð of heh ł of heofnu*m* inlihte
uiscera misericordiae d*e*i nostri in quib*us* uisitauit nos oriens ex alto 79 inluminare

ðæm ðaðe in ðiostru*m* ⁊ in scua deaðes sittas to rehtanne foet usra In we sibb
his qui in tenebris et in umbra mortis sedent ad dirigendos pedes nostros in uia pacis

se cnæht ðon*ne* gewox ⁊ gestrenced wæs gaste ⁊ wæs In woest*er*n oðð on dæg
80 puer autem crescebat et confortebatur sp*iritu* et erat in deserto usq*ue* in diem

ædeaunise his to isr*ae*l
ostensionis suae ad israhel

---

68. sie gibletsad drihten god israhela forðon gisohte ⁊ dyde lesnisse folches his 69. ⁊ ahof horn hælo us in huse dauiðes cnæhtes his 70. swa sprecende wæs ðerh muð haligra witgana hiora ðaðe fro*m* weorlde werun 71. ⁊ alesde usih from fiondum usu*m* ⁊ of hondu*m* alra ðaðe usih læddun 72. to doanne mild-heortnisse mið fædru*m* usum ⁊ gimyndge cyðnisse his halges 73. að ꝥte giswor ł ꝥte gisworen bið to abrahame feder usum walde gisella us 74. ꝥte buta ondo of honda fionda userra gifriad were here we him 75. in halignisse ⁊ soð-fæstnisse bifora him allum dagum usum 76. ⁊ ðu cnæht witga ðæs hesta giceged bist.... forðon fora onsione drihtnes georwige woegas his 77 ⁊ to sellanne wisdom hælo folche hisi n forgefnisse synna hiora 78. ðerh giðoht mild-heortnisse godes uses in ðæm gisohte usihariseð of heofnum 79. in lihte ðæm ðaðe in ðiostrum ⁊ in scua deoðes sittas ⁊ to rehtanne foet usra in woege sibbe 80. ðe cnæht ðon*ne* giwox ⁊ gistrongad wæs in gaste ⁊ wæs in woestern oððe on dæge æt-eownisse his ⁊ israhelum

CHAPTER II.

Ðis sceal on mydde wyntres mæssenyht to þære forman mæssan. A. Exiit edictum a cessare augusto. B.

1 Soþlice on þam dagum wæs geworden
gebod fram þam casere augusto.
ꝥ eall ymbe-hwyrft wǽre to-mearcod;
2 Þeos to-mearcodnes wæs æryst gewórd-
en fram þam deman syrige cirino.
3 ⁊ ealle hig eodon. ⁊ syndrie férdon on
hyra ceastre;
4 Ða ferde iosep fram galilea of þære
ceastre nazareth. on iudeisce ceastre dauides.
seo is genemned bethleem. forþam þe he
wæs of dauides húse. ⁊ hirede
5 ꝥ he férde mid marian þe him bewed-
dod wæs. ⁊ wæs geeacnod;
6 So[þ]lice wæs gewórden þa hi þar
wǽron. hire dagas wǽron gefyllede ꝥ heo
cende.
7 ⁊ heo cende hyre frum-cennedan sunu.
⁊ hine mid cild-cláþum bewánd. ⁊ hine on
binne aléde. forþam þe hig nǽfdon rúm on
cumena huse;
8 ⁊ hyrdas wǽron on þam ylcan ríce waciende. ⁊ niht-wæccan healdende ofer heora
heorda
9 þa stód drihtnes engel wiþ híg ⁊ godes
beorhtnes him ymbe-scean. ⁊ hi him mycelum ege adredon.
10 ⁊ se engel him to cwæð; Nelle ge eow
adrǽdan. soþlice nu ic eow bodie mycelne
gefean. se bið eallum folce.
11 forþam to-dǽg eow ys hælend acenned. se is drihten crist on dauides ceastre;

CHAPTER II.

1 Soðlice on þam dagen wæs ge-worðen
ge-bod fram þan caisere auguste.
þæt eall ymb-hwyrft wære to-mærcod.
2 Ðeos to-mearcednysse wæs ærest ge-
worðen. fram þan deman syrige cyrino.
3 ⁊ ealle hyo eoden ⁊ syndrie ferden on
heore ceastre.
4 Ða ferde ioseph fram galilea. of þare
ceastre nazareht. on iudeissce ceastre.
dauiðes syo is ge-nemned bethléém. for
þan þe he wæs of dauiðes huse ⁊ hyrde
5 þæt he ferde mid marian þe hym ge-
wedded wæs. ⁊ wæs ge-eacnod.
6 Soðlice wæs ge-worðan þa hyo þær
wæren. hyre dages wæren ge-fyllede þæt
hyo kende
7 ⁊ hyo þa akende hire frum-kennedan
sunu. ⁊ hine mid cyld-claþen be-wand. ⁊
hine on binne alegde. for þan þe hyo
næfden rum on cumene huse.
8 Ænd heordas wæren on þam ylcan
riche wakiende. ⁊ niht-wæccen healdende
ofer heore heorda.
9 Þa stod drihtnes ængel wið hyo ⁊ godes
brihtnysse heom ymbe-scan; ⁊ hyo heom
mychel eige adredden.
10 ⁊ se engel heom to cwæð. Nelle ge
eow on-dræden. soðlice nu ich eow bodige
mychele blisse syo beoð eallen folce.
11 for þan to dayg eow is hælend akenned. se is drihten crist on dauiðes ceastre.

Exiit edictum a cesare augusto.

Various Readings.

Ch. ii. v. 1. A. agusto. C. to-mearcon(!). 2. A. to-mearcodnys. A. ærest. A. syrie. 3. B. C. hi. A. synderlice. A. heora. 4. A. bethleæm; C. behleem. 5. C. beweddon(!). 6. Solice *in text;* A. Soðlice; B. C. Soþlice. A. hig þær. A. heora. 8. A. wacigende. C. niht-wæcan. 9. A. B. C. ymbe-scan. A. hig. A. myclum. A. ondredon. 10. A. ondrædan. A. bodige.

Various Readings.

Ch. ii. v. 1. RUBRIC; *so also in* R. dagum; ge-worden. 2. to-mearcednys; ge-worden. 3. hyra. 4. nasareth; iudeysce; dauides seo; þam. 5. be-wedded. 6. ge-worden; wæron [*first time*]; cende. 7. heo; acende; -cennedan; -clæðum; næfdon; cumena. 8. hyordas wæron; rice waciende; -wæccon; heora. 9. engel; bryhtnys; mycen (*sic*); adræden. 10. eom; adræden; ic; mycelne ge-fean se bið eallum. 11. halend acenned; dauides.

CAP. II.

aworden wæs ðonne on dagum ðæm foerde bod from cessares august ꝥ gemercad were
1 *Factum est autem in diebus illis exiit edictum a cesare agusto ut describeretur * V.

all ymb-hyrft ðios . gemercong forma aworden wæs from under-cynige syries ⁊
uniuersus orbis 2 haec describtio prima facta est á praeside syriae cyrino 3 et

gaað alle ꝥ fore-ondetande weron ða syndrigo ł æl syndrio In his ceastra astag ðonne æc
ibant omnes ut profiterentur singuli in suam ciuitatem 4 ascendit autem et

iohannes of galilea from ceastre nazareth in Iudea ceastre dauiðes ðio is ge-nemned
ioseph a galilaea de ciuitate nazareth in iudaeam ciuitatem dauid quae uocatur bethlem eo

forðon were from hus ⁊ higo dauides ꝥte fore-ondete were mið befæstad him wif
quod esset de domo et familia dauid 5 ut profiteretur cum maria desponsata sibi uxore

berende aworden wæs ðonne miððy weron ðer gefylled weron ða dagas ꝥte acende ł accenned were
praegnate. 6 factum est autem cum essent ibi impleti sunt dies ut pareret

⁊ cende sunu his frumcende ⁊ mið cild-claðum bewand ⁊ eft-gebeg hine In
7 et peperit filium suum primogenitum et pannis eum inuoluit et inclinauit eum in

binnæ forðon ne wæs him stoue in gest-hus ⁊ ða hiorde woeron on lond ꝥ ilca
praesepio quia non erat eis locus in diuersorio 8. et pastores erant in regione eadem

wæccende ⁊ haldendo wacana næhtes ofer edo his ⁊ heono engel drihtnes
uigilantes et custodientes uigilias noctis supra gregem suum 9 et ecce angelus domini

s[t]od æt ł neh ðæm ⁊ berhtnise godes ymb-secan hia ⁊ ondreardon mið ondo miclo ⁊
stetit iuxta illos et claritas dei circumfulsit illos et timuerunt timore magno 10 et

cuoeð ðæm se engel nallað ge ondrede heeno forðon ic bodigo iuh ge-fea mið miclum ꝥ
dixit illis angelus nolite timere ecce enim euangelizo uobis gaudium magnum quod

bið allum folce forðon accenned Is us to dæg hælend seðe is crist drihten in
erit omni populo 11 quia natus est nobis hodie saluator qui est christus dominus in

ceastre dauiðes
ciuitate dauid

CAP. II. 1. worden wæs wutudlice in dagum ðæm foerde bod from casere agustos ꝥte gimercad were all ymb-hwyrft 2. ðios mercung forma giworden wæs from undercynige syrres cyreno noma wæs 3. ⁊ gað alle ꝥte fore-ondetende werun ða syndrige in his cæstre 4. astag ðonne .... of galilea from cæstre .... in iudea cæstre dauiðes ðio is ginemned .... hio forðon were of huse ⁊ higo dauiðes 5. ꝥte fore-ondette werun mið .... bifæsted him wif berende 6. aworden wæs ðonne miððy werun ðer gifylled werun ða dagas ꝥte acenned were 7. ⁊ cende sunu his frum-cennedne ⁊ ða mið claðum hine biwand ⁊ efne gibeg hine in binne forðon ne wæs him stowwe in gest-huse 8. ⁊ ða hiordas werun in londe ðæt ilce wæccende ⁊ haldende wacone næhtes ofer ede his 9. ⁊ heonu engel drihtnes stod æt ł neh ðæm ⁊ berhtnisse godes ymb-scean hia ⁊ ondreordun mið ondo miclum 10. ⁊ cwæð ðæm ðe engel nallað ge ondreda heonu forðon ic bodigo iow gifeo micelne ðæt bið allum folche 11. forðon acenned is iow to dæge hælend ðeðe is crist drihten in cæstre dauiðes

12 And þis tácen eow byð; Ge ge-metað
án cild hreglum bewunden. ⁊ on binne
aled;
13 And þa wæs fǽringa geworden mid
þam engle mycelnes heofonlices werydes
god heriendra ⁊ þus cweþendra;
14 Gode sy wuldor on heahnesse ⁊ on
eorðan sybb mannum godes willan;
15 ⁊ hit wæs gewórden þa ða englas to
heofene férdon. þa hyrdas him betwynan
sprǽcon ⁊ cwædon; Utun faran to bethleem.
⁊ geseon ꝥ wórd þe gewórden is. ꝥ drihten
ús æt-ýwde;
16 ⁊ hig efstende comon. ⁊ gemetton
marían ⁊ iosep ⁊ ꝥ cild on binne aled;
17 Þa hi ꝥ gesáwon þa on-cneowon hig
be þam wórde þe him gesǽd wæs be þam
cilde;
18 ⁊ ealle þa ðe gehyrdon wundredon be
þam þe him þa hyrdas sǽdon;
19 María geheold ealle þas wórd on
hyre heortan smeagende;
20 Ða gewendon ham þa hyrdas god
wuldriende ⁊ heriende on eallum þam ðe
hi gehyrdon. ⁊ gesáwon; Swa to him
gecweden wæs;
Ðys sceal on þone ehtoðan mæsse-dæg to myddan wyntra. Postquam consumati sunt dies octo. A. Postquam impleti sunt dies octo. B.
21 ÆFter þam þe ehta dagas gefyllede
wæron ꝥ ðæt cild emsnyden
wǽre. his nama wæs hælend; Se wæs
fram engle genemned. ǽr he on innoðe
ge-eacnod wǽre;

Various Readings.

12. A. on cyld. C. hrægl*um*; A. claþ*um*. 13. A. mycelnys heofenlices weredes. A. herigendra. 14. A. syg. A. heahnysse. 15. B. C. heofone; A. heofen*um*. A. Uton. 16. A. efestende. 17. A. hig [*for* hi]. B. hí; C. hi [*for* hig]. 20. A. wuldrigende. A. hig. 21. A. ymb-snyden; B. msnyden (1*st letter erased*).

12 And þis taken eow beoð. Ge findað
an chyld ræglen be-wunden. ⁊ on binne
aleigð.
13 And þa wæs færinge ge-worðan mid
þam ængle myceles heofenlices weredes god
heriendra. ⁊ þus cweðende
14 gode syo wuldor on heahnysse. ⁊ on
eorðan sibbe mannen godes willan.
15 ⁊ hyt wæs ge-worðen þa þa ængles to
heofene ferden. Þa heordan heom be-
tweonen spræcen ⁊ cwæðen. Vton faren
to bethléém. ⁊ ge-seon þæt word þe ge-
worðen ys. þæt drihten us atywede.
16 ⁊ hyo efstende comen ⁊ ge-metton marian ⁊ Ioseph ænd þæt chyld on binne aleigd.
17 Ða hyo þæt ge-seagen þa on-cneowen
hyo be þam worden þe heom ge-sæd wæs.
be þam chylde.
18 Ænd ealle þa þe ge-herden wundreden
be þam. þe heom þa heordes saigdon.
19 Maria ge-heold ealle þas word on
hire heorte smeagende.
20 Ða ge-wenden ham þa heordes god
wuldriende. ⁊ heriende on eallen þan þe
hyo ge-herden ⁊ ge-seagen. Swa to heom
ge-cweðen wæs.
21 ÆFter þam þe ehta dages ge-felde Postquam i pleti sunt di octo.
wæren ꝥ þæt chyld embsnyðen
wære. Hys nama wæs hælend. Se wæs
fram ængle ge-nemned ær he on innoðe
ge-eacned wære.

Various Readings.

12. *Æ*nd; tacen; byð; ge-metað [*for* findað]; cyld hrægl*um*; alegd. 13. faringe ge-worden; engle; heofonlices; herigendra; cweðendre. 14. eorðon; mann*um*. 15. ge-worden; englas; heofone; hyrdas; be-tweonan spræcon; cwædon; faran; ge-worden; ætywde. 16. efestende; cyld; alegd. 17. ge-sawon; þan; cylde. 18. geherdon wundrededen (*sic*); hyrdas sægdon. 19. ge-heald; heorten. 20. hyrdas; herigende; all*um* þam; ge-hyrdon; ge-sawon. 21. RUBRIC; *so also in* R. Efter; ge-fulde wæron; emsnyðen ware; engle; ge-eacnod.

⁊ ðis iuh tacon ł becon gie gemoetes iñ ꝥ cild mið cild-claðu*m* iñbewunden ⁊ gesetted in
12 et hoc uobis signum inuenietis infante*m* pannis inuolutum et positum in

binne ⁊ sona aworden wæs mið engle menigo hiorodes heofonlic hergendra god
praesepio 13 ET subito facta est cum angelo multitudo militiae caelestis laudantium d*eum*

⁊ cuoeðendra wuldor In heannisu*m* gode ⁊ In eorðo sibb monnu*m* gôdes willo
et dicentium 14 gloria in altissimis deo et in terra pax hominib*us* bonæ uoluntatis

aworden Is ꝥte fearradon fro*m* him ða englas in heofne ða hiorda ge-sprecon bituih
15 factum est ut discesserunt ab eis angeli in caelum *Pastores loquebantur ad inuicem * VI.

of*er*-fære we oðð in beth*leem* ⁊ ge-sea woe ðis word ꝥte aworden wæs ðætte dyde se drihten
transeamus usq*ue* in bethlee*m* et uideamus hoc uerbu*m* quod factum est quod fecit d*ominus*

⁊ æd-eaude us ⁊ cuomon oefistande ⁊ gemoeton ⁊ ⁊ ꝥ cild
et ostendit nobis 16 et uenerunt festinantes et inuenerunt maria*m* et ioseph et infante*m*

gesetted in binna gesegon ðon*ne* ongeton fro*m* word ꝥte cuoeden wæs ðæm
positum in præsipio 17 uidentes autem cognouerunt de uerbo quod dictum erat illis

fro*m* cnæht ðisu*m* ⁊ alle ðaðe ge-herdon awundrade woeron ⁊ from ðæm ða ðe acuoeden weron
de puero hoc 18 et omnes qui audierunt mirati sunt et de his quae dicta erant

fro*m* hiordu*m* to ðæm ilcu*m* ðon geheald alle worda ðas lædon in
a pastoribus ad ipsos 19 maria autem conseruabat omnia uerba haec conferent in

hearta his ⁊ eft-cerdon ł cerde weron ða hiorde wuldrigendo ⁊ hergendo god in allu*m*
corde suo 20 et reuersi sunt pastores glorificantes et laudantes d*eum* in omnib*us*

ðaðe geherdon ⁊ gesegon sua cuoeden wæs to him ⁊ æft*er* ðon ge-endad weron
quae audierant et uiderant sicut dictum est ad illos 21 *ET postquam consummati sunt * VII.

dagas æhto ꝥte ymb-corfen were ge-ceigd wæs noma his se hæl*end* ꝥte ge-ceiged wæs fro*m* engel
dies octo ut circum-cideretur uocatum est nomen eius i*esus* quod uocatum est ab angelo

aer ðon Inna ge-ecnad were
prius-qua*m* in utero conciperetur

---

12. ⁊ ðis is iow tacun ł becun ge gimoetas ðæt cild mið claðum biwunden ⁊ giseted in binne 13. ⁊ sona aworden wæs mengu .... heofun-lic hergende god ⁊ cweðende 14. wuldor in heonissum gode ⁊ on eorðo sibb monnum godes willa 15. ⁊ aworden wæs ꝥte feorradun fro*m* him ða englas on heofnas ða hiordas wutud-[*lice*] gisprecun bitwih him fære we oððæt in bethlem ⁊ gisea we ðis word ðæt aworden wæs ðætte drih*ten* æt-eowde iow 16. ⁊ comun ł cymende werun .... ⁊ .... ⁊ ðæt cild giseted in binne 17. gisegun ðonne on-getun fro*m* worde ðætte cweden wæs ðæm from cnæhte ðissu*m* 18. ⁊ alle ðaðe giherdun awundrade werun ⁊ from ðæm ðaðe cweden werun from hiordum to ðæm ilcum 19. .... ðonne giheold alle word ðas læddun in heorte his 20. ⁊ eft gicerdun ł cerende werun ða hiordas wuldrende ⁊ hergende god in allum ðaðe giherdun ⁊ gisegun swa acweden wæs to him 21. ⁊ æfter ðon giendad werun dagas æhtowe ꝥte ymb-corfen were ðe cnæht giceged wæs noma his hæl*end* ðætt gicweden wæs from engle ær ðon in ionna giecnad were

Postquam impleti sunt dies purgationis mariæ. B.

22 ⁊ æfter þam þe hyre clænsunge dagas gefyllede wǽron. æfter moyses ǽ. hi læddon hyne on hierusalem ꝥ hi hine gode gesettun

23 swa swa on drihtnes ǽ. awriten is; ꝥ ælc wæpned gecýnd-lím. ontynende. byð drihtne halig genemned;

24 And ꝥ hig offrunge seáldon æfter þam þe drihtnes ǽ. gecweden is. twa turtlan. oððe twegen culfran briddas.

25 ⁊ þa wæs án man on hierusalem þæs nama wæs simeon ⁊ þes man wæs riht-wís ⁊ oþ israhela frofor geanbidiende. ⁊ háli gast him on wæs.

26 ⁊ he andsware fram þam halegan gaste onfeng. ꝥ he deað ne gesawe. buton he ǽr drihten crist gesawe;

27 And on gaste he on ꝥ tempel cóm. ⁊ þa his magas læddon þone hælend. ꝥ hig for him æfter þære .ǽ. gewunan dydon.

28 he onfeng hine mid his handum. ⁊ god bletsode ⁊ cwæð;

29 Drihten. nu þu lætst þinne þeow æfter þinum worde on sibbe;

30 Forðam míne eagan gesawon þine hæle.

31 ða þu ge-earwodest beforan ansyne eallra folca;

32 Leoht to þeoda awrigenesse ⁊ to þines folces wuldre ISRAHEL.

Ðis sceal on sunnan dæg betweox mydde wintres mæsse-dæge ⁊ twelftan dæge. Erat ioseph & maria. A. Erat pater iesu & mater mirantes super his que dicebantur de illo. B.

33 Ða wæs his fæder ⁊ his modor wundriende be þam þe be him gesǽde wǽron;

22 Æfter þam þe hire clænsing-dages ge-felde wæren. æfter moyses lage. hyo lædden hine on ierusalem þæt hyo hine gode setton

Postquam i[...] pleti sunt d[...] purgationis Marie.

23 swa swa [on] drihtnes lage awriten ys. Ðæt ælc wæpnyd ge-cyndlym untynende beoð drihtenes halig ge-nemned.

24 ⁊ þæt hyo offrunge sealden. æfter þan þe drihtnes læge ge-cweðen is. twa turtlan. oððe twa culfran briddes.

25 Ænd þa wæs an man on ierusalem þas name wæs symeon. ⁊ þes man wæs rihtwis ⁊ mid israele frofren ge-anbadiende. ⁊ halig gast him on wæs.

26 ⁊ he andswere of þam halgen gaste on-feng. þæt he deað ne ge-seage buton he ær drihten crist ge-seage.

27 Ænd on gaste he on þæt tempel com. ⁊ þa his mæges læddon þanne hælend. ꝥ hyo for hym æfter þare læge ge-wunan dyden.

28 Heo on-feng hine mid hys handen. ⁊ god bletsede. ⁊ cwæð.

29 Drihten nu þu lætst þinne þeow æfter þine worde on sibbe.

30 for þam mine eagen ge-seagen þine hæle.

31 þa þu ge-gearwudest be-foran alre folce ansiene.

32 leoht to þeoda awrigenysse. ⁊ to þines folces wuldre israele.

33 Þa wæs hys fæder ⁊ hys moder wundriende be þam þe be hym ge-saigde wæren.

Erat pater [...] mini & mat[...] mirantes super his q[...] dicebantur [...] illo.

Various Readings.

22. A. hig (*twice*). A. ge-setton. 23. B. C. wæpnyd. A. gecynde-lym. 24. B. C. hi. 25. A. *om.* oþ. A. frofre. A. B. C. halig. 26. A. *om.* þam. A. halgum. B. C. onfenc. 28. A. *inserts* ⁊ *before* he. 31. A. earwodest; B. C. ge-earwudést. A. B. C. ealra. 32. A. awrygenysse. 33. A. moder wundrigende.

Various Readings.

22. RUBRIC; *so also in* R. Efter; ge-fullede wæron; éa [*for* lage]. 23. on *supplied from* R.; ǽ [*for* lage]; byð. 24. þam þe drihtne (*sic*) ǽ. gecweden; twegen culfran. 25. ⁊ oð israhele frofer. 26. andswære fram þam halgan; ge-sawe (*twice*). 27. And; magas; þonne halend; þære æ. ge-wunan dydon. 28. He; bletsode. 30. eagan ge-seawen. 31. ge-earwudest; ansyne ealra folce. 32. israel. 33. RUBRIC; *so also in* R.; fader; wundrigende; ge-sagde wæron.

⁊ æfter ðon gefylled wer dagas clænsunges his æft*er* ae lædon hine
22 et postquam impleti sunt dies purgationis eius secundum legem mosi tulerunt illum

in hierusalem sua auritten is in ae drihtnes ꝥte eghuelc he ł woepen-mon to-untynes
in hierusalem 23 sicut scribtum est in lege d*omi*ni quia omne masculin*um* adaperiens

hrif ł wom ł i*n*na halig drih*tne* ge-ceiged ⁊ ꝥte saldon geafa ł asægdnise æft*er* ꝥte
uuluam s*anctu*m d*omi*no uocabitur 24 et ut darent hostiam secundum quod

acuoeden is in æ tuoe turturas ł tuoge birdas culfras ⁊ heono monn wæs in
dictum est in lege par turturum aut duos pullos columbarum 25 et ecce homo erat in

hierusal*em* ðæm noma simeon ⁊ monn ðes soðfæs ⁊ ondredend wæs bīdend frofor isr*ae*la
hierusalem cui nomen simeon et homo iste iustus et timoratus expectans consolationem israhel

⁊ gaast halig wæs In him ⁊ ond-suere on-feng fro*m* gast halig ne gesege
et sp*iritu*s s*anctu*s erat in eo 26 et responsum acceperat á sp*iritu* s*anct*o non uisurum

he deað buta ær gesege gecorene drihtnes ⁊ cuom In gast In temple ⁊ miððy
se mortem nisi prius uideret *christu*m d*omi*ni 27 et uenit in sp*iritu* in templum et cum

in-lǽddon ðone cnæht hæl*end* aldro his ꝥte dydon æft*er* gewuna aes fo*re* hine
inducerent puerum *iesu*m parentes eius ut facerent secundum consuetudinem legis pro eo

⁊ he onfeng him on armu*m* his ⁊ gebloedsade god ⁊ cuoeð nu fo*r*letes [ł] fo*r*gefes
28 et ipse accepit eum in ulnas suas et benedixit d*eu*m et dixit 29 nunc dimittis

esne ðin la drih*ten* æft*er* word ðin on sibb fo*r*ðon gesegon ego min
seruum tuum d*omi*ne secundu*m* uerbum tuum in pace 30 quia uiderunt oculi mei

hælo ł halwoende ð[in] ꝥ ðu gearuades ær ł fo*re* onsione alra folca leht to
salutare tuum 31 quod parasti ante faciem omnium populorum 32 lumen ad

æd-eaunise cynna ⁊ wulder folces ðines isr*ae*l ⁊ wæs fader his ⁊ moder
reuelatione*m* gentium et gloriam plebis tuae israhel 33 et erat pater eius et mater

wundrando of*er* ða ðaðe gecuoeden weron fro*m* hi*m*
mirantes super his quae dicebantur de illo

---

22. ⁊ æfter ðon gifylled werun dagas clænsunge his æfter æ moyses læddun hine .... ꝥte asettun hine drihten 23. swa awriten is in æ drihtnes ðætte eghwelc wepenmon to-untynes hrif ł wombe halig drihten giciegeð 24. ⁊ ꝥte saldun gæfel ł asægdnis æfter ðætte acweden wæs in æ drihtnes twoege turturas ł twoege birdas culfra 25. ⁊ heonu mon wæs in .... ðæm noma wæs simeon ⁊ mon ðes soðfæst ⁊ ondredende biddende frofre israhelas ⁊ gast halig wæs in him 26. ⁊ ondswore onfeng fro*m* gaste halgu*m* ne gisæh he him deað buta ær gisege gicorone drihtnes 27. ⁊ com in gaste in temple ⁊ miððy inlæddun ældru his ðone cnæht ðe hæl*end* ꝥte dydon æfter giwuna æs fore hine 28. ⁊ he onfeng hine on eormas his ⁊ bletsade god ⁊ cwæð 29. nu forletes ł fo*r*gefes esne ðinne drihten æfter worde ðinum in sibbe 30. forðon gisegun ego mine hælo ðine 31. ðætte ðu gigeorwades bifora onsione alra folca 32. leht to æteowednisse cynna ⁊ wuldur folches ðines israhel 33. ⁊ wæs fæder his ⁊ moder his wundrende ofer ða ðaðe gicweden werun from hi*m*

34 And þa bletsude hig simeon ⁊ cwæþ to marian his meder; Loca nu þes is on hryre. ⁊ on æryst asett manega on israhel. ⁊ on tacen þa*m* ðe wið-cweden byð;

35 And his swurd þine sawle þurh-færð. ꝥ geþohtas sȳn awrigene of manegum heortum;

36 And anna wæs witegystre fanueles dohtor of asséres mægðe þeos wunude manigne dǽg. ⁊ heo leofode mid hyre were seofan gḗr of hyre fæmn-hāde.

37 ⁊ heo wæs wudewe oð feower ⁊ hund-eahtatig geara; Seo of þa*m* temple ne gewat. dæges ⁊ nihtes þeowigende on fæstenum ⁊ on halsungu*m*.

38 And þeos ðǽre tīde becumende drihtne andette ⁊ be hi*m* spræc eallu*m* þa*m* þe ge-anbidedon hierusalem alysednesse;

39 ⁊ þa hi ealle þing gefyldon. æfter drihtnes .ǽ. hi ge-hwurfon on galilea*m* on heora ceastre nazareth;

40 Soðlice ꝥ cild weox ⁊ wæs gestrangod wīs-domes full. ⁊ godes gyfu wæs on him.

41 ⁊ his magas ferdon ælce gere to hierusale*m* on easter-dæges freols-tīde.

42 ⁊ þa he wæs twelf wintre hy fōron to hierusale*m* to þan easterlican freolse æfter hyra gewunan.

43 And gefylledum dagum þa hig agḗn-gehwurfon. belāf se hælend on hierusale*m*. ⁊ his magas ꝥ nyston.

34 And þa ge-bletsede hyo symeon. ⁊ cwæð to marian hys moder. loca nu þes is on hryre ⁊ on arist ge-sett. manegre on israele ⁊ on taken þam þe wið-cweðen byð.

35 Ænd his sweord þine sawle þurhferð. þæt ge-þohtes seon awrigene of manegen heorten.

36 And anna wæs witegestre fanueles dohter of asseres mægðe. þeos wunede manigene daig ⁊ hye lefede mid hire were sefe gear on hire femnehade

37 ⁊ hyo wæs wudewe oð feower ⁊ hund-eahtetig geare. Seo of þam temple ne ge-wat daiges ne nihtes. þeowiende on fæstene. ⁊ on halsunge.

38 And þeos þare tide be-cumende drihtne andette ⁊ be hym spræc. eallen þan þe ge-an-bided-en ierusalem alysednysse.

39 ⁊ þa hyo ealle þing ge-feldon æfter drihtenes lage. hyo hwurfon on galilēē on hire ceastre nazareth.

40 Soðlice þæt chyld weox ⁊ wæs ge-stranged wisdomes full. ⁊ godes geue wæs on him.

41 ⁊ his mæges ferden ælche geare to ierusalem on eastre daiges freols-tide.

42 ÞA he wæs twelf wintre. hyo foren to ierusalem to þam east-erlicen freolse. æfter hyre ge-wunenen (*sic*). Cum factum esset iesus annorum duodecim.

43 ⁊ þa ge-fylleden dagen. þa hyo agen ge-hwurfon be-laf se hælend on ierusale*m* ⁊ hys mæges þæt nyston.

Various Readings.

34. A. bletsode. A. hyre [*for* hryre]. A. aset. A. B. C. manegra. 35. A. sweord. 36. A. wytegestre. A. wunede mænigne. A. lyfede. A. seofen gear. 37. A. wuduwe. A. -ehtatig. A. þeowgende. 38. A. alysednysse. 39. A. hig (*twice*). B. C. hyra. 41. A. geare. 42. A. hig. A. þa*m*. A. heora. 43. A. on-gean-.

Various Readings.

34. asett manegra; isræl. 35. Ænd; þurh-færð; syn; manegu*m* heortv*m*. 36. wytegystre; dohtor; wunode manigne dæg; heo leofode; sefen; of [*for* on]; femnhade. 37. heo; eahtatig geara; ⁊ [*for* ne]; þeowiendu*m*; fæst-enu*m*; halsungu*m*. 38. Ænd; sprac eallu*m* þa*m*; ge-an-bydedon. 39. gefyldon; æ [*for* lage]; ge-wurfon; galileam. 40. cyld; ge-strangod; gyfe. 41. magas; ælce; easter-dages. 42. *Same rubric in* R. foron; hierusale*m*; easterlican; hyore gewuwunen (*sic*). 43. End; ge-fylledu*m* dagv*m*; nysten.

⁊ ge-bloedsade him ⁊ cuoeð to moder his heono geseted is ðes on
34 et benedixit illis simeon et dixit ad mariam matrem eius ecce positus est hic in

gefælnise ⁊ erist monigra ⁊ on taco ƚ on becon ðæm wið-cuoeden bið ⁊
ruinam et resurrectionem multorum in israhel et in signum cui contradicetur 35 et

ðin ðæs ƚ his sauel ðerh of*er*-færeð suord ꝥte æd-eaud were ƚ woeron of monigum heortum smeaungas
tuam ipsius anima*m* pertransibit gladius ut reuelentur ex multis cordib*us* cogitationes

⁊ wæs Anna ðio witga dohter fro*m* folc Aseres† ðios gefealle on dagum monigu*m* † i. iacobes sunu
36 et erat anna prophetissa filia phanuel de tribu aser haec processerat in dieb*us* multis

⁊ lifde mið wer hire wintru*m* seofo fro*m* hehstald-had hire ⁊ ðios widiua oðð
et uixerat cum uiro suo annis septem á uirginitate sua 37 et haec uidua usque

wintro ⁊ hund-hæhtatih feouer ðio ne of-foerde fro*m* temple mið fæst*er*nu*m* ⁊ gebeadum
annos octoginta quatuor quae non descedebat de · templo ieiuniis et obsecrationib*us*

hērde næht ⁊ dæge ⁊ ðio ilca tīd of*er*-cuom ge-onditteð drih*tne* ⁊ sprecend wæs
seruiens nocte ac die 38 et haec ipsa hora super-ueniens confitebatur d*omi*no et loquebatur

of him allum ðaðe ge-biodon ƚ bidendo woeron lesing ƚ lesnis hier*usalem* ⁊ ꝥte ðerh-dedon ƚ geen-
de illo omnib*us* qui expectabant redemtionem hierusalem 39 et ut perfece-

dadon alle æft*er* ae driht*nes* gecerdon ƚ awoende woeron on gali*lea* in ceastre his
runt omnia secundum legem d*omi*ni reuersi sunt in galilæa*m* in ciuitatem suam

nazar*eth* se cnæht ðon*ne* awox ⁊ gestrencged wæs full mið snyttro ⁊ geafa godes wæs in
nazareth 40 puer autem crescebat et confortabatur plenus sapientia et gratia d*e*i erat in

ðæm ⁊ foerdon aldro his ðerh alle wintro in hier*usalem* on dæge symbeles eastres
illo 41 et ibant parentes eius per omnes annos in hierusalem in die solemni paschae

⁊ miððy aworden were wintra tuoelf stigendu*m* ðæm on hier*usalem* æft*er*
42 *Et cum factus fuisset annorum duodecim ascendentib*us* illis in hierusolimam secundum * VIII.

gewuna dæges halges ƚ symb*les* ⁊ miððy geendade weron dagas miððy eft-cerdon eft-wunade
consuetudinem diei festi 43 consummatis-que dieb*us* cum redirent remansit

se cnæht hæl*end* in hier*usalem* ⁊ ne cuðon aldro his
puer i*esus* in hierusalem et non cognouerunt parentes eius

---

34. ⁊ gibletsade hiæ simeon ⁊ cwæð to .... moeder his heonu giseted is ðes on gæfelnisse ⁊ erist monigra in israhelum ⁊ on becnum ðæm wiðcweden bið 35. ⁊ ðin ðæs ƚ his sawel ðerh-fæereð ⁊ sword ðætte æteowed were of monigum heortum smeunges 36. ⁊ wæs anna ðio witga dohter fanueles from folche aseres ðios gifeoll on dagum monigum ⁊ lifde mið wer hire winter siofune from hehstaldhade hire 37. ⁊ ðios widwe oððe winter hund-æhtetig ðio ne offoerde from temple mið fæstennu*m*. ⁊ gibeadum herde gode næht ⁊ dæg 38. ⁊ ðio ilca tid ofercom giondetade drihtne ⁊ sprecende wæs of him allum ðaðe biddende werun lesinge ƚ lesnisse .... 39. ⁊ ꝥte ðerh-dedun alle æfter æ drihtnes gicerdun ƚ woemde werun .... in cæstre his nazarenes 40. ðe cnæht ðonne awox ⁊ gistrongad wæs full mið snytrum ⁊ gefe godes wæs mið ðæm 41. ⁊ foerdun ældro his ðerh alle wintru in hierusalem on dæge symbles eastra 42. ⁊ mið aworden were wintru twelfe stigendum ðæm on hierusalem æfter giwuna dæges halges ƚ symbles 43. ⁊ miððy giendade werun dagas miððy eftcerdun eftwunade ðe cnæht hælend in .... ⁊ ne cuðun ældro his

44 wendon ꝥ he on heora gefére wǽre. Þa cómon hig ánes dæges fær. ⁊ hine sohton betux his magas ⁊ his cuðan.

45 ða hig hyne ne fundon hig gewendun to hierusalem hyne secende;

46 Ða æfter þrim dagum hig fundon hine on þam temple sittende on middan þam lareowum. hlystende ⁊ hi ahsiende;

47 Þa wundrodon hig ealle þe gehyrdon be his gleaw-scipe. ⁊ hys ⁊-swarum;

48 Ða cwæþ his modor to him; Sunu hwi dydest þu unc ðus. þin fæder ⁊ ic sarigende þe sohton;

49 Ða cwæð he to him. hwæt is ꝥ gyt me sohton. nyste gyt ꝥ me gebyrað to beonne on þam ðingum ðe mínes fæder synt;

50 Ða ne ongéton híg ꝥ wórd þe he to him spræc;

51 Ða ferde he mid him ⁊ com to nazareth. ⁊ wæs him under-þeod; And his modor geheold ealle þas wórd on hyre heortan smeagende;

52 And se hælend þeah on wísdome ⁊ on ylde. ⁊ mid gyfe. mid gode ⁊ mid mannum

CHAPTER III.

Ðis ge-byrað on sætern-dæg to æw-fæstene ær myddan wyn-tra. Anno quinto de-cimo. A.

1 Soðlice þam fifteoðan geare þæs caseres anwealdes tiberíí. begymendum þam pontiscan pilate iudéa-þeode. feorðan dæles ríca galilée herode. filippo his breþer feorðan dæles ríca. Iturie. ⁊ þæs ríces traconitidis ⁊ lisania abilíne feorþan dæles ríca.

Various Readings.

44. B. C. hyra. A. betweox; B. betwux. 45. A. gewendon. B. C. secynde. 46. A. hig acsigende. 47. A. B. C. wundredon. 48. A. moder. A. hwig. 49. A. þingon. A. synd. 50. A. ongeaton. 51. C. *om.* his. A. moder.

Cap. iii. v. 1. B. anwaldes. A. galileæ. A. philyppo. C. forðan [*2nd time only.*]

44 wende þæt he on heore ge-ferrede wære. Ða comen hyo anes daiges feor. ⁊ hyo hine sohte be-tweoxe his mæges ⁊ hys cuðan.

45 þa hyo hine ne funden; hyo ge-wenton to ierusalem hine sechende.

46 Ða æfter þreom dagen. hyo funden hine on þam temple sittende. on middan þam lareowan. hlystende ⁊ hyo axiende.

47 Ða wundredon hyo ealle þe ge-hyrden be his gleawscype; ⁊ his ændsweren.

48 Ða cwæð his moder to him. Sune hwi dydest þu unc þus. þin fæder ⁊ íc sarigende þe sohten.

49 Þa cwæð he to heom. hwæt is þæt gyt me sohten. nyste gyt þæt me ge-byred to beonne on þam þingen þe mines fæder synde.

50 Ða ne on-geaton hyo þa word þe he to heom spræc.

51 Ða ferde he mid heom ⁊ com to nazareth. ⁊ wæs heom under-þeod. And hys moder ge-heold ealle þas word on hire heorte smeagende.

52 Ænd se hælend þeah on wisdome ⁊ on ylde. ⁊ mid gyfe mid gode ⁊ mid mannen.

CHAPTER III.

1 Soðlice þam fiftendan geare þas caiseres an-wealdes tyberij. be-ginnenden þam pontiscen pilate iudea þeode. feorðan dæles rice galilée herode. philippe hys broder. feorðan dæles rice iturie. ⁊ þas riche traconitidis. ⁊ lisania abiline feorðan dæles rica.

Anno quinto decimo tyber cesaris.

Various Readings.

44. wenden; hyra gefere; dæges fær; *om.* hyo; sohton be-tweox; magas. 45. ge-wendon; secynde. 46. ðrim dagum; fundon; lareowum; hi ahsiende. 47. ge-hyrdon; glewscype; andswarum. 48. modor; Sunu; sohton. 49. sohton; ge-byreð; synt. 51. heortan. 52. mannum.

Cap. iii. v. 1. *Same Rubric in* R. fifteoðan geara; beginnendum; feorðon; rica; filippon; broðor feorðes; rices [*for* rice]; rices [*for* riche].

woendon uutedlice hine ꝥte were hia mið fylgende cuomon geong dæges ⁊ eft sohton
44 existimantes autem illum esse in comitatu uenerunt iter diei et requirebant

hine betuih freondo ⁊ cuðo ⁊ ne gemoeton gecerdon ɫ gecerde woeron in hierus*alem*
eum inter cognatos et adnotos 45 et non inuenientes reuersi sunt in hierusalem

eft-sohton hine ⁊ aworden wæs æfter ðriim dogr*um* gemoeton hine on temple sittende on
requirentes eum 46 et factum est post triduum inuenerunt illum in templo sedentem in

middum ðara laraua herende hine ⁊ fraegnende astylton ðon alle ðaðe hine
medio doctorum audientem illos et interrogantem 47 *Stupebant autem omnes qui eum * 4. ii. mt. lxii. mr. xiii.

geherdon of*er* snytro ɫ hogoscip ⁊ ondsuearu*m* his ⁊ gesegon awundrade woeron ⁊ cueð
audiebant super prudentia et responsis eius 48 et uidentes ammirati sunt *Et dixit * 5. x.

ðio moder to hine la sunu huætd dydest ðu us heono fæder ðin ⁊ ic mænende we sohton ðec
mater ad illu*m* filii quid fecisti nobis ecce pater tuus et ego dolentes quaerebamus te

⁊ cuoeð to him huæd is ꝥte mec gie sohton ne cuðugie ꝥte in ðæm ðaðe fadores
49 et ait ad illos quid est quod me quaerebatis nesciebatis quia in his quae patres (*sic*)

mines sint gerisenlic me to wosanne ⁊ ða ne on-cneaun word ꝥte sprecend wæs to
mei sunt oportet me esse 50 et ipsi non intellexerunt uerbum quod locutus est ad

him ⁊ of-stag mið him ⁊ cuom to naza*reth* ⁊ wæs under-ðioded him ⁊ moder his
illos 51 et descendit cum eis et uenit nazareth et erat subditus illis et mater eius

geheælde ɫ gehaelde alle worda ðas in hearta his ⁊ se hæl*end* gewox mið snytro ⁊ ældo
conseruabat omnia uerba haec in corde suo 52 et i*esus* proficiebat sapientia [et] aetate

⁊ wuldur mið god ⁊ monnu*m*
et gratia apud d*eum* et homines

CAP. III.

ger ðon*ne* ðio fifteiðe hæses wæs scire-monn iudeas
1 *Anno autem quinto decimo imperii tiberii caesaris procurante pontio pilato iudaea * VIIII. [6. iii. mt. uii. io. ii. xxu.]

ðon*ne* broðere his ⁊
tetrarcha autem galilaeae herode philippo autem fratre eius tetrarcha itureae et trachonitidis

londes
regionis et lissaniae abilinae tetrarcha

---

44. woendun wutudl*ice* hine ꝥ he were hiæ mið fylgende comun gonga dæges ⁊ eftsohtun hine bitwih freonde ⁊ cyððo 45. ⁊ ne gimoettun gicerde werun in .... eftsohtun hine 46. ⁊ aworden wæs æfter ðrim dogru*m* gimoetun hine in temple sittende in middum ðara larwara herende hine ⁊ fregnende hine 47. astyltun ðonne alle ðaðe hine giherdun ofer snytro ⁊ ondsworum his 48. ⁊ gisegun awundrade werun ⁊ cwæð ðio moder his to him la sunu hwæt dydestu us swa heonu fæder ðin ⁊ ic mænende sohtun ðec 49. ⁊ cwæð to him hwæt is ðætte mec gisohtun ne cuðon ge ðæte in ðæm fædras mine sindun girisenlic me to wosanne 50. ⁊ ða ne oncneowun word ðætte sprecende wæs to him 51. ⁊ astag mið him ⁊ com to naza*reth* ⁊ wæs under-ðioded him ⁊ moder his gihælde alle word ðas in heorte his 52. ⁊ ðe hæl*end* giwox mið snytru ⁊ ældu ⁊ wuldur mið god ⁊ alle

Cap. III. 1. ger ðonne ðe fifteg ða he wæs tiberis ðæs caseres wæs sciremon .... iudea .... soðliche .... ðon*ne* broðer his .... ⁊ .... londes ....

2 under ðara sacerda ealdrum anna ⁊ caifā. godes word wæs geworden ofer zacharias sunu on westene

3 ⁊ he cōm into eall iordanes rīcæ bodiende dæd-bōte fulluht. ⁊ synna forgyfenesse.

4 swa hit awriten ys on isaias bec þæs witegan; Clypiende stēfen on westene. gegearwiað drihtnes weg. doð his siðas rihte;

5 Ælc denu bið gefylled. ⁊ ælc munt ⁊ beorh byð genyðerud. ⁊ þwuru beoð on gerihte. ⁊ ungerydu on smēðe wegas.

6 ⁊ ælc flæsc gesihð godes hǣle;

7 Soþlice he cwæð to þa*m* menegu*m* þe fērdon ꝥ hi wæron gefullode fra*m* him. eala næddrena cynn hwa æt-ywde eow ꝥ ge fleon fra*m* þam towerdan yrre;

8 Doð geornlice dæd-bōte wæst-mas ⁊ ne ongynne ge cweðan. we habbað us to fæder abraha*m*; Ic secge eow. ꝥ god is swa mihtig ꝥ he mæg of þysu*m* stānu*m* abrahames bearn aweccan;

9 Nu is seo æx asett. to ðæs treowes wyrtruman. witodlice ælc treow þe ne bryncð godne wæs[t]m. bið for-corfen ⁊ on fȳr aworpen;

10 Þa ahsodon hyne þa menegu ⁊ cwædon. hwæt do we;

11 Ða cwæð he to him. se þe hæfð twa tunecan sylle þam þe næfð. ⁊ þam gelice dō se þe mettas hæfþ;

2 under þare sacerde ealdres anna ⁊ chaifa. godes word wæs ge-worðan ofer zacharias sune on westene.

3 ⁊ he com into eall Iordanes riche bodiende. deadbote fulluht ⁊ synne for-gyfenesse

4 swa hit awriten ys on ysaias bech þas witegan. Clepiende stefn on westene. gegarewiað drihtenes weig dod his siðas rihte.

5 Ælch dane beoð ge-feld. ⁊ ælch munt ⁊ beorh beoð ge-niðered. ⁊ þwuru beoð on ge-rihte. ⁊ ungerydu on smeðe weges.

6 ⁊ ælc flæsc ge-sihð godes hæle.

7 Soðlice he cwæð to þam mægen þe ferden þæt hyo wæren fullode fram hym. Eale næddrene kyn hwa atewedo (*sic*) eow þæt ge fleon fram þam towearde eorre.

8 Doð eornestlice deadbote wæstmes. ⁊ ne on-ginnen ge cweðen. we hæbbed us to fader abraham. Ich segge eow þæt god is swa mihtig þæt he maig of þisen stanen abrahames bearn aweccan.

9 Nu ys syo æx asett. to þas treowas wirtrumen. Witodlice ælch treow þe ne brincd godne wæstme beoð for-corfan ⁊ on fyr aworpen.

10 Ða axoden hine þa manige ⁊ cwæðen; hwæt do we.

11 Þa cwæð he to heom. se þe hafð twege tunekan. sylle þam þe næfð. ⁊ þam ge-lice do se þe metes hæfð.

Various Readings.

2. A. þæra. A. westenne. 3. A. B. C. rice. A. bodigende. A. forgifenysse. 4. A. ysaies. A. B. C. Clypiendes stefn. A. westenne. 5. A. ge-nyðerod. A. þweoru. 6. A. hælo. 7. A. mænegu*m*. A. B. C. hig. A. *inserts* ge *after* eala. B. C. cyn. A. to-weardan. 8. A. *inserts* weorðlice *after* geornlice. C. gos [*sic; for* god]. A. þyssu*m*. 9. A. aset. A. bringð. A. B. wæstm; C...stm. 10. A. acsedon. A. mænegeo.

Various Readings.

2. þara sacerda; caifa; ge-worden. 3. rice; dædbote; forgyfenysse. 4. bec; witegen. Cleopiendes; drihtnes; doð. 5. Ælc; bið ge-fylled; ælc; byð ge-nyðered. 7. mægu*m*; ferdon; ge-fullode; cyn; ætywde; toweardo yrre. 8. geornlice [*for* eornestlice]; dædbote wæstmas; hæbbeð; fæder; Ic; mæg; þisum stanu*m*; bern. 9. treowes wyrtruman; ælc; brincð; wæstm byð. 10. mænge; cwaðen. 11. tuneken.

under aldormon*num* sac*erdum* ⁊ aworden wæs word drih*ten* of*er* ioh*anne*
2 sub principib*us* sacerdotum anna et caipha factum est uerbum d*omi*ni super iohannen

sunu on west*ern* ⁊ cuom on alle lond bodade ꝥ ful-wiht
zachariae filium in deserto 3 *Et uenit in omnem regionem iordanis praedicans baptism*um* * 7. i. mt. uiii. mr. ii. io. x.

hreaunise in f*or*gefnise synna sua awritten is in boc worda
paenitentiae in remisionem peccatorum 4 sicut scribtum est in libro sermonum esaiae

ðæs witges stefn cliopende on woest*ern* gearuað woeg drih*tnes* rehto wyrcas geongæs his eghuelc
prophetæ uox clamantis in deserto parate uiam d*omi*ni rectas facite semitas eius 5 omnis

pæð ł dene gefylled bið ⁊ eghuelc mor ⁊ hyll ge-beged bið ⁊ biðon un-ræhto ł woh in geongo*m* ⁊
uallis implebitur et omnis mons et collis humiliabitur et erunt praua in directa et

roeðo on woegu*m* smoeðu*m* ⁊ geseað eghuelc lichoma haluende godes cuoeð forðon to
aspera in uias planas 6 et uidebit omnis caro salutare dei 7 *Dicebat ergo ad * 8. u. mt. x.

ðread ðaðe foerdon ꝥte hia wero gefuluad fro*m* him cynna æterna hua eauað iuh
turbas quae exiebant ut baptizarentur ab ipso genimina uiperaru*m* quis ostendit uobis

geflea fro*m* tocymenda wraðe wyrcað f*or*ðon wæstm wyrðe to hreau*u*nise ⁊ ne beginnes cuoeða
fugire a uentura ira 8 facite ergo fructus dignus (*sic*) paenitentiae et ne coeperetis dicere

fader we habbað ic cueðo f*or*ðon iuh ꝥte mæge god fro*m* stanu*m* ðisu*m* awecce
patrem habemus abraham dico enim uobis quia potest d*eus* de lapidib*us* istis suscitare

sunu soðlice f*or*ðon acasa to wyrtruma treuana geseted is eghuelc f*or*ðon treeo ne
filios abrahae 9 iam enim securis ad radicem arboru*m* posita est omnis ergo arbor non

doeð wæstm ofcorfen bið ⁊ on fyr gesended ⁊ gefrugnon hine ðæt folc ł ða ðreatas
faciens fructum excidetur et in ignem mittitur 10 *Et interrogabant eum turbae * 9. x.

cuoeðendo huæd f*or*ðon we doað onduarde ða cuoeð him seðe hæfeð tuege cyrtlas
dicentes quid ergo faciemus 11 respondens autem dicebat illis qui habet duas tunicas

seleð ne ł ðæm næbbende ⁊ seðe hæfeð metto gelic doað
det non habenti et qui habet escas similiter faciat

---

2. under aldormonnum sacerda .... ⁊ .... aworden wæs word drihtnes ofer ioh*anne* .... ⁊ suno on woestenne 3. ⁊ com in alle lond bodade ðæt fulwiht hreownisse in forgefnisse synna 4. swa awriten is on bocum worda essaies ðæs witga stefn cliopende on woestenne georwigas woeg drih*t*nes rehte wyrcas stige his 5. eghwelc pæð ł dene gifylled bið ⁊ alle moras ⁊ hyll gibeged bioðon ⁊ bioðon unrehte ł woh in gongum. ⁊ roeðe on woege smoeðum 6. ⁊ giseað eghwelc lichoma halwendo godes 7. cwæð forðon to ðæm ðreote ðaðe foerdun ꝥte hie gifulwad were from him cynn æterne hwelc æteoweð iow gifleane from tocymende wraðra 8. wyrcað forðon wæstim wyrðne to hreownisse ⁊ ne biginnes cweoða fæder we habbas .... ic cwæðo forðon iow ðætte mægen is godes from stanum ðissum awecca sunu abrahames 9. soðlice forðon acase to wyrtruma treona giseted is eghwelc forðon treo ne does wæstim godne ðe of-corfen bið ⁊ on fyr sended 10. ⁊ gifrugnun hine ðe ðreot cweðende hwæt forðon doað we 11. ondworde ða cwæð him seðe hæfes twoege cyrtlas seleð ðæm næbbende ⁊ seðe hæfeð mett gilic doe ł wyrce

12 Ða comon þa mánfullan ꝥ hig aþwegene wæron. ⁊ cwǽdon to him. lareow hwæt do we;

13 Þa cwæð he ne do ge naht mare þon*ne* ꝥ eow geset is;

14 Ða ahsodon hine þa cempan ⁊ cwædon. ⁊ hwæt do we; Ða sǽde he him. ne sleage nanne; Ne tále ne doð. ⁊ beoð eð-hylde on eowrum andlyfenum;

15 Soðlice þam folce wenendum ⁊ eallu*m* on hyra heortan þencendum be iohanne hwæþer he crist wære;

16 Ða ⁊swarude iohannes him. eallu*m* secgende; Witodlice ic eow on wætere fullige; Soþlice cymð strengra þon*ne* ic. þæs ic ne eom wyrþe ꝥ ic hys sceo-þwancg ún-cnytte; He eow fullað on halgu*m* gaste ⁊ on fýre;

17 ⁊ his fann ys on his handa. ⁊ he feormað his bernes flóre. ⁊ gaderað hys hwǽte into his berne. ꝥ ceaf he for-bærnþ. on unácwencedlicu*m* fýre;

18 Manega oðre þing bodigende he ꝥ folc lǽrde;

19 Herodes se feorðan dæles ríca. þa he wæs fra*m* him geðread. be ðære herodiadiscan hys broðor wife. ⁊ be eallu*m* yfelu*m* þe herodes dyde;

20 ⁊ ofer eall ꝥ ge-icte ꝥ he be-clysde iohanne*m* on cwearterne;

21 Soðlice wæs geworden þa eall ꝥ folc wæs gefullod. ⁊ þa*m* hælende gefulledum ⁊ gebiddendu*m*. heofon wæs ge-openud

Various Readings.

14. A. acsedon. C. *repeats* ⁊ cwædon. A. nænne. A. stale [*for* tale]. 15. A. heora. 16. A. B. C. ⁊swarode. A. -þwang. 17. A. berenes. A. berene. A. *om.* on. 19. A. broðer. B. broður; C. broþur. C. yfellu*m*. 20. A. ꝥ he geycte. B. C. cwerterne. 21. A. wæs eall gefullad. A. ge-fullodu*m*. A. heofen. A. ge-openod.

12 Ða comen þa manfulle þæt hy aþwegene wæren. ⁊ cwæðen to hym lareow hwæt do we.

13 Þa cwæð he ne do ge naht mare þanne þæt eow ge-sett ys.

14 Ða axoseden (*sic*) hine þa cempan ⁊ cwæðen. ⁊ hwæt do we. Þa sæde he heom. ne sla ge nanne man. Ne tále ne doð. ⁊ beoð eð-healde on eowren andlyfenum.

15 Soðlice þam folce wenenden ⁊ eallen on heore heorten þencenden be Iohanne hwæder he crist wære.

16 Ða andswerede Iohannes heom eallen seggenden. Witodlice ic eow an watere fullige. Soðlice kymð strengre þanne ich; þas ich nem wurðe þæt ich hys scoþwang un-cnytte. Heo eow fulled on halgen gaste. ⁊ on fyre.

17 ⁊ his fann is on his handa. ⁊ he fermed hys bernes flore. ⁊ gadered hys hwæte in-to hys berne. þæt chæf he for-bernð on un-acwenctelice fyre.

18 Manega oðre þing bodiende. He þæt folc lærde.

19 Herodes se feorðan dæles rica þa he wæs fram him ge-þread. be þare herodiscan his broder wife ⁊ be eallen yfelen þe herodes dyde.

20 ⁊ ofer eall þæt ge-icte þæt he be-clysde Iohanne on cwarterne.

21 Soðlice wæs ge-worðan þa eall þæt folc wæs ge-fullod. ⁊ þam hælende ge-fulloden ⁊ ge-biddenden. heofene wæs ge-opened

Various Readings.

12. comon; manfullan; hyo. 13. þonne; ge-set. 14. ahsodon; cwæðon; sleage nanne (*sic*); *om.* man; eðealde; eowrum. 15. wenendu*m*; eallum; heora heortu*m* þencendu*m*; hweðer. 16. eallu*m* seggendu*m*; on wætere; cymð; þo*n*ne ic; ic næm; ic is (*sic*); He; fulloð; halgu*m*. 17. feormað; gaderað; ceaf; for-bærnð; unacwencendlice. 18. bodigende. 19. broðor; allu*m*. 20. iohanne*m*; cwærterne. 21. ge-worden; ge-fullodu*m* ge-biddendu*m*.

cuomon ða ⁊ bærsyn*nigo* ꝥte weron gefuluad ⁊ cuoedon to him la laruu huæd
12 uenerunt autem et publicani ut baptizarentur et dixerunt ad illum magister quid

we gedoað soð he cueð to him noht *for*ðor ðon*ne* ꝥ gesetted is iuh gie doað
faciemus 13 at ille dixit ad eos nihil amplius quam constitutum est uobis faciatis

frugnon ðon*ne* hine ⁊ cempo cuedon huæd doað we æc us ⁊ cuoeð him ne aenig mon*n*
14 interrogabant autem eum et milites dicentes quid faciemus et nos et ait illis neminem

gedroefað gie ⁊ ne telnise ł sceoma gedoað ⁊ ðæm wosað nestu*m* iurom miððy wōende
concutiatis neq*ue* calumnia*m* faciatis et contenti estote stipendiis uestris 15 existimante

ðon*ne* ꝥ folc ⁊ smeandu*m* allum in heortu*m* hiora fro*m* ioh*anne* eaða mage he were crist
autem populo et cogitantib*us* omnib*us* in cordib*us* suis de iohanne ne forte ipse esset *christus*

onduarde ioh*annes* cuoeð allum Ic æc soð of ł fro*m* wætre ic fulua iuh cymeð ðon*ne* strongra
16 respondit iohannes dicens omnib*us* *Ego quidem aqua baptizo uos ueniet autem fortior * 10. i. mt. xi. mr. iiii. io. ui.

mec ðæs ne am ic wyrðe to unbindanne ðuongas sceoea his he iuih gefuluað in
me cuius non sum dignus soluere corrigiam calciamentorum eius ipse uos baptizabit in

gast hal*ig* ⁊ mið fyr his fonnæ ł windgefon*næ* in hond his ⁊ clænseð ber-ern ł bereflor
sp*iritu* s*anct*o et igni 17 *Cuius uentilabrum in manu eius et purgauit aream * 11. v. mt. xii.

his ⁊ somnað huæte in ber-ern his ða halm ł ða windungo ða geberneð to fyre
suam et congregauit triticum in horreu*m* suum paleas autem comburet igni

unadrysnendlic meuigo æc ðon ⁊ oðero getru*m*made bodade ꝥ folc
inextinguibili 18 multa quidem et alia exortans euangelizabat populum 19 *Herodes * X. 12. ii. mt. cxliiii. mr. luiiii.

ðon*ne* miððy gerihðe from him fro*m* wife broðres his ⁊ fro*m* allum
autem tetrarcha cum corriperetur ab illo de herodiadae uxore fratris sui et de omnib*us*

yflum ðaðe dyde to-geecde ⁊ ðis of*er* alle ⁊ in-tynde ioh*annem* in carcern
malis quae fecit herodes 20 adiecit et hoc supra omnia et inclusit iohannem in carcere

aworden wæs ðon*ne* miððy gefuluad wæs all folc ⁊ se hæl*end* miððy wæs gefuluad ⁊ biddende
21 *Factum est autem cum baptizaretur omnis populus et i*esu* baptizato et orante * 13. i. mt. xiiii. mr. u. io. xu.

un-tyned wæs heofon
ápertum est caelum

---

12. comun ða wutudlice ⁊ bearswinige ꝥte were gifulwad ⁊ cwedun to him la larwa hwæt we gidoað 13. soð he cwæð to him noht forðor giseted is iow gidoað 14. wutudlice frugnun hine ⁊ ða cempo cwedun hwæt doað we ⁊ ec us ⁊ cwæð him ne ænigmon gidroefað ge ne tellnisse ł scomu doað ⁊ ðæm .... wosað nestum iowrum 15. miððy woende ðonne ðæt folc ⁊ smea[n]dum allum in heortum hiora from ioh*anne* eaðe mæge he were crist 16. ondsworade iohannis cwæð allum ic ec soð of wætere gifulwo iowih .... cumað ðonne strongra me ðæs ne am ic wyrðe to unbindanne ðwongas giscoes his he iowih gifulwas in gaste halgum ⁊ mið fyre 17. his fone ⁊ wind-fone in honda his ⁊ clænsað bereflor his ⁊ gisomnað hwæte his in ber-ern his ðæt halm ł winnunge ðon*ne* giberneð to fyre unadryssenlic 18. monige ec ðonne ⁊ oðre gitrymede bodona ðæt folc 19. .... ðonne .... miððy gerihte fro*m* him of .... from wif broðer his ⁊ from allum yflum ðaðe dyde herodes 20. to-giecte ⁊ ðis ofer alle ⁊ untynde ioh*annem* ðæt carcern 21. aworden wæs ðonne miððy gifulwad wæs all folc ⁊ ðe hæl*end* mið wæs gifulwad ⁊ biddende ontyned wæs heofun

22 ⁊ se halega gast astah lichamlicre ansyne on hyne swa án culfre. ⁊ stefen wæs of heofone geworden ⁊ þus cwæð; Ðu eart min gecorena sunu. on þe me gelicode.

23 ⁊ se hælend wæs on ylde swylce þritig wintre. ꝥ menn wendon ꝥ he wære iosepes sunu; Se wæs heliges sunu.

24—38 se wæs nazareth. swa of cneorysse on cneorysse oð adám; Se wæs godes sunu. oð fíf ⁊ hund-seofantig cneoryssa;

Various Readings.

22. A. B. C. halga. C. aastah. A. B. C. stefn. A. heofene. 23. A. þryttig; C. þrittig. A. B. C. men. A. helies. 24—38. B. C. cneoresse [*2nd time only*]. A. -seofentig.

22 ⁊ se halga gast astah lichamlicere an-syna on hine swa an culfre ⁊ stefne wæs of heofene ge-worðan ⁊ þus cwæð. Ðu ert min ge-corena sune on þe me ge-likeð.

23 ⁊ se hælend wæs on ylde swilce þrittige wintre. þæt men wenden þæt he wære Iosepes sune. Se wæs heliges sune.

24—38 se wæs nazareth. swa of cneornysse on cneornysse oððe ada*m*. Se wæs godes sunu oð fif ⁊ hund-seofentig cneornisse.

Various Readings.

22. stefn; hefone ge-worden; eart; ge-licode. 23. þrittig. 24—38. cneorysse on cneoresse; suna; -seofontig cneorissa.

⁊ adune astag gast se halig mið lic-homlic hui*u* suelce culfra on hine ⁊ stefn of heofne
22 et descendit sp*iritus* *sanctus* corporali specie sicut columba in ipsum et uox de caelo

aworden wæs ðu arð sunu min leaf ꝉ leofost on ðec licað me ⁊ he ꝉ se hæl*end* wæs
facta *est* tú és filius meus dilectus in te complacuit mihi 23 *Et ipse *iesus* erat * 14. iii. mt. i. io. i.

onginnende suelce wintra ðrittih ꝥte woende sunu iosep*es* seðe wæs heling se' w'
incipiens quasi annorum triginta ut putaretur filius ioseph qui fuit heli 24 qui fuit

mata' se' w' ꝉ se' w' meꝉ se' w' ia' se' w' io' se' w'
mattat qui fuit leui qui fuit melchi qui fuit iannae qui fuit ioseph 25 qui fuit

ma' se' w' am' se' w' na' se' w' es' se' w' na' se' w' ma'
mathathie qui fuit ámos qui fuit naum qui fuit ésli qui fuit naggae 26 qui fuit maath

se' w' math' se' w' se' se' w' io' se' w' iodaing se' w' io' se'
qui fuit mathathiæ qui fuit semei qui fuit iosec qui fuit ioda 27 qui fuit iohanna qui

w' resaing se' w' sorobabeling s' w' saꝉ s' w' nering s' w' m' s' w'
fuit resa qui fuit sorobabel qui fuit salathiel qui fuit neri 28 qui fuit melchi qui fuit

a' s' w' cos' s' w' heꝉ s' w' hering s' w' ihesuing s' w' eli'
addi qui fuit cosam qui fuit helmada*m* qui fuit her 29 qui fuit ihesu qui fuit eliezer

s' w' io' s' w' ma' s' w' leuing s' w' si' s' w' iu' s'
qui fuit iorim qui fuit matthad qui fuit leui 30 qui fuit symeon qui fuit iuda qui

w' io' s' w' ionaing s' w' eli' s' w' meꝉ s' w' men' s' w'
fuit ioseph qui fuit iona qui fuit eliachim 31 qui fuit melea qui fuit menna qui fuit

ma' s' w' nathaning s' w' da' s' w' iessing s' w' obeðing s' w' bo' s'
matthata qui fuit nathan qui fuit dauid 32 qui fuit iesse qui fuit obed qui fuit booz qui

w' sa' s' w' na' s' w' a' s' w' ar' s' w' es' s' w'
fuit salmon qui fuit naason 33 qui fuit aminadab qui fuit áran qui fuit esrom qui fuit

p' s' w' iu' s' w' ia' s' w' is' s' w' ab' s' w' th' s' w'
phares qui fuit iudae 34 qui fuit iacob qui fuit isaac qui fuit abrahã qui fuit thare qui fuit

na' s' w' se' s' w' ra' s' w' p' s' w' eb' s' w' sa' s'
nachor 35 qui fuit seruch qui fuit ragau qui fuit phalec qui fuit eber qui fuit sale 36 qui

w' cha' s' w' ar' s' w' s' s' w' n' s' w' ꝉ s' w'
fuit chainan qui fuit arfaxat qui fuit sem qui fuit noe qui fuit lamech 37 qui fuit

maðaling s' w' e' s' w' ia' s' w' m' s' w' ca' s' w'
matthusale qui fuit enoc qui fuit iared qui fuit malelehel qui fuit cainan 38 qui fuit

en' s' w' se' s' w' a*dam*ing s' w'
enos qui fuit seth qui fuit adam qui fuit d*ei*

---

22. ⁊ adune astag gast ðe haliga mið lichomlice megwlite swelce culfra on hine ⁊ stefn of heofnum giworden wæs ðu arð sunu min leof ꝉ leowusta on ðec licað me 23. ⁊ se hælend wæs onginnende swelce wintra ðritig ꝥte woende suno were iosephes seðe wæs eling 24. seðe wæs .... seðe wæs .... seðe wæs .... seðe wæs .... seðe wæs .... 25. seðe wæs .... seðe wæs .... seðe wæs ....

CHAPTER IV.

1 Soðlice se hælend wæs full halgu*m*
gáste ⁊ ferde fra*m* iordane. ⁊ he wæs fram
haligu*m* gaste gelæd. on sumum westene

2 feowertig daga. ⁊ wæs fram deofle
costod. ⁊ he on þa*m* dagum nān þing ne
æt; And þam dagu*m* gefylledu*m* hine hingrede;
3 Ða cwæð se deofol him to. gif þu sy
godes sunu sege þisu*m* stāne ꝥ he to hlafe
gewurðe;
4 Ða ⁊swarude him se hǽlend; Hit is
awriten ꝥ se man ne leofaþ be hlāfe anu*m*.
ac of ælcum godes wórde;
5 And þa lædde se deofol hyne. ⁊ ætywde
him ealle rīcu eorðan ymbe-hwyrftes. on
ānre byrhm-hwīle
6 ⁊ to him cwæð; Ealne þisne anweald
ic ðe sylle. ⁊ hyra wuldor. forþa*m* þe hi
me synt gesealde. ⁊ ic hi sylle þa*m* ðe ic
wylle;
7 Witodlice ealle hig beoð þine gif þu
geeað-metst beforan me;
8 Þa ⁊swarode him se hælend; Hit is
awriten. drihten þinne god ðu geead-metst.
⁊ him anum þeowast;
9 Ða lædde he hyne on hierusale*m* ⁊ gesette hine ofer þæs temples hricg. ⁊ hi*m*
to cwæð; Gyf þu sy godes sunu ásend þe
heonun nyþer;

CHAPTER IV.

1 Soðlice se hælend wæs full halgen
gaste ⁊ ferde fram iordane.
Se halend wæs fram halig gaste ge-læd
on sumen westene
2 feortig dagen. ⁊ wæs fra*m* deofol
costnod. ⁊ he on þam dagen nan þing
ne æt. And þam dagen ge-fylleden hine
hingrede.
3 Þa cwæð se deofel hym to. gyf þu
syo godes sunu. sæge þisen stanen þæt he
to hlafe ge-wurðe.
4 Ða andswerede him se hælend. Hit
ys awriten þæt se man ne leofeð be hlafe
anen. ác of ælcen godes worde.
5 And þa lædde se deofel hyne ⁊ atewede
hi*m* ealle þa rice eorðe ymbhwyrftes on
anre brihtan hwile.
6 ⁊ to hi*m* cwæð. Ealne þisne anweald
ic þe sylle ⁊ heora wuldor for þan þe hy
me synde ge-sealde. ⁊ ich hye sylle þan þe
ich wille.
7 Witodlice ealle hyo beoð þine gif þu
ge-eadmedest be-foran me.
8 Ða andswerede him se halend. Hit
is awriten. Drihten þinne god þu ge-
eadmest ⁊ hym ane þeowast.
9 Ða lædde he hyne on Ierusalem. ⁊
ge-sette hine ofer þas temples ricg ⁊ hym
to cwæð. Gyf þu syo godes sunu á-send
þe heonen nyder.

Ductus est *iesus* in de- sertum á s*ritu* ut ten taretur a diabolo.

Various Readings.

Cap. iv. v. 1. A. halgu*m*. 2. B. C. þinc. A. hyngrode. 3. A. sig. [*for* sy]. A. *inserts* to *after* sege. A. ge-weorðe. 4. A. ⁊swarode. A. lyfað. 5. A. B. byrhtm-; C. *hardly legible.* 6. A. heora. A. hyg. A. synd. A. hig. 7. A. ge-eadmedst; C. geaðmetst. 8. A. ge-eaðmetst. 9. C. hric. A. sig. A. heonen.

Various Readings.

Cap. iv. v. 1. halend; ful halgu*m*. *Same Rubric in* R. haligu*m*; sumu*m*. 2. feowertig dagu*m*; deofle costod; dagv*m*; dagu*m* gefylledum. 3. deofol; sy; sege þisum stane. 4. halend; leofað; anum; ælcum. 5. deofol; æt-ywde; *om.* þa; eorðan ymbe-hwyrftas; brihtm. 6. anweld; hyra; þa*m*; synt; ic hyo; þam; ic. 7. byð; ge-eadmest. 8. andswarode; anu*m*. 9. þæs; sune; heonon.

CAP. IV.

se hælend uutedlice full gast halig færend wæs from iordane ⁊ wæs doend on gast in
1 *Iesus autem plenus spiritu sancto regressus est ab iordane et agebatur in spiritu in * XI. 15. ii. mt. xu. mr. ui.

woestern dagum feortih ⁊ wæs gecosted from diab' ⁊ noht ge-ētt in dagum
desertum 2 diebus quadraginta et temtabatur á diabolo *Et nihil manducauit in diebus * 16. v. mt. xui.

ðæm ⁊ miððy geendad weron ða gehyngerde cuoeð uutedlice him se diob' gif sunu godes arð cuoeð
illis et consummatis illis esuriit 3 dixit autem illi diabolus si filius dei és dic

stano ðissum ꝥte hlaf sē ⁊ onduarde to him se hælend auritten Is ꝥte ne In hlafe
lapidi huic ut panis fiat 4 et respondit ad illum iesus scribtum est quia non in pane

ane lifes monn ah in eghuelc word godes ⁊ lædde hine se diab' ⁊ æd-eaude him alle
solo uiuet homo sed in omni uerbo dei 5 et duxit illum diabolus et ostendit illi omnia

ricu ymb-huirftes eorðes in huil tides ⁊ cueð him ðe ic sello mæht ðas ł ðios
regna orbis terrae in momento temporis 6 et ait ei tibi dabo potestatem hanc

all ⁊ wuldor hiora forðon me gesald aron ⁊ ðæm ic willo ic sello ðailca ðu forðon
uniuersam et gloriam illorum quia mihi tradita sunt et cui uolo dó illa 7 tú ergo

fallande gif ðu worðias fore me biðon ðinæ alle ⁊ ge-onduarde se hælend cuoeð him
procidens si adoraueris coram me erunt tua omnia 8 et respondens iesus dixit illi

awritten is drihten god ðin worða ðu ⁊ him anum geher ðu ⁊ lædde hine in
scribtum est dominum deum tuum adorabis et illi soli seruies 9 et duxit illum in

hierusalem ⁊ sette hine cfer hornpic temples ⁊ cuoeð him gif sunu godes arð Asend ðeh
hierusalem et statuit eum supra pinnam templi et dixit illi si filius dei es mitte té

heona ł ðona aduna
hinc deorsum

CAP. IV. 1. ðe hælend wutudlice full gaste seðe wæs goding halge færende wæs from iordane ⁊ wæs doende in gaste on woestenne 2. daga feowertigum ⁊ wæs gicostad from diofle ⁊ noht gieet on dagum ðæm ⁊ miððy giendad werun ða gihyncrede 3. cwæð wutudlice him ðe diawul gif ðu sunu godes arð cweð stane ðissum ꝥte hlafas se 4. giondsworade to him ðe hælend awriten is forðon ðætte ne on hlafe anum lifeð mon ah in eghwelcum worde godes 5. ⁊ lædde hine ðe diaful ⁊ æteowde him alle rice ymb-hwyrftes eorð in hwile tide 6. ⁊ cwæð to him ðe ic selo mæhte ðas alle ⁊ wuldor hiora forðon me gisald arun ⁊ ðæm ðe ic wyllo .... ðe ilca 7. ðu forðon gif ðu worðas bifora mec ⁊ bioðun ðine alle 8. ⁊ giondworde ðe hælend cwæð him awriten is drihten god ðinne wearða ðu ⁊ him anum giher ðu 9. ⁊ læde hine in .... ⁊ sette hine ofer horn-pic temples ⁊ cwæð to him gif sunu godes arð asend ðeh hiona ł ðona of-dune

10 Soðlice hyt is awriten. ꝥ he hys englum be þe bebyt ꝥ hig þe gehealdon.

11 ⁊ þæt hig þe mid handum nimon. þe-læs þu ðinne fot æt stāne æt-speorne ;

12 Ða cwæð se hælend him ⁊swariende ; Hyt is gecweden. ne costa þu drihten þinne god ;

13 ⁊ ealre þære costunge gefylledre. se deofol him sume hwile fram gewāt ;

14 Þa ferde se hælend on gastes mægene on galileam. ⁊ his hlisa be him ferde on eall ꝥ rīce.

15 ⁊ he lǣrde be hyra gesamnungum. ⁊ wæs fram eallum gemærsod ;

16 Ða cōm he to nazareth. þar he afed wæs. ⁊ he eode on reste-dæge on þa gesamnunge æfter his gewunan ⁊ he arās ꝥ he rædde.

17 ⁊ him wæs geseald isaias bōc þæs witegan ⁊ sona swa he þa boc unfēold þa funde he þar awriten.

18 drihtnes gast is ofer me. for-þam ðe hē smyrede mē. he sende me þearfum bodian. ⁊ gehæftum alysednesse. ⁊ blindum gesihþe. for-brocene ge-hælan

19 ⁊ bodian drihtnes and-fenge ger. ⁊ edleanes dæg ;

20 And þa he þa bōc befeold he hig þam ðēne agef ⁊ sæt. ⁊ ealra heora eagan on þære gesamnunge wæron on hyne behealdende ;

10 Soðlice hit ys awriten þæt he hys ænglen be þe be-beot ꝥ hyo þe ge-healden ;

11 ⁊ ꝥ hyo þe mid handen nymen þe læs þe þu þinne fot æt stane æt-sperne.

12 Ða cwæð se hælend him andswe̊riende. hyt is ge-cweðen ne costa þu drihten þinne god.

13 ⁊ ealle þare costlinge ge-fylledera. se deofel hym sume hwile fram ge-wat.

14 ÞA ferde se hælend on gastes mægne on galileam. ⁊ his hlise be him ferde on eall þæt riche.

15 ⁊ he lærde be heora samnunge. ⁊ wæs fram eallen ge-mearsod.

16 Ða com he to nazareth. þær he afed wæs. ⁊ he eode on reste-dāige on þa gesamnenge æfter his ge-wunen. ⁊ he aras ꝥ he rædde.

17 ⁊ hym wæs ge-seald ysaias boc þas witegan. ⁊ sona swa he þa boc unfeld þa funde he þær awriten ;

18 drihtnes gast is ofer me for þan he smerede me. He sende me þærfen bodian. ⁊ ge-hæften alysendnysse. ⁊ blinden gesihðe. for-brokene ge-hælen.

19 ⁊ bodian drihtnes anfenge gear ⁊ edleanes daig.

20 And þa he þa boc be-feold he hye þam þeigne sealde ⁊ agef ⁊ sæt. ⁊ ealre hire eagen on þare samnunge wæren on hine be-healdende.

Various Readings.

10. A. ge-healdan. 11. A. nyman þy-læs. A. æt-sporne. 12. A. costa, *altered to* costna. 13. A. costnunge. A. deoful. 14. B. C. mægne. 15. A. heora. C. *om.* eallum. 17. A. þær. 18. A. alysednysse. 19. A. gear. 20. A. ageaf. B. C. hyra.

Various Readings.

10. englum ; be-byt. 11. handum ; þine. 12. halend ; þine. 13. eallere ; costlinge (*so written, but apparently meant for* costunge); ge-fylledre ; deofol. 14. hlisa ; all ; rice. 15. ge-samnungum ; eallum ge-mærsod. 16. -dage ; ge-samnunge. 17. aseld (*altered to* ge-seld); un-feold. 18. smyrede ; ge-hæftum alysednysse ; blindvm ; forbrocene. 19. drihtenes ; ger ; dæg. 20. hy ; þegne ; *om.* ⁊ *before* ealra [*for* ealre]; hyora eagan.

aritten is forðon ꝥte englum his bebead from ðec ꝥte efne-gehereð ðe ⁊ forðon
10 scribtum est enim quod angelis suis mandabit de té ut conseruent té 11 et quia

In hondum læðeð ł niomað ðec eaðæ mæge ꝥte ðu wiðspurna to stane fot ðinne ⁊
in manibus tollent té ne forte offendas ad lapidem pedem tuum 12 et

ge-onduarde se hælend cuoeð him acuoeden is ne costa ðu drihten god ðin ⁊
respondens iesus ait illi dictum est non temtabis dominum deum tuum 13 et

geendad weron alle mið costunge-łwæs gecostad se diwob' eft-foerd from him wið to tid ⁊
consummata omnia (*sic*) temtatione diabolus recessit ab illo usque ad tempus 14 *Et * XII. 17. i. mt. xxiii. mr. xxuii. io. xlui.

færende wæs se hælend on mæht gastes in galilea ⁊ mersung foerde ðerh all lond
egressus est iesus in uirtute spiritus in galilaea et fama exiit per uniuersam regionem

of him ⁊ he lærde in somnungum hiora ⁊ gemiclad wæs from allum ⁊
de illo 15 et ipse docebat in synagogis eorum et magnificabatur ab omnibus 16 *Et * 18. x.

cuom to nazareth ðer wæs gefoeded ⁊ in-eade æfter ge-una his dæge sunnan in
uenit nazareth ubi erat nutritus et intrauit secundum consuetudinem suam die sabbati in

somnung ⁊ aras to redanne ⁊ gesald wæs him boc ðæs witges esaie ⁊ ꝥte ł miððy
synagogam et surrexit legere 17 et traditus est illi liber prophetae esaiae et ut

untynde ꝥ boc gemitte to stoue ðer awritten wæs gast drihtnes on mec forðon
reuoluit librum inuenit loco ubi scribtum erat 18 spiritus domini super me propter quod

gesmiride mec ł to sæccanne ðorfendum sende meh to bodianne ermingum ł gehæftendum forgefnise ⁊
unxit me euangelizare pauperibus misit me praedicare captiuis remissionem et

blindum gesihðo forleta ða gebroceno on forgefnise bodia gēr drihtnes ondfenge
cæcis uisum dimittere confractos in remissionem 19 praedicare annum domini acceptum

⁊ dæge eft-selenise ⁊ miððy gefeald ꝥ bōc agæf ðæm embeht-menn ⁊ saett ⁊
et diem retributionis 20 et cum plicuisset librum reddidit ministro et sedit et

allra on somnung ego woeron bihaldendo on hine
omnium in synagogam (*sic*) oculi erant intendentes in eum

---

10. awriten is forðon ðætte englas his bibeod from ðe ðætte efne-gihērað ðe 11. forðon in hondum ðinum lædað ł niomað ðec eoðe mæge ðætte ðu wiðspurne to stane fott ðinne 12. ⁊ giondworde ðe hælend cwæð him acweden is ne costa ðu drihten god ðinne 13. ⁊ giendad werun alle mið costunge ðe diafol eftfoerde from him wið to tide 14. ⁊ færende wæs ðe hælend on mæhte gastes in.... ⁊ mersung foerde ðerh alle lond of him 15. ⁊ he lærde in somnungum hiora ⁊ gimiclad wæs from allum 16. ⁊ com to nazareth ðer wæs gifoeded ⁊ ineode æfter efne-giwuna his dæge symbles in somnunge ⁊ aras to redanne 17. ⁊ gisald wæs him boc ðæs witga essaies ⁊ ontynde boc gimitte to stowwe ðer awriten wæs 18. gast drihtnes ofer mec forðon ðæt gismirede mec ł to soecanne ðorfendum sende mec to bodanne ermingum ł hæftedum forgefnisse ⁊ blindum gisihðe forleta ða gibrocono on forgefnisse 19. bodiga geras drihtnes onfenge ⁊ dæg eft-to-selenisse 20. ⁊ miððy gifylled wæs ðio boc agæf ðæm embihtmen ⁊ sætt ⁊ alle in somnungum egu werun bihaldende on hine

21 Ða ongan he him to cweðan; Soþlice to-dǽg þis gewrit is on eowrum earum gefylled;

22 ⁊ hig ealle wǽron þæs gecnǽwe. ⁊ wundredon be þam wordum þe of his muþe eode. ⁊ þus cwædun; Nys þes iosepes sunu.

23 ða cwæþ he. witodlice ge secgað me þas gelicnesse. eala lǽce. gehǽl ðe sylfne; Do hér on þinum earde. swa fela wundra swa we ge-hyrdon gedóne on cafarnaum;

24 Ða cwæð he soðlice ic eow secge ꝥ nán witega nis and-fenge on his eþele;

25 Soþlice ic eow secge manega wudewan wǽron on helías dagum on hisrahel. ða þa seo heofon wæs belocen þreo ger ⁊ syx monþas; Þa wæs gewórden mycel hunger on ealle eorðan

26 ⁊ to þara nanum næs helias asend. buton to anre wudewan on sarepta sidónie;

27 And manega licþroweras wǽron on israhel. under heliséo þam witegan. ⁊ hyra nán næs aclænsud buton náámán se sirisca;

28 Ða wurdon hig ealle on þære gesamnunge mid yrre gefylled. þas þing gehyrende;

29 ⁊ hig arison ⁊ scufon hine of ðære ceastre. ⁊ læddon hine ofer ðæs muntes cnæpp. ofer þone hyra buruh getimbrud wæs. ꝥ hi hyne nyðer bescufon.

30 þa ferde he þurh hyra midlen;

Various Readings.

21. A. heom. 22. A. ge-cnawe. A. eodon. A. cwædon. 23. B. C. witudlice. A. ge-lycnysse. A. fæla. A. capharnaum. 25. A. wudewa. A. ysrahel; B. israhel. A. heofen. A. gear. A. B. C. ealre. 26. A. þæra. 27. A. manege. A. heora. A. aclænsod. 28. A. he gehyrde [*for* gehyrende]. 29. A. heora. A. B. C. burh. A. getymbred. A. hig. 30. A. heora.

21 Ða on-gan he heom to cwædene. Soðlice to daig ys þis writ on eowren earen ge-fylled.

22 ⁊ hyo ealle wæren þis ge-cnawe ⁊ wundredon be þam worden þe of hys muðe eode. ⁊ þus cwæðen. Nis þes Iosepes sune.

23 Þa cwæð he. Witodlice ge seggeð me þas ge-licnysse. eala leche ge-hæl þe sylfne. Do her on þinen earde swa fela wundre swa we ge-hyrden ge-dóne on chapharnaum.

24 Ða cwæð he. soðlice ic eow segge þæt nan witege nis and-fenge on hys æðele.

25 Soðlice ic eow segge manega wudewan wæren on helias dagon on israel. þa þa seo heofena wæs be-loken þreo gear ⁊ six monþas. Þa wæs ge-worðan mycel hunger on ealre eorðan

26 ⁊ to þare nanun næs helias asend. buton to anre wudewan on sarepta sydonie.

27 And manega lichþrowæres wæron on israel under helyseo þam witegan; ⁊ heore nan næs æclænsed butan náá man se sciresan.

28 Þa wurðen hyo ealle on þare gesamnunge mid eorre ge-fylled. þas þing ge-herende.

29 ænd hyo arison ⁊ scufen hine of þare ceastre. ænd lædden hine ofer þas muntes cnæp ofer þane hyra burh ge-tymbred wæs þæt hyo hine nyðer be-scufan.

30 þa ferde he þurh hyra midlen.

Various Readings.

21. cwæðen; eawrum (*sic*) earum. 22. wæron; gecnæwe; wundrodon; wordum; cwæðon. 23. læce; þinum; wundra; gehyrdon. 24. secge; eðele. 25. wæron; heofana; be-locen; ge-worden. 26. nanum. 27. Ænd; licðroweras; isræl; hyora; æclænsud buton; sirisca. 28. wurdon; irre; ge-hyrende. 29. ⁊ [*for* ænd]; scufon; ⁊ læddon; þæs; cnæpp; þone hyora.

ongann uut*edlice* ɫ ða cuoaða to him ꝥte to dæg gefylled wæs ðios gewritt In earu*m*
21 coepit autem dicere ad illos quia hodie impleta est haec scriptura in aurib*us*

Iuru*m* ⁊ Alle cyðnisse him hia saldon ⁊ awundradon in wordu*m* wuldres ɫ wuldro
uestris 22 *Et omnes testimonium illi dabant et mirabantur in uerbis gratiae * 19. i. mt. cxli.

ðaðe fo*re*-cuomon fro*m* muðe his ɫ ðæs ⁊ cuoedon ahne ðes sunu Is ios*eph* ⁊ cuoeð mr. l.
quae procedebant de ore ipsius et dicebant nonne hic filius est ioseph 23 *Et ait io. luiiii. * 20. x.

ðæm uut*edlice* gie cuoeðað me ðios onlic-nesse la lece lecne ðec seolfne In monigo geherde we
illis utiq*ue* dicetis mihi hanc similitudinem medice cura te ipsum quanta audiuimus

awordeno i*n* ðær byrig do aec her on oeðel ðin he cuoeð ða soðlice ic cuoeðo iuh ꝥte
facta in capharnau*m* fac et hic in patria tua 24 *Ait autem amen dico uobis quia * 21. i. mt. cxlii.

ne ænig witga ondfenge wæs on oeðel his in soðfæstnise ic cuoeðo iuh monigo widua mr. li. io. xxxu.
nemo propheta acceptus est in patria sua 25 *In ueritate dico uobis multae uiduae * 22. x.

woeron on dagum helies in isr*ae*l ða betyned wæs se hefon geru*m* ðrím ⁊ moneðum sex
erant in dieb*us* heliae in isra*e*l quando clusum est caelum annis trib*us* et mensib*us* sex

miððy Aworden wæs hunger micel on alle eorðo ⁊ ne to ængu*m* ðara bur*i*ga asended wæs
cum facta est fames magna in omni terra 26 et ad nullam illarum misus est

buta in ðær byrig to ðæm wife widua ⁊ monigo hreafo weron
helias nisi in sareptha sidonæ ad mulierem uiduam 27 et multi leprosi erant in israhel

under ðæne witgo ⁊ ne ænig hiora geclænsad wæs buta neman . i . wæs lic-ðrower ðerisca ⁊
sub helisaeo propheta et nemo eorum mundatus est nisi nema sirus 28 et

gefylled woeron ða alle in somga mið wraðo ðas geherdon ⁊ arison ⁊ awurpon
repleti sunt omnes in synagoga ira haec audientes 29 et surrexerunt et eiecerunt

hine buta ðære ceastra ⁊ læddon hine oðð to ofer mores of*er* ðone ɫ ðio
illum extra ciuitatem et duxerunt illum usq*ue* ad super-cilium montis supra quem

ða burg hiora wæs getimbred ꝥte hia geglendradon hine he ðon*ne* of*er*foerde ɫ færende
ciuitas illorum erat aedificata ut praecipitarent eu*m* 30 ipse autem transiens

ðerh middum hiora geeode
per medium illorum ibat

---

21. ongan wutudl*ice* cweoða to him ðætte to dæge gifylled wæs ðis giwritt in eorum iowrum 22. ⁊ alle cyðnisse him hia saldun ⁊ wundradun on wordum wuldres ɫ wuldor ðaðe fore-comun from muðe his ɫ ðæs ⁊ cwedun ahne ðes sunu is ios*eph* 23. ⁊ cwæð ðæm wutudl*ice* ge cweoðas me ðas ongilicnisse la lece lecna ðec solfne hu monigu giherdun we awordne in . . . . ðær byrig doa ⁊ her on oedle ðinum 24. cwæð ðonne soðlice ic cweðo iow ðætte nænig witga onfongen wæs on oedle his 25. in soðfæstnisse ic cweðo iow monige widuwe werun on dagum helias in israhelum ða bityned wæs heofunn gerum ðrim ⁊ monoðas sexu. miððy giworden wæs hungor micel on alre eorðo 26. ⁊ ne to ængum ðara burga sended wæs buta in . . . . ðær byrig . . . . ⁊ to ðæm wife widwe 27. ⁊ monige hreofe werun in isr*ael* under helise ðæm witga ⁊ nænig hiora giclænsad wæs buta neman . . . . wæs licðrowere 28. ⁊ gifylled werun ða alle in somnungum mið wræððo ðas giherdun 29. ⁊ arioson ⁊ awurpun hine buta ða cæstre ⁊ læddun hine wið to ofer . . . . moras ofer ðon ðio burug [*Eight leaves are here lost in the* Rushworth MS.]

31 And he ferde to cafarnaum on galileisce ceastre. ⁊ hi þar on reste-dagum lærde

32 ⁊ hig wundredon be his lare. forþam his spæc on anwealde wæs;

33 And on hyra gesamnunge wæs sum man unclæne deofol hæbbende. ⁊ he hrymde micelre stefne

34 ⁊ cwæþ; Læt lá nadzarenisca hælend. hwæt is us ⁊ þe. com þu us to for-spillanne. ic wát ꝥ ðu eart godes halega;

35 And þa cidde him se hælend ⁊ cwæþ. adumba ⁊ ga him of; ⁊ þa he ut-adraf hine on heora midlene. he him fram-gewát. ⁊ him naht ne derude;

36 Ða wurdon hig ealle forhte ⁊ spræcon him betwynan. ⁊ cwædon. hwæt ys ꝥ word ꝥ he on mihte ⁊ on mægene un-clænum gastum bebyt ⁊ hig ut-gaþ;

37 Ða wæs his hlisa ge-widmærsod on ælcere stowe þæs rices;

Ðis sceal on þone þryddan þunres dæg innan lenctene ⁊ to pentecosten on sæternes dæg. Surgens iesus de sinagoga introiuit in domum simonis. A.

8 Soþlice he aras of heora gesamnunge ⁊ ferde on simones hus; Ða wæs simones sweger geswenced on mycelum feferum. ⁊ hig hyne for hyre bǽdon.

39 ⁊ he standende ofer hig þam fefore bebéad ⁊ he hig forlet ⁊ heo sóna aras and him þenode;

40 Soðlice þa sunne asáh ealle þe untrume wæron on mislicum adlum hig lǽddon him to ⁊ he syndrygum hys hánd on-settende híg gehælde;

Various Readings.

31. A. hig. 32. A. spræc [*but* B. C. spæc]. B. C. anwalde. 33. A. heora ge-somnunge. 34. A. *om.* lá. B. nadzarenisa, *altered to* nazarenisa. A. B. C. halga. 35. B. hyra. A. C. derede. 36. B. spæcon. 37. B. C. ælcre. 38. B C. hyra. B. C. swegr. A. bædun. 39. C. of [*for* ofer]. A. fefere.

31 And he ferde to kapharnaum on galileisce ceastre. ⁊ he þær on ræste-daigen lærde.

32 ⁊ hyo wundreden be his lare; for þan hys spræce on anwealde wæs.

33 And on hire samnunge wæs sum man un-clæne deofol hæbbende. ⁊ he hrymde michelere stefne

34 ⁊ cwæð. Læt la nazareisce hælend. hwæt is us ⁊ þe come þu us to for-spillene. ich wat þæt þu ert godes halga.

35 And þa cydde hym se hælend and cwæd. Adumba ⁊ ga hym of. ⁊ þa he ut adraf hine on hire midlene; ⁊ he hym fram ge-wat. and hym naht ne derede.

36 Ða wurðen hyo ealle forhte ⁊ spraeken heom be-tweonen. ⁊ cwæðen hwæt is þæt word þæt he on mihte ⁊ on mægne un-clænen gaste be-beot. ⁊ hyo ut gað.

37 Ða wæs hys hlise ge-wid-mærsod on ælcere stowe þas rices.

38 Soðlice he aras of here samnunga ⁊ ferde on symones hus. Ða wæs simones sweger ge-swenched on mycelen feofren. ⁊ hyo hine for hire bæden.

39 ⁊ he standende ofer hyo þam feofre be-bead. ⁊ he hyo for-let. ⁊ hyo sone aras. ⁊ hym þenede.

40 Soðlice þa sunne asah ealle þe untrume wæren on mistlicen adlen hyo lædden him to. ⁊ he sindrigen his hand on-settende hyo ge-helde.

Various Readings.

31. Ænd; cafarnaum; reoste-dagan. 32. wundroden; sprace; andwealde. 33. hyora; habbende; mycelere. 34. nazarenisca; for-spillenne; eart. 35. Ænd; cwæð; heora; *om.* ⁊ *after* midlene. 36. wurden; spæcen; betwenen; cwædon; un-clænum. 37. hlisa; ælcer. 38. heora; swegr ge-swenced; mycelum feofrum; bædon. 39. stændende; be-bed; heo sona; þenode. 40. wæron; mist-licum adlum; sindrigum; ge-hælde.

⁊ dune astag in caph*arnaum* ceastra gal*il*ies ⁊ ðær lærde hia on dagu*m* ⁊
31 *Et discendit in capharnaum ciuitatem galileae ibiq*ue* docebat illos sabbatis 32 †Et

* XIII. 23. uiii. mr. xii. † 24. ii. mt. lxii. mr. xiii. * 25. u[iii]. mr. xiiii. [MS. mt. xiiii.]

astyltdon on lar his for*ð*on in mæht wæs word his ł ðæs ⁊ on som*nunge* wæs
stupebant in doctrina eius quia in potestate erat sermo ipsius 33 *Et in synagoga erat

monn hæfde ðone dioul unclæne ⁊ gecliopade mið stefne micle cuoeðende *for*let ł blinn
homo habens daemonium inmundum et exclamauit uoce magna 34 dicens sine

huæd us ⁊ ðe hæl*end* nazarenesca ðu cuome to *for*doanne usig ic wat ðec ðuðe arð halig godes
quid nobis et tibi i*esus* nazarenae uenisti perdere nos scio té qui sis *sanctus* dei

⁊ geðreade him se hæl*end* cuoeð *for*e-suige ⁊ gaa of him ⁊ miððy awarp hine
35 et increpauit illi i*esus* dicens ommutesce et exi ab illo et cum proiecisset illum

ðone dioul in middu*m* foerde fro*m* him ⁊ noht hine ł him sceðde ⁊ aworden wæs fyrhto
daemonium in medium exiit ab illo nihilque illu*m* nocuit 36 et factus est pauor

in allum ⁊ efne-gesprecon bituih cuoedon ꝥ is ðis word ꝥte in mæhte ⁊
in omnib*us* et con-loquebantur adinuicem dicentes quod est hoc uerbum quia in potestate et

mægne gehateð gastu*m* unclænum ⁊ geongas ⁊ wæs gemersad mersong of him In all
uirtute imperat spiritib*us* inmundis et exeunt 37 et diuulgabatur fama de illo in omnem

stoue ðæs londes aras ða of somnung inneode In hus simo*nes* suær
locum regionis 38 *Surgens autem de sinagoga introiuit in domum symonis socrus

* XIIII. 26. ii. mt. lxuii. mr. xu.

ðon*ne* genu*m*men wæs miclu*m* feber-adlum ⁊ bedon hine *for*æ hia ⁊ stod of*er*
autem symonis tenebatur magnis febrib*us* et rogauerunt illum pro ea 39 et stans super

hia geheht ðæm febere ⁊ *for*leort hia ⁊ recone arās embehtade him miððy
illam imperauit febri et dimisit illam et continuo surgens ministrabat illis 40 cum

sunna uut*edlice* to set eade alle ðaðe hæfdon untrymigo missenlicu*m* adlum lædon hia to
sol autem occidisset omnes qui habebant infirmos uarís languorib*us* ducebant illos ad

him soð he anlapum [ł] syndrigum hond gesette lecnade hia ł ðailco
eum at ille singulis manus inponens curabat eos

[*Eight leaves lost in the* Rushworth MS.]

41 Ða ferdon þa deoflu of manegum hrymende ⁊ cweðende; Soðes þu eart godes sunu. ⁊ he ne geþafude ꝥ hig æni þing sprǣcon forþam þe wiston ꝥ he crist wæs;

42 Ða gewordenum dæge se hælend utgangende ferde on weste stṓwe. ⁊ þa meniu hine sohtun. ⁊ hi comon to him. ⁊ behæfdon hine. ꝥ he him fram ne gewite;

43 Þa sæde he him. soðlice me gedafænað oðrum ceastrum godes rice bodian. forþam. to þam ic eom asend

44 ⁊ he wæs bodigende on galilea gesamnungum;

CHAPTER V.

Ðis sceal on þone syxtan sunnan-dæg ofer pentecosten. *Cum turbe inruerent ad iesum.* A.

1 Soþlice wæs geworden þa ða menegu him to comon ꝥ hig godes word gehyrdon. he stṓd wið þone mere genesareth.

2 ⁊ he geseah twa scīpu standende wið þæne mere; Ða fisceras eodun ⁊ wohson heora nett;

3 He þa astigende on ān scyp. ꝥ wæs simones bæd hyne ꝥ he hit lyt-hwṓn fram lande tuge. ⁊ on þam scipe sittende he lærde þa menegu;

4 Ða he sprecan geswac he cwæþ to simone; Teoh hit on dypan ⁊ lætað eowre nett on þone fisc-wer;

---

41 Þa ferden þa deofle of manegen hremende. ⁊ cweðende. Sodes þu eart godes sune. ⁊ he ne ge-þafede þæt hye any þing spræcen. for þan he hyo wisten þæt he crist wæs.

42 Ða ge-wordenen daige se hælend utgangende ferde on westene stowe. ⁊ þa manega hine sohten. ⁊ hyo comen to hym. ⁊ be-hæfden hine; þæt he heom fram ne wite.

43 Ða sægde he heom. Soðlice me geþafened oþren ceastren godes riche bodian. for þan to þan ich eom asend

44 ⁊ he wæs bodiende on galilea gesamnunge.

CHAPTER V.

1 Soðlice wæs ge-worðen þa þa manege him to comen þæt hyo godes word ge-hyrden. he stod wið þane mere genesareth.

2 ⁊ he ge-seah twa scipe standende wið þanne mere. Ða fixeres eoden ⁊ wexon heore nett.

3 He þa astigende on an scyp; þæt wæs symones. bed hine þæt he hit lithwa*n* fram lande tuugen. ⁊ on þam scype sittende he lærde þa manega.

4 Ða he spræcen ge-swac he cwæð to symone. Teoh hit on deopan ⁊ læteð eowre nett on þanne fisc-wær.

Various Readings.

41. A. mænegu*m*. A. geþafode. A. ænig. B. C. þincg. A. *inserts* hig *before* wiston. 42. A. mænegu; B. C. menegu. A. sohton. A. hig. B. C. be-hæfdun. 43. A. B. C. gedafenað. 44. C. bodiende. A. gesomnungu*m*.

Cap. v. v. 1. A. mænegu. C. god [*for* godes]. B. C. þæne. 2. A. þone. A. eodon. A. woxon; B. C. wohsun. A. net. 3. A. mænigeo. 4. A. net.

Various Readings.

41. manegu*m* hrimende; Sodes (*as in* H.); hy; hy wæston (*sic*). 42. ge-wordenu*m*; halend; menega; sohton; comon; be-hæfdu*n*. 43. sæde; ge-ðafenað oþru*m* ceastru*m*; rice; forðam; þam; eam. 44. ge-samnungan.

Cap. v. v. 1. ge-worden; mænega; comon; ge-hyrdon; þene. 2. þonne; fisceras eodum (*sic*); weoxón heora. 3. bæd; lythwon; tuge; mænega. 4. þone fisc-wer.

foerdon *uutedlice* ða diowlas from menigum cliopende ⁊ cuoeðenda ꝥte ðu arð sunu godes ⁊
41 *Exiebant etiam daemonia á multis clamantia et dicentia quia tú és filius dei et * 27. uiii. mr. xui.

geðreade ne gelefde ða gesprecca forðon wiston hine ꝥte were crist a- ł ge-warð ða
increpans non sinebat ea loqui quia sciebant ipsum esse *christum* 42 *Facta autem * 28. uiii. mr. xuii.

dæge wæs færende eade on woestigum stowe ⁊ ða menigo sohton hine ⁊ cuomon wið to
die egressus ibat in desertum locum et turbae requirebant eum et uenerunt usque ad

him ⁊ gehealdon hine ꝥte ne fearrade from him ðæm he cuoeð forðon ⁊ oðrum
ipsum et detinebant illum ne discenderet ab eis 43 quibus ille ait quia et aliis

ceastrum gedæfneð mec bodia ríc godes ꝥte forðon gesended Am ⁊ wæs bod-
ciuitatibus oportet me euangelizare regnum dei quia ideo missus sum 44 et erat prae-

ande on somnungum *galiles*
dicans in synagogis galilaeae

CAP. V.

aworden wæs ðonne miððy ða menigo geræsdon ł giorndon on him ꝥte geherdon word godes ⁊
1 *Factum est autem cum turbae inruerent in eum ut audirent uerbum dei et * XV. 29. x.

he stod æt mere genesareth ⁊ gesæh tuoege ł tuu sciopo stondendo æt ðæm mere
ipse stabat secus stagnum genesareth 2 et uidit duas naues stantes secus stagnum

ða fiscaras ðonne of-astigon ⁊ geðuogon ꝥ nett Astag *uutedlice* in anum scip
piscatores autem descenderant et lauabant retiam (*sic*) 3 ascendens autem in unam nauem

ðio wæs simones gebæd ðonne hine from eorðo eft-læda huon ⁊ sætt lærde of
quae erat simonis rogauit autem eum á terra reducere pusillum et sedens docebat de

ðæm scipe ða menigo ꝥte geblann ðonne gespreaca cuoeð to simone læd on heanise ⁊ let
nauicula turbas 4 *Ut cessauit autem loqui dixit ad simonem duc in altum et laxa * 30. uiiii. io. ccxuiiii.

ða netto iuero on gefeng ł stællo
retia uestra in capturam

[*Eight leaves lost in the* Rushworth MS.]

5 þa cwæþ sīmon him ⁊swariende; Eala be-beodend ealle niht swincende we naht ne gefengon; Soðlice on þinum worde ic mīn nett ut-lǽte;

6 ⁊ þa hi ꝥ dydon hig betugon mycele menigeo fixa. ⁊ hyra net wæs to-brocen.

7 ⁊ hig bicnodon hyra geferan. þe on oðrum scipe wæron. ꝥ hi comun ⁊ him fylston; Ða comon hig ⁊ gefyldon butu þa scipu. swa ꝥ hi neh wæron besencte;

8 þa petrus ꝥ geseah he feoll to þæs hælendes cneowum ⁊ cwæð; Drihten. gewīt fram me forþam ic eom synfull mann.

9 ⁊ he wundrude ⁊ ealle þa ðe mid him wæron on þam were þara fixa þe hi gefengon;

10 Gelice iacobum ⁊ iohannem zebedeis suna. þa wæron simones geferan; Ða cwæþ se hælend to simone. ne ondrǽd þu þe; Heonon forð þu byst men gefonde;

11 ⁊ hig tugon hyra scypo to lande. ⁊ for-leton hig ⁊ folgodon þam hælende;

12 Ða he wæs on ānre ceastre þa wæs þar ān hreofla ⁊ þa he geseah þæne hælend þa astrehte he hine ⁊ bæd ⁊ þus cwæð; Drihten. gyf þu wylt þu miht me geclænsian;

13 And he æt-hrān hine his handa āþenede ⁊ cwæð; Ic wylle. si þu geclænsud; And sona se hreofla him fram fērde

5 Ða cwæd symon him andswerede. Ela be-bended (*sic*) ealle niht swikende we naht ne fengen. Soðlice on þinum worde ich min nett ut-læte.

6 ⁊ þa hyo þæt dydon. hyo be-tugen mycele maniga fixsca; ⁊ heore nett wæs to-broken.

7 ⁊ hyo becneden heore ge-feren; þe on oðren scypen wæren. ꝥ hyo comen ⁊ heom felsten. Ða comen hyo ⁊ ge-felden baðа þa scype swa þæt hyo neh wæren ge-sencten.

8 þa petrus þæt ge-seah he feoll to þas hælendes cneowen; ⁊ cwæð. Drihten gewit fram me for þam ich em sinful man

9 ⁊ he wundrede. ⁊ ealle þa þe mid hym wæren on þam wære þare fixsca þe hyo gefengen.

10 Gelice Iacobum ⁊ Iohannem Zebedeis sunes. þa wæren symones ge-feran. þa cwæð se hælend to symone. ne on-dræd þu þe. Heonen forð þu byst mēnn feonde.

11 ⁊ hyo tugen hyre scyp to lande. ⁊ for-læten hyo ⁊ folgedon þam hælende.

12 ÞA he wæs on anre ceastre þa wæs þær an hreofla. ⁊ þa he geseah þanne hælend þa astrahte he hine ⁊ bæd. ⁊ þus cwæð. Drihten gif þu wilt. þu miht me ge-clænsien.

13 Ǽnd he æt-hran hine his handa aþenede. ⁊ cwæð. Ic wille; syo þu geclænsed. Ǽnd sone se hreofla hym fram ferde.

Various Readings.

5. A. ⁊swarigende. A. net. 6. A. hig. A. mænigeo. A. heora. C. nett. 7. A. bicnedon heora. A. híg. A. C. comon. A. hig. 8. C. feol. A. synful man. 9. A. wundrode. A. þæra. A. hig. 10. A. zebedeus. A. heonen. 11. B. C. hi. A. heora scypu. A. folgedon. C. hælend. 12. A. þær. A. þone. 13. A. aþenigende. A. sig þu ge-clænsod.

Various Readings.

5. andsweriende; be-bedend; swincende; ge-fengon; ic. 6. meniga fixa; hyra net; to-brocen. 7. becnedon hyra ge-feran; oðrum scipum; comon; fylsten; gefuldon butu; scypa; hi; be-sencte. 8. cneowum; ic em synfull mann. 9. wundrode; wæron; were; fixa; gefengon. 10. suna; wæron; halend; Heonon; foende. 11. tugon hyra; for-leton; folgodon; halende. 12. þonne; astrehte; ge-clænsian. 13. ge-clænsod; And sona; hreofola.

⁊ ge-onduarde simon cuoeð him ðu haldormon ðerh alle næht we wunnon noht we fengon
5 et respondens simon dixit illi praeceptor per totam noctem laborantes nihil cepimus

on worde ðonne ðinum ic forlette net ⁊ miððy ðis dydon efne-gebegdon fiscana ꝥ meni-
in uerbo autem tuo laxabo rete 6 et cum hoc fecissent concluserunt piscium multitudi-

go monigfald to-slitten wæs ðonne ðæt nett hiora ⁊ becnadon ðæm foerum ðaðe weron on
nem copiosam rumpebatur autem retia eorum 7 et annuerunt sociis qui erant in

oðora scip ꝥte gecuomon ⁊ gehulpo hia ⁊ cuomon ⁊ gefyldon ða tuoge ł tuu sciopo suæ
alia naui ut uenirent et adiuuarent eos et uenerunt et impleuerunt ambas nauiculas ita

ꝥte gedruncnadon ł were ꝥ miððy gesege feol to cneuum ðæs hælendes
ut mergerentur 8 *Quod cum uideret simon petrus procidit ad genua iesu * 31. x.

cuoeð geong from me forðon monn synnfull Am drihten slep forðon ymb-salde hine
dicens exi a me quia homo peccator sum domine 9 stupor enim circum-dederat eum

⁊ Alle ðaðe mið him weron on gefeng fiscana ðone ł ꝥ genomon gelic ðonne
et omnes qui cum illo erant in captura piscium quam ceperant 10 similiter autem

⁊ sunu ðaðe woeron gefoero ⁊ cuoeð to simone se hælend
iacobum et iohannem filios zebedaei qui erant socii simonis *Et ait ad simonem iesus * 32. ii. mt. xxi. mr. x.

nælle ðu ondrede of ðis uutedlice menn bist ðu niomende ⁊ under-læded woeron to eorðo
noli timere ex hoc iam homines eris capiens 11 et subductis ad terram

scioppo forletno allum gefyligde weron hine ⁊ aworden wæs miððy wære on an
nauibus relictis omnibus secuti sunt illum 12 *Et factum est cum esset in una * XVI. 33. ii. mt. lxiii. mr. xuiii.

ðæra ceastrana ⁊ heono wer full hriofle ⁊ gesæh se hælend ⁊ feoll on onsione ⁊ bæd
ciuitatum et ecce uir plenus lepra et uidens iesum et procidens in faciem et rogauit

hine cuoeðende drihten gif ðu wilt ðu mæht meh geclænsia ⁊ aðenede hond gehran
eum dicens domine si uís potes me mundare 13 et extendens manum tetigit

hine cuoeð ic willo geclænsige ⁊ sona ðio hriofol offearrade from him
illum dicens uolo mundare et confestim lepra discessit ab illo

---

[*Eight leaves lost in the* Rushworth MS.]

14 ⁊ he bebead him ꝥ he hit nanum men
ne sæde. ac gá æt-yw þe þa*m* sacerde. ⁊
bring for þínre clænsunga swa moyses bebead him on gewitnesse;
15 Witodlice þæs þe má seo spræ̃c be
him férde ⁊ mycele menegeo comun ꝥ hi
ge-hyrdon ⁊ wurdon gehælede fram hyra
untru*m*nessu*m*;
16 He þa ferde on westen ⁊ hyne gebæd;

Ðis sceal on frige-dæg on þære pentecostenes wucan. Factu*m* est in una dieru*m* et *iesus* sedebat docens. A.

17 Ða wæs anum dæge geworden ꝥ he
sæt ⁊ hig lǽrde ⁊ þa wǽron þa farisḗi sittende ⁊ þære. ǽ.-lareow-was. þa comon of
ælcon castele galileǽ ⁊ iudeæ. ⁊ hierusalem ⁊ drihtnes mægen wæs hig to gehæl-
ene;
18 And þa bæron men on anum bedde
anne man. se wæs lama.
19 ⁊ hig ne mihton hine inbringan ⁊
alecgan beforan him. for þære menigo þe
mid þam hælende wæs; Þa astigon hig
uppan þæne hróf ⁊ þurh þa watelas hine mid
þa*m* bedde asende beforan þæne hælend;
20 Ða he ge-seah hyra geleafan he cwæð;
La mann þe synd þine synna forgyfene;

21 Þa agunnon þencan þa boceras ⁊ farisei ⁊ cwǽdon. hwæt is þes þe her sprycþ
woffunga; Hwa mæg synna for-gyfan buton
god ana;

14 ⁊ he bed him ꝥ he hit nanen men ne
saigde. ac ga ⁊ atewe þe þam sacerde.
ænd bring for þinre claensinge swa moyses
be-bead heom on ge-witnysse.
15 Witodlice þas þe má seo spræc be him
ferde ⁊ mycele menega comen þæt hyo ge-
hyrdon ⁊ wurðen ge-hælede fram heora
untrumnesse.
16 He þa ferde on westen ⁊ hine ge-bæd.
17 Þa wæs anen daige ge-worðen þæt
he sæt ⁊ hyo lærde. ⁊ þa wæren þa farisei
sittende ⁊ þare lage-lareow-wæs. þa comen
of ælche castelle galiléé ⁊ Iudéé ⁊ ierusalem. ⁊ drihten magen wæs hyo to ge-
hælene.
18 Ænd þa bæren men on anen bedde
enne man; se wæs lame.
19 ⁊ hyo ne mihten hine in-bringen ⁊
aleggen be-foran hym; for þare maniga þe
mid þam hælende wæs. Ða astigen hyo up
on þanne rof. ⁊ þurh þa watelas hine mid
þam bedde asende be-foran þam halende.
20 Ða he ge-seah heora ge-leafe. he
cwæð. La man þe synd þine sinne for-
gefene.
21 Ða agunnen þencen þa bokeres ⁊ farisei ⁊ cwæðen. hwæt is þes þe her sprecd
woffunga. hwa maig senna for-gefen buton
god ane.

Various Readings.

14. B. *inserts* ⁊ *after* gá. 15. A. mænigeo; C. menego. A. comon. A. hig. A. heora untru*m*nyssu*m*. 17. A. ǽlareowas (*all one word*); B. ǽ-lareow-wæs. A. ælcu*m* castellu*m*. C. galiléé. C. iudee. A. gehælanne; B. ge-hælenne; C. hælenne. 18. C. bæran. 19. A. mænio; B. menigeo; C. menegeo. A. asendon. B. bo-foran (*sic*). A. þone. 20. A. heora. A. mān; C. man. B. C. synt. 21. A. on-gunnon. A. cweðan. A. sprecð. B. C. butan.

Various Readings.

14. bead; nanum; sægde; æt-yw; clænsunge. 15. þæs; menegeo comon; wurdon; untru*m*-nessum. 17. anum; ge-worden; wæron; pharisei; æ-lareow-wæs; ælce; drihtnes; ge-hælenne. 18. And; bæron; anu*m*; ænne; lama. 19. myhton; aleggan; menegeo; halende; astigon; þonne; þonne hælend. 20. ge-leafan; mann; synt; for-gyfene. 21. agunnon þencan; boceras; sprecð; mæg synna forgyfan; ana.

ɿ he bebead him ꝥte ne ænigu*m* gecuoede ah geong æd-eaua ðec ðæm sacerde ɿ breng
14 et ipse praecepit illi ut nemini diceret sed uade ostende té sacerdoti et offer

fore clænsunge ðine suæ be-bead ł heht moses on cyðnise him ðerh-eode ł wæs geongende
pro emundatione tua sicut praecepit moses in testimonium illis 15 perambulabat

ðon*ne* suiðor word fro*m* him ɿ efne-cuomon ða menigo ł ð[a] feolo ꝥte geherdon ɿ ꝥte woeron gelecned
autem magis sermo de illo et conueniebant turbae multae ut audirent et curarentur

fro*m* untrymnisu*m* hiora he ða gesætt on wæs*tern* ɿ gebæd ɿ geworden
ab infirmitatibus suis 16 *Ipse autem sedebat in deserto et orabat 17 †Et factum

wæs on an ðara dagana ɿ he gesætt lærende ɿ woeron ða æ-lar*uu*as ł aldo-uuto sittendo ɿ æs
est in una dierum et ipse sedebat docens et erant pharisaei sedentes et legi[s]

* 35. i[i]. mt. cxluiiii. mr. lxui.
† XUII. 36. ii. mt. cliii. mr. lxuiiii.

laruas ða ðe cuomon fro*m* eghuelc ceastre gałi ɿ iu' ɿ hie*rusalem* ɿ mægen wæs
doctores qui uenerant ex omni castello galilaeae et iudae et hierusalem et uirtus erat

driht*nes* to hælenne hia ɿ heono wæras berende on bed ł on bēr monno seðe wæs
d*omi*ni ad sanandum eos 18 *Et ecce uiri portantes in lecto hominem qui erat

* 37. i. mt. lxx. mr. xx. io. xxxuiii.

eorð-crypel ɿ sohton hine gebrenge ɿ gesette f*o*ra hine ɿ ne gemoeton
paraliticus et quaerebant eum inferre et ponere ante eum 19 et non inuenientes

of huælcu*m* dæl hine gebrohton f*o*re ðæm folce astigon of*er* ł onufa hus ðerh ða watla ɿ duna
qua parte illum inferrent prae turba ascenderunt supra tectum per tegulas et summi-

sendon hine mið bed in middum f*o*re hæl*end* ðæra geleafa ꝥte gesæh cuoeð la monn
serunt illum cum lecto in medium ante i*esu*m 20 quorum fidem ut uidit dixit homo

f*or*gefen biðon ðe synna ðina ɿ ongunnun gesmeage wuðuto ɿ cuoeðende hua
remittuntur tibi peccata tua 21 et coeperunt cogitare scribae et pharisaei dicentes quis

is ðes seðe spreces ebolsongas hua mæge f*or*geafa synna buta ðe ana god
est hic qui loquitur blasphemia quis potest dimittere peccata nisi solus d*eus*

[*Eight leaves lost in the* Rushworth MS.]

22 Ða se hælend gecneow hyra geþancas he ⁊swariende cwæþ to him. hwæt þencege on eowrum heortu*m*.

23 hwæðer is eðre to cweþenne þe synd þine synna for-gyfene. hwæþer þe cweþan aris ⁊ ga.

24 ꝥ ge witon ꝥ mannes sunu on eorðan anwea[l]d hæfð synna to for-gyfanne ; And he sǽde þam laman. þe ic secge aris. nim þin bed. ⁊ ga on þin hūs ;

25 ⁊ he sona be-foran hīm aras. ⁊ nam ꝥ he on lǽg ⁊ to his huse ferde ⁊ god wuldrode.

26 ⁊ hig ealle wundredon ⁊ god mærsodon ⁊ wæron mid ege gefyllede. ⁊ cwǽdon. soðes we to-dæg wundru gesawon ;

27 Þa æfter þam he ut-eode ⁊ geseah publicanu*m* he wæs oþrum naman leuī gehaten æt ceap-sceamule sittende. ⁊ he cwæþ to hi*m* filig me ;

28 ⁊ he him þa filigde ⁊ ealle hys þing for-let ;

29 ⁊ leuī dyde hi*m* mycelne gebeorscype on his huse. ⁊ þar wæs mycel menegeo manfulra ⁊ oðerra þe mid him sǽton ;

30 Þa murcnodon þa farisei ⁊ þa boceras ⁊ cwædon to hys leorning-cnihtu*m*. hwi etege ⁊ drincað mid manfullum ⁊ synfullu*m* ;

31 Ða ⁊swarude se hælend ⁊ cwæþ to him ; Ne beþurfon læces þa ðe hale sȳnd. ac þa ðe unhælþe habbaþ ;

22 Ða seo hælend ge-cneow heora geþances ; he andsweriende cwæð to heom. Hwæt þence ge on eowre heorten

23 hwæðer is eþere to cweðene þe synt þine senne for-gefene ; hwaðer to cweðene aris ⁊ ga.

24 þæt ge witen þæt mannes sune on eordan anweald hafð synne to for-gefena. Ǽnd he sægde þam lamen. þe ich segge aris ; nym þin bed ⁊ ga on þin hus.

25 ⁊ he sone be-foren heom aras ; ⁊ nam þæt he on læig ⁊ to his huse eode. ⁊ god wuldrede.

26 ⁊ hyo ealle wundredon ⁊ god mærsedon ⁊ wæren mid eige ge-fylde. ⁊ cwæðen soðes we to-daig wundre ge-seagen.

27 ÞA æfter þan he ut-eode. ⁊ ge-seah publicanu*m* þe wæs oðer name leuj ge-haten. æt cheap-scamele sittende. ⁊ he cwæð to hym felge me.

28 ⁊ he hym þa felgede. ⁊ ealle hys þing for-let.

29 Ǽnd leuj dyde him michele ge-beorscipe on his huse. ⁊ þær wæs mycele manege manfulra ⁊ oðre þe mid him sæton.

30 Þa murcneden þa farisei ⁊ þa bokeres. ⁊ cwæðen to his leorning-cnihten. hwi æte ge. ⁊ drinkeð mid manfullen ⁊ senfullen.

31 Ða andswerede se hælend ⁊ cwæð to heom. Ne be-þurfen læches þa þe hale synde. ac þa þe un-hæle hæbbeð.

Various Readings.

22. A. heora. C. *om.* he. A. ⁊swarigende. A. B. C. þence ge (*two words*). 23. B. C. synt. 24. A. anweald ; B. C. anwald. 27. A. oðre nama. A. ceap-sceamele ; C. ceap-scemule. 29. A. mænigeo. A. oðra. 30. A. murcnedon. A. hwig. A. B. ete ge (*two words*). 31. A. ⁊swarode. A. beþurfun læcas. B. synt.

Various Readings.

22. se ; hyra ; andswerigende ; eowra heorta*n*. 23. synne for-gyfene ; hweðer ; cweðen. 24. witan ; eorðan ; synna ; for-gyfanne ; laman ; ic. 25. sona be-foran ; læg ; ferde [*for* eode] ; wuldrode. 26. wuldrodon ; mærsoden ; ge-fyllede ; dæg ; ge-sawen. 27. þam ; he [*for* þe] ; oðru*m* namen ; ceap-sceamele ; fylge. 28. fylgde. 29. mycele ; mycel menegeo. 30. murcnodon ; pharisei ; boceras ; cwæðon ; leor-cnihtum ; ete ; drincað ; manfullu*m* ; synfullu*m*. 31. andswarode ; læces ; synt ; un-hælðe hæbeð.

ꝥte ongætt ða se hael*end* smeaunga hiora ge-onduarde cuoeð to hi*m* ł ðæm huæd smeas gie
22 ut cognouit autem i*esus* cogitationes eorum respondens dixit ad illos quid cogitatis

in heart*um* iur*um* huoeðer is eaðor gecuoæða *for*gefen biðon ðe synna ł cuoeða
in cordib*us* uestris 23 quid est facillius dicere dimittuntur tibi peccata án dicere

aris ⁊ gaa ꝥte ðon*ne* gie wittæ ꝥte ꝥ sunu monnes mæht hafeð on eorðo
surge et ambula 24 ut autem sciatis quia filius hominis potestatem habet in terra

*for*geafa synna cuoeð ðæm cryple ðe ic cuoeðo aris nim beer ðin ⁊ gaa in hus
dimittere peccata ait paralytico tibi dico surge tolle lectum tuum et uade in domum

ðin ⁊ sona aras fo*r*e him genom on ðæm gelæg ⁊ foerde in hus his
tua*m* 25 et confestim surgens coram illis tulit in quo iacebat et abiit in domu*m* suam

ge-miclade god ⁊ feer-stylt genom ł *for*grap alle ⁊ Auundradon god ⁊ gefylled
magnificans d*eu*m 26 et stupor appraehendit omnes et magnificabant d*eu*m et repleti

woeron mið fyrhto cuoedon ꝥte we gesegon wundra to dæge ⁊ æft*er* ðas foerde ⁊ gesæh
sunt timore dicentes quia uidimus mirabilia hodie. 27 *Et post hoc exiit et uidit * XUIII. 38. ii. mt. lxxi. mr. xxi.

ðone bærsynnig genemned wæs sittende to ⁊ cuoeð him fylg mec ł soec mec ⁊
publicanu*m* nomine leui sedentem ad teloneum et ait illi sequere me 28 et

*for*leorte ł miððy allum *for*letno aras fylgende wæs him ⁊ dyde him farma ł gebearsgip
relictis omnibus surgens secutus est eum 29 *Et fecit ei conuiuium * 39. ii. mt. lxxii. mr. xxii.

micel se leui in hus his ⁊ wæs ðreat menigo ⁊ oðera ðaðe mið him
magnum leui in domo sua et erat turba multa publicanorum et aliorum qui cum illis

weron hlingend*um* ł hlingende ⁊ lyceton ⁊ hiora cuoedon to
erant discumbentes 30 et murmurabant pharisaei et scribae eorum dicentes ad

ðegn*um* his fo*r*hon mið ⁊ synnfull*um* gie ettas ⁊ gie drincas ⁊
discipulos eius quare cum publicanis et peccatori*bus* manducatis et bibitis 31 *Et * 40. ii. mt. lxxiii. mr. xxiii.

ondsuarade se hæl*end* cuoeð to him ne ðo[r]feð ðaðe halo sint to lece ah ða ðe yfle habbað
respondens i*esus* dixit ad illos non egent qui sani sunt medico sed qui male habent

---

[*Eight leaves lost in the* Rushworth MS.]

32 Ne com ic riht-wise clypian. ac synfulle on dædbote;

33 Ða cwædon hig to hi*m*. hwi fæstað iohannes leorning-cnihtas gelōmlice ⁊ halsunga doð. ⁊ eall-swa farisea. ⁊ þine etað ⁊ drincað;

34 Þa cwæð he cwystuþu magon þæs brydguman bearn fæstan swa lange swa se brydguma myd hi*m* ys;

35 Soþlice þa dagas cumaþ þon*ne* se brydguma him byð afyrred. þon*ne* fæstað hig on þam dagum;

36 Þa sæde he hi*m* an big-spell. ne asend nan mān scȳp of nīwum reafe on eald rēaf. elles ꝥ nīwe slīt. ⁊ se niwa scyp ne hylp þam ealdan;

37 Ne nan man ne sent nīwe wīn on ealde bytta. elles ꝥ nīwe wīn brycð þa bytta ⁊ ꝥ wīn byð agoten. ⁊ þa bytta forwurðað;

38 Ac nīwe wīn is to sendenne on nīwe bytta. þon*ne* beoð þa bytta gehealdene;

39 And ne drincð nān man eald wīn ⁊ wylle sona ꝥ nīwe. he cwyþ. ꝥ ealde is betere;

CHAPTER VI.

1 Soþlice wæs geworden on þa*m* æfteran reste-dæge. æryst þa he ferde þurh þa æceras hys leorning-cnihtas þa eār pluccedon ⁊ mid hyra handu*m* gnidon ⁊ æton;

Various Readings.

33. A. hwig. A. farisea (*alt. to* farisei). 34. A. cwyst ðu; B. C. cwyst þu. 36. A. byg-spel. A. asent. A. scep (*alt. to* scyp; *twice*). A. B. hylpð; C. hylpþ. 37. A. for-weorðað. 38. A. sendanne. 39. A. ꝥ ðæt [*for* ꝥ *before* ealde].

Cap. vi. v. 1. A. ærest. A. gear. A. heora.

32 Ne com ich rihtwise to clepian. ac synfulle on deadbote.

33 Ða cwæðen hyo to hym. hwi fæsted iohannes leorningcnihtes ge-lomlice ⁊ halsunge doð. ⁊ eal swa fariseen. ⁊ þine æteð ⁊ drinceð;

34 Þa cwæð he. cwedst þu magen þas bredgumen bearn fæsten. swa lange swa se bredgume mid heo*m* ys.

35 Soðlice þa dages cumeð þanne se bredgume heom beoð aferred. þanne fæsted hyo on þan dagen.

36 Ða sæde he heom an bispell. Ne asende nan man scyp on neowan reafe. on eald reaf elles þæt neowe slyt. ⁊ se neowe scyp ne helpd þan ealden.

37 Ne nan man ne synt niwe win on ealde butta elles þæt neowa win breceð þa butta ⁊ þæt win beoð agoten ⁊ þa butta forwurðed.

38 Ac neowe win is to asendenne on neowe butta þanne beoð þa butte ge-healdenne.

39 ⁊ ne drincð nan man eald win. ⁊ wille sona þæt neowe he cweð þæt ealde is betere.

CHAPTER VI.

1 Soðlice wæs ge-worðen on þam æfteren reste-daige; ærest þa ferde he þurh þa æceras hys leorning-cnihtes þa ear pluccoden. ⁊ miḍ heora handa gnidon ⁊ æten.

Various Readings.

32. R. *om.* to; clypian; dædbote. 33. fæsteð; -cnihtas; eallswa pharisen; etað; drincað. 34. cwyðst; brydguman; fæstan; langa; bridguma; eom. 35. cymað þonne; briðguma; byð afyrred þonne fæsteð; þam dagum. 36. eom; of niwum; niwe (*twice*); helpð þam ealdan. 37. sent; healde; niwe; brecð; bið; for-wurðað. 38. niwe; sendenne; nywe buttan þon*ne* bið; buttan. 39. niwe; cwyð.

Cap. vi. v. 1. ge-worden; æfteran; he ferde; -cnihtas; plucceden; hande.

ne cuom ic to ceiganne soðfæsto ah ða synnfullo in hreonise soð hia cuoedon to
32 non ueni uocare iustos sed peccatores in paenitentiam 33 at illi dixerunt ad

him forhuon ðegnas iohannes fæstað symble ⁊ gebeodo doað gelic ⁊
eum quare discipuli iohannis ieiunant frequenter et obsecrationes faciunt similiter et pharisae-

ðine ðonne eotað ⁊ drincað ðæm he cuoeð ahne magogie suno brydgumes
orum tui autem edunt et bibunt 34 quibus ipse ait numquid potestis filios sponsi

ða huil mið him is ꝉ bið se brydguma wyrca gefæsta cymað uutedlice ða dagas miððy genumen
dum cum illis est sponsus facere ieiunare 35 uenient autem dies cum ablatus

bið from him se brydguma ða gefæstað in ðæm dagum cuoeð ðonne ⁊ onlic-
fuerit ab illis sponsus tunc ieiunabunt in illis diebus 36 dicebat autem et similitu-

nise to him ꝥte ne aenig ꝥ ē-sceapa from woedo niuue onsendeð on gewedo ald
dinem ad illos quia nemo commissuram á uestimento nouo inmittit in uestimentum uetus

elcur nu ⁊ ꝥ niua toslitað ⁊ ðæm alde ne gehriseð ꝥ esceapa of ðæm niue ⁊ ne aenig
alio-quin et nouum rumpit et ueteri non conuenit commissura á nouo 37 ét nemo

sendeð win niua in byttum aldum elcur nu tosliteð ꝥ win niua ða aldo ⁊ ꝥ ilce
mittit uinum nouum in utres ueteres alio-quin rumpit uinum nouum utres et ipsum

agotten bið ⁊ ða byto lasað ah ꝥ win niua In byttum niuum to sendanne is ⁊
effunditur et utres peribunt 38 sed uinum nouum in utres nouos mittendum est et

egðer biðon gehaldan ⁊ ne aenig gedranc ꝥ alde sona wilnað ꝥ niua cuoeð forðon se alda
utraque conseruantur 39 et nemo bibens uetus statim uult nouum dicit enim uetus

betra is
melius est

CAP. VI.

aworden wæs ðonne on ðone æfterra daeg mið-ðy oferfoerdon ðerh gecoecton ðegnas
1 *Factum est autem in sabbato secundo cum transirent per sata uellebant discipuli * XIIII. 41. ii. mt. cxiii[i]. mr. xxiii.

his ða croppas ꝉ ehras ⁊ eton gebrecon mið hondum
eius spicas et manducabant confricantes manibus

[*Eight leaves lost in the* Rushworth MS.]

2 Ða cwǽdon sume of þan sundor-halgan. hwi do ge ꝥ eow alýfed nis on reste-dagon;

3 Þa ⁊swarode him se hælend ne rædde ge ꝥ. hwæt dauid dyde þa hine hingrede. ⁊ þa ðe mid hi*m* wæron.

4 hu he eode into godes huse. ⁊ nam þa offrung-hlafas ⁊ hig ǽt. ⁊ þa*m* sealde þe mid him wærun. þa nærun alyfede to etanne buton sacerdon anum;

5 And he sǽde him ꝥ drihten is mannes sunu. eac swylce reste-dæges;

6 Soðlice on oðrum reste-dæge wæs geworden ꝥ he on gesamnunge eode ⁊ lærde. ⁊ þar wæs sum man ⁊ his swyðre hand wæs for-scruncen;

7 Ða gymdon þa boceras ⁊ farisei hwæþer he on reste-dæge hælde. ꝥ hi hyne gewregdon;

8 Soþlice he wiste hyra geþancas. ⁊ he sǽde þam men þe ða for-scruncenan hand hæfde. arís ⁊ stánd her amiddan; þa arás he ⁊ stód;

9 Ða cwæþ se hælend to him; Ic ahsige eow alyfþ on reste-dagum wel don. oððe yfele. sawle hale gedon. hwæþer ðe forspillan;

10 And him eallu*m* gesceawodu*m* mid yrre he sæde þam men; Aþene þine hand. ⁊ he aþenode ⁊ his hand wæs ge-edniwod;

11 Þa wurdon hig mid unwisdóme gefyllede ⁊ spæcon betux him hwæt hig þa*m* hælende dydon;

Various Readings.

2. A. þa*m*; C. þam. A. sunder-halgu*m*. A. hwig. A. -dagu*m*. 3. A. hyngrade. 4. A. *omits from* hu *to* wærun. A. næron. A. sacerdu*m*. 7. A. hig. 8. A. heora. A. on-myddan. 9. A. acsige. 10. A. ge-sceawedu*m*. A. aðenede. 11. A. spræcon. A. betweox; B. C. betwux. C. halend.

2 Ða cwæðen sume of þam sunder-halgen. hwi do ge þæt eow alyfd nis on reste-dagen.

3 Ða andswerede se hælend heom ⁊ cwæð. Ne redde ge hwæt dauid dyde þa him hingrede. ⁊ þa þe mid him wæron

4 hu he eode into godes huse ⁊ nam þa offrenge-hlafes ⁊ hyo æt. ⁊ þam sealde þe mid him wæren. þa næren alyfde to ætene buton sacerden. anen.

5 Ænd he saigde heom þæt drihten is mannes sune. eac swilce reste-daiges.

6 Soðlice on oðrum reste-daige wæs geworðen. þæt he on ge-samnunge eode. ⁊ lærde. ⁊ þær wæs sum man. ⁊ his swiðre hand wæs for-scrunken.

7 Ða gemden þa bokeras ⁊ pharisei hwaðer he on reste-daige helde þæt hyo hine wreidon.

8 Soðlice he wiste heore þances ⁊ he saide þam men þe þa forscru*n*kene hand hafde. aris ⁊ stand her amidden. Ða aras he ⁊ stod.

9 Ða cwæð se hælend to hem*. Ich acsie eow alyfð on reste-dagon wel don oððe yfele sawle hæle ge-don hwæder þe forspillan.

10 And heom eallon ge-sceawedon mid eorre he saigde þam men. Aþene þine hand; ⁊ he aþenede ⁊ hys hand wæs ednywod.

11 Ða wurðen hyo mid unwisdome gefyllede ⁊ spræcen be-twux heom hwæt hyo þam hælende dydon.

* MS. him, *alt. to* hem.

Various Readings.

2. sundor-halgan; -dagon. 3. eom se hælend; hine. 4. offrung-; wæro*n*; næron; etanne; sacerdon anu*m*. 5. sægde; sunu; dæges. 6. -dæge; ge-worden; swyððre; for-scru*n*cen. 7. gymdon; boceras; hwæðer; -dæge hælde; wreiden. 8. hyra þancas; sæde; for-scruncena; stan. 9. him; Ic asxige (*sic*); hwæðer. 10. Ænd eom eallen ge-sceawedu*m*; yrre; sægde. 11. wurdon; spracen; halende.

sumo oðer* ðon*ne* cuoedon him huæd gie doeð ꝥte ne riseð on symbel-dagu*m*
2 quidam autem pharisaeorum dicebant illi quid facitis quod non licet in sabbatis

* oðer *is underlined, as if for expunction.*

⁊ onduearde se hæl*end* to him cuoeð ne ðis geleornadon ꝥte dyde dauið miððy hine gehyngerde
3 et respondens i*esus* ad eos dixit nec hoc legistis quod fecit dauid cum esurisset

he ⁊ ða ðe mið hine weron huu inn-eade in hus goddes ⁊ hlafas *fore*gegear-
ipse et qui cum eo erant 4 quomodo intrauit in domum d*e*i et panes propo-

uad ł getemesed ondfeng ⁊ ge-ett ⁊ salde ðæm ðaðe mið hine weron ðas ne is gelefed
sitionis sumsit et manducauit et dedit hís qui cum ipso erant quos non licet

to eattanne buta anu*m* sacerdum ⁊ cuoeð him ꝥte drihten is sunu monnes
manducare nisi tantum sacerdotib*us* 5 et dicebat illis quia d*omi*n*us* est filius hominis

uut*edlice* symbeldæges aworden wæs ðon*ne* ⁊ on oðero symbeldæge ꝥte in-foerde on somnung
etiam sabbati 6 *Factum est autem et in alio sabbato ut intraret in synagoga*m*

* XX. 42. ii. mt. cxui. mr. xxu.

⁊ lærde ⁊ wæs ðer monn ⁊ hond his ðiu suiðra gescruncan behealdon ðon*ne*
et doceret et erat ibi homo et manus eius dextra arida 7 obseruabant autem

ða uðuuto ⁊ gif on symbe[l]dæg he hælde ꝥte hia gemoete to telenne hine he uut*edlice*
scribae et pharisaei si sabbato curaret ut inuenirent accusare illum 8 ipse uero

wiste smeunga hiora ⁊ cuoeð ðæm menn seðe hæfde hond gescrengc*e* ł dryge aris ⁊
sciebat cogitationes eorum et ait homini qui habebat manum† aridam surge et

† MS. magnum, *with the gloss* micel; *altered to* manum, *with the gloss* hond.

sona on middum ⁊ aras astód cuoeð ðon*ne* to him se hæl*end* ic gefregno iuih gif is alefed
sta in medium et surgens stetit 9 ait autem ad illos i*esus* interrogo uos sí licet

on symbeldæg wel doa ł oððe yfle sawel hal doa ł oððe losiga ⁊ ymb-sceawandu*m*
sabbato bene facere án male animam saluam facere an perdere 10 et circum-spectis

allu*m* cuoeð ðæm menn aðen hond ðin ⁊ aðenide ⁊ eft-geniuað wæs hond his
omnib*us* dixit homini extende manum tuam et extendit et restituta est manus eius

ðailco uut*edlice* gefylled weron mið unsnytro ⁊ efne-sprecon bituih huæd for*ð*on dedon
11 ipsi autem repleti sunt insipientia et conloquebantur ad inuicem quidnam facerent

ðæm hæl*ende*
i*esu*

[*Eight leaves lost in the* Rushworth MS.]

12 Soþlice on þam dagum he férde on anne munt hine gebiddan. ⁊ wæs þar waciende on godes gebede;

13 And þa ðа dæg wæs he clypode hys leorning-cnihtas ⁊ geceas twelf of him. ⁊ þa he nemde apostolas;

14 Simonem þæne he nemde Petrus ⁊ his broðor andreas. Iacobum ⁊ Iohannem. Filippum. ⁊ Bartholomeum.

15 ⁊ Thomám. ⁊ Matheum. ⁊ Iacobum. alfei. ⁊ simonem. se is genemned zelotes.

16 Iudam. Iacobi. ⁊ iudam scarioð se wæs læwa;

17 And mid him farendum he stód on feld-lice stówe. ⁊ mycel wered his leorning-cnihta. ⁊ mycel menegeo fram ealra iudea ⁊ fram ierusalem. ⁊ ofer muþan ⁊ sǽ-gemæro tíri ⁊ sidónis. ðа coman ꝥ hi hyne gehyrdon. ⁊ wǽron of hyra adlum gehælede.

18 ⁊ þa ðe wǽron of unclænum gastum ge-drehte wærun gehælede;

19 And eal seo menigeo sohte hine tó æt-hrinenne. forþam þe mægen of him eode ⁊ he ealle gehælde;

20 Ða cwæþ se hælend beseonde to his leorning-cnihtum; Eadige synd ge þearfan on gaste forþam þe godes ríce is eower;

21 Eadige synd ge ðe hingriað nú. forþam þe ge beoð gefyllede; Eadige synt ge ðe nu wepað. forþam ge hlihaþ;

12 Soðlice on þam dagen he ferde on ænne munt. hine ge-byddan. ⁊ wæs þær wakiende on godes ge-bede.

13 Ænd þa þa hit daig wæs he cleopede his leorning-cnihtes ⁊ ge-cheas twelf of heom. ⁊ þa he nemnede apostles.

14 Simonem þanne he nemnede petrus. ⁊ his broðer andreas. Iacobum. ⁊ Iohannem. philippum ⁊ bartholomeum.

15 Thomam ⁊ Matheum. Iacobum alphei ⁊ symonem. se ys ge-nemned zelotes

16 Iudam Iacocobi (*sic*). ⁊ Iudam scarioth. se wæs læwa.

17 And mid heom farenden he stod on feldlicere stowe ⁊ micel werd hys leorning-cnihte ⁊ mycele manega fram alre iudea. ⁊ fram ierusalem ⁊ ofer muðan ⁊ sæ. ge-mare tyry ⁊ sydonis. þa comen þæt hyo hyne ge-hyrdon ⁊ wæren of heora adlen ge-hælde.

18 ⁊ þa þe waren of un-clænen gaste ge-drehte wæren ge-hælede.

19 Ænd seo manegeo sohte hine to æt-hrinnenne. for þam þe mægen of hym eode. ⁊ he ealle ge-hælde.

20 ÐA cwæð se hælend beo-seonde to hys leorning-cnihton. Eadige synde ge þearfen on gaste. for þan þe godes ríce is eower.

21 Eadige synde ge þe hingrieð nu. for þam ge beoð ge-fyllede. Eadige synde ge þe nu wepad; for þam ge hlyhað.

Various Readings.

12. A. B. C. wacigende. 13. A. twelfe. 14. A. andream. A. philippum; C. Filippus. C. bartholomeus. 15. A. B. C. *omit* ⁊ *before* Thomám *and* Iacobum. 17. A. B. feldlicre; C. flendlicre (*sic*). A. mænegeo. C. ealre. A. B. C. sǽ-gemære. A. comon; B. C. comun. A. hig. A. heora. 18. A. wæron. 19. A. *om.* eal. A. mænigeo. A. æt-hrynanne. C. *om.* ealle. 20. B. C. synt. 21. B. C. synt [*for* synd]. A. synd [*for* synt]. C. Eadie. A. hlihhað.

Various Readings.

12. dagum; wacyende. 13. R. *om.* hit; clypede; -cnihtas; ge-ceas; nemde apostlas. 14. þonne; nemde. 16. Iacobi. 17. Ænd; eom; farenden [*as in* Hatton MS.]; -cnihta; menega; alra; comon; wæron; adlum ge-hælede. 18. waron; unclænum; ge-halede. 19. Ænd eall syo menegeo. 20. halend; -cnihtum; Eadig synt ge þearfan; for-þam. 21. synt; hingriað; sint; wepað.

aworden wæs ðon*ne* on ðæm dagum foerde on more to gebidda*nne* ⁊ wæs ðerh-wæccende
12 *Factum est autem in illis diebus exiit in montem orare et erat pernoctans * 43. ii. mt. cxluiii[i]. mr. lxui. [MS. cxui.]

in gebed godes ⁊ mið ðy dæg aworden wæs geceigde ða ðegnas his ⁊ geceas tuoelf
in oratione d*e*i 13 *Et cum dies factus esset uocauit discipulos suos et elegit duodecim * 44. ii. mt. lxxx. mr. xxx.

of ðæm ða æc apos*tolas* genemde ðone simon ðone getor-nomade ł stan ⁊
ex ipsis quos et apostolos nominauit 14 simonem quem cognominauit petrum et

broðer his ⁊ ⁊ ⁊
andrean fratrem eius iacobum et iohannen philippum et bartholomeu*m* 15 matheum et

ðe huita ł ⁊ seðe is geceiged ⁊
thoman iacobum alphei et simonem qui uocatur zelotes 16 iudam iacobi et iudam

seðe wæs hlega ⁊ of-dune astag mið him astod on stou ⁊ menigo ł ðreat
scarioth qui fuit proditor 17 *Et descendens cum illis stetit in loco campestri et turba * 45. i. mt. xxiii. mr. xxuii. io. xlui.

ðegna his ⁊ ðio menigo monigfald folces of alle iud' ⁊ ⁊ ⁊
discipulorum eius et multitudo copiosa plebis ab omni iudaea et hierusalem et maritima et

⁊ ða ðe cuomon ꝥte geherdon hine ⁊ weron gehældo fro*m* adlu*m* hiora ⁊
tyri et sidonis qui uenerunt ut audirent eum et sanarentur á languoribus suis 18 et

ðaðe gecosted weron fro*m* gastu*m* unclænum woeron gelecnad ⁊ all ðread sohton
qui uexabantur á spiritib*us* inmundis curabantur 19 et omnis turba quaerebant

hine to ge*h*rinanne for*ð*on mæhto ł mægno of him foerdon ⁊ hælde alle ⁊ he ahebbendum
eum tangere quia uirtus de illo exiebant et sanabat omnes 20 *Et ipse eleuatis * XXI. 46. u. mt. xxu.

egum on ðegnum his cuoeð eadgo ða ðorfendo for*ð*on iuer is ríc godes eadgo
oculis in discipulos suos dicebat Beati pauperes quia uestrum est regnum d*e*i 21 *Beati * 47. u. mt. xxuiii.

ðaðe nu gehyncres for*ð*on gie biðon gehriorded eadgo ðaðe nu gie woepeð for*ð*on gie hlæheð
qui nunc esuritis quia saturabimini *Beati qui nunc fletis quia ridebitis * 48. u. mt. xxuii.

[*Eight leaves lost in the* Rushworth MS.]

22 Eadige beo ge. þone eow men hatiað ⁊ ehtað. ⁊ on-hiscaþ. ⁊ awurpað eowerne naman swa swa yfel for mannes suna;

23 Ge-blissiað ⁊ gefagniað on þa*m* dagu*m*. nu eower med is mycel on heofenu*m*; Soðlice æfter þissu*m* þingu*m* hyra fæderas dydon þa*m* witegum;

24 Þeah-hwæðere wā eow witegum. forþa*m* þe ge eowerne frofor habbað;

25 Wa eow þe ge-fyllede synt. forþam þe ge hingriað. Wa eow þe nu hlihað. forþa*m* þe ge heofað ⁊ wepað;

26 Wa eow þonne eow ealle men bletsiað. æfter þissum þingum hyra fæderas dydon þam witegum;

27 Ac ic eow sege forþa*m* þe ge gehyraþ. lufiað eowre fynd doþ þa*m* tala þe eow hatedon;

28 Bletsiað þa ðe eow wiriað. gebiddaþ for þa þe eow on-hisceað;

29 And þa*m* þe slihþ on þin gewenge wend oðer agēn. ⁊ þa*m* þe ðin reaf nymþ. ne for-beod him no þīne tunecan;

30 Syle ælcu*m* þe ðe bidde. ⁊ se ðe nimþ þa ðing þe ðīne synt ne mynega þu hyra;

31 And swa ge wyllaþ ꝥ eow men dōn doþ him gelice;

32 ⁊ hwylc þanc is eow gif ge lufiað þa þe eow lufiað; Soðlice synfulle lufiað þa þe hi lufiað;

Various Readings.

22. C. Eadie. A. þonn*e*. A. aworpað; C. wurpað. 23. A. ge-fægeniað. C. heofonu*m*. A. þysu*m*. A. heora. 24. A. frofer. 25. A. synd. A. hlyhhað. A. heofiað. 26. C. *om.* 2*nd* eow. A. heora. 27. B. C. secge. A. tæla. 28. A. wyrgeað. A. on-hyscað. 29. A. þe ðe slyhð. A. ongean. A. na. 30. A. synd. B. mynga; C. myng. A. hyne [*for* hyra]. 31. A. heom. 32. C. *inserts* swa *before* hwylc. A. hig. C. *omits from* Soðlice *to end of verse.*

22 Eadige beo ge þanne eow men hatiað ⁊ ehtað. ⁊ on-huscað. ⁊ awurped eowre namen swa swa yfel for mannes sune.

23 Ge-blissiad ⁊ ge-fageniad on þam dagen; nu eower mede is mycel on heofene. Soðlice æfter þisen þingen hyra faderes dydon þa*m* witegan.

24 Þeah-hwæðere wa eow witegan. for þan þe ge eowwerne frofer hæbbeð.

25 Wa eow þe ge-fylde sinde; for þan þe ge hingriað. Wa eow þe nu hlehgad for þan þe ge heofað ⁊ wepeð.

26 Wa eow þanne eow ealle men bletsiað æfter þisen þingen heora fæderes dyden þam witegen.

27 Ac ic eow segge for þam þe ge hyrad. Lufiað eowre feond doð þam tæle þe eow hatedon.

28 Bletsieð þa þe eow weregieð. Ge-biððed for þa*m* þe eow on-huscieð.

29 ⁊ þa*m* þe þe slehð on þa*m* wange. wend oðer agen. ⁊ þam þe þin reaf nymð ne for-beod him na þine tunecan.

30 Syle ælcen þe þe bidde. ⁊ se þe nymd þa þing þe þine synde ne munega þu hyra.

31 ⁊ swa eow willeð ꝥ eow men do; doð he*m* ge-lice.

32 ⁊ hwilc þanc is eow gyf ge lufieð þa þe eow lufieð. Soðlice senfulle lufieð; þa þe hy lufieð.

Various Readings.

22. þonne; on-hyscað; awurpeð; naman. 23. Ge-blissiað; ge-fageniað; dagv*m*; heofenu*m*; þyssum þingu*m*; fæderas; witegu*m*. 24. witegum; for-þa*m*; eowerne frofor habbað. 25. ge-fyllede sint; hlihhað; wepað. 26. þo*n*ne; þissu*m* þingu*m*; fæderas dydon; witegu*m*. 27. hyrað; tale. 28. Bletsiað; wyrgyað; ge-byddað; ða; on-hysceað. 29. slyhð; þin [*for* þa*m*]; ge-wenge. 30. ælcum; nimð; synt. 31. ge [*for* 1*st* eow]; willað; don [*for* do]; heom. 32. lufiað [*four times*]; synfulle; hyo.

eadgo gie biðon miððy iuih læðeð menn ⁊ miððy to-sceadon ł sceadas iuih ⁊ telað ł harm
22 *Beati eritis cum uos oderint homines et cum separauerint uos et exproba- * 49. u. mt. xxx.

cueðað ⁊ auorpað noma iuer suelce yfel ł apoltre *fore* sunu monnes gefeað
uerint et eiecerint nomen uestru*m* tam-quam malum propter filium hominis 23 gaudete

on ðæm dæge ⁊ wosað glæd heono *for*ðon mearda iura menigo on heofne æft*er* ðæs *for*ðon
in illa die et exultate ecce enim mercis uestra multa in caelo secundum haec enim

dydon witgum fadoras hiora soð huoeðre wæ iuh weligum *for*ðon gie habbað
faciebant prophetis patres eorum 24 *Uerum-tamen uáe uobis diuitib*us* quia habetis * 50. x.

froefernise iuer wæ iuh *for*ðon ge gefylled biðon *for*ðon biðongie hyngrendo wæ iuh
consolationem uestram 25 uáe uobis quia saturati estis quia esurietis uáe uobis

ðaðe gie hlæhas nū *for*ðon gie woepað wæ miððy wel iuh cuoæðað alle menn
qui ridetis nunc quia lugebitis 26 *uáe cum bene uobis dixerint omnes homines [* 51. x.]

æft*er* ðas dydon witgu*m* fador*as* hiora ah iuh ic cuoeðo ðaðe ge geherdon
secundum haec faciebant prophetis patres eorum 27 *Sed uobis dico qui auditis * 52. u. mt. xl.

lufigað fiondas Iura wel doeð ðæm ðaðe iuih læðað wel cueðas ł bloedsas ðæm
diligite inimicos uestros bene facite hiis qui uos oderunt 28 benedicite male-

woergendu*m* iuh gebiddað *fo*re ðæm harm-cuoedu*m* iuih ⁊ seðe ðec slaeð on cece
dicentib*us* uobis orate pro calumniantib*us* uos 29 *Et qui té percutit in maxillam *53. u. mt. xxxuiii.

agef æc ða oðero ⁊ of ðæm ł fro*m* him seðe genimeð ðe woedo æc ꝥ cyrtil nælle ðu
praebe et alteram et ab eo qui auferet tibi uestimentum etiam tunica[*m*] noli

*for*stonda ł *for*beada eghuelcu*m* uut*edlice* giugiende ðec sel ⁊ seðe ni*m*með ðaðe ðin sint ne
prohibere 30 omni autem petenti té tribue et q*ui* auferet q*ue* tua *sun*t ne

eft-bidde ðu ⁊ suæ gie wælle ꝥte gedoe iuh menn ⁊ gie doað him gelic
repetas 31 *Et pro-ut uultis ut faciant uobis homines et uos facite illis similiter * XXII. 54. u. mt. liiii.

⁊ gif gie lufað hia ðaðe iuih lufað ða ł huelc iuh is ðonc ł wuldor *for*ðon ⁊ synnfullo
32 *Et si diligitis eos qui uos diligunt quae uobis est gratia nam et peccatores * 55. u. mt. xli.

ða lufiande hia lufagiað
diligentes sé diligunt

[*Eight leaves lost in the* Rushworth MS.]

33 And gyf ge wel doð. þa*m* ðe eow wel doð. hwylc þanc is eow. witodlice ꝥ doð synfulle.

34 ⁊ gyf ge lænaþ þa*m* þe ge eft æt onfoð. hwylc þanc is eow; Soþlice synfulle synfullu*m* lænað. ꝥ hi gelice onfon.

35 þeah-hwæðere lufiað eowre fynd ⁊ hi*m* wel doð. ⁊ læne syllað nan þing þanun eft ge-hihtende. ⁊ eower med byþ [mycel] on heofone. ⁊ ge beoþ þæs hehstan bearn. forþa*m* þe he is gód ofer unþanc-fulle ⁊ ofer yfele;

Ðis ge-byrað on þone fiftan sunnan-dæg ofer pentecosten. Estote ergo misericordes. A.

36 Heornost-lice beoþ mild-heorte swa eower fæder is mild-heort;

37 Nelle ge deman. ⁊ ge ne beoð demede; Nelle ge ge-nyðerian. ⁊ ge ne beoð genyþerude; Forgyfaþ. ⁊ eow byð for-gyfen;

38 Syllað ⁊ eow byþ geseald gód gemet ⁊ full. geheapod ⁊ ofer-flowende hig syllaþ on eowerne bearm; þam sylfan gemete þe ge metað. eow byð gemeten;

39 Ða sæde he him sum bigspell; Segst þu. mæg se blinda þæne blindan lædan. hu ne feallaþ hig begen on þæne pytt;

40 Nis se leorning-cniht ofer þone lareow; Ælc byð fulfremed. gif he is swylce hys lareow;

41 Hwi gesihst þu þa egle on þines broþor eagan. ⁊ ne ge-sihst þæne beam on þinu*m* eagan;

33 And gif ge wel doð þan þe eow wel doð; hwilc þanc is eow. Witodlice þæt doð sinfulle.

34 ⁊ gyf ge leaneð þa*m* þe ge eft on-foð; hwilc þanc is eow. Soðlice sinfulle sinfulle leaneð. þæt hyo gelice on-fon.

35 Þeah-hwæðere lufiað eowre feond. ⁊ heom wel doð. ⁊ leane sylled nan þing þanum (*sic*) eft ge-hihtende. ⁊ eower mede beod mycel on heofene. ⁊ ge beoð þas hegesten bearn. for þam þe he ys god ofer unþanc-fulle ⁊ ofer yfele.

36 Eornestlice beoð mildheorte swa eower fader is mildheort.

37 Nelle ge demen. ⁊ ge ne beoð demede. Nelle ge nyðerien. ⁊ ge ne beoð ge-nyðereð. For-gyfeð; ænd eow beoð for-gefen.

38 Selleð ⁊ eow beoð ge-seald. gód gemet ⁊ full ⁊ ge-heapod. ⁊ ofer-flowende hyo sylled on eowrne bearm. Þam sylfen gemette þe ge meteð; eow beoð ge-metan.

39 Ða sæde he heom sum by-spell. Segst þu maig se blinde þane blinde læden. hu ne fealled hyo begen on þanne pet.

40 Nis se leorning-cniht ofer þanne lareow. ælc byð fulfremed gyf he is swilc hys lareow.

41 hwi ge-syhst þu þa eigle on þines broðer eagen. ⁊ ne syhst þænne beam on þynen eagen.

Various Readings.

33. A. deð [*for 2nd* doð]. 34. A. hig. 35. A. þanen. A. B. C. *insert* mycel, *which* Corpus MS. *omits.* 36. A. B. C. Eornostlice (*with coloured initial*). 37. A. genyðerode. 38. A. B. C. *insert* ⁊ *before* geheapod. 39. A. þone. A. ænne pytt. 40. A. se [*for* hys]. 41. A. hwig. A. broðer. A. þone. C. egan.

Various Readings.

33. þa*m*. 34. lænað; R. *inserts* æt *after* eft; Soððlice; lænað. 35. fynd; eom; læne syllað; þanun; med byð; heofone; þæs heahstan. 36. Eornostlice; fæder. 37. deman; byð ge-nyderede; For-gyfað; byð for-gyfan. 38. Syllað; byð ge-sealð; ge-heapoð; syllað; sylfan; gemetan [*as in* Hatton MS.]. 39. eom; bi-spel; mæg; þone; fealleð; pytt. 40. þonne læreow. 41. ge-sychst; broðor eagan; syhcst (*sic*) þæne; þinu*m* eagan.

⁊ gif wel gie doeð ðæm ðaðe iuh wel doeð huelc iuh is ðonc ðah-hueðre ⁊
33 et si bene-feceritis hiis qui uobis benefaciunt quae uobis est gratia siquidem et

synnfulle ðis doað ⁊ gif huerf gie sellas ðæm from ðæm gie hyhtað to onfoane huelc
peccatores hoc faciunt 34 et si mutu[u]m dederitis his á quibus speratis accipere quae

ðonc is iuh forðon ⁊ synnfullo synnfullum biðon gearwyrðed ꝥte onfoað efne ł
gratia est uobis nam et peccatores peccatoribus fænerantur ut recipiant aequalia

soð-hueðre lufiges fiondes iuera ⁊ wel doað ⁊ huoerf seallað noht on ðec hyhtendo
35 uerumtamen diligite inimicos uestros et benefacite et mutuum date nihil in té sperantes

⁊ bið meard iura micelo ⁊ gie biðon sunu ðæs heiste forðon he rũm-mõd is ofer unðoncfullum
et erit mercis uestra multa et eritis filii altissimi quia ipse benignus est super ingratos

⁊ yflum wosað gie forðon milt-heorte suæ ⁊ faeder iuer milt-heart is nellað gie
et malos 36 estote ergo misericordes sicut et pater uester misericors est 37 *Nolite * XXIII.56.ii. mt. l. mr. xli.

gedoema ⁊ ne ꝥte gie se gedoemed nællað gie gehniðra ⁊ ꝥte gie ne se gehniðrad forletas ⁊
iudicare et non iudicabimini nolite condemnare et non condemnabimini dimittite et

iuh bið forleten seallas ⁊ iuh bið sald gewoege ł gemet god efne-gebroht ⁊ ⁊
dimittimini 38 date et dabitur uobis mensuram bonam confertam et coagitatam et

ofer flouende hia sellað on barm iuer ðio ilco forðon gemet ꝥte metende gie biðon
super effluentem dabunt in sinum uestrum eadem quippe mensura qua mensi fueritis

eft-gemeten iuh bið cuoeð ðonne him ⁊ onlicnese hueðer mæg se blind
rementientur (*sic*) uobis 39 *Dicebat autem illis et similitudinem num-quid potest caecus * 57. u. mt. clui.

ðone blinde gelæda ahne boege on seaðe fallað ne is ł nesẽ discipul ofer magistre
caecum ducere nonne ambo in foueam cadent 40 *Non est discipulus super magistrum * 58. ii[i]. mt. xc. io. cxxxuiiii.

wis-fæst ðonne eghuelc bið gif ł sua laruu his huæd ðonne gesiist ðu ꝥ lytle mõt in
perfectus autem omnis erit sicut magister eius 41 *Quid autem uides festucam in * 59. u. mt. li.

ego broðres ðines ðone beam uutedlice ðio in ego ðinum is ne efne-sceauas ðu
oculo fratres (*sic*) tui trabem autem quae in oculo tuo est non consideras

---

[*Eight leaves lost in the* Rushworth MS.]

42 And hu miht þu segan þínu*m* breþer bróþor lǽt ꝥ ic ateo þa egle of þínu*m* eage. ⁊ þu sylf ne ge-syhst þæne beam on þinu*m* agenu*m* eagan; Eala licetere. teoh ærest þone beam of þinu*m* eage. ⁊ þon*ne* þu gesihst ꝥ ðu ateo þa egle of þines broðor eage;

43 Nys god treow þe yfelne wæstm deð. ne nis yfel treow. gódne wæstm donde;

44 Ælc treow is be his wæstme on-cnáwen; Ne hig of þornu*m* fíc-æppla ne gaderiaþ. ne winberian on gorste ne nimað;

45 God man of godu*m* gold-hórde. hys heortan. god forð-bringð. ⁊ yfel man of yfelu*m* gold-horde yfel forð-bringþ; Soðlice se muð spycð swa seo heorte þencð.

46 hwi clypege ge mé drihten drihten. ⁊ ne doð ꝥ ic eow secge;

47 Ælc þara þe to me cymþ ⁊ míne spræca gehyrð ⁊ þa deþ. ic him æt-ýwe hwa*m* he ge-lic is;

48 He ys gelic timbriendu*m* men his hús; Se dealf deopne ⁊ hys grund-weall ofer þæne stán asette; Soðlice gewordenu*m* flode hit fleow into þam huse. ⁊ hyt ne mihte ꝥ hus astirian. hit wæs ofer þæne stán getrymed;

49 Se ðe gehyrð ⁊ ne déþ. he is gelíc þa*m* timbriendan men his hus ofer þa eorþan butan grund-wealle. ⁊ ꝥ flod in-fleow. ⁊ hrædlice hyt afeoll ⁊ wearð mycel hryre þæs huses;

42 Ænd hu myht þu seggen þinen breðer. broðer læt þæt íc ateo þa eigle of þinen eage*n*. ⁊ ðu self ne ge-syhst þanne beam on þinen eagenen eagen. Eala licetere teoh ærest þanne beam of þinen eage. ⁊ þanne þu ge-syhst þæt þu ateo þa eigle of þines broðor eage.

43 Nís god treow þæt yfelne wæstm deð. ⁊ nis yfel treow godne wæstm doende.

44 Ælc treow is be hys wæstme oncnawen. Ne hyo of þornen fic-æppel ne gaderieð. ne winberian of gorste ne nymeð.

45 gód man of goden goldhorde; hys heorte god forð-brincð. ⁊ yfele men of yfele goldhorde yfel forð-bringeð. Soðlice se muð specð swa swa sye heorte þencð.

46 Hwy clepie ge me drihten drihten ⁊ ne doð þæt ic eow segge.

47 Ælc þare þe to me kymð. ⁊ mine spræce ge-hyrð ⁊ þa deð. ích hym átewie hwam he ge-lic ys.

48 He ys gelíc tymbriende men hys hus se dealf deopne ⁊ his grundwall ofer þanne stan asette. Soðlice ge-worðene flode hit fleow in-to þam huse. ⁊ hit ne mihte ꝥ hus astyrian hit wæs ofer þanne stan getrymed.

49 Se ðe ge-hyrð ⁊ ne deð; he is gelich þam tymbriende*n* men his hus ofer þa eorðen buton grundwalle. ⁊ ꝥ flod in-fleow ⁊ rædlice hit afeol ⁊ warð mycel ryre þas huses.

Various Readings.

42. A. B. C. secgan. C. ege [*for* 1*st* egle]. A. eagan [*for* 1*st* eage.] A. þone [*for* þæne]. B. C. æryst. A. broðer eagan. **44.** B. C. hi. A. of [*for* on]. **45.** A. forð-bryncð; C. forð-bring [2*nd time*]. A. sprycð. **46.** A. hwig. A. clypige; B. C. clypie. **47.** A. þæra. **48.** A. deope. A. þone (*twice*). **49.** C. timbriendum.

Various Readings.

42. þine; broðor [*for* broðer]; egle; þinu*m* eage; sylf; þænne; þinu*m* agenu*m* eagan; arest þonne; þinu*m*; þone; egle. 43. ne [*for* ⁊]; westm. 44. þornum fíc-æppla; gaderiað; on [*for* of]; nymað. 45. godu*m*; heortan; brýngð; yfel man; yfelum gold-horde; brincð; seo. 46. clepige me. 47. þaræ; cymð; ætywie. 48. tymbrigendu*m*; dælf; þonne; ge-wordene. 49. ge-lic; eorðan butan; -wealle; afeoll; werð.

⁊ hu mæht ðu cuoæða broðre ðinu*m* broðer *for*let þte ic aworpo ðone mot of ego ðinu*m*
42 et quomodo potes dicere fratri tuo frater sine eiciam festucam de oculo tuo

he in ego ðinu*m* þ beam ne gesiis ðu la legere aworp ærist ðone beam of ego ðinu*m* ⁊
ipse in oculo tuo trabem non uidens hypocrita eice primum trabem de oculo tuo et

ðon*ne* ðu eft-locas þte ðu ofgebrenge ðæt mot of ego broðres ðines ne is *for*ðon tree god
tunc respicies ut educas festucam de oculo fratris tui 43 *Non est enim arbor bona * 60. u. mt. luiii.

ðio doeð wæstma yfla ne tree yfla wyrcas wæstm god an suæ-huælc *for*ðon
quae facit fructos (*sic*) malos neq*ue* arbor mala faciens fructum bonum 44 unaquaeque enim

tree of wæstm his gecyðed bið ne *for*ðon of ðornu*m* gesomnað fic-beam ne of
arbor de fructu suo cognoscitur *Neq*ue* enim de spinis colligunt ficus neque de †rubo * 61. u. mt. lu[ii]. † *Over* rubo *are two glosses, nearly obliterated;* (1) word [*as if it were* uerbo]; (2) reado [*as if* rubro].

hia winigað ł monigfaldas þ winbeger ł þ cropp god mon of god strion heartes his ahefeð
uindemiant uuam 45 *Bonus homo de bono thesauro cordis sui profert

god ⁊ yfel monn of yfele ahebbeð yfel of monigfaldnise *for*ðon heartes muð spreces
bonum et malus homo de malo profert malum ex habundantia enim cordis ós loquitur * 62. u. mt. cxxu.

huæd ðon*ne* ceiges gie mec drih*ten* drih*ten* ⁊ ne doað gie ða ðe ic cuoeðo eghuoelc seðe
46 *Quid autem uocatis me d*omi*ne d*omi*ne et non facitis quae dico 47 †Omnis qui * 63. iii. mt. luiiii. io. cxui. † 64. u. mt. lxi.

cymeð to me ⁊ gehereð worda mina ⁊ doeð ða ł hia ic ad-eaua iuh huæm gelíc sie
uenit ad me et audit sermones meos et facit eos ostendam uobis cui similis est

gelic is ðæm menn timbrende hus seðe delfæð on heanise ⁊ gesette ða grundas of*er*
48 similis est homini aedificanti domum qui fodit in altum et posuit fundamenta supra

carr ł stan flod ł hreh miððy uut*edlice* awarð to-brocen wæs se stream ðæm huse ⁊ mæhte hia
petram inundatione autem facta inlisum est flumen domui illi et non potuit eam

gestyurige gesettet *for*ðon wæs on-ufa carr seðe ðon*ne* geherde ⁊ ne dyde gelic is
mouere fundata enim erat supra petram 49 qui autem audiuit et non fecit similis est

ðæm menn timbrende hus his on-ufa stan buta grund on ðon toslitten wæs þ stream
homini aedificanti domum suam supra petram sine fundamento in qua inlisus est fluuius

⁊ sona gefeall ⁊ aworden wæs faell huses ðæs micel
et continuo cecidit et facta est ruina domus illius magna

[*Eight leaves lost in the* Rushworth MS.]

CHAPTER VII.

1 Soþlice ða he ealle his wórd gyfylde
on þæs folces hlyste. he eode into
cafarnaum;
2 Þa wæs sumes hundred-mannes þeowa
untrum. se wæs sweltendlic. se wæs him
dýre;
3 And þa he gehyrde be þam hælende
he sende to him iudea ealdras ⁊ bæd ꝥ he
cóme. ⁊ hys þeow gehælde;
4 Þa hí to þam hælende comun. hi bǽdon hyne geornlice ⁊ þus cwǽdon; He is
wyrðe ꝥ ðu him tilige.
5 witodlice he lufað úre þeóde. ⁊ he us
úre samnunge getimbrode;
6 Þa ferde se hælend mid him. ⁊ þa he
wæs un-feor þam huse se hundred-mann
sende hys frýnd to him ⁊ cwæþ; Drihten
nelle þu beon gedreht. ne eom ic wyrðe ꝥ
ðu ga under míne þecene.
7 forþam ic ne tealde me sylfne ꝥ ic to
ðe cóme; Ac cweð þín wórd ⁊ min cniht
byð gehæled;
8 Ic ne (*sic*) eom an man under anwealde
gesett; Cempan under me hæbbende. ⁊ ic
secge þissum gá ⁊ he gæð. ⁊ ic secge þissum
cum þonne cymð he. ⁊ ic secge minum
þeowe. do þis ⁊ he deð;
9 Ða wundrude se hælend þam gehyred-
um. ⁊ cwæþ to þære menigeo bewend;
Soþlice ic secge eow ne funde ic on israhel
swa mycelne geleafan.

Various Readings.

Cap. vii. v. 1. A. B. C. gefylde. A. capharnaum. 2. B. hundred-manes. B. swetendlic, *alt. to* sweltendlic; C. swetendlic. 4. A. hyg. A. comon. A. hig. A. tylie. 5. A. ge-samnunge. A. tymbrode. 6. A. *inserts* fram *before* þam. A. -man. C. *om.* eom. 8. A. B. C. *om.* ne *after* Ic. 9. A. wundrode. A. mænio; B. C. menigo.

CHAPTER VII.

1 Soðlice þa he ealle his word gefylde
on þas folces hlyste. he eode in-to
capharnaum.
2 Ða wæs sum hundred-mannes þeowa
untrum se wæs swentendlic (*sic*). se wæs
him dyere.
3 Ænd þa he ge-hyrde be þam hælende.
he sende to him iudea aldres. ⁊ bed þæt
he come ⁊ his þeow ge-hælde.
4 Ða hyo to þam hælende coman. hyo
bæden hine geornlice ⁊ þus cwæðen. He
is wurðe þæt þu him telie.
5 Witodlice he lufeð ure þeode. ⁊ he
us ure samnunge ge-tymbrede.
6 Ða ferde se hælend mid heom. ⁊ þa
he wæs unfeor þam huse se hundredes
ealdor sende his frend to him and cwæð.
Drihten nelle þu beon ge-dreaht. ne eom
ích wurðe þæt þu ga under minne þechene;
7 for þan ích ne tealde me sylfne swa
wurð þæt ich to þe come. Ac cweð þin
word and mín cniht beoð ge-hæled.
8 Ic eom an man under anwealde ge-
sett; cæmpen under me hæbbende. ⁊ ích
segge þissen ga; ⁊ he gæð. ⁊ ích segge
þissen cum; þonne cymð he. ⁊ ích segge
mine þeowe þis do; ⁊ he hit deð.
9 Ða wundrede se hælend þam ge-hyrden.
⁊ cwæð. to þare manigeo be-wend. Soðlice ic segge eow ne funde ich on israel swa
mychele ge-leafen.

Various Readings.

Cap. vii. v. 1. þæs. 2. sweltendlic; dyre. 3. R. *om.* 2*nd* to; ealdras; bæd. 4. halende; coman [*as in* Hatton MS.]; bædon; hin (*sic*) tilige. 5. lufað. 6. halend; him; hundred-man; freond; ge-drect; mine þecene. 7. R. *om.* swa wurð; ic. 8. em; ge-set; campan; habbende; ic; þissum; ic; þissum; ic; þeowwe; R. *om.* hit. 9. halend; ge-hyrdum; menenigo (*sic*); ic; mycele geleafan.

CAP. VII.

miððy uut*edlice* gefyllde alle worda his in earu*m* folces infoerde in ꝥ burug
1 *Cum autem implesset omnia uerba sua in aures plebis intrauit capharnaum *XXIIII. 65. iii. [MS. lxx. x.]

ðæs aldor-monnes ðā sum esne yfle hæbbend wæs dead-lic seðe him wæs dior-wyrðe
2 centurionis autem cuiusdam seruus male habens erat moriturus qui illi erat pretiosus

⁊ mið-ðy geherde fro*m* ðæm hal*end* sende to hi*m* ældo-wuto baed hine ꝥte gecuome ⁊
3 et cum audisset de i*esu* misit ad eum seniores iudaeorum rogans eum ut ueniret et

haelde ðrael his soð hia miððy gecuomon to ðæm helend bedon hine geornlice
saluaret seruum eius 4 at illi cum uenissent ad i*esum* rogabant eum sollicite

cuoedon him ꝥte ł for*ð*on wyrðe is ꝥte ðis him ðu doe lufað for*ð*on cynn usra ⁊
dicentes ei quia dignus est ut hoc illi praestes 5 diligit enim gentem nostram et

somnung ł cirica he getimbrade us se hæl*end* uut*edlice* foerde mið him ⁊ miððy soðlice ne
synagogam ipse aedificauit nobis 6 i*esus* autem ibat cum illis et cum iam non

fearr wæs fro*m* hus sende to him se aldorm*an* freondas cuoeð drih*ten* nælle ðu firr-farra ł ne for*ð*on
longe esset á domo misit ad eum centurio amicos dicens d*omi*ne noli uexari non enim

wyrðe Am ꝥte under *h*rof minu*m* in*n*gae æc for*e*ðon ⁊ mec seolfne ne am ic
dignus sum ut sub tectum meum intres 7 propter quod et me ipsum non sum

wyrðe doemend am ꝥte ic cuome to ðe ah cuoeð mið worde ⁊ hal hið cnæht min for*ð*on
dignum arbitratus ut uenirem ad té sed dic uerbo et sanabitur puer meus 8 nam

⁊ ic monn am under mæht efne-gesettet hafo under mec here-menn ⁊ ic cuoeðo ðisu*m* gāa ⁊
et ego homo sum sub potestate constitutus habens sub me milites et dico huic uade et

gaeð ⁊ oðre cym ⁊ cymeð ⁊ ðræle minu*m* do ðis ⁊ doeð miððy geherde se hæl*end* aundrad wæs
uadit et alio ueni et uenit et seruo meo fac hoc et facit 9 quo audito i*esu* miratus est

⁊ efne-gecerde ł ymbwærlde ðæm æft*er*fylgendu*m* hine ðreatu*m* cuoeð soðlice ic cuoeðo iuh ne in isr*ael*
et conuersus sequentib*us* sé turbis dixit amen dico uobis nec in israhel

ðus micelo geleafo gemoete ic ł ne fund ic
tantam fidem inueni

[*Eight leaves lost in the* Rushworth MS.]

Ðys sceal on þone seofen-teoðan sunnan-dæg ofer pentecosten. Ibat *iesus* in ciuitatem quæ uocatur naim. A.

10 ⁊ þa ðá ham comon ðe asende wæron
hig gemetton halne þone þe ær untrum
wæs;
11 Þa wæs syððan gewórden he férde
on þa ceastre þe is genemned
naím. ⁊ mid him ferdun hys leorning-
cnihtas. ⁊ mycel menego;
12 Þa he ge-nealæhte þære ceastre gate
þa wæs þar án dead man geboren anre
wudewan sunu þe nanne oðerne næfde; ⁊
seo wudewe wæs þar. ⁊ mycel menegu
þære burhware mid hyre;
13 Þa se hælend hig ge-seah þa wæs he
mid mild-heortnesse ofer hig gefylled. ⁊
cwæþ to hyre. ne wep þu ná.
14 Ða genealæhte he ⁊ þa cyste æt-hran.
þa æt-stodon þa þe hyne bæron; Þa cwæþ
se hælend. eala geonga þe ic secge arís;
15 Ða arás se þe dead wæs. ⁊ ongan
sprecan. þa agef he hine hys meder;
16 Þa ofer-eode ege hig ealle. ⁊ hig god
mærsodon ⁊ cwædon. ꝥ mære witega on
us arás. ⁊ þæt god hys folc geneosude;

Misit iohannes duos de discipulis suis ad *iesum* dicens. Tu es qui uenturus és án alium expectamus. B.

17 Ða férde þeos spæc be him on ealle
iudea. ⁊ embe eall ꝥ ríce;
18 Ða cyddun iohannes leorning-cnihtas
him be eallum þysum þingum;
19 Þa clypode iohannes twegen of his
leorning-cnihtum. ⁊ sende to þam hælende.
⁊ þus cwæþ; Eart þu þe [to] cumene eart.
hwæðer þe we oþres scylon onbydan;

---

10 ⁊ þa þa ham comen þe asende wæren
hyo ge-metten halne þanne þe ær u[n]trum
wæs.
11 ÞA wæs syððen ge-worðen he ferde Ibat *iesus* ciuitatem uocatur na
on þa ceastre þe ys ge-nemned
naym; ⁊ mid hym ferden his leorning-
cnyhtes. ⁊ mycel manigeo.
12 Þa he ge-nehlahte þare ceastre gate
þa wæs þær an dead man ge-boren ane
wudewon sune. þe nænne oðerne næfde.
⁊ syo wudewe wæs þær. ⁊ mycel menigeo
þare burh-wære míd hire.
13 Ða se hælend hyo ge-seah. Ða wæs
he míd mildheortnysse ofer hyo ge-felled.
⁊ cwæð to hire. ne wep þu na.
14 Þa ge-nehleahte he ⁊ þa cheste ætran.
þa æt-stoden þa þe hine beren. Ða cwæð se
hælend. Eala geonge þe is (*sic*) segge aris.
15 Þa aras se þe dead wæs. ⁊ ongan
spræcen. þa agef he hine his moder.
16 Þa ofer-eode eyge hyo ealle. ⁊ hyo
god mersodon ⁊ cwæðen. ꝥ mare witega
on us aras. ⁊ þæt god his folce ge-neosode.
17 ÐA ferde þeos spræce be him on
eallen iudea ⁊ embe eall þæt rice.
18 Ða cyddan iohannes leorning-cnihtes
him be eallen þisen þingen.
19 ÐA cleopede iohannes twegen of Misit ioha nes duos d discipulis ad iesum d cens. tu es uenturus e an alium e pectamus.
his leorning-cnihten to hym. ⁊
sende to þam halende ⁊ þus cwæð. Ert þu
þe to cumene ert; hweðer þe we oðres
sculon on-bidon.

Various Readings.

11. A. ferdon. A. mænigeo. 12. A. wude, *altered to* wudewe. A. mænigeo. 13. A. myldheortnysse. 15. A. ageaf. 16. A. neosode. 17. A. spræc. A. ymbe. 18. A. cyðdon. 19. A. *inserts* to *after* þe. A. cumenne. A. sceolon; B. C. sculon.

Various Readings.

10. wæron; ge-metton; þonne; untru*m*. 11. syððan geworden; -cnihtas; menego. 12. ge-neahlæhte; ane wudewan; seo; menego; burh-ware. 13. halend; mud [*an error for* mid]; ge-fylled. 14. ge-neahlæhte; cyste; et-stoden; bæron; ic. 15. ðead [*an error for* dead]; sprecan; agaf; modor. 16. cwaðen. 17. ealle. 18. -cnihtas; eallum þissu*m* þingum. 19. cleopode; -cnihtu*m*; Eart [*for* 1*st* Ert]; on-bidan.

⁊ gecerdon ðaðe gesended woeron to hām ł hus gemoeton ðone esne seðe un-hal wæs hal
10 *Et reuersi qui missi fuerant domum inueniunt seruum qui languerat sanum * 66. u. mt. lxui.

⁊ aworden wæs æfter ðon foerde on ceastre ðiu is genemned naim ⁊ eadon mið hine
11 *Et factum est inceps ibat in ciuitatem quae uocatur naim et ibant cum illo * XXU. 67. x.

ðegnas his ⁊ folc monigo mið ðy ðonne geneolecte to durum ceastres ⁊ heono
discipuli eius et turba copiosa 12 cum autem apropinquaret portæ ciuitatis et ecce

dead wæs ferende sunu ancende moderes his ⁊ ðios widua wæs ⁊ folco ceastres monig
defunctus efferebatur filius unicus matris suae et haec uidua erat et turba ciuitatis multa

mið hia ꝧ ilca miððy gesege se drihten mið milt-heortnise gecerred ofer hia cuoeð hir to
cum illa 13 quam cum uidisset dominus misericordia motus super ea dixit illi

nælle ðu woepa ⁊ geneolecde ⁊ hran ꝧ ceiste ða uutedlice ðaðe beron stodon ⁊
noli flere 14 et accessit et tetigit loculum hi autem qui portabant steterunt et

cuoeð esne ðe ic cuoeðo aris ⁊ eft-sætt ł aras seðe wæs dead ⁊ ongann
ait adulescens tibi dico surge 15 et resedit qui fuerat mortuus et cepit

spreca ⁊ salde hine moeder his ondfeng uutedlice alle ondo ⁊ wundradon god
loqui et dedit illum matri suae 16 accepit autem omnes timor et magnificabant deum

cuoedon ꝧte witga micel aras in us ⁊ forðon god sohte folc his
dicentes quia propheta magnus surrexit in nobis et quia deus uisitauit plebem suam

⁊ eode ł foerde ðis word on all iudea ⁊ all ymb ꝧ lond ⁊
17 *Et exiit hic sermo in uniuersam iudaeam et omnem circa regionem 18 †Et * 68. x. † 69. u. mt. cii.

sægdon iohanne ðegnas his of allum ðæm ⁊ efne-geceigde tuoge from ðegnum
nuntiauerunt iohanni discipuli eius de omnibus hſs 19 *Et con-uocauit duos de discipulis * XXUI.

his iohannes ⁊ sende to drihtne cuoeð ðu arð ł arð ðu seðe tocymende wæs ł arð ł oðer
suis iohannes et misit ad dominum dicens tú és qui uenturus és an alium

we abídeð
expectamus

[*Eight leaves lost in the* Rushworth MS.]

20 Ða hig to him comun þus hig cwædon. Iohannes se fulluhtere us sende to þe ⁊ þus cwæð; Eart þu ðe to cumenne eart þe we sculon oðres onbidan;

21 Soðlice on þære tíde he ge-hælde manega of adlum. ge of wítu*m* ⁊ of yfelum gastum. ⁊ manegu*m* blíndum he ge-sihþe forgeaf;

22 Ða cwæþ se hælend; Faraþ ⁊ cyþað iohanne þa ðing þe ge ge-sáwon ⁊ ge-hyrdon; ꝥ blinde geseoð ⁊ healte gaþ. hreoflan synt gehælede. deafe gehyrað. deade arisaþ. þearfan bodiað.

23 ⁊ eadíg ys swa hwylc swa ne byð on me ge-untrywsud;

24 And þa þa iohannes ærend-dracan ferdon. þa cwæð se hælend to þa*m* folce be Iohanne; Hwi ferde ge on westene geseon ꝥ hreod þe byð mid wínde astyred;

25 Ac hwi ferde ge to seonne þone man mid hnescum reafum gescryddne; þa ðe synt on deorwurþum reafe ⁊ on estum;

26 Ac hwi ferde ge þæne witegan geseon. witodlice ic eow secge he is mara þon*ne* witega;

27 Ðes is be þa*m* þe awriten is. nu ic asende minne engel beforan þine ansyne. se ge-gearwað þinne weg beforan þe.

28 Soþlice ic eow secge. nis betwúx wífa bearnum nan mærra witega þon*ne* iohannes se fulluhtere; Se þe is læssa on godes ríce. se is his mara.

Various Readings.

20. A. comon. A. eart hwæðer þe we oðres sceolon. 21. C. *om.* ⁊ *before* manegum. 22. A. synd. 23. A. ge-untreowsod; B. C. ge-untreowsud. 24. A. ærendracan. A. hwig ferdon. A. westenne. 25. A. hwig. A. B. C. ge-seonne. A. B. C. gescrydne. A. synd. A. deorwyrðu*m*. A. B. C. *all the verse at* estum. 26. A. hwig. A. þone. 28. A. betweox. A. mara. [*for* mærra.]

20 Ða hyo to him comen þus hyo cwæðen. Iohannes se fulluhtere us sende to þe ⁊ þus cwæð. Ert þu þe to cumene ert. þe we sculon oðres on-bidan.

21 Soðlice on þare tide he ge-hælde manege of adlen. ge of witen. ⁊ of yfele gasten. ⁊ manegen blinden he ge-sihþe for-gef.

22 þa cwæð se hælend. Fareð end kydað Iohanne þa þing þe ge ge-seagen ⁊ ge-hyrden. ꝥ blinde ge-seoð. ⁊ healte gað. hrefle synde ge-helde. deafe ge-hereð. deade ariseð. þærfen bodiað.

23 ⁊ eadige beoð swa hwilc swa ne beoð on me ge-untreowsod.

24 And þa þa iohannes arend-dracan ferdon; þa cwæð se hælend to þam folce be Iohanne. hwi ferde ge on westene geseon ꝥ reod þe bieð mid winde astyred.

25 Ac hwi ferde ge. to ge-seonne þanne man mid hnescan reafen ge-scyrdne. þa þe sende on deorwurðe reafe ⁊ on esten.

26 Ac hwi ferde ge þanne witegan geseon witodlice ich eow segge he ys mare þanne witega.

27 þes is be þam þe awriten ís. nu ích asende minne ængel be-foran þine ansyene; se ge-gerewed þinne weig be-foran þe.

28 Soðlice ích eow segge nis be-tweox wife bearnen nan mare witegen. þanne iohannes se fulluhtere. Se þe ys læsse on godes rice; se is his mare;

Various Readings.

20. cweð; Eart; eart. 21. manega; adlum; witu*m*; yfelu*m* gastu*m*; manegu*m* blindu*m*; for-geaf. 22. Farað ⁊ cyðað; R. *om.* ge; ge-sawon; ge-hyrdon; gæð; synt ge-halde; ge-hyrað; a-risað; þærfan. 23. eadig byð; byð; ge-untreowsed. 24. ærind-; bið. 25. þonne; hnescum reafu*m* ge-scrydne; synt; estum. 26. þonne; ic; mara. 27. ic; ansyne; ge-gearweð; weg. 28. bitwux wifa bearnu*m*; mærra witega þonne; mara.

miððy uut*edlice* gecuomon to him wæras cuoedon ioh*annes* sende usih to ðe
20 cum autem uenissent ad eum uiri dixerunt iohannis baptista misit nos ad té

cuoeðende ðu arð seðe tocymende wæs ł arð ł oðer we abidas in ðailca ðon*ne* tid lecnade
dicens tú és qui uenturus és an alium expectamus 21 in ipsa autem hora curauit

monigo of adlu*m* ⁊ teissum ł cualmu*m* ⁊ of gastu*m* yflu*m* ⁊ blindum monigu*m* salde gesihðe
multos á languoribus et plagis et spiritibus malis et caecis multis donauit uisum

⁊ ondsuarede cuoeð to him geongas sægcas ioh*anne* ða ðing gie gesego ⁊ gie herdon ꝥte blindo
22 et respondens dixit illis euntes nuntiate iohanni quae uidistis et audistis quia caeci

geseað halto geongeð hreafo geclænsad aron ł sint deafo geherað deado arisað ðorfendo
uident claudi ambulant leprosi mundantur surdi audiunt mortui resurgunt pauperes

hia bodagæð ⁊ eadig is suahuælc seðe ne bið geondspurnad on mec ⁊
euangelizantur 23 et beatus est quicumq*ue* non fuerit scandalizatus in me 24 et

miððy fro*m*-foerdon erendwreco ioh*annes* ongann cuoeða of ioh*anne* to ðæm hergum ymb huæd ł *for*huon
cum discessissent nuntii iohannis coepit dicere de iohanne ad turbas quid

foerdongie on woest*ern* gesea hread ł gerd fro*m* wind gecèrred ah *for*hon foerdegie gesea
existis in desertum uidere harundinem uento moueri 25 sed quid existis uidere

monno *h*nescum gewoedum gegearuad heono seðe In woede diorwyrðe sint ⁊ in
hominem mollib*us* uestimentis indutum Ecce qui in ueste pretiosa sunt et deliciis in

huso cyninga sint ah ymb huæd foerdongie gesea ł to sceawnne witgo uut*edlice* ic cuoeðo
domib*us* regum sunt 26 sed quid existis uidere prophetam utique dico

iuh ⁊ *for*ðor ðon witgo ðis is of ðon awritten is ł wæs heono ic sendo engel
uobis et plus quam prophetam 27 *Hic est de quo scribtum est ecce mitto angelum * 70. ii. mt. ciii. mr. i.

min *fore* onsione ðin seðe *fore*-gearwaðe weg ðin *fore* ðec ic cuoeðo *for*ðon iuh mara
meum ante faciem tuam qui praeparabit uiam tuam ante te 28 *Dico enim uobis maior * 71. u. mt. ciii[i].

bituih sunvm wifa witgo fro*m* ioh*anne* ne ænig is ðæm ðe ðon*ne* leasa is in ric
inter natos mulierum propheta iohanne baptista nemo est cui autem minor est in regno

godes mara is him ł ðæm
dei maior est illo

[*Eight leaves lost in the* Rushworth MS.]

29 ⁊ eall folc þis gehyrende sundor-halgan god heredon ⁊ gefullede on iohannes fulluhte ;

30 Soþlice þa sundor-halgan ⁊ þa ǽ-gleawan forhogodon þæs hælendes geþeaht on hi*m* sylfon. na fram þa*m* hælende gefullode ;

31 Hwa*m* telle ic gelíce þisse cneorisse men. ⁊ h[w]a*m* synt hi gelice ;

32 Hi synt gelice cildum on stræte sittendu*m* ⁊ specendum betwux hi*m* ⁊ cweðendu*m* ; We sungon eow be hearpan. ⁊ ge ne saltudun. we heofdun ⁊ ge ne weopun ;

33 Soþlice iohannes cóm se fulluhtere hláf ne ǽtende ne wín drincende. ⁊ ge cweðað. deofol-seocnysse he hæfð ;

34 Mannes sunu cóm. etende ⁊ drincende. ⁊ ge cweþað þes man is swelgend ⁊ wín dringcende. mán-fullra and synfulra freond ;

35 And wisdom is geriht-wisud on eallu*m* his bearnu*m* ;

Ðis god-spel sceal to þa*m* ymbrene innan hærfaste on frige-dæg. Rogabat iesum. A.

36 Þa bæd hine sum of þa*m* sundor-halgu*m* ꝥ he mid him ǽte. ða eode he into þæs fariseiscan húse ⁊ gesæt ;

37 And þa ꝥ wíf þe wæs on þære ceastre synfull. þa heo on-cneow ꝥ he sæt on þæs fariseus húse. heo brohte hyre sealf-box.

38 ⁊ stód wið-æftan his fét. ⁊ ongan mid hyre tearu*m* hys fét þwean. ⁊ drigde mid hyre heafdes fexe. ⁊ cyste hys fét ⁊ mid sealfe smyrede ;

Various Readings.

29. A. eal. A. sunder-. A. ge-fullode. C. *om.* on. 30. A. sunder-. A. forhogedon. A. sylfu*m*. 31. A. C. hwâ*m*; *but* Corpus MS. *and* B. *have* ha*m*. A. synd hig. 32. A. hig synd. A. sprecendu*m*. A. betweox. A. sealtedon (*with* & non saltastis *above it*). A. heofdon. A. weopon. 33. A. etende; C. ētende. A. deofel-seocnyssa. 34. A. dryncende; B. C. drincende [*2nd time*]. A. C. manfulra; B. mânfulra. 35. A. geryht-wysod. 36. A. sunder-. 37. A. synful. A. ge on-cneow (*with* ge *underlined*). 38. C. *omits from* tearum *to* drigde mid hyre. B. C. feaxe.

29 ⁊ eall folc his herende sunder-halgen god heredon ⁊ ge-fullode on Iohannes fulluhte.

30 Soðlice þa sunder-halgen ⁊ þa lage-gleawen for-hugedon þas hælendes ge-þoht on heom sylfen. na fram þam hælende ge-fullode.

31 Hwan telle ic ge-lic þeosse cneorisse men. ⁊ hwam synde hi* ge-lice.

* hi *added above the line*

32 Hyo synde gelice cylden on strete sittende ⁊ sprecende be-tweox heom. ⁊ cwæðende. We sungen eow be harpen. ⁊ ge ne salteredon. we heofoden ⁊ ge ne weopen.

33 Soðlice Iohannes co*m* se fulluhtere hlaf ne etende ne win drinkende. ⁊ ge cweðed. deofel-seocnysse he hafð.

34 Mannes sune com etende ⁊ drinkende. ⁊ ge cweðað þes man ys swelgende ⁊ win drinkende. manfulra ⁊ senfulre freond.

35 And wisdom ís ge-rihtwised on eallen his bearnen.

36 ÞA bæd sum hine of þam sunder-halgen ꝥ he mid hym æte. Þa eode he in-to þas fariseiscen huse ⁊ ge-sæt.

37 And þa þæt wif þe wæs on þare ceastre synful þa hy on-cneow þæt he sæt on þas farisees huse. hyo brohte hire sealfe-box.

38 ⁊ stod wið-eften his fet. ⁊ on-gan mid hire tearen his fet þwean. ⁊ dreide mid hire heafdes fexe. ⁊ kyste hys fet. ⁊ mid sealfe smerede.

Various Readings.

29. sundor-halgan. 30. sundor-halgan; æ-gleawan for-hogodon; ge-þeaht; sylfum. 31. þisse; heom [*for* hwam]; sint. 32. synt; cildu*m*; stræte; specende; cweðendu*m*; sungon; hearpan; saltedon; heofodon; weopan. 33. drincende; cweðað deofol-. 34. drincende; swelgend; drincende; synfulra. 35. ge-riht-wisud; eallu*m*; bearnv*m*. 36. sundor-halgu*m*; eæte; phariseiscen. 37. synfull; heo; phariseus; heo. 38. wid-eftan; tearu*m*; drihgde; cyste.

⁊ all folc geherde ⁊ bærsynnig gesoð-fæstadon god weron gefulwad mið fulwiht
29 *Et omnis populus audiens et publicani iusticauerunt d*eu*m baptizati baptismo * 72. x.

ioh*annes* ða aeldo ðon*ne* ⁊ æs wuto ðæhtung godes teldon on him seolfum
iohannis 30 pharisaei autem et legis periti consilium d*e*i spreuerun*t* in semetipsos

ne woeron gefulwad fro*m* him huæm for*ð*on ongelic ic cuoeðo menn cneoreses ðisses ⁊
non baptizati ab eo 31 *Cui ergo similes dicam homines generationis huius et * 73. u. mt. cuii.

huæm ongelic sint ongelic sint cnaehtu*m* sittendu*m* on sprēc ⁊ sprecendu*m* bituih ⁊
cui similes sunt 32 similes sunt pueris sedentib*us* in foro et loquentib*us* adinuicem et

cuoeðendu*m* we gesungun iuh mið hwistlu*m* ⁊ ne plægade gie we hond-beafton ⁊ ne wæpde gie
dicentibus cantauimus uobis tibiis et non saltastis lamentauimus et non plorastis

cuom for*ð*on ioh*annes* ne eteð hlaf ne drincað win ⁊ gie cuoeðas
33 uenit enim iohannes baptista neq*ue* manducans panem neq*ue* bibens uinum et dicitis

diowl hæfeð cuom sunu monnes eteð ⁊ drincað ⁊ gie cuoeðað heono
dæmonium habet 34 uenit filius hominis manducans et bibens et dicitis ecce

monn ettere ⁊ drincað ꝥ win freond bærsynigra ⁊ synnfullra ⁊
homo deuorator et bibens uinum amicus publicanorum et peccatorum 35 et

gesoðfæstad wæs mið snytro fro*m* allu*m* sunu*m* his gebaed ða hine sum fro*m*
iustificata est sapientia ab omnib*us* filiis suis 36 *Rogabat autem illum quidam de * XXUII. 74. i. mt. cclxxui. mr. cluiii. io. xcuiii.

aelde-uutu*m* ꝥte geete mið hine ⁊ infoerde hus gehlionade ⁊ heono
pharisaeis ut manducaret cum illo et ingressus domum pharisaei discubuit 37 et ecce

wif ðio wæs in ceastra port-cuoene ł synnful ꝥte ongaet ꝥte hlionade in hus
mulier quae erat in ciuitate peccatrix ut cognouit quod accub*u*it in domo pharisaei

tō-brohte oele-fæt full smirinise ⁊ stod bihianda æt fotu*m* his mið tæheru*m* ł tearu*m*
attulit alabastrum ungenti 38 et stans retro secus pedes eius lacrimis

ongann geðuoa ł aðoa foet his ⁊ mið herum heafdes hiræ gedrygde ⁊ gecyste foet his ⁊
coepit rigare pedes eius et capillis capitis sui tergebat et osculabatur pedes eius et

mið smirinise aðuoh
ungento ungebat

[*Eight leaves lost in the* Rushworth MS.]

39 Ða se sundor-halga þe hyne ingelaðode ꝥ geseah. he cwæþ on hys geþance; Gyf þe man witega wære. witodlice he wiste hwæt. ⁊ hwylc þis wīf wǣre þe his æt-hrinþ ꝥ heo synful is;

40 Ða cwæð se hælend him andswariende; Symon ic hæbbe þe to secgenne sum ðing; þa cwæð he. lareow sege þænne;

41 Twegen gafol-gyldon wǣron sumum lænende. ān sceolde fīf hund penega. ⁊ oðer fiftig;

42 Ða hig næfdon hwanon hi hyt aguldon. he hit him bām forgef; Hwæþer lufode hyne swyðor;

43 þa andswarode simon. ic wene. se ðe he māre forgef. Ða cwæð he rihte. þu demdest;

44 þa be-wende he hyne to þam wīfe. ⁊ sæde simone; Ge-syhst þu þis wīf ic eode into þinum huse ne sealdest þu me wǣtan to minum fōtum; Ðeos mid hyre tearum mine fēt þwōh. ⁊ mid hyre loccum drigde;

45 Coss þu me ne sealdest. þeōs syððan ic in-eode. ne ge-swac ꝥ heo mine fēt ne cyste;

46 Min heafod þu mid ele ne smyredest. þeos smyrede mid sealfe mine fēt;

47 For-þam ic secge þe. hyre synt manega sinna forgyfene. for-þam heo me swyðe lufode; Læsse lufað þam ðe læsse forgyfen ys;

48 þa cwæþ he to hyre. þe sȳnt þine synna for-gyfenne;

Various Readings.

39. A. sunder-. A. ge-seh. A. þes man. 40. A. ⁊swarigende. A. secganne. C. sæge. A. þonne. 41. A. -gyldan. 42. A. hyg. A. for-geaf. A. lufede. 43. A. for-geaf. 44. A. wæter; B. wæten. 47. A. synd. 48. A. synd. A. forgyfene.

39 Ða se sunder-halge þe hine in-laðede þæt ge-seah; he cwæð on his ge-þance. Gif þes man witege wære. witodlice he wiste hwæt ⁊ hwilc þæt wif wære þe his æt-rind. þæt hyo synful īs.

40 Ða cwæð se hælend him andswer-iende. Simon īch hæbbe þe to seggene sum þing. Ða cw̄. he. Lareow sege þanne.

41 Twegen gafel-gyldon wæren sumen lænende; ⁊ scolde fif hund panege se an. ⁊ se oðer fiftig.

42 Ða hyo næfden mid hwy hyo hit agulden. he hit heom bam for-gef. hwader lufede hine swiðre.

43 Ða andswerede symon ic wene. se þe he mare for-gef. Ða cwæð he rihte þu demdest.

44 Ða be-wende he hine to þam wife. ⁊ sægde symone. Ge-syhst þu þis wif; īch eode in-to þinen huse. ne gefe þu me wæter to minen foten. þeos mid hire tearen mine fet þweag. ⁊ mid hire locken dreide.

45 Cos þu me ne gefe. þeos seððe īch īnn eode ne ge-swac þæt hyo mine fet ne kyste.

46 Min heafed þu mid ele ne smeredest. þeos smerede mid sealfe mine fet.

47 For þam īch segge þe; hyre synde manege synne for-gefene. for þan þe hio me swiðe lufede. læsse lufod þam þe læsse for-gyfen īs.

48 Ða cwæð he to hire. ðe synde þine seńne for-gefene.

Various Readings.

39. sundor-halga; in-læðede; witega ware; æt-rinð; sinfull. 40. andswerigende; ic habbe; seggenne; þonne. 41. wæron sumum; an [*for* ⁊ *before* scolde]; penega; R. *om.* se an; R. *om.* se *before* oðer. 42. næfdon; hwanon [*for* mid hwy]; aguldon; for-geaf; hwaðer lufode; swyðor. 43. andswarode; for-geaf. 44. ic; þinum; seldest [*for* gefe]; wæten; minum fotum; þwoh; loccum drigde. 45. Coss; sealdest [*for* gefe]; syððan ic in; heo; cyste. 46. heafod; hele; smyredest; smyrede. 47. ic; manega sine for-gyfene; lufode; lufað. 48. sint; sinne for-gyfene.

gesæh ða se alda-wuta seðe ge-ceigde hine cuoeð bituih him cuoeð ðes gif were
39 uidens autem pharisaeus qui uocauerat eum ait intra sé dicens hic si esset

witge wiste uut*edlice* i. ðailca ⁊ hulic wif were ðio gehrineð him ꝥte port-cuoene is
propheta sciret utique quae et qualis mulier esset quae tangit eum quia peccatrix est

⁊ onduearde se hæl*end* cuoeð to him ɫ ðæm ic hafo ðe huot-huoego to cuoeðanne soð he
40 et respondens *iesus* dixit ad illum simon habeo tibi aliquid dicere at ille

cuoeð laruu cuoeð tuoege scyldgo woeron sume rice menn an ahte to geldanne
ait magister dic 41 duo debitores erant cuidam feneratori unus debebat

penningas fif hũnd oðer fif-teih ne hæbbendum ðæm huona guldon *for*gaef
denarios quingentos alius quinquagenta 42 non habentib*us* illis unde redderent donauit

him baem ɫ eghðer huelc *for*ðon hine *for*ðor lufade geondsuarede cuoeð ic woeno ꝥte
utrisque quis ergo eum plus diliget 43 respondens simon dixit aestimo quia

of ðisu*m* ðæm *for*ðor ɫ mara *for*gaef soð he cuoeð him rehte ðu doemdest ⁊ ymb-wærlde to
hís cui plus donauit at ille dixit ei recte iudicasti 44 et conuersus ad

ðæm wife cuoeð to simon gesiistðu ðios wif ic infoerde in hus ðin ꝥ wæter fotu*m* minu*m*
mulierem dixit simoni uides hanc mulierem intraui in domum tuam aquam pedib*us* meis

ne saldest ðu ðios uut*edlice* mið tearu*m* ɫ tehru*m* aðuoh foet mine ⁊ mið herum hire geclænsade
non dedisti haec autem lacrimis rigauit pedes meos et capillis suis tersit

coss me ne saldest ðu ðios uut*edlice* of ðon ɫ siððа in ic foerde ne blann cossetunges ɫ foeta
45 osculum mihi non dedisti haec autem ex quo intraui non cessauit osculari pedes

mine mið smirinise heafod min ne ge-ðuoge ðu ðios uut*edlice* mið smirenise aðuogh foet min
meos 46 oleo capud meum non unxisti haec autem ungento unxit pedes meos

*for*eðon ic cuoeðo ðe *for*gefen biðon hiræ synno menigo *for*ðon lufade suiðe ɫ feolo ðæm
47 propter quod dico tibi remittentur ei peccata multa quoniam dilexit multum cui

uut*edlice* lyttel bið *for*gefen lyttel lufad ɫ lufade cuoeð ða to ðær ilca *for*gefen biðon ðe
autem minus dimittitur minus diligit 48 dixit autem ad illam remittuntur tibi

synna
peccata

[*Eight leaves lost in the* Rushworth MS.]

49 Ða begunnon þa ðe þar sæton betwux
him cweðan ; Hwæt is þes þe manna synna
forgyfð ;
50 Ða cwæþ he to þam wífe. þin geleafa þe dyde hále gá nú on sybbe ;

CHAPTER VIII.

1 Syððan wæs geworden ꝥ he ferde
þurh þa ceastre ⁊ ꝥ castel. godes
ríce prediciende ⁊ bodiende. ⁊ hi twelfe
mid [hym]
2 And sume wíf þe wæron gehælede of
awyrgdu*m* gastu*m*. ⁊ untrum-nessum. seo
magdalenisce maría of þære seofan deoflu
ut-eodon.
3 ⁊ iohanna chuzan wíf herodes gerefan.
⁊ susanna ⁊ manega oðre þe him of hyra
spédu*m* þenedon ;
4 Soþlice þa mycel menegeo com ⁊ of
þam ceastrum to him efstun. he sǽde him
án big-spel ;
5 Sum man his sæd seów. þa he ꝥ seow
sum feoll wið þæne weg ⁊ wearð for-treden.
⁊ heofones fugulas hyt fræton ;
6 And sum feoll ofer þæne stán ⁊ hit for-
scranc forþam þe hit wǽtan næfde ;
7 ⁊ sum feoll on þa þornas. ⁊ þa þornas
hyt forþrysmodon ;
8 And sum feoll on góde eorðan. ⁊
worhte hund-fealde wæs[t]m ; Þa clypode
he. ⁊ cwæð ; Ge-hýre se ðe earan hæbbe ;
9 Ða ahsodon hine hys leorning-cnihtas
hwæt ꝥ bigspel wære ;

49 Þa be-gunnen þa þe þær sæten be-twux
heom cweðen. hwæt is þes þe manne synne for-gyfð.
50 Þa cwæð he to þan wife. þin ge-
leafe þe dyde hal ga nu on sibbe.

CHAPTER VIII.

1 Syððon wæs ge-worðen þæt he ferde
þurh þa ceastren. ⁊ þa ceastle
godes rice predikende ⁊ bodiende. ⁊ hyo
twelf mide.
2 And sume wif þe wæren ge-helde of
awweregeden gasten ⁊ untrumnyssen. sye
magdalenisce Marie of þare seofan deofle
ut-eoden.
3 ⁊ iohann chuzan wif herodes ge-refen ;
⁊ susanna ⁊ manega oþre þe him of hyra
spede þenedon.
4 Soðlice þa mycel manige com ⁊ of þa
ceastren to hym efstum (*sic*) ; he saigde
heom an bispel.
5 Sum man hys sæd seow. þa he þæt
seow su*m* feoll wið þanne weig ⁊ warð for-
treden. ⁊ heofene fugeles hit fræton.
6 And sum feoll ofer þanne stan ⁊ hit
for-scranc for-þam-þe hyt wæten næfde.
7 ⁊ sum feol on þa þornas ; ⁊ þa þornes
hit for-þrysmeden.
8 And sum feoll on gode eorþan. ⁊
worhte hund-fealddne wæstme. Þa clypede
he ⁊ cwæð. Ge-here se þe earen hæbbe.
9 þa axseden hine hys leorning-cnihtes
hwæt ꝥ bispel wære.

Various Readings.

49. A. þær. A. be-tweox.
Cap. viii. 1. A. predeciende ; B. sprediciende (*with* s *erased*) ; C. spreende (*sic*). A. bodigende. A. hig. A. *inserts* hym, *which* B. C. *omit*. 2. A. awyrgedu*m*. A. seofen ; B. C. seofon. 4. A. mænigeo. 5. C. feol. A. þone. A. heofenes fugelas. 6. B. C. feol. A. þone. 7. B. C. feol. 8. C. feol. A. B. hundfealdne. A. B. C. wæstm. 9. A. acsodon.

Various Readings.

49. begunnon ; sæton ; cweðan. 50. þa*m*.
Cap. viii. 1. cestle ; predicende ; bodigende. 2. wæron ge-hælde ; awirgdu*m* gastu*m* ; untru*m*nyssum ; seo madalenisce maria ; ut-eodon. 3. ge-refan ; mænega ; spedum. 4. menegeo ; þam ceastrom ; efstum [*as in* H.] ; sæde ; big-spel. 5. þonne ; wearð ; heofones. 6. Ænd ; feol ; þænne ; wætan. 7. ðornas [*2nd time*] ; for-ðrysemedon. 8. Ænd ; hund-fealdne ; earan. 9. axsoden ; -cnihtas ; big-spel.

⁊ ongunnon ðaðe mið ætgeadre hliongende woeron gecuoeða betuih him huæt is ðes seðe
49 et coeperunt qui simul discumbebant dicere intra sé quis est hic qui

fæstlice synna *for*gefeð cuoeð ða to ðæm wife geleafo ðin ðeh hal dyde gaa
etiam peccata dimittit 50 dixit autem ad mulier*em* fides tua té saluam fecit uade

in sibbe
in pace

CAP. VIII.

⁊ aworden wæs æfter ðon ⁊ he geong dyde ðerh ceastra ⁊ woerc bodade
1 *Et factum est deinceps et ipse iter faciebat per ciuitatem et castellum praedicans * XXUIII. 75. x.

⁊ godspellade ric godes ⁊ tuoelfo mið hine ⁊ ða wifo ⁊ oðro ða ðe woeron
et euangelizans regnum d*e*i et duodecim cum illo 2 et mulieres aliq*ue* quae erant

gehæled fro*m* gastum wohfullu*m* ł yflu*m* ł unrehtwisu*m* ⁊ fro*m* untrymnisu*m* ðio is geceiged magda-
curatae ab spiritib*us* malignis et infirmitatib*us* maria quae uocatur magda-

lenesca of ðær diowlas seofo of-foerdon ⁊ wif chuzes ⁊
lene de qua demonia septem exierant 3 et iohanna uxor chuza procuratoris herodis et

⁊ oðero menigo ða ðe embehtadon ðæm of strionum hiora miððy ðon*ne*
susanna et aliae multae quae ministrabant eis de facultatib*us* suis 4 *Cum autem * 76. ii. mt. cxxxi. mr. xxxui.

ðreat menigo efne-cuome of ceastru*m* geneolecdon to him cuoeð ðerh onlicnese ł bisene
turba plurima conueniret de ciuitatib*us* properarent ad eum dixit per similitudinem

eade seðe saweð to sawenne sed his ⁊ miððy saweð oðer feall neh wege ⁊
5 exít qui seminat seminare semen suum et dum seminat aliud cecidit secus uiam et

ge-treden wæs ⁊ flegendo heofnes gefreten ꝥ ⁊ oðer feall of*er* stan ⁊
conculcatum est et uolucres caeli comederunt illud 6 et aliud cecidit supra petram et

ꝥ brord ł awisnade ł *for*drugade *for*ðon ne hæbde wetnise ⁊ oðer gefeall æt ðornu*m* ⁊
natum aruit quia non habebat umorem 7 et aliud cecidit secus spinas et

ongelic arison ðornas under-dulfon ł *for*dydon ꝥ ⁊ oðer feoll on eorðo god ⁊
simul exortae spinae suffocauerunt illud 8 et aliud cecidit in terra*m* bonam et

uphebbing dyde wæstm hunteantig siða monigfal*d* ðas cuoeðende ceigde seðe hæfeð earo hernises
ortum fecit fructum centumplum haec dicens clamabat qui habet aures audiendi

geherað gefrugnon ða hine ðegnas his huæt wære ðio biseno
audiat 9 interrogabant autem eum discipuli eius quae esset parabola

---

[*Eight leaves lost in the* Rushworth MS.]

10 Þa cwæð he eow is geseald ꝥ ge witun godes ríces geryne. ⁊ oðrum on big-spellu*m*. ꝥ hi geseonde ne geseon. ⁊ gehyrende ne ongyton ;

11 Soðlice þis is ꝥ bigspell. ꝥ sæd ys godes word.

12 þa ðe synt wið þæne weg. ꝥ synt þa þe gehyrað. syððan se deofol cymþ. ⁊ æt-bryt ꝥ wórd of hyra heortan ꝥ hig þurh þone geleafan hále ne ge-wurðað ;

13 Ða ðe synt ofer þǽne stan þa ꝥ wórd mid gefean onfoð. ⁊ þa nabbað wyrt-ruman forþa*m* þe hi hwilu*m* gelyfað. ⁊ awaciaþ on þære costnunge timan ;

14 Ðæt sæd þe feoll on þa ðornas ꝥ synt þa ðe gehyraþ. ⁊ of carum ⁊ of welu*m* ⁊ of lustu*m* þiss lifes synt for-þrysmede. ⁊ nanne wæstm ne bringað ;

15 ꝥ feoll on ða godán eorðan. ꝥ synt þa ðe on godre ⁊ on selestre heortan ge-hyrende ꝥ word healdað ⁊ wæstm on ge-þylde bringað ;

16 Ne ofer-wrihð nan man mid fæte his on-ælede leoht-fæt. oððe under bedd asett. ac ofer candel-stæf asett. ꝥ ða in-gangendan leoht geseon ;

17 Soðlice nis nán ðing digle ꝥ ne sy geswutelod. ne behydd. ꝥ ne sy cuþ. ⁊ open ;

18 Warniað hu ge ge-hyran. þam byð geseald ðe hæfð. ⁊ swa hwylc swa næfð ꝥ he wene ꝥ he hæbbe. him byð afyrred ;

10 Ða cwæð he eow is ge-seald ꝥ ge witen godes rices ge-ryne. ⁊ oðren on bi-spellen þaet hyo ge-seonde ne ge-seagen ⁊ ge-hyrende ne on-geoton.

11 Soðlice þis is þæt bispell. þæt sæd is godes word.

12 þa þe synd wið þanne weig. þæt synde þa þe ge-hyred. seoððen se deofel kymð and æt-briht ꝥ word. of heora heortan þæt hio þurh þane ge-leafen hale ne ge-wurðað.

13 þa þe sinde ofer þanne stan ; þa þæt word mid ge-fean on-foð. ⁊ þa næbbed wertrumen for-þan-þe hyo hwilon ge-leafen and awakieð on þare costnunge timen.

14 Þæt sæð ꝥ feoll on þa þornes þæt synde þa þe ge-hered. ⁊ of caren ⁊ of welen ⁊ of luston þys lifes synde for-þrysmede ⁊ nænne wæstme ne bringeð.

15 Þæt feoll on þa goden eorðan. ꝥ synde þa þe on godere ⁊ on selestre heortan ge-herende ꝥ word healdeð ænd wæstme on ge-þilde bringed.

16 Ne ofer-wercð nan man mid fæte his on-ælde leoht-fæt ; oððe under beoð aset. ac ofer candel-stef asett. þæt þa ingangende þæt leoht ge-seon.

17 Soðlice nis nan þing swa dygele þæt ne seo ge-swutelod. ne be-hyðð ; þæt ne syo cuð. ⁊ open.

18 Warniað hu ge ge-hyren ; þam beod ge-seald ðe hæfeð. ⁊ swa hwilc þe næfeð ꝥ he wene ꝥ he hæbbe him beoð afirred.

Various Readings.

10. A. wyton. A. hig. 11. A. bigspel. 12. A. synd. A. þone. A. synd. A. *om.* se. A. heora. B. C. hi. A. ge-weorðon. 13. A. synd. A. þone. A. hig. B. C. costunge. C. timat (*sic*). 14. A. synd. A. þyses. A. synd forþrysmode. A. nænne. 15. B. C. feol. A. synd. 16. A. *places* myd fæte *after* leoht-fæt. A. *om.* under. A. aset (*twice*). 7. A. sig (*twice*).

Various Readings.

10. witon ; oðrum ; bi-spellum ꝥ ; geseode (*sic*) ; ge-seon ; ne ge on-gyton (*sic*). 12. synt ; þæne ; synt ; ge-hyrað ; sið-þan ; deofol cymð ; æt-brigt ; hyra ; hy ; þon*n*e ge-leafan. 13. sint ; nabbað wrytruman (*sic*) ; þa*m* ; hwilu*m* geleafað ⁊ awaciað ; timan. 14. þe [*for* ꝥ] ; þornas ; sint ; ge-hyrað ; carum ; welu*m* ; þiss ; synt for-þrysemede ; bringað. 16. -wryhð ; bedd asett ; -stæf ; ingangenden. 17. R. *omits* swa ; dygle ; syo ; be-hydd ; sy. 18. ge-hyran ; byð ; hæfð ; næfð ; bið.

ðæm he cuoeð iuh gesald is to wuttanne ł ꝥ gie witte clæne ryne ł asægdnise rices
10 quibus ipse dixit uobis datum est nosse mysterium regni

godes oðrum uutedlice in geddungum ꝥte gesegon ne geseað ⁊ geherdon ne on-cnaueð
dei *Ceteris autem in parabolis ut uidentes non uideant et audientes non intellegant * 77. i. mt. cxxxiii. mr. xxxuii. io. cuiiii.

is ðonne ðios bisseno sed is word godes seðe uutedlice æt woeg sint
11 *Est autem haec parabola semen est uerbum dei 12 qui autem secus uiam sunt * 78. ii. mt. cxxxu. mr. xxxuiii.

ða ðe geherað æfter ðon cuom se diowl ⁊ genom ꝥ word of heorta hiora ne gelefas ꝥte hal
qui audiunt deinde uenit diabolus et tollit uerbum de corde eorum ne credentes salui

hia g[e]worða forðon seðe onufa stan ða ðe miððy geherað mið gefea ł glædnise onfoað
fiant 13 nam qui supra petram qui cum audierunt cum gaudio suscipiunt

word ⁊ ðas wyrtruma ne habbað ðaðe to tid ł to huil gelefað ⁊ in tid costunges
uerbum et hí radicem non habent qui ad tempus credunt et in tempore temtationis

hia fearrageð ł fleað ꝥte uutedlice in ðornum gefeall ðas sindon ðaðe geherdon ⁊ mið gemnissum
recedunt 14 quod autem in spinis cecidit hi sunt qui audierunt et sollicitudinibus

⁊ walum ⁊ willum lifes miððy geongas under-dolfen biðon ⁊ ne eft-brengeð wæstm
et diuitís et uoluptatibus uitae euntes suffocantur et non referunt fructum

ꝥte uutedlice on god eorðo ðas sint ðaðe In herte god ⁊ gecoren geherdon word
15 quod autem in bonam terram hí sunt qui in corde bono et optimo audientes uerbum

haldas ⁊ wæstm brengas in geðyld ne ænig *monn* ðonne leht-fæt ł ðæcilla miððy ge-bernes
retinent et fructum afferunt in patientia 16 *Nemo autem lucernam accendens * XXUIIII. 79. ii. mt. xxxii. mr. xxxuiiii.

awria ðailca mið fatte ł under bedd sette ah onufa leht-isrn sette ꝥte in-geongande ł infærende
operit eam uase aut subtus lectum ponit sed supra candelabrum ponit ut intrantes

hia gesea ꝥ leht ne forðon is degle ꝥte ne bið æd-eawad ne gehyded ł forholen
uideant lumen 17 *Non enim est occultum quod non manifestetur nec absconditum * 80. ii. mt. xcii. mr. xl.

ꝥte ne on-cnauen ł ongetten bid ⁊ on eawung cymed geseað forðon huu ge g[e]herdon
quod non cognoscatur et in palam ueniat 18 *Uidete ergo quomodo auditis * 81. u. mt. cxxxii.

seðe forðon hæfeð gesald bið him ⁊ sua hua seðe ne hæfeð uutedlice ꝥte woeneð hine ł he hæbbe
qui enim habet dabitur illi et. quicumque non habet etiam quod putat sé habere

genumen bið from him ł ðæm
auferetur ab illo

[*Eight leaves lost in the* Rushworth MS.]

19 His modor ⁊ his gebroðru. him to comun ⁊ hi ne mihton hine for þære menegu geneosian;

20 Þa wæs him gecyðed. þin modor ⁊ þine gebroðru standað her ūte. wyllað þe geseon;

21 Þa cwæð he to him. min modor and mīne gebroðru synt þa ðe gehyrað ⁊ doð godes word;

22 Soðlice anum dæge wæs geworden þa he on scyp eode ⁊ his leorning-cnihtas. þa cwæþ he to him; Utun seglian ofer þisne mere. ⁊ hig seglydan þa;

23 Þa hig reowun. þa slep hē; Ða com windi yst ⁊ hig forhtodon;

24 Þa genealæhton hig him to ⁊ cwǣdon. hlāford. we forwurðað; Ða aras he ⁊ ðreade þæne wīnd ⁊ þæs wæteres hreohnesse; Ða geswac se wīnd ⁊ wearð mycel smyltnes;

25 Ða cwæþ se hælend hwar is eower geleafa. þa adredon hig ⁊ wundredon ⁊ betwux him cwǣdon; Wenst þū hwæt is þes. ꝥ he be-byt ge windum ge sǣ. ⁊ hig him hyr-sumiað;

26 Þa reowon hig to gerasenorum rice. ꝥ is foran ongen galileam;

27 Þa he to lande com. him agen ārn sum man. se hæfde deofol-seocnesse lange tīde. ⁊ næs mid nanon reafe gescrydd. ⁊ ne mihte on huse gewunian ac on byrgenum;

Various Readings.

19. A. moder. A. gebroðra. A. comon. A. hig. A. for þære mænigeo hyne. 20. A. moder. 21. A. moder. A. synd. 22. A. Uton. A. segledon; B. C. seglydun. 23. A. reowon. A. wyndig. A. forhtedon. 24. A. *om.* to. A. for-weorþað. A. þone. A. hreohnysse. A. smyltnys. 25. A. be-tweox. C. yrsumiað. 26. B. C. reow. A. on-gean. 27. A. on-gean. A. deofel-seocnyssa; B. C. deofol-seocnysse. A. nanum. A. gescryd.

19 Hys moder ⁊ his ge-broðre him to comen. ⁊ hio ne mihte hine for þare manige ge-neoh-sian.

20 Þa wæs him ge-cydeð. Ðin moder ⁊ þine ge-brodre standeð her ute willeð þe ge-seon.

21 Þa cwæd he to heom. min moder ⁊ mine ge-brodre synde þa þe ge-hireð ⁊ doð godes word.

22 Soðlice anen daige wæs ge-worðen þa þe he on scyp eode. ⁊ his leorning-cnihtes; þa cwæd he to heom. Vton seiglien ofer þisne mere. ⁊ hyo segledon þa.

23 Þa þe hyo reowan þa slep he. Þa com windj east ⁊ hyo forteden.

24 Þa ge-nehlahten hyo him to ⁊ cwæðen hlaford we forwurðeð. Ða aras he ⁊ þreadde þane wind. ⁊ þas wæteres reðnysse. Ða ge-swac se wind ⁊ wærð mycel smoltnysse.

25 Þa cwæð se hælend hwær is eower ge-leafe. Þa andreddon hio ⁊ wundredon. end be-twuxe heom cwæðen. Wenst þu hwæt is þes. þæt he be-beot windon. ⁊ sæ; ⁊ hy him hersumieð.

26 Ða reowen hy to gerasenorum rice. ꝥ is foren on-gean galileam.

27 Ða he to lande com; him agen arn sum man se hæfde deofel-seocnysse lange tide. ⁊ næs mid nanen reafe ge-scrid. ⁊ ne mihte on huse ge-wunian ac on byregenen.

Various Readings.

19. ge-broðra; coman; hy; þara menige ge-neosian. 20. ge-cyðed; ge-broðre. 21. cwæð; modor; broðra synt; ge-hyrað. 22. anum; ge-worden; R. *omits* þe; -cnihtas; cwæð; seglian; seglydon. 23. windi ýst; forhtoden. 24. ge-neahlahton; cwadon; forwurðað; þreade þænne; wateres hrehnesse; wearð; smiltnysse. 25. halend; geleafa; adreddon; ⁊ be-twux; cwæðon; ge windum ge sæ; hyo; hyrsumiað. 26. reowan hyo; foran. 27. æge [*for* agen]; deofol-; nanon; gescrudd; byrgenum.

cuomon ðonne to him ł ðæm moder ⁊ broðro his ⁊ ne mæhton gecuma to him
19 *Uenerunt autem ad illum mater et fratres eius et non poterant adire ad eum * 82. ii. mt. cxxx. mr. xxxu.

fore ðæm here ⁊ asægd wæs him moder ðin ⁊ broðro ðine stondeð uta wallas ðec
prae turba 20 et nuntiatum est illi mater tua et fratres tui stant foris uolentes té

gesea seðe ondsuarede cuoeð to him ł ðæm moder min ⁊ broðro mine ðas sint ðaðe word
uidere 21 qui respondens dixit ad . eos mater mea et fratres mei hi sunt qui uerbum

godes geherað ⁊ doað aworden wæs ða on ân ðara dagana ⁊ he astag on an
dei audiunt et faciunt 22 *Factum est autem in una dierum et ipse ascendit in una * XXX. 83. ii. mt. lxuiiii. mr. xluii.

scipp ⁊ ðegnas his ⁊ cuoeð to him ł to ðæm ofer-cearfa we ł ofer ꝥ luh ⁊ astigōn
nauicula et discipuli eius et ait ad illos transfretemus trans stagnum et ascenderunt

*h*rowundu*m* ł miððy ge*h*rowun ðon*ne* ðæm slepde ⁊ ofduna astag hræs ł windes on luh ⁊
23 nauigantib*us* autem illis obdormiuit et descendit procella uenti in stagnum et

woeron gefylled ł ⁊ woeron afryhtad ł geneolecton uut*edlice* awoehton hine cuoeðende ł cwoedon
complebantur et periclitabantur 24 accedentes autem suscitauerunt eum dicentes

la haesere we losaiað so*ðlice* he aras geðreade ꝥ wind ⁊ hroeðnise ł unwoeder ðæs wætres ⁊ geblann
praeceptor perimus at ille surgens increpauit uentum et tempestatem aquae et cessauit

⁊ aworden wæs ðio smyltnise cuoeð uut*edlice* ðæm huoer is gehleafo iuera ðaðe gēe-ondredes awun-
et facta est tranquillitas 25 dixit autem illis ubi est fides uestra qui timentes mi-

dradon ł woeron Awundrad cuoedon bituih hua woenest ðu ðes is ꝥte ⁊ windum hatteð ⁊
rati sunt dicentes adinuicem quis putas hic est quia et uentis imperat et

sae ⁊ ge-herað him ðona gehrewun ða to londe ðara lioda ðio is
mari et oboediunt ei 26 *ENauigauerunt *autem* ad regionem gerasenor*um* quae est * XXXI.

fo*r*a ongægn gali*lea* ⁊ miððy færende woere to londe to-gægnes arn him wer sum seðe
contra galilaeam 27 et cum egressus esset ad terram occurrit illi uir quidam qui

hæfde ðone diowl fæstlice tidu*m* monigu*m* ⁊ mið woedo ne gegearuad wæs ne in hus
habebat dæmoniu*m* iam temporib*us* multis et uestimento non induebatur neq*ue* in domo

gewunade ah in byrgennu*m*
manebat sed in monumentis

[*Eight leaves lost in the* Rushworth MS.]

28 Þa he geseah þæne hælend he astrehte hyne to-foran him. ⁊ cwæþ mycelre stefne hrymende; Hwæt is me and þe. lá hælend þæs hehstan godes sunu; Ic halsige þe ꝥ ðu ne ðreage me;

29 Þa bead he þa*m* unclænan gaste ꝥ he of ðam men ferde; Soþlice lange tíde he hyne gegrap. ⁊ he wæs mid racenteagu*m* gebunden ⁊ mid fot-copsum gehealden. ⁊ toborstenu*m* bendum he wæs fram deofle on westen gelædd;

30 Ða ahsode se hælend hine. hwæt is þín nama; Þa cwæð he legio. ꝥ is on úre geþeode eored. for-þa*m* þe manega deoflu on hyne eodun;

31 Þa bǽdon hig hine ꝥ he him ne bude ꝥ hi on grund ne bescuton;

32 And þar wæs mycel heord swyna on þa*m* munte læsiendra. þa bædon hy ꝥ he lyfde him on þa gán. þa lyfde he him.

33 þa eodon hig of þa*m* men on þa swyn. þa ferde seo heord myculum ræse on ðæne mere ⁊ wearð þar adruncen;

34 Þa ða hyrdas ꝥ gesawon þa flugon hig ⁊ cyddon on þa ceastre ⁊ on tunum;

35 Þa eodon hig út ꝥ hig gesawon ꝥ ðar geworden wæs. þa comon hig to þam hælende. þa fundon hig ðæne man þe deofol of eode gescryddne ⁊ halum mode æt his fotu*m*. ⁊ hig adredon him;

36 Ða cyddon him þa ðe gesawon hu he wæs hál geworden of ðam eorede;

28 Þa he ge-seah þanne hælend he astrehte hine to-foren him ⁊ cwæð. michelere stefne hremende. Hwæt is me ⁊ þe la hælend þas hehestan godes sune. Ic halsige þe þæt þu ne ðreage me.

29 Þa bed he þa*m* unclænen gaste. þæt he of þam men ferde. Soðlice lange tide he hine grap ⁊ he wæs mid raketeagen gebunden ⁊ mid fot-copsen ge-healden. ⁊ toborstenen benden he wæs fram deofle on westen ge-lædd.

30 Ða axoden se hælend hine hwæt is þin name. Ða cwæð he legio; þæt is on ure ge-þeode eored; for-þan-þe manege deofle on hine eodon.

31 Ða bæden hyo hine þæt he heom ne bude ꝥ hy on grund ne be-scuton.

32 And þær wæs mycel heord swine on þam munte læsiendre. Ða bæden hio þæt he lefde heom on þam gan; þa lefde he heom.

33 Þa eoden hyo of þam menn on þa swin. þa ferde se heord michelen raese on þane mere. ⁊ warð þær adruncen.

34 Þa þa heorden þæt ge-seagen þa flugen hyo ⁊ kyddan on þa ceastre ⁊ on þa tunan.

35 Ða eoden hio ut þæt hyo ge-seagen ꝥ þær ge-worðen wæs. Þa comen hyo to þam hælende þa funden hyo þanne man þe deofel of eode ge-scridne ⁊ halen mode æt his fote. ⁊ hyo adredden heom.

36 Ða kyddan heom þa þe ge-seagen hu he wæs hal ge-worden of þam heorde.

Various Readings.

28. A. þone. A. stemne. 29. A. ge-læd. 30. A. acsode. A. leio. A. eodon. 31. A. hig (*twice*). B. C. bescutun. 32. A. læswigende. A. hig. 33. A. mycelu*m*. A. þone. 35. A. þone. A. B. gescrydne. A. ondredon. 36. A. eorode.

Various Readings.

28. þonne halend; astrechte; to-foran; mycelere; hrymende; hehstan. 29. bead; unclænum; racen-teagan; fot-copsum; toborstenu*m* bendu*m*. 30. asxode; nama; manega deofla. 32. Æpd; læsiendra; lyfde [1*st time only*]. 33. men; mycelu*m* ræse; ðæne; wearð; adru*n*can. 34. heordes; ge-sawen; flugon; cyddan. 35. ge-sawen; ge-worden wæs [*in handwriting of scribe of* H.]; halende; þonne; deofol; halum; fotu*m*; adreddon. 36. cyddan; ge-seawen hwu.

ðes ꝥte gesæh ðone hæl*end* gefeall bef*or*a him ⁊ ceigde ł cliopade stefne micla cuoeð huæd me
28 is ut uidit i*esu*m procidit ante illum et exclamans uoce magna dixit quid mihi

⁊ ðe is hæl*end* sunu godes ðæs hæsta ic biddo ðec ne mec ðrouiga ł ꝥte ðu mec ne gegroeta ł ne pinia
et tibi est i*es*u fili d*e*i altissimi obsecro té ne me torqueas

bebeade f*or*ðon ðæm unclæne gaste ꝥte foerde of ðæm menn monigum f*or*ðon tidum
29 praecipiebat enim spiritui inmundo ut exiret ab homine multis enim temporibus

f*or*nom hine ⁊ gebunden wæs mið raccentegu*m* ⁊ mið fatru*m* gehalden wæs ⁊ miððy geslitten weron
arripiebat illum et uinciebatur catenis et compedib*us* custoditus et ruptis

ða bendo gedrifen wæs fro*m* diowlæ on woest*er*nu*m* gefraign ða hine se hæl*end* cuoeð
uinculis ágebatur á dæmonio in deserta 30 interrogauit autem illu*m* i*esu*s dicens

huæd ðe noma is soð he cuoeð here f*or*ðon in-eadon diowlas monigo in him ⁊
quod tibi nomen est at ille dixit legio quia intrauerunt daemonia multa in eum 31 et

bedon hine ꝥte ne gehehte him ꝥte in niolnise gefoerdon hia wæs ðon*ne* ðer ede ł sunor
rogabant eum ne imperaret illis ut in abissum irent 32 erat autem ibi grex

bergana monigo foedendra ł lesuuandra on more ⁊ bedon hine ꝥte gelefde him In ðæm
porcorum multorum pascentium in monte et rogabant eum ut permitteret eis in illos

ingeonga ⁊ gelefde him foerdon f*or*ðon ða diowblas of ðæmenn ⁊ infoerdon In bergu*m*
ingredi et permisit illis 33 exierunt ergo daemonia ab homine et intrauerunt in porcos

⁊ mið fer-ræs eode ꝥ sunor oefistlice on luh ⁊ f*or*doen wæs ꝥte sua ꝥ gesegon
et impetu abiit grex per praeceps in stagnum et suffocatus est 34 quod ut uiderunt

aworden ł awarð ðaðe gelesuadon flugon ⁊ sægdon in ða burug ⁊ in londu*m* foerdon
factum qui pascebant fugerunt et nuntiauerunt in ciuitatem et in uillas 35 exierunt

ðon*ne* gesea ꝥte auorden wæs ⁊ cuomon to ðæm hæl*ende* ⁊ gemoeton ðone monno sittende
autem uidere quod factum est et uenerunt ad i*esu*m et inuenerunt hominem sedentem

of ðæm ða diowlas foerdon ge-wēded ⁊ hal ðoht*e* to fotu*m* his ⁊ on-dreardon sæg-
á quo dæmonia exierant uestitum ac sana mente ad pedes eius et timuerun*t* 36 nun-

don ða ðæm ⁊ ðaðe gesegon huu hal Aworden wæs fro*m* diowla here
tiauerunt *autem* illis et qui uiderant quomod*o* sanus factus esset á legione

---

[*Eight leaves lost in the* Rushworth MS.]

37 Þa bæd hine eall menego þæs rices gerasenorum ꝥ he fram him gewite. forþam hig mycelum ege gehæfte wærun. Ða wende he on scype agén

38 þa bæd hyne se man ðe se deofol of eode ꝥ he mid him wunede; Þa for-let se hælend hyne ⁊ cwæð to him.

39 wend to þinum huse ⁊ cyð hu mycel þe god gedón hæfð; Ða ferde he into eall þa ceastre. ⁊ cyðde hu mycel se hælend him gedón hæfde;

Ðis sceal on frige-dæg on þære pentecostenes wucan to þam ymbrene. Uenit ad i*esum* uir cui nom*en* iairus. A.

40 Soðlice wæs geworden þa se hælend agén-cóm. seo menegeo hine on-feng. ealle hig gebidon his;

41 And þa com án man þæs nama wæs iáirus. se wæs þære gesamnunge ealdor; Ða feoll he to þæs hælendes fotun ⁊ bæd hyne ꝥ he ferde to hys huse.

42 for-þa*m* he hæfde áne dohtor. nean twelf wintre ⁊ seo forð-ferde; þa ge-byrede hyt þa he ferde of ðam menegum he wæs of-þrungen;

43 Ða wæs sum wíf on blod-ryne twelf gér; Seo for-dælde on læcas eall ꝥ heo ahte. ⁊ ne mihte þeah of ænegum beon ge-hælyd;

44 Ða ge-nealæhte heo wið-æftan ⁊ æt-hrán hys reafes fnæd. Ða æt-stod sona þæs blodes ryne;

45 Þa cwæð se hælend. hwæt is se ðe me æt-hrán; Ða hig ealle æt-socon. þa cwæð petrus ⁊ þa ðe mid him wæron; Eala hlaford. þas menegeo þe ðringað ⁊ geswencað. ⁊ þu segst hwa hwa æt-hran me;

37 Ða bæd hine eall syo manege þas rice gerasenorum ꝥ he fram heom ge-wite. for þam hyo micelen eige ge-hæfte wæren. Ða wende he on scype on-gen.

38 Ða bæð hine se man ðe se deofel of eode þæt he mid hym wunede. Þa for-let se hælend hine ⁊ cwæð to hym.

39 wend to þinen huse. ⁊ kyd hu mycel god þe ge-don hæfð. Þa ferde he in to eall þa ceastre ⁊ kydde hu mycel se hælend him ge-don hæfde.

40 Soðlice wæs ge-worðen þa se hælend agen co*m* seo manege hine onfeng. ealle hyo on-bidan hys.

41 Ænd þa com an man þæs name wæs jairus; se wæs þare ge-samnunge ealdor. Þa feoll he to þæs hælendes foten. ⁊ bæd hine þæt he ferde to his huse;

42 for-þan he hæfde ane dohter neoh on twelf wintre ⁊ syo forð-ferde. Ða ge-byrede hit. þa he ferde of þam manegen he wæs of-þrungen.

43 Ða wæs sum wif of blodrine twelf gear. syo for-dælde on læces eall þæt hyo ahte. ⁊ ne mihte hire þeah of anygen beon ge-hæld.

44 Ða ge-nehlahte hyo wið-æften. ⁊ æt-ran hys reafes fined (*sic*). Ða æt-stod sone þas blodes rine.

45 Ða cwæð se hælend. hwæt ys se þe me ætran. þa hyo ealle æt-soken; þa cwæð petrus ⁊ þa þe mid hym wæren. eale hlaford þas manigeo þe þringað. ⁊ geswenced. ⁊ þu sægst hwa æt-ran me.

Various Readings.

37. A. eall seo mænigeo. A. ge-swencte [*for* gehæfte] wæron. A. on-geán. 38. A. wunode. 39. A. hæfð gedon. 40. A. on-gean. A. mænigeo; C. menego. B. C. gebidun. 41. A. fotu*m*; *but* B. C. fotun. 42. A. neah. A. mænegu*m*. 43. A. gear. A. eal. A. þeh. A. gehæled. 45. A. mænegeo; B. C. menego. A. B. C. *have* hwa *once only*.

Various Readings.

37. R. *om.* syo; menega þæs rices; hy mycelu*m* ege; agen. 38. deofol; haled (*sic*). 39. cyð; þe god ge-don hafð; cydde; halend. 40. ge-worden; menegeo; on-bydon. 41. And; nama; þara; halendes fotum. 42. hafde; dohtor neh; menegu*m*; of-drungen. 43. on [*for* of]; Seo; hahte; anegum. 44. ge-neahlæchte; fned; sona þæs. 45. cweð; halend; æt-hran; æt-socen; wæron; Eala; mænega; ge-swænceð; secgst; æt-hran.

⁊ beðon hine all ðio menigo londes ðara lioda ꝥte gefearrade from ðæm
37 et rogauerunt illum omnis multitudo regionis gerasenorum ut discederet ab ipsis

forðon mið fyrhto miclo woeron gehalden he ðonne astag ꝥ scipp eft-cerde ł cerrende ⁊
quia timore magno tenebantur *IPSE autem ascendens nauem reuersus est 38 et * 84. uiii. mr. xluiii.

gebaed hine se weor of ðæm ða diowblas foerdon ꝥte mið hine were forleort ða hine se hæl*end*
rogabat illum uir a quo daemonia exierant ut cum eo esset dimisit autem eum *iesus*

cuoeð eft-fær to huse ðinu*m* ⁊ sæge huu micla ðe dyde god ⁊ eode ðerh
dicens 39 redi domum tuam et narra quanta tibi fecit d*eus* et abiit per

alle ða ceastra bodade hu micla him dyde se hæl*end* aworden wæs ðon*ne* mið-ðy
uniuersam ciuitatem praedicans quanta illi fecisset *iesus* 40 *Factum est autem cum * XXXII. 85. ii. mt. lxxiiii. mr. xluiiii.

eft-cuom se hæl*end* onfeng hine ðio ðread woeron for*ð*on alle bidende hine ⁊ heono
redisset *iesus* excepit illum turba erant enim omnes exspectantes eum 41 et ecce

cuom se wer ðæm noma wæs ⁊ he aldormon somnunges wæs ⁊ feall to fotu*m* hæl*endes*
uenit uir cui nomen iairus et ipse princeps synagogae erat et cecidit ad pedes *iesu*

gebæd hine ꝥte inn-eode In hus his for*ð*on dohter an-cende wæs him woeno ic wintro
rogans eum ut intraret in domum eius 42 quia filia unica erat illi fere annorum

tuoelfo ⁊ ðios deadade ⁊ gelamp mið-ðy eode fro*m* ðæm here wæs geðringed ł geðrungen
duodecim et haec moriebatur et contigit dum iret á turba comprimebatur

⁊ wif sum wæs in flowing blodes fro*m* wintrum tuoelfum ðio on lecum
43 et mulier quaedam erat in fluxu sanguinis ab annis duodecim quae in medicos

fro*m*-salde all feh hire ne fro*m* ænigu*m* mæhte gelecnæge ł wosa gelecned geneolecde
erogauerat omnem substantiam suam nec ab ullo potuit curari 44 accessit

behianda ⁊ gehran fasne wedes his ⁊ sona Astod ꝥ flowing blodes hire
retro et tetigit fimbriam uestimenti ei*us* et confestim stetit fluxus sanguinis eius

⁊ cuoeð se hæl*end* hua wæs seðe mec gehran onsæccendu*m* ðon*ne* allu*m* cuoeð pet*rus*
45 et ait *iesus* quis est qui me tetigit negantib*us* autem omnib*us* dixit petrus

⁊ ðaðe mið him woeron haesere ða menigo ðec geðringað ⁊ woerdað ł ⁊ ðu cuoeðas hua
et qui cum illo erant praeceptor turbae te comprimunt et affligunt et dicis quis

mec gehran
me tetigit

---

38. .... ðe wer of ðæm ða diowulo foerdun ꝥte mið hine were forleort ða hine ðe hæl*end* cwæð 39. eft-fær to huse ðinum ⁊ sæge hu micle ðe dyde drih*ten* ⁊ eode ðerh alle ða cæstre bodade hu micle him dyde drih*ten* 40. aworden wæs wutudlice miððy eft-com ðe hæl*end* onfeng hine ða ðreatas werun wutudlice alle biddende hine 41. ⁊ heonu com ðe wer gongende ⁊ he of aldormenn somnunge wæs ⁊ gifeol ⁊ to fotum him gibed hine ðætte foerde in hus his 42. forðon dohter uncenned (*sic*) wæs him ic woenu wintro twelfe ðios deodade ⁊ gilamp miððy eode from ðæm berge wæs giðring ł giðrungun 43. ⁊ wifum ðæm ðe wæs in flowing blodes from wintrum twelfum ðio in lecum for-salde all feh hire ne in ængum mæhte gihæla ł lecniga 44. ⁊ gineolicade bihionda ⁊ gihran fæste wedum ⁊ sona astod ðio flownis blodes his 45. cwæð ðe hæl*end* hwelc is seðe mec gihran ne sæccende ðonne allum cwæð .... ⁊ ðaðe mið hine werun hæsere ðio mengo ðec giðringað ⁊ weorðað ⁊ ðus cweoðas hwelc mec gihran

46 Þa cwæþ he sum me æt-hran. ic wiste. ꝥ mægen of me eode ;

47 Ða ꝥ wíf geseah ꝥ hit him næs dyrne. heo com forht ⁊ astrehte híg to his fotum ⁊ ge-swutulude beforan eallu*m* folce. for hwylcu*m* þinge heo hit æt-hrán. ⁊ hu heo wearð sona hál ;

48 Þa cwæð he to hyre ; Dohtor þin geleafa þe hale gedyde. ga nú on sybbe ;

49 Him þa gyt specendum. þa com sum man to þære gesamnunge ealdre ⁊ cwæð to hi*m*. ne drece þu hyne ;

50 Þa se hælend ꝥ word gehyrde he ⁊swarude. þæs mædenes fæder ; Ne ondræd þu ðe. gelýf wotodlice. ⁊ heo bið hal ;

51 And þa ðe he to þa*m* huse cóm. ne let hê nanne mid him in-gán buton petrum ⁊ Iohanne*m* ⁊ iacobum. ⁊ þæs mædenes fæder. ⁊ hyre modor ;

52 Þa weopon hig ealle ⁊ heofodon hi ; Ða cwæþ he. ne wepe ge ; Soþlice nis þis mæden dead. ac heo slæpð ;

53 Ða tældon hig hyne ⁊ wiston ꝥ heo dead wæs ;

54 Ða nam he hyre hánd ⁊ cwæð ; Mǽden. þe ic secge arís ;

55 Þa gehwearf hyre gast agen ⁊ heo sona aras. ⁊ he het hyre syllan etan ;

56 Ða wundredon hyre magas þa bead he þam ꝥ hi hit nanum men ne sædon ꝥ þar geden wæs ;

Various Readings.

47. A. ge-swutelode. A. hym [*for* hit]. 48. A. dohter. 49. A. sprecendu*m*. A. ge-somnunge. 50. A. ⁊swarode. A. B. C. witodlice. 51. A. ða [*for* ðe]. A. nænne. C. hyr. A. moder. 52. B. C. hi. A. heofedon hig. 55. A. on-gean. 56. A. hig. A. B. C. gedon.

46 Þa cwæð he sum me æt-ran. ic wiste þæt maing me of eode.

47 Ða þæt wif ge-seah þæt hit him næs derne ; hyo com forð. ⁊ astrehte hyo to his foten ⁊ ge-swutelede be-foren ealle folce. for hwilcen þingen hyo hine æt-hran. ⁊ hu hyo warð sone hall.

48 Ða cwæð he to hire. Dohter þin geleafe þe hal ge-dyde. ga nu on sibbe.

49 Him þa gýt sprecenden þa com sum man to þare ge-samnenge ealdre ⁊ cwæð to him ; ne drece þu hine.

50 Ða se hælend þæt word ge-hyrde he andswerede þas mædenes fader. Ne ondræð þu þe. ge-lef witodlice. ⁊ hyo beod hal.

51 Ǽnd þa he to þan huse com ; ne let he nenne mid him in-gán buton petrum ⁊ Iohanne*m* ⁊ Iacobu*m*. ⁊ þas mædenes fæder ⁊ hire moder.

52 Ða weopen hyo ealle ⁊ heofodon hyo. Ða cwæð he ne wepe ge. soðlice nis þis mæden dead ac hyo slepð.

53 Þa tælden hyo hine. ⁊ wiston þæt hyo deað wes.

54 Ða nam he hire hand ⁊ cwæð. Mæden þe ic segge aris.

55 Ða ge-hwarp hire gast agen ⁊ hyo sona aras. ⁊ he het hire syllan æten.

56 Ða wundreden hire mages. þa bed he þan þæt hyo hit nanen menn ne sægdon. þæt þær ge-don wæs.

Various Readings.

46. æt-hran ; mægn of me. 47. dyrne hy ; forht (*sic*) ; fotum ; ge-swutolode be-foran eallu*m* ; þinge ; werð sona hal. 48. Dohtor. 49. geat sprecendu*m* ; gesamnu*n*ge. 50. þæs medenes fæder ; on-dræd ; ge-lif ; bið. 51. End ; þæs ; modor. 52. cweð ; slæpð. 53. tældon ; he dead wæs. 55. ge-hwearf ; heo ; etan. 56. wundrodon ; magas ; bead ; þam ; nanu*m* men.

⁊ cuoeð se hæl*end* gehran mec huoelc huoege for*ð*on ic wiste mæht from mec eode
46 et dixit *iesus* tetigit me aliquis nam ego noui uirtutem de me exisse

gesæh ðon*ne* ꝥ wif ꝥte ne ge-degelde cuaccende cuom ⁊ gefeall fore fotu*m* ðæs ł his ⁊
47 uidens autem mulier quia non latuit tremens uenit et procidit ante pedes illius et

fo*re* ðæm Inting gehrine hrine (*sic*) becnade fo*ra* allum folce ⁊ huu sona
ob quam causam tetigerit eum indicauit coram om[n]i populo et quem-ammodum confestim

gehæled wæs soð he cuoeð him dohter geleafa ðin ðec hal dyde gaa In sipp
sanata sit
48 at ipse dixit illi filia fides tua té saluam fecit uade in pace

ðageane hine spreccende from aldormonn somnunges cuoeð him ꝥte dead is doht*er* ðin
49 athuc illo loquente uen*it* a principe synagogae dicens ei quia mortua est filia tua

nælle ðu gestyrege hine se hæl*end* ða miððy geherde ðis word geondsuarede feder ðæræ mædne
noli uexare illum
50 *iesus* autem audito hoc uerbo respondit patri·. puellae

nælle ðu ðe ondrede gelef ana ⁊ hal hio bið ⁊ miððy gecuome to hame ne gelefde
noli timere crede tantu*m* et salua erit
51 et cum uenisset domum non permisit

ingeonga mið ænig buta ⁊ ⁊ ⁊ fader ⁊ moder
intrare secum quem-quam nisi petrum iacobum et iohannem et patrem et matrem

ðæræ mægdne gewaepon ðon*ne* alle ⁊ mændon ðailca soð he cuoeð nallað go woepa ne
puellae
52 flebant autem omnes et plangebant illam at ille dixit nolite flere non

Is dead Ah slepeð ⁊ hlogun ł teldon hine hia wiston ꝥte dead were he
est mortua sed dormit
53 et deridebant eum scientes quia mortua esset
54 ipse

ða geheald hond his cliopade cuoeðende la mægden aris ⁊ eft-awoende wæs gaast
autem tenens manu*m* eius clamauit dicens puella surge
55 et reuersus est sp*iritus*

hire ł ðæra ⁊ aras recone ⁊ heht hir sealla eatta ⁊ wundradon ł gestyldon
eius et surrexit continuo et iussit illi dari manducare
56 et stupuerunt

aldro ðæm bebead ꝥte ne ænigu*m* hia gecoedon ꝥte Aworden wæs
parentes quib*us* praecipit ne alicui dicerent quod factum erat

---

46. ⁊ cwæð ðe hæl*end* gihran me hwæt ł hwelchwoegu for*ð*on ⁊ ic wiste mæhte from me eode 47. gisæh ðonne ꝥ wif ðætte ne deglde cwacende com ⁊ gifeoll bifora fotum his ⁊ for ðæm intinga gihran him gibecnade bifora allum folche ⁊ hu efne sona gihæled wæs 48. ⁊ he cwæð him dohter gileofa ðin ðec hale dyde gaa in sibbe 49. geona hine sprecende com from aldormonnu*m* somnungum cwæð him ðætte deod is dohter min nelle ðu gihrina hir 50. ðe hæl*end* ðonne giherde ðis word giondsworade feder ðæs mægdnes nelle ðu ondreda gilef ana ⁊ hal bið 51. ⁊ miððy gicomon to hame ne gelefde in-gonga hine mið ænigne buta . . . . ⁊ . . . . ⁊ . . . . ⁊ fæder ⁊ moder ðæs mægdnes 52. giweopun ðonne alle ⁊ mændun ða ilca soð he cwæð nelle giwoepa ne is deod ah slepeð 53. ⁊ hlogun ⁊ teldun hine wiste forðon ðæt deod were 54. he ða gihælde hiæ honda his ⁊ cliopade cweðende mægden aris 55. ⁊ efteowende wæs gast his ⁊ aras recone ⁊ heht sella hir eota 56. ⁊ stylton ł wundradun ældro hire ðæm bibeod ðæt ne ængu*m* gicwede ðæt giworden wæs

CHAPTER IX.

Ðys sceal on þunres dæg on þære pentecostenes wucan. Conuocatis *iesus* duodeci*m* discipulis dedit illis potesta*tem*. A.

1 Þa clypode he to-gædere his twelf apostolas. ⁊ sealde him mihte. ⁊ anweald ofer ealle deofol-seocnessa. ⁊ ꝥ adla hi ge-hældon.

2 ⁊ he sende hig to bodianne godes ríce. ⁊ untrume gehælan;

3 Ða cwæþ he to him. ne nyme ge nan þing on wege. ne gyrde. ne codd. ne hláf. ne feoh. ne ge ne ge (*sic*) nabbon. twa tunecan.

4 ⁊ on swa hwylc hus swa ge ingað wuniað þar oð ge út-gán.

5 ⁊ swa hwylce swa eow ne on-foð. þon*ne* ge of þære ceastre gað asceacað eower fota dúst ofer hig on witnesse.

6 Ða ferdon hig þurh þa burhga bodiende ⁊ æghwar hælende;

7 Þa gehyrde herodes se feorðan dæles ríca ealle þa ðing þe be hi*m* wærun geworden; Ða twynude him forþam þe sume sǽdon ꝥ iohannes of deaðe árás.

8 sume sǽdon ꝥ helias æt-ywde; Sume sǽdon eald witega árás;

9 Ða cwæþ herodes. iohanne*m* ic beheafdude hwæt is þes. be þa*m* ic þilc gehyre; Ða smeade he ꝥ he hine gesawe;

10 Þa cyddun him ða apostolas swa hwæt swa hig dydon; Ða nam he hig ⁊ ferde onsundron on weste stówe seo is bethsaida;

11 Ða ða menego ꝥ wiston þa filidon híg him. þa onfeng he hig ⁊ spæc to hi*m* be godes ríce. ⁊ þa he gehælde ðe lacnunga beþorftun;

CHAPTER IX.

1 ÞA cleopede he to-gædere his twelf apostles ⁊ sealde heom mihte. ⁊ anweald ofer ealle deofel-seocnysse. ⁊ þæt adle hyo ge-healden.

2 ⁊ he senð hy to bodienne godes rice. ⁊ un-trume gehælen.

3 Ða cwæð he to heom. ne nyme ge nan þing on weige. ne gyrde ne cod ne hlaf ne feoh ne ge næbben twa tunecan.

4 ⁊ on swa hwilce huse swa ge in gad wunied þær oððe ge ut-gan.

5 ⁊ swa hwilce swa eow ne on-fod þanne ge of þare ceastre gad asacað eowre fota dust ofer hyo on witnysse.

6 Ða ferden hyo þurh þa burga bodiende. ⁊ æghwær hælende.

7 Ða ge-herde herodes se ferðen dæles rice ealle þa þing þe be him wæren geworðene. Ða tweonede him for-þan þe sume sægdon ꝥ ioha*n*nes of deaðe aras

8 sume sædon þæt helias atewde. sume þæt an eald witega aras.

9 Ða cwæð herodes. iohannem ich beheafdede hwæt is þes. be hwam ic þellic gehire. Ða smægde he þæt he hine geseage.

10 Ða cyððan hym þa apostles swa hwæt swa hyo dyden. Þa nam he hyo ⁊ ferde on-sunder on weste stowe syo is bethsaida.

11 Ða þa manige þæt wisten þa felgeden hyo hym; þa onfeng he hyo ⁊ spræc to heom be godes rice. ⁊ þa he ge-hælde þa læcnunge be-þorten.

Various Readings.

Cap. ix. 1. A. deofel-seocnyssa. A. hig adla. A. bodigende [*for* to bodianne]. 3. A. B. C. ne ge (*once*). C. nabban. 4. A. *inserts* ꝥ *after* oð. 5. C. hylce (*sic*). A. ge-wytnysse. 6. A. burh, *altered to* burha. A. bodigende. 7. A. wæron. A. tweonode. 8. A. B. C. ꝥ an eald [*for* sǽdon eald]. 9. A. Iohannes. A. beheafdode. A. þæs. 10. A. C. cyddon. C. *om.* him. A. on-sundru*m*. 11. A. mænigeo. A. fyligdon. A. spræc. A. be-þorfton.

Various Readings.

Cap. ix. 1. clypede; to-gadere; apostlas; deofol-; adla; ge-halden. 2. sende hyo; bodianne; ge-halen. 3. codd; næbban. 4. hwylc hus; in-gað wuniað þar. 5. on-foð þo*n*ne; gað. 6. burhgo bodigende. 7. gehyrde; ferðan; rica; waren ge-worden; twynude; þam; sædon. 8. ætywde. 9. ic be-heafdode; þa*m* [*for* hwam]; þylc; smeagde; ge-sawe. 10. cyddan; apostolas; dydon; on-sundrion; seo. 11. menigeo; wyston; fylidon; spæc; þe [*for* þa *before* læcnunge]; be-þorfton.

CAP. IX.

miððy geceiged woeron uutedlice tuoelfo ða apostolas salde ðæm mægn ⁊ mæht ofer
1 *Conuocatis autem duodecim apostolis dedit illis uirtutem et potestatem super * XXXIII. 86. ii.

Alle diowlas ⁊ ꝥte ða untrymigo gelecnades ⁊ sende hia bodia ł to bodianne ric godes mt. lxxuiiii.
omnia daemonia et ut languores curarent 2 et misit illos praedicare regnum dei mr. xxuiiii.

⁊ hæla ða un-stronga ⁊ cuoeð to ðæm noht gie nime on woege ne gerd ne
et sanare infirmos 3 *Et ait ad illos nihil tuleritis in uia neque uirgam neque * 87. ii. mt. lxxxii.

pocca ł posa ne hlaf ne feh ne tuoege cyrtlas habas gie ⁊ in suahuel- mr. liii.
peram neque panem neque pecuniam neque duas tunicas habeatis 4 et in quam-cum-

cum hus gie inn-gae ðer wunað ⁊ ðona ne færes gie ⁊ seðe suahua ne onfoeð
que domum intraueritis ibi manete et inde ne exeatis 5 *Et quicumque non receper[i]nt * 88. ii. mt. lxxxu.

iuh færað from ceastra ðæ ilca fæstlice ꝥ asca fota Iura asceaccað on cyðnise mr. lu.
uos exeuntes de ciuitate illa etiam puluerem pedum uestrorum excutite in testimonium

onufa ðæm ilcom foerdon ðonne ymb-eadon ðerh ða ceastra bodande ⁊ lecnande
supra illos 6 *Egressi autem circumibant per castella euangelizantes et curantes * 89. uiii. mr. lu[i].

eghuer ge-herde ða se cynig alle ða ðe weron aworden from him ⁊ tuiade
ubique 7 *Audiuit autem herodes tetrarcha omnia quae fiebant ab eo et haesitabat * XXXIIII. 90. ii.

forðon wæs acuoeden from summum ꝥte iohannes aras from deadum from summum mt. cxliii.
eo quod diceretur á quibusdam quia iohannes surrexit á mortuis 8 á quibusdam mr. luii.

æc forðon ł ꝥte helias ædeaude from oðrum ðonne ꝥte se witgæ an from witgum aras
uero quia helias apparuit ab aliis autem quia propheta unus de antiquis surrexit

⁊ cuoeð se cynig ic ofcearf huelc ðonne is ðes of ðæm gehero ic ðuslico ⁊
9 et ait herodes iohannem ego decollaui quis autem est iste de quo audio ego talia et

sohte to gesceanne hine ⁊ eft-cerdon ða ðegnas sægdon him ðaðe sua huæd hia dydon
querebat uidere eum 10 *Et reuersi apostoli narrauerunt illi quaecumque fecerunt * 91. uiii. mr. lxi.

⁊ miððy onfenge woeron hia foerde syndria on woestigum stou seðe is ðæt burug ꝥte
*Et assumtis illis secessit seorsum in locum desertum qui est bethsaida 11 quod * 92. ii[i]. mt. cxlui.

miððy ongeton ða menigo gefylgendo woeron hine ⁊ genom hia ⁊ spræcc him of ric io. xluii.
cum cognouissent turbæ secutae sunt illum et excepit illos et loquebatur illis de regno

godes ⁊ ðailco ðaðe gemnise behofadon gehælde
dei et eos qui cura indigebant sanabat

Cap. IX. 1. miððy gicegdun wutudlice twelfe apostolas salde ðæm mæhte ⁊ mægen ofer alle diowlas ⁊ ꝥ ðio untrymigu gilecnadun 2. ⁊ sende hiæ to bodiganne rice godes ⁊ hæle ða unstronga 3. ⁊ cwæð to ðæm noht ginime iow on woege ne in gerde ne in pohha ne hlafas ne feh ne twoege cyrtlas habbas ge 4. ⁊ swa hwelcum huse ge in-gæ ðer wunigað ⁊ ðona ne faras ge 5. ⁊ swa hwelc swa ne on-foeð iow farað from cæstre ðær ilca fæstlice ða asca foeta iowra asceacað on cyðnisse ofer hiæ 6. foerdun ðonne ymb-eodun ðerh ða cæstre bodende ⁊ lecnadun eg-hwer 7. giherde ða cynig..... alle ðaðe werun aworden from him ⁊ twiade of him ðætte wæs gicweden 8. from sumum ec forðon.... æt-eowde from oðrum ðonne forðon witga an from witgum aras 9. ⁊ cwæð ðe cynig.... ic of-ceorf hwelc ðonne is ðes of ðæm ic ðus-lico doema ⁊ sohte to seanne hine ł ðæt he gisege 10. ⁊ eft-cerdun ða ðegnas sægdun him ðaðe swa hwæt hiæ dydun ⁊ miððy ond-fonge hiæ foerdun syndrige on stowwe on woestern seðe is ðio burug 11. ðætte miððy swa ongetun ða mengo fylgende werun him ⁊ on-gan hiæ ⁊ spræc wæs him of rice godes ⁊ ðailco ðaðe gemnisse bihofadun gihælde

Ðis sceal on wodnes dæg on þære pentecostenes wucan to þam ymbrene. Dimitte turbas ut euntes in castella. A.

12 Þa gewat se dæg forð. ⁊ hig twelfe him genealæhton ⁊ sædon him; Læt þas menego ꝥ hig farun on þas castelu ⁊ on þas tunas þe her abutan synt; ⁊ him mete findon. for-þa*m* þe we synt her on westere stṓwe;

13 Ða cwæð he to him. sylle ge him etan; Ða cwædon híg we nabbað buton fíf hlafas ⁊ twegen fixas. buton we gan ⁊ ús mete bicgon ⁊ eallum þissu*m* werede;

14 Þar wæron neah fif þusenda wera; Ða cwæþ he to his leorning-cnihtun; Doþ ꝥ hig sitton. þurh gebeorscypas fiftegum.

15 ⁊ hig swa dydon ⁊ hi ealle sæton;

16 Ða nam he þa fíf hlafas ⁊ þa twegen fixas. ⁊ on þone heofon beseah ⁊ bletsude hig ⁊ bræc. ⁊ dælde his leorning-cnihtum. ꝥ hig asetton hig beforan þam menegum;

17 Þa æton hig ealle ⁊ wurdon gefyllede. ⁊ man nam þa gebrotu þe þar belifon twelf cypan fulle;

18 Ða wæs geworden þa se hælend wæs ana hine gebiddende. hys leorning-cnihtas wǽron mid him; Þa ahsode he hig hwæt secgð þis folc ꝥ ic sy;

19 Ða ⁊swarudon hig ⁊ cwædon; Iohannes baptistam. sume heliam. sume ꝥ sum witega of ðam ealdu*m* arás;

20 Ða sæde he him hwæt secge ge ꝥ ic sy; Þa andswarude petrus. ðu eart crist godes sunu;

21 Ða þreade he hig ⁊ bead ꝥ hig hit nanum men ne sædon.

Various Readings.

12. A. mænygeo. B. C. hi. A. faron. A. synd (*twice*). A. westre; C. westene. 13. A. þis. 14. A. cnyhtu*m*. B. C. hi. 15. A. B. C. hig [*for* hi]. 16. A. B. C. heofen. A. be-seh. A. bletsode. A. mænegu*m*. 17. A. læfde (*alt. to* læfede) wæron [*for* belifon]. 18. A. acsode. A. segð. A. sig. 19. A. B. C. ⁊swaredon. A. Iohanne*m*. 20. A. sig. A. ⁊swarode.

12 Þa ge-wat se daig forð. ⁊ hyo twelfe neh-lacte hym. ⁊ sæden to hym. Læt þas manige þæt hyo faran on þas castelles. ⁊ on þas tunas þe her abuton sinde. ⁊ heom mete finden. for-þam we sinde her on westene stowe.

13 Þa cwæð he to heom. sylle ge heom etan. Ða cwæðen hyo we næbbeð buten fif hlafes. ⁊ twegen fixsas. buton we gan ⁊ us mete beggen ⁊ eallen þissen werede.

14 Þær wæren neh fif þusend were. Þa cwæð he to hys leorning-cnihton. Doð þæt hyo sitten þurh ge-beorscypas fiftegum

15 ⁊ hyo swa dydon. ⁊ hyo ealle sæten.

16 Ða nam he þa fif hlafes. ⁊ þa twegen fixas. ⁊ on þanne heofen be-seah ⁊ bletsode hyo ⁊ bræc. ⁊ dælde his leorning-cnihten. þæt hyo asetten hyo be-foran þam manigeo.

17 Ða æten hyo ealle. ⁊ wurðen ge-fylde. ⁊ man nam þa ge-brute þe þær wære ⁊ fylde twelf kypan fulle.

18 Ða wæs ge-worðen þa se hælend wæs ane hine ge-biddende. his leorning-cnihtes wæren mid him. Ða axsode he hyo. hwæt sægð þis folc þæt ich syo.

19 Ða andsweredon hyo ⁊ cwæðen. Iohannes baptistam. sume Heliam. sume þæt sum witege of þam ealden aras.

20 Ða saigde he heom. hwæt segge ge þæt ich syo. Þa andswerede petrus. þu ert crist godes sune.

21 Þa þreadde he hyo ⁊ bæd. þæt hyo hit nanen men ne saigden.

Various Readings.

12. ge-neahlæchton; sægdon; menega; castella; synt; findon; sint. 13. buton; fixas; biggan; eallu*m* þissu*m*. 14. þusenda wera; -cnihtan; sitton. 15. sæton. 16. fisxas; þonne heofon; -cnihtum; be-foram (*sic*); menigeo. 17. eato (*sic*); wurdon ge-fyllede; ge-brotu; belifon [*for* wære]; R. *om.* ⁊ fylde; cypan. 18. ge-worden; -cnihtas wæron; ahsode; segð; ic. 19. andswaredon; cwæðon; Iohannēs (*sic*); witegan; ealdu*m*. 20. sæde; ic sy; cart. 21. bead; nanu*m*; sægdon.

se dæg ða ongann gefara ł gebege ⁊ geneolecdon ða tuoelfo cuoedon him *for*let ða hergas
12 *Dies autem coeperat declinare et accedentes duodecim dixerunt illi dimitte turbas * XXXU. 93. i. mt. cxlvii.

ꝥte geeadon in ða ceastra ⁊ londo ðaðe ymb sint of-cerdon ðæt-te hia gemoeton metto *for*ðon her mr. lxiiii.
ut euntes in castella uillasq*ue* quae circa sunt deuertant et inueniant escas quia hic io. xluiiii.

in stowe woestig woe sindon cuoeð ða to ðæm gie seallað ðæm eatta soð hia cuoedon
in loco deserto sumus 13 ait autem ad illos uos date illis manducare at illi dixerunt

ne sint us mara ðon fif hlafo ⁊ tuoege fiscas buta woenunga us we gefæra ⁊ we gebygce
non sunt nobis plus quam quinq*ue* panes et duos pisces nisi forte nos eamus et emamus

on Alle ðiosne here metto woeron ðon*ne* ic woeno wæras fif ðusendo cuoeð ðon*ne*
in omnem hanc turbam esces (*sic*) 14 erant autem fere uiri quinque milia ait autem

to ðegnum his doað ðæm to dælu*m* ł ðerh gebearscipo fif hund ⁊ sua dedon
ad discipulos suos facite illos discumbere per conuiuia quinquagenos 15 et ita fecerunt

⁊ todælni*sse* ł dydon Alle onfengo woeron uut*edlice* fif hlafum ⁊ tuæm
et discumbere fecerunt omnes 16 acceptis autem quinq*ue* panib*us* et duob*us*

fiscu*m* eft-locade on heofne ⁊ gebloedsade him ⁊ gebræcc ⁊ todælde ðegnu*m* his ꝥte hia gesete
piscib*us* respexit in caelum et benedixit illis et fregit et distribuit discipulis suis ut ponerent

f*ore* ðæm hergum ⁊ eton alle ⁊ gefylde woeron ⁊ ge-numen wæs ꝥte gehlaefde
ante turbas 17 et manducauerunt omnes et saturati sunt et sublatum est quod superfuit

ðæm scraedungra ceaolas tuoelfo ⁊ aworden wæs miððy ana woere gebiddenda
illis fragmentorum cophinos duodecim 18 *ET factum est cum solus esset orans * XXXUI. 94. i. mt. clxui.

woeron mið hine aec ða ðegnas ⁊ gefrægn ðailco cuoeðende huælcne mec cuoeðas ꝥ ic se ðas hergas mr. lxxxii.
erant cum illo et discipuli et interrogauit illos dicens quem me dicunt esse turbae io. lxxiiii.

soð hia ondsuaredon ⁊ cuoedon ioh*annem* oðero uut*edlice* oðero ꝥte witga
19 at illi responderunt et dixerunt iohannem baptistam álii autem heliam álii quia propheta

an of ðæm ærr*um* aras cuoeð ða ðæm gie ðon*ne* huelcne mec ꝥte ic se cuoaðas
unus de priorib*us* surrexit 20 dixit autem illis uos autem quem me esse dicitis

geondsuarede cuoeð gecoren godes soðlice he geðreade hia bebead
respondens simon petrus dixit *christu*m dei 21 *At ille increpans illos praecipit * 95. ii. mt. clxuiii. mr. lxxxiii.

ꝥte ne ænigum gecuoedon ðis
ne cui dicerent hoc

---

12. ðe dæg ða ongan gifara ł gibega ⁊ gineolicadun twelfe cwedun him forlett ða hergas ꝥte eodun in ða cæstre ⁊ lond ðaðe ymb sindun of-cerdun ꝥ hiæ gimoettun metas forðon her in stowwe woestigne we sindun 13. cwæð ða to ðæm ge sellas ðæm to eotanne soð hiæ cwedun ne sint us mara ðonne fif hlafas ⁊ twoege fiscas buta woenunga us we gifære ⁊ we gibycce in allum ðisse herge mett 14. werun ðone ic woeno weara fif ðusend cwæð to ðegnum his.... 15. ....to dalum dydon alle 16. onfenge werun wutudl*ice* fif hlafum ⁊ twæm fiscum eft-loccade on heofne ⁊ bletsade cwæð him ⁊ bræc ⁊ todælde ðegnum his ꝥte hiæ gisette foræ ðæm hergum 17. ⁊ etun alle ⁊ gifylde werun ⁊ ginimen wæs ðætte ofer-læfed wæs him screadungum ceoflas twelfe 18. ⁊ aworden wæs miððy ane were ⁊ bidende werun ⁊ miððy hine ðegnas his ⁊ gifrægn ða ilca cwæðende hwelcne mec cweoðas eadge 19. ða ond-sworadun ⁊ cwedun....ðæm fulwihtere oðer wutudl*ice* elie oðer ðætte witga ann of ðæm ærrum aras 20. cwæð ða ðæm ge ðonne hwelc were ah cweoðas ond-sworade........cwæð ðæm gast godes 21. soð he giðreode hiæ bibeod ðætte ængum ne cwedun

22 for-þam þe hit gebyreð ꝥ mannes sunu fela þinga þolige. ⁊ beo aworpen fram ealdrum ⁊ ealdor-mannum ⁊ fram bocerum. ⁊ beon ofslegen. þriddan dæge arísan;

Si quis uult uenire post me abneget semet ipsum. B.

23 Þa cwæð he to eallum; Gyf hwa wyle æfter me cuman. æt-sace hine sylfne ⁊ nime his cwylminge ⁊ me folgige;

24 Se þe wyle hys sawle hale gedon. se hig for-spilþ. witodlice se ðe his sawle for me for-spilð he hi gehæleð;

25 Hwæt fremað ænegum men þeah he ealne middan-eard on æht begite. ⁊ hyne sylfne for-spille; And his for-wýrd wyrce;

26 Se ðe me ⁊ mine spæca forsyhþ. þæne mannes sunu for-syhþ. þonne he cymð on his mægen-þrymme ⁊ hys fæder ⁊ halegra engla;

27 Ic secge eow soðlice. her synd sume standende þa deade ne wurðaþ. ær hig godes ríce geseon;

28 Ða wæs gewórden æfter þam wordum nean eahta dagas. ꝥ he nam petrum ⁊ Iohannem. ⁊ Iacobum. ⁊ eode on anne munt. ꝥ he hyne gebæde;

29 Þa he hine gebæd þa wæs hys ansyn oþres híwes. ⁊ his réaf hwit scinende;

30 Þa spǽcon twegen weras wið hyne moyses ⁊ helias

31 gesewene on mægen-þrymme. ⁊ sǽdon his gewitend-nesse þe he to gefyllende wæs on hierusalem;

22 for-þam-þe hit ge-byred þæt mannes sune fele þinge þolie. ⁊ beo aworpen fram ealdren mannen. ⁊ fram boker. ⁊ beon ofslagen. ⁊ ðridden daige arisan.

23 ÞA cwæð he to eallen. Gyf hwa wile æfter me cuman; æt-sake hine sylfne. ⁊ nime his cwelminge ⁊ me folgie.

Si quis u[illegible] uenire po[illegible] me, abneg[illegible] semet ips[illegible]

24 Se þe wile his sawle hæle ge-don; se hyo for-spilð. Witodlice se þe his sawle for me for-spilð. he hyo ge-hæleð.

25 hwæt fremed anig men þeah he alne midden-eard on ehte be-geote. ⁊ hine sylfne for-spille. and his for-wurd werche.

26 Se þe me ⁊ mine spæce for-sihð. þanne mannes sune for-sihð þane He kemð on his magen-þrimnesse ⁊ his fader ⁊ halgra ængle.

27 Ic segge eow soðlice he (*sic*) sende sume standende þe deade ne wurðað ær hyo godes rice ge-seon.

28 Ða wæs ge-worðen æfter þam worden neoh ehte dagas. þæt he nam petrum. ⁊ Iohannem. ⁊ Iacobum. ⁊ eode on enne munt. þæt he hine ge-bæde.

29 Ða he hine ge-bæd þa wæs his ansiene ge-worðen oðres hiowes. ⁊ his reaf hwit scynende.

30 Ða spæken twegen weres wið hine. moyses ⁊ helias.

31 ge-sogene on magen-þrimnesse. ⁊ sæden his witendnysse þe he to ge-fellende wæs on ierusalem.

Various Readings.

22. A. fæla þynga þolie. A. ealder-. A. beo ofslagen. ⁊ þryddan dæge aryse. 23. *Rubric in* B.; *not in* A. A. folgie. 24. A. se hig ge-hælð. 25. A. myddan-geard. 26. A. spræca. A. þone [*for* þæne]. 27. B. C. synt. A. weorðað. 28. A. neah ehta. A. ænne. 30. A. spræcon. 31. A. gesawene. A. ge-wytnesse; *but* B. C. gewitendnesse. A. to gefyllenne; *but* B. C. to gefyllende.

Various Readings.

22. ge-byreð; fela þinga þolige; ealdrum ⁊ ealdormannum; bocerum; of-sleagen; ðriddan dæge. 23. *Rubric as in* H. eallum; hwile [*for* wile]; æt-sæce. 24. hale; for-spillð [*2nd time*]. 25. fremeð anigum; hehte begete; Ænd [*for* and]; forwird wirce. 26. þonne; þænne He [*with capital, as in* H.] cymð; mægen-þrimnysse; eangla. 27. her sint; wyrðað. 28. wordum neah eahta. 29. ansyne ge-worden; hywes; wit (*sic*). 30. spæcen; weras. 31. ge-sewene; mægn-þrimnysse; sædend (*sic*); ge-fyllende.

cuoeð ꝥte Ariseð sunu monnes feolo ł micelo geðolia ł geðrowia ⁊ for*cumm*ā fro*m* ald*um* ł
22 dicens quia oportet filium hominis multa pati et reprobari á seni-

fro*m* ðæm ældest*um* ⁊ aldormonn*um* sacerda ⁊ uðwut*um* ⁊ ofslaa ł ꝥte sē ofslægen ⁊ ðe ðirddan ðæg
orib*us* et principib*us* sacerdotum et scribis et occidi et tertia die

Arisa cuoeð he ða to Allu gif hua wil*e* æft*er* mec gecyme onsæccað him seolf*um* ⁊
resurgere 23 *Dicebat autem ad omnes si quis uult post me uenire abneget séipsum et * 96. ii. mt. clxx. mr. lxxxu.

lædað ðrowung his dæge gehuæmlice ⁊ fylgeð me ł soec*e* mec seðe for*ð*on wælle sauel his
tollat crucem suam cotidie et sequatur me 24 qui enim uoluerit animam suam

hal gewyrca losað ðailca for*ð*on seðe losað sawel bis for*e* mec hal doað ðailca
salua*m* facere perdet illam nam qui perdiderit animam suam propter me saluam faciet illam

huæd for*ð*on for*s*tondað monn gif he strioneð allne middang*eard* hine ðon*ne* seolfne losað ⁊
25 quid enim proficit homo si lucretur uniuersum mundum sé autem ipsum perdat et

losuist his gewyrcað for*ð*on seðe mec gesceomigað ⁊ mino wordo ðiosne sunu
detrimentum sui faciat 26 *Nam qui me erubuerit et meos sermones hunc filius * 97. ii. mt. xciiii. mr. lxxxui.

monnes gesceomiað miððy cymeð iu ðrymm his ⁊ fadores ⁊ haligra engla
hominis erubescit cum uenerit in maiestate sua et patris et s*anct*orum angelorum

ic cuoeðo uut*edlice* iuh soðlice sint sume oðera her stondað ðaðe ne gebergeð ðone deað oðð-dæt
27 *Dico autem uobis uere sunt aliqui hic stantes qui non gustabunt mortem donec * XXXUII. 98. ii. mt. clxxii. mr. lxxxuii.

geseað ríc godes aworden wæs ða æft*er* ðasu*m* wordu*m* ic woeno dagas æhto ⁊ genom
uideant regnum d*e*i 28 factum est autem post haec uerba fere dies octo et assumsit

⁊ ⁊ ⁊ astag on more ꝥte gebede ⁊ aworden wæs
petrum et iacobum et iohanne*m* et ascendit in montem ut oraret 29 et factum est

miððy gebæd mægwlit onsione his oðoro ⁊ gewoedo his huit swiðe gescean ⁊ heono tuoege
dum oraret species uultus eius altera et uestitus eius albus refulgens 30 et ecce duo

wæras gesprecon mið hine woeron uut*edlice* ⁊ woeron gesene in ðrymm ⁊
uiri loq*ue*bantur cum illo erant autem moses et helias 31 uisi in maiestate et

cuoedon to-fær ł his ðone scealde gefylled wosa ł wæs in hie*rusalem*
dicebant excessum eius quem completurus erat in hierusalem

---

22. cwæð ðætte ariseð sunu monnes feolu ł monige giðolas ⁊ from-cumen from ældum ⁊ aldor-monnum ða sacerda ⁊ uð-wutum ⁊ ofslað ⁊ ðe ðirda dæge arises 23. cwæð he ða to ðæm allum gif hwa wyl æfter me cuma ne sæceð him solfum ⁊ lædað ðrowunge his dæg-hwæmlice ⁊ fyllgeð ł soeces mec 24. seðe forðon welle sawle his halle doa losað ða ilca ⁊ seðe losað sawle his fore mec hale gidoað ða ilca 25. hwæt forstondeð ł forstod ðæm men gif he strioneð alne middengeord hine ðonne solfne losað ⁊ los-west wyrcað 26. forðon seðe mec giscomigað ⁊ mine word ðiosne sunu monnes giscomigað miððy cymeð in ðrymme his ⁊ fædras ⁊ haligra hengla 27. ic cweðo wutudlice iow soðlice sindun oðro her stondað ðaðe ne gi-bergað deoð oððæt hiæ giseað rice godes 28. aworden wæs ða æfter ðissum worde ic woenu daga æhtowe ⁊ ginom ....⁊....⁊....⁊ astag on mor ꝥte gibede 29. ⁊ aworden wæs miððy gibæd meg-wlitt onsione his oðre ⁊ giwedu his hwitu swiðe giscionun 30. ⁊ heonu twoege wearas sprecende mið hine wæs ....⁊.... 31. werun gisene in ðrymme ⁊ cwedun ðætte ofer his gifylled wosa ł wæs in hierusal*em*

32 Petrus ⁊ þa þe mid him wǽron wurdon mid slæpe gehefegude; And þa hi onwæcnedun hi gesawun his mægen-þrym. ⁊ twegen weras þe mid him stodun;

33 And hi him fram eodun. petrus cwæð to him; Eala bebeodend. god is ꝥ we her beon ⁊ uton wyrcan þreo eardung-stowa. ane þe. ⁊ áne moyse. ⁊ ane hælie. ⁊ he nyste hwæt he cwæð;

34 Ða he þis spæc. ða wearð genip ⁊ ofer-sceadude hig. ⁊ hi ondredon him gangende on ꝥ genip;

35 Ða cóm stefen of þam genipe and cwæð; Þes ys mín leofa sunu. gehyrað hyne;

36 Ða seo stefn wæs gehyred þa wæs se hælend gemett ana. ⁊ hi suwodun ⁊ ne sædun nanum men on þam dagum nan þing þæs ðe hi ge-sawun.

37 Oðrum dæge him of þam munte farendum him agen arn mycel menego.

38 þa clypode án wer of þære menego ⁊ cwæð; Láreow ic halsie þe. ge-seoh minne sunu forþam he is mín ánlica sunu.

39 ⁊ nu se unclæna gást hine æt-hrinð. ⁊ he færlice hrymð ⁊ for-nimð hyne ⁊ fæmð. ⁊ hyne tyrð ⁊ slít.

40 ⁊ ic bæd þine leorning-cnihtas ꝥ hig hine ut-adrifon ⁊ hig ne mihton;

41 Þa cwæð se hælend him to ⁊sware; Eala ungeleafulle. ⁊ þwure cneores; Swa lange swa ic beo mid eow. ⁊ eow þolie; Læd hider þinne sunu;

Various Readings.

32. A. ge-hefegode. A. hig on-wæcnodon. hig gesawon. A. stodon. 33. A. hig. A. eodon. A. helie. 34. A. he cw̄. þis. A. ofer-sceadede. A hig. 35. B. C. stefn. C. leafa. 36. A. stefen. A. gemet. A. hig suwedon. A. sædon. A. hig ge-sawon. 37. A. ongean. A. mænigeo. 38. B. C. clypede. A. mænegeo; B. C. menegu. A. halsige. A. ænega [*for* ánlica]. 40. B. hi (*first time*). 41. A. ungeleaffulle. A. þweore.

32 Petrus ⁊ þa þe mid him wæren wurðen mid slape ge-hefegede. And þa hyo onwakeden; hyo ge-seagen his maing-þrim. ⁊ twegen weres þe mid hym stoden.

33 And hyo hym fram eoden; petrus cwæð to him. Eala be-beodend; god is þæt we her beon. ⁊ uten wercan þreo eardung-stowen ane þe. ⁊ ane moysese. ⁊ ane helie. ⁊ he nyste hwæt he cwæð.

34 Þa he þis spæc; þa warð ge-nip ⁊ ofer-scadede hyo. ⁊ hyo on-drædden him gangende on þæt ge-nip.

35 Ða com stefn of þam ge-nip ⁊ cwæð. Þes is min leofa sune ge-hered hine.

36 Ða seo stefen wæs ge-hyrd. þa wæs se hælend ge-met áne; ⁊ hyo swegedon. ⁊ ne sæden nanen men on þam daige nan þing. þas þe hyo ge-sægen.

37 Oðren daige him of þan munte farende hym agen arn mycel manegeo.

38 þa cleopede an wer of þare manigeo ⁊ cwæð. Lareow ic hælsige þe ge-seoh minne sune. for-þan he ys min anliche sune.

39 ⁊ nu se un-clæne gast hine æt-rind; ⁊ he færlice hrimd. ⁊ for-nymd hine. ⁊ fæmð. ⁊ hine tyrð. ⁊ slit;

40 ⁊ ic bæd þine leorning-cnihtes þæt hyo hine ut adrifen ⁊ hyo ne mihton.

41 Ða cwæð se hælend him to andswere. Eala un-ge-leafulle ⁊ þwore cneores. Swa lange swa ic beo mid eow. ⁊ eow þolie. læd hider þinne sune.

Various Readings.

32. wurdon; slæpe; Ǽnd; on-wacenedon; ge-sæwen; mægen-þrim; weras. 33. Ǽnd; eodon; cweð; utan wyrcan; -stowa; moyse. 34. wearð; -sceadede; hi on-dredon. 35. ge-hyrað. 36. syo; ge-hered; halend gemett ana; hi swuwodon; sædon nanum; dagum; gesawun. 37. Oðrum; þam; farendum; menegeo. 38. cleopode; menege; halsige; minum; þam; an-lica. 39. æt-rinð; hrymð; fornymð. 40. -cnihtas. 41. andsware; þwure; þine.

ðec ⁊ ðaðe mið hine gehefigad woeron fro*m* slepe ⁊ awæhton gesegon ðrymm
32 petrus uero et qui cum illo grauati erant somno et uigilantes uiderunt maiestatem

his ⁊ tuoege wæras ðaðe stodon mið him ⁊ aworden wæs miððy foerdon fro*m* him
eius et duos uiros qui stabant cum illo 33 et factum est dum discederent ab illo

cuoeð to ðæm hæl*ende* la bodare god is us her to wosanne ⁊ wyrca we ðrea hus
ait petrus ad *iesum* praeceptor bonum est nos hic esse et faciamus tria tabernacula

an ðe ⁊ an ⁊ an ne wiste huæd gec*u*oeðe ðas ða hine
unum tibi et unum mosi et unum heliae nesciens quid diceret 34 haec autem illo

sprecende aworden wæs wolcen ⁊ of*er*-brædde hia ⁊ ondreardon geongendu*m* him in ꝥ wolcen
loquente facta est nubis et obumbrauit eos et timuerunt intrantib*us* illis in nubem

⁊ stefn aworden wæs of ðæm wolcne cuoeðende ðes is sunu mîn leof hine ł ðene geherað
35 et uox facta est de nube dicens hic est filius meus dilectus ipsum audite

⁊ miððy wæs se stefn gemoetad wæs se hæl*end* he ana ⁊ hia suigdon ⁊ ne ænigu*m* gecuoedon in
36 et dum fieret uox inuentus est *iesus* solus et ipsi tacuerunt et nemini dixerunt in

ðæm dagum æniht of ðæm ðaðe gesegon geworden wæs ðon*ne* on ðæm æft*er*ra doege
illis dieb*us* quicquam ex hís quae uiderant 37 *Factum est autem in sequenti die * XXXUIII. 99. ii.

ofdune Astigendu*m* ðæm of ðæm more Arn togægnes him here micelo ⁊ heono woer of ðæm here mt. clxxiiii.
descendentib*us* illis de monte occurrit illi turba multa 38 et ecce uir de turba mr. xci.

gecliopade cuoeð la laruu ic biddo ðec besæh on sunu minu*m* for*ð*on an-cende is me
exclamauit dicens magister obsecro té respice in filium meum quia unicus est mihi

⁊ heono gast gegrippde hine ⁊ ferlice cliopiað ⁊ bites ⁊ fo*r*doað hine mið
39 et ecce sp*iritu*s appraehendit illum et subito clamat et elidit et dissipat eum cum

famæ ⁊ ned ł hefia fearras to-sliteð hine ⁊ ic bædd ðegnas ðine ⁊ awurpon hine
spuma et uix discedit dilanians eum 40 et rogaui discipulos tuos et (*sic*) eicerent illum

⁊ ne mæhton ondsuarede ðon*ne* se hæl*end* cuoeð la cneoreso ungeleafull ⁊ woh-full hu
et non potuerunt 41 respondens autem *iesus* dixit o generatio infidelis et peruersa usq*ue*

longe ic biom mið iuh ⁊ ic ðola iuih tolæd sunu ðinne
quo ero apud uos et patiar uos adduc filium tuum

---

32. . . . . ec ⁊ ðaðe mið hine gihefgade werun from slepe ⁊ awæhtun gisegun ðrym his ⁊ twoege weoras ðaðe stodun mið him 33. ⁊ aworden wæs miððy foerdun fro*m* him ꝥte . . . . to ðæm hæl*ende* bodere god is us her to wosane wyrce we ðrio hus an ðe ⁊ an moyse ⁊ an heliæ ne wiste hwæt he cwede 34. ðas ða him sprece giwörden wæs wolcen ⁊ ofer-brædde hiæ ⁊ ondreordun ge-on-gægdum (*sic*) him in ðæt wolcen 35. ⁊ stefn giworden wæs of wolcne cweðende ðis is sunu min leof in gaste giherað 36. ⁊ miððy wæs stefn gimoeted wæs ðe hæl*end* ana ⁊ hiæ swigadun ⁊ nænigum gicwedun in ðæm dagum æniht of ðæm ðaðe gisegun 37. giworden wæs ðonne on ðæm æfterra dæge of-dune astigende ðæm of more ⁊ arn togægnes ⁊ ðe ðreott micel 38. ⁊ heono wer of ðæm herge gicliopade la larwa ic biddo ðec loca on mec drihten forðon ancende is me 39. ⁊ heonu gast gigrap hine ⁊ ferlice cliopað ⁊ bites ⁊ slites hine mið swate ⁊ nede fearras to-slitas hine 40. ⁊ ic bæd his ðegnas ł ðine ðætte hiæ awurpun hine ⁊ ne mæhtun 41. ond-sworade ðon*ne* cwæð la cneoreswa ungileof-ful ⁊ woh-full hulonge ic biom mið iowih ⁊ ic ðolo iow to-læd sunu ðinne

42 And þa he hyne lædde him to. se deofol hine for-nam ⁊ fordyde. Ða nydde se hælend þone unclænan gast út. ⁊ gehælde. þæne cnapan ⁊ agef hine his fæder;

43 Þa wundredon hig ealle be godes mærðe. ⁊ eallu*m* wundriendu*m* be þa*m* þingum þe gewurdun. he cwæð to his leorning-cnihtum;

44 Asettað þas spæca on eowrum heortu*m*. hit ys towerd ꝥ mannes sunu si geseald on manna handa;

45 Ða þohton hig þis word ⁊ hit wæs bewrigen beforan hi*m* ꝥ hi hit ne ongeton. ⁊ hi ne dorston hine be þam wórde ahsian;

46 Soðlice ꝥ ge-þanc eode on híg. hwylc hyra yldest wǽre;

47 Ða se hælend geseh hyra heortan geþancas he ge-sette þæne cnapan wiþ hine

48 ⁊ cwæþ to hi*m*; Se ðe þysne cnapan on mínum naman onfehð. se me onfehð; And se þe me onfehð he onfehð þæne þe me sende; Witudlice se ðe is læst betwex eow ealle. se is mara;

49 Ða ⁊swarode iohannes. bebeodend. we gesawon sumne on þinum naman deofolseocnessa út-drifende ⁊ we hine for-budon. for-þam he mid us ne fylygð;

50 Ða cwæð he. ne for-beode ge; Se ðe nis ongen eow se is for eow;

51 Soðlice wæs geworden þa his andfenga dagas wæron gefyllede. he ge-trymede hys ansyne ꝥ he ferde to hierusalem;

42 And he þa lædde hine hi*m* to; se deofol hine nam ⁊ for-dyde. Ða nædde se hælend þanne unclæne gast ut. ⁊ ge-hælde þanne cnapan. ⁊ agef hine his fæder.

43 Ða wundredon hyo ealle be godes mærðe. ⁊ eallen wundrenden be þam þingen; þe ge-wurðen ware. He cwæd to his leorning-cnihten.

44 Asetteð þas spræce on eowren heorten; hit is to-ward þæt mannes sune syo ge-seald on mannes handen.

45 Þa þohten hyo þis word. ⁊ hit wæs be-wrigen be-foren heom þæt hyo hit ne ongeaton. ⁊ hyo ne dorsten hine be þa*m* worde ahsian.

46 Soðlice þæt þanc eode on hyo hwilc heora yldest wære.

47 Þa se hælend þis ge-hyrde he ge-seah here heortan ge-þances he ge-sette þanne cnapen wið hine;

48 ⁊ cwæð to heo*m*. Se þe þisne cnape on minen naman on-fehð; he on-fehð me. ⁊ se þe on-fehð me; he on-fehð þane þe me sente. Witodlice se þe is læst be-tweox eow ealle; se is mara.

49 Þa andswerede Iohannes. be-beodend we ge-seage sumne on þinen naman deofelseocnysse ut-drifende. ⁊ we hine for-buden; for-þam he mid ús ne fylgieð.

50 Ða cwæð he ne for-beode ge. Se þe nis on-gean eow se is forð mid eow.

51 Soðlice wæs ge-worðen þa hys anfengen dages wæren ge-worðene ge-fellede; he getremede his ansiene ꝥ he ferde to ierusalem.

Various Readings.

42. A. þone (*twice*). A. ageaf. 43. A. ge-wurdon. 44. A. spræca. A. toweard. A. sig. 45. A. hig. A. on-geaton. C. *om.* ⁊ *before* hi. A. hig. A. acsian. 46. A. heora. 47. A. ge-seah heora. A. þone. 48. C. ofehð (*first time*). A. þone. A. Witodlice. A. betweox. 49. B. C. ⁊swarude. A. -seocnyssa. A. ut adryfende. 50. A. on-gean.

Various Readings.

42. þa he hine lædde; nydde; þonne (*twice*). 43. alle; marðe; eallum wundriendu*m*; ðyngu*m*; ge-wurdon; R. *om.* ware; -cnihtu*m*. 44. eowru*m* heortum; his [*for* is] to-weard; mannu*m* (*sic; 2nd time*). 45. þohton; be-foran hi*m*; hi; dorston. 46. hyra. 47. halend; heora; ge-þancas. 48. cnapan; minv*m*; þoene; sende. 49. ge-sawon; þinu*m*; for-budon; fyligð. 50. for [*for* forð mid]. 51. ge-worden; anfenga; ge-worden ge-fyllede; ge-trymede; ansyne.

⁊ miððy geneolecde agroette hine se diowl ⁊ losade ł ⁊ geðreade se hæl*end* ðone gast
42 et cum accederet elisit illum daemonium et dissipauit et increpauit i*esus* sp*iritu*m

unclænne ⁊ gehælde ðone cnæht ⁊ Agæf hine fæder his gewundradon soðlice alle
inmundum et sanauit puerum et reddidit illum patri eius 43 *Stupebant autem omnes * 100. uiii. mr. lxxu.

on suiðe micelnisse godes Allum ða ilco undrandu on allum ðaðe he dyde cuoeð to ðegnum
in magnitudine d*e*i omnib*us* quae mirantib*us* in omnib*us* quæ faciebat *Dixit ad discipulos * XXXUIIII. 101. ii. mt. clxxui. mr. xciii.

his settes gie in heortu*m* iuru*m* wordo ðas sunu for*ð*on monnes to-waerd is
suos 44 ponite uos in cordib*us* uestris sermones istos filius enim hominis futurus est

ꝥte gesald bið in hond monna soð hia ne on-cneaun word ðis ⁊ wæs awrigen
ut tradatur in manus hominum 45 at illi ignorabant uerbum istud et erat uelatum

fore hia ꝥte ne ðohton ꝥ ⁊ ondreardon to frægnanne hine of*er* ðis word in-eode
ante eos ut non sentirent illud et timebant interrogare eum de hoc uerbo 46 *INtrauit * 102. ii. mt. clxxuiii. mr. xcu.

ut*edlice* smeaung in him huælc hiora mara were ða se hæl*end* gesaeh smeaungas heartes
autem cogitatio in eos quis eorum maior esset 47 at i*esus* uidens cogitationes cordis

hiora gelahte cnæht sette hine neh him ⁊ cuoeð ðæm ilco*m* ðegnu*m* seðe sua chuælc
illorum adprehendens puerum statuit eum secus sé 48 et ait illis quicumq*ue*

onfoæð cnæhte ðissu*m* on noma minum mec onfoað ⁊ seðe sua hua mec onfoað onfoað
susceperit puerum istum in nomine meo me recipit et quicumq*ue* me recipit recipit

ðone ilca seðe mec sende for*ð*on seðe leasā is bituih allum iuh ðes maasta is ondsuarede
eum qui me misit nam qui minor est inter omnes uos hic maior est 49 *Respondens * 103. uiii. mr. xcuii.

ioh*annes* cuoeð la hæsere woe gesegon sum oðer in noma ðinu*m* aworpende ða dioblas ⁊
autem iohannes dixit praeceptor uidimus quaendam in nomine tuo eicientem daemonia et

we for*b*udon him for*ð*on ne fylges usig mið ⁊ cuoeð to him se hæl*end* nallað gie
prohibuimus eum quia non sequitur nobiscum 50 et ait ad illum i*esus* nolite

forbeadæ seðe for*ð*on ne Is wið iuih for*e* iuih is aworden wæs ða miððy
prohibere qui enim non est aduersus uos pro uobis est 51 *Factum est autem dum * XL. 104. x.

gefylled woeron dagas ondfenges ł geliornises his ⁊ he onsione his getrumade ꝥte foerde hie*rusalem*
complerentur dies assumtionis eius et ipse faciem suam firmauit ut iret hierusalem

---

42. ⁊ miððy gineolicade agroette hine ðe diowul ⁊ giðreade ⁊ ðreade ðe hæl*end* gast unclænne ⁊ gihælde ðone cnæht ⁊ agæf hine fæder his 43. giwundradun soðlice alle on swiðe micelnisse godes alle ðailco wundradun in allum ðæmðe dyde cwæð to ðegnum his 44. sette ge i*nc* (*sic*) heortum iowrum word ðas sunu min ł monnes toword is ꝥte gisald bið in hond monnes 45. soð hiæ ne on-cneowun word ðas ⁊ wæs awriten is fore hiæ ⁊ ðætte ne ðohtun ðæt ne ondredanne to fregnanne hine of ðissu*m* worde 46. in-eode wutudl*ice* smeoung in him hwelc hiora..... 47. ...to-gilahte ðone cnæht sete hine neh him 48. ⁊ cwæð ðæm seðe swa hwelc onfoeð ðone cnæht ðissum on noma minum mec onfoeð ⁊ swa hwelc swa mec onfoeð onfoeð ðone ilcu seðe mec sende onfoeð hine forðon seðe mara is bitwih allum iow ðes mara is 49. ond-sworade wutudl*ice* ioh*annes* la hæsere we gisegun sume oðre in noma minum aworpende ða diowla ⁊ we for-budun him forðon ne fylgeð usih mið 50. ⁊ cwæð to him ðe hæl*end* nallað ge for-beada seðe forðon ne is wið iowih fore iowih is 51. aworden wæs ða miððy gifylled werun dægas to on-fonges ł liornisse his ⁊ he onsione his gitrymme (*sic*) ꝥte foerde in hierusalem

52 Ða sende he bodan beforan his ansyne. þa eodon hig on þa ceastre samaritanorum þæt hi him gegearwodon.

53 ⁊ hig ne onfengon hine forþam þe he wolde faran to hierusalem ;

54 Ða his leorning-cnihtas ꝥ gesawon. iacobus. ⁊ Iohannes. þa cwædon hig; Drīhten. wyltu we secgað ꝥ fȳr cume of heofone ⁊ for-nime hig ;

55 And hine bewende he hig þreade.

56 ⁊ hig ferdon on oþer castel ;

57 Ða hi ferdon on wege. sum him to cwæð ; Ic fylige þe swa hwyder swa þu færst ;

58 Ða cwæþ se hælend. foxas habbað holu ⁊ heofones fuglas nestþ ; Soðlice mannes sunu næfþ hwar he hys heafod ahylde ;

59 Ða cwæþ he to oðrum filig me ; Ða cwæþ he drihten alyf me æryst bebyrigean minne fæder ;

60 Ða cwæþ se hælend. læt þa dead byrigan hyra deadan. ga ðu ⁊ boda godes rīce ;

61 Ða cwæð oðer ic fylige þe drihten. ac læt me æryst hit cyþan þa*m* ðe æt ham synt ;

52 þa sente he boden be-foren his ansiene. þa eoden hyo on þa cestre Samaritanorum þæt hyo him ge-geareweden.

53 ⁊ hyo ne on-fengen hine for-þam þe he wolde faran to ierusalem.

54 Ða his leorning-cnihtes þæt ge-herden. Iacobus. ⁊ Iohannes. þa cwæðen hyo. Drihten wilt þu ꝥ we seggen þæt fer cume of heofene ⁊ for-nyme hyo.

55 ⁊ he be-wente hine ⁊ hyo þreatede.

56 ⁊ hyo ferde on oðerne castel.

57 þa hyo ferden on wēi sume him to cwæðe. Ic felgie þe swa hwider swa þu ferst.

58 Ða cwæð se hælend. foxas hæbbeð hole. ⁊ heofene fugeles nystas. soðlice mannes sune næfð hwær he hys heafed ahylde.

59 Ða cwæð he to oðren felgieð me. Ða cwæð he drihten alyf me ærest berien minne fader.

60 þa cwæð se hælend. læt þa deade berigen heora deaden. ga þu ⁊ bode godes rice.

61 Ða cwæð se oðer. ic felgie þe drihten. æc læt me arest hit kyðan þam þe æt ha*m* synden.

Various Readings.

52. A. hig (*twice*). 54. A. wylt þu. A. heofene. 55. A. ⁊ he hyne be-wende. ⁊ hig. B. C. bewend. 57. A. hig. 58. A. heofenes fugolas. A. nest; *but* B. C. nestþ. 59. A. ærest. A. byrian; B. C. byrigean. 60. A. deadan byrgean heora. 61. A. ærest. A. synd.

Various Readings.

52. sende; bodan beforan; ansyne; eodon; ceastre; ge-gearewedon. 54. -cnihtas; gesawen [*for* ge-herden]; secgað; fyr; heofone. 55. bewende; þredde (*sic*). 56. ferden; oðer. 57. hi ferdon; wege sum; cwæð; fylgige; færst. 58. halend; holu; hefone; heafod. 59. oðrv*m* fylgið; arest byrigean; fæder. 60. dead byrigan hyora deadan. 61. R. *om.* se; fylige; aryst; cyðan; synt.

⁊ sende erendureca *fore* gesigðe his ⁊ miððy foerdon In-eadon in ða ceastræ
52 et misit nuntios ante conspectum suum et euntes intrauerunt in ciuitatem

ðara lioda ꝥte *fore*-gearuadon him ⁊ ne ondfengon hine *for*ðon onsione his wæs færendes
samaritanorum ut pararent illi 53 et non receperunt eum quia facies eius erat euntis

hier*usalem* miððy gesegon ðegnas his ⁊ cuoedon drih*ten* wilt ðu
hierusalem 54 cum uidissent discipuli eius iacob*us* et iohannes dixerunt d*omi*ne uís

ꝥte we coeða ꝥte fyr ofduna astige of heofnum ⁊ *for*nime hia ⁊ ymbwælde geðreade
dicimus ut ignis descendat de caelo et consumat illos 55 et conuersus increpauit

ða ilco ł hia ⁊ foerdon in oðer*um* woerc aworden wæs ðon*ne* geongend*um*
illos 56 et abierunt in aliud castellum 57 *Factum est autem ambulantib*us* * 105. u. mt. lxuiii.

him on woeg cuoeð sum oðer to him ic fylgo ðec suæhuiddir ðu fære ⁊ cuoeð him se hæl*end*
illis in uia dixit quidam ad illum sequar té quocumq*ue* ieris 58 et ait illi i*esus*

foxas holas habbað ⁊ flegendo heofnes nesto hab*bað* sunu uut*edlice* monnes ne hæfeð ðer ł hűer
uulpes foueas habent et uolucres caeli nidos filius autem hominis non habet ubi

heafud gebega cuoeð ða to oðr*um* sőec ł fylg mec he ða coeð drih*ten*
caput reclinet 59 *Ait autem ad alterum sequere me ille autem dixit d*omi*ne * 106. x.

*for*gef ł gelef me ærist geonga ⁊ ꝥ ic byrga fæder min ⁊ cuoeð se hæl*end* *for*let
permitte mihi primum ire et sepelire patrem meum 60 dixitque i*esus* sine

ꝥte ða deado bebyrgað deado hiora ðu uut*edlice* gaa saeg ríc godes ⁊
ut mortui sepeliant mortuos suos tú autem uade annuntia regnum dei 61 et

cuoeð oðer ic fylgo ðec drih*ten* ah ærist gelef me eft-sæcga ðæm ðaðe æd hām
ait alter sequar te d*omi*ne sed primum permitte mihi renuntiare hís qui domi

sint
sunt

---

52. ⁊ sende erend-wreacu fora gisihðe his ꝥte foerdun in-eodun in ða cæstre ðara lioda .... ꝥte fore georwadun him 53. ⁊ ne onfengun hine forðon onsione his wæs færende in hier*usalem* 54. miððy gisegun wutudl*ice* ðegnas his .... ⁊ .... cwedun drih*ten* wiltu ðæt we cweðe ꝥte fyrr ofdune astige of heofnum ⁊ for-nime hiæ 55. ⁊ ymb-wærlde ðe hæl*end* giðreade ðaillco ⁊ cwæð .... 56. .... ⁊ foerdun in oðer werc 57. aworden wæs ðon*ne* gongendum him on woege cwæð sum oðer to him ic fylgo swa hwider swa ðu fære 58. ⁊ cwæð hi*m* ðe hæl*end* foxes holo habbás ⁊ flegendé heófnes nest sunu wutudl*ice* monnes ne hæfeð hwer he heofud his gibege 59. cwæð ða to oðrum fylig ł folga me he ða cwæð drihten forgef ł lef me ærest gonga ⁊ ðæt ih byrge fæder minne 60. cwæð ða him ðe hæl*end* forlett ða deodu bibyrgað deodu hiora ðu gaa ⁊ sæge in rice godes 61. ⁊ cwæð oðer ic fylge ðe drihten ah ðerh ærist gong eft sæcga ðæm ðaðe æt huse sindun

62 Đa cwæþ se hælend him to. nan mann þe hys hand asett on hys sulh. ⁊ onbæc besyhð nys and-fenge godes rice;

CHAPTER X.

Ðis godspel sceal to anes apostoles mæssan. Designauit *dominus* & alios septuaginta duos. A. Designauit *dominus iesus* & alios septuaginta duos & misit illos binos ante facie*m* suam. B.

1 ÆFter þam se hælend gemearcude oðre twa ⁊ hund-seofantig and sende hig twam beforan his ansyne on ælce ceastre. ⁊ stōwe þe he to cumenne wæs.

2 ⁊ cwæð to him her is mycel rīp. ⁊ feawa wyrhtan. biddað þæs ripes hlaford ꝥ he sende wyrhtan to his ripe;

3 Farað nu. nu ic eow sende swa swa lamb betwux wulfas;

4 Ne bere ge sacc. ne codd. ne gescy. ne nanne man be wege ne gretað;

5 On swa hwylc hus swa ge in-gað. cweðaþ æryst. sib si þisse hiw-ræddenne;

6 And gyf þar beoð sybbe bearn. reste þar eower sib. gif hit elles sy. heo sy to eow gecyrred;

7 Wunigaþ on þam ylcan huse. ⁊ etað ⁊ drincað þa þing þe hig habbað; Soðlice se wyrhta is his mēde wyrðe; Ne fare ge fra*m* hūse to hūse.

8 ac on swa hwylce ceastre swa ge ingað ⁊ hig eow onfoð. etað ꝥ eow toforan aset ys.

9 ⁊ ge-hælað þa un-truman þe on þam huse synt. ⁊ secgað him. godes rice to eow genealæcð.

Various Readings.

62. A. B. C. man. A. rices.

Cap. x. 1. A. gemearcode. A. -seofentig. 2. A. wyrhtena. 3. A. betweox. 4. A. ge-scig. A. nænne. 5. A. sig. A. hyw-rædene; B. hiw-rædene. 6. A. ge-sybbe. A. syg. A. syg. 7. A. Wuniað; B. C. Wunigeaþ. 8. A. hwylcere. 9. A. synd.

62 Đa cwæð se hælend hyem to. nan man þe his hand asett on his sluh (*sic*) ⁊ on his bæch be-sihð. nis and-fenge godes rice.

CHAPTER X.

Designauit *dominus iesus et* alios septuaginta duos [&] misit illos binos ante faciem suam.

1 After þan se hælend ge-mearcude oðre twa and hund-seofentig. ⁊ sente hyo twam ⁊ twam beforan his ansiene on ælce ceastre ⁊ stowe þe he to cumenne wæs.

2 ⁊ cwæð to heom her is micel rip ⁊ feawe wirhtan byddeð þas ripes hlaford ꝥ he sende wirhten to his ripe.

3 Fared nu; nu ich eow sende swa swa lamb be-twux wulfes.

4 Ne bere ge sech. ne cod. ne ne scy (*sic*). ne nenne man be weige ne greteð.

5 On swa hwilce huse swa ge in-gad; cweðed arest. sib syo þisse hiwrædene.

6 And gyf þær beoð sibbe bearn. reste þær eower sibbe. Gif hit elles syo. ⁊ hyo syo to eow ge-cerred;

7 wunieð on þam ylcan huse ⁊ etad ⁊ drinkeð þa þing þe hyo hæbbeð on þam ilken huse. Sodlice se werchte is his mede wurðe. Ne fare ge fram huse to huse.

8 ac on swa hwilce ceastre ge in-gað ⁊ hyo eow on-foð. æteð þæt eow æt-foren aset is.

9 ⁊ ge-hæleð þa u[n]trumen þe on þam huse sende. ⁊ seggað heom; godes rice to eow geneohlaeceð.

Various Readings.

62. him; sulh; on-bæc.

Cap. x. 1. *Rubric as in* H. -seofontig; sende; ansyne; ealce. 2. him; biddað; wyrhta. 3. Farað; ic; wulfas. 4. secc; nænne. 5. hwylc; in-gað; cweðað. 6. sibb [*2nd time*]. 7. wuniað; etad (*sic*); drincað; habbað ⁊ on þa*m* ilcan huse (*repeated as in* H.); Soðlice; wyrhta. 8. etað; aforen. 9. gehalað; untruman; synt; eom; eeow ge-nealaecð.

cuoeð to him se hæl*end* ne ænig sende hond his on sulh ⁊ behaldas on bæcg
62 ait ad illum ie*sus* nemo mittens manum suam in aratrum et respiciens retro

gecoren is to ríc godes
aptus est regno d*ei*

CAP. X.

æft*er* ðas ðon*ne* of-gemercade drih*ten* ⁊ oðoro hund-seofontig tuoege ⁊ sende hia tuoege
1 *Post haec autem designauit d*ominus* et alios septuaginta duos et misit illos binos * XLI. 107. x.

fo*r*a onsione his on alle ceastra ⁊ ꝥ stydd ðæm wæs he tocymende ⁊ cuoeð
ante faciem suam in omnem ciuitatem et locum quo erat ipse uenturus 2 et dicebat

him hrippes soðlice feolo wyrcendra uut*edlice* huon biddað for*ð*on drih*ten* ðære hrippes ꝥte gesende
illis *Messis quidem multa operari autem pauci rogate ergo d*ominum* messis ut mittat * 108. u. mt. lxxuiii.

woercmenn on ohtrippe his gaað heono ic sendo iuih sua lombro bi-tuih ulfu*m*
operarios in messem suam 3 *Ite ecce ego mitto uos sicut agnos inter lupos * 109. u. mt. lxxxui.

nællað gie gebeara seam ne posa ne sceoe ⁊ ne ænigne *monn* ðerh woege gie groetað
4 *Nolite portare sacculum neq*ue* peram neq*ue* calciamenta et neminem per uiam salutaueritis * 110. ii. mt. lxxxii. mr. liii.

on sua huelcne hus gie ingæeð ærist cuoeðað sibb ðissu*m* huse ⁊ gif ðer sie sunu
5 *In quam-cumq*ue* domum intraueritis primum dicite pax huic domui 6 et si ibi fuerit filius * 111. u. mt. lxxxiiii.

sibbes wunað of*er* hia sibb iuera gif ðon*ne* to iuh eft-gecerreð in ðæm ilca ðon*ne*
pacis requiescit super illam pax uestra sin *autem* ad uos reuertetur 7 *IN eadem *autem* * 112. ii. mt. lxxxiii. mr. liiii.

hus wunað eattas ⁊ drincas ða mið him sint wyrðe for*ð*on is se woercmonn mearde
domo manete edentes et bibentes quae apud illos sunt dignus enim est operarius mercede

his nallað gie of*er*-fara of huse in hus ⁊ in suæ-huælc ceastra gie in-færeð ⁊
sua nolite transire de domo in domum 8 *ET in quam-cumq*ue* ciuitatem intraueritis et * 113. x.

on-foað iuh eattas ða to-gesetted biðon iuh ⁊ gemað ða un-trymigo ðaðe *in* ðær sint
susceperint uos manducate quae apponuntur uobis 9 et curate infirmos qui in illa sunt

⁊ cuoeðað him geneolecde in iuh ríc godes
et dicite illis appropinquauit in uos regnum d*ei*

---

62. cwæð to him ðe hæl*end* ne ænig sende honda his on s*u*luh ⁊ bi-haldes onbæc gicoren is to rice godes

Cap. X. 1. æfter ðas ðonne of-gimercade drihten ⁊ oðro tu ⁊ hund-sifontig ⁊ sende hiæ twoege fore onsione his on alle cæstre ⁊ stowwe ðæm wæs he to cymende 2. ⁊ cwæð ðæm ripes soðlice feolu wyrcende wutudlice hwon biddað forðon drihten ripes ꝥte sende werc-men in oht-rip his 3. gað heono ic sendo iowih swa lombor bitwih wulfum 4. nallað fo*r*ðon gibeara seom ne posa ne gi-scoe ⁊ ne ænig mon ðerh woeg ge gigroetað 5. ....æres cweoðas sibb ðissu*m* huse 6. ⁊ gif ðer bið ł sie sunu sibbes wunigað ofer hia sibbe iower gif ðonne to iow eft-gicerrað 7. in ðæm ilca huse wunigað eotas ⁊ drincas ðaðe mið him sindun wyrðe is forðon ðe werc-monn metes his nallað ge ofer-fara of huse in hus 8. ⁊ in swa hwelce cæstre ge ingongas ⁊ on-foeð iowih eotas to-gisete bioðun iow 9. ⁊ gemað ða untrymigo ðaðe in ðær sindun cweoðas him to-gineolicade to iow rice godes

10 on swa hwylce ceastre swa ge ingað. ⁊ hig ne onfoð eow gaþ on hyra stræta ⁊ cweðaþ;

11 ꝥ dust ꝥ of eowre ceastre on urum fotum clifode. we drigeaþ on eow. witað þeah ꝥ godes ríce genealæcð;

12 Ic eow secge ꝥ sodom-waron on þam dæge bið forgyfenlicre þon*ne* þære ceastre;

13 Wa þe corozam. wa þe bethsáida. forþam gif on tyro ⁊ on sidóne gewordene wæron þa menegu þe on eow gedone synt. gefyrn hig on hǽran ⁊ on axan hreowsunge dydon;

14 Đeah-hwæþere tíro ⁊ sydóne on þam dæge byð forgyfenlicre þonne eow;

15 And þu cafarnaum oð heofon upahafen. þu byst oþ helle gesenced;

16 Me gehyrð se ðe eow gehyrð. ⁊ me ofer-hogaþ se ðe eow ofer-hogað; Se þe me ofer-hogað. he ofer-hogað þæne þe me sende;

17 Đa ge-cyrdon þa twa ⁊ hundseofantig mid gefean ⁊ cwǽdon; Đrihten deofol-seocnessa us synt on þinum naman underþeodde;

18 Đa sæde he him. ic geseah satanan swa swa lig-ræsc of heofone feallende.

19 ⁊ nu ic sealde eow anweald to tredenne ofer næddran. ⁊ snacan ⁊ ofer ælc feondes mægen. ⁊ nan þing eow ne derað;

10 on swa hwilce ceastre swa ge ingað; ⁊ hyo ne on-foð eow; gað on heore stræte ⁊ cwedeð.

11 Đæt dust þæt of eowre ceastre on uren foten clefede. we dreigeð on eow. triteð þeah ꝥ godes rice neohlæceð.

12 Ich eow segge þæt sodome-wæren on þam dagen beoð for-geofendlicere þanne þare ceastre ge-ware.

13 Wa þe corozaim wa þe bethsaida. for-þam gyf on tire ⁊ on sidone ge-worðene wæren þa manege þe on eow ge-done synde. ge-fern hyo on heren. ⁊ on escan reowsunge dydon.

14 Þeah-hwæðere tyre ⁊ sydone on þam daige beoð for-geofendlicere þanne eow.

15 Ǽnd þu capharnaum oð heofen upahafen; þu beost oð helle be-senceð.

16 Me ge-hyrð se þe eow ge-herð. ⁊ me ofer-hugeð; se þe eow ofer-hugeð. se þe me ofer-hugeð; he ofer-hugeð þane þe me sente.

17 Þa ge-cyrde þa twa ⁊ hund-sefentig mid ge-fean ⁊ cwæðen. Drihten deofelseocnysse us synden on þinen namen underþeode.

18 Þa saide he heo*m*. ic ge-seah satana swa swa legeræsc of heofene fallende.

19 ⁊ nu ich sealde eow anweald to tredenne ofer næddren ⁊ snaken ⁊ ofer ælc feondes mægen ⁊ nan þing eow ne dereð.

Various Readings.

10. B. C. cestre. A. heora. 11. A. driað. 12. A. -waru*m*. 13. A. corozaim. A. mænegu. A. synd. A. hā́ran. 14. A. Þeah-hwæðre. A. *om.* dæge. A. forgifenlicere. 15. A. heofen. A. B. C. besenced. 16. A. B. C. þone. 17. A. -seofentig. A. -nyssa. A. synd. 18. A. ligetræsct. A. heofene.

Various Readings.

10. goð; hyora; cweðað. 11. uru*m* fotu*m* clyofede; drygeað; witað; nealæcð. 12. waron; dagu*m* bið for-gefenlicere. 13. tyro ge-wordene waren; menega (*sic*); synt; ge-fyrn; hæran; axan hreowsunge. 14. Đæh-hweðere tyro; byð for-gifenlice þonne. 15. heofon; bist; be-senced. 16. ge-hyrð (*2nd time*); ofer-hugað (*last 3 times*); þonne; gesende. 17. ge-cyrdon; -seofentig; cwæðon; deofol-; synt; þinu*m* namon underþeodde. 18. sagde; him; satanan; lygeræsc; heofone. 19. ic; anweld; nædran; snacan; elc; deoreð.

in suahuelc ceastra gie ingæð ⁊ ne onfoæð iuh færað on plæcum hire
10 *IN quam-cumque ciuitatem intraueritis et non receperint uos exeuntes in plateas eius * 114. ii. mt. lxxxu. mr. lu.

cuoeðað æc soð ꝥ asca seðe æt-hran us from ceastra Iuera of we drygdon on iuih
dicite 11 etiam pulurem qui adhaesit nobis de ciuitate uestra extergimus in uos

soðlice ðis wutað gie ꝥte geneolacað ric godes ic cuoeðo iuh ꝥte sodomom
tamen hoc scitote quia appropinquauit regnum dei 12 dico uobis quia sodomis

on dæge ðæm forgefenra ł eaðor to forgeafanne bið ðon ðær ceastra wæ ðe ꝥ is burug wæ
in die illa remissius erit quam illi ciuitati. 13 *Uáe tibi corazain uáe * 115. u. mt. cuiii.

ðe ꝥ is æc burg forðon gif in ⁊ awordna woeron ða mæhto ðaðe in iuih awordeno woeron
tibi bethsaida quia si in tyro et sidone factæ fuissent uirtutes quae in uobis facte sunt

forlonge in huitum hrægle ⁊ on asca hia waldon sitta ꝥte hea gehreawsadon ł geboeton soðlice huoeðre
olim in cilicio et cinere sedentes pæniterent 14 uerumtamen tyro

⁊ forgefenra bið eaðor in dóm ðon iuh ⁊ ðu ꝥ is burg oðð
et sidoni remissius erit in iudicio quam uobis 15 et tú capharnaum usque in

heofon ahefen oðð to helle gedrencged seðe iuih gehereð mec gehereð ⁊ seðe iuih
caelum exaltata usque ad infernum demergeris 16 *Qui uos audit me audit et qui uos * 116. i. mt. xcuiii. mr. xcui. io. cxi. xl.

teleð ł geheneð mec henes seðe uutedlice mec henes geheneð ðone seðe mec sende
spernit me spernit qui autem me spernit spernit eum qui me misit

eftcerdon ł awoendo woeron ða tuu ⁊ hundseofontig mið glædnise cuoedon drihten soðlice
17 *Reuersi sunt autem septuaginta duo cum gaudio dicentes domine etiam * 117. x.

diowlas sint under-ðioded us on noma ðinum ⁊ cuoeð him ic ge-sæh ðone wiðerworda
daemonia subiciuntur nobis in nomine tuo 18 et ait illis uidebam satanan

suelce legeðslæht of heofnum fallende heono ic salde iuh mæht henisæs ł hniðrunges ł
sicut fulgor de caelo cadentem 19 ecce dedi uobis potestatem calcandi

on-ufa nedrum ⁊ ⁊ on-ufa all mæht fiondes ⁊ noht iuh
supra serpentes et scorpiones et supra omnem uirtutem inimici et nihil uobis

gesceðeð
nocebit

---

10. in swa hwelce cæstre ge in-gongas ⁊ ne on-foað iowih farað on plætsa his ⁊ cweoðað 11. ec soð ðætte to-gineolicað forðon rice godes 12. ic cweðo iow ðætte sodomom on dæge ðæm forgefen bið ðonne ðio cæstre ðer 13. wæ ðe ꝥ is burug wæ ðe ꝥ is æc burug forðon gif in tyrom ða mæhte ðaðe in iow awordne werun forlonge in hwitum hrægle ⁊ on asca hiæ waldun sitta ꝥ hiæ gihreowsadun 14. soðlice hweðre ⁊ .... forgefenra bið on dome ðonne iow 15. ⁊ ðu capharnaum oððe heofun ahæfen oððe to helle ðu arð gidrenceð 16. seðe iowih giheres mec giheres ⁊ seðe iowih teleð ł heneð mec teleð ł heneð ⁊ seðe witudlice mec heneð heneð ł teleð hine seðe mec sende 17. eft-cerrende werun ða tu ⁊ hund-sifuntig mið glædnisse cwedon drihten soðlice diowlas sind under-ðioded us on noma ðinum 18. ⁊ cwæð him ic gisæh ðone wiðerworda swa legeð of heofne fallende 19. heonu ic saldo iow mæhte hennisse ł niðrunge ofer nedre ⁊ .... ⁊ on-ufa alle mæht fiondes ⁊ noht iow gisceð-ðas

20 Þeah-hwæðere ne blissige ge on þa*m* þe eow synt gastas under-þeodde; Ge-blissiað ꝥ eower naman synt on heofonum awritene;

21 On þære tíde he on halgum gaste geblissode ⁊ cwæð; Ic andete þe fæder. drihten heofones ⁊ eorðan. forþam þe ðu þas ðing wisum ⁊ gleáwu*m* behyddest. ⁊ lytlingu*m* awruge. forþa*m* hit beforan þe swa gelicode;

22 Ealle þing me synt fra*m* minu*m* fæder gesealde. ⁊ nan man nat hwylc is se sunu buton se fæder. ne hwylc si ðe fæder buton se sunu. ⁊ se ðe se sunu hit awreon wyle;

Ðis sceal on þære feowerteoðan wucan ofer pentecosten. Beati oculi qui uident quæ uos uidetis. A. Beati oculi qui uiderunt quæ uos uidetis. B.

23 Þa cwæþ he to his leorningcnihtu*m* bewend; Eadige synt þa eagan þe geseoð þa ðing þe ge ge-seoð;

24 Soðlice ic eow secge ꝥ manega witegan ⁊ cyningas woldon geseon ꝥ ge ge-seoþ ⁊ hig hit ne gesawon. ⁊ woldon gehyran ꝥ ge gehyraþ. ⁊ hig hit ne gehyrdon;

25 Ðá áras sum ǽ-glæw man. ⁊ fandode his ⁊ cwæð; Lareow. hwæt do ic ꝥ ic ece líf hæbbe;

26 Ða cwæþ he to hi*m*. hwæt is gewriten on þære ǽ. hu rætst þu;

27 Ða ⁊swarude he. lufa drihten þinne god of ealre þinre heortan. ⁊ of ealre þinre sawle. ⁊ of eallum þínum mihtu*m* ⁊ of eallu*m* þinum mægene. ⁊ þinne nehstan swa ðe sylfne;

Various Readings.

20. A. synd. A. synd. A. heofenu*m*. 21. A. andette. A. B. C. heofenes. 22. A. synd. A. ys (*with* sy *above; for* si). A. onwreon. 23. A. synd. 25. A. æ-gleaw. 26. A. awryten. A. ræddest. 27. A. ⁊swarode. A. mægne.

20 Ðah-hwæðere ne blissie ge on þam þe eow sende gastes under-þedde. Geblissieð þæt eower námen synden on heofene awritene.

21 On þare tide he on halgen gaste blissede ⁊ cwæð. Ich andette þe fæder. drihten heofenes ⁊ eorðan. for-þan-þe þu þas þing wisen ⁊ gleawen be-heddest. ⁊ litlengen un-awruge. for-þam hit be-foran þe swa gelicode.

22 Ealle þingm e synde fram mine fader ge-sealde. ⁊ namman nat hwilc is se sune buton se fæder. ne hwilc sye se fæder buton se sune. ⁊ se þe se sune hit unawreon wile.

23 Þa cwæð he to his leorning-cnihton be-wend. Eadig synð þa eagen þe ge-seoð þa þing þe ge ge-seoð. Beati oculi que uideru que uos uid tis.

24 Soðlice ich eow segge þæt manigé witegan ⁊ kynges wolden ge-seon þæt þæt ge ge-seoð. ⁊ hi hit ne ge-seagen. ⁊ wolden ge-heren þæt ge ge-hereð ⁊ hi hit ne ge-herdon.

25 Ða aras sum ægleow man ⁊ fandede his ⁊ cwæð. Lareow hwæt do ic þæt ich eche lif hæbbe.

26 Ða cwæð he to him. hwæt is gewriten on þare lage. hu ræstdst (*sic*) þu.

27 Ða andswerede he. Lufe drihten þinne god. on ealre þinre heorte. ⁊ on alre þinre sawle. ⁊ on eallen þinen mihte. ⁊ of eallen þinen magene. ⁊ þiné nehstan swa swa þe sylfne.

Various Readings.

20. -hweðere; blissige; synt; under-þeodde; Ge-blissiað; naman synt; heofone. 21. halgu*m*; for-þa*m*-þe; wisum; gleawu*m* behyddast; lytlingu*m*. 22. sint; nan man; sy; fader; un-awrean. 23. synt; egan. 24. manega; cyngas; R. *has* þæt *once only*; hyo; ge-sawon; ge-hyran; ge-hyrað; hyo; ge-hyrdon. 25. æ-gleaw; ic ece; habbe. 26. þære; æ [*for* lage]; rætst. 27. Lufa; ðine; of [*for* on; 3 *times*]; ealra þi*n*ne heortan; eallu*m* þinu*m* mihtu*m*; eallu*m* þinu*m* mægene; sylfan.

soðlice huoeðre ðis nallað gie ge-feage for*ðon* se gastæs iuh under-ðioded sint gefeað ðon*ne*
20 uerumtamen hoc nolite gaudere quia sp*iritus* uobis subiciuntur gaudete autem

ꝥte noma iuera awritteno sint on heofnu*m* in ðæm tíd gefeade gaste hal*ige*
quod nomina uestra scribta sunt in caelis 21 *In ipsa hora exultauit sp*iritu* s*ancto* * XLII. 118. u. mt. cx.

⁊ cuoeð ic ondeto ðe fæder drih*ten* heofnes ⁊ eorðes ꝥte ðu gehyddest ðas fro*m* snottru*m* ⁊
et dixit confiteor tibi pater d*omin*e caeli et terrae quod abscondisti haec á sapientib*us* et

hogu*m* ⁊ æd-eauades ða ðam lytlu*m* soðlice la fæder for*ð*on suæ gelicade bef*o*re ðec Alle
prudentib*us* et reuelasti ea paruulis etiam pater quia sic placuit ante te 22 *Omnia * 119. iii. mt. cxi. io. cxluiii.

me gesald sint fro*m* feder ⁊ neænig wat huelc is sunu buta se fæder ⁊ huelc is se fæder buta
mihi tradita sunt á patre et nemo scit qui sit filius nisi pater et qui sit pater nisi

se sunu ⁊ huæm wælle se sunu æd-eaua ⁊ ym-wærlde to ðegnu*m* his cuoeð eadgo
filius et cui uoluerit filius reuelare 23 *Et conuersus ad discipulos suos dixit beati * 120. u. mt. cxxxiiii.

ða ego ðaðe geseað ðaðe geseas gie ic cuoeðo for*ð*on iuh ꝥte menigo witgo waldon gesea
oculi qui uident quae uidetis 24 dico enim uobis quod multi prophetae uoluerunt uidere

ðaðe gie geseað ⁊ ne gesegon ⁊ ge-hera ðaðe gie geherdon ł geherað ⁊ ne geherdon
quae uos uidetis et non uiderunt et audire quae auditis et non audierunt

⁊ heono sum æs laruu aras cunnade hine ⁊ cuoeð laruu huæd ł hu mið dẽd
25 *Et ecce quidam legis peritus surrexit temtans eum et dicens magister quid faciendo * XLIII. 121. ii. mt. cxciii. mr. cuii.

líf ǽce mæg ic bya ł ic agnage mæg soð h[e] cuoeð to him in æ huæd awritten
uitam aeternam possidebo 26 at ille dixit ad eum in lege quid scribtum

is hu leornas ðu he ondsuarede cuoeð lufa drih*ten* god ðin of
est quomodo legis 27 ille respondens dixit diliges d*ominu*m d*eu*m tuum ex

allra heorta ðin ⁊ of allra sauele ðin ⁊ of allu*m* mægnum ðinu*m* ⁊ of alle ðohte ðine ⁊
toto corde tuo et ex tota anima tua et ex omnib*us* uirib*us* tuis et ex omni mente tua et

ðe neste ðin sua ðec seolfe
proximum tuum sicut téipsum

[*A leaf lost in the* Rushworth MS.]

28 Þa cwæð he. rihte þu ⁊swarodest. do ꝥ. þonne leofast þu;

29 Ða cwæþ he to þa*m* hælende. ⁊ wolde hine sylfne geriht-wisian; And hwylc is min nehsta;

30 Ða cwæþ se hælend hine úpbeseonde; Sum man ferde fram hierusalem to hiericho ⁊ becom on þa sceaðan. þa hine bereafodon; ⁊ tintregodon hine. ⁊ for-leton hine samcucene.

31 Þa gebyrode hit ꝥ sum sacerd férde on þam ylcan wege ⁊ þa he ꝥ geseah he hine for-beh.

32 ⁊ eall-swa se diácon. þa he wæs wið þa stówe ⁊ ꝥ geseah he hyne eac forbeah;

33 Ða ferde sum samaritanisc man wið hine. þa he hine geseah þa wearð he mid mild-heortnesse ofer hine astyred

34 þa genealæhte he ⁊ wrað his wunda ⁊ on-agét ele ⁊ wín. ⁊ hine on hys nýten sette ⁊ gelædde on his lǽce-hus. ⁊ hine lacnude

35 ⁊ brohte oðru*m* dæge twegen penegas ⁊ sealde þa*m* læce. ⁊ þus cwæð; Begym hys. ⁊ swa hwæt swa þu mare to-gedest. þon*ne* ic cume ic hit forgylde þe;

36 Hwylc þara þreora þyncð þe ꝥ sy þæs mæg. þe on ða sceaðan befeoll;

37 Ða cwæð he. Se ðe him mild-heortnesse on dyde; Ða cwæþ se hælend gá. ⁊ do eall-swa;

28 Ða cwæð he. rihte þu andsweredest. do þæt. þanne lefest þu.

29 Ða cwæð he to þam hælende. ⁊ wolde hine selfne rihtwisian. And hwilc is min nehsta.

30 Ða cwæð se hælend hine up be-seonde. Sum man ferde fram ierusalem to ierico. ⁊ be-com on þam scaðan. þa hine be-reafeden. ⁊ tintregedon hine ⁊ for-læten hine samcweocne.

31 Þa ge-byrede hit. þæt sum sacerde ferde on þan ylken weige. ⁊ þa he þæt geseah he hine for-beah.

32 ⁊ eall swa se diacone. þa he wæs wið þa stowe. ⁊ þæt ge-seah he hine eac for-beah.

33 Ða ferde sum samaritanisc man wið hine. þa he hine ge-seah. þa warð he mid mild-heortnysse ofer hine astyred.

34 Ða ge-nehlahte he ⁊ wrad his wunden. ⁊ þron geat ele ⁊ win. ⁊ hine on his neten sette. ⁊ ge-lædde on his læche-hus ⁊ hine læcnede.

35 ⁊ brohte oðren daige twegen paneges ⁊ sealde þam læce ⁊ þus cwæð. Begeam his. ⁊ swa hwæt swa þu mare to ge-dest; þanne ich cume ich hit for-gelde þe.

36 hwilc þare þreora þincd þe þæt syo þæs mæg þe on þa scaðan be-feoll.

37 Ða cwæð he. se þe him mildheortnysse on dæde. Ða cwæð se hælend; ga ⁊ do eal-swa.

Various Readings.

28. B. C. ⁊swarudest. A. lyfast. 30. A. be-reafedon. A. *om.* ⁊ *before* tintregodon. 31. A. gebyrede. A. forbeah; B. C. forbieh. 32. A. eal-swa. A. deacon. A. *om.* eac. 33. A. myldheortnysse. 34. A. on-geat; C. onagên (*sic*). A. win ⁊ ele. A. asette. A. gelacnode. 35. A. *om.* þe. 36. A. þæra. A. sig. 37. A. myldheortnysse.

Various Readings.

28. þon*n*e leofast. 29. silfne; Ænd. 30. halend; be-reofoden; for-leten; sam-cwecne. 31. sacerd; þam ylcan. 32. diacon. 33. wearð. 34. ge-nehlæhte; wrað; wunda; on-ageat; nyten; lace-. 35. oðru*m* dæge; pæneges; ic (*twice*); for-gylde. 36. þara; þyncð; sceaðan. 37. dyde.

⁊ cuoeð him rehtlice ðu geond-suaredes ðis dő ꝥte ðu gelifige he ðon*ne* walde
28 dixitque illi recte respondisti hoc fac et uiues 29 *Ille autem uolens * 122. x.

gesoðfæstiga hine seolfne cuoeð to ðæm hæl*ende* ⁊ huelc is min ðe neestæ ondfeng
iustificare séipsum dixit ad ie*sum* et quis est meus proximus 30 suscipiens

ða se hæl*end* cuoeð monn sum adune astigade ł cuo*m* from hie*rusalem* in ðær byrig ⁊ befoerde ł becuo*m*
autem ie*sus* dixit homo quidam descendebat ab hierusalem in hiericho et incidit

on ða ðeafas ðaðe uut*edlice* bereofadon hin ⁊ mið wundu*m* on-settenu*m* fro*m*-foerdon half cwic ł lifigiende fo*r*leten
in latrones qui etiam despoliauerunt et plagis impositis abierunt semi-uiuo relicto

gelamp ðon*ne* ꝥte sac*erd* sum foerde ðailca woege ⁊ gesene hine bi-wærlde
31 accidit *autem* ut sacerdos quidam descenderet eadem uia et uiso illo præteriuit

ongelic ⁊ se diacon miððy wæs neh ꝥ stou ⁊ gesege hine of*er*-foerde samarita*nus* ꝥ
32 similiter et leuita cum esset secus locum et uideret eum transiit 33 sama-

is hæðinmonn ða su*m*m geong ł fær of*er*-eade cuom neh him ⁊ gesæh hine mið miltheart*nisse*
ritanus autem quidam iter transiens uenit secus eum et uidens eum misericordia

gecerred wæs ⁊ ge-neolecde geband ł wundo his to ł on-dælde oele ⁊ win ⁊
motus est 34 et appropians alligauit uulnera eius infundens oleum et uinu*m* et

gesette hine on netne his læddo in leçe-hũs ⁊ gemnise his dyde ⁊
imponens illum in iumentum suum duxit in stabulum et curam eius egit 35 et

oðero dæge fo*r*ebrohte tuoege peñd ⁊ salde ðæm lece ł ⁊ coeð gemnise ðæs hæfe ⁊
altera die protulit duos denarios et dedit stabulario et ait curam illius habe et

ꝥ suahuæd of*er* ðu giuas ic miððy eft-cerro ic fo*r*geldo ðe huelc ðisra ðreana
quod-cumq*ue* supererogaberis ego cum rediero redda*m* tibi 36 quis horum trium

is gesene ł ðyncge ðe se neesta woere ðæm ł him seðe in-foerde on ða ðaðeafas (*sic*) soð he cuoeð
uidetur tibi proximus fuisse illi qui incidit in latrones 37 at ille dixit

seðe dyde ꝥ miltheart*nis* on him ⁊ cuoeð him se hæl*end* gaa ⁊ ðu dőo ongelic
qui fecit misericordia*m* in illum et ait illi ie*sus* uade et tú fac similiter

---

[*A leaf lost in the* Rushworth MS.]

Ðys sceal to Assumptione s*anc*te marie. ⁊ sætern-dagu*m* be maria. Intrauit i*esus* in quoddam castellu*m*. A.

38 Soðlice hit wæs geworden þa hig
ferdon. se hælend eode on sum
castel ⁊ sum wíf on naman martha onfeng
hyne on hyre hús.
39 ⁊ þære swustur wæs maria seo eac
sæt wið þæs hælendes fét ⁊ his word ge-
hyrde;
40 Soþlice martha geornlice him þenode;
þa stod heo ⁊ cwæþ. drihten. nis þe nán
caru ꝥ min swustur let me ǽnlipie þenian
sege hyre ꝥ heo fylste me;
41 Ða cwæþ se hælend. martha martha.
geornfull þu eart ⁊ embe fela þinga ge-
drefed;
42 Ge-wislice an þing is nied-behefe.
maría geces þæne selestan dæl se hyre ne
byð afyrred;

CHAPTER XI.

1 Soðlice wæs geworden þa he wæs on
sumere stowe hine gebiddende.
þa þa he geswac. him to cwæð an his
leorning-cnihta; Drihten. lǽr ús. us ge-
biddan. swa iohannes his leorning-cnihtas
lærde;
2 Ða cwæþ he to him. cweðað þus.
þonne ge eow gebiddað; Ure fæder þu ðe
on heofone eart. si þin nama gehalgod tó-
cume þin ríce. gewurðe ðin willa on heofone ⁊ on eorþan.
3 syle us to-dæg urne dæg-hwamlican
hláf.

Various Readings.

38. A. *inserts* seo wæs *after* wyf. 39. A. swuster. 40. A. eornlice. A. swuster. A. æn-lypige; B. C. ǽnlypie. 41. A. geornful. A. fæla. 42. A. nyd-behefe; C. nied-behefe *or* med-behefe (*indistinct*). A. ge-ceas. þone.

Cap. xi. 2. A. heofenu*m*. A. sig. A. ge-weorðe. A. heofene.

38 Soðlice hit wæs ge-worden þa hyo
ferden se hælend eode on sum
castel. ⁊ sum wif on name martha on-feng
hine on hire huse.
39 ⁊ þare swuster wæs Marie seo eac
sæt wið þas hælendes fet. ⁊ his word ge-
hyrde.
40 Soðlice martha geornlice him þenode.
Ða stod hyo ⁊ cwæð. drihten nis þe nan
care þæt min swuster læt me anlepige
þenian. sege hire þæt hyo felste me.
41 Ða cwæð se hælend; martha martha
geornfull þu ert ⁊ emb fele þinge ge-drefed.
42 Ge-wislice an þing is neod-be-hefe;
marie ge-cheas þanne sælesten dael se hire
ne beoð afirred.

CHAPTER XI.

1 Soðlice wæs ge-worðen þa he wæs
on summer stowe hine be-biddende.
þa þa he ge-swac. hi*m* to cwæð an his
leorning-cnihten. Drihten lær us. us to
ge-biddan. swa iohannes his leorning-
cnihtes lærde.
2 þa cwæð he to heom. cweðed þus
þanne ge eow ge-biddað. Ure fæder þu þe
on heofene eart syo þin name ge-haleged.
to-cume þin rice. ge-worðe þin wille on
heofene ⁊ on eorðe.
3 syle us to-daig urne daig-hwamlicne
hlaf.

Various Readings.

38. ferdon; halend; naman. 39. maria; halendes. 40. carv; swustor let; ænlypige; heo fylste. 41. halend; eart; embe fela þinga. 42. nied-; maria ge-ches þonne selestan dæl; byð.

Cap. xi. 1. sumere; on; leoning-cnihtan (*sic*); R. *om.* to *after* us; ge-bidden; -cnihtans (*sic*). 2. cweðað; þonne; heofon; ge-halgad; ge-wurðe; heofane; eorðan. 3. dæg-hwamlican.

aworden wæs ða miððy foerdon ⁊ he in-eade in summe woerc ⁊ wif
38 *Factum est autem dum irent et ipse intrauit in quoddam castellum et mulier * XLIIII.

sum oðero marða wæs genemned genom hine in hus hire ⁊ ðisser wæs suoest*er*
quaedam martha nomine excepit illum in domu*m* suam 39 et huic erat soror

wæs genemned maria ðio uut*edlice* gesætt ætt fotu*m* drih*tnes* geherde word ðæs ɫ his
nomine maria quae etiam sedens secus pedes d*omi*ni audiebat uerbum illius

ðon*ne* wel dyde ymb oft embehte ðio astod ⁊ coeð drih*ten* ne
40 martha autem satagebat circa frequens ministerium quae stetit et ait d*omi*ne non

is ðe gemnise ꝥte soest*er* min fo*r*leort mec ana geembehta cuoeð *for*ðon hir ꝥte fultume ɫ gehel*pe*
est tibi curae quod soror mea reliquit me solam ministrare dı́c ergo illi ut adiuuet

mec ⁊ onduarde cuoeð hir se drih*ten* geornfull ɫ arð ⁊ ðu bist astyred
me 41 et respondens dixit illi d*omi*n*us* martha martha sollicita és et turbaris

ymb ða menigo soðlice ɫ an is nedðarf ɫ be*h*oflic gecoren dæl geceas
circa plurima 42 porro unum est necessarium mariam (*sic*) optimam patrem (*sic*) elegit

ðio ɫ ða ne bið genumen fro*m* hir
quae non auferetur ab ea

CAP. XI.

⁊ aworden wæs miððy were in stowe sum*re* gebiddende ꝥte geblann cuoeð an of
1 *ET Factum est cum esset in loco quodam orans ut cessauit dixit unus ex * XLU. 123. u. mt. xliii.

ðegnu*m* his to him drih*ten* lær usih ꝥ we gebidde sua ⁊ gelærde ðegnas his
discipulis suis ad eu*m* d*omi*ne doce nos orare sicut et iohannes docuit discipulos suos

⁊ cuoeð him miððy gie gebiddað cuoeðað fader gehalgad sie noma ðin to-cymæð rı́c
2 et ait illis cum oratis dicite pater *sanct*ificetur nomen tuum adueniat regnum

ðin hlaf userne dæg-huæmlice sel us eghuelc dæge
tuum 3 panem nostrum cotidian*u*m da nobis cotidie

---

38. .... oðer wæs ... nemned ginom hine in hus hire 39. ⁊ ðisser wæs swester nemned .... ðio ðe gisætt æt fotum drih*tnes* giherde word ðæs 40. .... ðonne wel dyde ymb oft embihte ðio stod ⁊ cwæð drihten ne is gemnisse ðe ðætte swester min for-leort mec ana giembihta cwæð forðon hir ꝥte mec hæle ɫ fulleste me 41. ondsworade cwæð hi*m* ðe hæl*end* .... georn-ful is ⁊ ðu bist astyred forðon monige 42. soðlice an is ned-ðarf ɫ bi-hoefe .... ðonne gicoren dæl giceos ðio ne bið ginumen fro*m* hir

Cap. XI. 1. ⁊ aworden wæs miððy were on stowwe sumre gibiddende ꝥte giblann cwæð an of ðegnum his to him drihten lær mec ɫ usih ðæt we gibidde swa ... lærde ðegnas his 2. ⁊ cwæð him miððy gibiddas cweoðas fæder user seðe is on heofnum gihalgad bið noma ðin to-cymeð rice ðin sie willa ðin sie swa on heofne ⁊ on eorðo 3. hlaf userne dæg-hwæmlice sel us to dæge

4 ⁊ forgyf us ure gyltas. swa we forgyfað ælcum þara þe wið us agyltað. ⁊ ne læd þu us on costunge. ac alȳs ūs fra*m* yfele;

* Ðis sceal to gang-dagon þæge twegen dagas. Quis uestru*m* habebit amicu*m*. A.

5 Ða cwæþ he to him; * Hwylc eower hæfð sumne freond. ⁊ gæþ to midre nihte to hi*m*. ⁊ cwyð to him; La freond lǣn me þry hlafas.

6 For-þa*m* mīn freond com of wēge to me. ⁊ ic næbbe hwæt ic him to-foran lecge;

7 And he þon*ne* hi*m* þus ⁊swarige. ne beo þu me gram nu min duru is belocen. ⁊ mine cnihtas synt on reste mid me. ne mæg ic arīsan nū ⁊ syllan þe;

8 Gyf he þonne þurh-wunað cnucigiende. ic eow secge gyf he [ne] arist ⁊ him sylð þon*ne* forþa*m* þe he his freond ys. þeahhwæþere for hys onhrope he arist ⁊ sylð him his neode;

9 And ic eow secge. biddað. ⁊ eow byð seald. secað. ⁊ ge findað. cnuciað. ⁊ eow byð untyned.

10 ælc þara þe bitt onfehð. ⁊ se ðe secð he fint. ⁊ cnuciendum byð untyned;

11 Hwylc eower bitt his fæder hlafes. segst þu sylð he him stān. oððe gif he byt fisces sylð he hi*m* næddran for fisce.

12 oððe gyf he bit ǣg. segst þu ræcð he him scorpione*m*. ꝥ is an wyrm-cynn.

13 Witodlice gyf he (*sic*) þon*ne* þe synt yfele cunnun syllan gōde sylene eowrum bearnu*m* swa mycele ma eower fæder of heofone sylð godne gast þam þe hyne biddað;

Various Readings.

4. A. þæra. A. B. C. agylt. A. costnunge. 5. A. Hwylc *with large blue* H, *with rubric before it.* A. myddre. 7. A. ⁊swarie. A. cnyhtas, *with the gloss* ł cnapa *above.* A. synd. 8. A. cnuciende. A. B. C. *and* Corp. *all omit* ne. A. -hwæðre. C. syld. 9. A. ge-seald. A. ontyned. 10. A. þæra. B. C. cnucigendu*m*. A. ontyned. 11. A. bytt (*twice*). A. nædran. 12. A. bytt. A. wyrmcynn, *with the gloss* . i . þrowend *above.* 13. A. B. C. ge [*for* he]. A. synd. A. cunnon. A. on heofenu*m*.

4 ⁊ for-gyf us ure geltes swa we forgyfað ælcen þare þe wið us agylteð. ⁊ ne læd þu us on costnunge. ac alys us fram yfele.

5 Ða cwæð he to heom. Hwilc eowre hafed sumne freond ⁊ gæð to middre nihte to him. ⁊ cwæð to hym. La freond læn me þreo hlafes.

6 for þan min freond com of weige to me. ⁊ ic næbbe hwæt ic him to-foran legge.

7 Ænd he him þanne þus andswerige. ne beo þu me gram nu min dure is be-cosen. ⁊ mine cnihtes synde on reste mid me ne maig ich arisan nu ⁊ sillen ðe.

8 Gyf he þanne þurh-wuned cnokigende; ic eow segge gyf he arist ⁊ him sylleð; þanne for þan þe he his freond is. þeahhwæðere for hys on-rope he arist ⁊ sylð him his neode.

9 And ich eow segge byddað. ⁊ eow beoð seald. secheð ⁊ ge findað. cnokieð ⁊ eow beoð un-tynd.

10 Ælc þare þe bitt on-fehð. ⁊ se þe secð he fint. ⁊ cnokiende byð un-tyned.

11 hwilc eower bit his fader hlafes. segest þu seld he him stan. oððe gyf he bit fissces sylð he him næddren for fissces.

12 oððe gyf he hym bytt aig. segst þu ræcd he him scorpionem þæt is an wermkyn.

13 Witodlice gyf ge þanne þe synt yfele cunnan syllan gode sylene eowren bearnen; swa micele ma eower fader of heofene sylð godne gast þam þe hine biddað.

Various Readings.

4. gyltas; ælcum þara; agyltað. 5. hæfð; frend; gað; cweð; hlafas. 6. for-þa*m*. 7. þonne; duru; becosen (*as in* H.); cnihtas synt; mæg ic; sillan. 8. þonne þurh-wunað cnucygende; gif he arist (*as in* H.); sylð þonne; -hweðere. 9. ic; byð; secað; cnucyað; untyned. 10. þara; bidt; cnuciende. 11. fæder; segst; sylð; fysces; fisces. 12. R. *om.* hym; bit æg; ræcð; wyrm-cyn. 13. þonne; eowru*m* bearnu*m*; heofone.

⁊ forgef us synna usra gif fæstlice æc we forgefæs eghuelc scyldge us* ⁊

4 et dimitte nobis peccata nostra sí quidem et ipsi dimittimus omni debenti nobis et

ne usic onlæd ðu in costunge ⁊ cuoeð to him ɫ ðæm sua huelc iuer hæbbe ɫ hæfeð friond

ne nos inducas in temtationem 5 * Et ait ad illos quis uestrum habebit amicum

⁊ gaeð to him æd middernæht ⁊ cuoeðes him la freond lih ɫ sel me ðreo *h*lafas forðon

et ibit ad illum media nocte et dicit illi ámice commoda mihi tres panes 6 quoniam

friond min cuom of woeg to me ⁊ ne hæfic ꝥte ic sette befora hine ⁊ he

amicus meus uenit de uia ad me et non habeo quod ponam ante illum 7 et ille

of inne cuoeð nælle ðu me woede ɫ hefig wosa forðon ðe dura beloccen is ⁊ cnæhtas mino

de intus dicat noli mihi molestus esse iam ostium clausum est et pueri mei

mec mið sint in cotte ne mæge ic arisa ⁊ sealla ðe ic cuoeðo iuh ⁊ gif ne selles

mecum sunt in cubili non possum surgere et dare tibi 8 dico uobis etsi non dabit

him ariseð forðon friond his bið fore scendla ɫ scending ɫ giornise huoeðre his ariseð ⁊

illi surgens eo quod amicus eius sit propter inprobitatem tamen eius surget et

seleð him ꝥte hæfeð ned-ðarfo*m* ɫ behoflice ⁊ ic iuh cuoeðo giuiað ⁊ gesald bið iuh

dabit illi quod habet necessarios (*sic*) 9 * Et ego uobis dico petite et dabitur uobis

soecað ⁊ gie gemoetað cnyllsað ⁊ untyned bið iuh eghuelc forðon seðe giuiað onfoað

quaerite et inuenietis pulsate et áperietur uobis 10 omnis enim qui petit accipit

⁊ seðe soecað gemoetað ⁊ ðæm cnylsanda untyned huelc ðon*ne* of iuh ðone fader giueð

et qui quærit inuenit et pulsanti aperietur 11 quis autem ex uobis patrem petit

hlaf hueðer stan seleð him ɫ gif fisc hueðer fore fisc nedra selleð him

panem num-quid lapidem dabit illi aut si piscem num-quid pro pisce serpentem dabit illi

ɫ gif giuað ꝥ æg hueðer ræceð him scorpiōn gif forðon iuih miððy gie biðon

12 aut si petierit ouum num-quid porrigit illi scorpionem 13 si ergo uos cum sitis

yflo wutað gie gōdo sellendo gesealla sunum Iuer*um* mara woen faeder iuer of heofnum sellað

mali nostis bona data dare filiis uestris quanto magis pater uester de caelo dabit

gast god giuendu*m* ɫ biddenda

sp*iritu*m bonum petentib*us* sé

* forgef*æs* *repeated here by mistake.*

* XLVI. 124. [x].

* 125. u. mt. liii.

---

4. ⁊ for-gef us synne use swa fæstlice ⁊ ec he ɫ we for-geofas eghwelce scylde user ⁊ ne usih on-læd ðu in costunge ah afria usih fro*m* yfle 5. ⁊ cwæð to ðæm hwelc iower hæfeð freond ⁊ gæð to him æt midder næht ⁊ cweðes him la freond lih ɫ sel me ðria hlafas 6. forðon freond com minu of woege to me ⁊ ne hafo ic hwæt ic sette ɫ lecce fora hine 7. ⁊ he of inne ond-sworade cwæð nelle ðu me moeðe ɫ hefig wosa forðon ðe dura bilocen is ⁊ cnæht min mec mið sint in cote ne mæg ic arisa ⁊ sella ðe 8. ⁊.... ....ic cweðo iow ⁊ gif ne sellas him arises for*ð*on ðætte freond his bið scendla [ɫ] giornisse hweðre freondes his ariseð ⁊ seleð him ðæt ðætte hæfeð ða ned-ðarfe ɫ bihoefe 9. ⁊ heono ic cweðo iow giowigas ⁊ sald bið iow soecað ⁊ ge gimoetað cyllað ⁊ ontyned bið iow 10. eghwelc forðon seðe giowað onfoeð ⁊ seðe soeceð gimoeteð ⁊ ðæm cnyllende ontyned bið 11. hwelc forðon of iow sunu ðone fæder giowað hlaf hweðer stan seleð ɫ gif fisces hweðer fore fisce nedre seleð him 12. ɫ gif giowað ðæt æg hweðre ræceð him scorphion 13. gif forðon iowih miððy ge bioðon yfle wutað godo sellende sunum iowrum mara woen is fæder iower of heofne seleð gast godne giowendu*m* ɫ biddendu*m* him

Ðis god-spel ge-byraᵭ on þone þryddan sunnan-dæg innan lenctene. Erat *iesus* eiciens demonium. A.

14 Ða wæs se hælend ut-adrifende sume deofol-seocnysse. ⁊ seo wæs dumb; And þa he ut-dráf þa deofol-seocnesse þa spræc se dumba. ⁊ þa menego wundredon;

15 Sume cwǽdon on bel-zebub deofla ealdre he ut-adrifᵭ þa deofol-seocnessa;

16 And sume his fandodon ⁊ gyrndon of heofone tacnys of hi*m*;

17 Ða he geseah hyra geᵭancas he cwæᵭ; Ælc ríce on hyt sylf to-dæled byᵭ. toworpen ⁊ ꝥ hus ofer ꝥ hus fealᵭ;

18 Gyf satanas is todæled on hine sylfne. hu stent his ríce. for-þa*m*-þe ge secgaᵭ ꝥ ic on bel-zebub deofol-seocnessa ut-adrife;

19 Gif ic on bel-zebub deofla ut-drífe. on hwa*m* ut-adrifaᵭ eower bearn. forþam hig beoᵭ eowere déman;

20 Gewislice gif ic on godes fingre deofla ut-adrífe. eallunga godes ríce on eow becymᵭ;

21 Ðonne se stranga gewæpnud his cafertun gehealt. þon*ne* beoᵭ on sibbe þa ᵭing þe he ah;

22 Gyf þon*ne* strengra ofer hine cymᵭ. ⁊ hine ofer-winᵭ. ealle his wæpnu þe he on truwude he him afyrᵭ. ⁊ to-dælþ his here-reaf;

23 Se þe nis mid me se is ongen me; And se þe ne gaderaᵭ mid me. se hit tostret;

14 Þa wæs se hælende ut-adrifende sume deofel-seocnysse. ⁊ seo wæs dumb. And þa he ut-adraf þa deofel-seocnisse. þa spræc se dumbe. ⁊ þa manega wundreden.

15 Sume cwæᵭen on beelzebub deofle ealdre he ut-adraf þa deofel-seocnysse.

16 And sume his fandedon ⁊ geornden of heofene tacnys of him.

17 Ða he ge-seah heora þances he cwæᵭ. Ælc rice on hit sylf to-dæled byᵭ to-worpen. ⁊ þæt hus ofer þæt hus fald.

18 Gif satanas is to-daeled on hine sylfne hu stent his rice for-ᵭan-þe ge seggeᵭ þæt ich on beelzebub deofel-seocnysse ut-adrife.

19 Gyf ich on beelzebub deofle ut-adrife. on hwam ut-adrifeᵭ eowre bearn. for-ᵭan hyo beoᵭ eowre deman.

20 Ge-wislice gyf ic on godes fingre deofle ut-adrife; ealle godes rice on eow be-kymᵭ.

21 Þanne se strange ge-wæpned his cæfertun ge-healt. þonne beoᵭ on sibbe þa þing þe he ahᵭ.

22 Gyf þanne strengre ofer hine cymᵭ. ⁊ hine ofer-swiᵭ; ealle his wæpne þe he on truwede he hym afyrᵭ. ⁊ to-dælᵭ his here-reaf.

23 Se þe nis mid me. he is on-gen me. And se ne gadered mid me; se hit to-stret.

Various Readings.

14. A. deofel- (*twice*). A. mænigeo. 15. A. deofelseocnyssa. 16. C. is [*for* his]. A. fandedon. A. heofene tacnes. 17. A. heora. A. *inserts* ⁊ *before* to-worpen. A. fealleᵭ. 18. A. stynt. A. deofelseocnyssa. 19. A. deoflu ut adryfe. A. B. C. eowre [*for* eowere]. 21. A. ge-wæpneda (*sic*). 22. A. ofer-swyᵭ; B. C. ofer-swiᵭ. A. eall. A. truwode. 23. A. on-gean.

Various Readings.

14. halend; deofol-; deofol-; dumba; menega wundredon. 15. cwædon; belzebub deofla ealdræ; adrifᵭ; deofol-. 16. Ænd; fandodon; gyrndon; heofone. 17. Elc; fealᵭ. 18. to-dæled; secgaᵭ; ic; belzebub deofol-. 19. ic; ut-drife; eowra; byᵭ. 20. eallun (*sic*); be-cymᵭ. 21. Ðonne; ge-halt; hah [*for* ahᵭ]. 22. þonne. 23. ongean; Ænd se ᵭe ne gaderaᵭ.

⁊ wæs worpende diowbles ⁊ ꝥ wæs dumþ ⁊ miððy aworpe ꝥ diowl sprecend
14 *ET erat eiciens daemonium et illud erat mutum et cum eicisset dæmonium locutus * XLIII. 126. v. mt. cxiiii.

wæs se dumb ⁊ awundrade weron ða menigo sume ðon of ðæm cuoedon
est mutus et ammiratae *sunt* turbae 15 *Quidam autem ex eis dixerunt in beelzebub * 127. ii. mt. cxxi. mr. xxxii.

on ðone aldōr diowla aworpeð diowlas ⁊ oðero costadon becon of heofne sohton
principem daemoniorum eicit daemonia 16 *Et alii temtantes signum de caelo quaerebant * 128. ii. mt. cxxiii.

fro*m* him he ða ꝥte gesæh smeawungas hiora cuoeð him eghuelc rīc in him seolf*um*
ab eo 17 *IPSE autem ut uidit cogitationes eorum dixit eis omne regnum in se ipso * 129. ii. mt. cxxii. mr. xxxiii.

to-dæled to-slitten bið ⁊ hus on-ufa hus falleð gif ðon*ne* ⁊ se wiðerworda In hine seolfne
diuisum desolatur et domus supra domum cadet 18 si autem et satanas in se ipsum

to-dæled wæs huu stondeð rīc his *for*ðon gie cuoeðas geworpa mec diowblas
diuisus est quomodo stabit regnum eius quia dicitis in beelzebub eicere me daemonia

gif ðon*ne* ic on aworpo diowlas suno iuero on huon aworpeð f*or*ðon gie ł ðailco
19 si autem ego in beelzebub eicio daemonia filii uestri in quo eiciunt ideo ipsi

doemō Iuero biðon soðlice gif on finger godes ic aworpo diowblas uut*edlice* f*ore*-cymeð in iuih
iudices uestri erun*t* 20 porro si in digito d*ei* eicio daemonia profecto prae-uenit in uos

rīc godes mið-ðy se stronga woepen-berend gehealdað ceafertun his in sibb biðon ða ðaðe
regnum d*ei* 21 cum fortis armatus custodit átrium suum in pace sunt ea quae

agnageð gif ðon*ne* bið strongra him se of*er*cymmend gebindeð ł f*ore*-cymeð hine alla woepeno
possidet 22 si autem fortior illo sup*er*ueniens uicerit eum uniuersa arma

his genimeð on ðæm gelefde ⁊ reafo his todælde seðe ne is mec mið
eius auferet in quib*us* confidebat et spolia eius distribuit 23 qui non est mecum

wið mec is ⁊ seðe ne somnigað mec mið to-straegdæð
aduersum me est et qui non colligit mecum dispergit

---

14. ⁊ wæs worpende diowlas ⁊ ðæt wæs dumdba (*sic*) ⁊ miððy aworpe ðæt diowul sprecende wæs ðe dumba ⁊ awundrade werun ðio mengu 15. alle ł sume ðonne of ðæm ælð. cwedun in belze*bub* on ðone aldor diowla aworpas ða diowlas 16. ⁊ oðre costadun becun ł tacon sohtun of heofnum fro*m* him 17. he ða ꝥte gisæh smeounge hiora cwæð him eghwelc rice in him solfu*m* todæled tosliten bið ⁊ hus ofer-ufa huse fallet 18. gif ðonne ⁊ ðe wiðerworda satan awarp in him solfum to-dæled wæs huu stondeð rice his forðon ge cweoðas . . . . giworpa diowlas 19. . . . . suno iowre of hwon aworpeð forðon ða ilco doemu iowre bioðon 20. soðlice gif on finger godes ic worpe diowlas wutud-lice forecumað in iowih rice godes 21. miððy ðe stronga wepend-berend gihaldað cæfer-tun his in sibbe bioðon ða ðaðe agnigað 22. gif ðonne strongra him ofer-cymes gibinde ł forcyme hine alle wepeno his ginimeð on ðæm gilefde ⁊ reof his to-dæleð 23. seðe ne is mec mið wið mec is ⁊ seðe ne somnað mec mið to-stregdes

24 Ðon*ne* se un-clæna gast gæð of þam men. he gæð þurh un-wæterie stówa reste secende ⁊ nane ne gemet þon*ne* cwyð he; Ic gewende eft to mínum huse þe ic of eode.

25 ⁊ þænne he cymð. he hit gemet æmtig mid besmu*m* afeormod;

26 Þon*ne* gæð he ⁊ nimð seofan oðre gastas wyrsan þon*ne* he ⁊ ingað. ⁊ þar eardiað. þon*ne* synt þæs mannes endas wyrsan þam ærrum;

27 Soðlice wæs geworden þa he ðis sǽde. sum wíf him to cwæþ; Eadig is se innoð þe þe bær. ⁊ þa breost þe ðu suce;

28 Ða cwæð he. eadige synt þa ðe godes word ge-hyrað ⁊ ꝥ ge-healdaþ;

29 Ða hyra manega to-gædere comon he cwæþ to hi*m*; Ðeos cneorys is manfull cneorys. heo secð tacen. ⁊ hyre ne bið nán geseald buton Ionan tacen;

30 Swa swa iona wæs tacen niniuetu*m*. swa bið mannes sunu tacen þisse cneorisse;

31 Suð-dæles cwén arist on dome mid þisse cneorysse mannu*m* ⁊ genyðerað hig forþa*m* þe heo com of eorðan endum to gehyranne salomones wisdom; And efne þes is mára þonne salomon;

32 Niniuetisce men arísaþ on dóme mid þisse cneorysse ⁊ genyðeriað hig. for-þa*m* þe hig dæd-bóte dydon. æt ionam bodunge. ⁊ þes is mara þon*ne* ioná;

24 Þanne se un-clæne gast gæð of þam men; he gæð þurh un-wæterie stowe reste secende. ⁊ nane ne ge-mett. Þanne cweð he. Ic wende æft to minen huse þe ich of eode.

25 ⁊ þanne he kymð he hit ge-mett emtig mid besme afermed.

26 Þanne gæð he ⁊ nymð seofan oðre gastes wirsan þanne he. ⁊ in-gæð ⁊ þær eardieð. Þanne synt þas mannes ændes werse þanne þam earren.

27 Soðlice wæs ge-worðen þa he þis saigde; sum wif him to cwæð. Eadig is se innoð þe þe bær. ⁊ þa breost þe þu suke.

28 Þa cwæð he. Eadige sinde þa þe godes word ge-hereð ⁊ þæt ge-healdeð.

29 Þa hyra manega to-gadere coman he cwæð to heom. Þeos cneoris is manful cneoris; he secd taken ⁊ hire ne beoð nan ge-seald buton Ionas taken.

30 Swa swa iona wæs taken Niniueten swa beoð ma*n*nes sune taken þise cneorisse.

31 Sud-dale cwen arist on dome mid þise cneorisse mannen ⁊ ge-nyðereð hyo for-ðan hyo com of eorðan endum to geheren Salomones wisdom. Ænd efne þes is mare þanne salomon.

32 Niniuetisce men arised on dome mid þisse cneornisse. ⁊ ge-ne-ðeriað hyo. forþan þe hyo deadbote dyden. æt Iona*n* bodegunge. ⁊ þes is mare þanne jona.

Various Readings.

24. A. un-wæterige. 25. A. þonn*e*. 26. A. seofen; C. seofon. A. synd. 28. A. synd. 29. A. manful. 32. A. ⁊ ionan [*for* æt ionam].

Various Readings.

24. Ðonne; geð; gað; ge-met; þo*n*ne cwyð; eft; minu*m*; ic. 25. þonne; cymð; ge-met; afeormod. 26. Ðonne; þonne; eardiað; þon*ne*; þæs; endas wirsun þo*n*ne; earrum. 27. ge-worden; sægde; suce. 28. Eadig sinð; ge-hyrað. 29. mænega; manfull; secð tacen; byð; Ionan tacen. 30. tacen niniuetu*m*; bið; tacen þisse. 31. Suð-dæles; þysse; mannum; ge-herenne; þonne. 32. arisað; cneorisse; ge-niðeriað; Ionan bodunge; þo*n*ne.

miððy se unclæne gaast ge-eode from ðæm menn ðerh-eode ł gãð ðerh stowa wæterleasa
24 *Cum immundus spiritus exierit de homine perambulat per loca inaquosa * 130 u. mt. cxxuiiii.

soecende ł sohte ræst ⁊ ne gemoete cuoeð eft ic cerro In hus min ðona ic foerde
quaerens requiem et non inueniens dicit reuertar in domum meam unde exiui

⁊ miððy cwome gemoete mið besmum geclænsad ⁊ ða gaeð ł eade ⁊ genom ł onfeng
25 et cum uenerit inuenit scopis mundatam 26 et tunc uadit et assumit

seofono oðoro gaastas wohfullre him ⁊ in-foerdon gebydon ðer ⁊ woeron ða endo monnes
septem alios spiritos (*sic*) nequiores sé et ingressi habitant ibi et sunt nouissima hominis

ðæs wuyrso ðæm ærrum aworden wæs ða miððy ðas gecuoæð ahof ðone stefn
illius peiora prioribus 27 *Factum est autem cum haec diceret extollens uocem * XLUIII. 131. x.

sum wif of ðæm here cuoeð him eadig womb ł hrif seðe ðec gebær ⁊ ða titto ł ða breosto
quædam mulier de turba dixit illi beatus uenter qui té portauit et ubera

ða ðu gediides soð he cuoeð alluncga suæ hit his eadgo biðon ðaðe geherað word godes ⁊
quae suxisti 28 at ille dixit quippini beati qui audiunt uerbum dei et

gehaldas hergum ða efne-Iornendum ongann coeða cneoreso ðios cneoreso woh-full
custodiunt 29 *Turbis *autem* concurrentibus coepit dicere generatio haec generatio nequam * 132. v. mt. ccxxuiii.

is becon soecað ⁊ becon ne bið sald him buta becon iones. i. ðæs witgo forðon suæ
est signum quaerit et signum non dabitur illi nisi signum ionae 30 nam sicut

wæs becon ðære burge suæ bið ⁊ sunu monnes cneoreso ðissum coen
ionas fuit signum nineuitis ita erit et filius hominis generationi isti 31 regina

suð-ernæs ł suð-dæles ariseð on dóm mið werum cneoreso ðisses ⁊ geheneð hia forðon
a[u]stri surget in iudicio cum uiris generationis huius et condemnabit illos quia

cuom from gemærum eorðes to geheranne snyttro salomones ⁊ heono maro salomone ðes ł her wæras
uenit á finibus terrae audire sapientiam salomonis et ecce plus salomone hic 32 uiri

ðær byrig arisað on dome mið cneoreso ðios ⁊ hia gehenað ða ilca forðon hreonise
nineuitae surgent in iudicio cum generatione hac et condemnabunt illam quia paenitentiam

dydon to bod ⁊ heono mara ðes
egerunt ad praedicationem ionæ et ecce plus iona hic

---

24. miððy ðe unclæne gast gieode from ðæm men ðerh-eode ł gæð ðerh stowe wæter-lease soecende ræste ⁊ ne gimoette cwæð eft ic cerre in hus min ðona ic cerde 25. ⁊ miððy ic come ic gimoete mið bisenum (*sic*) giclænsad ⁊ . . . . 26. ⁊ ða eode ⁊ ginom ł onfeng siofone oðre gastas woh-fulra him ⁊ infoerdun gibyedun ðer ⁊ ðer werun ðende monnes ðæs wyrsa ðæm ærrum 27. aworden wæs ðonne miððy ðas gicwæð ahof ða stefne sum wif of ðæm herge cwæð him eadig womb seðe ðec gibær ⁊ ða tito ł ða breost ða ðu deðedes 28. soð he cwæð to him . . . . eadge bioðon ðaðe giherað word godes ⁊ gihaldes 29. hergum ða iornendum ongan cweoða cneoreswe ðios cneoreswe woh-ful is becun soeceð ⁊ becun ne bið sald him buta becun iones ðæs witga 30. forðon swa ionas becun wæs ðære burge swa bið ⁊ sunu monnes cneoreswa ðissum 31. cwoen suðerne ariseð on dome mið weorum cneoreswo ðisser ⁊ giheneð hia forðon com from gimærum eorðo to giheranne snytro . . . . ⁊ heono mara salamon ðes 32. weoras in ðær byrig arisað on dome mið cneoreswum ðios ⁊ hiæ giherað ðailco forðon hreownisse dydon to bibode iones ⁊ heono mara . . . . ðes

33 Ne on-ælþ nān man his leoht-fæt ⁊ sett on diglum. ne under bydene ac ofer candel-stæf. ꝥ ðа þe in-gаð leoht geseon;

34 Ðin eage is þines lichaman leoht-fæt; Gif þin eage bið hluttor ðonne bið eall þin lichama beorht; Gif hit byð deorc. eall þin lichama byð þystre;

35 Warna ꝥ ꝥ leoht þe ðe on is. ne syn þystru;

36 Gyf þin lichama eall bið beorht and næfþ nanne dæl þystra þonne byð he eall beorht. ⁊ þe on-lyht swa ꝥ leoht-fæt þæs lig-ræsces;

Ðys godspel ge-byrað on frige-dæg on þære teoðan wucan ofer pentecosten. Rogabat iesum quidam phariseus ut pranderet apud se. A.

37 Þa bæd hine sum fariseisc man ꝥ he ǣte mid him ⁊ he ineode ⁊ sæt;

38 Ða ongan se fariseisca on him smeagan ⁊ cweðan; Hwi he ge-þwogen nære ær his gereorde;

39 Ða cwæð drihten to him nu ge farisei ꝥ ute is calices ⁊ disces geclænsiað ꝥ eow innan is. ꝥ is full reaf-lace ⁊ unriht-wisnesse;

40 La dysegan hu ne worhte ꝥ ꝥ inne is. se ðe worhte ꝥ ūte is.

41 þeah-hwæþere ꝥ to lafe is syllað ælmessan þonne beoð eow ealle þing clǣne;

42 Ac wā eow fariseum ge þe teoþiað mintan ⁊ rūdan. ⁊ ælce wyrte ⁊ ge for-bugað dōm ⁊ godes lufe; Þas þing eow gebyrede to donne. ⁊ þa þing ne for-lætan;

Various Readings.

37. A. phariseisc. 38. A. phariseisca. A. smeagean. A. Hwig. A. ge-þwagen. 39. A. pharisei. A. ynne [*for* innan]. A. reaflaces. A. unryhtwysnysse. 40. B. C. worht [*2nd time only*]. 41. A. ælmyssan. 42. A. phariseum.

33 Ne on-ælð nan man his leoht-fett ⁊ sett on diglen. ne under bedene. ac ofer candel-stef. þæt þe ingað leoht geseon.

34 Þin eage is þines lichames leoht-fæt. Gif þin eage beoð hluttor; þanne beoð eall þin licháme briht. Gif hit beoð deorc; eall þin lichame beoð þeostre.

35 Warne þæt ꝥ leoht þe þe on is; ne syo þeostra.

36 Gif þin lichame eall beoð breoht; ⁊ næfd nænne dæl þeostre; þanne beoð he eall breoht. ⁊ þe on-liht swa þæt leoht-fæt þas lægræsces.

37 Ða bæd hine sum fariseisc man þæt he æte mid him. ⁊ he in-eode ⁊ sætt.

38 Ða on-gan se fariseisce on him smeagen ⁊ cwæðan. Hwi he ge-þwogen nære ær his ge-reorde.

39 Ða cwæð drihten to him. nu ge farisei þæt ute is calices ⁊ disces ge-clænsieð ꝥ eow innan is. þæt is ful reaflake ⁊ unrihtwisnysse.

40 La desige hu ne worhten (*sic*) ꝥ ꝥ inne is. se þe worhte þæt ute is.

41 þeah-hwaðere þæt to lafe is sellað ælmessan þanne beoð eow ealle þing clæne.

42 Ac wa eow fariseum ge þe teoðiað mintan ⁊ rudan ⁊ ælce wirte. ⁊ ge forbugeð dom ⁊ godes lufe. Þas þing eow geberede to donne. ⁊ þa þing ne for-læten.

Various Readings.

33. -fet; set; diglum; -stæf; R. *inserts* þa *before* þe. 34. byð lutter þonne byð; breoht; byð; þystre. 35. syn þystra. 36. lichama; næfð; þystra þonne byð; þæs lygræsces. 37. ete; R. *om.* *2nd* he; sett. 38. fariseisca; smeagan; cweðan. 39. pharisei; ge-clænsiað; reaflace. 40. dysegan; worhte (*twice*). 41. -hwæðere; syllað; þonne. 42. ge-byrede; for-læton.

ne ænig ðæccilla gebernað ⁊ in degelnise setteð ne under mitto ah on-ufa leht-
33 *Nemo lucerna accendit et in abscondito ponit neq*ue* sub modio sed supra candela- * XLUIIII. 133. ii. mt. xxxii. mr. xxxuiiii.

fæte ꝥte ða ðe in-geongas leht hia gesea ðæccilla lic-homes ðines is ego ðin
brum ut qui ingrediuntur lumen uideant
34 *Lucerna corporis tui est oculus tuus * 134. n. mt. xluii.

gif ego ðin bið milde ł bliðe ł bilwit all lic-homa ðin leht bið gif ðon*ne* wohfull sie
si oculus tuus fuerit simplex totum corpus tuum lucidum erit si autem nequam fuerit

uut*edlice* lichoma ðin ðiostrig bið geseh f*or*ðon Ne leht ꝥ in ðec is ðiostro ꝥte sie
etiam corpus tuum tenebrosum erit
35 uide ergo ne lumen quod in te est tenebrae sint

gif f*or*ðon lichoma ðin all leht bið ne hæbbe sum dæl ðiostriona bið
36 si ergo corpus tuum totum lucidum fuerit non habens aliquam partem tenebrarum erit

leht all ⁊ sua leht legeð inlehtað ðec ⁊ mið-ðy gespræc baed
lucidum totum et sicut lucerna fulgoris inluminabit té
37 *ET cum loqueretur rogauit * L. 135. u. mt. ccxxxui.

hine sum ælde-wuto ꝥte gehriordade ł gebrece mið hine ⁊ in-eade gehlionade
illum quidam pharisaeus ut pranderet apud sé et ingressus recubuit
38 pharisaeus

ðon*ne* agann bituih him getalade to coæðanne f*or*huon ne gefulwad were ær ge*h*riorda
autem coepit intra sé reputans dicere quare non baptizatus esset ante prandium

⁊ cuoeð drih*ten* to hine nu gie ældouuto ꝥ ūtteweard is calices ⁊ disces
39 et ait d*omi*n*us* ad illum nunc uos pharisaei quod de foris est calicis et catini

gie clænsað ꝥte ðon*ne* inweard is iuer full is mið nednimincg ⁊ mið unrehtwisnise
mundatis quod autem intus est uestrum plenum est rapina et iniquitate

unwiso Ahne seðe dyde ꝥte wuteard is uut*edlice* ꝥ ꝥte of inweard is dyde
40 stulti nonne qui fecit quod de foris est etiam id quod de intus est fecit

soðlic huoeðre ꝥte of*er*-hlæfeð ł ꝥte wona is seallað ælmissa ⁊ heono alle clæno biðon
41 uerum-tamen quod super-est date elemosynam et ecce omnia munda sunt

iuh ah wæ iuh æl*dum* f*or*ðon giæ teigðas meric ł ⁊ cunela ł ⁊ ælc wyrt
uobis
42 *Sed uǽ uobis pharisaei quia decimatis mentam et rutam et omne holus * 136 u. mt. ccxxxiiii.

⁊ bi-wærlas ꝥ dom ⁊ lufo ł broðerscip godes ðas uut*edlice* geras to wyrcanne ⁊ ðailco ne
et praeteritis iudicium et caritatem dei haec autem oportuit facere et illa non

to f*or*hycganne
omittere

---

33. ne ænig ðæcele giberneð ⁊ in degolnisse seteð ne under mitta ah on-ufa leht-fæt ꝥte ðaðe in-gongas leht hiæ giseað 34. ðæcela lic-homa ðines is ego ðin gif ego ðin biað milde ł bliðe all lichoma ðin leht bið gif ðonne woh-ful siæ wutudl*ice* ⁊ lic-homa ðiostor bið 35. gisæh forðon ne leht ðætte in ðiostrum sint 36. gif forðon lic-homa ðin all leht bið ne hæbbe sumne dæll ðiostrana leht bið all ⁊ swa leht legedes in-lihteð ðec 37. ⁊ miððy sprecende bið bæd hine sum ælde uðwuta ꝥte giriordade mið hine ⁊ in-eode giblionade 38. .... ðon*ne* ongan bitwih him gitalade to cweoðanne forwhon ne ærist .... were ær giriordum 39. ⁊ cwæð drih*ten* to him nu ge ælde-wutu ærist ðætte uta-word is calices ⁊ disces giclænsas ðætte ðonne ionnaword is iower full is mið ned-nime ⁊ mið unrehte 40. unwise ah ne seðe dyde utaword is soðlice ðætte of ionna-word*um* is dyde 41. soð hweðre ðætte ofer is sellað elmessa ⁊ heono alle clæne bioðon iow 42. ah wæ iow ældum forðon ge tegðigas merece ⁊ cunela ⁊ alle wyrte ⁊ biwærlas ðone dom ⁊ lufo-broðorscip godes ðæs wutudlice giras to wyrcanne ⁊ ða ilco ne to forhycganne

43 Wā eow fariseum ge þe lufiað þa forman heah-setl on ge-samnungum ⁊ gretinga
on strǣte ;
44 Wa eow for-þam þe ge synt swylce þa
byrgena þe man innan ne sceawað ; And
þa men nyton þe him on-ufan gað ;
45 Ða ⁊swarode him sum ægleaw. lareow teonan þu wyrhcst [us] mid þisse sage ;
46 Þa cwæþ he ; Wa eow ægleawum
forþam þe ge symað men mid þam byr-
þenum þe hig aberan ne magon. ⁊ ge ne
ahrinað þa seamas mid eowrum anum
fingre ;
47 Wa eow ge þe timbriað witegena
byrgena. eower fæderas hig of-slōgon
48 eallunga ge cyðað. ⁊ ge þafiað eower
fædera weorcum. forþam hig ofslogon hig.
⁊ ge timbriað hira byrgena ;
49 Forþam cwæð godes wisdōm. ic sende
to him witegan ⁊ apostolas. ⁊ hig of-sleað
hig. ⁊ ehtað
50 ꝥ ealra witegena blod sy ge-soht. þe
wæs agoten of middan-geardes fruman. fram
þisse cneorysse.
51 fram abeles blode oð zachariam blod.
se forwearð betux þam altare ⁊ þam temple.
ic eow secge. swa bið ge-soht fram þisse
cneorysse ;
52 Wa eow ægleawum for-þam þe ge
ætbrudun þæs ingehydes cæge. ge in ne
eodun ⁊ ge forbudon þa þe in-eodun ;

43 Wa eow fariseen ge þe lufieð þa
formen heahsetlen on ge-samnungen ⁊ gretinge on stræten.
44 Wa eow for-þan-þe ge sende swilce
þa byrigenna þe man innan ne sceawed. ⁊
þa men nyten þe heom on ufen gad.
45 Ða andswerede him sum lage-gleaw.
lareow teonan þu wercst us mid þisse sage.
46 Ða cwæð he Wa eow lagewisen for-
þan ge semeð menn mid þam byrdenen þe
hyo aberen ne mugen. ⁊ ge ne æthrinað
þa seames mid eowren anen fingren.

47 Wa eow þe timbrieð witegena byri-
gena ; eowre faderes hyo of-slogen
48 eallunge. ge kyðed ⁊ ge þafieð eowre
fader weorces. for-þam hyo slogen hyo. ⁊
ge timbrieð heore berigena.
49 For-þam cweð godes wisdom. Ic
sende to heom witegen ⁊ þa apostles ; ⁊ hyo
of-slæð hyo ⁊ æhtað
50 þæt ealra witegene blod syo ge-soht ;
þe wæs agoten of midden-eardes fruman ;
fram þisse cneorisse
51 fram abeles blode oð zacharias blod.
se for-warð be-tweox þam altare ⁊ þam
temple. Ic eow segge swa beoð ge-soht
fram þisse cneornysse.
52 Wa eow lage-gleawe for-þam-þe ge
ætbruden þas inge-heades ceyge ge in ne
ge-heodden. ⁊ ge for-budon þa þe in-eoden.

Various Readings.

43. A. heh-. A. stræt*um*. 44. A. synd. 45. B. ⁊swarude. A. wyrcst ; B. C. wyrhcst. A. *om.* us. 47. A. Wa (*with large blue capital*). 48. A. heora. 50. A. sig. A. myddan-eārdes. 51. A. betweox ; B. C. betwux. 52. A. æt-brudon. A. eodon (*twice*). A. *wrongly inserts* ne *before* forbudon.

Various Readings.

43. fariseu*m* ; lufiað ; forman ; heah-setl ; gesamnu*n*gum ; stræte. 44. synt ; byrgena ; sceawað ; on-ufan gað. 45. ea-gleaw ; werhcst. 46. ea-glæwen [*for* lagewisen] ; men mid ; byrþenu*m* ; abeoren ; magen ; ahrinað ; seamas ; eowru*m* anum fingrum. 47. timbriað ; eower fæderes. 48. eallunga ; cydað (*sic*) ; þafiað ; fædera weorcon ; timbriað heora byrigenna. 49. cwæð ; eom witegan ; apostlas ; of-slæað ; ehtað. 50. witegena ; sy ; middan-eardas. 51. zacharia*m* ; for-werð be-twux ; byð ; cneorysse. 52. æ-glæwu*m* [*for* lage-gleawe] ; forþan þe ; cæge ; geheodu*m* ; in-eodum (*sic*).

wæ iuh al*dum* ðaðe gie lufað ða f*or*ma seatlas on somnungu*m* ⁊ ða groetencgo on
43 *Uáe uobis pharisaeis qui diligitis primas cathedras in synagogis et salutationes in * 137. ii. mt. ccxxuiiii. mr. cxxxu.

sprēc wæ iuh f*or*ðon gie aron suælcæ byrgenna ðaðe ne foedað ł ne alað ł adeauæð ⁊ ꝥte menn
foro 44 *Uáe uobis quia estis ut monumenta quae non parent et homines * 138. u. mt. ccxxuii.

geonges on-ufa ne wuton geondueardo ða sum fro*m* æs wisistu*m* cuoeð him
ambulantes supra nesciunt 45 *Respondens autem quidam ex legis peritis ait illi * LI. 139. u. mt. ccxxuiii.

laruu ðas coeð uut*edlice* us sceoma ðu does ł wyrcas soð he cuoeð ⁊ iuh æs
magister haec dicens etiam nobis contumiliam facis 46 at ille ait et uobis legis

wisestu*m* wæ f*or*ðon gie sēmað menn mið seamu*m* ðaðe gebeara ne magon ⁊ gie seolf anum fingre
peritis uáe quia oneratis homines oneribus quae portari non possunt et ipsi uno digito

mið iuer ne gehrinað ðæm hond-hæfu*m* we iwh f*or*ðon gie timbras byrgenna ðara witgana
uestro non tangitis sarcinas 47 *Uáe uobis quia ædificatis munumenta prophetarum * 140. u. mt. ccxxuiii.

fadores ðon*ne* iueres ofslogon hia soðlice gie getrymeð ł ꝥte ge geneolecað ł woerc*um*
patres autem uestri occiderunt illos 48 profecto testificamini quod consentitis operibus

fadora iuera f*or*ðon æc gie hia ofslogon gie ða getimbras hiora
patrum uestrorum quoniam quidem ipsi eos occiderunt uos autem ædificatis eor*um*

byrgenna f*or*ðon ⁊ snyttro godes cuoeð ic sendo to iuh iwtgo (*sic*) ⁊ apos*tolas*
sepulchra 49 *Propter-ea et sapientia d*e*i dixit mittam ad illos prophetas et apostolus (*sic*) * 141. u. mt. ccxl.

⁊ of ðæm ofslæð ⁊ oehtad biðon ꝥte ge-soht bið blōd allra witgana
et ex illis occident et persequentur 50 ut inquiratur sanguis omnium prophetaru*m*

seðe agotten wæs fro*m* onsetnise middan*geardes* of cneureso ðisa from blod abeles
qui effusus est á constitutione mundi á ge[ne]ratione ista 51 á sanguine abel

wið to blod zachariæs seðe losade ł bitwih wigbed ⁊ ꝥ waghræl*e* ł sua ic cuoeðo to iuh gesoht bið
usq*ue* ad sanguinem zachariae qui periit inter altare et aedem ita dico uobis requiretur

fro*m* ðissu*m* cneoreso wæ iuh æs uutu*m* f*or*ðon gie nomon cægo wisdomes gie
ab hac generatione 52 *Uáe uobis legis peritis quia tulistis clauem scientiae ipsi * 142. u. mt. ccxxxii.

ne in-foerdon ł ne in-eodegie ⁊ ða ðaðe in-foerdon f*or*estemdongie ł gie bewoeredon
non introistis et eos qui introiebant prohibuistis

---

43. wæ iow ældum forðon ðaðe lufigas ða forma seatlas in somnungum ⁊ ða groetinge on sprece 44. wæ iow f*or*ðon ge arun swelce byrgenne ðaðe ne foedað ł aleð ⁊ ꝥte menn geongas of*er*ufa ða ne wutun 45. giondworde ða sum from æs wisistum cwæð him larow ðas cwæð wutudl*ice* us scomu ðu does ł dydes 46. soð he cwæð ⁊ iow æs wisistum wæ iow forðon gisemað menn mið seomum ðaðe gibeara ne magun ⁊ ge solfa anum fingre iowrum ne gi-hrinas ðæm hond-hafum ðæræ 47. wæ iow forðo ge timbrias byrgenne witgana ðara fædras ðonne iowre ofslogun hiæ 48. soðlice ge gitry*mm*að gineolicade werca fædra iowra forðon hiæ ge ofslogun iow ða gitimbro byrgenne 49. ⁊ forðon ⁊ snytro godes cwæð ic sende to iow witgo ⁊ apos*tolas* ⁊ of ðæm of-slað ⁊ oehteð 50. ꝥte gisoht bið blod alra witgana seðe agoten wæs from onsetnisse midden-geordes fro*m* cneoreswo ðisser 51. from blode abeles wið to to (*sic*) blode zacharies ⁊ seðe losade bitwih wibide ⁊ ðæm wæg-hrægle swa ic cweðo iow gisoht bið fro*m* ðæsser cneowreswe 52. wæ iow æs wutum forðon genomun cægo wis-domes ⁊ he ł ge ne in-foerdun ⁊ ða ðaðe in-foerdun for-stemdon ge

53 Ða he him þis to cwæð. þa ongunnun ða farisei ⁊ þa ægleawan hefilice him agen standan ⁊ his muð dyttan

54 ⁊ embe hine syrwan. secende su*m* þing of his muðe ꝥ hig hine wregdun.

CHAPTER XII.

1 mycelum weredu*m* him embe standendu*m* ꝥ hig hine trǽdun; Ða cwæð he to his leorning-cnihtum warniað wið farisea lare ꝥ is licetung;

2 Soðlice nis nan þing ofer-heled. þe ne beo un-heled. ne be-hydd ꝥ ne sy witen.

3 forþam þe ꝥ ge secgað on þystrum beoð on leohte sæde ⁊ þæt ge on earum spræcu*n* on bedd-cofu*m* bið on hrofum bodud;

4 Ic secge eow minu*m* freondu*m* ne beo ge bregyde fra*m* þam þe þone lichaman of-sleað. ⁊ nabbað syþþan hwæt hig mā dōn;

5 Ic eow æt-ywe hwæne ge on-dredon. adrædað þone þe anweald hæfð. seððan he ofslyhð on helle asendan. þus ic eow secge adrædað þone.

6 ne becypað hīg fīf spearwan to helflinge. ⁊ an nis of þa*m* ofer-gyten beforan gōde.

7 ac ealle eowres heafdes loccas synt getealde; Ne adrǽde ge eow ge synt beteran manegum spearwum;

53 ÞA he heom þis to cwæð. þa ongunnen þa farisej ⁊ þa lage-wisan hefilice him agēn standen ⁊ his muð dettan.

54 ⁊ ymbe hine syrwan; sechende sum þing of his muðe þæt hyo hine wreidon

CHAPTER XII.

1 micelen wereden hym embe-standende. þæt hyo hine træden. Ða cwæð he to his leorning-cnihten warnieð eow wið farisea lare þæt is licetung.

2 Soðlice nis nan þing ofer-heled; þe ne beoð un-heled. ne be-hed; þe ne sye gewyten.

3 For-þan-þe þæt ge seggeð on þeostren beoð on leohte saigde. ⁊ þæt ge on earen spræcon on bedd-cofum beoð on rofen boded.

4 Ich segge eow minen freonden ne beo ge brygede fram þam þe þanne lichamen of-sleað. ⁊ næbbeð syððan. hwæt hyo ma don.

5 Ic eow atewige hwane ge on-dræden. adredeð þane þe anweald hæfð. seððan he of-slehð; on hellen asenden; þus ich eow segge; adredeð þane.

6 ne be-cypað hyo fif sparewen to halpenige. ⁊ an nis of þam ofer-gyten be-fore gode.

7 ac ealle eowres heafdes loccas sende getealde. Ne on-dræde ge eow ge sende beteren þan manegen sparewen.

Various Readings.

53. A. ongunnon. A. hefiglice. A. ongean. 54. A. ymbe. A. syrwdon. A. wregdon.

Cap. xii. 1. A. ymbe. A. trædon. B. C. warnigeað. A. licetung (*alt. to* liccetung). 2. A. sig. 3. A. gearu*m*. A. spræcon; B. C. spræcum (*sic*). A. bed-. 4. A. beoð ge bregede. 5. A. B. C. ondrædon. A. ondrædað. A. syððan. 6. A. ælflinge. 7. A. synd. A. ondræde. A. synd.

Various Readings.

53. him; ongunnun; farisei; eaglewan [*for* lage-wissan; dyttan. 54. embe; secende; wreigdon.

Cap. xii. 1. mycelu*m* weredu*m*; -standenden; trædun; -cnihtum; warniað. 2. beo un-heolod; be-hydd; sy. 3. seggað; þystron byð; sægde; earu*m* spracon; byð; rofu*m* bodud. 4. Ic; minu*m* freondv*m*; bregyde; þonne. 5. ætywe hwæne; adrædeð þonne; andweald; of-slyhð; asendan; ic; adrædeð þone. 6. sparewan; helflinge. 7. synt; synt beateran (*sic*); manegum spearewum.

mið-ðy ðas to him ge-cuoeð ongunnun ða ældu ⁊ æs unto pislice ł hefiglice wið-stonda
53 *Cum haec ad illos diceret coeperunt pharisaei et legis periti grauiter insistere * 143. x.

⁊ muð his for-ðrycga of monigum sẽtnungum ł ⁊ sohton to niomanne huoelc-huoego of
et ós eius opprimere de multis 54 insidiantes et quaerentes capere aliquid ex

muðe his ꝥte hea gehendon hine
ore eius ut accusarent eum

CAP. XII.

menigum ðonne ł ða hergum ymb-stondendum suæ ꝥte hia him bituih geteldon ongann cuoeða
1 multis autem turbis circumstantibus ita ut sé inuicem conculcarent coepit dicere

to ðegnum his behaldað gie iuih from dærste ꝥ is esuicnise noht
ad discipulos suos *Attendite á fermento pharisaeorum quod est hypocrisis 2 †Nihil * 144. ii. mt. clxiiii. mr. lxxuiiii.

ðonne awrigen is ꝥte ne ædeauad bið ne gehyded ł gedegled ꝥte ne bið geypped forðon
autem opertum est quod non reueletur neque absconditum quod non sciatur 3 quoniam † 145. u. mt. xciii.

ðaðe in ðiostrum gie cuoedon in leht biðon gecoeden ⁊ ꝥte in eare sprecend gie woeron in cottum
quae in tenebris dixistis in lumine dicentur et quod in aurem locuti estis in cubiculis

aboden bið on hrofum ic cuoeðo ða ł ðonne iuh friondum minum ꝥte gie ne se afyrhtad from ðæm
praedicabitur in tectis 4 dico autem uobis ámicis meis ne terreamini ab his

ðaðe ofslæð ꝥ lichoma ⁊ æfter ðas ne habbas forðor ꝥte doað ic ad-eawu ðonne
qui occidunt corpus et post haec non habent amplius quod faciant 5 ostendam autem

iuh ðone gie ondrede ondredas ðene seðe æfter ðon ofslaeð hæfeð mæht gesenda ł to ge-
uobis quem timeatis timete eum qui postquam occiderit habet potestatem mit-

sendanne in tintergo suæ ic cuoeðo iuh ðionne ondredeð ahne fifo staras ł cymeð
tere in gehennam ita dico uobis hunc timete 6 nonne quinque passeres ueniunt (*sic*)

⁊ an of ðæm ne is on ofergetnise ł fora godæ ah ⁊ æc hero
* depundio et unus ex illis non est in obliuione coram deo 7 sed et capilli * i. duo minuta ł (*in margin*).

heafdes iweres alle getalad aron nallað gie forðon ondrede monigum forðoro ł maro
capitis uestri omnes numerati sunt nolite ergo timere multis passeribus plures

gie sint ł biðon
estis

---

53. miððy ðas to him cwæða on-gunnun ða ældu ⁊ æs witgu pislice wið-stonde ⁊ muð his for-ðrycca of monigum 54. setnungum him ⁊ sohtun to niomanne welc-hwoegnu of muðe his ꝥte hiæ gihendun hine

Cap. XII. 1. monige ðonne hergum ymb-stonda swa ꝥte hiæ him bitwih giteldun ongunnun cweoða to ðegnum his ærist bihaldas ge iowih for dærstum ældum hiora ðæt is es-swicnis 2. noht ðonne awrigen is ðætte ne eowed bið ne gihyded ł gidegled ðætte ne bið giypped 3. forðon ðaðe in ðiostrum giherdun in lehte gicweden bið ⁊ ðætte in earum giherdest ⁊ sprecende gewerun in cotum abodad bið on hrofum ⁊.... 4. ic cweðo ðonne iow friondas mine ðætte ge ne se gifyrhted from him ðaðe ofslað ðonne lichoma ⁊ æfter ðas ne haldas forðor ðætte doeð 5. ic æt-eowo ðonne iow ðone ge on-drede on-dredas ðone seðe æfter ðon of-slað hæfeð mæhte gisende in tintergu swa ic cwæð iow ðonne ondredað 6. ah ne stearas fife comun twoege.... ⁊ an of him ne is on ofer-getnisse fora gode 7. ah ⁊ ec her heofdes iowres alle gitalad arun nallað ge forðon on-dreda monigum.... forðor ł mara ge sindun ł bioðon

8 Soðlice ic eow secge swa hwylc swa me andet beforan mannum. þone mannes sunu andet beforan godes englum;

9 Se þe me wið-sæcð beforan mannum. se byð wið-sacen beforan godes englum.

10 ⁊ ælc þe segð ænig word agēn mannes sunu þam bið for-gyfen; Ðam þe wiðer-sacað ongen haligne gast. ne bið þam forgyfen;

Ðis sceal on frige-dæg ofer pentecosten. Cum autem inducerent uos in sinagogis. A.

11 Þonne hig lædað eow on gesamnunga ⁊ to dugeðe-ealdrum. ⁊ to anwealdum. ne beo ge embe-þencynde. hū oððe hwæt ge specon. oððe ⁊swarian.

12 halig gast eow lærð on þære tīde þa þing þe eow specan gebyrað;

13 Ða cwæð sum of þam menegum; Lāreow. sege minum breðer ꝥ he dæle uncer æhta wið me;

14 Ða cwæð he. lā mān. hwa sette me dēman. oððe dælend ofer īnc;

15 Þa cwæð he. gymað ⁊ warniað. wið ælce gytsunge. forþam þe nys nanes mannes līf on gytsunge of þam þe he ah;

16 Ða sæde he him sum big-spel; Sumes weliges mannes æcer brohte forð gōde wæstmas.

17 þa ðohte he on him sylfum. ⁊ cwæð; Hwæt do ic forþam ic næbbe hwyder ic mīne wæstmas gadrige;

18 Ða cwæþ he þus ic do. ic towurpe mīne bernu ⁊ ic wyrce māran. ⁊ ic gaderige þyder eall ꝥ me ge-wexen ys. ⁊ mīne gōd

8 Soðlice ic eow segge swa hwilc swa me andeat be-foren mannen. þanne mannes sune andeat be-foren godes ængles.

9 Se þe me wið-secð be-foren mannen. se beoð wið-saken be-foran godes ænglen.

10 ⁊ ælc þe saigð ani word agen mannes sune. þam beoð for-gefen. Þam þe wiðer-sakeð on-gen halgen gast. ne beoð þam for-gyfen.

11 Þanne hyo lædeð eow on ge-samnunge. ⁊ to dugeðe ealdren. ⁊ to anwealden ne beo ge ymbe-þencende hu oððe hwæt ge spæcen oððe andswerien.

12 halig gast eow lærð on þare tide þa þing þe eow spæcan ge-byreð.

13 þa cwæð sum of þam manigeo. Lareow sege mine breðer þæt he dæle unker ehte wið me.

14 Ða cwæð he la man hwa sette me deman; oððe dælend ofer hine (*sic*)

15 Þa cwæð he. gymeð ⁊ warnieð wið ælce gitsunge. for-þan-þe nis nanes mannes lyf on gytsunge of þam þe he ah.

16 Ða sæde he heom sum bispel. Sumes weliges mannes acer brohte forð gode wæstmes.

17 þa þohte he on him sylfen ⁊ cwæð. hwæt do ic for-þan ich næbbe hwider ich mine wæstmes gaderie.

18 Ða cwæð he þus ich do. ic to-werpe mine berne. ⁊ ich werche hyo mare ⁊ ic gaderie þider eall þæt me wexen is. ⁊ mine god.

Various Readings.

8. A. ⁊dett. A. andett. 10. A. ongean (*twice*). 11. A. ge-samnunge. A. dugoðe-. A. ymbe-þencende. A. sprecon. A. B. ⁊swarion. 12. A. sprecan. 13. A. mænegum. 14. A. ync. 15. A. gimað. A. *om.* þe *be-fore* nys. 17. A. gaderige. 18. A. toweorpe. A. berenu. A. gaderie. A. geweaxen.

Various Readings.

8. andett be-foran mannum. þonne; andett be-foran; engles. 9. be-foran mannum; -sacen; englum. 10. segð ænig; sunu; byð; -sacað ongean halgne; byð. 11. Ðonne; ge-samnunga; ealdrum; anwealdum; embe-þencynde; specen. 12. specen. 13. menegu; Lærew; uncer æhte. 14. hinc. 15. gymað; warniað; -þam-; manes. 16. eom; big-spel; wæstmas. 17. on him sylfum *is repeated in* R.; forðam ic; ic; wæstmas gaderige. 18. ic; to-wyrpe; bernu; ic wyrce maran [*omitting* hyo]; gaderige; ge-wexen.

ic cuoeðo ðon*ne* iuh eghuelc seðe suahuelc ondetende bið on mec bef*ora* monnu*m* ⁊ sunu
8 dico autem uobis omnis quicumq*ue* confessus fuerit in me coram hominib*us* et filius

monnes geondetað bið on ðæm f*or*e englu*m* godes seðe uut*edlice* onsæccað mec f*or*e
hominis confitebitur in illo coram angelis d*e*i 9 *Qui autem negauerit me coram * 146. ii. mt. xciiii. mr. lxxxui.

monnu*m* oncæccen (*sic*) bið f*or*e englum godes ⁊ alle seðe cuoeðas word on sunu
hominib*us* denegabitur coram angelis d*e*i 10 *Et omnes (*sic*) qui dicit uerb*um* in filium * 147. ii. mt. cxxiii. mr. xxxiii [i].

monnes eft f*or*gefen bið ðæm ðæm uut*edlice* seðe on halig gast ebolsað ne bið him f*or*gefen
hominis remittetur illi ei autem qui in sp*iritu*m s*anc*tu*m* blasphemauerit non remittetur

miððy uut*edlice* inlædæð gie in somnungum ⁊ to laruum ⁊ mæhtum nallað gie
11 *Cum autem inducent uos in synagogas et ad magistratus et potestates nolite * 148. ii. mt. lxxxuiii. mr. cxli.

gem*a* ł gearnfulle ł hōgo wosa huu ł huæd gie geonduearde gast f*or*ðon halig gelæreð
solliciti esse qualiter aut quid respondeatis 12 sp*iritu*s enim s*anc*tus docebit

iuih on ðæm tíd ðaðe behofað ł gehriseð to cuoeðanne cuoeð ða sum him of ðæm here
uos in ipsa hora quae oporteat dicere 13 *Ait autem quidam ei de turba * LII. 149. x.

laruu cuoeð broðre minu*m* ꝥte gedæla mec mið ꝥ erfe soð he cuoeð him la monn
magister dic fratri meo ut diuidat mecum hereditatem 14 at ille dixit ei homo

hua mec gesette doema ł dælend of*er* iuih ⁊ cuoeð to him geseað ⁊
quis me constituit iudicem aut diuisore*m* supra uos 15 dixitq*ue* ad illos uidete et

behaldað fro*m* eghuelcu*m* gitsuncge f*or*ðon ne on monigfaldnise æniges lif his is of ðæm ðaðe
cauete ab omni auaritia quia non in abundantia cuius-quam uita eius *est* ex his quae

agnigeð cuoeð ða onlicnesse to him cuoeð monnes summes wloncas monigfaldo
possidet 16 dixit autem similitudine*m* ad illos dicens hominis cuiusdam diuitis ubcres

wæstmas lond to-brohte ⁊ smeade bituih him cuoeð huæd ic doa ꝥte ne hæfo ic
fructus ager attulit 17 et cogitabat intra sé dicens quid faciam quod non habeo

ðer ic somnigo wæstmo min ⁊ cuoeð ðis ic g[e]dóm ic to-slíto bererno mino ⁊ ða mara
quo congregem fructus meos 18 et dixit hoc faciam destruam horrea mea et maiora

ic doam ⁊ ðer ic somniga willo alle ðaðe gewæxen sint me ⁊ godo mino
faciam et illuc congregabo omnia quae nata sunt mihi et bona mea

---

8. ic cweðo ðonne iow eghwelc seðe swa ondetende bið on mec fora monnum ⁊ sunu monnes gi-ondetad bið
in him fore englum godes 9. seðe wutudl*ice* ne onsæces me fora monnum onsæcen bið fora englum
godes 10. alle ðaðe cweoðað word on suno monnes eft for-gefen bið him ðæm wutudl*ice* seðe on gaste
halgum eofol-sigað ne bið forgefen him ⁊ eghwelc seðe cweðes word on sunu monnes for-gefen bið him
11. miððy wutudl*ice* inlædað ge in somnungum ⁊ to larwum ⁊ mæhte nallað ge gema ł hogo wosa huu ł hwæt
gi-ondworde ł hwæt ge cweðe 12. gast forðon halig gilareð iowih in ðær tide ðaðe bi-hofað to cweoðanne
13. cwæð ða him sum wer of ðæm herge larow cwæð broðer min ꝥte he gi-dæle mec mið ꝥ erfe 14.
soð he cwæð him la mon hwa mec gisette doema ł dælend ofer iowih 15. cwæð ða to ðæm giseað
⁊ bihaldað fro*m* eghwelcum gitsungum forðon ne on monig-faldnisse ænges lif his is of ðæm ðaðe agnigað
16. cwæð ða onlicnisse to him cwæð monnes sumes wlonches monigfalde wæstmas on londe to-brohte
17. ⁊ smeode bitwih him cwæð hwæt ic doa ðætte ne hafo ic ðer ic somnigo wæstmas mine 18. ⁊
cwæð ðis ic dom ic to-slito berern min ⁊ ða mara ic dom ⁊ ðer ic somniga wyllo alle ðaðe wexne sindun
me ⁊ godo mine

19 ⁊ ic secge minre sawle eala sawel þu hæfst mycele gód. asette to manegum gearum. gerest þe. ét. ⁊ drínc ⁊ gewísta;

20 Ða cwæð god to him; La dysega on þisse nihte hig fecca𝒹 þine sawle fram þe. hwæs beoð þa ðing þe ðu ge-gearwudest;

21 Swa is se ðe him sylfum strynð. ⁊ nis welig mid gode;

22 Þa cwæð he to his leorning-cnihtum. forþam ic eow secge ne beo ge ymbe-hydige eowre sawle hwæt ge étan. ne eowrum lichaman hwæt ge scrydun;

23 Seo sawul ys ma þonne se lichama. ⁊ se lichama má þon*ne* ꝥ reaf;

24 Besceawiað þa hrefnas ꝥ hig ne sawað. ne ne ripað. nabbað hig heddern ne bern. ac god hig fett. þæs þe má ge synt hyra selran;

25 Hwylc eower mæg þencende ican áne elne. to his anlicnesse.

26 gyf ge ꝥ læsse ne magon. hwy synt ge be oðru*m* þingum ymbe-hydige;

27 Sceawiaþ þa lilian hu hi wexað. hi ne swincað ne ne spinnað; Soðlice ic eow secge ꝥ salomon on eallum hys wuldre næs gescrydd. swa þissa án;

28 Gyf god scrytt ꝥ híg. ðe ys to-dæg on æcere. ⁊ to-morgen forscrincð; swa mycele ma gód scryt eow ge-hwædes ge-leafan;

19 ⁊ ich segge minre sawle. eale sawel þu hafst mycele god. Asette to manegen gearen. ge-rest þe. æt ⁊ drinc ⁊ ge-wista.

20 Ða cwæð god to hym. La desige on þisse nihte hyo fecceð þine sawle fram þe. hwæs beoð þa þi*n*g. þe þu gærewedest.

21 Swa is se þe him sylfen strenþeð ⁊ nis welig mid gode.

22 Þa cwæð he to his leorning-cnihten. for-þan ich eow segge. ne beo ge ymbehedige eowre sawle hwæt ge etan. ne owren lichaman hwæt ge scrydan.

23 Seo sawle is mare þanne se lichame. ⁊ se lichame mare þanne þæt reaf.

24 Be-sceawiað þa refnes þæt hyo ne sawað ne ne ripað. næbbað hyo heddern ne bern. ac god hyo fet þas þe ma. ge synde heore selre.

25 hwilc eower mæg þencende echan ane elne to his anlichnysse.

26 gyf ge þæt læsse ne magen hwy synde ge be oðren þingen ymbe-hedige.

27 Scewieð þa lilien hu hyo wexeð. hyo ne swinceð ne ne spinnəð. Soðlíce ic eow segge þæt Salomon on eallen his wuldre næs ge-scryd swa þis án.

28 Gif god scrytd ꝥ héy þe is to-daig on æcere ⁊ to-morgen for-scrincð. Swa mycele ma god scrit eow ge-hwædes ge-leafen.

Various Readings.

19. A. gereste. 20. A. ge-gearwodest. 22. A. B. C. scrydon. 23. A. sawel. A. mare. A. lychama ys mare. 24. B. C. Bescewiað. A. beren. A. fet. A. synd heora. 25. A. ge-ycan. A. anlycnysse. 26. A. hwig synd. 27. A. hig (*twice*). A. gescryd. 28. A. scryt. A. to-mergen.

Various Readings.

19. ic; hafest; manegu*m* georen; et. 20. dysige; feccað. 21. silfv*m* strenð. 22. -cnihtu*m*; ic; eowren [*for* owren]. 23. þo*n*ne; lichama; lichama; þonne. 24. Bescewiað; ræfnes; þæs; synt; hyora sylrei (*sic; partly rewritten in later hand*). 25. ecan; anlicnysse. 26. magon; sint; oðru*m* þingu*m* ymbe-hydige. 27. Scewiað; lilian; wexað; swyncað; spinnað; allu*m*; ge-scrudd; þissa. 28. scritt; eig [*for* héy]; to-dæig; ge-leafan.

⁊ ic coeðo sawle mine la sawel ðu hæfeð monigo ꝉ feolo godo gesettedo on geru*m* monigu*m*
19 et dicam animae meae anima habes multa bona posita in annos plurimos

ræst bruce dring ge*h*riordig cuoeð ðon*ne* him god la unwis ðisser næht saul
requiesce comede bibe epulare 20 dixit autem illi d*eus* stulte hac nocte anima*m*

ðin eft wilnað fro*m* ðe ðaðe ðon*ne* ðu ge-gearuades ðæs ꝉ huæs biðon ꝉ woeron suæ is seðe ðe
tuam repetunt á te quae autem parasti cuius erunt 21 sic est qui tibi

gestrionað ⁊ ne is in god welig ꝉ wlonc ⁊ cuoeð to ðegnu*m* his fo*r*ðon ic cuoeð iuh
thesaurizat et non est in d*eum* diues 22 *Dixitq*ue* ad discipulos suos ideo dico uobis * 150. u. mt. xluiiii.

nallað gie geornfullo wosa mið ðohte huæd gie geette ne to lichoma huæd gie ge-gearuad se sauel
nolite solliciti esse animae quid manducetis neq*ue* corpori quid uestiamini 23 anima

mara is ðon mett ⁊ lichoma ðon wŏede behaldað ða ræfnas ꝥte ne
plus est quam esca et corpus quam uestimentum 24 considerate corbos quia non

sawæð ne *h*riopað ðæm ne is hordern ne ber-ern ⁊ god foedeð hia micla
seminant neq*ue* metunt quib*us* non est cellarium neq*ue* horreum et d*eus* pascet illos quanto

mara gie fo*r*ðor aron ðæm huælc ðon*ne* iuer mið smeawung mæge geĕce to
magis uos plures estis illis 25 quis autem uestrum cogitando potest adicere ad

leng ꝉ his elne an gif fo*r*ðon ne ꝥte leassæst is magogie huæd of
staturam suam cubitum unum 26 si ergo neq*ue* quod minimum est potestis quid de

oðru*m* færwit-fulla menn ꝉ geornfullo gie sint behaldað ða wyrta huu wæxað ne winnað
ceteris solliciti estis 27 considerate lilia quomodo crescunt non laborant

ne nestað ic cuoeðo ðon*ne* iuh ne salo*mon* on alle wuldor his woere gegearuad ꝉ gewoedad suelce
non neunt (*sic*) dico autem uobis nec salomon in omni gloria sua uestiebatur sicut

an fro*m* ðissu*m* gif ðon*ne* ꝥ gærs ꝥ to dæge on lond is ⁊ tomorgen
unum ex istis 28 si autem faenum quod hodie in agro est et cras in clibanum

geseuded bið god suæ gegearuað mara micla ꝉ gie huono ꝉ lytlo geleafas
mittitur d*eus* sic uestit quanto magis uos pussillae fidei

---

19. ⁊ ic cweðo sawle minę hæfes monig ꝉ feolu goda gisetedo on gerum monigum ræst bryce riording drince giriordinge 20. cwæð ðonne him god la unwis ðisser næht sawel ðin eft wilnað fro*m* ðe ðaðe ðonne ðu georwades ðæs ꝉ hwæs bioðon ꝉ werun 21. swa is seðe ðe gistrioneð ⁊ ne is in god weolig 22. cwæð ða to ðegnum his forðon ic cwæð iow nallað ge geornfulle wosa mið ðohte hwæt ge giete ne to lichoma hwæt ge gigerwed sie 23. sawel mara is ðonne mett ⁊ lichoma mara ðonne giwedo 24. bihaldas hræfnas ðaðe ne sawað ne riopað ðæm ne is hordern ne bere-ern ⁊ god foedeð hia micle mara ge ⁊ forðor aron ðæm 25. hwelc forðon iower mið smeunge mæge ge-ece to lengu his elne ane 26. gif ðonne ne ðætte læssa is magun ge hwæt of oðrum ferwett-fulle men ge sint 27. bihaldað ða wyrte lilia hu hio wexeð ne winneð ne nestað ic cweðo ðonne iow ne . . . . on alle wuldre his were gigeorwad swa ana from ðissum 28. gif ðonne ðæt gers ðæt to-dæge on londe ⁊ to-morgenne on ofon gisended bið gode swa gegeorwad mara micle hwon ꝉ lytle ꝉ læssa gileofa

29 And nelle ge secean hwæt ge eton oððe drincon. ⁊ ne beo ge up-ahafene

30 ealle þas þing þeoda seceað; Eower fæder wat ꝥ ge þises beþurfon;

31 Þeah-hwæþere seceað godes rīce ⁊ ealle þas þing eow beoþ ge-ihte;

32 Ne ondræd þu þe la lytle heord. forþam eowrum fæder gelicode eow rīce syllan;

33 Syllaþ ꝥ ge agon ⁊ syllað ælmessan. wyrcað seodas þa ðe ne for-ealdigeað. ungeteorudne gold-hord on heofenum. þyder ðeof ne ge-nealæcð. ne ne (*sic*) moððe ne ge-wemð;

34 Ðar eower gold-hord is. þar byð eower heorte;

Dis god-spel ge-byrað to mæniges confessores mæsse-dæge. Sint lumbi *uestri* precincti. A.

35 Sin eower lendenu begyrde ⁊ leohtfatu byrnende.

36 ⁊ beo gelice þam mannum þe hyra hlafordes abidað hwænne he sy fram gyftum gecyrred. ꝥ hig him sona ontynon þon*ne* he cymð ⁊ cnucað;

37 Eadige synt þa þeowas þe se hlaford wæccende gemet þon*ne* he cymð; Soðlice ic eow secge ꝥ he begyrt hine ⁊ deð ꝥ hig sittað. ⁊ gangende hi*m* þenað;

38 And gif he cymð on þære æfteran wæccan. oððe on þære þriddan ⁊ þus gemet. eadige synt þa þeowas;

39 Witað ꝥ gif se hiredes ealdor wiste hwænne se þeof cuman wolde. witodlice he wacude ⁊ ne geþafude ꝥ man his hus under-dulfe;

29 Ænd nelle sechan hwæt ge etan oððe drincan. ⁊ ne beo ge up-ahafene.

30 ealle þas þing þeode secheð. eower fader wat þæt ge þises be-þurfen.

31 Ðeah-hwæðere secheð godes rice ⁊ ealle þas þing eow beoð ge-icte.

32 Ne on-dræd þu þeah litle heord. forþan eowren hefenlic fader licode eow rice syllen.

33 Syllað þæt ge agen ⁊ sylleð ælmessen. Wereeð seaðes þa þe ne for-ealdiged. unge-teorudne goldhord on heofene. þiðer þeof ne ge-neohlaceð. ne mogðe ne gewemd.

34 Ðær eower goldhord is þær beoð eower heorte.

35 Syen eower lendene be-gyrde ⁊ leohtfate bearnende.

36 ⁊ beoð ge-lice þam mannen þe hyore hlaforde abideð hwanne he syo fra*m* gyftan ge-cherred. þæt hyo him sona un-tyne þanne he cymð ⁊ cnokeð.

37 Eadige synde þa þeowes þe se hlaford waciende ge-fint. þanne he kymð. Soðlice ic eow segge þæt he be-gyrt hine. ⁊ deð þæt hyo sitteð ⁊ gangende heom þenað.

38 Ænd gyf he kymð on þare æftran wæccen. oððe on þare þridden ⁊ þus gemet. Eadig synde þa þeowes.

39 Witeð þæt gyf se hyrdes hlaford wiste hwanne se þeof cumen wolde. witodlice he wacode. ⁊ ge ne þafede (*sic*) þæt man his hus under-dulfe.

Various Readings.

29. A. secan. A. etan. A. dryncan. A. up-ahafen. 30. A. secað. 31. A. secað. A. ge-yhte; B. C. ge-icte. 33. A. ælmyssan. A. B. C. wyrceað. A. for-ealdiað. A. unge-teorodne. A. B. C. *have* ne *only once before* moððe. 36. A. ge ge-lyce [*for* gelice]. A. heora. A. hlafordas (*sic*). A. sig. 37. A. Eadie synd. 38. A. synd. 39. A. wacode. A. ge-þafode.

Various Readings.

29. secan, *alt. to* secean; R. *repeats* hwæt ge eton. 30. þeoda seaceð; be-þurfon. 31. seacað. 32. þeal [*for* þeah; *in margin*]; eowru*m*; R. *om.* hefenlic; ge-licode; syllan. 33. syllað ælmessan. Wyrcað seodas; for-ealdigeað; heofonu*m*; ge-nealæcð; moððe; ge-wemð. 35. Syn [*with red capital*]; byrnende. 36. mannu*m*; hyora; abydað hwænne; gecyrred; untyneð þo*n*ne; cnoceð. 37. Eadig synt; þeowas; ge-met [*for* ge-fint] þonne; cymst [*for* kymð]. 38. End; cymð; þæra; wæccan; ðriddan; Eadig synt; þeowas. 39. Witað; hyredes; ealdor [*for* hlaford]; hwænne; ge ne þafode (*sic*).

⁊ gie nællað gesoeca huæd gie geēte ł huæd gie gedringe ⁊ ne wællað gie in heannise
29 et uos nolite quaerere quid manducetis aut quid bibatis et nolite in sublime

genime ðas *for*ðon alle hædno ł cynno middang*eardes* soecað fæder uut*edlice* iuer wat
tolli 30 haec enim omnia gentes mundi quærunt pater autem uester scit

ꝥte ðissu*m* ł ðas gie behofað soðlic huoeðre soecas ric godes ⁊ ðas alle togēced biðon iuh
quoniam his indigetis 31 uerum-tamen quaerite regnum d*e*i et haec omnia adicientur uobis

ne wællaðge ondrede ꝥ lytel ēdæ *for*ðon gelicade woel feder iuer gesealla iuh ꝥ rīc
32 *Nolite timere pusillus grex quia complacuit patri uestro dare uobis regnum * LIII. 151. x.

bebycgeð ðaðe gie agnegeð ł agon ⁊ seallas ælmiss*e* wyrcas iuh seado ł of*er*seamas ðaðe ne
33 *Uendite quae possidetis et date elemosynam †Facite uobis sacculos qui non * 152. ii. mt. cxciiii. mr. cuiii.

aldagiað strion un-scortende in heofnu*m* ðer ðeaf ne geneoleceð ne mohða
ueterescunt thesaurum non deficientem in caelis quo fur non appropriat neq*ue* tinea + 153. u. mt. xlui.

gescendes ł suahuer *for*ðon strion iuer wæs ł is ðer ⁊ hearta iuer bið sie
corrumpit 34 ubi enim thesaurus uester est ibi et cór uestrum erit 35 *Sint * 154. x.

sido iuero *fore*-gegyrdedo* ⁊ ðæccillæ bernendo ⁊ gie ongelic monnu*m*
lumbi uestri praecincti et lucernae ardentes 36 et uos similes hominib*us* * i. mið gódum dedu*m* (*margin*).

abīdendu*m* hlaferd hiora ðon*ne* ge-cerres fro*m* symblu*m* ꝥte miððy cymeð ⁊ cnyllsað
expectantib*us* dominum suum quando reuertatur á nuptis ut cum uenerit et pulsauerit

sona untynað him eadgo biðon esnas ða ðaðe miððy cymes se drih*ten* gemoetað
confesti*m* áperiant ei 37 *Beati serui illi quos cum uenerit d*ominus* inuenerit * 155. u. mt. cclxui.

wæccendo soðlice ic cuoeðo to iuh ꝥte gegyrdeð hine ⁊ doæð hia gehriordagæ ł ⁊ of*er*foerde ł gaeð
uigilantes amen dico uobis quod praecingit sé et faciet illos discumbere et transiens

embehtað ł ðæm ⁊ gif cymeð on ða æft*er*ra waccane ⁊ gif on ða ðirdda wacan ge-cymeð ⁊
ministrabit illis 38 et sí uenerit in secunda uigilia et sí in tertia uigilia uenerit et

ðus ł suæ gemoetað eadgo biðon esnas ða ðis ðon*ne* wuteð gie ꝥte gif wiste fæder
ita inuenerit beati serui illi 39 *Hoc autem scitote quoniam sí sciret pater * 156. ii. mt. cclxiiii. mr. clu.

hiogwuisc ł hirodes fad*er* huelc tīd se ðeaf cwome walde wæca uut*edlice* ⁊ ne walde lēta ðerh-delfa
familias qua hora fúr ueniet uigilaret utiq*ue* et non sineret perfodi

hus his
domum suam

---

29. ⁊ ge nallað ge-soeca hwæt ge gi-ete ł hwæt gidrince ⁊ nallað ge in heonisse of-ginioma 30. ðas forðon alle hæðno middengeord soecað fæder wutudlice iower watt ðæt ðis ge bi-hofigas 31. soðlice hweðre soecað forðon ærest rice godes ⁊ ðas alle to-æt-eced iow 32. ne wallað ge on-dreda ðæt lytle eode forðon gilicade well feder iowrum seleð iow rice 33. bihyccað (*sic*) ðaðe habbað ⁊ sellas almesse wyrcas iow seadas ł of*er*seme ðaðe ne aldigað gistrion unscortende on heofnum ðer ðeof ne gi-neolicað ne mohða gisceððas 34. swa hwer gistrion goldes iower is ðer ⁊ heorte bið 35. ðe wutudl*ice* sidu iower fora-gigyrdedo ⁊ ðæcela iower berende (*sic*) 36. ⁊ ge onlic monnum abiddende hlaford hiora ðonne gicerras from symblum ðætte miððy cymeð ⁊ cnyllað sona ontyned bið him 37. eadge bioðon esnas ðæs ðaðe miððy cymeð ðe drih*ten* wæcende soðlice ic cwæð iow ðætte gegyrdað hine ⁊ doað hiæ giriordinge ⁊ ofer-foerde embehtas his 38. ⁊ gif on ða æfterra wacone ⁊ gif on ða ðirda cymeð ⁊ ðus ł swa gimoetað eadge bioðon esnas ða 39. ðas ðonne wutas ge ðætte gif ge-wiste ðe fæder hiowisc ðætte tide ðe ðeof come walde wæcce wutudl*ice* ⁊ ne walde leta ðerh-delfa hus his

40 And beo ge wære forþam þe mannes sunu cymð þære tíde þe ge ne wenað;

41 Þa cwæþ petrus drihten. segst þu þis big-spell to us hwæþer þe to eallum;

42 Ða cwæþ drihten. hwa wenst þu ꝥ sy getrywe ⁊ gleaw dihtnere. þæne se hlaford geset ofer hys hired ꝥ he him hwætes gemet on tíman sylle;

43 Eadig is se þeow þe his hlaford gemet þus donde þonne he cymð;

44 Soðlice ic secge eow ꝥ he gesett hine ofer eall ꝥ he ah;

45 Gyf þon*ne* se þeow cwyð on hys heortan mín hlaford úferaþ hys cyme. ⁊ agynð beatan þa cnihtas ⁊ þa þinena. ⁊ etan ⁊ drincan ⁊ beon ofer-druncen.

46 þon*ne* cymþ · þæs þeowan hlaford on þā*m* dæge þe he ne wenð. ⁊ þære tíde þe he nát. ⁊ to-dælþ hine ⁊ sett his dæl mid þa*m* ungetreowum;

47 Soþlice þæne þeow þe his hlafordes willan wiste ⁊ ne dyde æfter his hlafordes willan. he biþ witnad manegum witum;

48 Ðone þeow þe his willan nyste ⁊ þeah dyde he bit witnad feawum witum; Ælcum þe mycel geseald is. hi*m* man mycel to-secð. ⁊ æt þa*m* þe hig micel befæstun hig mycel biddað;

49 Fyr ic sende on eorþan ⁊ hwæt wylle ic buton ꝥ hit bærne;

50 Ic hæbbe on fulluhte beon gefullod. ⁊ wēnege. hu beo ic geþread. oð hyt sý gefyllyd.

40 Ænd beoð ge ware for-þam-þe mannes sune kymð þare tyde þe ge ne wenað.

41 Ða cwæð petrus drihten. segest þu þis bispell to ús. hwæðer to eallen.

42 Ða cwæð drihten; hwa wenst þu þæt is ge-treowe ⁊ gleaw dihtnere; þane se hlaford ge-sett ofer his hyrd þæt he hym hwætes ge-mett on timen sylle.

43 Eadig is se þeow þe his hlaford ge-met þus doende. þanne he kymð.

44 Soðlice ic segge eow þæt he sett hine ofer eall þæt he ah.

45 Gyf þanne se þeow cweð on his heorten min hlaford ufereð his cyme; ⁊ agind beaten þa cnihtes. ⁊ þa þinene. ⁊ etan ⁊ drincan. ⁊ beon ofer-druncan.

46 þanne kymð þas þeowe hlaford on þam daige þe he ne wenð. ⁊ þare tide þe he nat. ⁊ to-dælð hine. ⁊ sett his dæl mid þam un-ge-treowen.

47 Soðlice þane þeow þe his hlafordes wille wiste ⁊ ne dyde æfter his willen; he beoð witned manegen witen.

48 Þane þeow þe his wille nyste. ⁊ þeah dyde he beoð witned feawen witen. Ælcen þe mycel ge-seald is. him man mychel to-secð. ⁊ et þam þe hyo mycel be-fæsten hyo mychel byddeð.

49 Fyr ich sende on eorðan ⁊ hwæt wille ich buton ꝥ hyt bærne.

50 Ich hæbbe on fulluhte beon ge-fullod. ⁊ wene ge hu byo ich ge-þread. oððe hyt syo ge-fyld.

Various Readings.

42. A. B. C. ys [*for* sy]; A. þone. A. ge-sett. 43. B. C. dondne. 44. A. ge-sette. 45. A. etað. ⁊ dryncað. ⁊ beoð ofer-druncene. 47. A. þone. C. is [*for* his]. A. wytnod. 48. A. byð; B. C. bið [*for* bit]. A. wytnod. A. be-fæston. B. hi. 49. A. byrne. 50. A. wene ge; B. wēne ge. A. sig. A. ge-fylled; B. gefyllyd (*with 2nd* y *partly erased*).

Various Readings.

40. wære; cymð. 41. segst; eallu*m*. 42. ge-trywe; þæne; ge-set; heom; ge-met; timan. 43. þonne; cymð. 44. þet; set; hah. 45. þonne; heortan; uferað; aginð beatan; cnihtas; þinena; -druncen. 46. þonne cymð; set; un-getrewen. 47. þæne; willen [*for* wille]; his hlafordes willan; bið; manegu*m* witu*m*. 48. ðone; is [*for* his]; byð; feawu*m* witum; Ælcum; mycel (*four times*); æt; befæstum (*sic*); byddað. 49. ic (*twice*). 50. Ic habbe; beo ic; oð hit sy gefylld.

⁊ gie wosað gearuu f*or*ðon ðio tíd ne gie woenað sunu monnes cymeð cuoeð
40 et uos estote parati quia qua hora non putatis filius hominis ueniet 41 *Ait * 157. u. mt. cclxu.

ða him petr*us* drih*ten* to us cuoeðest ðu ðas bispell ɫ to allum cuoeð
autem ei petrus d*omi*ne ad nos dicis hanc parabolam án ad omnes 42 dixit

ðon*ne* se driht*en* huælc woenes ðu is geleaffull sgiire-*monn* ɫ feh*u*geroefa ⁊ hoga ðone gesettes
autem d*omi*n*us* quis putas est fidelis dispensator et prudens quem constituet

drih*ten* ɫ se hlaf*ord* ofer higo his ꝥte sellæ him In tíd huætes hrippe eadig
d*omi*n*us* super familiam sua*m* ut det illis' in tempore tritici mensuram 43 beatus

ðe esne ɫ ðræl ðone miððy cymeð se hlaf*ord* gemoetað sua ɫ ðus doende so*ðlice* ic cuoeðo
ille seruus quem cum uenerit d*omi*n*us* inuenerit ita facientem 44 uere dico

iuh ꝥte of*er* alle ðaðe agnegæð ɫ ah gesettes hine *ꝥte* gife cuoeðæs esne
uobis quia supra omnia quae possidet constituet illum 45 *Quod si dixerit seruus * 158. u. mt. cclxuii.

ðe In heorta his hlatto ɫ doað hlaf*ord* min to cu*m*manne ɫ ⁊ onginneð miððy slaa ða cnæhtas ⁊
ille in corde suo mora*m* facit d*omi*n*us* meus uenire et coeperit percutere pueros et

ðiuwas ⁊ ætta ⁊ drinca ⁊ druncgnia ɫ ꝥte se druncenig cymeð drih*ten* ðrælles ðæs
ancillas et edere et bibere et inebriari 46 ueniet d*omi*n*us* serui illius

on dæge ðy ɫ ðe ne hyhtað ɫ woenað ⁊ ðio tid ðe ɫ ne wat ⁊ todæleð hine ⁊ dæl his mið
in die qua non sperat et hora qua nescit et diuidet eum partemque eius cum

ungehleaffullu*m* setteð ðe ðon*ne* esne seðe ongætt willo drih*tnes* his ⁊
infidelib*us* ponet 47 *Ille autem seruus qui cognouit uoluntatem d*omi*ni sui et * 159. x.

ꝥte ne *for*egearuade ⁊ ꝥte ne dydo æft*er* willa his ges*u*uincgde ɫ gemænde menigo ɫ seðe
non praeparauit et non fecit secundum uoluntatem eius uapulabit multis 48 qui

ðon*ne* ne ongætt ⁊ ne dyde ða gerisno ɫ ða wȳrðo w*u*ræccum geswuing lytlum ɫ huon eghuoelcum
autem non cognouit et non fecit digna plagis uapulabit paucis omni

ðon*ne* ɫ uut*edlice* ðæm fealo ɫ micel gesald wæs micel bið gesoht fro*m* him ɫ ðæm ⁊ ðæm bebodadon
autem cui multum datum est multum quaeretur ab eo et cui commen-

ɫ gefeast*adon* feolo ɫ micel *for*ðor ɫ mara hia willniað ɫ giuað of ðæm fyr ic cwom to sendanne on
dauerunt multum plus petunt ab eo 49 *Ignem ueni mittere in * LIIII. 160. u. mt. xcu.

eorðo ⁊ huæd willo ic gif aberned bið fulw*u*iht ðon*ne* ɫ uut*edlice* ic hafo ꝥte ic se geful*u*wad ⁊
terram et quid uolo si accendat*ur* 50 baptisma autem habeo baptizari et

hu suiðe ic am gebeged ɫ gehaðrad am wið ɫ oðð ða hwil ge-endad sie
quomodo coarctor usq*ue* dum perficiatur

---

40. ⁊ ge wosað gitriowe forðon ðio tid ne ge-woenað sunu monnes tocymende is 41. cwæð ða petrus drihten to us cweðestu ðu bispell to us allum 42. cwæð ðonne drihten hwelc woenestu is gileof-ful scire-mon ɫ fehgroefa ⁊ hoga ðone gesetes drihten ofer higo his ꝥte selle him on tide hwætes ripes 43. eadig esne ɫ ðræl ðone miððy cymeð drihten gimoeteð swa doende 44. soð ic cwæðo iow ðæt ofer alle ðaðe ængað ɫ ah gisetes hine 45. ðætte gif cweðes esne ðe in heorte his cweðes læte doeð drih*ten* min to cumanne ⁊ onginneð miððy slaa ða cnæhtas ⁊ ða ðiowe eota ⁊ drinca ⁊ druncniga 46. cymeð drihten ðræles ðæs on dæge ðe ne hyhtað ⁊ tide ðaðe ne watt ⁊ todæleð hine ⁊ dæl ðe his mið ungi-leofa ɫ leoffullu*m* setet 47. ðe ðonne esne seðe ongæt willo drih*tnes* his ⁊ ðætte fore-georwade ⁊ ðætte ne dyde æfter willo his giswicte ɫ mænde menigu 48. seðe ðonne ne on-geotað ⁊ ne dyde ða gi-riseno wræccum giswenctum lytlum eghwelc ðonne ðæm feolo ɫ micel gisald wæs micel gisoht bið fro*m* him ⁊ ðæm bibodadum micle mara hiæ wilnigað from him 49. fyr ic com to sendanne on eorðo ⁊ hwæt willo ic gif aberned bið 50. fulwiht ðonne from him ic se gifulwad ⁊ hu swiðe ic am gi-beged oððe ða hwyle giendad sie

51 forþa*m* þe ic com sybbe on eorþan sendan. ne secge ic eow ac to-dǽl;

52 Heonon-forð beoð fife on anum húse to-dǽlede. þry on twegen. ⁊ twegen on þry.

53 beoð to-dælede; Fæder on sunu ⁊ sunu on his fæder. modor on dohtor ⁊ dohtor on hyre modor; Swegr on hyre snore. ⁊ snoru on hyre swegere;

54 ⁊ he cwæþ to þa*m* folce. þon*ne* ge ge-seoð þa lyfte cumende on west-dæle. sona ge cweðað storm cymð ⁊ hit swa byð;

55 And þon*ne* ge geseoð suðan blawan ge secgaþ ꝥ is tówerd ⁊ hit byð;

56 Lá liceteras cunnege afandian heofones ansyne ⁊ eorþan. humeta na afandige ge þas tíde;

57 Hwi ne demege of eow-sylfum ꝥ riht is;

58 Đonne þu gæst on wege mid þinum wiðer-winnan to hwylcu*m* ealdre. do ꝥ ðu beo fra*m* hi*m* alysed. þe-læs he þé sylle þa*m* déman. ⁊ se déma þa*m* bydele. ⁊ se bydel þe sende on cwertern;

59 Ic secge þe ne gæst þu þanone ær þu agylde þone ytemystan feorð-ling;

CHAPTER XIII.

1 Þar wæron sume on þǽre tíde of galileu*m* him cyþende. þara blod pilatus mengde mid hyra offrungum;

Various Readings.

52. A. heonen-forð. A. þreo (*2nd time*). 53. A. *om.* his. A. moder on dehter ⁊ dohter on hyre moder. Sweger. A. swegre. 55. A. tó-weard. 56. B. C. afandigean. A. heofenes. A. hu meta ne afandie. 57. A. hwig. A. deme ge. 58. A. þy-læs. A. cweartern. 59. A. þanene; C. þanon.

Cap. xiii. 1. A. þæra. A. heora.

51 for-þan-þe ich com sibbe on eorðe sænden; ne segge ich eow ac to-dæl.

52 heonen-forð byð fife on anen huse to-dælede. þreo on twegen. ⁊ twegen on þreo.

53 beoð to-dælede. Fader on sune. ⁊ sune on his fader. moder on dohter. ⁊ dohter on hire moder. Sweger on hire snore. ⁊ snore on hire swegere.

54 And he cwæð to þam folce. Þanne ge ge-seoð þa lifte cumende. on wæst-dæle. sone ge cweðeð storm kymð. ⁊ hit swa beoð.

55 And þanne ge ge-seoð suðan blawen ge seggeð þæt þe (*sic*) is toward ⁊ hit beoð.

56 La liceteres cunne ge afandigen heofenes ansiene ⁊ eorðan. Hu mæte na afandige ge þas tide.

57 hwi ne deme ge of eow sylfen þæt riht ys.

58 Þanne ðu gæst on weige mid þinen wiðer-winnen to hwilcen ealdre. do þæt þu beo fram him alised; þe-læs he þe sylle þam deman. ⁊ se dema þam bydelen. ⁊ se bedel þe sende on cwarterne.

59 Ic þe segge ne gæst þu þanen ær þu agylde þanne ytemestan ferðing.

CHAPTER XIII.

1 ÞÆr wæren sume on þare tide of galiléén hym keðende. þara blod pilates mengde mid hyre offrunge.

Various Readings.

51. ic; eorðan sændan; ic; to-dal. 52. henon-; anu*m*; þry [*1st time*]. 53. Fæder; fæder; modor [*1st time*]; dohtor (*twice*); Swegr; snoru [*2nd time*]. 54. þonne; west-; sona; cweðað; cymð; byð. 55. þonne; blawan; seggað; R. *om.* þe; towerd; byð. 56. afandigean heofones ansyne. 57. sylfu*m*; his [*for* ys]. 58. Đonne; wege; þinu*m* wiðer-winnan; hwylcu*m*; bydelu*m*; bydel; cwartern. 59. þanane; þo*n*ne; fyrðþing.

Cap. xiii. 1. wæron; galileu*m*; cyþende; pilatus; heora offrungv*m*.

woenað gie ꝥte sibb ic cuom to seallanne on eorðo ne cueðo ic iuh to ah ꝥ gesceād ł
51 putatis quia pacem ueni dare in terram non dico uobis sed separationem

biðon f*orð*on of*er* ðis fifo in hus ān todæled biðon ðrio on twæm ł ⁊ tuoege In ðrio ł
52 erunt enim ex hoc quinq*ue* in domo una diuisi tres in duo et duo in tres

biðon todæled fader on sunu ⁊ sunu on fæder his moder on doehter ⁊ dohter on
53 diuidentur pater in filium et filius in patrem suum mater in filiam et filia in

moeder suegir on snoru hire ⁊ snoru on suoegir hire cuoeð ða ⁊ to
matrem socrus in nurum suam et nurus in socrum suam 54 * Dicebat autem et ad * 161. u. mt. clxii.

ðæm hergum miððy gie geseað ꝥ wolcen upp-stigende fra*m* sunn-sett sona gie cuoeðað scyūr cymeð ⁊ sua
turbas cum uideritis nubem orientem ab occasu statim dicitis nimb*us* uenit et ita

bið ⁊ miððy suð wind gie cuoeðas ꝥte wind bið ⁊ bið legeras
fit 55 et cum austrum flante*m* dicitis quia uentus erit et fit 56 hypocritae

on-sione earðes ⁊ heofnes wutað gie gecunnia ł ꝥte sēe gecostad ðis uut*edlice* tid huu nege
faciem terrae et caeli nostis probare hoc autem tempus quomodo non

cunnað gie huæd ðon*ne* ⁊ fro*m* iuh seolfu*m* ne gedoemað huæd soðfæst is mið-ðy
probatis 57 quid autem et á uobis ipsis non iudicatis quid iustum est 58 * Cum * 162. u. mt. xxxui.

uut*edlice* ðu gast ł gegað mið wiðerworde ðinu*m* to aldormen on woeg sel geornlice ꝥte ðu se gefreod
autem uadis cum aduersario tuo ad principem in uia dá operam liberari

fro*m* him eaðemæg ł ðylæs genime ðec mið doema ł ł gelædæ ðec to dome ⁊ se doemere seleð ðec
ab illo ne forte trahat té apud iudicem et iudex tradat té

ðæm æf-groefe ⁊ se æf-groefa sendað ðec in carcern ic cuoeðo ðe ne gaes ðu ðona oðð
exactori et exactor mittat té in carcerem 59 dico tibi non exies inde donec

uut*edlice* ðone hlætmesto pricclu ł ꝥte ðu f*or*gelde
etiam nouissimu*m* minutum reddas

CAP. XIII.

to-cuomon ða sumo ðæm on tīd sægdon ða ł him of gali*lea* ðæm ł ðara
1 * ADerant autem quidam ipso in tempore nuntiantes illi de galilaeis * LU. 163. x.

ðara ł hiora blōd gemengde mið asægdnisu*m* hiora
quorum sanguinem pilatus miscuit cum sacrificiis eorum

---

51. woenað ge ðætte sibbe ic come to sellanne on eorðo ne cweðo ic iow to ah ðætte ge gisceodne 52. bioðun ł werun forðon of ðisse fife in hus an todæled bioðun ðria in tuo ⁊ tuo in ðrio 53. todæled bioðon fæder on suno ⁊ suno on fæder his moder in dohter ⁊ dohter on moder sweger on snora hire ⁊ snora on swegre hire 54. cwæð ða ł ðon*ne* ⁊ to ðæm hergum miððy ge giseað ðæt wolcen upstigende fro*m* sunsete sona ge cweoðað scur cymeð ⁊ swa bið 55. ⁊ miððy suð winde ge cweoðas ðætte wind bið ⁊ bið 56. .... onsione eorðo ⁊ heofnes wittas ge gicunniga ðisis wutudl*ice* tide huu ne gi-cunigas ge 57. hwæt ðonne ⁊ from iow solfum ne gi-doemað ðætte soð-fæst is 58. miððy wutudl*ice* ðu gæst mið wiðerwordne ðinne to aldor-men on woeg sel geornlice ðætte ðu se gilesed fro*m* him nemæg ł ðylæs he ge-nime ðeh in carcern ⁊ ðe æf-groefa sendeð ðec in carc-ern 59. ic cweðo ðe ne gi-gæstu ðona oðð*æt* wutudl*ice* ðone lætemestu pricla ðu forgelde

Cap. XIII. 1. to-comun ða sume on tide ðæm sægdun ðæm of galilea ðara ł hiora blod .... gimengde mið asægd-nissum hiora

2 þa cwæð he him ⁊swarigende. wenege wǽron þá galileiscan synfulle to-foran eallu*m* galileiscum. for-þa*m* þe hig swylc þoledon;

3 Ne secge ic na. ac ealle ge gelíce forwurðaþ. buton ge dæd-bote dón.

4 swa þa ehta-týne. ofer þa feoll se stýpel on siloá ⁊ hig of-sloh; Wenege ꝥ hig wæron scyldige ofer ealle menn þe on hierusalem wunedon;

5 Ne secge ic. ac swá gé forwurðaþ. buton ge dæd-bote dón;

Ðis god-spel sceal to þa*m* ymbrene innan hærefeste on sætern-dæg. Dicebat i*esus* turbis similitudine*m* hanc. Arbore*m* fici habebat quidam. A.

6 Ða sǽde he him þis bigspel. sum man hæfde án fíc-treow geplantod on his win-gearde. þa com he ⁊ sohte his wæstmas on hi*m* þa ne funde he nanne;

7 Þa cwæþ he to þa*m* hyrde nu synt þreo ger syðþan ic com wæstm secende on þissum fíc-treowe. ⁊ ic ne funde; For-ceorf hine hwi of-þricð he ꝥ land;

8 Ða cwæð he hlaford. læt hine gyt þis gear. oð ic hine bedelfe ⁊ ic hine bewurpe mid meoxe.

9 ⁊ witodlice he wæstmas bringð; Gif hit elles hwæt byð ceorf hine syððan;

10 Ða wæs he reste-dagu*m* on hyra gesamnunge lærende.

11 þa wæs þar sum wif seo hæfde untrumnesse gast ehtatyne gear. ⁊ heo wæs abógen. ne heo eallunga ne mihte upbeseon;

2 Þa cwæð he heom andsweriende. wene ge wæren þa galileiscan synfulle to-foran eallen galileiscan. for-þan-þe hyo swylc þoleden.

3 Ne segge ic na. ac ealle ge gelice forwurðeð. buton ge deadbote don;

4 swa þa ehte-tyna. ofer þa feoll se stepel on syloa. ⁊ hyo of-sloh. Wene ge þæt hyo wæren scyldige ofer ealle menn þe on ierusalem wunedon.

5 Ne segge ic ac swa ge for-wurðed. bute ge deadbote don.

6 Ða sæde he heom þis bispell. Summan hæfde an fic-treow ge-plantod on his win-gearde. þa com he ⁊ sohte his wæstmes on hym. þa ne fand he nane.

7 Þa cwæð he to þam hyrde nu synde þreo gear seððan ich com wæstme secende on þissen fic-treowe. ⁊ ic ne funde. For-scrif (*sic*) hine hwy ofer-stricð (*sic*) he þæt land.

8 Ða cwæð he. hlaford læt hine geat þis gear oð Ic hine be-delfe. ⁊ ic hine beweorpe mid dunge.

9 ⁊ witodlice he wæstmes bringeð. Gif hit elles hwæt beoð. for-scrif hine syððan.

10 Ða wæs he reste-dagen on hiore gesamnunge; lærende.

11 þa wæs þær sum wif seo hafde untrumnysse gast ehtetyne gear. ⁊ hyo wæs abogen ne hyo allunge ne mihte up beseon.

Various Readings.

2. A. ⁊swariende. A. B. wene ge. A. swylic. 3. A. na eac. A. for-weorþað. 4. A. syloé. A. men. 5. A. for-weorðað. A. ded-bóte. 6. B. C. hi [*sic; for* he]. A. big-spell. 7. A. synd. A. geár; B. C. gear. A. hwig. 8. A. beweorpe. 10. A. heora. 11. A. untru*m*nysse.

Various Readings.

2. andswerigende; wæron; eallu*m* galileiscum. 3. forwurðað. buten; dæd-bote. 4. ehta-; of-slogh; wæron; men; hierusalem wundon. 5. forwurðað. buton; dæd-bote. 6. bigspell; wæstmas; nænne. 7. synt; syððan ic; wæstm; þissum; For-cyrf; of-þricð. 8. meoxe [*for* dunge]. 9. wæstmas bringað; bið; for-ceof (*sic*); seððan. 10. -dagum; hyora. 11. ehtatyna; heo [*2nd time*]; eallu*n*ga.

⁊ geond-uarde cuoeð ðæm woenað gie ꝥte ðas galilesco *fore* allum galilesc*um* synfullo
2 et respondens dixit illis putatis quod hi galilaei prae omnib*us* galilaeis peccatores

biðon ł woeron *for*ðon ł ꝥte ðuslico ðrowendo weron ł biðon ne cuoeðo iuh Ah buta hreonisse
fuerunt quia talia passi sunt 3 non · dico uobis sed nisi paenitentiam

gie hæbbe Alle gelic gie sciolo losiga suæ ða teno ⁊ ða aehtou on-ufa ðæm gefeall
habueritis omnes similiter peribitis 4 sicut illi decem et octo supra quos cecidit

se torr in ðær byrig ⁊ of-slog ðailco woenað gie ꝥte æc ðailco scyldgo woeron bi Allum
turris in siloam et occidit eos putatis quia et ipsi debitores fuerunt praeter omnes

monnum byedon in hier*usalem* ne coeðo ic iuh ah hueðre gif hreonise gie ne doeð
homines habitantes in hierusalem 5 non dico uobis sed si non paenitentia*m* egeritis

Alle gelíc gie sciolon losiga ge-cuoeð he uut*edlice* ł ða ðios ł ðus geddung ł onlicnise ł bisene tree fic-beames
omnes similiter peribitis 6 *Dicebat autem hanc similitudinem arborem fici * LUI. 164. x.

hæfde sum *monn* geplontad ł gesetet in wingearde his ⁊ cuom sohte wæstm on ðær ilco ⁊
habebat quidam plantatam in uinea sua et uenit quaerens fructum in illa et

ne fand ł ne gemoete cuoeð ða to bigencga ł to ðæm bi-geon-le (*sic*) ðæs wingeardas heono gēro
non inuenit 7 dixit autem ad cultore*m* uineae ecce anni

ðrio sint of ðon ł soðða ic cuom sohte wæstm on fic-beame ðisser ⁊ ne ic fand ł ne gemoete ic
tres sunt ex quo uenio quaerens fructum in ficulnea hac et non inuenio

hrendas ł scearfað *for*ðon ðailca ł hia to huon uut*edlice* eorðo gi-ōnetað ł gemerras soð he onduarde
succidite ergo illam ut quid etiam terram occupat 8 at ille respondens

cuoeð to ðæm ł him driht*en* *for*let hia ⁊ ł æc ðios gēr wið ꝥ mið-ðy ic delfo ymb hia ⁊
dixit illi d*omi*ne dimitte illam et hoc anno usq*ue* dum fodia*m* circa illam et

ic sendo micxseno* ⁊ gif soðlice gedoeð wæstm gif ne doeð uut*edlice* in ðæm toweard ger ge-scearfa ðu * on ꝥ trē *is added in the margin.*
mittam stercora 9 et si-quidem fecerit fructu*m* sin autem in futurum succides

hia wæs uut*edlice* lærend in somnong hiora on symbeldagum ⁊ heono ꝥ wif
eam 10 erat autem docens in synagoga eorum sabbatis 11 et ecce mulier

ðio hæfde gast untrymnises gēru*m* teno ⁊ æhto ⁊ wæs *for*ðhald ł gebeged ne æfra ł allunga
quae habebat sp*iritu*m infirmitatis annis decem et octo et erat inclinata nec omnino

mæhte upp eft-lociga ł gesea
poterat sursum respicere

---

2. ⁊ giondsworade cwæð ðæm woenað ge ðætte ðes galilesco fore allum galilescum synnfulle bioðon ł werun forðon ðuslico ðrowende werun 3. ne cweðo ic iow ah buta hreownisse ge hæbbe alle gilice ge sciolun losige 4. swa ⁊ ða teno ⁊ æhtowe onufa ðæm gifeoll ðe torr in ðær byrig ⁊ ofslog ðailco woenað ge ðætte ⁊ ðailco scyldge werun bifore allum monnu*m* byedun.... 5. ne ic cweðo iow ah hweðre gif hreownisse ge ne doað gilice ge sciolun loesga 6. gicwæð he wutudlice ðas geddunga onlicnesse ł bisene treona ficbeomes hæfde sumum gi-plontad in win-georde his ⁊ com sohte wæstem on ðæm ilca ⁊ ne in-fand 7. cwæð ða to ð*æm* bigengum ðæs wingeordes heono ger ðrio sindun of ðæm ic com to soecanne wæstem in fic-beome ðissu*m* ⁊ ne fand ic ł ne moette ceorfas ł rendas forðon ðailco ꝥte hwon ⁊ wutudlice eorðo gi-onetað 8. soð he ond-worde cwæð to ðæm drihten forlet ða ł hiæ ⁊ ec ðis ger wiððæt miððy ic delfo ymb ðailca ⁊ ic sendo mixenne 9. gif soðlice ge-doað wæstem gif ne doeð wutudl*ice* in ðæm to-worda giceorf ða ł hia 10. wutudl*ice* wæs lærende on somnungu*m* hiora symbel-dagum 11. ⁊ heono wif ðio hæfde gast un-trymnisse geres tene ⁊ æhtowe ⁊ wæs forð-hald ł gibeged ne æfre allunga mæhte upp locgiga ł gisea

12 þa se hælend hig geseah he clypode hig to him. ⁊ sǽde hyre; Wíf. þu eart for-læten of þinre untrumnesse.

13 ⁊ his hand hyre on sette. þa wæs heo sona up aræred. ⁊ heo god wuldrode;

14 Ða ge-bealh se duguðe-ealdor hine forþa*m* þe se hælend on reste-dæge hǽlde ⁊ sǽde þa*m* menegum; Syx dagas synt on þa*m* gebyrað ꝥ man wyrce. cumaþ on þa*m* ⁊ beoð gehælede. ⁊ na on reste-dæge;

15 Ða ⁊swarude se hælend ⁊ cwæð; Lá lícteras. ne un-tigð eower ælc on reste-dæge his oxan oððe assan. fram þære binne ⁊ læt to wætere;

16 þas abrahames dohtor þe satanas geband nu eahta-tyne gear. ne gebyrede hyre beon unbunden of þissu*m* bende on reste-dæge;

17 þa he þis sǽde. þa sceamode ealle his wiðer-winnan. ⁊ eall folc geblissode on eallu*m* þa*m* ðe wuldor-fullice fra*m* hi*m* ge-wurdon;

18 Soðlice he cwæþ. hwam is godes. ríce gelíc. ⁊ hwam wene ic ꝥ hit beo gelíc.

19 hit ys gelic senepes corne ꝥ se man onfenc ⁊ seow on his wyrtun ⁊ hit weox ⁊ wearð mycel treow. ⁊ heofenes fuhlas restun on his bogum;

20 And eft he cwæð. hwa*m* wene ic ꝥ godes ríce si gelic.

Various Readings.

12. A. untrumnysse. 13. A. arǽred. 14. A. mænegu*m*. A. synd. 15. A. ⁊swarode. A. B. C. líceteras [*but* Corp. lícteras]. 16. A. þeos. A. dohter. A. ehtatyne eár. 19. A. onfeng. A. wyrt-tun. B. C. heofones. A. fugelas reston. 20. A. sig.

12 Ða se hælend hyo ge-seah he cleopede hyo to him. ⁊ saide hire. Wif þu ert for-læten of þinre untrumnysse.

13 ⁊ his hand hire on sette. þa wæs hyo sona up arerd. ⁊ hyo god wuldrede.

14 Ða ge-bealh se duguðe ealder hine for-þan þe se hælend on reste-daige helde ⁊ sæde þam manigeo. Syx dages synde on þam ge-bereð þæt man wyrce. cumeð on þam ⁊ beoð ge-hælde. ⁊ na on reste daige.

15 þa andswerede se hælend ⁊ cwæð. La liceteras ne un-tygð eower ælc on reste-daige his oxen oððe assen fram þare binne ⁊ læt to wætere.

16 Ðas abrahames dohter þe satanas geband nu ehtetyna gear. ne beryde hire beon un-bundon of þisen benden on reste-daige.

17 Ða he þis saide þa scamede eallen his wiðer-winnan. ⁊ eall folc ge-blissode on eallen þan þe wunderfullice fra*m* him ge-wurðon.

18 Soðlice he cwæð. hwam is godes rice gelic; ⁊ hwam wene ic þæt hit beo gelich.

19 hit is gelic sepenes (*sic*) corne þe se man onfeng ⁊ seow on his wertun. ⁊ hit weox ⁊ warð mycel treow ⁊ heofene fugeles resten on his bogen.

20 Ænd eft he cwæð. hwam wene ic þæt godes rice seo gelic.

Various Readings.

12. halend; clypode; sæde; eart for-læton. 13. aræerd; heo; wuldrode. 14. ealdor; -dæge hælde; menegum; dagas synt; ge-byrað; cumað; -dæge. 15. -dæge; oxan; assan. 16. dohtor; ge-byrede; þysum bende; -dæge. 17. sægde; scamode ealle; eallu*m* þa*m*; wuldorfullice; ge-wurdon. 18. his [*for* is]; ge-lic (*twice*). 19. senepes; ꝥ [*for* þe]; wyrtun; wearð; heofone fugelas reston; bogu*m*. 20. syo.

ðailca miððy gesege se hæl*end* geceigde to him ⁊ cuoeð to hir la wif *for*leten arð fro*m* untrymnis
12 quam cum uidisset ie*sus* uocauit ad se et ait illi mulier dimissa és ab infirmitate

ðin ⁊ gesette hir hónd ⁊ sona ahefen wæs ł gerehtad ⁊ geworðade ł gewul*drade*
tua 13 et imposuit illi manus et confestim erecta est et glorificabat

god ondsuarade ða ðæs folces aldormon wraððe *for*ðon on symbeldagu*m* gehælde
d*eum* 14 *Respondens autem arche-synagogus indignans quia sabbato curasset * 165. ii. mt. cxu [i].

se hæl*end* cuoeð He ðæm folce ł ðæm here sex dagas sint on ðæm geriseð ł is gelefed to wyrcanne ł þ
ie*sus* dicebat turbae sex dies sunt in quibus oportet ope-

gie wyrce on ðæm *for*ðon cymað ⁊ lecnegeð ⁊ ne in dæg symbles geonduearde ða
rari in his ergo uenite et curamini et non in die sabbati 15 respondens *autem*

to him drih*ten* ⁊ cuoeð gie eswico an eghuelc iuer on symbel-doeg ne unbindeð ł woxo his
ad illum d*ominus* et dixit hypocritae unusquisq*ue* uestrum sabbato non soluit bouem suum

ł assald of bósih ⁊ lædes to wætranne ðios uut*edlice* doht*er* abrahames ðailca
aut ásinum á præsepio et ducit ad aquare 16 hanc autem filia abrahae quam

gebänd ðe wiðerworda heono teno ⁊ æhto gēru*m* ne were gerisnelic ł reht to unbindanne ł to undoanne of
alligauit satanas ecce decem et octo annis non oportuit solui á

bend ðissu*m* dæge symb*les* ⁊ miððy ðas gecueð gesceomadon alle fiondas ł wiðer-worda
uinculo isto die sabbati 17 *Et cum haec diceret erubescebant omnes aduersarí * 166. x.

his ⁊ all þ folc gefeade ł wæs glæd on allu*m* ðæm wundr*um* ðaðe wundorlice woeron fro him
eius et omnis populus gaudebat in uniuersis quae gloriosae fiebant ab eo

cueð he soðlice to huæm ongelíc is ríc godes ⁊ huæm ongelic woere ic woenó ł ic leto ł ic doemo
18 *Dicebat ergo cui simile est regnum d*ei* et cui simile esse existimabo * 167. ii. mt. cxxxuii. mr. xliiii.

þ ongelic is corne senepes þte genu*mm*en wæs monn sende in lehtune his ⁊
illud 19 simile est grano synapis quod acceptum homo misit in hortum suum et

awox ⁊ aworden wæs on trēo miclu*m* ⁊ flegendo heofnes gehræston on telgum his
creuit et factum est in arborem magnam et uolucres caeli requieuerunt in ramis eius

⁊ eft*er*sona cuoeð huæm ongelic ic woeno ł ic wælle lēta ric godes ⁊ huæm ongelic is
20 *Et iterum dixit cui similem (*sic*) aestimabo regnum d*ei* et cui simile est * 168. u. mt. cxxxuiii.

---

12. ðailco miððy gisegun ðone hæl*end* gicegde to him ⁊ cwæð him la wif ðu arð forleten from untrymnisse ðinre 13. ⁊ gesette hir hond ⁊ sona ahæfen wæs ⁊ gewuldrad wæs god 14. ond-sworade ða ðæs folches aldor wraðe forðon on symbeldæge gihælde ðe hæl*end* cwæð he ðæm folche forðon sex dagas sint in ðæm girises to wyrcanne on ðæm forðon cymeð ⁊ lecnigað ⁊ ne on dæge symbles 15. giondworde ða to him drih*ten* ⁊ cwæð ge eswicu an eghwelc iower on symbel-dæge ne on-bindeð oxo his ł easald of bosge ⁊ lædes to wætranne 16. ðios wutudl*ice* dohter abrahames ða ilca giband ðe wiðerworda heono teno ⁊ æhtowe geras ne were girisen ł reht to unbindanne of bendu*m* ðissum dæge symbles 17. ⁊ miððy ðas gicwæð ge-scomedun alle wiðer-worde ł fiondas his ⁊ all ðæt folc gifeade 18. forðon ðæm gilic is rice godes ⁊ ðæm gilic were ic leto ðon*ne* ðæt 19. ongilic is corne senepes ðætte ginumen wæs menn sende in lehtun his ⁊ wox ⁊ aworden wæs on tree miclum ⁊ flegende heofnes gi-restun on telgum his 20. ⁊ efter-sona cwæð hwæm ongelic is woeno ðæt ic welle leta rice godes

21 hit is gelic *þam* beorman þe ꝥ wīf onfengc. ⁊ be-hydde on *þam* melewe þreo gemetu. oð hit wearð eall ahafen;

22 Ða ferde he þurh ceastra ⁊ castelu to hierusalem ⁊ þar lærde

23 Ða cwæð su*m* man to hi*m* drihten. feawa synt þe synt gehælede; þa cwæþ he to hi*m*.

24 efstað ꝥ ge gangen þurh ꝥ nearwe get forþa*m* ic secge eow manega secað ꝥ hig ingan ⁊ hi ne magon;

25 Ðon*ne* se hiredes ealdor ingæð ⁊ his duru beclyst ge standaþ þær ūte ⁊ þa duru cnuciað ⁊ cweðaþ. drihten atyn us; þon*ne* cwyð he to eow; Ne can ic eow. nat ic hwanon ge synt;

26 Ðon*ne* ongynne ge cweþan wē æton ⁊ druncon beforan þe. ⁊ on urum strætu*m* þu lærdest.

27 þon*ne* segð he eow. ne cann īc hwanon ge synt gewitað fram me ealle unriht-wyrhtan.

28 þar bið wop ⁊ toþa gryst-lung; Ðænne ge geseoþ abraham. ⁊ isaac. ⁊ iacob. ⁊ ealle witegan on godes rīce. ⁊ ge beoð ut-adrifene

29 ⁊ hig cumað fram east-dǣle ⁊ west-dæle. ⁊ norþ-dǣle. ⁊ sittað on godes rīce.

30 ⁊ efne synt yte-meste þa ðe beoð fyrmyste. ⁊ synt fyrmyste þa ðe beoð ytemeste;

Various Readings.

21. A. onfeng. A. meluwe. 23. A. synd þe synd. 24. A. gangon. A. geat. B. C. hig. 25. A. us [*sic; for 1st* eow]. A. hwanen. A. synd. 27. A. can. A. hwanen. A. synd. 28. þonn*e*. 30. A. synd ytemyste. A. B. C. fyrmeste. A. synd. A. B. C. fyrmeste. A. ytemyste.

21 hit ys gelic þam beorman þe þæt wif onfeng ⁊ be-hedde on þam melewe þreo ge-mitte. oððe hit warð eall ahafen.

22 Ða ferde he þurh ceastre ⁊ castella to ierusalem ⁊ þær lærde.

23 Ða cwæð sum man to him. drihten feawe synde þe synde ge-hælede. Ða cwæð he to heom.

24 efstað þet ge gangen þurh þa nærewe gate for-þan ich segge eow manege secað þæt hyo ingan ⁊ hyo ne magen.

25 þanne se hirdes ealdor ingæð ⁊ his dure be-clyst. ge standeð þær ute ⁊ þa dure cnokieð ⁊ cweðað. Ðrihten atyn us. þanne cweð he to eow. Ne can ich eow naht (*sic*) ich hwanen ge synde.

26 þanne on-ginnen ge cweðen. we æten ⁊ druncen be-foren þe ⁊ on uren stræten þu lærdest.

27 þanne saið he eow ne can ic hwanen ge synde. ge-writeð fram me ealle unriht-wyrhten.

28 þær beoð wop ⁊ toðe gristbihung*. þanne ge ge-seoð abraham ⁊ ysáác. ⁊ iacob ⁊ ealle witegen on godes rice. ⁊ ge beoð ut adrifene.

29 ⁊ hyo cumeð fram east-dæle ⁊ west-dæle. ⁊ suð-dæle. ⁊ sittað on godes rice.

30 ⁊ efne synde ytemeste þa þe beoð fyrmeste ⁊ synde fyrmeste þa þe beoð ytemeste.

* MS. grist-hung (*sic*), *with* bi *writt above.*

Various Readings.

21. be-hyde (*sic*); oð; werð. 22. castre; synt; synt ge-halede; eom. 24. ꝥ nærwe gat; for-þam ic; manega. 25. Ðone; cnucyað; Ðonne; ic; nat ic hwanon; synt. 26. Ðonne on-ginne; æton; druncon be-foran; urum stræton. 27. þo*nne* segð; cen; hwanon; synt. ge-witað; -wyrhtan. 28. þar byð; gristlung. Ðonne; witegan; geo (*sic*). 29. suð-dale. 30. synt (*twice*); byð (*2nd time*).

dærste ꝥ miððy onfoaeð wif gehydeð in meolo mitto ł ðrio oððæt sie gedærsted ł
21 fermento quod acceptum mulier abscondit in farinae sata tria donec fermenta-

gecnoeden All ⁊ foerde ðerh ceastro ⁊ woerco lærende ⁊ geong dyde in hierusalem
retur totum 22 *ET ibat per ciuitates et castella docens et iter faciens in hierusalem * 169. ii. mt. lxxui. mr. lii.

cuoeð ða him sum monn drihten gif huon sint ł lytle worado aron ðaðe gihæled biðon he ða
23 *Ait autem illi quidam domine si pauci sunt qui saluantur ipse autem * 170. v. mt. lu.

cuoeð to ðæm ilcom geðrincgas ł to ingeonganne ðerh nearo gætt ꝥte menigo ic cuoeðo
dixit ad illos 24 contendite intrare per angustam portam quia multi dico

iuh soecas ł biddas to inngeonganne ⁊ ne mæhton miððy ðonne ł uutedlice Inngaeð se fæder hiuuisc
uobis quaerunt intrare et non poterunt 25 *Cum autem intrauerit pater- * 171. v. mt. lx.

ł hiorodes fæder ł higna fæder ⁊ tyneð ꝥ duro ł dor ⁊ gie onginnes uuta stonda ⁊ cnylsiga ꝥ dor
familias et cluserit ostium et incipietis foris stare et pulsare ostium

ðus cuoeðendo drihten untȳn ūs ⁊ ondsuarænde cuoeðeð iuh ne connic iuih huona gie aron
dicentes domine áperi nobis et respondens dicet uobis nescio uos unde sitis

ðonne ł ða gie onginnes cuoeða we brecon ł ēton fora ðec ⁊ we drunccon ⁊ in placcum ł ūsum
26 tunc incipietis dicere manducauimus coram té et bibimus et in plateis nostris

ðu lærdes ł we gelærdon ⁊ cuoeðes iuh to ne connic huona arongie afearrað from me alle
docuisti 27 et dicet uobis nescio uos unde sitis discedite á me omnes

ða wyrcendo unreht-wisnises ðer bið wōp ⁊ grist-bittung toðana miððy gee geseað abraham
operari iniquitatis 28 ibi erit fletus et stridor dentium *Cum uideritis abraham * 172. u. mt. lxii.

⁊ ⁊ ⁊ alle witgo inngeonga in rīc godes gie uutedlice fordrifeno buta ł uta
et isaac et iacob et omnes prophetas introire in regno dei uos autem expelli foras

⁊ cymeð easta ⁊ woesta ⁊ norða ⁊ suða ⁊ hliniga ð ł hræstað in ric
29 et uenient ab oriente et occidente et aquilone et austro et accumbent in regno

godes ⁊ heono biðon hlætmesto ðaðe woeron forðmesto ⁊ biðon forðmesto ða woeron
dei 30 *ET ecce sunt nouissimi qui erunt primi et sunt primi qui erunt * 173. ii. mt. cxcuii mr. cxi.

hlætmesto
nouissimi

---

21. gilic is dærstum ðætte miððy onfoeð wif wif (*sic*) gihydeð in meolwe mitto ł ðria oððæt sie gidærstad ł cneden all 22. ⁊ foerde ðerh cæstre ⁊ werc lærende ⁊ gong dyde.... 23. cwæð ða him sum mon drihten gif hwon sint ðaðe eghwelcum bioðun he ða cwæð to ðæm ilcum 24. ge-ðringas to onginnanne ðerh naru gætt ðætte monige ic cweðo iow to soecas ł biddas to ingonganne ⁊ ne mæhtun 25. miððy ðonne wutudlice incode ł foerde fæder hiorodes ł higna ⁊ ontyneðð ða duro ł dor ⁊ ge ingongas uta stonda ⁊ clyniga ðæt dor ðus cweðende drihten untyn us ⁊ ond-sworade cweðeð iow ne con ic iowih hwona ge arun 26.... 27.... afearriað from me alle ðaðe wyrcað unrehtnisse 28. ðer bið wop ⁊ grist-bitung toða miððy ge giseað.....⁊.....⁊.....⁊ alle witgu in rice godes ge wutudlice fordrifne buta ł ute 29. ⁊ cymeð eostan ⁊ westa ⁊ norða ⁊ suða ⁊ hlionigað ł restað in rice godes 30. ⁊ heono bioðon læte-mesto ðaðe werun foerðmest ⁊ bioðon foermest ðaðe werun læte-mest

31 On þa*m* dæge hi*m* genealæhton sume
farisei ⁊ hi*m* sædon; Far ⁊ ga heonon for-
þam þe herodes þe wyle ofslean;
32 And þa cwæð he to him. gað ⁊
secgað þa*m* foxe. deofol-seocnessa ic út-
adrífe. ⁊ ic hæla gefre*m*me to-dǽg ⁊ to-
morhgen ⁊ þriddan dæge ic beo for-numen;
33 Đeah-hwæðere me gebyreþ to-dæg ⁊
to-morhgen. ⁊ þy æfteran dæge gán. for-
þa*m* þe ne gebyreð ꝥ se witega for-wurðe
bútan hierusalem;
34 Eala hierusale*m* hierusale*m*. þu ðe þa
witegan of-slyhst. ⁊ hænst. þa ðe to þe
asende synt. hu oft ic wolde þíne bearn
gegaderian swa se fugel deð his nest under
his fiðerum ⁊ þu noldest;
35 Nu bið eower hus eow for-læten;
Soðlice ic eow secge ꝥ ge mé ne geseoð
ærþa*m* þe cume se þon*ne* ge cweðað. ge-
bletsod sy se ðe cóm on drihtnes naman;

CHAPTER XIV.

Đys god-spel gebyrað on þære nygonteoðan wucan ofer pentecosten. Cu*m* intraret i*esus* in domu*m* cuiusda*m* principis phariseoru*m*. A. Intrauit i*esus* in domu*m* cuiusda*m* principis phariseoru*m* sabbato manducare pane*m*. B.

1 Þa wæs geworden þa he eode on
sumes farisea ealdres hus on
reste-dæge ꝥ he hlaf ǽte. ⁊ hig begymdon
hine
2 ða wæs þar sum wæter-seoc man beforan hi*m*;
3 Đa cwæþ se hælend to þa*m* ǽ.-gleawu*m*
⁊ fariseu*m*; Ys hit alyfed ꝥ man on reste-
dagu*m* hæle;

Various Readings.

32. deofel-seocnyssa. A. hælo. A. to-morgen. 33. A. to-mergen. A. ge-byrað. A. for-weorðe. 34. A. hynst. A. B. C. synd. 35. A. *om.* se *after* cume. A. syg.

31 On þam daige him ge-neohlacten sume
farisei ⁊ him saigdon. Far ⁊ ga heonon.
for-þam þe herodes þe wile of-slean.
32 And þa cwæð he to heom. Gað ⁊
segge𝔡 þam foxe. deofel-seocnysse ich ut
adrife. ⁊ ic hæle ge-fremme to-daig ⁊ to-
morgen ⁊ ðridden daige ich beo for-numen.
33 Þeah-hwæðere me ge-bereð to-daig
⁊ to-morgen. ⁊ þy æftere daige gan. for-
þan ne béreð þæt se witega for-wurðe buton
ierusalem.
34 Eale ierusalem ierusalem. þu þe þa
witegen of-sleahst. ⁊ hænst þa þe to þe
asent synden. hu ofte ic wolde þine bearn
ge-gaderian. swa se fugel doð his nyst
under his fyðeren ⁊ þu noldest.
35 Nu beoð eower hus eow for-lætan.
Soðlice ic eow segge ꝥ ge me ne ge-seoð
ær þan þe cume se þanne ge cweðed ge-
bletsod syo se þe com on drihtnes namen.

CHAPTER XIV.

1 ĐA wæs ge-worðen þa he eode on
sumes phariseas ealdres hus on
ræste-daige. þæt he hlaf æte. ⁊ hyo be-
gymden hine.
2 þa wæs þær sum wæter-seoc mann be-
foran hym.
3 Đa cwæð se hælend to þam lage-
gleawen. ⁊ farisean. is hit alyfed þæt
man on reste-dagen hæle.

[I] Ntrauit i*esus* in do-mu*m* cuius-dam princi[p]-sacerdotu*m* sabbato ma[n]-ducare pa-nem.

Various Readings.

31. ge-neahlacton; sægdon. 32. seggað; deofol-seocnyssa ic; dridden (*sic*); ic. 33. -hweðere; ge-byreð; to-morhgen; æfteran dæge; byreð; butan. 34. Eala; hierusalem (*2nd time*); witegan; asend synd. hwu; deð; fyðerum. 35. for-læton; seoð; þa*m*; þonne; cweðað; naman.

Cap. xiv. 1. *Rubric as in* H.; ge-worden; -dæge; ete; be-gymdon. 2. man. 3. halend; ea-glewum; alefd -dagu*m*.

on ðæm dæge geneolecdon summo ðara ældrā cuoeðendo him gaa ꝉ fær ⁊ geong heona
31 *IN ipsa die accesserunt quidam pharisaeorum dicentes illi exi et uade hinc * LUII. 174. x.

forðon herodes will ðec ofslaa ⁊ cuoeð ðæm gað cuoeðað foxe ðæm heono ic aworpo
quia herodes uult té occidere 32 et ait illis ite dicite uulpi illi ecce eicio

diwle ⁊ hælo ic ðerh-doe ꝉ endigo todæg ⁊ tomērne ⁊ ðæm ðirde dæge ic beom ge-endad
daemonio (*sic*) et sanitates perficio hodie et cras et tertio consummor

soð hueðre gehriseð ꝉ gedæfneð me to-dæg ⁊ tomerne ⁊ ðæm æfterfylgende geonga forðon ne
33 uerum-tamen oportet me hodie et cras et sequenti ambulare quia non

nimeð witge losia buta hierusalem ðu ofslæst ða witgo
capit prophetam perire extra hierusalem 34 *Hierusalem hierusalem quae occidis prophetas * 175. u. mt. ccxli.

⁊ ðu stænað ða ðaðe ge-sendad biðon to ðe suæ suiðe ic walde gesomnia suno ðino suelce
et lapidas eos qui mittuntur ad té quotiens uolui congregare filios tuos quemammodum

fugul nest his under feðrum ⁊ ne waldest ðu heono forleten bið iuh hūs iuera
áuis nidum suum sub pinnis et noluisti 35 ecce relinquitur uobis domus uestra

ic cuoeðo ða ꝉ uutedlice iuh forðon ꝉ ꝥte gie ne geseað mec oððæt cyme mið-ðy gie cuoeðo sē gebloedsad
dico autem uobis quia non uidebitis me donec ueniat cum dicetis benedictus

seðe cuom in noma drihtnes
qui uenit in nomine domini

CAP. XIV.

⁊ Aworden wæs mið-ðy innfoerde in hus summes aldormonnes on symbel-dæg
1 *ET factum est cum intraret in domum cuiusdam principes (*sic*) pharisaeorum sabbato * LUIII. 176. x.

to brucanne hlāf ⁊ ða-ilco behealdon hine ⁊ heono monn sum unhal ꝉ wæs
manducare panem et ipsi obseruabant eum 2 et ecce homo quidam hydropicus erat

fore hine ⁊ ondsuærede se hælend cuoeð to æs wistum ⁊ is gelefed
ante illum 3 *ET respondens iesus dixit ad legis peritos et pharisaeos licet * 177. ii. mt. cxui.

on symbeldæge ge-lecnia
sabbato curare

---

31. on ðæm dæge geneolicadun sume ðara aldormonna hiora cweðende him gaa ⁊ gong hiona forðon herodes walde ðec ofsla 32. ⁊ cwæð ðæm gað ⁊ cweoðað foxe ðæm heono ic aworpe diowul ⁊ hælo ih ðerh-wuno to-dæge ⁊ on merne ⁊ ðæm ðirda dæge ic biom gi-endad 33. soð hweðre giriseð to dæge ⁊ on merne ⁊ ðæm æfter fylgende forðon ne nimeð witga losiga buta hierusalem 34. hierusalem hierusalem ðu of-slæs ða witgu ⁊ ðu stænes ða ðaðe gisended bioðun to ðe swa swiðe ic walde gisomniga suno ðine ðaðe swelce fugol nest his under feðrum gisomneð ⁊ ne waldes ðu 35. heono forleten iow hus iower woestige ic cweðo ða wutudlice iow forðon ꝥte ge ne giseað mec oððæt cyme miððy ge cweðe se gibletsad seðe com in noma drihtnes

Cap. XIV. 1. ⁊ aworden wæs miððy infoerde in hus sumes aldor-monnes ðara uðwutuna hiora on symbel-dæge to bruccanne hlaf ⁊ ða ilca biheoldun hine 2. ⁊ heono monn sum unhal wæs bifora hine 3. ⁊ ondsworade ðe hælend cwæð to æs witgum ⁊ aldormonnium hiæ cwedun gif gilefed is on symbel-dæge ðe gilecniga ł no

4 Ða suwudon hig. þa nam he hine ⁊ gehælde ⁊ for-let hyne;

5 Þa cwæð he to him ⁊swariende. hwylces eowres assa oððe oxa befealþ on anne pytt ⁊ ne tihþ he hyne hrædlice up on restedæge;

6 Ða ne mihton hig agen þis hi*m* geandwyrdan;

7 Ða sǽde he su*m* big-spel be þa*m* ingelaðudan. gymende hu hig þa fyrmestan setl gecuron ⁊ þus cwæð;

8 Ðon*ne* þu byst to gyftu*m* gelaþod ne site þu on þam fyrmestan setle. þelæs wenunga sum wurð-fulra [sig yngelaðod fram hym.

9 ⁊ þonne] cu͞me se þe ðe in-gelaþode ⁊ secge ðe rym þysu*m* men setl. ⁊ þu ðænne mid sceame nyme ꝥ yte-meste setl;

10 Ac þon*ne* þu geclypod byst. gá ⁊ site on þa*m* ytemestan setle. ꝥ se ðe þe ingelaðude þænne he cymð cweþe to þe. la fréond. site ufur. þon*ne* byð þe wurðmynt be-foran mid-sittendum;

11 For-þam ælc þe hine úp-ahefð. bið genyðerud. ⁊ se ðe hine nyðerað se bið up-ahafen;

12 Ða cwæð he to þa*m* þe hine inlaðode. þon*ne* þu dest wiste oððe feorme ne clypa þu þine frynd ne þíne gebroðru. ne ðine cuðan ne þine welegan nehheburas. þe-læs hi ðe agen laðiun. ⁊ þu hæbbe ed-lean;

4 Ða swegedon hyo. þa nam he hine ⁊ hælde ⁊ for-let hine.

5 Ða cwæð he to heom andsweriende. Hwilces eowres asse oððe oxa be-feald on ænne pyt. ⁊ ne teod he hine rædlice up on reste daige.

6 Ða ne mihton hyo agen þis hym geandswerian.

7 Þa saigde he heom sum bispell. be þam inge-laðedon gymende hu hyo þa fyrmestan setle ge-curan. ⁊ þus cwæð.

8 Þanne þu beost to gyften ge-laðed. ne site þu on þa fyrmeste settle þi-læs wenunga su*m* wurðfulra cume.

9 ⁊ se þe inge-laðede segge þe rem þisen menn settl. ⁊ þu þanne mid scame nyme ꝥ ytemesten settle.

10 Ac þanne þu ge-clyped beost. ga ⁊ site on þam ytemesten settle. þæt se þe inge-laðode þanne he kymð cweðe to þe. La freond; site ufor. þanne beoð þe wurðment beforan mid-sittenden.

11 For-þan ælc þe hine up-ahefð byð ge-nyðered. ⁊ se þe hine niðered se beoð up-ahafen.

12 Þa cwæð he to þam þe hine in laðede. Þanne þu dest wyste oððe ferme. ne cleope þu þine freond ne þine broðre. ne þine cuðan. ne þine welegen. nehhebures. þelæs hyo þe agen laðian ⁊ þu hæbbe edlean.

Various Readings.

4. A. suwedon. 5. A. assan. A. ænne. 6. A. ongean. 7. A. big-spell. A. inge-laðedon. C. gecuran. 8. A. weorð-fulra. (*The words* sig yngelaðod fram hym. ⁊ þonne *occur in* A. *only.*) 9. A. þonn*e*. A. ytemyste. 10. C. *om.* gá. A. ytemystan. A. ingelaðode. þonn*e*. A. ufer. A. weorð-mynd. 11. A. ge-nyþerod. 12. A. ingelaðode. A. þy-læs hig þe ongean laðion.

Various Readings.

4. swugedon. 5. eom; assa; befealð; teoð. 7. sægde; eom; in-gelaðedan; ge-curen. 8. Ðonne; byst; gyftu*m* ge-laðod; þa*m*; setle þe-læs. 9. ingelæðede secge; rym þysum men setl; ytemeste setle. 10. þonne; byst; ytemestan setle; ðe þe [*for* þe] ingelæðode þænne; cymð; þo*n*ne byð; wurðmynt; -sittendu*m*. 11. For-þam; bið up-ahafan. 12. Ðenne; clype; broðeru; welegan nehheburas; eadlen.

soð hia ł ða suigdon he uut*edlice* ge*h*lahte gehælde ⁊ *for*leort ⁊ geondsuaræde
4 at illi tacuerunt ipse uero apprehensum sanauit ac dimisit 5 et respondens

to ðæm cuoeð huelc ł huæs iueres asald ł oxa in seað falleð ⁊ ne sona of-doeð
ad illos dixit cuius uestrum ásinus aut bos in puteum cadet et non continuo extrahet

hine doeg symbele*s* ⁊ ne mæhton to ðassu*m* geondueарde him cuoeð ða
illum die sabbati 6 et non potuerunt ad hæc respondere illi 7 *Dicebat autem * 178. x.

⁊ to ðæm laðendum ꝥ bisen beheald huu ða *for*mo hræsto hia geceason cuoeð to
et ad inuitatos parabola*m* intendens quomodo primos accubitos eligerent dicens ad

him mið-ðy gehlaðed ðu bist to færmum ne hlina ðu in ða *for*ma stoue eoðe mæge
illos 8 cum inuitatus fueris ad nuptias non dis-cumbas in primo loco ne forte

wyrðro ðec sie geneded ł gehlaðad fro*m* ðæm ⁊ cymeð ðeilco seðe ðec ⁊ hine ge-ceigeð ł
honoratior té sit inuitatus ab eo 9 et ueniens is qui té et illum uoca-

ge-ceigde cuoeðes ðe sel ðissu*m* ꝥ stou ⁊ ðon*ne* ðu inginnas mið sceoma ꝥ hlætmesto stoue gehalda
uit dicat tibi dá huic locu*m* et tunc incipias cum rubore nouissimum locum tenere

ah miððy geceiged ðu bist gaa hlinig on ꝥ hlætmesto stou ꝥte mið-ðy gecymeð seðe ðec
10 sed cum uocatus fueris uade recumbe in nouissimo loco ut cum uenerit qui té

gehlaðade cuoeðað ðe freond astig ufor ðon*ne* bið ðe wuldor ł gefea *for*a ðæm gelic
inuitauit dicat tibi ámice ascende superius tunc erit tibi gloria coram simul

hlingendu*m* *for*ðon eghuelc seðe hine ahebbað ge-hniðrad bið ⁊ seðe hine gebegað
discumbentib*us* 11 *Quia omnis qui sé exaltat humiliabitur et qui sé humiliat * 179. u. mt. ccxxi

gehefen bið cuoeð ða ⁊ ðæm seðe hine gehlaðade miððy ðu gedoeð hriord ł
exaltabitur 12 *Dicebat *autem* et ei qui sé inuitauerat cum facis prandium aut * 180. x.

symbel nelle ðu geceiga friondas ðina ne broðro ðino ne sibbo ł cuðo menn ne neheburas
caenam noli uocare ámicos tuos neq*ue* fratres tuos neq*ue* cognatos neq*ue* uicinos

weligo eaðamæge ⁊ ða ilco ðec eft-hlaðas ⁊ sie ðe eft-selenise
diuites ne forte et ipsi té ré-inuitent et fiat tibi retributio

---

4. soð hiæ swigadun he wutudl*ice* gilahte gihælde ł gihælde (*sic*) hine ⁊ for-leort 5. ⁊ giondsworade cwæð hwelc iower asald ł oxa in seað falleð ⁊ ne sona of of-doeð hine dæge symbles 6. ⁊ ne mæhtun to ðassu*m* gi⁊-sworade him 7. cwæð ða to ðæm lædendum ða bisine bihald hwa ða forma onfoe hie gifeasan (*sic*) cwæð to him 8. miððy bið laðad ðu bist to feormum ne hliona in ðær forma stowwe æðe mæg wyrðro ðec ł ðe sie gineded fro*m* him 9. ⁊ cymeð ðeilco seðe ðec ⁊ hine gicegeð cweoðas ðe sel ðissum stowwe ⁊ ðonne ðu on-ginnes mið scomo stowe ða lætemestu ge-halda 10. ah miððy gicegeð ðu bist gaa hlioniga on ða lætemestu stowwe ꝥ mið-ðy cymeð seðe ðec gilade cweoðað ðe friond astig ufor ðon*ne* bið ðe wuldor bi-fora ðæm gilice hlingendum 11. forðon eghwelc seðe hine ahefeð giniðrad bið ⁊ seðe hine abegeð gihæfen bið 12. cwæð ða ðæm ł him seðe hine gilaðade miððy ðu does riordo ł symbel nelle ðu gicegan friond ðinne ne broðor ðinne ne gisibbe cuðe men ne neh-giburas wealige ðaðe eaðe mæge ⁊ ða ilcu ðec gilaðiga ⁊ doe ðe eft-sel-nisse

13 Ac þænne þu ge-beor-scype dó. clypa þearfan ⁊ wanhale. ⁊ healte. ⁊ blinde.

14 þon*ne* bist þu eadig. for-þa*m* ðe hi nabbað hwanun hig hit þe forgyldon; Soðlice hit byð þe forgolden on riht-wisra æriste;

15 Ða þis gehyrde sum of þa*m* sittendu*m* þa cwæð he. eadig is se ðe hlaf ytt on godes rice;

Ðys god-spel ge-byrað on þone þryddan sunnandæg ofer pentecosten. Homo quida*m* fecit cena*m* magna*m*. A.

16 Ða sæde he hi*m*. su*m* man worhte mycele feorme ⁊ manega gelaðode.

17 þa sende he his þeowan to þære feorme timan ꝥ he sæde þa*m* gelaðedu*m* ꝥ hig comun forþa*m* þe ealle þing gearwe wæron;

18 þa ongunnon hig ealle hig beladian; Se forma hi*m* sæde. ic bohte ænne tún. ic hæbbe neode ꝥ ic fare ⁊ hine geseo. ic bidde þe ꝥ ðu me beladige;

19 Ða cwæþ se oþer. ic bohte án getyme oxena. nu wille ic faran ⁊ fandian hyra nu bidde ic þe beláda me;

20 Ða cwæð sum ic lædde wíf ha*m*. for-þa*m* ic ne mæg cuman;

21 þa cyrde se þeowa ⁊ cydde his hlaforde ꝥ; Ða cwæð se hlaford mid yrre to þa*m* þeowan; Gá hraþe on þa strǽta ⁊ on wic þisse ceastre ⁊ þearfan ⁊ wanhale. ⁊ blinde ⁊ healte lǽd hider ín;

Various Readings.

13. A. þonne. 14. A. hig. A. hwanon. C. for-goldon [*for* forgolden]. 15. B. C. yt. 17. A. comon. 18. B. C. beladie. 19. A. ge-tymðe. 21. A. raðe.

13 Ac þanne þu beorscype do; cleope þearfen ⁊ wanhæften ⁊ healte ⁊ blinde.

14 þanne beost þu eadig. for-þan þe hyo næbbed hwanen hyo hit þe folgeldon (*sic*). Soðlice hit beoð þe for-golden on riht-wisra ariste.

15 Ða þis ge-herde sum of þam sittenden. þa cwæð he. eadig is se þe hlaf æt on godes riche.

16 þa sægde he heom su*m* man worhte mycele ferme ⁊ manega ge-laðode.

17 þa sente he his þeowen to þare ferme timan. þæt he saide þam ge-laðedon þæt hyo coman. for-þan þe ealle þing gearewe wæren.

18 Ða ongamnan (*sic*) hyo ealle hyo be-laðedian. Se forme hym saigde ic bohte ænne tun; ich hæbbe neode þæt ic fare ⁊ hine ge-seo. ic bidde þe þæt þu me be-ladie.

19 Ða cwæð se oðer. ich bohte an ge-teme oxana. nu wille ich faren ⁊ fandian hyre. nu bidde ic þe be-lade me.

20 Ða cwæð sum ich ladde wif ham. for-þam ic ne mæg cuman.

21 Ða cyrde se þeowa ⁊ kydde his hlaforde þæt. Ða cwæð se hlaford mid yrre to þam þeowan. Ga raðe on þa stræte. ⁊ on wic þissere cestere. ⁊ þærfan ⁊ wan-hæften. ⁊ blinde. ⁊ healte. ⁊ læð (*sic*) hider in.

Various Readings.

13. þonne; clype þearfan; wan-hafen. 14. þo*n*ne bist; næbbeð hwanun; forgyldon; bið. 15. ge-hirde; et; rice. 16. com; feorme. 17. sende; þeowan; feorme; saegde; ge-laðedan; forða*m*; wæron. 18. ongunnan; be-laðian; sægde; ic [*for* ich]. 19. ic; ge-tyme; ic faran. 20. ic lædde. 21. cydde; þisse ceastre; wan-hafan.

ah mið-ðy ðu doest gebærscip ge-ceig ðorfendum unhalum haltum blindum ⁊ eadig
13 sed cum facis conuiuium uoca pauperes debiles clodos caecos 14 et beatus

ðu bist forðon hia ne habbað eft to seallane ðe eft bið gesald forðon ðe on erist soðfæstra
eris quia non habent retribuere tibi retribuetur enim tibi in resurrectionem (*sic*) iustorum

ðas mið-ðy geherde sume of ðæm mið ł gelic hlingendum cuoeð him eadig bið seðe ettað ł brucað
15 haec cum audisset quidam de simul discumbentibus dixit ei beatus qui manducauit

hlaf In ríc godes soð he cuoeð him ł ðæm monn sum dyde farma micelo ⁊
panem in regno dei 16 at ipse dixit ei *Homo quidam fecit cenam magnam et * LUIIII. 181. u. mt. ccxxi.

ceigde menigo ⁊ sende esne his tíd farmes to gecuoeðenne gehlaðas gê ꝥte
uocauit multos 17 et misit seruum suum hora caenae dicere inuitatis ut

hia cyme forðon uutedlice gegearuad sint alle ⁊ ongunnon gelíc alle onsacca ł
uenirent quia iam parata sunt omnia 18 et coeperunt simul omnes excusare

se æresta cuoeð him lônd ic bohte ⁊ nêd-ðarf ic hafo ꝥ ic geonga ⁊ gesea ꝥ ilca ic biddo ðec hæfe mec
primus dixit ei uillam emi et necesse habeo exire et uidere illam rogo té habe me

onsæcne ł ⁊ oðer cuoeð dæl ł oxna dæl fifo ⁊ ic geongo to cunnanne ða ilca ic biddo ðec
excusatum 19 et alter dixit iuga boum emi quinque et eo probare illa rogo té

hæfe mec gelefen ł ⁊ oðer cuoeð wif ic læde ł brohte ⁊ forðon ne mæg ic cume
habe me excusatum 20 et alius dixit uxorem duxi et ideo non possum uenire

⁊ eft-cerde se esne sægde ðas drihtne his ða wrað wæs se fæder hiuuisc cuoeð ðegne his
21 et reuersus seruus nuntiauit haec domino suo tunc iratus pater-familias dixit seruo suo

gaa recone in plǽcum ⁊ mærum ðære ceastre ⁊ ðorfendum ⁊ unhalum ⁊ blindum ⁊ haltum
exi cito in plateas et uicos ciuitatis et pauperes ac debiles et caecos et clodos

inn-lǽd
intro-duc

---

13. ah miððy does gibear-scip giceg ðorfendum un-halum halte blinde 14. ⁊ eadig ðu bist forðon hiæ ne habað eft to sellanne ðe eft bið sald forðon ðe in eriste soð-fæstra 15. ðas miððy giherde sum of ðæm dyde mið ðæm hlioniendum cwæð ðæm eadig seðe eteð hlaf in rice godes 16. ⁊ hee cwæð him mon sum dyde feorme micle ⁊ cede monigum 17. ⁊ sende esne his tide feorme to cweðanne giladigas ge ðætte hia cyme forðon wutudlice gigeorwad sindun alle 18. ⁊ ongunnun gilic alle onsaca ðe ærista cwæð him lond ih bohte forðon ⁊ nedðærfe ic hafo ꝥ ic gongo ⁊ gisie ðæt ilce ic biddo ðec hæfe mec on-sæcne 19. ⁊ oðer cwæð dæl cyna ic bohte fife ⁊ ic gongo to cunnanne ðailco ic biddo ðec hæfe mec gilefenne 20. ⁊ oðer cwæð wif ic lædo ⁊ forðon ne mæg ic cuma 21. ⁊ eft-cerde ðe esne sægde ðas drihtne his ða wrað wæs ðe fæder ðæs hiorodes cwæð esne his gaa recone in plætsa ⁊ mæro ðære cæstre ⁊ ðorfendum ⁊ un-halum ⁊ blinde ⁊ halte inlæd hider

22 Ða cwæð se þeowa. hlaford. hit ys gedón swa þu bude. ⁊ nu gyt her is æmtig stów;

23 Þa cwæð se hlaford þa gyt to þam þeowan; Gá geond þas wegas ⁊ hegas. ⁊ nyd hig ꝥ hig gān in. ꝥ min hus si gefylled;

24 Soðlice ic eow secge ꝥ nan þara manna þe geclypode synt ne onbyrigeað minre feorme;

Ðys godspel sceal to *sanctus* hermetis ⁊ to *sanctus* agustinus mæssan. Si quis uenit ad me & non odit patre*m* suu*m* & matre*m*. A.

25 Soðlice mid hi*m* ferde mycel menego. þa cwæð he to hi*m* bewend;

26 Gyf hwa to me cymð ⁊ ne hatað his fæder ⁊ moder ⁊ wíf ⁊ bearn ⁊ broþru ⁊ swustra. ⁊ þænne gyt his sawle ne mæg he beon min leorning-cniht;

27 ⁊ se þe ne byrð hys cwylminge ⁊ cymð æfter me. ne mæg he beon min leorning-cniht;

28 Hwylc eower wyle timbrian anne stypel. hu ne sytt he ærest ⁊ teleð þa andfengas þe hi*m* behefe synt. hwæðer he hæbbe hine to full-fre*m*menne

29 þe-læs syððan he þæne grund-weall legð. ⁊ ne mæg hine full-fre*m*man. ealle þe hit geseoð agynnað hine tælan

30 ⁊ cweðan; Hwæt þes man agan timbrian ⁊ ne mihte hit ge-endian;

Various Readings.

23. A. eond. A. sig. 24. A. þæra. A. synd. A. onbyriað. 25. A. mænego. 26. B. C. modor. A. þonne. 28. A. ænne. A. ful-fremmanne. 29. A. þy-læs. A. þone. C. grud-weall (*sic*). A. agynnon; B. C. agynnan. 30. A. ongan.

22 Ða cwæð se þeowa. Hlaford hit is ge-don swa þu bæde. ⁊ nu gyt her is emtig stowe.

23 Ða cwæð se hlaford gyt þa to þam þeowan. Ga geond þas wegas ⁊ hegas ⁊ nyd hyo ꝥ hyo gan in. ꝥ min hus syo gefelled.

24 Soðlice ic eow segge ꝥ nan þare manna þe ge-clepede synde. ne on-byriad mire (*sic*) ferme.

Si quis uen[it] ad me. ⁊ no[n] odit patrem suu*m* ⁊ matre*m*. ⁊ filio[s] ⁊ *fratres*. ⁊ sorores. adhuc ⁊ anima[m] sua*m*; non potest m*eus* esse discipulus.

25 Soðlice mid him ferde micel menige. þa cw̄. he to heom be-wend.

26 Gyf hwa to me cymð ⁊ ne hated hys fader ⁊ moder. ⁊ wif ⁊ bearn. ⁊ broðre ⁊ swustre. ⁊ þanne geot his sawle ne maig he beon min leorni*n*g-cniht.

27 ⁊ se þe ne bered hys cwelmenge ⁊ cymð efter me ne maig he beon min leorning-cniht.

28 hwylc eower wile timbrian ænne stepel. hu ne sit he arest ⁊ teleð þa andfenges þe him be-hefe synde. hwæðer he haebbe hine to fulfremenne.

29 þe-læs siððan he þanne grund-wall leigð. ⁊ ne maig hine fulfremman. ealle þe hit ge-seoð aginned hine tælen.

30 ⁊ cweðen. hwæt þes man agan tymbrian. ⁊ ne mihte hit ge-endian.

Various Readings.

22. bude; stow. 23. ge-fylled. 24. ge-clypede synt; on-byriað minre feorme. 25. *Rubric as in* H.; menego. 26. hatað; modor; broðra; sustra; geat; sawla; mæg. 27. byrð; cwelminge; æfter; mæg. 28. synt; habbe; full-fre*m*menne. 29. þenne; legð; mæg; agynnan. 30. cweðan.

⁊ cuoeð se ēsne drih*ten* aworden wæs ł is suæ ðu ge-hehtes ⁊ forðor ðaget sprecend wæs ⁊
22 et ait seruus d*omi*ne factum est ut imperasti et athuc locutus est (*sic*) 23 et

cuoeð se drih*ten* ðem ðegne fær on woegu*m* ⁊ woercu*m* ł ⁊ ge-nēd to in-geonganne ꝥte sie gefylled hus
ait d*ominus* seruo exi in uias et sepes et com-pelle intrare ut impleatur domus

min ic cuoeðo ðon*ne* ł uut*edlice* iuh ꝥte ne aenig warana ðara ðaðe geceigedo weron
mea 24 dico autem uobis quod nemo uiuorum (*sic*) illorum qui uocati sunt

ge-birgað farma mīn foerdon ða hergas mænigo mið hine ⁊ efne awoennde wæs cuæð
gustauit (*sic*) cenam meam 25 *Ibant autem turbae multae cum eo et conuersus dixit * LX. 182. u. mt. xcui.

to ðæm gif hua cymeð to me ⁊ ne læð*ues* ł ne fiunges fæder his ⁊ moder
ad illos 26 si quis uenit ad me et non odit patrem suu*m* et matrem

⁊ wif ⁊ sunu ⁊ broðro ⁊ suoestro *for*ðor ðaget ðā ⁊ sauel his ne mæge
et uxorem et filios et fratres et sorores athuc *autem* et anima*m* sua*m* non potest

min wosa ðegn ⁊ seðe ne beres ł ðroung his ⁊ cymeð æft*er* mec ne
meus esse discipulus 27 et qui non baiulat crucem suam et uenit post me non

mæge wosa min ðegn huælc *for*ðon fro*m* iuh wælle ł walde torr getimbra
potest esse meus discipulus 28 * Quis enim ex uobis uolens turrem ædificare * 183. x.

ahne aerist sitteð ł sittende getelles mið to geniomanne ða ðe ned-ðarf sindon ł behoflico sint gif hæfeð
nonne prius sedens com-putat sumtus qui necessari sunt si habet

to ge-endanne ꝥte ne æft*er* ðon gesette ꝥ grūnd ⁊ ne mæhte ge-ēndiga
ad perficiend*um* 29 ne post-ea-quam posuerit fundamentu*m* et non poterit perficere

Alle ða ðe geseas onginnað bismeria him ðus cuoeðendo *for*ðon ł ꝥte ðes monn ongann
omnes qui uident incipiant inludere ei 30 dicentes quia hic homo coepit

getimbra ⁊ ne mæhte ge-endia
aedificare et non potuit cons*umma*re

---

22. ⁊ cwæð ðe esne drih*ten* aworden wæs swa ðu gi-hehtes ⁊ forðor ðagett sprecende wæs 23. drihten cwæð ðegne ðæm gong on woegas ⁊ werc ⁊ gined in to gonganne swa hwelcne swa ðu finde ꝥ sie gifylled hus min 24. ic cweðo ðonne iow ðætte nænig weorona ðara ðaðe gicegde wērun gi-birgeð feorme mine 25. foerdun ða hergas monige mið hine ⁊ efne æt-edwed wæs cwæð to ðæm 26. gif hwelc cymið to me ⁊ ne lædes fæder his ⁊ moder ⁊ wif ⁊ suno ⁊ broðor ⁊ swester forðor ðagett sawle his ne mæg min wosa ðegn 27. ⁊ seðe ne beres ðrowunge his ⁊ cymeð æfter me ne mæg min wosa ðegn 28. hwelc forðon of iow welle tor gitimbra ahne ærist siteð gitelleð mið to giniomanne ðaðe ned-ðarfe sindun gif hæfeð to gi-endanne 29. ðæt ne æfter ðon gisette ðon*ne* grund ⁊ ne mæhte giendiga alle ðaðe giseað on-ginnað bismeriga hine 30. ðus cweðende forðon ꝥte ðes mon ongan gitimbria ne mæhte giendiga

31 Oððe gyf hwylc cynincg wyle faran ⁊ feohtan agen oðerne cyning hu ne sit he ær ⁊ þencð hwæðer he mæge mid tyn þusendu*m* cuman agen þone þe hi*m* agen cymð mid twentigum þusendu*m*.

32 ⁊ gif he þon*ne* wið hine gefeohtan ne mæg. he sent ærynd-racan ⁊ bitt sibbe;

33 Witodlice swa is ælc of eow þe ne wið-sæcð eallu*m* þingum þe he ah. ne mæg he beon min leorning-cniht;

34 Gőd ys sealt gif hit awyrð on þa*m* þe hit gesylt bið.

35 nis hyt nyt ne on eorþan ne on myxene. ac hyt bið űt-aworpen; Gehyre se þe earan hæbbe to ge-hyrenne;

CHAPTER XV.

Ðys godspel sceal on þone feorðan sunnan-dæg ofer pentec*osten*. Era*nt* adpr*o*pinquantes ad i*esu*m publicani & peccatores. A. Era*nt* a*utem* appropinq*u*antes ad i*esu*m publicani ⁊ peccatores. B.

1 Soðlice hi*m* genealæhtun manfulle ⁊ synfulle ꝥ hig his word gehyrdon;

2 Ða murcnedon þa farisei ⁊ þa boceras ⁊ cwædon; Ðes onfehð synfulle ⁊ mid hi*m* ytt;

3 Þa cwæþ he þis big-spel to þa*m*;

4 Hwylc man is of eow þe hæfð hund sceapa. ⁊ gif he for-lyst ān of þa*m*. hu ne for-læt he þon*ne* nigon ⁊ hund-nigontig on þa*m* westene. ⁊ gæð to þa*m* þe for-wearð oð he hit fint.

5 ⁊ þon*ne* he hit fint he hitt set on his exla geblissiende.

Various Readings.

31. C. Oðð. A. cyning. A. ongean. A. sytt. C. hwæder. A. ongean. A. on-gean. 32. C. bið [*for* wið]. A. ærend-racan. 35. A. gehyranne.

Cap. xv. 1. A. ge-nealæhton. B. C. gehyron. 5. A. hyt [*2nd time; but* B. C. hitt]. A. ge-blyssigende.

31 Oððe gyf hwilc kyning wile faran ⁊ feohten on-gean oðerne kyng. hu ne sit he ær ⁊ þencd hwaðer he mage mid teon þusenden cumen agen þane þe him agen kymð mid twentigen þusenden.

32 ⁊ gyf he þanne wið hine fihten ne maig; he sent erendraken ⁊ bit sibbe.

33 Witodlice swa ys ælc of eow þe ne wið-sæcð ealle þingen þe he ah; ne maig he beon min leorning-cniht.

34 Gőd is salt gif hit awurð on þam þe hit ge-selt beoð.

35 nys hyt nyt. ne on eorðen ne on mixene. ac hit beoð ut-aworpen. Gehere se ðe earen hæbbe. to ge-herene.

CHAPTER XV.

1 Soðlice him ge-nehlahte manfulle ⁊ synfulle. þæt hyo his word ge-hyron.

2 Ða murcneden þa farisei ⁊ þa bokeres ⁊ cwæðen. þes on-fegð synfulle ⁊ mid heo*m* ett.

3 Ða cwæð he þis bispell to þam.

4 hwilc man is of eow þe hafed hund scepa. ⁊ gif he leost an of þam; hu ne for-læt he þa nigen ⁊ hund-nigentig on þam wæstene. ⁊ gæð to þan þe for-warð oððe he hit fint.

5 ⁊ þanne he hit fint. he hit sett on his eaxle ge-blissiende.

Various Readings.

31. hwyc (*sic*) cyning; feohtan; cyning; þencð hweðer; þusendum cuman; þanne; cymð; twentigu*m* þusendum. 32. þo*n*ne; mag; erndracan. 33. eallu*m* þingu*m*; hah; mæg; beo. 34. sealt. 35. eorðan; byð; Ge-hyre; earu*n* habbe; ge-herenne.

Cap. xv. 1. ge-neahlahton. 2. murcnedon; boceras; cwæðon; on-fehð; eom et. 3. big-spell. 4. hafð; sceopa; lyst; for-let; nygon; -nigeontig; gað; þa*m*; for-wearð. 5. þo*n*ne; set; oxla.

ꝉ huælc cynig bið færende to gesendanne ꝉ to gesettanne ꝉ feht wið oðerne cynig ahne
31 aut quis rex iturus committere bellum aduersum alium regem non

sitteð ærist smeað ꝉ ðencgað gifhueðer maeg mið teum ꝉ tenum ðusendum iorna togægnes him seðe mið
sedens prius cogitat si possit cum decem milibus occurrere ei qui cum

tuoentigum ðusendum cymeð to him oðero ðingo ꝉ ða get him longe ꝉ fearre doend erendureca
uiginti milibus uenit ad sé 32 alio-quin athuc illo longe ágente legationem

sende gebiddeð ða ðaðe sibbes sint suæ forðon eghuelc from iuh seðe ne eft-sægeð ꝉ ne
mittens rogat ea quae pacis sunt 33 * Sic ergo omnis ex uobis qui non renun- * 184. u. mt. xcui.

onsæcæð Allum ðæm ðe Agniges ꝉ ah ne mæg min wosa ðegn god is se salt
tiat omnibus quae possidet non potest meus esse discipulus 34 * Bonum est sál * 185. ii. mt. xxxi. mr. cii.

gif ðonne se salt æc ðon· forduinde ꝉ forduineð in ðon ꝉ in ðæm bið besmitten ꝉ gehyded ne
si autem sál quoque euanuerit in quo condietur 35 neque

on eorðo ne in feltune ꝉ mixen ðorfæst is ah ũta gesended bið seðe hæfeð earo to heranne ꝉ
in terram neque in sterculinium utile est sed foras mittetur qui habet aures audi-

hernises gehereð
endi audiat

CAP. XV.

woeron ða geneolecdon him bær-synnigo ⁊ synnfullo ꝥte geherdon hine ⁊
1 * Erant autem appropinquantes ei publicani et peccatores ut audirent illum 2 et * LXI. 186. ii. mt. lxxii. mr. xxii.

gehyrston ꝉ ⁊ uð-uto cuoeðendo ꝥte ðes ða synnfullo onfoeð ⁊ etað mið
murmurabant pharisaei et scribae dicentes quia hic peccatores recipit et manducat cum

him ⁊ cuoeð to ðæm geddung ðios cuoeð huoelc from iuh monn seðe hæfeð
illis 3 * Et ait ad illos parabolam istam dicens 4 quis ex uobis homo qui habet * 187. u. mt. clxxxii

hundrað scip ⁊ gif forlorað ꝉ losað enne of ðæm ah ne forleteð ða nigona ⁊ hund-neontig on woestern
centum oues et si perdiderit unam ex illis nonne dimittit nonaginta nouem in deserto

⁊ gaað to ðær ilca ða ðe ꝉ ðio losade oð ðæt gemoete ða ilca ⁊ miððy gemoetað hia
et uadit ad illam quae perierat donec inueniat illam 5 et cum inuenerit illam

on-settað on scyldrum his gefeande
imponit in umeros suos gaudentes (*sic*)

---

31. ꝉ hwelc cynig bið færende to settanne gifeht wið oðerne cynig ahne sites æris (*sic*) smeoð gif hweðer mæg mið ten ðusendum iorna togægnes him ðæm cynige seðe mið twoegentigum ðusenda cymeð to him 32. oðer ðingo ða get longe him doende erend-wracu sende gibideð ða ðaðe sibbe sint 33. swa forðon eghwelc of iow seðe ne eft-sægeð allum ðaðe ægnigað ne mæg min wosa ðegn 34. god is ðæt salt gif wutedlice salt ec ðonne forðineð in ðon ꝉ ðæm bismiten bið 35. ne on eorðo ne in fel-tune ꝉ on mixenne ðorfæst is ah utt asended bið seðe hæfeð earo to giheranne giherað

Cap. XV. 1. werun ða to gineolicadun him bear-swinigo ⁊ synn-fulle ðætte giherdun hine 2. ⁊ gi-hyrston aldormen ⁊ uð-wutu cweðende ðætte ðes ða synfulle onfoeð ⁊ eteð miððy 3. ⁊ cwæð ðæm geddunge ðios cwæð 4. hwelc of iowih mon seðe hæfeð hundreð scipa ⁊ gif for-leaseð an of ðæm ahne forleteð ða hund-niontig ⁊ nione on weosterne ⁊ gað to ðer ilca ðaðe losigað oððæt gimoette ða ilco 5. ⁊ miððy gimoeteð hiæ on-settað ofer scyldrum his gifeande

6 ⁊ þon*ne* he ha*m* cymð he to-somne
clypað hys frynd ⁊ his nehheburas. ⁊
cwyð; Blissiað mid me for-þa*m* ic funde
min scep þe for-wearð;
7 Ic secge eow ꝥ swa byð on heofone
blis be anu*m* synfullum þe dædbote deð.
ma þonne ofer nigon ⁊ nigontigum riht-
wisra þe dæd-bote ne beðurfon;
8 Oððe hwilc wif hæfð tyn scyllingas.
gif heo forlyst anne scylling. hu ne on-ælð
heo hyre leoht-fæt. ⁊ awent hyre hus ⁊
secð geornlice oð heo hine fint;
9 ⁊ þonne heo hine fint heo clypað hyre
frynd ⁊ nehhe-byryna ⁊ cwyð. blyssiað mid
me forþa*m* ic funde minne scylling þe ic
forleas;
10 Ic secge eow swa bið blis beforan
godes englu*m* be anu*m* synfullu*m* þe dæd-
bote dēð;

Ðys god-spel gebyrað on sæternes dæg on þære oðre lencten wucan. Homo quida*m* duos filios habuit & dix*it* adolescentior. A. Homo quida*m* habebat duos filios & dixit iunior patri suo pater da mihi parte*m* substanciæ que me co*n*tingit. B.

11 He cwæð. soðlice su*m* man hæfde
twegen suna.
12 þa cwæð se yldra to his fæder; Fǽder. syle me minne dæl minre æhte þe me
to ge-byreþ. þa dælde he him his æhte;
13 Ða æfter feawa dagu*m* ealle his þing
gegaderude se gingra sunu. ⁊ ferde wræc-
lice on feorlen rice. ⁊ for-spilde þar his æhta
lybbende on his gǽlsan;
14 Ða he hig hæfde ealle amyrrede þa
wearð mycel hunger on þa*m* rīce ⁊ he wearð
wædla;

Various Readings.

6. A. sceap; *but* B. C. scep. 7. A. blyss. 8. A. ænne. A. eornlice. 9. A. nehhe-byrna. 10. A. blyss. A. doð. 12. A. B. C. yldra (*as in text*). A. æhta [2*nd time*]. 13. A. ge-gaderode. A. þær for-spylde.

6 ⁊ þanne he ham cymð. he to-somne
cleopeð hys freond. ⁊ his nehhe-bures. ⁊
cweð. Blissiað mid me for-þam ich funde
min scep þe for-warð.
7 Ich segge eow ꝥ swa beoð on heofene
blisse be anen synfullen ðe deadbote deð;
ma þanne ofer nigen ⁊ nigentig rithwisere
(*sic*) þe deadbote ne be-þurfon.
8 Oððe hwilc wif hæfed tyen scillenges.
gyf hyo for-leost ænne scilling. hu ne on-
elð hyo hire leoht-fet. ⁊ awent hire hus
⁊ secð geornlice oððe hyo hine fint.
9 Ænd þanne hyo hine fint; hyo cleopeð
hire freond ⁊ nehhe-bures ⁊ cweð blissieð
mid me. for-þam ich funde minne scilling
þe ich for-leas.
10 Ich segge eow swa beoð blisse be-
foran godes ænglen be anen senfulle þe
deadbote deð.
11 He cwæð soðlice. Sum man
hæfde twege sunes.

Homo quidam habebat duos filios. & dixit iunior patri suo. Pater da michi partem substantie que me contingit.

12 þa cwæð se ylder to his fader. Fader
syle me minne dæl minre ehte. þe me to
gé-byreð. Ða dælde he him his ehte.
13 Ða æfter feawa dagen ealle his þing
ge-gaderede se gingre sune. ⁊ ferde wræc-
lice on feor landen. ⁊ for-spilde þær his
ehte libbende on his gælsan.
14 Ða he hyo hæfde ealle amerde. þa
warð mycel hunger on þam rice. ⁊ he
warð wædle.

Various Readings.

6. þon*n*e; clypað; -buras; ic; sceap; for-wearð. 7. ,Ic; hefone; anum synfullum; þonne; riht-wisere. 8. hafð tyn scillingas; for-lyst anne; -fæt; georlice (*sic*). 9. ⁊ þonne; clypað; -buras; cwið blissiað; ic; mine; ic. 10. Ic; byð blis; englv*m*; anum synfullu*m*. 11. hafde; sunas. 12. yldra; Fæder (2*nd time*); heom. 13. fewa; ge-gaderude; gingra sunu; feorlen rice. 14. amerede; wearð; wearð wædla.

⁊ cuom to hus ł to ham geceigeð ł geceigde friondum ⁊ nehebur*um* cuoeð ðæm efne geðoncaiges
6 et ueniens domum conuocat amicos et uicinos dicens illis congratulamini

me forðon ic gemoete scip min ðio losade ic cuoeðo iuh ꝥte on ðā wisa gefea
mihi quia inueni ouem mea*m* quae perierat 7 dico uobis quod ita gaudium

bið on heofnu*m* of*er* enne ł an synn-fullne hreonise hæbbende ðon of*er* ða nigone ⁊ hund-neantig
erit in cælo super uno peccatore paenitentiam habentem (*sic*) quam super nonaginta nouem

soðfæstu*m* ł soðfæst*o* ða ðe ne beðorfeð to hreonise ł ðio wif hæfde ł hæbbe fif sceattas
iustis qui non indigent paenitentia 8 * Aut quae mulier habens dragmas * 188. x.

tea siðu*m* gif losað casering enne ah ne berneð ðæccilla ⁊ ymbstyreð ꝥ hus ⁊ soecað
decem si perdiderit dragma*m* unam nonne accendit lucerna*m* et euertit domum et querit

georne oððæt gemoete ⁊ mið ðy gefindes efne geceigað ða wif friondas ⁊ nehebyrildas
diligenter donec inueniat 9 et cum inuenerit conuocans amicas et uicinas

ðus cuoeðendo efne geðongigas me forðon ic fãnd ꝥ scilling ðæt ł ðio ic forleas ł ic forlure on ðā wisa
dicens congratulamini mihi quia inueni dragma*m* quam perdideram 10 * Ita * 189. v. mt. clxxxii.

ic cuoeðo iuh gefea bið befora englu*m* godes of*er* enne synn-fullne hreonisse doend
dico uobis gaudium erit coram angelis dei super uno peccatore paenitentiam agentem (*sic*)

cuoeð ða monn sum *monn* hæfde tuoege suno ⁊ cuoeð se giungra ł ðe giungesta of ðæm
11 * Ait autem homo quidam habuit duos filios 12 et dixit adulescentior ex illis * LXII. 190. x.

ðæm fæder fæder sel me dæl ł hlodd fæes ł striones ðio ł ðaðe mec gebyre ⁊ dælde ðæm
patri pater dá mihi portione*m* substantiae quæ me contingit et diuisit illis

ꝥ feh ⁊ ne æft*er* menigu*m* dagu*m* miððy gesomnandu*m* allu*m* se giungra sunu
substantia*m* 13 et non post multos dies congregatis omnib*us* adulescentior filius

ellðeodigde ł fearr færende wæs in lond un-neh ł ⁊ ðer gispilde feh his mið life
peregre profectus est in regionem longinqua*m* et ibi dissipauit substantiam suam uiuendo

lustfullice ł ðernelegere ł ⁊ æft*er* ðon Alle ge-endade Aworden wæs hunger suiðe strong on
luxoriose 14 et post-quam omnia consummasset facta est fames ualida in

lond ðæm ⁊ he ongann un-trymmia ł
regione illa et ipse coepit egere

---

6. ⁊ com to huse gicegde friondum ⁊ neh-gibur*um* cwæð ðæm efne giðongias me forðon ic gimoette scip min ðætte losed wæs 7. ic cweðo iow ðætte on ða wisa gifea bið on heofnu*m* of*er* enne synfulne hreownisse hæbbende ðonn*e* of*er* hund-niontig ⁊ nione soðfæste seðe ne biðorfeð to hreownise 8. ł ðæt wif hæfde fif sceattas teasiðum gif losað casering enne ahne berneð ðæcela ⁊ instyreð ꝥ hus ⁊ sooceð georne oððæt gimoeteð 9. ⁊ miððy in-findes giceas ða wif-friondas ⁊ ða nehgiburas ðus cwæð efne-giðonccigas me forðon ic fand ðon*e* scilling ðon*e* ic for-leos 10. on ðasso ic cweðo iow gifea bið bifora englum godes ofer enne synnfulne hreownisse doende 11. cwæð ða mon sum hæfde twoege suno 12. ⁊ cwæð se gingra of ðæm to feder fæder sel me ꝥ hlott feas ł gistriones ðætte mec gibyreð ⁊ dælde ðæm feh ł ða gistrion 13. ⁊ ne æfter monigum dagum miððy gisomnadun allum ðe gingra suno elðiodge ł fear-foerende wæs in londe

[*Here* two leaves *are lost in the* Rushworth MS.]

15 Þa ferde he ⁊ folgude ánum burh-sittendan men þæs rices. Ꝺa sende he hine to his tune ꝥ he heolde his swyn;

16 Ða ge-wilnode he his wambe gefyllan of þa*m* bien-coddun þe Ꝺa swyn ǽton. ⁊ hi*m* man ne sealde;

17 Þa beþohte he hine ⁊ cwæꝺ; Eala hu fela yrꝺlinga on mines fæder huse hláf genohne habbaꝺ ⁊ ic her on hungre for-wurꝺe;

18 Ic aríse. ⁊ ic fare to mínum fæder. ⁊ ic secge hi*m*; Eála fæder ic syngode on heofenas. ⁊ beforan þe.

19 nu ic neom wyrꝺe ꝥ ic beo þin sunu nemned. do me swa anne of þinu*m* yrꝺlingu*m*;

20 ⁊ he aras þa ⁊ com to his fæder. ⁊ þa gyt þa he wæs feorr his fæder he hyne geseah ⁊ wearꝺ mid mild-heortnesse astyrod ⁊ agen hine árn ⁊ hine beclypte ⁊ cyste hine;

21 Ða cwæꝺ his sunu; Fæder. ic syngude on heofon. ⁊ beforan Ꝺe. nu ic ne eom wyrþe ꝥ ic þin sunu beo genemned;

22 Ða cwæþ se fæder to his þeowu*m*; Bringaꝺ raꝺe þæne selestan gegyrelan ⁊ scrydaꝺ hyne ⁊ syllaꝺ him hring on his hand. ⁊ gescý to his fotu*m*.

23 ⁊ bringaꝺ an fætt styric ⁊ of-sleaꝺ ⁊ utun etan ⁊ gewist-fullian.

Various Readings.

15. A. folgode. A. -syttendu*m*. 16. A. bean-coddu*m*; B. bien-coddun; C. biencoddan. 17. A. hyrlinga. A. for-weorꝺe. 18. B. C. heofonas. 19. A. ne eom. A. ge-nemned. A. ænne. A. hyrlingu*m*. 20. A. feor. A. myd; C. *om.* mid. A. myldheortnysse astyred. A. ongean. 21. A. syngode. A. heofen. C. neom. 22. A. þone. A. gegyrlan. 23. C. fæt. A. uton.

15 Ða ferde he ⁊ folgede anen burh-sittenden men on þare rice. þa sende he hine to his tune þæt he heolde his swin.

16 Ða ge-wilnede he his wa*m*be fellen of þam bean-coddan þe þa swin æten. ⁊ him man ne sealde.

17 Ða be-þohte he hine ⁊ cwæꝺ. Eala hwu fela erdlinga on mines fæder huse hlaf ge-noh * hæbbeꝺ. ⁊ ich her on hungre for-wurꝺe.

* MS. ge-nohne, *altered to* ge-noh.

18 Ich arise ⁊ ich fare to minen fæder ⁊ ich segge him. Eala fader ic synegede on heofenas. ⁊ be-foran þe;

19 nu ich ne eom wurꝺe. ꝥ ic beo þin sune ge-nemned. do me swa ane of þinen yrꝺlingen.

20 ⁊ he aras þa ⁊ com to his fader. ⁊ þa gyt þa he wæs feor his fæder he hine ge-seah. ⁊ warꝺ mid mildheortnysse astyred. ⁊ agen hine earn ⁊ hine be-clypte ⁊ cyste hine.

21 Ða cwæꝺ hys suna. Fader ic synegede on heofene ⁊ be-foran þe. nu ic ne eom wurꝺe þæt ic þin sune beo ge-nemned.

22 Ða cwæꝺ se fader to his þeowan. bringeꝺ raꝺe þanne sæleste gegyrlan ⁊ scridaꝺ hine ⁊ sylleꝺ hym ring on his hand. ⁊ ge-scy to his foten.

23 ⁊ bringaꝺ an fet styric ⁊ of-sleaꝺ. ⁊ uten æten. ⁊ gewist-fullian;

Various Readings.

15. anu*m*; -sittende; þas rices. 16. ge-wilnode; fyllan; etan. 17. erꝺlinga; fader; genohne habbeꝺ; ic. 18. Ic; ic; minu*m*; ic; fæder; singode; heofonas; be-foren. 19. ic; suna; anne; ꝺinu*m* yrꝺlingum. 20. fæder; wearꝺ; R. *omits* mid; arn. 21. sunu; Fæder; syngude; heofan; neom wyrꝺe; be. 22. fæder; þeowum. Bringaꝺ; þane selestan; syllaꝺ; fotum. 23. bringeꝺ; uton eten.

⁊ ðona eode ⁊ æt-ran ł genehuade anum ðara burgawarã londes ðæs ⁊ sende hine ł ðene on
15 et abiit et adhaesit uni ciuium regionis illius et misit illum in

lond his ꝥte gelesuade ł gefoede ða bergas ł ða suino ⁊ wilnade gefylle womb his
uillam suam ut pasceret porcos 16 et cupiebat implere uentrem suum

of bean-bælgum ł pisum hosum ðaðe ða suin ge-ēton ⁊ ne ænig *monn* him salde on hine seol*fne*
de siliquis quas porci manducabant et nemo illi dabat 17 in sé

ða gewoende ł gecerde cuoeð huu menigo ða celmertmenn fadores mines monigfaldas mið hlafum
autem reuersus dixit quanti mercennarii patris mei abundant panibus

ic uut*edlice* her mið hungre ic losigo ic ariso ⁊ ic gae ł geonga to feder minum ⁊ ic cuoeðo
Ego *autem* hic fame pereo 18 surgam et ibo ad patrem meum et dicam

him la fader ic synngade on heofne ⁊ fo*ra* ðec soðlice ne am ic wyrðe ꝥ ic sē geceiged
illi pater peccaui in cælum et coram té 19 etiam non sum dignus uocari

sunu ðin do mec suelce enne ł suæ ānum from celmertmonnum ðinum ⁊ arās
filius tuus fac me sicut unum de mercennarís tuis 20 et surgens

cuom to feder his miððy uut*edlice* ða get fearra wæs ł wære gesæh hine fæder his ⁊
uenit ad patrem suum cum autem athuc longe esset uidit illum pater ipsius et

mið milt-heortnise gestyred wæs ł gecer*red* wæs ⁊ arn gefeall on-ufa suira his ⁊
misericordia motus est et occurrens cecidit super collum eius et

cyssende wæs hine ⁊ cuoeð him se sunu fader ic synngade in heof*on* ⁊ fo*ra* ðec
osculatus est eum 21 dixitq*ue* ei filius pater peccaui in cælum et coram té

uut*edlice* ne am ic wyrðe ꝥ ic se geceiged sunu ðin cuoeð ða se fæder to esnum his
iam non sum dignus uocari filius tuus 22 dixit autem pater ad seruos suos

recon*ne* fo*ra*breng ꝥ stol æriste ⁊ ge-wōedað ł hine ⁊ sellað hring on hond his ⁊
cito proferte stolam primam et induite illum et date anulum in manum eius et

scoeas on fot*um* ⁊ lædað ging oxo fætt ⁊ ofslaeð ⁊ ꝥte woe ēte ⁊
calceamenta in pedes 23 et ad-ducite uitulum saginatum et occidite et manducemus et

ꝥ we se ge*h*riordad
epulemur

[*Two leaves lost in the* Rushworth MS.]

24 for-þa*m* þes min sunu wæs dead ⁊ he ge-edcucude. he for-wearð ⁊ he is gemet; Ða ongunnon hig gewist-læcan

25 Soðlice hys yldra sunu wæs on æcere ⁊ he cōm. ⁊ þa he þa*m* huse genealæhte he ge-hyrde þæne sweg ⁊ ꝥ weryd.

26 þa clypode he anne þeow ⁊ axode hine hwæt ꝥ wære;

27 Ða cwæð he þin broðor com. ⁊ þin fæder of-sloh ān fæt celf for-þam þe he hyne halne on-feng;

28 Ða bealh he hine ⁊ nolde ingan; þa eode his fæder ūt ⁊ ongan hine biddan;

29 Ða cwæþ he his fæder ⁊swarigende; Efne swa fela geara ic þe þeowude ⁊ ic næfre þin bebod ne forgymde. ⁊ ne sealdest þu me næfre an ticcen ꝥ ic mid minu*m* freondu*m* gewist-fullude;

30 Ac syððan þes þin sunu com. þe hys spēde mid myltystru*m* amyrde. þu ofsloge hi*m* fǽtt celf;

31 Ða cwæþ he sunu. þu eart symle mid me. ⁊ ealle mine þing synt þīne

32 þe ge-byrede gewist-fullian ⁊ geblissian for-þa*m* þes þin broðor wæs dead ⁊ he ge-edcucede he for-wearð ⁊ he is gemet;

24 for-þan þes min sune wæs dead. ⁊ he ge-edcuðede (*sic*). he for-warð ⁊ he is gefunden. Ða ongunnan hyo wistleacen.

25 Soðlice his yldre sune wæs on akere ⁊ he com ham. ⁊ þa he þam huse genehlahte he ge-herde þanne sweig ⁊ þæt wyrd.

26 Ða cleopede he ænne þeow ⁊ axode hine hwæt þæt wære.

27 Ða cwæð he þin broðer is come. ⁊ þin fader of-sloh an fet chalf for-þan þe he hine halne on-feng.

28 þa balh he hine ⁊ nolde ingan. Ða eode his fader ut ⁊ angan hine biddan.

29 Ða cwæð he to his fæder andsweriende. Efne swa fela geare ic þe þeoweda. ⁊ ic næfre þin bebod ne forgymde; ⁊ ne sealdest þu me næfre an tycchen. ꝥ ic mid minen freonden ge-wistfullode.

30 Ac seoððan þes þin sune com þe his spede mid miltystren amerde; þu of-sloge him an fet chalf.

31 Ða cwæð he. sune þu ert symle mid me. ⁊ ealle mine þing synde þine.

32 þe ge-byrede ge-wistfullien ⁊ geblissian for-þan þes þin broðer wæs dead. ⁊ he ge-edcuðede (*sic*). he for-wearð. ⁊ ys gefunden.

Various Readings.

24. C. wæd dead (*sic*). A. ge-ed-cucode. 25. A. yldran (*sic*). A. þone. A. wered. 26. A. ænne. A. acsode. 27. A. broðer. A. fætt cealf. 28. A. ge-bealh. 29. A. B. C. ⁊swariende. A. fæla. A. þeowode. A. ge-wyst-fullode. 30. A. speda. A. myltestru*m*. A. fætt; B. C. fǽt. A. cealf. 31. A. synd. 32. A. broðer. A. ge-ed-cucedo.

Various Readings.

24. ge-edcucude; for-wearð; met [*for* ge-funden]; wist-læcan. 25. yldra sunu; æccre; R. *om.* ham; geneahlæhte; ge-hyrde þonn*e*; weryd. 27. com [*for* is come]; of-slog; chealf. 28. fæder; hin. 29. R. *om.* to; feola geara; þeowude; tyccen; minu*m* freondu*m* ge-wist-fullude. 30. syððon; sunu; myltystrum; R. *om.* an; cealf. 31. eart; synt. 32. gewistfullian; for-þa*m*; broðor; ge-ed-cucude; ⁊ he is ge-met.

for*ð*on ðes sunu mīn dead wæs ⁊ eft-liofeð ɫ lifde gelosade ⁊ ge-moeted is ⁊
24 quia hic filius meus mortuus erat et reuixit perierat et inuentus est et

ongannon hriordagæ wæs ða sunu his ældra on lond ⁊ miððy gec*u*ome ⁊
coeperunt aepulari 25 erat autem filius eius senior in agro et cum ueniret et

geneolecde to huse geherde huislung ⁊ þ song ɫ ⁊ ge-ceigde enne of ðæm ðrælum
appropinquaret domui audiuit simphoniam et chorum 26 et uocauit unum de seruis

⁊ gefraignde huætd ða woeron ⁊ ðe ilca cuoeð him broðer ðin cuom ⁊ ofslog fader
et interrogauit quae haec essent 27 ísq*ue* dixit illi frater tuus uenit et occidit pater

ðin ging oxa fætt for*ð*on hal hine on-feng wrað wæs uut*edlice* ⁊ ne ualde
tuus uitulum saginatum quia saluum eum recepit 28 indignatus est autem et nolebat

inn-geonga fader for*ð*on his foerde ongann gebidda hine soð he ondsuarede cuoeð feder his
introire pater ergo illius egressus coepit rogare illum 29 at ille respondens dixit patri suo

heono feolo ɫ menigu*m* ger*um* ic hero ðē ⁊ næfre bebod ðin ic for*h*eald ⁊ ne æfra
ecce tot annis seruio tibi et num-quam mandatu*m* tuum praeterii et num-quam

gesaldes me ticgen þte mið friondu*m* minu*m* ic were gehriorded ah æft*er* ðon sunu ðin
dedisti mihi haedum ut cum ámicis meis epularer 30 sed postquam filius tuus

ðes seðe gefrett feh his mið port-cuoenu*m* cuom ðu ofsloge him ging oxo fætt
hic qui deuorauit sub-stantiam suam cum meretricib*us* uenit occidisti illi uitulum saginatum

⁊ he cuoe[ð] him sune ðu symble mec mið arð ⁊ alle mino ðino sint to hriordanne
31 at ipse dixit illi fili tú semper mecum és et omnia mea tua sunt 32 epulari

uut*edlice* ⁊ gefeage gehrisnelic woere for*ð*on broðer ðin ðes dead wæs ⁊ eft-lifde for*l*oren wæs ⁊
autem et gauder*e* oportebat quia frater tuus hic mortuus erat et reuixit perierat et

gemoetad is
inuentus est

[*Two leaves lost in the* Rushworth MS.]

CHAPTER XVI.

Ðys god-spel ge-byraꝺ on þære teoꝺan wucan ofer pentecosten. Homo quida*m* erat diues q*u*i habebat uillicu*m*. & hic. A. Homo quida*m* erat diues qui habebat uillicu*m* & hic diffamatus e*st* aput illu*m* quasi dissipas*set* bona ipsius. B.

1 Ða cwæꝺ he to his leorning-cnihtum Sum welig man wæs hæfde sumne gerefan se wearꝺ wiꝺ hine for-wreged swylce he his gód for-spilde.

2 þa clypode he hine ⁊ sǽde him; Hwi ge-hyre ic þis be þe. agyf þine scíre ne miht þu lencg tún-scíre bewitan;

3 Ða cwæþ se gerefa on his geþance; Hwæt do ic for-þa*m* þe min hlaford míne gerefscire fra*m* me nymꝺ; Ne mæg ic delfan. me sceamaꝺ ꝥ ic wædlige.

4 ic wát hwæt ic do ꝥ hig me on hyra hus onfón þon*ne* ic be-scíred beo fra*m* tunscíre;

5 Ða þa gafol-gyldan gegaderude wæron þa sǽde he þam forman. hu mycel scealt þú minu*m* hlaforde;

6 Ða sæde he hund sestra eles. þa sæde he hi*m*. nim þine feꝺere ⁊ site hraꝺe ⁊ writ fiftig;

7 Ða sæde he oꝺru*m* hu mycel scealt þu. þa cwæþ he hund mittena hwætes; Ða cwæꝺ he. ni*m* þine stafas ⁊ writ hundeahtatig;

8 Ða herede se hlaford þære unriht-wisnesse tungerefan. forþa*m* þe he gleawlice dyde. forþa*m* ꝺe ꝺisse worulde bearn. synd gleawran þises leohtes bearnum on þisse cneoresse;

Various Readings.

Cap. xvi. 1. A. *inserts* se *before* hæfde. 2. A. hwig. A. leng. 4. A. heora. 5. A. gegaderode. 6. A *inserts* hym *before* hund A. fyꝺere, *altered to* feꝺere. A. raꝺe. 8. unryht-wysnysse. (*The words* For-þam þe he gleawlice dede (*sic*) *have been supplied in* A. *in a late hand.*) B. C. synt. A. þysses. A. cneorysse.

CHAPTER XVI.

1 ÐA cwæꝺ he to his leorning cnihten Sum welig man wæs. se hæfde sumne ge-refe. se warꝺ wiꝺ hine forwreiged swilce he is god for-spilde.

Homo quida erat diues qu habebat uilli cum & hic di famatus est apud illum quasi dissipasset bona ipsius.

2 Ða cleopede he hine ⁊ saide him. Hwi here ich þis be þe. agyf þine scyre. ne miht þu leng tun-scyre be-witen.

3 Ða cwæd se ge-refe. on his ge-þanke. Hwæt do ic for-þan þe min hlaford mine gerefscype fram me nymd. Ne maig ic delfen. me scamed þæt ic wædlie.

4 Ich wat hwæt ic do þæt hyo me on heore hus on-fon. þanne ic be-scyred beo fram tun-scyre.

5 þa þa gafel-gyldo ge-gaderede wæren; þa saide he þam formen. hu michel scealt þu minen hlaforde.

6 þa saide he hund sestres eles. þa saide he him. nym þine feꝺere ⁊ site raꝺe ⁊ writ fiftig.

7 Ða saide he oꝺren. hu mycel scelt þu. þa cwæꝺ he. hund mittene hwætes. Ða cwæꝺ he nym þine stafes ⁊ writ hundehtetig.

8 Ða herede se hlaford þare unrihtwisnesse tun-ge-refen. for-þam þe he gleawlice dede. For-þan þe þisse worulde bearn synde gleawre þissere leohtes bearnen on þisse cneornysse.

Various Readings.

Cap. xvi. 1. *Rubric as in* H. -cnihtum; R. *om.* se (1*st time*); ge-reafe; wearꝺ; his god for-spillde. 2. clypode; sæde; ic; be-witon. 3. cwæꝺ; ge-þance; gereaf-scyre; nymꝺ; mæg; delfan; scameꝺ; wædlige. 4. hwat; heora; þonne. 5. gafol-; wæron; sægde; forman; mycel; minu*m*. 6. segde; sæde. 7. sægde; oꝺrum; scalt; mittena wætes; stafas; -eahtitig. 8. unrihtwisnysse; ge-reafan; dyde; synt; þisse [*for* þissere]; bearnv*m*; cneorysse.

CAP. XVI.

cuoeð ða æc to ðegnu*m* his monn sum wæs welig seðe hæfde geroefa
1 *Dicebat autem et ad discipulos suos homo quidam erat diues qui habebat uilicum * LXIII.

⁊ ðes gemersað wæs mið hine suoelce gespilde godo his ⁊ ceigde hine ⁊
et hic diffamatus est apud illum quasi dissipasset bona ipsius 2 et uocauit illum et

cuoeð him huætd ðis ic hero fro*m* ðe agef ɫ *for*geld rehto groefscíre ðines ųut*edlice* *for*ðon ne
ait illi quid hoc audio de té redde rationem uilicationis tuae iam enim non

mæht ðu gescira ɫ cuoð ða se groefa bituih him huætd ic doa*m* *for*ðon drih*ten* min benimeð
poteris uilicare 3 ait *autem* uilicus intra sé quid faciam quia d*ominus* meus aufert

fro*m* me ꝥ groefscire delfa ne mæg ic to giornanne ɫ to fær*anne* on ælme*ssum* ic sceomigo mín ic wat
á me uilicationem fodere non ualeo mendicare erubesco 4 scio

huæt ic doam ꝥte miððy of-adrifen ic biom fro*m* ðæm groefscire eft onfoað mec in husum híora miððy
quid faciam ut cum amotus fuero á uilicatione recipiant me in domos suas 5 con-

weron geceigedo *for*ðon syndrigu*m* scyldgum hlaferdes his cuoæð ðæm *for*ðmesto huu micel aht ðu
uocatis igitur singulis debitorib*us* domini sui dicebat primo quantu*m*

to geldan*ne* hlaferde minu*m* soð he cuoeð hundteantih ombras ɫ oeles ⁊ cuoeð him onfoh
debes domino meo 6 at ille dixit centum cados olei dixitque illi accipe

hleaf-gewritten ɫ unawritten ðín ⁊ sitt recone awritt fiftih æft*er* ðon to oðr*um* cuoeð ðu
cautionem tuam et sede cito scribe quinquaginta 7 deinde alio dixit tú

aec huu feolo aht ðu to seðe cuoeð hundtean*tih* i.xxx. mitto huætes cuæð ðæm onfoh stafas ðino ⁊
uero quantum debes qui ait centum choros tritici ait illi accipe literas tuas et

awrit .lxxx. ⁊ geherede se hlaford g*e*roefo unrehtwisnisses ꝥte hoglice dyde ɫ doend
scribe octoginta 8 et laudabit (*sic*) d*ominus* uilicum iniquitatis quia prudenter fecisset

*for*ðon suno ðisses woruldes betro hogo ɫ sunu*m* lehtes on cneoreso hiora sint
quia filii huius sæculi prudentiores filiis lucis in generatione sua sunt

---

[*Two leaves lost in the* Rushworth MS.]

9 ⁊ ic secge eow. wyrcað eow frynd of þisse worulde-welan unriht-wisnesse ꝥ hig onfon eow on ece eardung-stōwe þonne ge ge-teoriað;

Ðys gebyrað on wodnesdæg on þære teoðan ucan ofer pentecosten. Qui fidelis est in mynimo & maiore fidelis est. Si ergo & iniquo mammone fideles non fuistis. A.

10 Se þe ys on lytlum getrywe. se ys on maran getrywe ⁊ se þe ys on lytlum unriht-wis se ys eac on maran unrihtwis;

11 Gif ge on unriht-wisum weoruld-welan næron getrywe hwa betæhð eow ꝥ eower ys;

12 And gyf ge on fremedum nǣron getrywe hwa sylþ eow ꝥ eower ys;

13 Ne mæg nan þeow twam hlafordum þeowian. oððe he anne hatað ⁊ oðerne lufað. oððe he anum folgað ⁊ oðerne for-hogað; And ge ne magon gode þeowian ⁊ woruld-welan;

14 Ðas ðing ealle þa farisei gehyrdon þa ðe gifre wǣron. ⁊ hig hine tældon;

15 Þa cwæð he to him. ge synt þe eow sylfe beforan mannum geriht-wisiaþ. soðlice god can eowre heortan forþam þe beforan gode ys ascuniendlic ꝥ mannum heah ȳs;

16 Seo ǣ. ⁊ witegan oð iohannem. ⁊ of him is bodud godes rīce. ⁊ ealle on ꝥ strang-nysse wyrcað;

17 Eaðre is ꝥ heofen ⁊ eorðe gewiton þonne ān stæf of þære ǣ. fealle;

9 And ic segge eow wyrceð eow freond of þisse werold-weolen unrihtwisnesse. þæt hyo un-fon eow on echen earding-stowen þonne ge ge-teoriað.

10 Se þe is on litlen ge-treowe. se is on mare ge-treowe. Ænd se þe is on litlen unrihtwis. se is eac on maren unriht-wis.

Qui fidelis e[st] in minimo & maiore fideli[s] est.

11 Gyf ge on unrihtwisen weordwelan næren ge-treowe. hwa be-tæcð eow þæt eower is.

12 Ænd gyf ge on fremden næren ge-treowe. hwa syld eow þæt eower is.

13 Ne maig nan þeow twam hlaforden þewian. oððe he ænne hated. ⁊ oðerne lufeð. oððe he anen folgeð ⁊ oðer forhugeð. ⁊ ge ne muge gode þewian ⁊ weorlde-welan.

14 Ðas...

Various Readings.

9. A. weorulde-. A. un-ryhtwysnysse. 10. A. lytlum þingum ge-treowe. A. ge-tryowe. 11. A. *omits* on. 13. A. ænne. A. weoruld-. 14. *After* ðing, B. *has lost a leaf, down to* leorning-cnihtum *in v.* 1 *of Cap.* xvi. *The missing portion is supplied in a late hand.* 15. A. synd. B. þreow (*miswritten for* þe eow). A. ascunod. 16. A. strannysse.

Various Readings.

9. Ænd; wyrcað; -weolan; un-rihtwisnysse; ecan; -stowe. 10. *Rubric as in* H. littlum; getrywe (*2nd time*); littlum. 11. -wisum woruldwelan; getreawe; be-tachð. 12. fremdon næron; sylð. 13. mæg; þewyan; hatað; lufað; anum folgað; oðrum for-hugað. End; mage; weoruld-welan. 14. Ðas þing (*after which, without any break, follows* un-mihtlic, *which see in* Cap. xvii. 1. *The word* þing *has been erased in* H).

⁊ ic iuh cuoeðo doað ł wyrcas iuh friondas of wælom ł* unrehtwisnisses ꝥte miððy
9 et ego uobis dico facite uobis amicos de mamona iniquitatis ut cum

* . I. sirisc spréc.

gē losigað hia onfoað iuh in ða ēco huso seðe geleaf-ful is on lytelum ⁊ in
defeceritis recipiant uos in æterna tabernacula
10 qui fidelis est in minimo et in

marum geleaffull is ⁊ seðe in lytlum unreht is ⁊ in marum unrehtwis is gif forðon
maiori fidelis est et qui in modico iniquus *est* et in maiori iniqus est
11 si ergo

in un-rehtwiso .i. ðæt is diwl-gittsungo treofæsto gie ne weron ꝥte soð is hua gelefeð iuh
in iniquo mamonæ fideles non fuistis quod uerum est quis credit uobis

⁊ gif on uta-cund treofest gie ne wero ꝥ soð is hua seleð iuh ne ænig
12 et si in alieno fideles non fuistis quod uestrum est quis dabit uobis
13 *Nemo

* LXIII[I]. 191. v. mt. xluiii.

esne mæg tuæm hlaferdum gehera ł forðon enne gefiweð ł ⁊ oðerne lufæð ł anum
seruus potest duobus dominis seruire aut enim unum odiet et alterum diligit aut uni

æthrineð ł genehuað ⁊ oðerne forhogeð ł ne mago gie gode hera ⁊ ðæm diwle geherdon
adhaerebit et alterum condemnet non potestis deo seruire et mamonae
14 *Audiebant

* 192. x.

uutedlice alle ðas ða aeldo ðaðe weron gitsaras ⁊ teldon ł hlogon hine ⁊ cuoeð him gie
autem omnia haec pharisaei qui erant auari et deridebant illum
15 et ait illis uos

sindon ða ðe gie soðfæstigeð iuih foræ monnum god uutedlice wāt hearta iura forðon ꝥte
estis qui iustificatis uos coram hominibus deus *autem* nouit corda uestra quia quod

monnum heh ł worð is fracoð ł laað is mið gode æ ⁊ witgo oðð to
hominibus altum est abominatio est apud deum
16 *Lex et prophetae usque ad

* 193. u. mt. cu.

iohanne from ðæm ríc godes gemersad bið ł aboden bið ⁊ all in ꝥ hefig ł wyrcas
iohannen ex eo regnum dei euangelizatur et omnis in illud uím facit
17

eaðor is uutedlice ꝥ heofon ⁊ ꝥ eorðo ꝥte foregeleore ðon of æ ān merce ł stæfes heafud
*Facilius est autem caelum et terram praeterire quam de lege unum apicem

* 194. u. mt. xxx[iiii].

gefalla
cadere

[*Two leaves lost in the* Rushworth MS.]

18 Ælc man þe his wīf for-læt ⁊ oþer nimð se unriht-hæmð; ⁊ se ðe ꝥ forlætene wīf nimð se unriht-hæmð;

Ðis godspel ge-byrað on þone oðerne sunnan-dæg ofer pente-costen. Homo quida*m* erat diues. A.

19 Sum welig man wæs. ⁊ he wæs gescrydd mid purpuran ⁊ mid twine. ⁊ dæghwa*m*lice riclice gewist-fullude;

20 And sum wædla wæs on naman lazarus. se læg on his dura swyðe for-wundon.

21 ⁊ wilnode ꝥ he hine of his crumu*m* gefylde þe of his beode feollu*n*. ⁊ hi*m* nan man ne sealde. ac hundas comon ⁊ his wunda liccodon;

22 Ða wæs geworden ꝥ se wædla forð-ferde ⁊ hine englas bæron on habrahames greadan; þa wearð se welega dead ⁊ wæs on helle bebyrged;

23 Ða ahof he his eagan upp þa he on þa*m* tintregu*m* wæs. ⁊ geseah feorran abraha*m* ⁊ lazaru*m* on his greadan;

24 Ða hrymde he ⁊ cwæð. eala fæder abraha*m* gemilsa me. ⁊ send lazarum ꝥ he dyppe his fingres lið on wætere. ⁊ mine tungan gehǣle. forþa*m* þe ic eom on þis līge cwylmed;

25 Ða cwæð abraha*m*. eala sunu geþenc ꝥ þu god onfenge on þinu*m* līfe. ⁊ gelīce lazarus on-feng yfel. nu ys þes gefrefryd ⁊ þu eart cwylmed;

26 And on eallu*m* þissu*m* betwux ūs ⁊ eow is mycel dwolma getrymed. þa ðe willað heonon to eow faran ne magon. ne þanun faran hidere;

Various Readings.

18—26. *Lost in* B., *and supplied in a late hand.* 19. A. weliman [*for* welig man]. A. gescryd. A. gewystful-lode. 20. A. wedla. A. B. C. forwundod. 21. A. feollon; B. feollum (*sic*). B. *omits* ne. A. liccedon. 22. A. C. abrahames. 23. A. up. 24. A. ge-myltsa; C. gemiltsa. 24. A. gehæle, *altered to* gecæle. 25. A. gefre-frod. 26. A. betweox. B. eowe (*miswritten*). A. heonen; C. heonan. A. þanen.

eghuelc seðe *for*letas wif his ⁊ lædes oðero he syngiges ⁊ seðe ða ɫ ðio *for*leteno bið
18 *Omnis qui mittit uxorem suam et ducit alteram moechatur et qui dimissam * 195. [ii]. mt. exc. mr. cu.

fro*m* were ·lædeð he synngeð monn sum wæs welig ⁊ wæs gegearuad mið fellereade ⁊
a uiro ducit moechatur 19 *Homo quidam fuit diues et induebatur purpura et * LXU. 196. x.

mið linneno*m* ⁊ gehriordade dæg-huæm fegerlice ɫ licsendo ⁊ wæs sum ðærfe ɫ ðofond ðæs noma wæs
bysso et epulabatur cotidie splendide 20 et erat quidam mendicus nomine

lazarus seðe gelæg to dura his wundum full wilnade ꝥte were gefylled of screadungu*m* ða ðe
lazarus qui iacebat ad ianua*m* eius ulcerib*us* plenus 21 cupiens saturari de micis quae

gefeallon of bead ɫ disc ðæs wlonces ah huoeðre ⁊ ða hundas gecuomon ⁊ liccedon wund hund (*sic*)
cadeban*t* de mensa diuitis sed et canes ueniebant et lingebant ulcera eius

aworden wæs ða ꝥte wæs dead se ðorfendo ⁊ wero gelæded fro*m* englu*m* on barme abrahames
22 factum est autem ut moreretur mendicus et portaretur ab angelis in sinum abrahae

dead wæs ða æc se welig ɫ wlonc ⁊ bebyrged wæs in helle ahof ða ēgo his
mortuus est autem et diues et sepultus est 23 in inferno eleuans autem oculos suos

miððy were in tintergu*m* ɫ gesæh ab*raham* fearra ⁊ on barme his ⁊ he
cum esset in tormentis uidebat abraham á longe et lazarum in sinum eius 24 et ipse

cliopade cuoeð fæder ab*raham* gemiltsa me ⁊ send la*zarum* ꝥte in-depe ɫ hrinæ utaweard fingeres
clamans dixit pater abraham miserere mei et mitte lazarum ut intinguat extremum digiti

ðines In wætre ꝥte geceola tunga mīn ðe ic ðrouigo in ðisser lēgo ⁊ cuoeð
tui in aquam ut refrigeret linguam meam qui crucior in hac flamma 25 et dixit

him ab*raham* la sunu eft-ðencg ɫ gemona ꝥte ðu on-fenge gōda in life ðinu*m* ⁊ la*zarus* ongelic ða wyflo
illi abraham fili recordare quia recepisti bona in uita tua et lazarus similiter mala

nu ðon*ne* ðēs gefroefred bið ðu ǣc ðu bist geðro*u*ad ⁊ in ðissu*m* allu*m* bituih iuih
nunc *autem* hic consolatur tú uero cruciaris 26 et in his omnib*us* inter uos

⁊ usih dene ɫ pæð micel gefæstnad is ꝥte ða ðaðe wallað heona of*er*fara to iuh ne magon
et nos chaos* magnum firmatum est ut hi qui uolunt hinc transire ad uos non possint * L. chas, *altered by glossator to* chaos.

ne ðona hider of*er*cerre
neq*ue* inde huc transmeare

[*Two leaves lost in the* Rushworth MS.]

25. .... ðes gi-froefred bið ðu soðlice ðrowas ðu nu 26. ⁊ in ðæm allum bitwih iow ⁊ usih ðon*ne* pæð miclum cele gifæstnad is ꝥte ða seðe wilnað hiona ofer-fara to iow ne magun ne on dæge ðona hider ofer-fara ɫ cerra

27 Ða cwæð he fæder. ic bidde þe ꝥ ðu sende hine to mines fæder hūse.

28 ic hæbbe fíf gebroþru ꝥ he cyðe him ꝥ hig ne cumon on þissa tintrega stowe;

29 Þa sæde abraham him. híg habbað moysen ⁊ witegan. hig hlyston him;

30 Ða cwæð he. nese fæder abraham. ac hig doð dædbote gif hwylc of deaðe to him færð;

31 Ða cwæð he. gif hig ne gehyraþ moysen ⁊ þa witegan. ne hig ne gelyfað þeah hwylc of deaðe aríse;

CHAPTER XVII.

Ðys god-spel ge-byrað on þone oðerne frige-dæg ofer pentecosten. Inpossibile est ut non ueniant scandala. A. B. *adds*—Sed uæ homini per quem ueniunt, &c.

1 Ða cwæð he to his leorning-cnihtum un-mihtlic is ꝥ gedrefednyssa ne cuman. wa þam þe hig þurh cumað.

2 nyttre him wære ꝥ an cweorn-stan sy ge-cnytt abutan his swūran ⁊ sí on sǽ beworpen ðonne he gedréfe anne of þissum lytlingum;

3 Warniað eow. gyf þin broðor syngað cíd him;

4 And gif he on dæg seofan siþun syngað. ⁊ seofan siþun to þe on dæg gecyrred byð. ⁊ cwyð; Hit me of-þincð. forgyf hit him;

5 Ða cwæðon (*sic*) his apostolas drihten. ge-íc urne geleafan;

6 Ða cwæþ drihten gif ge hæfdon geleafan swa senepes corn. ge sædun þissun treowe sy ðu awyrt-walud ⁊ aplantud on sǽ. ⁊ hit hyrsumode eow;

Various Readings.

27—31. *Lost in* B., *and supplied in a late hand.* 28. A. heom. 30. C. habraham. B. færðe (*miswritten*).

Cap. xvii. 1. *The old text in* B. *begins again with* unmihtlic. A. cumon. 2. C. ac [*sic; for* an]. A. sig gecnyt. A. sweoran. A. sig [*for* sí]. A. gedrefde ænne. B. þysum. 4. A. seofen; C. seofon (1*st time*). A. syðum; *but* B. C. siþun (1*st time*). A. seofen syðum (2*nd time*). A. ofþyngð. A. me [*for* him]. 5. A. B. C. cwædon. 6. A. sædon. A. þyssum; B. þissun; C. þissum. A. sig. A. -walod. A. aplantod.

CHAPTER XVII.

1 . . . . un-mihtlich ys þæt ge-dræfednysse ne cunnen. wa þam þe hyo þurh cumað.

2 nytre hym wære þæt an cweornstan syo ge-cniht on-buten his sweoren. ⁊ syo on sæ ge-worpen þanne he ge-drefe ænne of þisen litlingen.

3 Warnied eow gyf þin broðer senegeð kyð him.

4 And gif he on ane daige seofe syðen senegeð. ⁊ seofen syðan to þe on daig gecyrred beoð. ⁊ cweð hit me of-þincð. forgif hit hym.

5 Þa cwæðen his apostles. drihten geeac urne ge-leafen.

6 Ða cwæð drihten. gyf ge hafden geleafen swa micel swa an senepes corn. ⁊ ge sæden þise treowe syo þu awirt-waled. ⁊ aplanted on sæ. ⁊ hit hersumede eow.

Various Readings.

Cap. xvii. 1. *The* Royal MS. *begins again with* unmihtlic ys þæt ge-drefednysse ne cuman. 2. ge-cnyt abuton; swuran; be-worpen þone; þysum lytlingum. 3. Warnið (*sic*); syngeað chyd. 4. Ǽnd; R. *om.* ane; daig seofan syðan synegað; seofon; byð; cwæð. 5. apostlas; ge-leafan. 6. hafdon ge-leafan; R. *om.* micel swa; senepas; R. *om.* ⁊ *before* ge; sædon þissum; awyrt-walud; aplantod.

⁊ cuoeð ic biddo *for*ðon ðec la fæder ꝥ ðu sende hine in hus fadores mines ic hafo
27 et ait rogo ergo té pater ut mittas eum in dom*um* patris mei 28 habeo

*for*ðon fifo broðro ꝥte gecyðed him ne æ̃c ða ꝥte hia cymo in stoue ðis cursungra ⁊
enim quinq*ue* fratres ut testetur illis ne et ipsi ueniant in locum hunc tormentorum 29 et

cuoeð him ab*raham* habbað mo*sen* ⁊ witgo gehere hia ðæm ilco*m* soð he cuoeð næsæ
ait illi abraham habent mosen et prophetas audiant illos 30 at ille dixit non

la fader ab*raham* ah gif huælc ł from deadu*m* færes to him hreonisse hia doeð cuoeð
pater abraham sed si quis ex mortuis ierit ad eos pænitentiam agent 31 ait

ða him gif mo*sen* ⁊ ða wit*go* ne geherað ł ne ðah gif huelc of deadu*m* arises
autem illi si mosen et prophetas non audiunt neq*ue* si quis ex mortuis surrexerit

gelefæð
credent

CAP. XVII.

⁊ to ðegnu*m* his cuoeð unmæhtiglic is ꝥte ne cymo ða ondspyrniso wæ ðon*ne* ðæm
1 *ET ad discipulos suos ait inpossibile est ut non ueniunt scandala uáe autem illi * LXUI. 197. ii. mt. clxxuiiii. mr. xcuiiii.

ðerh ðone hia cymes ðarflicro is him gif stan coern geseted se ymb suira his ⁊
per que*m* ueniunt 2 utillius (*sic*) est illi si lapis molaris inponatur circa collum eius et

ꝥte se geworpen in sæ̃ ðon ꝥte geondspyrne enne of lytlu*m* ðis behaldas iuih gif
proiciatur in mare quam ut scandalizet unum de pusillis istis 3 *Attendite uobis si * 198. u. mt. clxxxiii.

sinngigað se broðer ðin geðrea hine ⁊ gif hreonise doeð *for*gef him ⁊ gif ł ðæh
peccauerit frater tuus increpa illum et si pænitentiam egerit dimitte illi 4 *Et si * 199. u. mt. clxxxuii.

seofo siða gesynngiga in ðec ⁊ seofa siða on dæge gecerred bið ł gewoendet bið to ðe
septies in die peccauerit in té et septies in die conuersus fuerit ad té

cuoeðende gehreues mec *for*gef him ⁊ cuoedon ða ðegnas driht*ne* togeẽc ús geleafo
dicens paenitet me dimitte illi 5 *ET dixerunt apostoli d*omi*no adauge nobis fidem * LXUII. 200. u. mt. clxxu.

cuoeð ða drih*ten* gif gie hæfde geleafa suelce corn senep*es* gie cuoede ðisu*m* tree .i. heart-breer
6 dixit autem d*omi*n*us* si haberetis fidem sicut granum sinapis diceretis huic arbori moro

ofwy[*r*]trumia ł ⁊ of*er*-plontia ł gesette on sæ ⁊ hērsumiað iuh
eradicare et transplantare in mare et obediret uobis

---

27. ⁊ cwæð ic biddo *for*ðon ðec fæder ꝥte ðu sende hine in hus fædres mines 28. ic hafo *for*ðon fife gi-broðor ꝥte gi-cyðeð him ne ⁊ ec ða ðæt hiæ cyme in stowwe ðasse cursungra 29. ⁊ cwæð ðæm ł hi*m* abraha*m* hæfde moys*en* ⁊ witgu giherde hia 30. soð he cwæð nese la fæder . . . . ah gif hwelc from deadum færeð to him hreownisse hiæ ðoað 31. cweð ða him gif moysen ⁊ ða witgu ne giherdun ahne gif hwelc of deoðe ariseð gilefað

Cap. XVII. 1. ⁊ to ðegnum his cwæð unmæhtiglic is ꝥte ne cyme ða ondspyrnisse wæ ðon*ne* ðæm ðerh ðone cymeð 2. ðarof-licra is him gif stan cern inseted se ymb swira his ⁊ ꝥte se giworpen in sæ ðonne ðætte ge-ondspyrne enne of ðissum lytlum 3. bihaldas wutudl*ice* iowih gif synnige ðe broðer ðin giðreata hine ⁊ gif hreownisse doeð forgef him 4. ⁊ gif ðu siofo siðum on dæge gisyngað in ðec ⁊ siofo siðum on dæge gi-cerred bið to ðe cweðende giherað mec ⁊ forgef him 5. ⁊ cwedun ða ðegnas drihtnes ge-ec us gileofu 6. cwæð ða drih*ten* gif ge hæfde gileofu swa corn senepes ge cwede ðissum tree heort-brere of wyrtrumum ⁊ of plontu*m* gisette on sæ ⁊ her-sumigað iow

7 Hwylc eower hæfþ eregendne þeow;
Oððe scep læsgendne þam of þam ǽcere
ge-hworfenum. he him sona segð gá ⁊ site.

8 ⁊ ne segþ him gearw ꝥ íc éte ⁊ gyrt þe
⁊ þéna me þa hwile. þe ic éte ⁊ drince ⁊
syððan þu ytst ⁊ drincst;

9 Wenst þu hæfð se þeowa ænigne þanc.
forþam ðe he dyde ꝥ him beboden wæs. ne
wene ic;

10 Swa ys eow þonne ge doð eall ꝥ eow
beboden ys. cweþað unnytte þeowas we
synt we dydon ꝥ we dón sceolon;

Ðys gebyrað on þære syxteoðan wucan ofter pentecosten. Dum *iret iesus* in hierusalem transiebat per mediam. A. B. *adds*—samariam & galiam (*sic*).

11 ÐA he ferde to hierusalem. he eode
þurh midde samarian ⁊ galileam;

12 ⁊ þa he eode on sum castel him agén
urnon tyn hreofe weras. þa stodon hig feorran

13 ⁊ hyra stefna úp-ahofon ⁊ cwǽdon;
Hælend. bebeodend gemiltsa ús;

14 Ða he hig geseah þa cwæþ he; Gað
⁊ æt-ywað eow þam sacerdum; þa hig
ferdun hig wurdon geclænsude;

15 Ða hyra án geseah ꝥ he geclænsud
wæs þa cyrde he mid mycelre stéfne god
mærsiende.

16 ⁊ feoll to hys fotum. ⁊ him þancode ⁊
þes wæs samaritanisc;

17 Þa cwæþ se hælend him ⁊swariende;
Hu ne synt týn geclænsude hwær synt þa
nigone.

18 næs gemett se ðe agén-hwurfe. ⁊
gode wuldor sealde. buton þes ælfremeda;

Various Readings.

7. A. hergendne. C. læsgendene. 8. A. earwa [*for* gearw]. A. gyrd. 10. A. synd. A. B. C. sceoldon. 12. C. þe [*for* þa he]. A. ongean. 13. A. heora. B. C. stefne. 14. A. ferdon. A. geclænsode. 15. A. heora. A. ge-clænsod. A. mærsigende. 17. A. synd (*twice*). A. geclænsode. A. C. hwar. A. nygene. 18. A. ge-met. A. ongean-. A. eall-fremeda.

7 Hwilc eower hafd eriendne þeow. oððe
sceap læsgendne. þam of þam akere ge-
hworfene he him sone saigð gá ⁊ site.

8 ⁊ ne saigð hym gearewe þæt ich ete.
⁊ gert þe ⁊ þene me þa hwile þe ic ete ⁊
drinke. ⁊ seððan þu ætst ⁊ drincst.

9 wenst þu hafð se þeowe anig þanc for-
ðan þe he dyde þæt him be-boden wæs; ne
wene ich.

10 Swa is eow þanne ge doð eal þæt
eow beboden is. Cweðed un-nytte þeowes.
we synde. we dyden þæt we don scolden.

Dum iret *iesus* in ierusalem transiebat per mediam samariam & galileam.

11 ÞA he ferde to ierusalem he eode
þurh midde samariam ⁊ galileam.

12 ⁊ þa he eode on sum castel ⁊ him
agen urnen teon reofle weres. þa stoden
hio forren.

13 ⁊ heore stefne up-ahofen. ⁊ cwæðen.
hælend be-beodende ge-miltse us.

14 Þa he hyo ge-seah þa cwæð he. Gað
⁊ ateowiad eow þam sacerden. Ða hyo
ferden. hyo wurden ge-clænsede.

15 Ða heore an ge-seah þæt he ge-clænsed
wæs. þa cyrde he mid micelere stefne god
heriende.

16 ⁊ feoll to his foten. ⁊ him þancode.
⁊ þes wæs samaritanisc.

17 Þa cwæð se hælend hym andsweriende.
Hu ne synden teon ge-clænsede. hwær
synden þa nigene.

18 næs ge-mett se ðe agen-hwurfe. ⁊
gode wulder sealde buten þes ælfremede.

Various Readings.

7. hæfð eregendne; scep; æcere ge-hworfenum; segð. 8. se ð; gearwe; ic; girt; wile; drince; siððan; ytst. 9. hæfð; forðam; ic. 10. þonne; eall; bebodon; Cweðað; þeowas; synt; didon. 11. *Rubric;* Cum [*for* Dum]. 12. R. *om.* ⁊ *before* him; tyn reofe; hyo feorran. 13. hyora; cwædon; bebeodand ge-miltsa. 14. ateowiað; sacerdum; fyrdon; wurðen ge-clænsode. 15. heora; ge-clænsod; mersiende [*for* heriende]. 16. fotum. 17. andswerigende; sint tyn ge-clænsode; synd. 18. wuldor; butan.

huel ðon*ne* iuerra hafeð esne eriende ł foedende ł lesuande seðe miððy gecerde of
7 *Quis autem uestrum habens seruum arantem aut pascentem qui regresso de * 201. x.

londe cuoeðeð him sona of*er*-fær gehlinig ⁊ ne cuoeðeð him gearua ꝥte ic hriordege ⁊
agro dicet illi statim transi recumbe 8 et non dicet ei para quod cenem et

fore-gyrd ł ðec ⁊ embihta me ða huile ł ic ēto ⁊ drinco ⁊ æft*er* ðas ðu ge-ētes ⁊
praecinge té et ministra mihi donec manducem et bibam et post haec tú manducabis et

dringes ðu ahne ðonc hafeð esne ðæm for*ð*on dyde ða ðe him gehaten hæfde ł geheht
bibes 9 numquid gratiam habet seruo illi quia fecit quae sibi imperauerat

ne woeno ic sua æc iuih miððy gedoað alle ða ðe bebodeno sint iuh cuoeðas esnas
non puto 10 sic et uos cum feceritis omnia quae praecepta sunt uobis dicite serui

ðorleaso we sind*on* ꝥte us reht wæs ł to doane we dydon ⁊ aworden wæs miððy eode in
inutiles sumus quod debuimus facere fecimus 11 *Et factum est dum iret in * LXUIII.

hier*usalem* of*er*-foerde ðerh middu*m* ða lioda ⁊ ⁊ mið-ðy innfoerde sum oðer
hierusalem transiebat per media*m* samariam et gallilæa*m* 12 et cum ingrederetur quod-dam

werc togægnes urnon him tea wæras hreafo ða stodon fearra ⁊ ahofon
castellum occurrerunt ei decem uiri leprosi qui steterunt á longe 13 et leuauerunt

ꝥ stefn cuoeðendo hæl*end* hæsere ł milsa user ða ꝥte gesæh cuoeð gaað æd-eauað
uocem dicentes *iesu* praeceptor miserere nostri 14. quos ut uidit dixit ite ostendité

iuih ðæm sacerdu*m* ⁊ aworden wæs mið-ðy foerdon geclænsad woeron an uut*edlice* of ðæm
uos sacerdotibus et factum est dum irent mundati sunt 15 unus autem ex illis

ꝥ ł suæ ge-sæh ꝥte geclænsad wæs eft-færende wæs mið miclo stefne gemiclade ł ðone god
ut uidit quia mundatus est regressus est cum magna uoce magnificans d*eum*

⁊ gefeall on onsione f*or*a fotu*m* his ðoncungo dyde ł doend ⁊ ðes wæs hæðin
16 et cecidit in faciem ante pedes eius gratias agens et hic erat samaritanus

geonduarde ða se hæl*end* cuoeð ahne teno geclænsad woeron ⁊ ða nigona huer sint
17 respondens autem *iesus* dixit nonne decem mundati sunt et nouem ubi sunt

ne is gemoetet seðe eft-cuome ⁊ salde wuldor ł ðongu*n*ng gode buta ðes utacunda ł ellðiodig
18 non est inuentus qui rediret et daret gloriam d*eo* nisi hic alienigena

---

7. hwelc ðon*ne* iower hæfeð esne eriende ł scip foedende seðe gicerde of londe cwæð him sona ofer-fær gihlionunga 8. ⁊ ne cweoðað gearwa me ðætte ic giriordige ⁊ for-gyrd ðec ⁊ embihta me ða hwile ic ete ⁊ ic drince ⁊ æfter ðas ðu gi-etes ⁊ drinces 9. ahne ðonc hæfeð esne ðæm forðon dyde ðaðe him gihaten hæfde ne woeno ic 10. swa ⁊ iowih miððy ge doas alle ðaðe bibodene sindun iow cweoðas esnas ðorleose we sindun ðætte unreht wæs to doanne we dydon 11. ⁊ aworden wæs miððy eode in hier*usa-lem* of*er*-foerde ðerh midne ða liode ⁊ . . . 12. ⁊ miððy infoerde sum oðer werc togægnes urnon him tea wearas hreofe ða stodun fearra 13. ⁊ ahofon stefne cweðende hæl*end* hæsere milsa user 14. ða ðæt gisæh cwæð gað æt-eowað iowih ðæm sacerdum ⁊ aworden wæs miððy foerdun giclænsade werun 15. an wutudl*ice* of ðæm ꝥ gi-sæh ðætte giclænsad wæs eft-færende wæs mið micelre stefne gimicladun ðone god 16. gifeoll on onsione fore fotum his ðancunge dyde ⁊ ðes wæs hæðen 17. giondworde ða hæl*end* ah ne teno giclænsade werun ⁊ nione hwer sindun 18. ne is gimoeted seðe eft-come ⁊ salde wuldor gode buta ðes utacunda ł elðiodig

19 Ða cwæð he. arís ⁊ gá forþam þe ðin geleafa þe halne gedyde;

Interrogabant *iesum* pharisei quando uenit regnum *dei*.

20 Þa ahsodon hine þa farisei hwænne godes ríce cóme; Ða ⁊swarude he ⁊ cwæð. ne cymð godes [ríce] mid begymene

21 ne hig ne cweðaþ efne her hyt ys. oððe þar. godes ríce is betwynan eow;

22 Þa cwæð he to his leorning-cnihtu*m*. þa dagas cumað þon*ne* ge gewilniað ꝥ ge geseon anne dæg mannes sunu ⁊ ge ne geseoð.

23 ⁊ hig secgað eow her he is. ⁊ þar he is. ne farege ne ne fyliað;

24 Witodlice swa se líg-ræsc lyhtende scinð under heofone on þa ðing þe under heofone synt. swa bið mannes sunu on his dæge;

25 Æryst hi*m* gebyreð ꝥ he fela þinga þolige. ⁊ beon fram þisse cneorysse aworpen.

26 ⁊ swa on noes dagum wæs gewórden swa beoð mannes suna to-cyme.

27 hig ǽtun. ⁊ drúncon. ⁊ wifodon. ⁊ wæron to gyftu*m* gesealde. oð þæne dæg þe noe on erke* eode. ⁊ flód cóm ⁊ ealle forspilde;

* *over an erasure.*

28 Eall-swa wæs geworden on loðes dagu*m* hig ǽtun. ⁊ druncon. ⁊ bohton. ⁊ sealdon. ⁊ plantedon. ⁊ timbrudon;

29 Soðlice on þa*m* dæge þe loð eode of sodoma hyt rínde fýr ⁊ swefl of heofone. ⁊ ealle forspilde;

19 Ða cwæd he aris ⁊ ga. for-þan þin ge-leafe þe halne ge-dyde.

Interrogab[ant] iesum phar[isei] quando u[enit] regnum de[i].

20 ÞA axoden hine þa farisej hwanne godes rice come. Ða andswerede he ⁊ cwæð ne cymd godes rice mid be-gemene.

21 ne hyo ne cweðað. efne her hit is. oððe þær; godes rice is be-twenan eow.

22 Þa cwæð he to his leorning-cnihten. þa dages cumæð þanne ge ge-wilnieð þæt ge ge-seon ænne daig mannes sunu. ⁊ ge ne seoð.

23 ⁊ hy seggeð eow her he ys. ⁊ þær he is. ne fare ge ne ne felgieð.

24 Witoðlice swa se leitres* lihtende scind under heofene on þa þing þe under heofene synde. swa byð mannes sune on his daige.

* H. leitre[s] *with* c *ex*[*pu*]*ncted.*

25 Ærest him ge-byreð þæt he fela þinge þolie ⁊ beon fram þisse cneorisse aworpen.

26 ⁊ swa on noes dagen wæs ge-worðen. swa beoð mannes sune to-kyme.

27 Hyo æten ⁊ druncan ⁊ wifeden ⁊ wæren to gyfte ge-sealde. oððe þane daig þe noe to earke eode; ⁊ flod com ⁊ ealle for-spilde.

28 Eall-swa wæs ge-worðen on lothes dagen ⁊ hyo æten ⁊ druncan. ⁊ bohten ⁊ sealden. ⁊ planteden ⁊ tymbreden.

29 Soðlice on þam daige þe loth eode of sodome hit rinde fyr ⁊ swefl of heofene. ⁊ ealle for-spilde.

Various Readings.

19. A. *om.* þe *before* ðín. 20. A. B. C. acsodon. A. ⁊swarode. A. B. C. *retain* ríce, *which the* Corpus MS. *omits.* 22. A. ænne. A. ⁊ þar he ys ⁊ þar he ys (*repeated*). A. fare ge; B. C. farege. A. B. C. fyligeað. 24. A. synd. 25. A. Ærest. A. fæla. 26. A. byð. 27. A. æton. A. wyfedon. A. þone. A. earce; B. erhe, *alt. to* erce; C. erke. 28. A. æton. A. timbredon; B. C. timbrudun.

Various Readings.

19. cwæð; geleafa. 20. (*In rubric,* d*e*i); axodon; cymð; begymene. 21. betwynan. 22. -cnihtum; dagas cumað þonne; ge-wilniað; anne dæg. 23. hyo segged; fyligeað. 24. lyg-ræsc; scynð; heofone (*twice*); synt. 25. þolige. 26. dagun; ge-worden; byð; suna to-cyme. 27. ætun; wifoden; wæron; gyfton; þo*n*ne dæg; on erke [*for* to earke]. 28. ge-worden; dagon; R. *om.* ⁊ *before* hyo æten; druncon; bohton; sealdon; plantodon; timbredon. 29. sodoma; heofonum.

ʒ cuoeð ðæm aris gaa forðon geleafo ðin ðec hal dyde gefrognen wæs ðonne * LXUIIII
19 et ait illi surge uade quia fides tua té saluum fecit 20 *INterrogatus autem 202. u. mt. cclu.

from huoenne cymmeð ríc godes ondsuarede him ʒ cuoeð ne cymeð ric godes mið
á pharisaeis quando uenit regnum dei respondit eis et dixit non uenit regnum dei cum

ofer ł fora-gemnise ne cuoeðas heono her ł heono ðer heono forðon ríc godes bituih iuh
obseruatione 21 neque dicent ecce hic aut ecce illic ecce enim regnum dei intra uos

is ʒ cuoeð to ðegnum cymeð dagas ðonne gie wilnias gesea enne doeg sunu
est 22 *Et ait ad discipulos uenient dies quando desideretis uidere unum diem filii * 203. x.

monnes ʒ ne geseað ʒ hia cuoeðað iuh heono her heono ðer nallað gie gâa ne
hominis et non uidebitis 23 *Et dicent uobis ecce hic ecce illic nolite ire neque * 204. ii. mt. ccliii. mr. cxluiii.

ge-fylges gie forðon ł sua legeð-slæht scímande (*sic*) ł of heofnum on ða ða ðe under heofne sind
sectemini 24 *Nam sicut fulgor coruscans de sub cælo in ea quae sub cælo sunt * 205. u. mt. cclui.

scineð on ða wisa bið sunu monnes on dæge his ærist uutedlice gehriseð him feolo
fulget ita erit filius hominis in die sua 25 *Primum autem oportet illum multa * 206. ii. mt. clxuiii. mr. lxxxiii.

geðrouia ł geðolia ʒ þte he se forcumen from cneoreso ðasum ʒ suæ aworden wæs on dagum
pati et reprobari á generatione hac 26 *Et sicut factum est in diebus * 207. u. mt. cclxi.

noes suæ bið æc on dæg sunu monnes brecon ʒ druncon wifo lædon ʒ
noe ita erit et in die filii hominis 27 edebant et bibebant uxores ducebant et

weron sald to brydloppum oðð on dæg of ðæm inn-eade in ærce ʒ cuom þ flód ʒ
dabantur ad nuptias usque in diem qua intrauit noe in arcam et uenit diluuium et

losade ł spilde alle ongelic sua aworden wæs on dagum lothes êton ʒ druncon
perdidit omnes 28 *Similiter sicut factum est in diebus loth edebant et bibebant * 208. x.

bohton ʒ bebohton gesetton ł getimberdon ðæm dæg ðonne foerde of ðæm burgum
emebant et uendebant plantabant aedificabant 29 qua die autem exiit loth á sodomis

feall þ fyr ʒ þ cuic-fyr of heofnum ʒ alle gespilde
pluit ignem et sulphur de caelo et omnes perdidit

---

19. ʒ cwæð ðæm aris ʒ gaa forðon gileofo ðin ðec halne gidoeð 20. gifrognen wæs ðonne from aldormonnum hwenne cymeð rice godes ondsworade him ʒ cwæð 21. ne cymeð rice godes mið ofergefnisse ne cweoðas heono her ł heono ðer heono forðon rice godes bitwih iow is 22. ʒ cwæð to ðegnum his cumað dagas ðonne ge wilnigas gisea enne dæg sunu monnes ʒ ne giseað 23. ʒ cweðeð iow heono iow her ʒ heono ðer nallað ge gaa ne ge-fylgas ge 24. forðon swa legeð-slæht scinende of heofne in hir (*sic*) ðaðe of heofne sint scineð on ða wise bið sunu monnes on dæge swa 25. ærist wutudlice giriseð him feolu gi-ðrowiga ʒ ðætte forcumen from cneoreswum ðassum 26. ʒ swa aworden wæs on dagum noes swa bið ʒ.... suno monnes 27. brecon ʒ drincon ʒ wif læddon ʒ werun sald to brydhlopum oððe on dæge of ðæm in-eode noe in erce ʒ com ðe flod ʒ spilde alle 28. ongilic swa aworden wæs on dagum lothes etun ʒ druncon bohton ʒ bibohtun gisettun ʒ gi-timbradun 29. ðæm dagum ðonne foerde loð of ðæm burgum.... gifeoll ðæt fyr ʒ cwic-fyr of heofne ʒ alle gispilde

30 Æfter þysum þingum bið on þam dæge þe mannes sunu onwrigen bið

31 on ðam dæge se ðe bið on þécene ⁊ his fatu on húse. ne stihð he nyðer ꝥ he hig nime; And se ðe bið on æcere. ne went he on-bæc;

32 Beoð gemyndige loðes wífes.

33 swa hwylc swa secð his sawle ge-dón hále se hig for-spilþ; ⁊ swa hwylc swa hig forspilþ se hig gelif-fæstað;

34 Soðlice ic eow secge on þære nihte beoð twegen on bedde an byð genumen ⁊ oðer bið for-læten;

35 Twa beoð ætgædere grindende. an bið genumen ⁊ oðer læfed;

36 Twegen beoð æt æcere. an bið genumen ⁊ oðer bið læfed;

37 Þa cwædon hig to him. hwar drihten; Ða cwæþ he. swa hwar swa se lichama bið þyder beoð earnas gegaderud;

CHAPTER XVIII.

[Iu]dex quidam erat [in] ciuitate qui [de]um non timuit neque [h]ominem. B.

1 Ða sæde he him sum big-spel ꝥ hit ys riht ꝥ man symle gebidde ⁊ na geteorige

2 ⁊ þus cwæð; Sum déma wæs on sumere ceastre se god ne ondred ne nanne man ne onþracude;

3 Ða wæs sum wudewe on þære ceastre. þa com heo to him ⁊ cwæð; Wrec me wið minne wiðer-winnan;

Various Readings.

34. B. C. twegyn. A. læfed [*for* bið for-læten]. 35. A. oðer byð læfed. 36. A. on [*for* æt]. 37. A. gegaderod.

Cap. xviii. 1. A. big-spell. A. symble. 2. A. sumre. A. onþracode. 3. C. *om.* sum. A. wuduwe.

30 Æfter þisen þingen byð on þam daige þe mannes sune un-wrogen beoð.

31 ⁊ on þam daige se þe byð on þecene ⁊ his fate on huse. ne stihgð he niðer þæt he hyo nyme. ⁊ se þe byð on akere; ne went he on-bæc.

32 Beoð ge-myndige lothes wifes.

33 swa hwilc swa secð his sawle ge-don hæle. he hyo for-spilð. ⁊ swa hwilc swa hyo for-spilð; seo hyo ge-liffest.

34 Soðlice ic eow segge on þare nihte beoð twegen on bedde. an beoð ge-numen ⁊ oþer for-læten.

35 Twa byð æt-gadere grindende. an beoð ge-numen ⁊ oðer lefed.

36 Twegen byð æt akere an byð ge-numen ⁊ oðer beoð lefed.

37 Ða cwæðen hyo to hym. hwær drihten. Ða cwæð he swa hwær swa se lichama byð þyder beoð earnes ge-gadered.

CHAPTER XVIII.

1 ÞA saigde he heom sum byspell þæt hit is riht þæt man symle ge-bidden. ⁊ na ge-teorige.

Iudex quidam erat in ciuitate qui deum timuit nec hominem.

2 and þus cwæð. Sume dema wæs on sumer cestre. se god ne on-dredde ne nenne man ne on-þracode.

3 Ða wæs sum wudewa on þare cestre; þa com hyo to him ⁊ cwæð. Wrec me wið minne wiðer-winne.

Various Readings.

30. Efter þisum þingum; un-wrygen bið. 31. R. *om.* ⁊ *before* on; stihð; æcere. 33. se hyo ge-lif-fæsteð. 34. bið (*twice*); for-læton. 35. bið (*twice*); læfed. 36. bið (*thrice*); acere; læfed. 37. hwar; bið (*for* byð); beoð (*as in* H.).

Cap. xviii. 1. *Rubric as in* H. sægde; byg-spell; gebidde. 2. Sum; sumere ceastre; on-drædde; nanne. 3. ceastre; -winnen.

æfterr ðas bið ðæm dæg sunu ðe monnes æd-eaued bið on ðær tíd ða ðe
30 secundum haec erit qua die filius hominis reuelabitur 31 *IN illa hora qui * 209. ii. mt. ccxluiii. mr. cxliii.

biðon in hrof ⁊ fato his in hus ne ofdune stigeð to niomanne ða ⁊ seðe on lónd ongelíc
fuerint in tecto et uasa eius in domo ne descendat tollere illa et qui in agro similiter

ne awoendað on-bæcc gemyndigo wosað wif lothes seðe suahuelc soecað sauel
non redeant retro 32 *Memores estote uxoris loth 33 †Quicumque quaesierit animam * 210. x. † 211. iii. mt. xcuii. io. cu.

his hal gewyrca spilleð hia ⁊ seðe sua gespilleð hia gelif-fæstað hia ic cuoeðo
suam saluam facere perdet illam et quicumque perdiderit illam uiuificauit eam 34 *Dico * 212. u. mt. cclxi [i].

iuh ðæm næht biðon tuoege in hrofe anum an genumen bið ⁊ oðer forleten bið
uobis illa nocte erunt duo in tecto uno unus assumetur et alter relinquetur

tuoege biðon ge-timbras ł grindas on an an ge-onfenge bið ⁊ oðero forleten bið tuoege
35 duae erunt molentes in unum una assumetur et altera relinquetur 36 duo

on lond an bið genumen ⁊ oðer forleten bið onduardon ł cuoedon him huer drihten seðe
in agro unus assumetur et alter relinquetur 37 *Respondentes dicunt illi ubi domine qui * 213. u. mt. cclnii.

cuoeð him suæ huer bið ðe lichoma ðer gesomnad biðon earnas
dixit eis ubi-cumque fuerit corpus illuc congregabuntur aquilae

CAP. XVIII.

cuoeð ða æc ðæt biseno to him ꝥte ł forðon gehriseð ł behoflic is symble gebidda ⁊
1 *Dicebat autem et parabolam ad illos quomodo oportet semper orare et * LXX. 214. x.

ne gesuica cuoeð doema sum wæs in summe ceastra seðe god ne ondrearde
non deficere 2 dicens iudex quidam erat in quadam ciuitatem (*sic*) qui deum non timebat

⁊ ðone monno ne sceomade ł widiua uutedlice sum wæs in ceastra ðær ⁊ gecymeð ł cuome
et hominem non reuerebatur 3 uidua autem quaedam erat in ciuitate illa et ueniebat

to him cuoeð wræc ðu mec of wiðerwordo minum
ad eum dicens uindica me de aduersario meo

---

30. æfter ðisse bið ðæm dæge sunu monnes æt-eowed bið 31. on ðær tide ðaðe bioðon on hrofe ⁊ fato his in huse ne dune astigeð to niomanne ða ⁊ seðe on londe ongelic ne āwendeð on-bæc 32. gimyndge wosað wif lothes 33. seðe swa hwelc ðonne soeceð sawle his hale doeð spillet hia ⁊ seðe miððy swa gispilleð gilif-fæstað hia 34. ic cweðo ðonne iow on ðær næht bioðun twoege on hrofe anum an ginumen bið ⁊ oðer for-leten bið 35. twoege grundas bioðon on anum an on-fenge bið ⁊ oðer forleten bið 36. twoege on londe an ginumen bið ⁊ oðer forleten bið 37. giondwordun cwedun him hwer drihten seðe ⁊sworað him swa hwer ðonne bið ðe lichoma ðer gisomna bioðon earnas

Cap. XVIII. 1. cwæð ða ðonne ⁊ ða bisine to him ðætte forðon giriseð symle gebidda ⁊ ne giswica 2. cwæð ðe doema bereð (*sic*) sum wæs in sumre cæstre seðe god ne on-dreord ⁊ ðone monno ne scomade 3. widuwe wutedlice sum wæs in cæstre ðær ⁊ gi-comun to hir cwæð wrec ðu mec of wiðer-wordra ðinum (*sic*)

4 Ða nolde he langre tide. æfter *þam* þa cwæþ he. þeah ic god ne ondræde. ne ic mán ne onþracige

5 þeah forþ*am* þe ðeos wuduwe me is gra*m* ic wrece hig. þe-læs heo æt neahstan cume me behropende;

6 Ða cwæð drihten. gehyrað hwæt se unriht-wisa dema cwyð;

7 Soþlice ne deð god his gecorenra wrace clypiendra to hi*m* dæges ⁊ nihtes. ⁊ he geþyld on hi*m* hæfþ;

8 Ic eow secge ꝥ he raþe hyra wrace deð; Ðeah-hwæþere wenst þu ðænne mannes sunu cymð. gemét he geleafan on eorðan;

9 Ða cwæð he to sumu*m* þis big-spel þe on hig sylfe truwedon ⁊ oðre for-hogodon;

Ðys ge-byrað on þære endlyftan wucan ofter pentecosten. Duo homines ascenderunt in templu*m*. A. Duo homines ascendebant in templu*m* ut orarent. B.

10 Twegen men ferdun to sumu*m* temple ꝥ hig hig gebædun an sundor-halga ⁊ oðer man-full;

11 Ða stód se fariséus ⁊ hine þus gebæd. god. þe ic þancas dó. for-þam þe ic ne eom swylce oðre men. reaferas unriht-wise. unriht-hæmeras. oððe eac swylce þes mánfulla;

12 Ic fæste tuwa on ucan. ic sylle teoþunga ealles þæs þe ic hæbbe;

13 Ða stód se man-fulla feorran ⁊ nolde furðun his eagan ahebban úp. to *þam* heofone ac he beot his breost ⁊ cwæþ; God beo þu milde me syn-fullu*m*;

4 Þa nolde ne langere tide. Æfter þam þa cw̄. he.

5 þeah ich god ne on-dræde. ne ic man ne on-þracige. þeah for-þan þe þeos wudewe me is gram. ich wreke hyo. þe-læs hyo æt nextan cume me be-ropende.

6 Þa cwæð drihten. ge-hyreð hwæt se unrihtwise deme cweeð (*sic*).

7 Soðlice ne deeð god his ge-corenra wrace cleopiende to hym daiges ⁊ nihtes; ⁊ he ðeld on him hafð.

8 Ich eow segge þæt he raðe heore wræce deð. Þeah-hwæðere wenst þu þanne mannes sune cymð. ge-met he ge-leafen on eorðan.

9 Ða cwæð he to sumen þis by-spell. þe on hyo selfe truweden. ⁊ oðrum for-hugodon.

10 Twegen men ferden to sume temple ꝥ ꝥ hyo; hyo ge-bæden. an sunderhalge. ⁊ an manfull.

Duo homines ascendebant in templ*u*m ut orarent.

11 Ða stod se phariseus ⁊ hine þus gebed. god þe ich þances do. for-þan ich ne em swilche odre men. reaferes unrihtwise. unriht-hameðes. oððe eac swylc þes manfulle.

12 Ic faeste twige on wuca. ic gife teondunge ealles þas þe ich hæbbe.

13 Ða stod se manfulla feorran ⁊ nolde for-ðan his eagen ahebben up to þam heofene. ac he beot his breost ⁊ cwæð. God beo þu milde me senfulle.

Various Readings.

4. A. men. A. onþracie. 5. A. þeh. A. wudewe. A. þy-læs. A. nycstan. 7. A. clypigendra. 8. A. heora. A. þonne. 9. A. B. C. for-hogedon. 10. A. ferdon. A. gebædon. A. sunder-. 11. C. neom [*for* ne eom]. 12. A. wucan. 13. A. forþan.

Various Readings.

4. langre. 5. þeh ic; for-þam; weduwe; ic wrece. 6. un-ritwisa dema cwyð. 7. deð; ge-corenenra (*sic*); clypiende; dæges; ge-ðeld; hæfð. 8. Ic; hyra; þonne; ge-leafan. 9. sumu*m*; big-spell; sylfe truwoden. 10. *Rubric as in* H.; ferdon; sumu*m*; sundor-halga; manful. 11. gebæd; ic; for-ðan þe ic ne eom; oðre; reaferas; unriht-hameras oðð; swylce; manfulla. 12. feste twuge; wucan; ic sylle teoþunga; þæs; ic habbe. 13. eagan ahæbben; heofone; bet; sinfullum.

⁊ ne walde ðerh menigo ł miclo ł feolo tíd ł æft*er* ðas ða cuoeð bituih hi*m** ⁊ ðah god
4 et nolebat per multum tempus post haec autem dixit intra sé etsi d*eu*m *. i. se doema.

ne ondredo ic ne monno sceomigo huoeðre *for*ðon woedo ł hefig wæs me ðio ł ðas widiua
non timeo nec hominem reuereor 5 tamen quia molesta est mihi haec uidua

ic wræco ðailco ꝥte on endo ł æt nesta cymeð geteleð ł mec cuoeð ða se hlafard
uindicabo illam né in nouissimo ueniens suggillet me 6 ait autem d*omin*us

geherað huæd se doema un-rehtwisnise cuoeð god ne doeð ꝥ wræcco ðara gecorenra
audite quid iudex iniquitatis dixit 7 d*omin*us autem non faciet uindictam electorum

his cliopendra to him dæge ⁊ næht ⁊ geðuild hæfeð on ðæm ic cuoeðo iuh
suorum clamantium ad se die ac nocte et patientiam habebit in illis 8 dico uobis

ꝥte ræðe doeð wræcce ðara soð huoeðre sunu monnes miððy cymes woenist ðu ꝥte gemoete
quia cito faciet uindictam illorum uerum-tamen filius hominis ueniens putas inue-

ł infinde geleafo on eorðo cuoeð ða æc to su*mmum* ðaðe on him gelefdon ł getreoudon
niet fidem in terra 9 *Dixit autem et ad quosdam qui in sé confidebant * LXXI.

suæ soðfæsto ⁊ aweredon ł teldon ða oðoro geddung ðios tuoege menn astigon
tamquam iusti et aspernabantur ceteros parabolam istam 10 duo homines ascenderunt

in temple ꝥte gebedon an wæs ⁊ oðer wæs bærsynig se stód ðas
in templum ut orarent unus pharisaeus et alter publicanus 11 pharisaeus stans hæc

mið him gebæd gode ðoncungo ic dóe ðe ꝥte neam ic suæ ða oðoro monna ned-niomo
apud sé orabat d*e*o gratias ago tibi quia non sum sicut ceteri hominum raptores

unsoð-fæsto dernel*icgende* suælce uut*edlice* ðes bærsyn*igo* ic fæsto tuigo in wico teigðuncgas
iniusti adulteri uelut etiam hic publicanus 12 ieiuno bís in sabbato decimas

ic sello allra ðaðe ic ah ł agnigo ⁊ ðe bærsyn*nigo* fearra to gestod ne walde ne ða ego
dó omnium quae possideo 13 et publicanus á longe stans nolebat nec oculos

to heofne ahebba ah geslog breost his cuoeðende god milt-heort ł wæs ðu me
ad cælum leuare sed percutiebat pectus suum dicens d*eu*s propitius esto mihi

synnful*lum*
peccatori

---

4. ⁊ ne walde ðerh monige tide æfter ðisse ða cwæð bitwih him ⁊ gif god ne on-dredo ic ne monno scomiga 5. forðon wedo hefig is ł wæs me ðios widwe ic wreco ðailco ðætte ne ende cymeð giteleð mec 6. cwæð ða drih*ten* giherað hwæt se doema unrehtwisnisse cwæð 7. god ða ne doeð ⁊ ða wraco ðara gicorenra hiora cliopendra to him dæg ⁊ nocte (*sic*) ⁊ giðyld hæfeð in ðæm 8. ic cweðo ðonne iow ðætte hræðe doeð wraco ðara soð hweðre suno monnes cymeð miððy ꝥte gimitte gileofo on eorðo 9. cwæð ða ⁊ ec to sumum ðaðe on hine gilefdun swa swa soðfæste ⁊ aweredon ł teldon ða oðre geddunge ðios 10. twoege men astigun on tempel ðæt gebedun an wæs ældra ⁊ oðer bear-swinig 11. se phar*iseus* stod ðes mið him gibæd god ðoncunc ic doe ðe *for*ðon ne am ic swa oðre menn ned-nioma unsoðfæste ðon*ne* lice (*sic*) swelce wutudl*ice* ðes bear-swinigo 12. ic fæsto twige on wica tegðunge gode alra ðaðe ic ah 13. ⁊ ðe bear-swinigo fearra stod ne walde ne ða ego to heofne ahebba ah sloge breost his ic cweðo (*sic*) god mild-heort wes ðu me synfullu*m*

14 Sóþlíce ic eow secge ꝥ þes ferde geriht-wisud to his huse. for-þam þe ælc þe hine úpp-áhefð bið genyðerud. ⁊ se þe hine nyðerað byð úpp-ahafen;

15 Ða brohton hig cild to him ꝥ he hig æt-hrine; þa his leorning-cnihtas hig gesawon híg ciddon him;

16 Ða clypode se hælend hig to him. ⁊ cwæð; Lǽtað þa lytlingas to me cuman ⁊ ne for-beode ge hig swylcera ys godes ríce;

17 Soðlice ic eow secge swa hwylc swa ne on-fehð godes ríce swa swa cild. ne gæð he on godes ríce;

18 Ða ahsode hyne sum ealdor. lareow. hwæt do ic ꝥ ic ece lif hæbbe;

19 Þa cwæð se hælend hwi segst þú mé góde. nis nán man god buton god ána;

20 Canst þu þa bebodu. ne of-slyh ðu. ne fyrena þu. ne stel þu. ne leoh þu; Wurþa þinne fæder ⁊ þine modor;

21 Ða cwæð he eall þis ic heold of mínre geoguþe;

22 Ða cwæð se hælend án þing þé is wana. syle eall ꝥ ðu hæfst. ⁊ syle eall ꝥ þearfum. þonne hæfst þu gold-hord on heofone. ⁊ cum ⁊ folga me;

23 Ða he þas word gehyrde he wearð ge-unrét. for-þam þe he wæs swiðe welig;

24 Ða se hælend hine unrotne geseah he cwæð; Eala hu earfoðlice on godes ríce gað þa ðe feoh habbað.

14 Soðlice ich eow segge þæt þes ferde ge-rihtwised to his huse. for-þan þe ælc þe hine up-ahefd beoð ge-nyðered. ⁊ se þe hine nyðered byoð up-ahafen.

15 Ða brohten hyo cyldre to hym þæt he hyo ætrine. Ða his leorning-cnihtes hyo ge-seagen hyo cydden heom.

16 Ða cleopede se hælend hyo to hym. ⁊ cwæð. Læteð þa litlinges to me cumen ⁊ ne for-beode ge heo swylcere ys godes rice.

17 Soðlice ic eow segge swa hwilc swa ne on-fegð godes rice swa swa cyld. ne gæð he on godes rice.

18 Ða axode hine sum aldor. godne lareow hwæt do ich þæt ich eche lyf hæbbe.

19 Ða cwæð se hælend hwi segest þu me godne. nis nan man god buten god ane.

20 Canst þu þa be-bode; ne of-sleh þu. ne fyrena þu. ne stell þu. ne leoh þu. wurðe þinne fader ⁊ þine moder.

21 Ða cwæð he eal þis ic heold. of minre geogeðe.

22 Ða cwæð se hælend an þing þe is wane. syle eall ꝥ þu hafst. ⁊ gyf eall ꝥ þearfen. þanne hafst þu gold-hord on heofene. ⁊ cum and folge me.

23 Ða he þas word ge-hyrde he warð ge-un-rot. for-þam þe he wæs swiðe welig.

24 Ða se hælend hine unrotne ge-seah he cwæð. Eale hu earfodlice gæð on godes rice þa þe feoh hæbbed.

Various Readings.

14. A. geryhtwysod. A. up-ahefð. A. genyþerod. A. up-ahafen. 18. A. acsode. A. ealder. A. B. godne *inserted before* lareow, *in very late hand.* 19. A. hwig. 20. A. ofsleh. A. weorða. A. moder. 21. A. geogoðe. 22. A. heofene. 24. B. gode (*wrongly*).

Various Readings.

14. ic; ge-rihtwisod; up-ahefð bið; nyþerað bið. 15. brohton; cild; athrine; -cnihtas; ge-sawon; ciddan him. 16. halend; litlingas; hyo [*for* heo]. 17. on-fehð. 18. axsode; ealdor; R. *om.* godne; hwat; ic; ic ece; habbe. 19. halend; segst; buton. 20. Cænst; leah; fæder; modor. 21. eall. 22. halend; his [*for* is] wana; syle [*for* gyf] all þæt þearfan. þonne hæfst; heofone. 23. werð. 24. Eala; earfoðlice; habbað.

ic cuoeðo iuh of-astag ðes wæs gesoðfæstad in hus his from ðæm forðon eghuoelc seðe
14 dico uobis descendit hic iustificatus in domum suam ab illo *Quia omnis qui * 215. u. mt. cccxxi.

hine ahebbað gebeged bið ⁊ seðe hine gebegeð ahofen bið gebrohton ða to
sé exaltat humiliabitur et qui sé humiliat exaltabitur 15 *Afferebant autem ad * LXXII. 216. ii. mt. cxcii. mr. clii. [*read* cuii].

him æc ða cildo þte hia gehrinade þ mið ðy gesegon ða ðegnas geðreadon ɫ hia se hælend
illum et infantes ut eos tangeret quod cum uiderent discipuli increpabant illos 16 *iesus*.

ða þfne-geceigde hia cuoeð lētas ða cnaihtes cuma to me ⁊ ne wallað hia ɫ ða awoerda ɫ ðuslicra
autem conuocans illos dixit sinite pueros uenire ad me et nolite eos uetare talium

is forðon rīc godes soðlice ic cuoeðo iuh seðe sua huælc ne on-foeð rīc god
est enim regnum d*e*i 17 *Amen dico uobis qui-cumq*ue* non acceperit regnum d*e*i * 217. ii. mt. clxxuiii. mr. xcu.

suæ þ cnæht ne in-cymeð in ðæt ilce ⁊ gefrægn hine sum Aldormon cuoeð
sicut puer non intrabit in illud 18 *ET interrogauit eum quidam princeps dicens * LXXIII. 218. ii. mt. cxciii. mr. cuii.

laruu la gōd huæd ic dōe lif ēce þte ic āga cuoeð ða him se hæl*end*
magister bone quid faciens uitam aeternam possidebo 19 dixit autem ei *iesus*

huæd ɫ forhuon cuoeðes ðu gōd ne ænig is gōd butan ðe ana god bodo ðu wast ne
quid me dicis bonum nemo bonus nisi solus d*eus* 20 mandata nosti non

of-slah ðu ne synnge ðu ɫ ne ðiofonto ðu doe ne leas witneso ɫ cyðneso ðu cuoeða worðig fader
occides non moechaberis non furtum facies non falsum testimonium dices honora patrem

ðin ⁊ moder seðe cuoeð ðas alle ic geheald of minum from gigoðe
tuum et matrem 21 qui ait haec omnia custodiui á iuuentute mea

miððy þ geherde se hæl*end* cuoeð him ða get an ðe is wona Alle ða ðe suahuelc ðu hæfeð bebyg
22 *Quo audito *iesus* ait ei athuc unum tibi deest omnia quae habes uende * 219. ii. mt. cxciiii. mr. cuiii.

⁊ sel ðorfendum ⁊ ðu hæfes strion in heofnum ⁊ cym fylg ɫ soēc mec ðas he
et dá pauperib*us* et habebis thesaurum in caelo et ueni sequere me 23 *His ille * 220. ii. mt. cxcu. mr. cuiiii.

miððy geherde gewūn-rōtsad wæs forðon wuelig wæs suiðe gesæh ða ɫ gere hine se hæl*end*
auditis contristatus est quia diues erat ualde 24 uidens autem illum *iesus*

unrōt aworden cuoeð suiðe hēfig ɫ ūneaðe ɫ suiðe ūnmæghtiglic ða ðe striono ɫ habbað in rīc
tristem factu*m* dixit quam difficile qui pecunias habent in regnum

godes inn-geongað
d*e*i intrabunt

---

14. ic cweðo iow astag ðes wæs gisoð-fæstad in huse his from him forðon eghwelc seðe hine ahefeð gibeged bið ⁊ seðe hine edmodað ahæfen bið 15. to-gibrohtun ða to him ⁊ ða cild þ hiæ gihrine ðætte miððy gisegun ðegnas giðreadun hia 16. ðe hælend ða efne-cegde ðailco cwæð letas ða lytla cuma to me ⁊ ne wallað hiæ werda ðuslicra is forðon rice godes 17. . . . swa ðe cnæht ne incymeð in ðæt ilce 18. gifrægn hine sum aldormon cwæð larow god hwæt ic doe to life ecum ðæt ic age 19. cwæð ða ðe hæl*end* hwæt me cweðestu god ne ænig is god buta ana god 20. godes bibodu ðu wast ne of-slah ðu ne synga ðu ne stel ðu ɫ does stalo ne leose witnisse ðu cweðe worða fæder ðinne ⁊ moder 21. seðe cwæð ðas alle ic hæld from gigoð-hada minum 22. miððy giherde ðe hæl*end* cwæð him ða gett an ðe wona is alle swa hwelc swa hæfes bibyge ⁊ sel ðarfum ɫ ðorfendu*m* ⁊ ðu hæfes gi-strion on heofne ⁊ cym fylig ɫ soec mec 23. ðas he miððy giherde giunrotsad wæs forðon weolig wæs swiðe 24. gisæh ða hine ðe hæl*end* unrott giworden cwæð swiðe hefge ðaðe gistriono hæfde in rice godes ingað

25 eaðelicor mæg se olfend gān þurh
are [*sic*] nǣdle eage. þon*ne* se welega on
godes rīce;
26 Ða cwǣdon þa ðe þis gehyrdon. ⁊ hwa
mæg hal beon;
27 Ða sǣde he hi*m*. gode synt mihtelice
þa ðing þe mannu*m* synt unmihtelice;
28 Þa cwæð petrus. ealle þing we for-
leton ⁊ folgodon þe;
29 Ða cwæþ he. soþlice ic eow secge.
nis nan man þe his hus forlæt oððe magas.
oððe broþru. oððe wīf. oððe bearn. for
godes rīce.
30 þe ne onfō mycele mare on þysse tīde.
⁊ ece līf on towerdre worulde;
31 Þa nam se hælend his leorning-
cnihtas ⁊ cwæð to hi*m*. faraþ
to hierusale*m*. ⁊ ealle þing beoð gefyllede
þe be mannes suna þurh witegan awritene
synt;
32 He byð þeodu*m* geseald ⁊ bið
bysmrud ⁊ geswungen. ⁊ on-spæt.
33 ⁊ æfter þa*m* þe hig hine swingað hig
hine ofsleað. ⁊ he þriddan dǣge arist
34 ⁊ hig naht þæs ongeton ⁊ hi*m* þis word
wæs behydd;
35 Þa he genealæhte hiericho. sum blind
man sæt wið þæne weg wædligende.
36 ⁊ þa he ge-hyrde þa menego farende.
he ahsude hwæt þ wære;

Assu*m*sit *iesus* discipulos suos secreto & ait illis. Ecce ascendimus. B.

Cu*m* appropinqua[ret] *iesus* hiericho cecus quida*m* sedebat [secus] uia*m* me*n*dicans. B.

25 eðelicor mæg se olfend gan þurh
anre nedle eage. þanne se welige on godes
riche.
26 Ða cwæðen þa þe þis ge-hyrden. ⁊
hwa mæg hal beon.
27 þa saide he heom. Gode beoð mihti-
lice þa þing þe mannen synde un-mihtilice.
28 Þa cwæð petrus. Ealle þing we forleten ⁊ folgedon þe.
29 Ða cwæð he. Soðlice ic eow segge
nis nan mann þe his hus for-læt. oððe
mæges oððe broðre. oððe wif. oððe
bearn; for godes rice.
30 ðe ne on-foð michele mare on þisse
tide. ⁊ ece lyf on towearde worelde.
31 ÞA nam se hælend his leorning-
cnihtes. ⁊ cwæð to heom. Fareð
to ierusalem. ⁊ ealle þing beoð ge-fylde
þe be mannes sune þurh witegene awritene
synde.
32 He beoð þeoden ge-seald ⁊ byoð bis-
mereð. ⁊ ge-swungen. ⁊ on-spætt.
33 ⁊ æfter þa*m* þe hyo hine swingeð
hyo hine of-slead. ⁊ he ðridde daige arist.
34 ⁊ hyo naht þas on-geatan. ⁊ heom
wæs þis word be-hydd.
35 ÞA he neahlahte jerico sum blind
man sæt wið þane weig wæd-
liende.
36 ⁊ þa he ge-hyrde þa manigeo farende.
he axode hwæt þ wære.

Assumpsit iesus discipulos suos secreto & ait illis. Ecce ascendimus.

Cum appropinq*ua*ret iericho.

Various Readings.

25. A. anre; *but* B. C. are. 27. A. synd (*twice*). 28. B. C. forletun. A. folgedon. 29. A. *om.* man. 30. A. toweardre. 31. A. synd. 32. A. ge-bysmerod. 33. B. swigað (*by error*). 34. A. ongeaton. 35. A. þone. 36. A. mænigeo. A. acsode.

Various Readings.

25. are nædle; þonne; weolige; rice. 26. ge-hyrdon. 27. sægde; mannum sint. 28. þint (*sic*); forleton; folgodon. 29. man; magas; bear (*sic*). 30. micele; ecce; to-worde woruldе. 31. *Rubric as in* H.; -cnihtas; him. Farað; ge-fyllede; witegan; synt. 32. bið þeodu*m*; bið bismored; on-spett. 33. swingað; of-sleað; dridde (*sic*). 35. *Rubric as in* H.; nealahte hiericho; þonne; wædligende; menego.

eaðor ł is *for*ðon se camal ꝥ micla dear ðerh ðyrl ł ego nēdles ꝥte gefære ðon se welig geonga
25 facilius est enim camelum per foramen acus transire quam diuitem intrare

in rīc godes ⁊ cuoedon ðaðe ꝥ geherdon ⁊ hua mæg hāl wosa cuoeð
in regnum d*ei* 26 et dixerunt qui audiebant et quis potest saluus fieri 27 ait

him ða ðing ūn-mæhtigo sindon mið mounum mæhtigo sindon mið gode cuoeð uut*edlice*
illis quae inpossibilia sunt apud homines possibilia sunt apud d*eum* 28 ait autem

pet*rus* heono we *for*leorton alle ⁊ fylgdon ł fylgendo we sindon ðe seðe cuoeð him
petrus ecce nos dimisimus omnia et secuti sumus té 29 *Qui dixit eis * 221. ii. mt. cxcuiii. mr. cx.

soð is ꝥ ic cuoeðo iuh ne ænig is seðe *for*letes hus ł ham ł aldro ł broðro ł wif
amen dico uobis nemo est qui reliquit domum aut parentes aut fratres aut uxorem

ł suno *fore* rīc godes ⁊ ꝥte ne oNfoe micla mara ł ðisser tīd
aut filios propter regnum dei 30 et non recipiat multo plura in hoc tempore

⁊ In world tocymende ł toweard lif ēce genōm ł onfēng ða se hæl*end* ða tuoelfo
et in saeculo futuro uitam aeternam 31 *Assumsit autem i*esus* duodecim * LXXIIII. 222. ii. mt. cci. mr. cxii.

⁊ cuoeð ðæm heono we astigeð ða burg ,⁊ ge-endad biðon alle ða ðe awriteno
et ait illis ecce ascendimus hierusolymam et consumabuntur omnia quae scribta

sindon ðerh witgo of sunu monnes gesāld bið *for*ðon hæðnu*m* ⁊ gebismered bið ł getēled
sunt per prophetas de filio hominis 32 tradetur enim gentib*us* et inludetur

⁊ ges*u*ungun ł gesuinceged bið ⁊ gespeoftad bið ł gehoræd bið ⁊ æft*er* ðon ł siððа gesuingeð hia
et flagillabitur (*sic*) et conspuetur 33 et post-quam flagellauerint

ofslæ̅s hine ⁊ dæge se ðirddan arīsað ⁊ ðailco ne ænig ðara † ongēton ⁊ wæs
occedent (*sic*) eum et die tertia resurget 34 *ET ipsi nihil horum intellexerunt et erat * 223. x. †.i. wordo.

word ðis ge-deglad fro*m* hi*m* ⁊ ne geton ða ðe gecuoeden woeron aworden
uerbum istud absconditum ab eis et non intellegebant quae dicebantur 35 *Factum * LXXU. 224. ii. mt. ccu. mr. cxui.

wæs ða mið ðy geneolecde ðære byrig blīnd sum gesætt æt ðæm woege giornde ł bæd
est autem cum appropinquaret hiericho caecus quidam sedebat secus uiam mendicans

⁊ miððy geherde ꝥ here bi-færende ł gefrægnade huæd ðis ł ꝥ were
36 et cum audiret turbam praeter-euntem interrogabat quid hoc esset

---

25. eðor is *for*ðon ðæm camele ðerh ðyrel nedle ꝥ he gefære ðon*ne* ðe weoliga ingonge in rice godes
26. ⁊ cwedun ðaðe giherdun ⁊ hwa mæg hal wosa 27. cwæð him ða ðing unmæhtge sindun mið monnu*m*...
28. cwæð wutudl*ice* .... heono we forleortun alle ⁊ fyligdun ðe 29. seðe cwæð him soð ic cweðo iow
nænig is seðe *for*leteð hus ł ældro ł broðer ł wif ł suno ł lond *fore* rice godes 30. ⁊ ne on-foeð micle
mara in ðisser tide ⁊ in weorlde tocymende in lif ece giseted bið 31. ginom ł onfeng ða ðe hæl*end* ða
twelfe ⁊ cwæð ðæm heono we astigas hierusalem ⁊ giendad bioðon alle ðaðe awritene sindun ðerh witgo of
suno monnes 32. gisald bið mið hæðnum ⁊ gibismerad bið ⁊ swungen bið ⁊ gispitted bið 33. ⁊
æfter ðon giswungen bið of-slas hine ⁊ ðy ðirda dæge arises 34. ⁊ ðailca nænig ðara ongægn (*sic*) ⁊ wæs
word ðis gidegled from him ⁊ ne ongeton ðaðe gicweden werun 35. aworden wæs ða miððy gineolicadun
.... ðær byrig bliud sum sætt æt woege giornde 36. ⁊ miððy gi-herde ðon*ne* ðreatt bifærende gifrægn
hwæt ðis were

37 Ða sædon hig ꝥ þær ferde se nazareniscea hælend ;

38 Þa hrymde he ⁊ cwæð ; Eala hælend dauides sunu gemiltsa me ;

39 ⁊ þa ðe fore-stopun hine þreadon ꝥ he suwude ; Ðæs þe ma he clypode. dauides sunu gemiltsa me ;

40 Ða stód se hælend ⁊ het hine lædan to him ; Þa he ge-nealæhte he ahsude hine

41 hwæt wylt ðu ꝥ ic ðe dó ; Ða cwæð he. drihten. ꝥ ic geseo ;

42 Ða cwæþ se hælend beseoh þin ge-leafa þe ge-hælde ;

43 And he sona geseah. ⁊ him folgode god wuldrigende ⁊ eall folc gode lof sealde þa hig ꝥ gesawon ;

CHAPTER XIX.

1 Ða eode he geond iericho.

2 þa wæs þar sum man on naman zacheus. se wæs welig

3 ⁊ he wolde geseon hwylc se hælend wǽre. þa ne mihte he for ðære menegu. forþam þe he wæs lytel on wæstmum.

4 þa arn he beforan ⁊ stah up on ân treow. sicomorum ꝥ he hine gesawe. forþam þe he wolde þanon faran ;

5 Þa he com to þære stówe þa ge-seah se hælend hine ⁊ cwæð ; Zacheus efst to þínum huse for-þam þe ic wylle to-dæg on þínum huse wunian ;

6 Ða efste he ⁊ hine bliþelice onfengc ;

Various Readings.

37. A. ðar ; B. C. þar. A. nazarenisca. 39. A. -stopon. A. swigode. A. He þæs ðe ma cleopode. 40. A. lædan hyne. A. acsode. 43. C. wuldriende. C. sawon.

Cap. xix. 1. A. eond. 3. A. mænegu. 5. A. *inserts* to hym *after* cwæð. 6. A. onfeng.

37 þa saigden hyo þæt þær ferde se nazarenisce hælend.

38 Þa remde he ⁊ cwæð. Eale hælend dauiðes sune ge-miltsce me.

39 ⁊ þa þe fore-stopen hine þredden þæt he swugede. þas þe mære he clypede. Dauides sune ge-miltse me.

40 Ða stod se hælend. ⁊ het hine læden to him. Ða he nehlahte he axode hine.

41 hwæt wilt þu þæt ic þe dó. Ða cwæð he. Drihten ꝥ ich ge-seo.

42 Ða cwæð se hælend. ge-seoh. þin ge-leafe þe ge-hælde.

43 ⁊ he sone ge-seah. ⁊ hym fylgde. god wuldriende. ⁊ eall folc god lof sealde. þæt hyo ꝥ ge-seawen.

CHAPTER XIX.

1 Ða eode he geond jerico.

2 Ða wæs þær sum man on namen zacheus. se wæs welig.

3 ⁊ he wolde ge-seon hwilc se hælend wære. þa ne mihte he for þare manige. for-þan þe he wæs litel on wæstme.

4 Ða arn he be-foren ⁊ stah up an treow sicomorum ꝥ he hine ge-seage. for-þan he wolde þanen faren.

5 Ða he com to þare stowe þa ge-seah se hælend hine ⁊ cw̄. Zacheus efste to þinen huse. for-þan þe ic wille to-daig on þinen huse wunien.

6 Ða efstede he ⁊ hine bliðelice on-feng.

Various Readings.

37. saigdon ; halend. 38. Eala halend dauides ; ge-miltze (*sic*). 39. swugode ; ma [*for* mære] ; clypode ; ge-miltdse (*sic*). 40. halend ; neh-lachte. 41. ic (*twice*). 42. halend ; ge-lefe. 43. sona ; folgede ; wuldrigende ; þa [*for* þæt] ; ge-sæwon.

Cap. xix. 1. ierico. 2. naman. 3. halend ware ; menigeo. for-þam. 4. be-foran ; ge-sawe ; faran. 5. efst ; þinum ; forþam ; to-dæg ; þinum ; wunian. 6. efste.

cuoedon ðа him ꝥte se hælend nazarenisca ł* ofer-foerde ⁊ cliopade cuoeð * ðe bebbisca .i. allsua monn cuoeðas.
37 dixerunt autem ei quod iesus nazarenus transiret 38 et clamauit dicens

la hælend sunu dauiðes milsa me ł mines ⁊ ða ðe fore-eodon geðreadon hine ꝥte gesuigade
iesu fili dauid miserere mei 39 et qui prae-ibant increpabant eum ut taceret

he forðon micle mara ł cliopade sunu dauiðes mildsa me stōd ða se hælend geheht
ipse uero multo magis clamauit fili dauid miserere mei 40 stans autem iesus iussit

hine to-læda hine ⁊ mið ðy geneolecde gefrægn hine cuoeð huæd ðe wilt ðu
illum adduci sé et cum appropinquasset interrogauit illum 41 dicens quid tibi uís

ꝥ ic doam ł gedoe soð he cuoeð la drihten ꝥte ic gesii ł gesea mæge ⁊ se hælend cuoeð him besæh
faciam at ille dixit domine ut uideam 42 et iesus dixit illi re-

ł loca geleafo ðin ðec hal dyde ⁊ sona gesæh ⁊ fylgde hine wundrade ł miclade
spice fides tua té saluum fecit 43 et confestim uidit et sequebatur illum magnificans

god ⁊ all ꝥ folc ꝥte gesæh gesalde lof ł gode
deum et omnis plebs ut uidit dedit laudem deo

CAP. XIX.

⁊ infoerde ðerh-eode ða burg ⁊ heono wer ðæs noma wæs ⁊ ðes wæs
1 *ET ingressus perambulabat hiericho 2 et ecce uir nomine saccheus et hic erat * LXXUI. 225. x.

Aldormonn ł foruost ⁊ he wæs welig ⁊ sohte to geseanne ðone hælend huelc were
princeps publicanorum et ipse diues 3 et quærebat uidere iesum quis esset

⁊ ne mæhte fore ðæm here forðon on lencgo lyttel wæs ⁊ fore-arn astāg in
et non poterat præ turba quia statura pussillus erat 4 et prae-currens ascendit in

treē heard* ꝥte gesege hine forðon ðona wæs færende ⁊ mið ðy gecuome to * .i. gelic ficbeame.
arborem sico-morum ut uideret illum quia inde erat transiturus 5 et cum uenisset ad

ðæm stōue onfeng se hælend gesæh hine ⁊ cuoeð to him ł to ðæm zache oefesta ł oefistlice adūne stig
locum suscipiens iesus uidit illum et dixit ad eum zacchee festinans descende

forðon to dæge In hus ðīn gedæfned is me to wunianne ł gewunia ⁊ oefistade of-stag adune ⁊
quia hodie in domo tua oportet me manere 6 et festinans descendit et

on-feng hine gefeande
excepit illum gaudiens (sic)

---

37. cwedun ða him ðæt ðe hælend nazarenisca ofer-foerde 38. ⁊ cliopadun cwæð la hælend sunu dauiðes milsa me 39. ⁊ ðaðe fore-eadun gi-ðreotodun hine ꝥte he swigde he forðon micle marom cliopade suna dauiðes milsa me 40. stod ða ðe hælend heht hine læde to him ⁊ mið ðy ge-nealocade gefrægn hine 41. cwæð hwæt ðe wilt ðu ic doe soð he cwæð drihten ðæt ic ge-sii 42. ⁊ ðe hælend cwæð him bisæh ł locco geleofa ðin ðec halne gidyde 43. ⁊ sona gisæh ⁊ fylgde him wundrade ł miclade god ⁊ all ꝥ folc gisæh gesalde lof gode

Cap. XIX. 1. ⁊ foerde ðerh-eode in ða burg.... 2. ⁊ heono wer wæs ðæs noma zacheus ⁊ ðæs wæs aldormon beor-swinigra ⁊ he wæs weolig 3. ⁊ sohte to geseana ðone hælend hwelc he were ⁊ ne mæhte for ðæm herge forðon on lengo lytel wæs 4. ⁊ bifore arun astag on treo heord onlic fic-beome ꝥte gisege hine forðon ðona wæs færende 5. ⁊ miððy ge-come to stowwe on-feng ðe hælend gesæh hine ⁊ cwæð to him zache eofesta adune stig forðon to-dæge in hus ðin gidæfned is me to wuniganne 6. ⁊ eofestade ofdune astag ⁊ onfeng hine gifeaande

7 Þa hig ꝥ gesawon þa murcnudun hig ealle. ⁊ cwǽdon ꝥ he to synfullum men gecyrde;

8 Ða stód zacheus ⁊ cwæð to drihtne; Nu ic sylle ðearfum healfe mine æhta. ⁊ gif ic ænigne bereafode ic hit be feowerfealdum agyfe;

9 Ða cwæð se hælend to him to-dæg þisse hiw-ræddene ys hæl gewórden forþam he wæs habrahames bearn;

10 Mannes sunu com secean ⁊ hal dón ꝥ forwearð;

11 Þa hig þis gehyrdon þa ge-ichte he sum big-spell forþam þe he wæs neh ierusalem. ⁊ forþam þe hig wéndon ꝥ hrædlice godes ríce geswutelud wǽre;

Ðys godspel sceal on sancte gregorius mæsse-dæg. Homo quidam nobilis abiit in regionem longinquam. A. Homo quidam nobilis habiit in regionem longinquam accipere sibi regnum & reuerti. B.

12 Witodlice he cwæð. sum æþelboren man ferde on fyrlen land ꝥ he him ríce onfenge ⁊ eft agén come;

13 Ða clypode he his tyn þeowas ⁊ sealde tyn pund him. ⁊ cwæð to him; Ceapiaþ oððꝥ ic cume;

14 Ða hatedon hine his leóde ⁊ sendon ærend-racan æfter him ⁊ cwædon; We nyllað ꝥ þes ofer ús rixie;

15 Ða he agén cóm ⁊ ꝥ ríce onfengc. he het clypian his þeowas þe he ꝥ feoh selde. ꝥ he wiste hu mycel gehwylc gemangode;

16 Ða com se forma ⁊ cwæð. hláford. þis pund gestrynde tyn pund;

7 Þa hyo ꝥ ge-seagen þa murcneden hyo ealle ⁊ cwæðen. þæt he to synful men gecyrde.

8 Ða stod zacheus ⁊ cwæð to drihton. Nu ic selle þearfen half mine ehte. ⁊ gef ich anigne be-reafode ic hyt be feowerfealden agyfe.

9 Ða cw̄. se hælend to hym. to-daig þisse heow-rædene is hæle ge-worðen. forþam he wæs abrahames bearn.

10 Mannes sune com secan. ⁊ halde ꝥ for-warð.

11 Þa hyo þis ge-hyrden þa ge-ehte he sum bispell. for-þam þe he wæs neoh ierusalem. ⁊ for-þan þe hyo wenden þæt rædlice godes rice ge-swuteled wære.

12 Witodlice he cwæð. Sum æthelboren man ferde on ferren land. ⁊ he him rice on-fenge. ⁊ eft ongean com.

Homo quid… nobilis abii… regionem l… ginquam ac… pere sibi re… num & reue…

13 Ða cleopede he hys teon þeowas ⁊ sealde teon pund heom. ⁊ cw̄. to heom. Cheapiað oððæt ic cume.

14 Ða hatedon hine his leoden. ⁊ sænden arendraken æfter hym. ⁊ cwæðen. We nelleð þæt þes ofer us rixie.

15 Ða he on-gen com ⁊ ꝥ rice on-feng; he het cleopian his þeowas þe he ꝥ feoh sealde. ꝥ he wiste hu mycel ge æghwilc ge-mangeden.

16 Ða com se forme ⁊ cwæð. Hlaford þin pund strenede tyen pund.

Various Readings.

7. A. murcnodon. 9. A. hyw-rædene. A. *inserts* ðe *after* forþam. A. B. C. abrahames. 10. A. B. C. secan. 11. A. ge-yhte. A. big-spel. A. ge-swutelod. 12. A. ongean. 14. A. nellað. A. ricsie ofer us. 15. A. ongean. A. on-feng. A. hys feoh [*for* ꝥ feoh]. A. B. sealde; *cut off in* C. A. mangode. 16. A. þyn [*for* þis].

Various Readings.

7. ge-sawen; murcnodon; cwæðon; synfullon (*sic*). 8. drihton (*as in* H.); sylle; gif ic ænigne; -fealdon. 9. halend; hiw-rædene; ge-worden. 10. haldon; forwearð. 11. ge-hyrdon; ge-echte; big-spell; neh; forþam; hrædlice; ge-swutelod ware. 12. *Rubric as in* H.; æðel-; ferlen; ⁊ he (*as in* H.); come. 13. clepode; tyn (*twice*); eom (*2nd time*); Ceapiað. 14. leode; sændon ærendracan. cwæðon; nylleð. 15. agen; clypian; mycel ge-hwylc ge-mangode. 16. forma; strende tyn.

⁊ miððy gesegon alle huuæstredon ł yfle ymb-sprecon cuoedon ꝥte to menn synnfullum
7 et cum uiderent omnes murmurabant dicentes quod ad hominem peccatorem

gecerde gesto uutedlice cuoeð to ðæm hælende heono half godra mīnra
diuertisset 8 stans autem zaccheus dixit ad dominum ecce demedium bonorum meorum

drihten ic sello ðorfendum ⁊ gif huæd ænigne ic besuāc ic forgeldo fear-fald ł feorsiðum cuoeð
domine dó pauperibus et si quid aliquem de-fraudaui reddo quadruplum 9 ait

se hælend to him ꝥte ł forðon to dæge hælo huse ðissum aworden Is forðon ⁊ he sunu is ł bið
iesus ad eum quia hodie salus domui huic facta est eo quod et ipse filius sit

abrahames cwom forðon sunu monnes to soecanne ł ⁊ to hælenne ꝥte losade ł losad wæs ðas
abrahae 10 *Uenit enim filius hominis quaerere et saluare quod perierat 11 †Haec * 226. u. mt. cluiii. † 227. x.

ðæm geherendum to-geēcde cuoeð ꝥ geddung forðon wære neh hierusalem ⁊ forðon hia woendon
illis audientibus ádiciens dixit parabolam eo quod esset prope hierusalem et quia existimarent

ꝥte sona ríc godes were æd-eauad cuoeð ðā monn sum wel-boren foerde on
quod confestim regnum dei manifestaretur 12 *Dixit ergo homo quidam nobilis abiit in * LXXUII. 228. ii. mt. cclxuiiii. mr. cliiii.

lond ūn-neh ł suiðe fearr to on-foanne him ric ⁊ eft he to cerranne woeron gecegid ðonne teno
regionem longinquam accipere sibi regnum et reuerti 13 uocatis autem decim

ðrælas his salde ðæm tea oro i. libras ⁊ cuoeð to ðæm cēapigas oð ꝥ ic cymo
seruis suis *Dedit illis decem mnas et ait ad illos negotiamini dum uenio * 229. u. mt. cclxx.

burg-waras uutedlice his gefiadon hine ⁊ sendon bod ł erendureca æfter him cuoedon ꝥ nallo we
14 ciues autem eius oderant illum et miserunt legationem post illum dicentes nolumus

ðiosne ꝥte gerixage ofer usic ⁊ aworden wæs ꝥte eft-cuom ł awoende mið-ðy onfeng to ríc
hunc regnare super nos 15 et factum est ut rediret accepto regno

⁊ heht geceiga ðæm esnum ł ða esnas ðæm gesalde ꝥ feh ꝥte wiste huu feolo ł eghuelc
et iussit uocari seruos quibus dedit pecuniam ut sciret quantum quisque

geceopad were cuom ða ðe forma cuoeðende drihten libras tuoege teno libras*
negotiatus esset 16 uenit autem primus dicens domine mna tua decem mnas * i. oro.

gesohte ł
adquisiuit

---

7. ⁊ miððy gesegon alle hwispredon ł yfle ˹sprecon cwedon ꝥte to men synnfullum ge-cerde 8. ge-stod ða zacheus cwæð to ðæm hælende heono hlaf (*sic*) godra mīnra drihten ic selle ðorfendum ⁊ gif hwæt ænige ic biswac ic forgeldo feoðor-fald 9. cwæð ðe hælend to him forðon to dæge hælo huse ðissum aworden wæs forðon ⁊ he is sunu abrahames 10. com forðon suuo monnes to soecenne ⁊ to hælenne ł wyrce ꝥte losade ł losad wæs 11. ðæm ðas giherdun togeecte cwæð ða geddunge forðon ꝥte were neh hierusalem ⁊ forðon hia woendun ꝥte sona rice godes nere æt-æwed 12. cwæð ða mon sum wel-boren foerde on londe unneh ł swiðe feor to onfoanne him rice ⁊ eft to cerranne 13. weron giceged ðonne ðræles tene salde ðæm teo oro ⁊ cwæð to ðæn ceopigas oð ꝥ ic cyme 14. burugweras wutudlice his gifiadun hine ⁊ sendun bod ł erendwreoca æfter him cwedon nallan we ðiosne ꝥte rixige ofer usih 15. ⁊ giworden wæs ꝥte eft com ł wende miððy onfeng rice ⁊ heht cega ðæm esnum ðæm ge-salde ðæt feh ꝥte wiste hu feolu eghwelc geceapad were 16. com ða ðe forma cweðende drihten liðre (*sic*) ðine teo oro ge-sohte

17 þa cwæð sé hláford gęblissa þú góda
þeowa. forþ*am* þe ðu wǽre on lytlu*m*
getrywe. þu byst and-weald hæbbende ofer
tyn ceastra ;
18 Ða co*m* oðer ⁊ cwæð. hláford. þin
pund gestrynde fíf pund ;
19 Ða cwæþ he to þ*am*. ⁊ beo þu ofer fíf
ceastra ;
20 Ða co*m* oþer ⁊ cwæð. hlaford. her
ys þin pund þe ic hæfde on swát-lín aléd.
21 ic ðe adred forþ*am* þe ðu eart stið
man. þu nimst ꝥ ðu ne settest. ⁊ þu ripst
ꝥ ðu ne seowe ;
22 Ða cwæð he to hi*m*. of þinu*m* muðe
ic ðe déme. la lyðra þeowa ; Ðu wistest
ꝥ ic eom stið man. ꝥ ic nime ꝥ ic ne sette
⁊ ripe ꝥ ic ne seow ;
23 And hwi ne sealdest þú min feoh to
hýre. ⁊ þon*ne* ic cóme ic hit witodlice mid
gestreone onfenge ;
24 Ða cwæð he to þ*am* þe hi*m* abútan
stódon. nimað ꝥ pund fra*m* hi*m* ⁊ syllað
þ*am* þe hæfð án pund ;
25 Ða cwǽdon hig to hi*m* hlaford. he
hæfð tyn pund ;
26 Soðlice ic secge eow ꝥ ælcu*m* hæbben-
du*m* bið geseald fra*m* þam þe næfð. ge
ꝥ ꝥ he hæfð hi*m* byð afyrred ;

17 þa cw̄. se hlaford. ge-blissa þu gode
þeowa. for-þan þe þu on litlen wære ge-
treowa þu beost anweald hæbbende ofer
teon cestren.
18 Ða com oðer ⁊ cw̄. hlaford þin pund
strynde fif pund.
19 þa cw̄. he to þan. ⁊ byo þu ofer fif
cestren.
20 Ða com oðer. ⁊ cw̄. Hlaford her is
þin pund þe ich hæfde on swat-lin aleigd.
21 Ich þe on-dredde for-þan þe þu ert
stið man. þu nymst þæt þu ne settst. ⁊
þu ripst þæt þu ne seowe.
22 þa cwæð he to him. of þinen muðe
ich þe deme la leðra þeowa. Ðu wistest ꝥ
ich eom stið man. ꝥ ic nyme ꝥ ich ne sette.
⁊ ripe þæt ic ne seow.
23 And hwi ne sealdest þu min feoh to
hyre. ⁊ þanne ic come ic hit witodlice mid
ge-streone on-fenge.
24 Ða cw̄. he to þam þe him abuten
stoden. anymed þæt pund fram him ⁊
sylled þam þe hæfð tin pund.
25 þa cwæðen hyo to hi*m*. hlaford he
hæfd teon pund.
26 Soðlice ich segge eow. þæt ælchen
hæbbenden beoð ge-seald. fram þan þe
næfð. ge ꝥ ꝥ he hæfð hym beoð afyrred.

⁊ cuoeð him gefæg wel la god esne for*ð*on on lytl*um* geleaffull ɫ treoufæst ðu were ðu bist
17 et ait illi euge bone serue quia in modico fidelis fuisti eris

mæht ɫ onwæld hæbbende on-ufa ɫ of*er* ten*um* ceastr*um* ⁊ oðer cuom cuoeð drih*ten* libras
potestatem habens supra decem ciuitates 18 et alter uenit dicens d*omi*ne mna

ðino dyde fif libras ⁊ ðiss*um* cuoeð ⁊ ðu wæs of*er* fif burgas ⁊
tua fecit quinq*ue* mnas 19 et huic ait et tú esto supra quinque ciuitates 20 et

oðer cuom cuoeð drih*ten* heono libra ðin ðone ic hæfde eft-Asettet in halsado ic ondreard
alter uenit dicens d*omi*ne ecce mna tua quam habui repositam in sudario 21 timui

for*ð*on ꝥte ꝥte scripen ɫ gearu*u*tol ɫ ðu arð ðu nimes ꝥte ne settes ⁊ hrippes ꝥ ðu ne
enim quia homo austerus és tollis quod non posuisti et metis quod non

gesaudesd cuoeð him of muðe ðinu*m* ðec ic doeomo la esne wohfull ðu wistes ꝥ ic
seminasti 22 dicit ei de ore tuo té iudico serue nequam sciebas quod ego

gearnfull ɫ gearuutol monn am nimmes ꝥ ic ne gesett ⁊ hrippes ꝥte ðu (*sic*) ne gesaudeð ⁊
austerus homo sum tollens quod non possui et metens quod non seminaui 23 et

for*h*uon ne saldes ðu feh meh to wege ɫ to disc ⁊ ic miððy cuome mið agnettu*m* ɫ uut*edlice*
quare non dedisti pecuniam meam ad mensam et ego ueniens cum usuris utiq*ue*

ic giude ɫ walde giuge ꝥ ⁊ ðæm stondendu*m* cuoeð genimmeð fro*m* him libra*m* ⁊ seallað ðæm
exigissem illud 24 et adstantib*us* dixit auferte ab illo mnam et date illi

seðe teno libras hæfeð ⁊ cuoedon him drih*ten* hæfis tea libr*as* ic cuoeð
qui decem mnas habet 25 et dixerunt ei d*omi*ne habet decem mnas 26 *Dico * 230. ii. mt. cclxxi. mr. xlii.

uut*edlice* iuh ꝥte eghuelcu*m* hæbbende ɫ ðæm ðe hæfeð g[isald bið] fro*m* ðæm uut*edlice* seðe ne hæfes
autem uobis quia omni habenti dabitur ab eo autem qui non habet

⁊ ꝥ hæfeð genumen bið fro*m* him soð-huæðre fiondas mino ða ðaðe ne waldon
et quod habet auferetur ab eo 27 *Uerum-tamen inimicos meos illos qui noluerunt * 231. u. mt. cclxxii.

mec rixage of*er* him to-brenges hider ⁊ cearfas bef*or*a mec
me regnare super sé adducite huc et inter-ficite ante me

---

17. ⁊ cwæð him gehwelc good esne forðon on lytlum gileofful ɫ tr*eow*f*æst* ðu were ðu bist mæht ɫ onwæld hæbbende onufa ɫ of*er* teo cæstre 18. ⁊ oðer com cwæð drih*ten* libras ðine dyde fif libras 19. ⁊ ðissum cwæð ⁊ ðu wæs ofer fif cæstre 20. ⁊ oðer com cwæð drih*ten* heono libras ðine ðone ic hæfde eft asetet in halsado 21. ic ondreord for*ð*on ðe ꝥte mon scripende is ðu nimes ꝥte ðu nege-setes ⁊ ripes nege-sæwe 22. cwæð him of muðe ðinom ðe ic doeme leasne wohfull ðu wistes ðæt ic mon georn-full am nimes ꝥte ðu ne settes ⁊ ripes ꝥte ðu ne sæwe 23. ⁊ for*h*won ne saldest ðu feh min to wege ɫ to disce ⁊ ic miððy come wutud*lice* ic giowade ɫ giowigia wal*de* ꝥte mið egnetnum 24. ⁊ ðæm stondendum cwæð geneniomað (*sic*) from him libram ⁊ seollað ðæm ðe hæfeð teo libras 25. ⁊ cwedon him drih*ten* hæfeð teo libras 26 ic cweðo wutud*lice* iow seðe alle hæbbende gisald bið fro*m* ðæm wutudl*ice* seðe ne hæfeð ⁊ ðæt hæfeð ginumen bið fro*m* him 27. soð-hweðre fiondas mine ða ðeðe ne waldun mec rixiga ofer him to-brengas hider ⁊ ceorfas bifora me

28 ⁊ þysum gecwedenum he férde to hierusalem;

Ðys gebyrað feower wucon ær middan wyntra ⁊ on palm-sunnan-dæg. Cum adpropinquasset iesus hierosolimis & uenisset bethfagie. A.

29 Ða he ge-nealæhte bethfage ⁊ bethanía to þam munte þe is genemned olíueti. he sende his twegen cnihtas

30 ⁊ cwæð; Faraþ on ꝥ castel þe ongen inc ys. on þam gyt gemetað assan folan getiged. on þam nan man gyt ne sæt. untigað hyne. ⁊ lædað to me;

31 ⁊ gif inc hwa ahsað hwi gyt hyne untigeað secgað him drihten hæfð his neode;

32 Ða férdon þa ðe asende wǽron ⁊ fundon swa he him sæde þæne folan stándan;

33 Ða hig hine untígdon þa cwǽdon þa hlafordas hwi untige ge þæne folan;

34 Ða cwædon hig for-þam þe drihten hæfð his neode;

35 Þa læddon hig hine to þam hælende. ⁊ hyra reaf wurpon ofer þæne folan. ⁊ þæne hælend on-ufan setton.

36 ⁊ þa he for. hi strehton under hine hyra réaf on þam wege.

37 ⁊ þa he ge-nealæhte to oliuétes muntes nyðer-stíge. þa ongunnon ealle þa menego geblissian. ⁊ mid mycelre stefne god heredon be eallum þam mihtum þe hig gesawun.

38 ⁊ cwǽdon; Gebletsud sy se cyning þe com on drihtnes naman. syb sy on heófenum. ⁊ wuldor on heahnessum;

28 ⁊ þisen ge-cweðen he ferde to ierusalem.

29 ÐA he ge-neahlahte bethphage ⁊ bethanie to þam munte þe is ge-nemned oliuetj. he sænde his twegen cnihtes

30 ⁊ cwæð. Fareð on ꝥ castel þe ongean inc ys on ðam gyt meteð assan folen ge-tegeð; on þam nan man geot ne sæt. untygeð hine ⁊ læðeð to me.

31 ⁊ gyf hwa eow axeð hwi gyt hine untegeð seggeð heom drihten hæfd his neode.

32 Ða ferden þa þe asende wæren ⁊ funden swa he heom saide þane folen standen.

33 Þa hyo hine unteigden. þa cwæðen þa hlafordes hwi un-teige ge þanne fole.

34 Ða cwæðen hyo for-þan þe drihten hæfð his neode.

35 Ða lædden hyo hine to þam hælende. ⁊ heora reaf wurpen ofer þanne folan. ⁊ þane hælend of-ufen setten.

36 ⁊ þa he for; hyo strehten under hine heore reaf on þam weige.

37 ⁊ þa he ge-neahlahte to oliuetes muntes niðer-stige. þa on-gunnen ealle þa menigeo ge-blissian ⁊ mid mychelere stefne god heredon be eallen þam mihten þe hyo sægen.

38 ⁊ cwæðen. Ge-bletsod syo se kyng þe com on drihtenes name. syb sy on heofene ⁊ wuldor on heahnysse.

Various Readings.

28. A. þyssum. 29. A. nemned. 30. A. on-gean. A. untygað; B. C. untigeað. 31. A. acsað. A. hwig. A. untigeon. C. secgeað. A. dryhten, *glossed by* se hlaford. 32. A. þone. 33. A. cwædon hys hlafordas. hwig. A. þone. 35. A. heora. A. þone (*twice*). 36. A. hig. A. heora. 37. A. mænegeo. A. gesawon. 38. A. Gebletsod sig. A. syg [*for* sy]. A. heahnyssum.

Various Readings.

28. þysum. 29. ge-neahlæcte bethfage; bethania; olíueti; cnihtas. 30. Farað; folan ge-tyged; gyt. 31. axsoð; un-tigeað seggað; hafð. 32. ferde; wæron; fundon; sægde; folan. 33. untygdon; cwaðon; hlafordas; un-tyge; þane folan. 34. cwæden; nyode. 35. læddon; halende; hyora; wurpon; þonne [*for* þanne]; þæne [*for* þane]; on-ufon setton. 36. hy strehton; heora; weyge. 37. ge-neahlachte; menego; mycelere; allum þam myhton; sawen. 38. cwæðon; cyning; drihtene (*sic*) naman; syo; heofonum; wuldon (*sic*); heahnyssum.

⁊ miððy ðas woeron gecuoedno *fora*-foerde astag hier*usalem* ⁊ aworden wæs
28 et his dictis praecedebat ascendens hierosolyma 29 *ET factum est * LXXUIII. 232. ii. mt. ccui. mr. cxuii.

miððy geneolecde to ⁊ to ðær byrig to more seðe geceiged is oelebearuu sende
quum appropinquasset ad bethpage et bethania ad montem qui uocatur olíueti misit

tuoege ðegnas his cuoeð gaas in woerc ꝥ ongeaegn is in ðæt miððy gie ingaeð
duos discipulos suos 30 dicens ite in castellum quod contra est in quod introeuntes

gie gemoetað folo asaldes gebunden ðæm ne ænig æfra monna gesætt undoeð ł unbindas
inuenietis pullum assinae alligatum cui nemo um-quam hominum sedit soluite

hine ⁊ to me lædes ⁊ gif hua iuih gefraignas *for*huon unbundongie sua cuoeðas him ł ðæm
illum et adducite 31 et si quis uos interrogauerit quare soluitis sic dicetis ei

*for*ðon se hlaferd woerco his willniað ðona foerdon uut*edlice* ðaðe gesendat woeron ⁊ gemoeton
quia d*ominus* opera eius desiderat 32 *Abierunt autem qui missi erant et inuenerunt * 233. ii. mt. ccuiii. mr. cxuiii.

sua cuoeð him ðone stonde folo miððy undoendu*m* ðon*ne* ðæm ðone folo cuoedon hlaferdas
sicut dixit illis stantem pullum 33 soluentib*us* autem illis pullum dixerunt domini

his to ðæm huæd ł *for*huon undoað gie ꝥ folo soð ðā cuoedon *for*ðon drih*ten* hine
eius ad illos quid soluitis pullum 34 at illi dixerunt quia d*ominus* eum

ned-ðarf hæfeð ⁊ lædon hine to ðæm hæl*ende* ⁊ wurpon gewoedo hiora
necessarium habet 35 et duxerunt illum ad i*esum* et iactantes uestimenta sua

onufa ðone folo on-setton ðone hæl*end* færende ðon*ne* hine under-brædden ł legdon gegerclo
supra pullum inposuerunt i*esum* 36 eunte autem illo substernebant uestimenta

hiora on woege ⁊ mið-ðy geneolecde ł gee to æfdæll ł stigniss*o* mōres oliuetes ongunnun
sua in uia 37 *ET cum appropinquaret iam ad descensum montis olíueti coeperunt * 234. i. mt. ccuiiii. mr. cxuiiii. io. c.

Alle ða menigo ofstigendra ł gefeadon ł gefeande to herganno god mið stefne micla of*er* Allu*m*
omnes turbae discendentiu*m* gaudentes laudare d*eum* uoce magna super omnibus

ða gesegen hæfdon ðæ*m* mæhtu*m* cuoeðende se gebloedsad seðe cuom cynig In noma drih*tnes*
quas uiderant uirtutib*us* 38 dicentes benedictus qui uenit rex in nomine d*omi*ni

sibb in heofnu*m* ⁊ wuldor in heanissu*m*
pax in caelo et gloria in excelsis

---

28. ⁊ miððy cweoðas gicwedeno astag hierusalem 29. giworden wæs miððy to-gineolicade to beth*ania* ⁊ to more seðe giceged is.... sende twoege ðegnas his 30. cwæð gaað in cæs*tel* ðæt fora ongægn us is in ðæt miððy ge in-gað ge gimoetas fola asaldes gibundenne ðæm nægnig (*sic*) æfre monna on gisætt undoað hine ⁊ to-gelædað 31. ⁊ gif hwelc iowih gifregne *for*hwon undoað swa cweoðas him *for*ðon drih*ten* wero his wilniað 32. ðona foerdun wutudl*ice* ðaðe sended werun ⁊ gimoettun swa cwæd him ðon*ne* ston*de* ðone fola 33. miððy undydon wutudl*ice* ðæ*m* ðon*e* fola cwedun hlafardas his to ðæm hwæt un-doað ge ðon*e* fola 34. soð hiæ cwedun *for*ðon drih*ten* hine nedðærfe hæfeð 35. ⁊ læddun hine to ðæ*m* hæl*ende* ⁊ wurpon giwedo his on-ufa ðone fola on-settun ðon*e* hæl*end* 36. færende ðonne hine unbræddun ł legdun giwedo hiora on woeg 37. ⁊ miððy to-gi-neolicadun to æfdelle mores oliuetes on-gunnun alle ðio mengu of-stigende gifeadun to herganne drih*ten* stefne micler of*er* allum ða gisegun ðæm mæhtum 38. cweðende sie gibletsad seðe com in noma drih*tnes* sibb on heofne ⁊ wuldor in heonisse gode

39 Ða cwædon sume of þa*m* fariseum to hi*m* ; Lāreow. cid þinu*m* leorningcnihtu*m* ;

40 Ða cwæþ he to hi*m*. Ic eow secge þeah þas suwigen stanas clypiaδ ;

Ðys godspel gebyraδ on þære endlyftan wucan ofer pente*costen*. Cu*m* adp*ro*pinquaret i*esus* hierosolima*m* uidens ciuitate*m* fleuit sup*er* illam. A.

41 ⁊ þa he ge-nealæhte ⁊ geseah þa ceastre. he weop ofer hig

42 ⁊ cwæδ ; Eala. gif þu wistest ⁊ witodlice on þysu*m* þinu*m* dæge þe δe to sybbe synt. nu hig synt fra*m* þinum eagu*m* behydde.

43 forþa*m* δe þa dagas to δe cumaδ. ⁊ þīne fynd þe betrymiaþ. ⁊ behabbaδ þe. ⁊ genyrwaδ þe æghwanun.

44 ⁊ to eorþan afyllaδ þe ⁊ þine bearn þe on δe synt. ⁊ hig ne læfaδ on þe stān ofer stāne. forþa*m* þe δu ne on-cneowe þa tīde þīnre geneosunge ;

45 Ða ongan he of þa*m* temple ut-drīfan þa syllendan ⁊ δa bicgendan.

46 ⁊ hi*m* to cwæδ ; Hit ys awriten ꝥ min hus ys gebed-hūs. ge hit worhton to sceaδena scræfe.

47 ⁊ he wæs dæg-hwa*m*lice on þa*m* te*m*ple lærende ;

Soþlice þara sacerda ealdras ⁊ þa boceras ⁊ þæs folces ealdor-men smeadon hu hig hine fordon mihton.

48 ⁊ hig ne fundon hwæt hi him to gylte dydon ; Soδlice eall folc wæs abysgod þe be hi*m* gehyrde secgan ;

39 Ða cwæδ sum of þam farisei to him Lareow kyδ þinen leorning-cnihten.

40 þa cwæδ he to heom. Ich eow segge þeah þas swugieδ stanes cleopieδ.

41 ⁊ þa he ge-neahlacte ⁊ ge-seah þa ceastre. þa weop he ofer hyo

42 ⁊ cwæδ. Eale gyf þu wistest ⁊ witedlice on þisen þinen dagen. þe þe to sibbe synde. nu hyo synden fran þinen eagen be-hydde.

43 for-þan þa dages to þe cumeδ. ⁊ þine feond þe be-trymieδ. ⁊ be-hæbbeδ þe. ⁊ be-nærewiaδ þe aighwanen.

44 ⁊ to eorδan afelled þe. ⁊ þine bearn þe on [þe] synde. ⁊ hi ne lefeδ on þe stan ofer stane. for-þan þe þu ne on-cneowe þa tide þinre ge-neosunge.

45 Ða on-gan he of þam temple ut-drifen þa syllende ⁊ þa biggende

46 ⁊ heom to cwæδ. Hit is awriten. ꝥ min hus is ge-bed-hus. ge hit worhten to scæδena scræfen.

47 ⁊ he wæs daighwamlice on þam temple lærende.

Soδlice þare sacerde ealdres ⁊ þa bokeres ⁊ þas folkes ealder-men. smægdon hu hi hine for-don mihten.

48 ⁊ hyo ne funden hwæt hyo hym to gylte dyden. Soδlice eal folc wæs abysgod þæt be hym ge-hyrde seggen.

Various Readings.

40. A. suwion. 42. A. synd (*twice*). 43. A. cumaδ to δe. A. æghwanon. 44. A. afyllδ. A. synd. 47. A. þæra. 48. A. hig [*for* hi].

Various Readings.

39. cwaδon sume; pharisei; cyδ þinu*m*; -cnihtu*m*. 40. Ic; þeh; swugian; cleopiaδ. 41. ge-neahlæcte; he weop [*for* þa weop he]. 42. Eala; witodlice; þysum þinu*m* dagum; synt; synt fra*m* þinu*m* eagan. 43. Forda*m* (*sic*); dagas; cumaδ; be-trymiaδ; be-habbaδ; ge-nearawiaδ. 44. afyllaδ; on þe sint; hyo; læfeδ. 45. ut-drifan. 46. eom; worhton; sceδena scræfe. 47. dæghwa*m*lice; þara sacerda; boceras; folces ealdor-men smeagdon hwu hyo; mihton. 48. fun (*sic*); eall; þe [*for* þæt]; seggan.

⁊ sumo ðara of hergum cuoedon to him laruu geðreat ðegnas
39 *ET quidam pharisaeorum de turbis dixerunt ad illum magister increpa discipulos * 235. u. mt. ccxiii.

ðino ðæm he cuoeð ic sægo iuh ꝥte gif ðas gesuigas stanas clioppogað
tuos 40 quibus ipse ait dico uobis quia si hi tacuerint lapides clamabunt

⁊ ꝥte ł miððy geneolecde gesæh ðæt ceastra geweæp ofer ðær cuoeð forðon gif
41 *ET ut propinquauit uidens ciuitatem fleuit super illa 42 dicens quia si * LXXUIIII. 236. x.

ðu wistes æc ðú ⁊ soðlice in ðissum dæg ðino ðaðe to sibbe ðe sint nu uutedlice
cognouisses et tú et quidem in hac die tua quae ad pacem tibi nunc autem

gedegledo ł gehyded sindon from égum ðinum forðon cymeð dagas on ðec ⁊ ymbselleð ł
abscondita sunt ab oculis tuis 43 quia uenient dies in té et circum-dabunt

ðec fiondas ðino mið dícg ⁊ ymbsettas ł ðec ⁊ efne-gehaðrigas ł ðec eghuuonan to
té inimici tui uallo et circum-dabunt té et coangustabunt té undique 44 ad

eorðo gelecgas ł ðec ⁊ ða suno ðaðe in ðec biðon ⁊ ne forletas ł in ðec stan ofer
terram prosternent te et filios qui in té sunt *ET non relinquent in té lapidem super * 237. ii. mt. ccxlii. mr. cxxxuiii.

stan forðon ne oncneu ðu tid socnises ðines ⁊ in-foerde in tempel
lapidem eo quod non cognoueris tempus uisitationis tuæ 45 *ET ingressus in templum * 238. i. mt. ccxi. mr. cxxi. io. xxi.

ongann aworpa ða bebyccendra in ðæm ⁊ ða bycgendo cuoeð ðæm awritten is forðon ł ꝥte hús
coepit eicere uendentes in illo et ementes 46 dicens illis scribtum est quia domus

min hus gebeddes is gie uutedlice gedydon hia cofa hreafera ⁊ wæs
mea domus orationis est uos autem fecistis illam speluncam latronum 47 *ET erat * 239. i. mt. ccxx. mr. cxxii. io. lxxxu.

lærend dæg-hæm in tempel ða aldormen ða sacerdas ⁊ uðuuto ⁊ aldormenn ðæs folces soh-
docens cotidie in templo principes autem sacerdotum et scribæ et princeps (*sic*) plebis quae-

ton hine to spillanne ⁊ ne gemoeton ł ne fundon ꝥte dydon him all forðon ꝥ folc
rebant illum perdere 48 et non inueniebant quod facerent illi omnis enim populus

hlosnende wæs geherde hine
suspensus erat audiens illum

---

39. ⁊ sume ðara ældra of hergum cwedun to him larow giðreata ðegnas ðine 40. ðæm he cwæð ic cweðo iow ðætte gif ðas swigas stanas cliopigað 41. ⁊ to-gineolicade gisæh cæstre giweop ofer ða 42. cwæð forðon gif ðu wistes ec ðu ⁊ soðlice on ðassum dæge ðine ðaðe to sibbe ðe nu wutudlice gidegled ł gihyded sint from egum ðinum 43. forðon cumað in ðec dagas ⁊ ymb-sellað ðec ⁊ efne gihaðrigað ðec fiondas ðine mið dice ⁊ ymbsellað ðec eghwona 44. ⁊ to eorðo gileccas ⁊ suno ðine ðaðe in ðe sint ⁊ ne forletas in ðec stan ofer stane forðon ðæt ne on-cnaw ðu tide soecnisse ðine 45. ⁊ infoerde ðe hælend in tempel ongan aworpa ða bibycgende in templo ⁊ ða bibycgende 46. cwæð ðæm awriten is forðon hus min hus gibedes is gif ge wutudlice dydon hia cofa reofera 47. ⁊ wæs lærende dæghwæmlice on templo aldor-men ða sacerdas ⁊ uð-wutu ⁊ ældro ðæs folces sohton hine to slaånne 48. ⁊ ne gimittun ł ne fundun hwæt dydon him alle forðon ðæt folc hlosnende wæs giherde hine

CHAPTER XX.

Cum intrasset *iesus* in templum. accesserunt ad eum principes sacerdotum & seniores populi dicentes In qua potestate hec facis. B.

1 Ða wæs anu*m* dæge geworden þa he ꝥ folc on þa*m* temple lǽrde ⁊ hi*m* bodude þa comun þara sacerda ealdras ⁊ þa boceras

2 ⁊ to hi*m* cwǽdon; Sege us on hwylcu*m* anwalde wyrcst þu ðas þing. oððe hwæt ys se ðe þe þisne anwald sealde;

3 Ða cwæþ he hi*m* to ⁊sware; ⁊ ic ahsige eow ân word ⁊swariað me.

4 wæs iohannes fulluht of heofone. hwæðer þe of mannu*m*;

5 Ða þohton hig betwux hi*m* ⁊ cwædon; Gŷf we secgað ꝥ he sy of heofone. he cwyð to ûs hwi ne gelyfde ge hi*m*;

6 Gyf we secgað ꝥ he sy of mannu*m*. eall folc us hænð hi wiston gere ꝥ iohannes wæs witega;

7 Ða ⁊swaredon hig ꝥ hig nyston hwanun he wæs;

8 Ða cwæð se hælend hi*m* to ne ic eow ne secge on hwylcu*m* anwalde ic þas þing wyrce;

Dixit *iesus* discipulis suis parabola*m* hanc. Homo quidam plantauit uinea*m* & locauit ea*m* agricolis. B.

9 He ongan þa ðis big-spel to þa*m* folce cweðan; Su*m* man plantude hi*m* wingeard ⁊ hine gesette mid tiliu*m*. ⁊ he wæs hi*m* feor manegu*m* tidu*m*;

10 Ða on tide he sende hys þeow to þa*m* tiliu*m* ꝥ hig hi*m* sealdon of þæs wingeardes wæstme. þa swungon hig þæne ⁊ idelne hine for-leton;

Various Readings.

Cap. xx. 1. A. lærde on þa*m* temple. A. comon þæra. 2. A. anwealde. A. anweald. 3. A. acsie. 4. A. heofene. 5. B. C. þohtun. A. betweox. A. *omits from* Gŷf *to* him. 6. A. sig. A. hig. A. geare. 7. A. hwanon. 8. A. anwealde. 9. A. plantode. 10. A. þone.

CHAPTER XX.

Cum intrasset *dominus* in templum. accesserunt ad eum principes sacerdotum & seniores populi dicentes. In qua potestate hec facis

1 ÞA wæs ane daige ge-worden. þa he ꝥ folc on þa*m* temple lærde. ⁊ heom bodede. þa comen þare sacerde ealdres. ⁊ þa bokeres

2 ⁊ to him cwæðen. Sege us on hwilcen anwealde wyrcst þu þas þing. oððe hwæt is se ðe þisne anweald þe sealde.

3 Þa cwæð he heom to andswere. ⁊ ich acsige eow an word. andswerieð me;

4 wæs iohannes fulluht of heofene hwæðer þe of mannen.

5 Ða þohten hyo be-tweox heo*m* ⁊ cwæðen. Gyf we seggeð þæt he syo of heofene. he cweð to ûs hwi ne ge-lyfde ge hym.

6 Gif we seggeð þæt he syo of mannen eall folc us hænð. hyo wisten gere ꝥ johannes wæs witege.

7 Þa andswereden hyo ꝥ hyo nesten hwanen he wæs.

8 Ða cwæð se hælend to heom. ne ic eow ne segge on hwilcen anwealde ich þas þing werche.

9 He on-gan þa þis bispell to þam folke cwæðen.

Homo quidam plantauit uinea*m* et locauit agricolas.

Sum man plantede wingeard. ⁊ hine sette mid tilien. ⁊ he wæs heom feor manegen tide.

10 Ða on oðre tide he sende his þeow to þam tilian ꝥ hyo hym sealden of þas wingeardes wæstme. þa swugedon (*sic*) hyo þanne ⁊ ydelne hine for-leten.

Various Readings.

Cap. xx. 1. *Rubric as in* H.; anu*m*; coman þara sacerda ealdras; boceras. 2. cwædon; hus; hwylcu*m* anwalde; ðo þe [*for* se ðe]; R. *om.* þe *before* sealde. 3. him; andsware; ic; andswериað. 4. heofone hweðer; mannu*m*. 5. cwæðon; heofone. 6. secgeð; sy; mannum; hi wiston gare; Iohannes; witega. 7. andswaroden; nysten. 8. halend heom to; hwilcu*m*; ic; wyrce. 9. big-spel; folce cweðan; *rubric as in* H.; plantode him wingeard; manegu*m*. 10. R. *om.* oðre; weastme; swungon; þonne.

CAP. XX.

⁊ aworden wæs on anum ðara dagana lærende hine ꝥ folc in temple ⁊ bodande
1 *ET factum est in una dierum docente illo populum in templo et euangelizante * LXXX. 240. ii. mt. ccxuii. mr. cxxuii.
efne-cuomon ða alldormenn sacerdo ⁊ uðuuto mið ðæm ældestum ⁊ sægdon cuoeðendo ðus to
conuenerunt principes sacerdotum et scribae cum senioribus 2 et aiunt dicentes ad
him cuoeð us in huælc mæht ðas ðu doest ł huelc is seðe gesalde ðe ðios mæht
illum dic nobis in qua potestate haec facis aut quis est qui dedit tibi hanc potestatem
ondsuarede ða cuoeð to ðæm wællo fregna iuih ⁊ ic anum worde ondsuaraide ł ondsuareð
3 respondens autem dixit ad illos interrogabo uos et ego unum uerbum respondete
me fuluiht iohannis of heofnum wæs ł from monnum soð hia gesmeaudon
mihi 4 baptismum iohannis de caelo erat án ex hominibus 5 at illi cogitabant
bituih him cuoeðende forðon gif we cuoeðas of heofnu cuoeðeð he forhuon forðon ne gelefdegie him
inter sé dicentes quia si dixerimus de cælo dicet quare ergo non credidistis ei
gif ðonne we cuoeðas from monnum ꝥ folc all gestæNað usig untuendlic sind forðon
6 sin autem dixerimus ex hominibus plebs uniuersa lapidabit nos certi sunt enim
from iohanne witga ꝥte woere ⁊ geondsuaredon ꝥ hia ne wiston huona woere ⁊
iohannen prophetam esse 7 et responderunt sé nescire unde esset 8 et
se hælend cuoeð ðæm ne ic cuoeðo iuh in huoelc mæht ðas ic dóm on-gann he
iesus ait illis neque ego dico uobis in qua potestate haec facio 9 *Coepit * LXXXI. 241. ii. mt. ccxuiiii. mr. cxxuiii.
ða cuoeða to ðæm folce geddung ðios monn gesette wingeard ⁊ agæf ł hia ðæm buendum
autem dicere ad plebem parabolam hanc homo plantauit uineam et locauit eam colonis
⁊ he suiðe fearr wæs monigum tidum ⁊ in tíd sende to bigengum esne
et ipse peregre fuit multis temporibus 10 et in tempore misit ad cultores seruum
ꝥte of wæstm ðæs wingeardas ꝥte saldon him ðaðe geðorscen forleorton hine Idelhende
ut de fructu uineae darent illi qui caesum dimiserunt eum inanem

---

Cap. XX. 1. ⁊ giworden wæs on anum dæge ðara lærde hine ðæt folc in temple ⁊ bodende efne-comun ða aldormen sacerda ⁊ uð-wuta mið ðæm ældrum 2. cweðende to him cwæð us in hwelcer mæhte ðas ðu does ⁊ hwelc is seðe seleð ðe ðas mæhte 3. ondsworade ða cwæð to ðæm welle fregna iowih ⁊ ic worde giondsworigað me 4. fulwiht iohannis of heofne wæs ł from monnum 5. soð hiæ gismeadun bitwih him cweðende forðon gif we cweoðas of heofne cweðes us forhwon forðon negi-lefdon ge him 6. gif ðonne we cweoðas from monnum ꝥ folc all gistæneð usih wutudlice sindun forðon from iohanne witga ꝥte were 7. ⁊ ond-sworade him ne wistun hwona were 8. ⁊ ðe hælend cwæð him ne ic cweðo iow in swa hwelce mæhte ðas ic dom 9. ongan ða cweoða to ðæm folche geddunge ðas mon gisette wingeard ⁊ agef hine ðæm byendum ⁊ he swiðe fear wæs monigum tidum 10. ⁊ to tide sende to bigengum esne ꝥte of wæstmum win-geardeȝ ꝥte saldo him ðaðe giðorscen forleortun hine idel-hende

11 Ða sende he oðerne þeow þa beoton hig ðæne ⁊ mid teonu*m* gewæcende hine forleton idelne;

12 Þa sende he þridan. þa wurpon hig ut þæne gewundudne;

13 Ða cwæð þæs wingeardes hlaford hwæt do ic. ic asende minne leofan sunu wenunga hine hig for-wandiað þon*ne* hig hine geseoþ;

14 Ða hine þa tilian gesawun hig þohton betwux him ⁊ cwædon; Her ys se yrfeweard. cumaþ uton hine ofslean ꝥ seo æht ure sy;

15 ⁊ hig hine of þa*m* wingearde awurpon ofslegene; Hwæt deð þæs wingeardes hlaford.

16 he cymð. ⁊ for-spilð þa tilian. ⁊ sylþ þæne wingeard oðru*m*; Híg cwædon þa hig þis gehyrdon ꝥ ne gewurþe;

17 Ða beheold he hig ⁊ cwæð; Hwæt is ꝥ awriten is. þone stan þe ða wyrhtan awurpon. þés is geworden on þære hyrnan heafod;

18 Ælc þe fylþ ofer þæne stán byð forbryt. ofer þæne þe he fylð. he to-cwyst;

19 Ða sohton þara sacerda ealdras ⁊ þa boceras hyra handa on þære tíde on hine wurpun. ⁊ hig adredon hi*m* ꝥ folc; Soðlice hi ongeton ꝥ he þis big-spell to hi*m* cwæð;

11 Ða sende he oðerne þeow. þa byeton hyo hine and mid teonen ge-wæcende hine for-leten ydelne.

12 Þa sende he þridden. þa wurpen hyo ut þæne ge-wundenne.

13 Ða cwæð þas win-geardes hlaford hwæt do ich. ich asende minne leofne sune wenunge hine hyo for-wandiað þanne hyo hine ge-seoð.

14 Ða hine þa tilian ge-seagen hyo þohten be-tweoxe heom. and cwæðen. Her ys se earfednyme; cumeð uton hine of-slean. þæt syo ehte ure byo.

15 ⁊ hyo hine of þa*m* wingearde awurpen ut of-slægen. Hwæt deð þes wingeardes hlaford.

16 He cymd ⁊ for-spilð þa tilien ⁊ syld þane wingeard oðrum. Hyo cwæðen þa hyo þis ge-hyrden ꝥ ne ge ne (*sic*) wurðe.

17 Þa be-heold he hyo ⁊ cwæð. Hwæt is ꝥ awriten ys. þane stan þe þa werhtan awurpen. þes is ge-worðen on þare hernen heafod.

18 Elc þe fyld ofer þane stan byð forberst; ofer þane þe he fyld. he to-cwest.

19 Ða sohten þare sacerda ealdres ⁊ þa bokeres heora handa on þa tide on hine wurpen. ⁊ hyo adredden heom ꝥ folc. Soðlice hyo on-gæten ꝥ he þis bispel to heom cwæð.

Various Readings.

11. A. þone. 12. A. þryddan; B. C. þriddan. A. þone gewundodne. 13. A. wyn-eardes. 14. A. gesawon. A. betweox. A. sig. 15 .A. wyn-earde. A. ofslagene; B. ofslege (*sic*). A. wyn-eardes. 16. A. þone wyn-eard. A. ge-weorðe. 17. C. awrityn. A. heafde. 18. A. þone (*2nd time only*). 19. A. þæra. A. heora. A. wurpan; *but* B. C. wurpon. B. hi [*for* hig]. A. ondredon. A. hig on-geaton. A. big-spel.

Various Readings.

11. beoton; þone [*for* hine]; teonu*m*. 12. þriden; wurpan; gewundedne. 13. ic; leofe; wenunga; þon*ne*. 14. ge-sawen; be-twux; yrfeweard. cumað; eht; sy [*for* byo]. 15. awurpon of-slege; þæs. 16. cymð; tilian; sylð þæne; cwæðon; ge-hyrdon; ne ge-wurðe. 17. þone; wyrhtan awurpan; ge-worden; hyrnan. 18. fylð; þone; for-bryt; þonne; fylð; to-cwyst. 19. sohtan þara; boceras hyra; wurpon; adreden; on-geoton; eom.

⁊ to-geëcde oðerne esne to sendanne ðailco uut*edlice* ðone æc geðu*ur*scon ⁊ awoerdon ɫ
11 Et addidit alterum seruum mittere illi autem hunc quoq*ue* caedentes et afficientes

mið teancuidu*m* ɫ *for*leorton idil[h]ende ⁊ to-geëcde ðone ðirdde to sendanne ða æc ðone geuun-
contumelia dimiserunt inanem 12 et addidit tertium mittere qui et illum uulne-

dadon awurpon cuoeð ða ɫ uut*edlice* hlaferd ðæs wingeardes huæd ic do ic sendo suno
rantes eiecerunt 13 dixit autem d*ominus* uineæ quid faciam mittam filium

min leof*ne* woen is ɫ uut*edlice* miððy ðone ilca gesegon gesceomadon ɫ ðone miððy gesegon
meum dilectum forsitan cum hunc uiderint uerebuntur 14 quem cum uidissent

ða buendo gesmeadon in hi*m* cuoedon ðes is erfuard wutu*n* ofslæ̂ hine ꝥte usra sie ɫ
coloni cogitauerunt in sé dicentes hic est heres occidamus illum ut nostra fiat

ðio erfuardnise ⁊ awoerpen wæs hine buta ðæm wingearde ofslogon huæd *for*ðon does
hereditas 15 et eiectum illum extra uineam occiderunt quid ergo faciet

ðæm hlaf*ord* ðæs wingeardes cymeð ⁊ spilleð buendo ðas ⁊ selleð ꝥ wingeard
illis d*ominus* uineae 16 ueniet et perdet colonos istos et dabit uineam

oð*rum* mon*num* miððy ꝥ wæs gehered cuoedon hia ne sie suæ he ða beheald hia cuoeð
aliis quo audito dixerunt illi absit 17 ille autem aspiciens eos dixit

huæd is æc ɫ ðis ꝥte awritten is stan ðone *for*cuomon ɫ eðwitadon timbrende ðes Aworden
quid est ergo hoc quod scribtum est lapidem quem reprobauerunt aedificantes hic factus

wæs on heafud ðæs huo*m*mes eghuoelc seðe gefalleð on-ufa ðæm stane efne-gequoeccad bið
est in capud anguli 18 omnis qui ceciderit supra illum lapide*m* conquassabitur

on-ufa ðone ðon*ne* ɫ uut*edlice* bið gefælled gegrindæs ɫ hine ⁊ sohton aldorm*en*
supra quem autem ceciderit comminuet illum 19 *Et quaerebant principes * 242. i. mt. ccxx. mr. cxxuiiii. io. lxxxuiii.

ðara sac*erda* ⁊ ða uðuto to sendanne in hine hondo ðæm tid ⁊ ondreardon ꝥ folc ongetton
sacerdotu*m* et scribae mittere in illum manus illa hora et timuerunt populu*m* cognouerunt

*for*ðon ꝥte to ðæm ɫ to him seol*fum* gecuoede onlicnise ɫ ðios
enim quod ad ipsos dixerit similitudinem istam

---

11. [*verse omitted*] 12. ⁊ to-gieode (*sic*) ðirdan siðe to sendanne ðaðe ⁊ ðailco giwundadun aworpun 13. cwæð ða ðe hlafard ðæs wingeardes hwæt ic dom ic sendo suno minne leofne woen is ɫ wutud*lice* miððy ðon*e* ilco gegisegun giscomadun 14. ðon*e* miððy gisegun ða byende gismeodun bitwih him cweðende ðes is erfeword wutudl*ice* ofsla we hine ⁊ userra erfeweard siæ 15. ⁊ aworpen wæs hine buta ða cæstre ofslogun hwæt forðon doeð ðæm ðe hlafard ðæs wingeardes 16. cymeð ⁊ spilleð byende ðas ⁊ seleð ðæne wingeard oðru*m* miððy ꝥ wæs gihered cwedun hia ne sie swa 17. he ða biheold hiæ cwæð hwæt is forðon ðis ꝥ awriten is stan ðon*e* fore-comun edwitadun timbrende ðis giworden wæs on heofud ðæs hwommes 18. eghwelc seðe gifalleð on-ufa ðæm stane efne-gicwæceð bið ofer ðone ðonne bið gifælled gigrindes hine 19. ⁊ sohtun aldor-men ðara sac*erda* ⁊ uð-wutu to sendanne on hine hond in ðær tide ⁊ ondreordun ꝥ folc ongetun forðon ꝥte to ðæm cwæð onlicnisse ðios

20 Ða sendun hig mid searwu*m* þa ðe riht-wise léton ꝥ hig hine gescyldgudun ⁊ ꝥ hig hine gesealdon þa*m* ealdron to dóme ⁊ to þæs deman anwalde to fordemanne;

21 Ða ahsodon hig hine ⁊ cwǽdon. lá-reow. we witun ꝥ þu rihte sprycst ⁊ lærest. ⁊ for nanon men ne wandast. ac godes weg on soðfæst-nesse lærst.

22 Ys hit riht ꝥ man þa*m* casere gafol sylle þé ná;

23 Þa cwæð he to hi*m* þa he hyra fácen onget; Hwi fandige mín;

24 Ywaþ me anne peninc hwæs anlicnesse hæfþ he. ⁊ ofer-gewrit; Ða cwædon hig þæs caseres;

25 Ða cwæð he to hi*m*; Agyfað þa*m* casere þa ðing þe ðæs caseres synt. ⁊ gode þa ðing þe godes synt.

26 Ða ne mihton hig his word befón beforan þa*m* folce. þa suwudon hig wundrigende be his ⁊sware;

Ðys god-spel sceal on wodnes dæg ofer pente-costen. Accesserunt ad *iesum* quidam saduceorum qui negant esse resurrectionem. A.

27 Ða genealæhton sume of saduceu*m*. þa ætsacað þæs æristest (*sic*) ⁊ ahsodon hine

28 ⁊ cwǽdon; Lάreow moyses us wrat gif hwæs broðor byð dead ⁊ wíf hæbbe. ⁊ se byð butan bearnu*m* ꝥ his broðor nime his wíf ⁊ hys broþor sǽd awecce;

29 Seofon gebroðru wæron ⁊ se forma na*m* wíf. ⁊ wæs dead butan bearnu*m*;

30 Ða nam oðer hig ⁊ wæs dead butan bearne;

20 ÞA senden hyo mid searwun þa þe hyo rithwise læten ꝥ hyo hine ge-scyldeden. ⁊ ꝥ hyo hine sealden þan ealdren to dome ⁊ to þas deman anwealde to for-demænne.

21 Ða axoden hyo hine ⁊ cwæðen. Lareow we wite ꝥ þu rihte specst. ⁊ lærst. ⁊ for nanen men ne wandest. ac godes weig on soðfæstnysse lærst.

22 is hit riht ꝥ man þam caisere gafol sylle þe na.

23 Ða cwæð he to heom. þa he heore facen on-geat. Hwy fandige min.

24 Tewiæð me ænne panig. hwas anlicnysse hafd he; ⁊ ofer-ge-writ. Ða cwæðen hyo þas caiseres.

25 Ða cwæð he to heom. Agyfeð þam caisere þa þi*n*g þe þas caiseres sende. ⁊ gode þa þing þe godes synde.

26 Þa ne mihten hyo his word be-fon be-foran þa*m* folce. þa swugedon hyo wundriende be his andswere.

27 Þa ge-nehlacten sume of þam sadu-céén. þa æt-saceð þas æristes. ⁊ axoden hine

28 ⁊ cwæðen. Lareow moyses ut-wrat gyf hwas broðer byð dead ⁊ wif hæbbe ⁊ sye byð buten bearne þæt his broðer nyme hys wif ⁊ his broðer sæd a-wecce.

29 Seofen broðren wæren ⁊ se forme na*m* wif ⁊ wæs dead buton bearne.

30 Ða nam se oðer hye; ænd wæs dead buten bearne.

Various Readings.

20. A. sendon. A. *inserts* hig *after* þa ðe. A. gescyldegodon; *but* B. C. gescyldgudun. A. anwealde. 21. A. acsodon. A. wyton. A. B. C. lærst. A. nanu*m*. A. -nysse. 23. A. heora. A. hwig fandie ge myn. 24. A. Eowiað. A. penig. A. -nysse. 25. A. synd (*twice*). 26. A. suwedon; B. C. suwudun. A. wundriende. 27. A. ærystes; B. C. æristes. A. acsedon. 28. A. broðer (1*st time only*). 29. C. buton. A. bearne.

Various Readings.

20. leson; gescyldgudu*n*; gesealdon þa*m* ealdran; þæs; for-demanne. 21. hy; cwædon; witon; sprycst; nanon; wandast; weyg. 22. casere. 23. heora. 24. Ywað [*for* Tewiæð]; pennic. hwæs; hæfð; cwædon; þæs caseres. 25. Agyfað; casere; þæs caseres synt; synt. 26. mihton; andsware. 27. ge-nehlæcton; R. *om.* þam; saduceu*m*; æt-sacað; aristes. 28. hwæs broðor; deað (*sic*); habbe; se [*for* sye]; butan; broðor (*twice*). 29. broðru wæron; butan bearnum. 30. hyo; butan bearnu*m*.

⁊ behealdon sendon sēteras ɫ ðaðe hia soðfæsto worhton ɫ teledon ɫ bebrugdon ꝥte
20 *ET obseruantes miserunt insidiatores qui sé iustos simularent ut * LXXXII. 243. ii. mt. ccxxiii. mr. cxxx.

genomo hine on wōrd ⁊ ꝥte saldon hine ðæm aldordōm ⁊ to onwælde ðæs under-cyninges
caperent eum in sermone et traderent eum principatui et potestati præsidis

⁊ gefrugnon hine cuoeðendo laaruu we wutton ꝥte recte (*sic*) ðu cuoeðes ⁊ læres ⁊ ne
21 et interrogauerunt illum dicentes magister scimus quia recte dicis et doces et non

onfoæs ōnsion ɫ ah in soðfæstnisse woege godes ðu læres is reht ɫ us to seallanne ꝥ geafel
accipis person*am* sed in ueritate uiam d*e*i doces 22 licet nobis dare tributum

ðæm caseri ɫ nō sceauade ɫ beheald ða facen ɫ esuicnise hiora cuoeð to him fo*r*huon ɫ mec
caesari án non 23 considerans autem dolum illorum dixit ad eos quid me

gie costages æd-eauæð me ꝥ penning ɫ huæs hæfeð onlicnessa ⁊ ōn-mercung ɫ i*n*n-awritting
temtatis 24 ostendite mihi denariu*m* cuius habet imaginem et inscribtionem

ondsuaredon ɫ cuoedon ðæs caseres ⁊ cuoeð ðæm agefað ɫ ageldas fo*r*ðon ða ðe ðæs caseres
respondentes dixerunt caesaris 25 et ait illis reddite ergo quae caesaris

sindon ðæm casere ⁊ ða ðe godes sindon gode ⁊ ne mæghton word his getela ɫ
sunt cæsari et quae d*e*i sunt d*e*o 26 et non potuerunt uerbum eius repraehendere

fo*r*a ðæm folce ⁊ awundradon In ondsuær*um* his gesuigdon ɫ geneolecdon ðon*ne* su*m*mo
coram plebem et mirati in responsis eius tacuerunt 27 *Accesserunt aute*m* quidam * LXXXIII.

ðara ða ðe onsæccað ꝥte se erest ɫ ⁊ frugnun hine cuoeðendo
saducaeorum qui negant esse resurrectionem et interrogauerunt eum 28 dicentes

laruu mo*ses* Awrāt ūs gif broðer huoelc huoeges dead bið ɫ sē ꝥte hæbbe wif ⁊ ðes
magister moses scribsit nobis si frater alicuius mortuus fuerit habens uxorēm et hic

butta sunu bið ꝥte onfoe hia broðer his þæm wife awæcce sēd broðre his
sine filiis fuerit ut acciperet eam frater eius uxorem suscitet semen fratri suo

seofono fo*r*ðon broðero woeron ⁊ se fo*r*ma onfeng ɫ genom ꝥ wif ⁊ dead wæs buta sunu*m*
29 septem ergo fratres erant et primus accepit uxorem et mortuus est sine filiis

⁊ sohte ɫ fylgde onfeng ða il*ca* ⁊ he ɫ ðe dead wæs buta sunu
30 et sequens accepit illa*m* et ipse mortuus est sine filio

---

20. ⁊ biheoldun sendun stearas (*sic*) ðaðe hiæ soðfæste worhtun ꝥte geongunne hine on worde ⁊ ꝥte saldun hine ðæm aldor-dome ⁊ to onwælde ðæs undercyniges 21. ⁊ gifrugnon hine cweðende larow we wutun ðætte reht ðu læres ⁊ cweðes ⁊ ne onfoas onsione an (*sic*) in soðfæstnisse woege godes ðu læres 22. is reht us to sellanne ðon*e* gerlo ðæm casere ɫ noo 23. sceawade ɫ biheald ða eswic hiora cwæð to ðæm hwæt mec ge costigas. 24 æt-eowað me ðone pening hwæs hæfes onlicnisse ⁊ onmercunge ⁊ onwritinge ondsworadun cwedun ðæs caseres 25. ⁊ cwæð ðæm ageofað forðon ðaðe ðæs caseres sindun ðæm casere ⁊ ðaðe godes sindun gode 26. ⁊ ne mæhtun word his gi-tela bifora ðæm folche ⁊ awundrade on ond-swore his ⁊ swigadun 27. gineolicadun ðon*ne* sum ðara hiora ðaðe ne on-sæccað ðætte sie erest ⁊ gifrægn hine 28. cweðende moyses wrat us gif broðer hwelces hwogu dead bið ðe hæfde wif ⁊ ðes buta suno bið ꝥte on-foe ða broðer ðæm wife ⁊ awecce sed broðor his 29. siofune forðon broðor his (*sic*) weron ⁊ ðe forma onfeng wif ðæt ⁊ deod wæs buta suno*m* 30. ⁊ sohte ɫ fyligde onfeng ða ilco [*omission*]

31 Ða nam se þridda hig. ⁊ swa ealle seofone. ⁊ nán sǽd ne lǽfdon ⁊ wæron deade.

32 þa ealra ytemest wæs ꝥ wíf dead;

33 On þ*am* æryste hwylces hyra wíf biþ ꝥ;

34 Ða cwæþ se hælend to hi*m*. þysse worulde bearn wifiað ⁊ beoð to giftu*m* gesealde;

35 Ða ðe synt þære worulde wyrðe. ⁊ ærystes of deaðu*m* ne giftigeaþ hi ne wif ne lǽdað

36 ne ofer ꝥ sweltan ne magon. hig synt soðlice englu*m* gelice. ⁊ hig synt godes bearn þon*ne* hig synt ærystys bearn.

37 for-þa*m* þe soðlice déade arisað. ⁊ moyses æt-ywde wið anne beig-beam swa he cwæð; Drihten abraha*m*mes god. ⁊ isaaces god. ⁊ iacobes god.

38 nys god deadra ac lybbendra. ealle hig hi*m* lybbað;

39 Ða ⁊swarudon hi*m* sume þara bocera ⁊ cwǽdon. láreow. wel þu cwǽde.

40 ⁊ hig hine leng ne dorston ænig þing ahsian;

41 þa cwæð he to hi*m*; Hwi secgað hig ꝥ crist sy dauides sunu.

42 ⁊ dauid cwyð on þa*m* sealme. drihten sǽde to minu*m* drihtne site on mine swiðran healfe.

31 þa nam se þridde hy ⁊ wæs dead
buton bearne. ⁊ swa ealle seofene ⁊ nán* sæd ne lefden ⁊ wæren deade buton.

32 þa ealre ytemest wæs ꝥ wif dead.

33 On þam æriste hwilces heores wif byð ꝥ.

34 þa cwæð se hælend to heom þisse worulde bearn wifieð ⁊ byð to gyfton gesealde.

35 ða ðe synde þare werulde wurðe. ⁊ æristes of deaðe ne gyftiað hy** ne wif ne lædeð.

36 ne ofer ꝥ sweltan ne magen. ⁊ hyo synden soðlice ænglen ge-lice ⁊ hyo synden godes bearn. þanne hyo synden æristes bearn.

37 for-þam þe soðlice deade ariseð. ⁊ moyses atewde wið ænne beig-beam. swa he cwæð. Drihten abrahames god. ⁊ ysaacs god. ⁊ iacobes god.

38 nys god deadre ac libbendra; ealle hyo him libbeð.

39 Ða andswerede hi*m* su*m* þare bokere ⁊ cwæðen. lareow; wel þu cwæðe.

40 ⁊ hyo hine leng ne dorston ænig þing axien.

41 Ða cw̄. he to heom. Hwi seggeð hyo ꝥ crist sy dauiðes sune.

42 ⁊ dauid cweð on þam sealme. Drihten sæde to minen drihtne. site on minen swiðren healfe

* MS. nád.

** MS. hyo, *alt. to* hy.

Various Readings.

31. A. seofene. 33. A. heora. 34. A. weorulde. 35. A. synd. A. weorulde. A. giftiað. A. *om.* hi. 36. A. synd (*thrice*). A. ærystes; *but* B. C. ærystys. 37. A. bei-bea*m*. A. B. C. abrahames. 38. A. deaddra god. 39. A. ⁊swaredon. A. þæra. 40. A. acsian. 41. A. hwig. A. sig. 42. A. *om.* to.

Various Readings.

31. þrydda hyo; butan bearnu*m*; seofone; nan; læfdon. 32. ealra. 33. hyora. 34. hale*n*d; weorulde; wifiað; gyfton (*as in* H.). 35. weorulde; aristes; deadu*m*; hyo; lædað. 36. swelten; R. *om.* ⁊ *after* magen; synt (*thrice*); englu*m*; þon*ne* hi; æristis (*sic*). 37. arisað; æt-ywde; anne; beig-beam (*as in* H.); isááces. 38. deadra; libendra; libbað. 39. andswaraden; sume þara bocera; cwædon. 40. dorton (*sic*); axsoian (*sic*). 41. seggað; dauides. 42. minu*m* (1*st time*); swiðran.

ɔ se ðirdda genom hia ongelīc ɔ alle seofono ɔ ne *for*leorton sēd
31 et tertius accepit illam similiter et omnes septem et non relinquaerunt semen

ɔ dēadō woeron ɫ hio æt nesta ɫ hlætme*sta* allra hio deado wæs æc ꝥ wif in
et mortui sunt 32 nouissima omnium mortua est et mulier 33 in

erest *for*ðon*ne* huæs ðara ɫ hiora bið ꝥ wif æft*er* ðon ða seofono hæfdon hia ɫ ꝥ ilca wif
resurrectione ergo cuius eorum erit uxor siquidem septem habuerunt eam uxorem

ɔ cuoeð ðæm se hæl*end* suno woreldes ðisses gesiniga*ð* ɔ sald biðon to bryd-lopum ɫ ða
34 et ait illis *iesus* filii saeculi huius nubunt et traduntur ad nuptias 35 illi

uut*edlice* ðað[e] wyrðo habbað ɫ wyrðe biðon worulde ðæm ɔ erest fro*m* dead*um* ne siniga*ð* ɫ
autem qui digni habebuntur saeculo illo et resurrectione ex mortuis neq*ue* nubunt

ne lædeð ɫ fatas wifo ne *for*ðon leng ɫ of*er* ꝥ deadage ɫ magon gemæcca ɫ gelīco, *for*ðon
neq*ue* ducunt uxores 36 neq*ue* enim ultra mori poterint aequales enim

englu*m* biðon ɔ sunu biðon godes mið ðy biðon suno eristes *for*ðon ɫ soðlice ɫ arisað
angelis sunt et filii sunt d*e*i cum sint filii resurrectionis 37 quia uero resurgant

ða deado ɔ mos*es* adeaude ætt ðæm heape ɫ suæ cuoeð drih*ten* god abraham ɔ god
mortui et moses ostendit secum rubum sicut dicit d*ominum* d*eum* abraham et d*eum*

isaces ɔ god iacobes god ðon*ne* ɫ uut*edlice* ne is deadra ah hlifigiendra alle
isaac et d*eum* iacob 38 d*eus* autem non est mortuorum sed uiuorum omnes

*for*ðon *h*lifigað him ondsuaredon ða sumo ðara uduutana cuoedon laruu wel
enim uiuunt ei 39 respondentes autem quidam scribarum dixerunt magister bene

ðu cuoede ɔ leng ɫ *for*ðor ne darston hine ænight ɫ gefrægne cuoeð
dixisti 40 *Et amplius non audebant eum quicquam interrogare 41 †Dixit *

uut*edlice* ɫ ðon*ne* to ðæm huu cuoeðas crist sunu dauiðes ꝥte seē ɔ se ilca
autem ad illos quomodo dicunt *christum* filium dauid esse 42 et ipse

dauið cuoeð on boēc ðara salma cuoeð drih*ten* drihtne minu*m* sitt to suiðru*m* mi*n*um
dauid dicit in libro psalmorum dixit d*ominus* d*omino* meo sede á dextris meis

---

31. ...gi-lice ɔ alle ða siofune ɔ ne for-leortun sed ɔ deode werun 32. hio æt nesta ɫ lætemest ða alra deod wæs ɔ wif ꝥ 33. in eriste forðon wæs hiora ɫ ðara bið ꝥ wif gif æfterðon ða siofune hæfdun hia 34. ɔ cwæð ðæm ðe hæl*end* suno weorulde ðisse gisinnigo ɔ sald bioðon to bryd-hlopum 35. ða wutudl*ice* ðaðe wyrðe habbað ɫ wyrðe bioðon weorlde ðær ɔ on eriste from deaðe ne synnigað ne lædas ɫ ne foas wif ða 36. ne *for*ðon leng deadiga magan gimæcce *for*ðon englas sindun ɔ sunu sindun godes miððy bioðo suno erestes 37. *for*ðon soðlice ariseð ða deade.... æt-eowde heope.... sva cwæð drih*ten* god abrahames ɔ god.... ɔ god.... 38. god wutudl*ice* ne is deodra ah lifgendra alle forðon lufigað him 39. onsworade sum ðara uðwutuna cwæð wel ðu cwede 40. ɔ leng ɫ forðor ne darstun hine gifregna æniht 41. cwæð ða to ðæm huu cweoðas ge crist sunu were dauiðes 42. ɔ he dauið cwæð on boec ðara salmana cwæð drih*ten* drih*t*ne minu*m* sitt to swiðra min

43 oð ꝥ ic asette þīne fynd to fot-sceamole þinra fota;

44 Dauid hine clypað drihten ⁊ humeta ys he hys sunu;

45 Ða sæde he hys leorning-cniht*um*. eall*um* folce gehyrendum;

46 Warniað wið þa boceras ða þe wyllað on gegyrl*um* gān. ⁊ lufiað gretinga on stræte. ⁊ þa yldstan setl on gesamnung*um* ⁊ þa forman hlininga on gebeorscypum.

47 þa forswelgað wydywyna hus. hiwgende lang gebed. þa onfoð maran genyþerunge;

CHAPTER XXI.

1 Ða he hīne beseah he ge-seh þa welegan hyra lāc sendan on þone sceoppan.

2 þa geseah he sume earme wydewan bringan twegen feorð-lingas;

3 Ða cwæð he soð ic eow secge ꝥ ðeos earme wudewe ealra mæst brohte;

4 Soðes ealle þas brohton gode lāc of hyra mycelan welan. þeos wudewe brohte of þ*am* þe heo hæfde ealle hyre andlyfene;

5 ⁊ þa cwæð he to þ*am* þe sædon be þ*am* te*m*ple. ꝥ hit wǣre geglenged mid gōd*um* stān*um* ⁊ god*um* gif*um*.

6 Þas þing þe ge geseoð þa dagas cumað on þ*am* ne bið stan læfed ofer stan. þe ne beo to-worpen;

7 Þa ahsodon hig hine la bebeodend hwænne beoð þas þing. ⁊ hwylce tacna beoð þon*ne* þas þing gewurðaþ;

Various Readings.

43. A. fot-sceamele. 46. A. yldestan. A. hleonunga; B. hlinunga; C. hlininga (*as in text*). 47. A. wudewena. A. hiwigende. A. ge-nyþerunga.

Cap. xxi. 1. A. beseh. A. heora. 2. A. B. C. wudewan. 4. A. heora. 7. A. acsedon. A. tacen. A. geweorþað.

43 od ꝥ ic asette þine feond to fotscamele þinre fote.

44 Dauid hine cleopeð drihten. ⁊ hu mæte is he his sune.

45 Þa saigde he his leorning-cnihten ealle folce ge-herende.

46 Warnieð eow wið þa bokeres. þa þe willeð on ge-gyrlan gan. ⁊ lufige gretunge on stræte. ⁊ þa yldest settl on ge-samnu[*n*]-gan. ⁊ þa formen þeninge on ge-beorscipen.

47 þa for-swelgeð wudewena* us hiwgende lang ge-bed. þa on-foð mare ge-nyðerunge.

* na *is repeated here above the line.*

CHAPTER XXI.

1 Þa he hine be-seah; he ge-seah þa welian heore lac senden on þane sceoppan.

2 Ða ge-seah he sume earme wudewan bringen twegen ferðinges.

3 Þa cwæð he soð ic eow segge þæt þeos earme wudewe ælre mæst brohte.

4 Sodes ealle þas brohten gode lac of heore micelen welen. þeos wudewe brohte of þam þe hyo hafde ealle hire andlyfene.

5 ⁊ þa cwæð he to þam þe saiden be þam te*m*ple ꝥ hit wære ge-glenged mid goden stanen ⁊ goden gyfen.

6 Ðas þing þe ge ge-seoð. þa dages cumeð on þan ne beoð stan lefed ofer stan; þe ne beo to-worpen.

7 Þa axoden hyo hine. La be-beodend. hwanne beoð þas þing. ⁊ hwilcne tacne beoð þanne þas þing ge-wurðeð.

Various Readings.

43. oð; þinra fota. 44. clypað. 45. sæde; -cniht-u*m*; ge-hyrendu*m*. 46. Warnið; boceras; wyllað; ge-gyrlu*m*; lufiað gretunga; yldestan secl (*sic*); ge-samnungu*m*; forman hlininga; ge-beorscypu*m*. 47. for-swelgað wydewena; us (*as in* H.).

Cap. xxi. 1. welegan hira; sendan; þone. 2. firð-lingas. 3. ealre. 4. Soðes; hyora mycelan weolan; heo. 5. sægdon; ware; godu*m* stanum; godu*m* gyfu*m*. 6. cymað; þam; byð; læfed. 7. hwænne; hwylce; þonne; ge-wurðað.

oðð ꝥte ic setto fiondas ðine to fot-scoemel fota ðinra forðon drih*ten*
43 donec ponam inimicos tuos scabellum pedum tuorum 44 dauid ergo d*omi*n*um*

ðeilco ɫ ðone ceigeð ⁊ huu sunu his is miððy wæs gehered ða allu*m* folce cuoeð
illum uocat et quomodo filius eius est 45 *Audiente autem omni populo dixit * 246. ii. mt. ccxxuiiii. mr. cxxxu.

ðegnu*m* his be-haldað iuih fro*m* uð-ut*um* ða ðe wallað geonga In stolu*m* ɫ on ofe*r*slopu*m*
discipulis suis 46 attendite á scribis qui uolunt ambulare in stolis

⁊ lufas groetingo in sprēc ⁊ ða fo*r*ma seatlas in somnungu*m* ⁊ ða fo*r*mo sēdlo in
et amant salutationes in foro et primas cathedras in synagogis et primos discubitos in

gēbearsciopu*m* ða ðe fo*r*suelgas ɫ hūso ða wid*u*ena wyrcas ɫ ꝥ long gebed ðas ɫ ða onfoæð ɫ
conuiuis 47 *Qui deuorant domos uiduarum simulantes longam orationem hi accipient * 247. u [iii]. mr. [MS. mt.] cxxxui.

cursung ꝥ mara ɫ ꝥ maasto
damnationem maiorem

CAP. XXI.

eft beheald ða ɫ ðon*ne* gesæh ða ðaðe gesendon ðingo hiora weligo
1 respiciens autem uidit eos qui mittebant munera sua in gazophilacium diuites

gesæh ðon*ne* ⁊ sum oðer ɫ an widua ðorfondlico sendende mæslenno feorð*ungas* tuoeg ɫ an feorðunge
2 uidit autem et qua[*n*]da*m* uiduam paupercula*m* mittentem aera minuta duo

⁊ cuoeð soð is ꝥ ic cuoeðo iuh ꝥte wid*ua* ðios ɫ ðas ðarfe fo*r*ðor ðon alle sende
3 et dixit uere dico uobis quia uidua haec pauper plus quam omnes misit

fo*r*ðon Alle ðas ɫ ða of monigfaldnise him sendon in ðingu*m* godes ðios uut*edlice* of ðon
4 nam omnes hí ex abundantia sibi miserunt in munera dei haec autem ex eo

ꝥte wona is ɫ fo*r*loren is ɫ wæs hire all lifoðæn hire ðone ɫ ꝥ hæfde sende ⁊
quod deest illi omnem uictum suum quem habuit misit 5 *Et * LXXXU. 248. ii. mt. ccxlii. m. cxxxuii.

ðara sum cuoeðendu*m* of temple ꝥte mið gōdu*m* stanu*m* ⁊ geafu*m* gehrined were cuoeð
quib*us*dam dicentib*us* de templo quod lapidib*us* bonis et donis ornatum esset dixit

ðas ða ðe gie gesegon ɫ geseað cymað dagas on ðæm ne bið fo*r*leten stan ofe*r* stane seðe
6 haec quae uidetis uenient dies in quibus non relinquetur lapis super lapidem qui

ne bið tostrogden gefrugnon ðon*ne* hine cuoeðendo hæsere ɫ huoenne ðas ɫ ða biðon
non destruatur 7 *Interrogauerunt autem illum dicentes praeceptor quando haec erunt * 249. ii. mt. ccxliii. mr. cxxxuiii.

⁊ huoelc ɫ huæd becon ɫ tacon miððy geworða ɫ ꝥte sie ɫ to wosanne onginnað
et quod signum cum fieri incipient

---

43. oððæt ic sette fiondas ðine scomel fota ðinra 44. .... forðon drihten ðeilca giceeð ⁊ huu sunu his is 45. miððy wæs gi-hered ða allum folche cwæð ðegnum his 46. bihaldas fro*m* uðwutum ðaðe wallað gonga on stollum ⁊ lufas groetinge on sprece ⁊ ða forma seatlas on somnungu*m* ⁊ ða forma sedlo in gibeorscipe 47. ðaðe fo*r*swelgað hus widwa wyrcas ꝥ longe gibed ðas onfoað ðæt mara ɫ mast cursunge

Cap. XXI. 1. eft biheold ðon*ne* gisæh ða ðaðe gisendun ar (*sic*) ðing hiora in gazo*philacium* weolige 2. giseh ðon*ne* sum oðer widwe ðorfendlico sendende mæsleno feorðungas twoego 3. ⁊ cwæð soð is ðæt ic cweðo iow ðætte widwe ðios ðorfende forðor ðon alle sende 4. forðon ðæs ða alle of monigfaldnisse him sendun on ðincgum, godes ðios wutudl*ice* of ðon ðætte wona is hir all lif hire ðæt hio hæfde hio sende 5. ⁊ ðara sum cweðendu*m* of temple ðætte mið stanum godum ⁊ geofum girinad were cwæð 6. ðios ðaðe gisegun cymeð dagas on ðæm ne bið forleten stan ofer stane seðe ne bið strogden 7. gifrugnun ðon*ne* hine cweðende hæsere hwenne ðas bioðon ⁊ hwelc gif becun miððy bið ðæt he (*sic*) onginneð

8 Ða cwæþ he warniað ꝥ ge ne syn beswicene. manege cumað on minum naman. ⁊ cweðað; Ic hit eom ⁊ tīd genealæcð; ne fare ge æfter him

9 ne beo gė bregede þonne ge geseoð gefeoht and twy-rædnessa; Ðas þing gebyrigeað ærystac nys þonne gyt ende;

10 Ða cwæð he to him þeod arist agen þeode ⁊ rice agen rīce

11 ⁊ beoð mycele eorþan styrunga geond stowa. ⁊ cwealmas ⁊ hungor. ⁊ egsan of heofone ⁊ mycele tacna beoð.

12 ac toforan eallum þissum hig nimað eow ⁊ ehtað ⁊ syððan eow on gesamnunga. ⁊ on hyrdnyssa ⁊ lædaþ eow to cyningum ⁊ to demum for mīnum naman.

13 þis eow gebyrað on gewitnesse;

14 Ne sceole ge on eowrum heortum fore-smeagan hu ge ⁊swarian.

15 ic sylle eow muð ⁊ wīsdom. þam ne magon ealle eower wiðer-winnan wiðstāndan ⁊ wið-cweðan;

16 Ge beoð gesealde fram māgum ⁊ gebroðrum ⁊ cuðum ⁊ freondum. ⁊ hig eow to deaðe geswencað.

17 ⁊ ge beoð eallum on hatunga. for minum naman.

18 ⁊ ne for-wyrð a locc of eowrum heafde;

19 On eowrum geþylde ge gehealdað eowre sawla;

Ðys godspell gebyrað on wodnes dæg on þære .xi. ucan ofer pen-

20 Þonne ge geseoð hierusalem mid here betrymede. witað ꝥ hyre toworpennes genealæcð.

Various eadings.

8. A. Manige. 9. A. ge ge-bregede. A. twyrædnyssa. A. ge-byriað ærest. 10. A. ongean (*twice*). 11. A. eond. A. hunger. A. egesan. A. heofene. A. B. C. tacnu. 13. A. gebyreð. A. ge-wytnysse. 14. A. scyle. A. B. C. -smeagean. A. ⁊swarion; B. C. ⁊swarigean. 18. A. ān; *but* B. C. a (*as in text*). *In* A., locc *is glossed by* hær. B. C. heafode. 19. A. sawle. 20. A. toworpenys.

8 Ða cwæð he warnieð eow ꝥ ge ne byon be-swikene. manege cumað on minen namen ⁊ cweðed. Ic hit eom. ⁊ tid genehlæceð. ne fare ge æfter heom.

9 ne beo ge bregede þanne ge ge-seoð ge-feoht ⁊ twirednyssa. Ðas þing ge-byriað ærest. ac nys þanne gyot ende.

10 Ða cwæð he to heom. Þeode arist agen þeode. ⁊ rice agen rice.

11 ⁊ beoð mycele eorðe steriunge. geond stowa; ⁊ cwalmes. ⁊ hunger ⁊ egsan on heofene ⁊ mychele tacne beoð.

12 ac to-foren eallen þisen hyo nymeð eow ⁊ ehteð ⁊ syððan eow on ge-samnunge. ⁊ on hyrdnyssa. ⁊ ladeð eow to kyningen. ⁊ to demen for minen namen.

13 þis eow ge-byrieð on ge-witnesse.

14 Ne scule ge on eowren heorten forsmeagen hu ge andswerien;

15 ic selle eow muð ⁊ wisdom. þam ne magen ealle eower wiðer-winnan wiðstanden ⁊ wið-cweðan.

16 Ge beoð ge-sealde fram magen ⁊ ge-broðren. ⁊ cuðen. ⁊ freonden. ⁊ hyo eow to deaðe ge-swenced.

17 ⁊ ge byoð eallen on hatigenga for minen name.

18 ⁊ ne for-wurð a locc of eowren hæfde.

19 On eowren ge-þelde ge ge-healded eowre sawle.

20 Þanne ge ge-seoð ierusalem mid here be-tremed. witeð ꝥ heore to-worpnysse ge-neohlæcð.

Cum uiderit ierusalem ci cumdarj ab exercitu.

Various Readings.

8. warniað; seon beo-swicene. manega; minum namon; cweðað; ge-neahlæcð. 9. þonne; arest; þonne gyt. 10. eom. þeod. 11. steriunga; hungor; heofone; mycele tacnu. 12. to-foran eallum þissun; nymað; ehtað; lædoð (*sic*); cyningum; demum; minum naman. 13. ge-byrað; gewitnysse. 14. sceole; eowrum heortum fore-smeagean ge hwu ge andswarian. 15. sylle; magon; wið-standan. 16. magum; ge-broðrum; cuðum; freondum; ge-swenceð. 17. eallum; hatinga; minum namen. 18. for-wyrð; eowrum hafde. 19. eowrum ge-þylde; ge-healdað; sawla. 20. *Rubric as in* H.; Ðonne (*with red initial*); hierusalem; be-trymede. witað; hyre toworpnes geneahlacð.

seðe cuoeð geseað ꝥte gie ne se bisuicen ɫ menigo for*ð*on hia cymað on noma minu*m* cuoeðendo
8 qui dixit uidete ne seducamini multi enim uenient in nomine meo dicentes

ꝥ ic am ⁊ ðio tíd geneoleceð ɫ geneolecde nallað gie for*ð*on geonga æft*er* hi*m* ɫ ðæ*m* mið ðy
quia ego sum et tempus appropinquauit nolite ergo ire post illos 9 cum

uut*edlice* gie gehereð gefehto ⁊ ymbsetnungo .i. ymbburgu*m* nallað iuih forhtiga ɫ gedæfned is ærist ðas
autem audieritis proelia et seditiones nolite terreri oportet primum haec

to wosanne Ah huoeðre ne sona ꝥ ende ða gecuoeð ðæm arisað cynn wið ɫ ongægn cynne
fieri sed non statim finis 10 tunc dicebat illis surget gens contra gentem

⁊ ríc wið ríc eorð-hroernisso miclo biðon ðerh stoua ⁊ deað-bernisse ɫ un-
et regnum aduersus regnum 11 terrae motus magni erunt per loca et pesti-

cuðo ádlo ⁊ hungro ⁊ fyrht-nisso of heofnu*m* ⁊ becono micelo biðon ah aér ðas Alle
lentiae et fames terrores-que de caelo et signa magna erunt 12 *Sed antė haec omnia * 250. i. mt. ccxliiii.

on-worpað ɫ iuh honda hiora ⁊ aoehtad gē biðon iuih sellas in somnungu*m* ⁊ hæftu*m* ɫ iuih seallað mr. cxxxuiiii.
inicient uobis manus suas et persequentur tradentes in synagogas et custodias tradentes io. cxlui.

æc cyninges ⁊ to under-cyningu*m* ɫ f*or*e noma minu*m* gelimpeð ɫ ðon*ne* iuh on cyðnise ɫ
et reges et ad praesides propter nomen meu*m* 13 continget autem uobis in testimonium

geset teð for*ð*on In Iuerum heortum ne gie f*or*e-ðencgæ huu ɫ suæ gie ondsuariga ɫ onduarde ic
14 *Ponite ergo in cordib*us* uestris non praemeditari quemammodum respondeatis 15 ego * 251. ii. mt. lxxxuiii.

for*ð*on sello iuh muð ⁊ æc snyttro ðæm ne magon hia wið-stonda ɫ ⁊ wið-cuoeða ɫ ongcaegn Alle mr. cxli.
enim dabo uobis ós et sapientiam cui non poterint resistere et contradicere omnes

wiðiwordas ɫ fiondas iura gesáld gie biðon uut*edlice* fro*m* aldru*m* ɫ ⁊ broðru*m* ⁊ friondu*m* ⁊
aduersarii uestri 16 trademini autem á parentib*us* et fratrib*us* et cognatis et

megu*m* ⁊ to deaðe acuoellað ɫ fro*m* iuh ɫ of iuih ⁊ gie biðon lað allum *monnum* f*or*e
amicis et morte afficient ex uobis 17 et eritis odio omnib*us* propter

noma mín ⁊ hēr of heafdo Iuero ne bið f*or*loren ɫ ne losað ⁊ on
nomen meum 18 et capillus de capite uestro non peribit 19 et in

ðýld iuera gie byeð ɫ gie agnigað sauelo iuero mið ðy ðon*ne* geseað gie ɫ gie geseas
patientia uestra possidebitis animas uestras 20 *Cum autem uideritis * LXXXUI. 252. x.

ꝥte sē ymbsald ɫ ymbsetet fro*m* here hier*usalem* ðon*ne* wutas gie ꝥte geneolecað f*or*letnisse ɫ woestonis*se* hire
circumdari ab exercitu hierusalem tunc scitote quia appropinquabit desolatio eius

---

8. seðe cwæð giseað ðætte ge [ne] se biswicen monige forðon cumað in noma minum cweðende forðon ic am crist ⁊ ðio tid togineolicað nallað ge forðon gonga æfter ðæm 9. mið wutudl*ice* ge giherað gifeht ⁊ ymbsetnunge nallað giforhtiga gidæfne is ærist ðas to wosanne ah hweðre ne sona ðe ende 10. ða ge-cweoðað ðæm ariseð cynn ɫ ongægn cynne ⁊ rice wið rice 11. ⁊ eorðo hroernis micelo bioðon ðerh stowwe ⁊ doeð-bernisse ⁊ hungor fyrhtnisse of heofnum ⁊ becono micelo bioðon 12. ah ær ðas alle onginneð iowih honda ⁊ gioehted ge bioðon sellas iowih in somnungu*m* ⁊ in hæftun (*sic*) iowih sellas to cynigas ⁊ under-cyniges fore noma minu*m* 13. gilimpe ðon*ne* iow on cyðnisse 14. gisettað mec f*or*ðon in heortum iowrum ne ge for-ðence hu ɫ swa ge ondsworigað 15. ic f*or*ðon selo iow muð ⁊ snytru ðæm ne magun hia giondsworia ⁊ wið-cweoða alle wiðer-worda iowre 16. gisald ge bioðon ðon*ne* from aldru*m* ⁊ broðrom ⁊ frio[n]dom ⁊ megum ⁊ to deaðe acwellað of iow 17. ⁊ ge bioðon laðe allum f*or*e noma minum 18. ⁊ her of heofde iowrum ne bið f*or*loren 19. ⁊ on ðylde iowre settas ge sawle iowre 20. miððy ðonne giseað ge ðætte ymb-sald from herge hierus*alem* ðon*ne* wutas ge ðætte gineolicað f*or*letnis ɫ awest-nisse hire

tecosten. Respondens *iesus* dixit discipulis suis. Cu*m* aute*m* uideritis circu*m*dari ab exercitu. A. Cum uideritis, &c. B.

21 þon*ne* fleoð on muntas þa ðe on iudea synt ⁊ nyðer ne astigað þa ðe on hyre middele synt. ⁊ into hyre ne magon þa ðe þar-ute synt

22 forþa*m* ðe þis synt wrace dagas ꝥ ealle þing syn gefyllede þe awritene synt;

23 Soðlice wā eacnigendu*m* wīfe ⁊ fedendu*m* on þa*m* dagu*m* þon*ne* bið mycel ofþriccednys ofer eorðan. ⁊ yrre þisu*m* folce.

24 ⁊ hig fealláð on swurdes ecge. ⁊ beoð hæftlingas on ealle þeoda; Hierusale*m* bið fra*m* þeodu*m* fortreden oð mægða tīda synt gefyllede;

25 And beoð tacna on sunnan ⁊ on monan ⁊ on steorru*m* ⁊ on eorðan. þeoda forþriccednys. for gedrefednesse sǽs swēges. ⁊ yða

26 bifigendu*m* mannu*m*. for ege ⁊ anbide þe eallu*m* ymbe-hwyrfte to-becumað; Đon*ne* beoð heofones myhta astyrede.

27 ⁊ þon*ne* hig geseoð mannes sunu on lyfte cum*en*de mid mycelu*m* anwalde ⁊ mægen-þry*m*me;

28 Đon*ne* þas þing agynnað beseoð ⁊ eowre heafdu ūp-ahebbaþ. forþa*m* ðe eower alysednes geNealæcð;

29 Đa sæde he hi*m* su*m* big-spel. behealdað þæne fic-bea*m* ⁊ ealle trywu

30 þon*ne* hig wæstm bringcað. ge witun ꝥ sumor ys gehende;

31 And þon*ne* ge þas þing geseoð witað ꝥ godes rīce is gehende;

Various Readings.

21. A. heora mydlene synd. A. synd (*twice*). 22. A. synd (*twice*). 23. A. eacniendu*m*. A. þyssu*m*. 24. C. fellað. A. sweordes. A. B. C. syn. 25. A. tacnu. 26. A. byfiendu*m*. B. C. astyrude. 27. A. anwealde. 28. A. *om.* ðe. A. alysednys. 29. A. þone. A. treowa. 30. A. wyton.

21 þanne fleod on muntes þa þe on iudea synde. ⁊ niðer ne astigeð þa þe on hire midlene synd. ⁊ in-to here* hus ne mugen þa þe þær-ute synden.

* H. hire, *alt. to* here.

22 for-þan þe þis synden wræce dages. ꝥ ealle þing seon ge-fylde. þe awritene synde.

23 Soðlice wa eacnigenden wife ⁊ fedenden on þam dagen þanne beoð mychel ofþricodnys. ofer eorðen. ⁊ yrre þisen folce.

24 ⁊ hyo falleð on sweordes egge. ⁊ beoð hæftlinges on eallen þeodan. Ierusalem beoð fram þeoden for-treden oð mægþa tide syen ge-fyllede.

25 And beoð tacne on sunnen ⁊ on monan ⁊ on steorren. ⁊ on eorðan þeoda for-þrecednyss. for ge-drefednysse. sæs sweges ⁊ yrða (*sic*)

26 byfigengan mannen for eige ⁊ an-bide ealle þa ymbbe-hrifte (*sic*) to be-cumað. þanne byð heofenes mihte astirede.

27 ⁊ þanne hyo ge-seoð mannes sune on lifte cumende mid michelen an-wealde ⁊ mægen-þrimme.

28 þanne þas þing aginneð be-seoð ⁊ eowre heafde up ahebbeð. for-þam þe eower alysednesse ge-neahlæceð.

29 Đa saigde he heom sum byspell. behealdeð þanne fic-beam. ⁊ ealle treowa.

30 þanne hyo wæstme bringeð ge witeð ꝥ sumer is ge-hende.

31 Ænd þone ge þas þing ge-seoð witað ꝥ godes rice is ge-hende.

Various Readings.

21. þon fleoð; muntas; synt; astigað; middele synt; hire; R. *om.* hus; magen; synt. 22. for-þa*m*; synt; wrace dagas; syn ge-fyllede; synt. 23. eacnigendu*m*; fedondu*m*; dagu*m*; þonne bið mycel of-þriccednys; eorðan; þisu*m*. 24. hie feallað; swurdes ecge; ealle þeoda. Hierusalem bið; deodu*m* (*sic*); od (*sic*); tida syn. 25. sunnan; steorru*m*; for-þricednys; iða. 26. bifigendu*m* mannu*m*; þe ealle [*for* ealle þa]; ymbehwyrfte; þon*ne*; heofones mihta astiride (*sic*). 27. þonne; michelum. 28. Đon*ne*; aginað; hæfde; alysednes. 29. sægde; big-spell. be-healdað þonne. 30. þone; bringað. 31. þo*n*ne.

ðon*ne* ða ðe In iuðea sindon ł biðon fleað In mor*um* ⁊ ða ðe on middum hire of-stigæð
21 *Tunc qui in iudæa sunt fugiant in montes et qui in medio eius desce[*n*]dant * 253. ii. mt. ccxluiii. mr. cxliii.

⁊ ða ðe In lond*um* biðon no in-gaað in ðær for*ð*on dagas wræccenise ða biðon ꝥte se gefylledo
et qui in regionib*us* non intrent in eam 22 quia dies ultionis hí sunt ut impleantur

alle ðaðe auritteno sindon wæ ðon*ne* ðæm berend*um* ⁊ foedend*um* on ðæm dagum·
omnia quae scribta sunt 23 *Uáe autem praegnantib*us* et nutrientib*us* in illis diebus * 254. ii. mt. ccxluiiii. mr. cxliiii.

·bið for*ð*on of*er*-suiðniss*o* ł micelo on-ufa eorðo ⁊ wræððo folce ðiss*um* ⁊ gefallas hia In muðe
*ERit enim praesura magna supra terra*m* et ira populo huic 24 †Et cadent in ore * 255. ii. mt. ccli. mr. cxlui. † 256. x.

suordes ⁊ geðeodo geláeded biðon in alle cynno ł hædno ⁊ hie*rusalem* ahēned bið ł gehniðrad bið fro*m* hædnu*m*
gladii et captiui ducentur in omnes gentes et hierusalem calcabitur á gentibus

oððæt se gefylled tído· ðara cynna ⁊ biðon beceno on sunna ⁊ mona ⁊ on tungl*um*
donec impleantur tempora nationum 25 *ET erunt signa in sole et luna et in stellis * 257. ii. mt. ccluiii. mr. cl.

⁊ on eorðum of*er*suiðnisse ł hædno ł hæðinra mið fo*re*-scending ł suegungniss*o* ł sæs ⁊ ðara yðana
et in terra pressura gentium prae confussione sonitus maris et fluctuum

ðæm for*cummenum* ł monnu*m* for*e* egisa ⁊ bídes ł basnung ða ðe of*er*-cymmas allu*m*
26 arescentib*us* hominib*us* prae timorem et expectatione quae superueniunt uniuerso

ymbhuirfte for*ð*on mægno heofna gestyredo ł biðon ⁊ ða geseað sunu monnes
orbi nam uirtutes caeloru*m* mouebuntur 27 *ET tunc uidebunt filium hominis * 258. ii. mt. ccluiiii. mr. cli.

cymende In wolcne mið onwæld micla ⁊ ðrymm ðæm ⁊ ðas uut*edlice* to wosanne
uenientem in nube cum potestate magna et maiestate 28 hís autem fieri

onginnendu*m* eft-locað ł ⁊ ahebbað heafda iuera for*ð*on geneolaceð onlesnisse iuera
incipientib*us* *Respicite et leuate capita uestra quoniam appropinquat redemtio uestra * LXXXUII.

⁊ cuoeð him onlicnisse ł geseað ꝥ fic-beam ⁊ alle treo miððy fo*ra*-brengað
29 et dixit illis similitudinem uidete ficulneam et omnes arbores 30 cum producunt

uut*edlice* of him wæstm witteð gie ꝥte neh is ðe su*m*mer ón ða wisa æc gie miððy
iam ex sé fructum scitis quoniam prope est aestas 31 ita et uos cum

gie geseað ðas ꝥte aworðe ł ꝥte hia se aworden wuttað gie ꝥte neh is ł bið ríc godes
uideritis haec fieri scitote quoniam prope est regnum d*ei*

21. ðon*ne* ðaðe in iudeu*m* sindun fleas on moras ⁊ ðaðe on middum hire ne astigeð ⁊ ðaðe on londum ne ingongas in ða 22. for*ð*on dagas wrecnisse ðas sindun ꝥ se gifylled alle ðaðe awriteno sindun 23. wæ ðonne ðæm berendum ⁊ foedendu*m* in ðæm dagum bið for*ð*on of-swiðnissum micelre of*er* eorðo ⁊ wræððo folche ðissu*m* 24. ⁊ fallað hiæ in muð swordana ⁊ giðiode to-dæled bioðon in alle cynn ⁊ ahened bið fro*m* hæðnu*m* ðeodu*m* oððæt sie gifylled ðio tid ðara cynna 25. ⁊ bioðon beceno on sunna ⁊ mona ⁊ steorra ⁊ on eorðo ofer-swiðnisse hæðnana mið forscendinge swinsunge ⁊ sæs ⁊ ðara yðana 26. ðæm for-cumnum monnum fo*re* egsa ⁊ bides [ł] basnunge ðaðe ofer-cumað allu*m* hwyrfte for*ð*on mægen heofna onwended bið 27. ⁊ ða giseað sunu monnes cymende in wolcnum mið onwælde miclum ⁊ ðrymme 28. ðæm wutudl*ice* onginnendum eft-locciigað ⁊ ahebbað heofodo iowre for*ð*on neolicað onlesnisse iowrum 29. cwæð him onlicnisse giseað ðon*e* fic-beom ⁊ alle treo 30. miððy fo*re*brengað wut*edlice* of him wæstim wutað ge ðætte neh is ðe sumor 31. on ða wise ⁊ ge miððy giseað ðas wosa wutað ge ꝥte neh bið rice godes

32 Soðlice ic eow secge ꝥ þeos cneores ne gewit ærþam þe ealle þas ðing ge-
wurþon;
33 Heofen ⁊ eorðe gewitaþ soðlice mine
word ne gewitað;

Ðys godspel gebyrað on frige-dæg on þære end-leftan wucan ofer pente-costen. A. B. Adtendite uobis ne grauentur corda uestra in crapula & ebrietate & curis. A.

34 Warniaþ eow þe-læs eower heortan
gehefegude syn on ofer-fylle ⁊ on druncen-
nesse ⁊ þises lifes carum ⁊ on eow se færlica
dæg be-cume
35 swa swa grin; He be-cymþ on ealle
þa ðe sittað ofer eorðan ansyne;
36 Waciað on ælcere tíde ⁊ bidað ꝥ ge
wurðe syn. ꝥ ge þas towerdan þing for-
fleon. ⁊ standan beforan mannes suna;
37 Soðlice he wæs on dæg on þam temple lærende. ⁊ on niht he eode ⁊ wunode
on þam munte þe ys gecweden olíueti
38 ⁊ eall folc on morgen com to him. to
þam temple ꝥ hi hine gehyrdon;

CHAPTER XXII.

Ðes passio gebyrað on wodnes dæg on þære palm-wucan. A. B. Adpropinquabat autem dies festus. A.

1 ÐA soðlice genealæhte freols-dǽg
azimorum se is gecweden eastre.
2 ⁊ þara sacerda ealdras ⁊ þa boceras
smeadon hu hig hine forspildon; [Soðlice
hig adredon him ꝥ folc;]
3 Ða eode satanas on iudam. se wæs
oðre naman scarioth. an of þam twelfum.
4 þa ferde he ⁊ spæc mid þara sacerda
ealdor-mannum ⁊ duguðe ealdrum hu he
híne him gesealde;

Various Readings.

32. A. cneorys. A. geweorðan. 33. B. C. Heofon. 34. A. þy-læs. A. ge-hefegode. A. druncennysse. A. þysses. 36. A. byddað. A. weorðe. A. toweardan. 37. B. C. lærynde. 38. A. mergen. A. hyg; B. C. hig.

Cap. xxii. 1. C. Sa [*for* Ða, *by mistake*]. A. eastron. 2. C. *om.* ⁊ *before* þara. A. þæra. Corpus MS. *omits from* Soðlice *to* folc, *which is supplied from* B. C.; A. *has* Soðlice hig ondredon hym ꝥ folc. 4. A. spræc. A. þæra. A. dugoðe.

32 Soðlice ich eow segge ꝥ þeos cneores
ne ge-wit ær þam þe ealle þas þing ge-
wurðon.
33 Heofene ⁊ eorþe ge-witeð; soðlice
mine word ne ge-witað.
34 Wærnieð eow þi-læs eower heorten
ge-hefegede synd on ofer-fylle ⁊ on drunce-
nesse ⁊ þises lifes carun ⁊ on eow syo se
færlice daig be-cume
35 swa swa grin. He be-cymð on ealle
þa þe sitteð ofer eorðan ansiene.
36 wakieð on ælcere tide ⁊ biddað ꝥ ge
wurðe syn. ꝥ ge þas to-wearde þing for-
flean ⁊ standen be-foran mannes sune.
37 Soðlice he wæs on daig on þam temple
lærende. ⁊ on niht he eode ⁊ wunede on
þam munte þe ys cweðen oliuetj.
38 ⁊ eall folc com on morgen to him to
þam temple þæt hyo hine ge-hyrdon.

CHAPTER XXII.

1 ÞA soðlice ge-neahlacte freols-daige
azimorum se ys ge-cweðen eastre.
2 ⁊ þare sacerda ealdres ⁊ þa bokeres
smægdon hu hyo hine forspildon. Soðlice
hyo adredden heom ꝥ folc.
3 Ða eode sathanas on iudam se wæs
oðre name scariot an of þam twelfen.
4 þa ferde he ⁊ spræce mid þare sacerde
ealdre mannen. ⁊ ðugede (*sic*) ealdren
hu he hine heo*m* sealde.

Various Readings.

32. ic; cnereos (*sic*); alle. 33. ge-witað (*twice*). 34. Warniað; þe-læs; heortan gehefegude synt; druncennysse; carum; dag. 35. sittáð; eorðam (*sic*) ansyne. 36. waciað. 37. þe his ge-cweðen olíueti.

Cap. xxii. 1. ge-neahlachte; -dæga. 2. þara; ealdras; boceras smeagdon; adreden. 3. satanas; nama; twelfum. 4. spræc; sacerda ealdor-mannum; ðugede (*as in* H.); ealdrum; eom sælde.

soð is ꝥ ic cuoeðo iuh ꝥte ne gelioreð ɫ cneoreso ðios oðð ꝥ alle hia se aworden heofon
32 amen dico uobis quia non praeteribit generatio haec donec omnia fiant 33 caelum

⁊ eorðo geliorad biðon wordo uut*edlice* míno ne of*er*-liorað behaldað ðon*ne* iuih
et terra transibunt uerba autem mea non transient 34 *Attendite autem uobis * 259. x.

caðe mæge ɫ ꝥte ne sie ahefigad hearto iuero on of*er*fyllo ⁊ mið druuncen ⁊ gemnisu*m* ðisses lifes ⁊
ne forte grauentur corda uestra in crapula et ebrietate et curis huius uitae et

of*er*-cymað on Iuih feer-lic ɫ dæge ðio ɫ ðe *dæg* suelce sâdo for*ð*on of*er*-cymeð
superueniant in uos repentina dies illa 35 tamquam laqueus enim super-ueniet

on allum ðaðe sittað of*er* onsione all corðes wæccæs for*ð*on alle tíde
in omnes qui sedent super faciem omnis terrae 36 uigilate itaq*ue* omni tempore

gebiddande ꝥte gie se wyrðo to habbanne gefleanne ðas alle ða ðe to-cymendo sint ɫ ⁊ stonda fo*r*a
orantes ut digni habeamini fugere ista omnia quae futura sunt et stare ante

sune monnes wæs ðon*ne* dagu*m* lærende in temple næhtu*m* æc foerde ɫ gewunade ɫ
filium hominis 37 erat autem diebus docens in templo noctib*us* uero exiens morabatur

on more seðe geceigd is olebearu mo*re* ⁊ all ꝥ folc to him In temple
in monte qui uocatur olilueti 38 et omnis populus manicauat ad eum in templo

to heranne hine
audire eum

CAP. XXII.

geneolecað ɫ ðon*ne* dæg symbel dærstana seðe gecuooden is eostro ⁊
1 *Appropinquabat autem dies festus azymorum qui dicitur pascha 2 †Et * 260. i. mt. cclxxiiii. mr. clui.

sohton aldorm*onno* sace*rda* ⁊ ða uð-uto hûu hine acuoella mæghton ondreardon for*ð*on
quaerebant principes sacerdotu*m* et scribae quomodo eum interficerent timebant uero io. xluiii. † 261. i. mt. ccxx.

ꝥ folc in-foerde ðon*ne* se wiðerworda in iudas seðe is geceiged scarioth an of ðæm
plebem 3 *INtrauit autem satanas in iudam qui uocatur scarioth unum de duo- mr. cxxii. io. lxxuii. * LXXXUIII. 262. uiiii.

tuoel*fum* ⁊ foerde ⁊ sprecend wæs mið aldormon*num* sac*erda* ⁊ lâruu*m*
decim 4 *ET abiit et locutus est cum principib*us* sacerdotum et magistratib*us* io. cxiii. * 263. ii. mt. cclxxuiii. mr. clx.

huu hine mæhte gesealla him
quem-ammodum illu*m* traderet eis

---

32. soð ic cweðo iow ꝥte ne gi-lioreð cneoreswe ðios oððæt alle hia se aworden 33. heofun ⁊ eorðo giliored bioðon word wutudl*ice* min ne ofer-lioreð 34. bihaldas ðonne iowih eaða mæge ꝥte ne se ahefgad heorte iowre on of*er*fyllo ⁊ druncennisse ⁊ gemnisse ðisses lifes ⁊ ofer-cumað on iowih ferlice dagas ðæm 35. swelce sade fo*rð*on of*er*cymeð on alle ðaðe sittað of*er* onsione alle corðo 36. wæccas forðon alle tide gibiddende ꝥte ge sie wyrðe to fleanne ðas alle ðaðe tocymende sindun ⁊ stondað fore sunu monnes 37. wæs ðon*ne* on dagum lærende on templo næhtum ec foerde giwunade on more seðe giceged bið.... 38. ⁊ all ðæt folc comun ar to him in tempil

Cap. XXII. 1. gineolicað wut*edlice* dæg symbles ðara dærstana ðæt giceged bið eostru 2. ⁊ sohtun from aldor-sacerdom ⁊ uðwutu*m* hu hine acwelle mæhtun ondreordun fo*rð*on ꝥ folc 3. infoerde ðon*ne* ðe wiðerworda i*n* iudeas seðe giceged is scariothisca an of ðæm twelfu*m* 4. ⁊ foerde ⁊ sprecende wæs mið aldor-monnum ðara sacerda ⁊ larwum hu hine mæhte hine (*sic*) sella him

5 And hig fagenydun ⁊ hi*m* weddedon feoh to syllenne.

6 ⁊ he behet ⁊ he sohte hu he eaðelicust hine be-æftan þære menego gesealde;

7 Ða co*m* se dǽg azimoru*m* on þa*m* hi woldon hyra eastron gewyrcan

8 ⁊ he sende petru*m*. ⁊ iohanne*m* ⁊ cwæð to hi*m* farað ⁊ gearwiað us ꝥ we ure eastron gewyrcon;

9 Ða cwædon hig hwar wylt tu ꝥ we gearwion

10 ⁊ he cwæð to him; Nu þænne ge on þa ceastre gað eow agen yrnð an man mid wæter-buce. filigeað hi*m* on ꝥ hus þe he in-gæð.

11 ⁊ secgeað þa*m* hus-hlaforde; Ure lareow þe segð hwar ys cumena hus. þar ic mine eastron wyrce mid minon leorning-cnihtu*m*;

12 And he eow betæcð mycele healle gedæfte. gegearwiað þara;

13 Ða ferdun hig ⁊ gemettun swa he hi*m* sæde. ⁊ hig gegearwudun eastrun;

14 And þa tima wæs he sæt ⁊ his twelfe apostolas mid hi*m*

15 ⁊ he sǽde hi*m*; Of gewilnunge ic gewilnude etan mid eow þas eastron ær ic forð-fare;

16 Ic eow secge ꝥ ic heonon-forð ne ète. ær hyt sy on godes rîce gefylled;

---

5 And hyo fagenedon ⁊ hym weddeden feoh to syllene.

6 ⁊ he be-het. ⁊ he sohte hu he æðelicest hine beften þare manigeo ge-sealde.

7 Ða com se daig azimorum on þam hyo wolden heore eastren ge-wyrcan

8 ⁊ he sende petre ⁊ iohanne. ⁊ cwæð to heom. fared ⁊ gearewiað us ꝥ we ure eastren ge-wyrcen.

9 Ða cwæðen hyo. hwær wilt þu þæt we gearewien.

10 ⁊ he cwæð to heom. Nu þanne ge on þa cestre gað; eow an-gen eornð an man mid wæter-buke. fylgieð hym on ꝥ hus þe he ingað;

11 ⁊ seggeð þam hus-hlaforde. vre lareow þe segð. hwær ys cumena hus þær yc min eastren wyrce mid mjnen leorning-cnihten.

12 ⁊ he eow be-tæcð mycele healle ge-dæfte ge-garewiad þara.

13 Ða ferden hyo ⁊ ge-metten swa he heom saigde. ⁊ hyo gearewedon eastren.

14 Ǽnd þa time wæs he sett ⁊ his twelf apostles mid hym.

15 ⁊ he saigde heom. Of ge-wilnenge ic ge-wilnede mid eow æten þas eastren ær ich forð-fare.

16 Ic eow segge þæt ic heonen-forð ne eta. ær hyt syo on godes rice ge-fylled.

Various Readings.

5. A. fagnedon. A. syllanne. 6. A. *puts* hyne *after* hu he. A. eaðelicost; B. C. eaðelucust. A. mænio. 7. A. adzimoru*m*. A hig. A. heora. 8. A. earwiað. A. gewyrcan. 9. A. ðu [*for* tu]. A. gegearwion; C. gearwian. 10. A. þonn*e*. A. ongean. A. ⁊ filiað [*for* filigeað]. 11. A. secgað. A. ic nyme eastron. ⁊ wyrce myd mynu*m*. 13. A. ferdon. A. gemetton. A. earwedon eastron. 14. A. twelf. 15. A. gewylnode. 16. A. sig.

Various Readings.

5. Ǽnd; fagenydon; weddedon; syllenne. 6. eaðe-lucust; bæftan; menego. 7. hyra eastron. 8. petru*m*; Iohanne*m*; farað; gearwiað; eastron gewyrcan. 9. cwæ-ðon; þet; geawian (*sic*). 10. þænne; ceastre; agen yrnð; -buce. fyligeð. 11. seggað; hwar; ic mine æstron; minen leornig-cnihtan (*sic*). 12. gegarewiad þara (*as in* H.). 13. ge-metton; sægde; gearewudun eastran. 14. tima; twelfe apostlas. 15. sæde; gewilnunge; etan; eastron; ic forð-fara. 16. secge; heonon-; ete.

⁊ gefeando woeron ⁊ ðafando ł woeron feh him to seallanne ł geseall*anne* ⁊ geheht ⁊
5 et gauisi sunt et pacti sunt pecuniam illi dare 6 et spopondit et

sohte ꝥ tidlicnisse ꝥte mæhte seal*la* hine buta ðæm hergu*m* cuo*m* ðon*ne* ł dæge dærstana
quaerebat oportunitatem ut traderet illum sine turbis 7 uenit autem dies azymorum

in ðæm ł nēd-ðarf wæs ꝥte were geslægen ł eostro ⁊ sende petru*m* ⁊ ioh*annen* ge-cuoeð
in qua necesse erat occidi pascha 8 et misit petrum et iohannen dicens

geongað gearuas us eostro ꝥte we ētte soð hia cuoedon huoer wilt ðu ꝥte woe gearuia
euntes parate nobis pascha ut manducemus 9 at illi dixerunt ubi uís paremus

⁊ cuoeð to ðæm heono I*nn*-færendu*m* iuh ł iw In ða ceastra to-gægne Iorneð iuh monn ombor ł full
10 et dixit ad eos ecce intro-euntib*us* uobis in ciuitatem occurrit uobis homo amphoram

wætres berende fylgeð ðone in hūs in ðæm inga*a*ð ⁊ cuoeðas gie ðæm fædir hiu*u*isc ł
aquae portans sequimini eum in domu*m* in qua intrat 11 et dicetis patri-

hiorodes hus he coeðes ðe laruu huer is ꝥ gest-ern ðer eostro mið ðegnu*m*
famelias domus dicet tibi magister ubi est diuersorium ubi pascha cum discipulis

minu*m* ic brucco ⁊ he iuh æd-eauað symbel-hus ł micel bedd ł song ⁊ ðēr
meis manducem 12 et ipse uobis ostendet cenaculum magnum stratum et ibi

ge-gearuað mið ðy foerdon gemoetton sua cuoeð ðæm ł him · ⁊ gegearuadon eostro
parate 13 euntes autem inuenerunt sicut dixit illis et parauerunt pascha

⁊ mið ðy aworden woere ł wæs ðio tīd gesætt ł gehlinade ⁊ toelfo apos*tolo* mið hine ⁊
14 et cum facta esset hora discubuit et duo-decim apostoli cum eo 15 *ET * 264. x.

cuoeð him willu*m* ic wilnade ðis eostro gebrucca ł to eattanne iuih mið ær ðon ic ðrowiga ł ic ðolega
ait illis desiderio desideraui hoc pascha manducare uobiscu*m* ante-quam patiar

ic coeðo for*ð*on iuh ꝥte from ðis ne brucco ic ꝥ oðð ꝥte gefylledo biðon in ríc
16 *Dico enim uobis quia ex hoc non manducabo illud donec impleantur in regno * 265. ii. mt. cclxxxu. mr. clxui.

godes
dei

---

5. ⁊ gifeande werun ⁊ ða gifeande werun feh him to sellanne 6. ⁊ gi-heht ⁊ sohte ðætte tidlice ꝥte mæhte sellan hine butan ðæm hergu*m* 7. com ðonne dæg ðara dærstana in ðæm ned-ðarf wæs ꝥte were gislægen eostru 8. ⁊ sende .... ⁊ .... cwæð gongað georwigað us eostru ꝥte we ete 9. soð hiæ cwedun hwer wyltu we georwiga 10. ⁊ cwæð to him ⁊ heono in-færendum iowih in ðær cæstre togægnes iorneð iow monn ombor fulne wætres berende fylgað ge him in hus ðæm ingað 11. ⁊ cweoðað ge ðæm feder hiorodes hus he cweðes ðe larow hwer is ðæt gest-ern ðer eostru mið ðegnum minum ic brucco 12. ⁊ he æt-eoweð iow symbel-hus micel bedd ⁊ ðer gegeorwigað 13. foerdun miððy gimoettun swa cwæð ðe hæl*end* *him* ⁊ georwadun eostru 14. ⁊ miððy aworden were ðio tid gisæt ł hlionade ⁊ twelfe apos*tolo* mið hine 15. ⁊ cwæð ðæm willu*m* ic wilnade ðas eostru to bruccanne iowih mið ærðon ic ðrowigo 16. ic cweðo *forð*on iow ðætte of ðisse ne bruco ic ðæt oððæt gifylled bioðon in rice godes

17 And onfeng calice ⁊ þancas dyde ⁊ cwæð; Onfoð ⁊ dælað betwux eow.

18 Soðlice ic eow secge ꝥ ic ne drince of þises win-geardes cynne ær godes rīce cume;

19 And he onfengc hlafe ⁊ þancude ⁊ him sealde. ⁊ cwæð; Ðis is min lichama. se is for eow geseald doð þis on min gemynd;

20 And swa eac þæne calic. syððan he ge-eten hæfde ⁊ cwæð; Ðes calic is niwe cyðnys on minum blode se bið for eow agoten;

21 Ðeah-hwæðere her is þæs lǣwan hand mid me on mysan.

22 ⁊ witodlice mannes sunu gæð æ[f]ter þam ðe him fore-stihtud wæs. þeah-hwæðere wa þam men þe he þurh geseald bið;

23 And hi agunnon betwux him smeagan hwylc of him ꝥ to donne wære;

24 ⁊ hi flitun betwux him hwylc hyra wǣre yldest;

25 þa sǣde he him cyningas wealdað hyra þeoda. ⁊ ða ðe anweald ofer hig habbað synt frem-fulle genemned.

26 ac ne beo ge na swa; Ac gewurðe he swa swa gingra se þe yldra ys betwux eow; And se þe fore-stæppend ys beo he swylce he þēn sy;

27 Hwæðer ys yldra þe se þe ðenað þe se ðe sitt. witudlice se ðe sitt; Ic eom on eowrum midlene swa swa se þe ðenað;

17 ænd on-feng calice. ⁊ þances dede ⁊ cwæð. On-foð ⁊ dæled be-tweoxe eow.

18 Soðlice ic eow segge ꝥ ich ne drinke of þises wingearde kynne ær godes rice cume.

19 And he on-feng hlaf ⁊ þancode ⁊ heom sealde ⁊ cwæð. þis ys myn lichame se is for eow ge-seald. doð þis on minen ge-mynde.

20 Ænd swa eac þanne calic; syððen he ge-eten hafde ⁊ cwæð. þes calic is niwe cyðnis on minen blode se beoð for eow agoten.

21 Ðah-hwædere her ys þes læwen hand mid me on myssan.

22 ⁊ witodlice manne (*sic*) sune gæð æfter þam þe him for-stihteð wæs. Ðeah-hwæðere wa þam men þe he þurh geseald beoð.

23 And hyo ongunnen be-tweox heom smægen hwilc of heom ꝥ to donne wære.

24 Ænd hyo fliten be-tweoxe heom hwilc heore wære yldest.

25 Ða saide he heom kyninges wealded heore ðeode. And þa þe anweald ofer hyo hæbbeð synde fremfulle ge-nemnede

26 ac ne beo ge na swa. Ac ge-wurðe he swa swa gingre se ðe yldre ys be-tweox eow. And se forsteppend ys beo he swilce he þein syo.

27 Hwæðer ys yldre se ðe ðenað þe se þe sytt. witodlice se þe sit. Ic eom on eowren midlene swa swa se þe þenað.

Various Readings.

17. A. betweox. 18. A. wyn-eardes. 19. A. onfeng. A. þancode. 20. A. þone. B. C. cyðnes; A. gecyðnys, *alt. to* cyðnys. 22. A. B. C. æfter. A. -stihtod. 23. A. hig. A. betweox. 24. A. hig flyton betweox. A. heora. A. yldost. 25. A. heora. A. synd. 26. A. geweorðe. A. betweox. A. fore-stæppende. A. sig þen [*for* þēn sy]. 27. A. syt (*twice*). A. wytodlice. A. *omits* 2*nd* swa.

Various Readings.

17. þancas dyde; dæleð be-tweox. 18. ic ne drince; wingeardes cynne. 19. Ænd; laf; þancude; min gemynd. 20. þonne; syððam; hæfde; minum. 21. Ðeah-hwæðere; þæs læwan; mysan. 22. mannes; for-stihted. 23. ongunnon be-twux; smeagan. 24. betwux. 25. sægde; cynningas wealdeð hyora ðeade; habbað synt. 26. gingra; yldra; betwux; Ænd; þen sy. 27. Hweðer; yldra; sitt [*for* sit]; eowrum.

⁊ miððy onfeng ðæm cælce ðoncgunga dyde ⁊ cuoeð onfoað ⁊ todælas bituen ł iuih ł
17 et accepto calice gratias egit et dixit accipite et diuidite inter uos

ic cuoeðo *for*ðon iuh ꝥte ne drinco ic of cynne ł cneoreso wingeardes oð ꝥ ríc godes
18 dico enim uobis quod non bibam de generatione uitis donec regnum d*e*i

gecyme ⁊ miððy onfeng hlaf ðoncgunga dyde ⁊ gebræcg ⁊ salde him coeðende ðus ðis is
ueniat 19 *Et accepto pane gratias egit et fregit et dedit eis dicens hoc est * 266. i. mt. cclxxxiiii. mr. clxu. io. lu.

lichoma mín ꝥ *for*e iuh sald bið ðis doað on minu*m* efne-gemynd ł ongelíc
corpus meum quod pro uobis datur hoc facite in meam commemorationem 20 *Similiter * 267. ii. mt. cclxxxu. mr. clxui.

⁊ ðone cælic æft*er* ðon ðe gehriordade cuoeð ðis is cælc niwa cyðnisse ł in blóde minu*m*
et calicem postquam cenauit dicens hic est calix nouum testamentum in sanguine meo

ꝥte *for*e iuh agotten soð-huoeðre hoeðre hond ðæs sellenndes mec mec mið is on disc ł
quod pro uobis fundetur 21 *Uerum-tamen ecce manus tradentis me mecum est in mensa * 268. ii. mt. cclxxxi. mr. clxiii.

⁊ æc soð sunu monnes æft*er* ꝥte geendat ł is gaeð ł soð-huoeðre wæ ðæm menn
22 et quidem filius hominis secundum quod definitum est uadit uerum-tamen uáe illi homini

ðerh ðone gesald bið ⁊ ða ł hia ongunnon soeca bituih him huelc were of him seðe ðis
per quem tradetur 23 *Et ipsi coeperunt quaerere inter sé quis esset ex eis qui hoc * 269. i. mt. cclxxx. mr. clxii. io. cxxii.

doend were aworden wæs ða ⁊ geflít bituih him huelc hiora geseen woere
facturus esset 24 *Facta est autem et contentio inter eos quis eorum uideretur esse *LXXXUIIII. 270. ii. mt. cciii. mr. cxiii[i].

mara ł cuoeð ða him cyningas hæðna geonwældad biðon ł rixað hiora ⁊ ðaðe onwæld ł
maior 25 dixit autem eis reges gentium dominantur eorum et qui potes-

mæht habbað of*er* hia wel-fremmende ł geceiged biðon gie uut*edlice* ne suæ ah seðe hera ł mara
tatem habent super eos benefici uocantur 26 uos autem non sic sed qui maior

is in iuih sie suæ ðe gingesta ł ⁊ seðe *for*e-latuu ł is suelce embehtere *for*ðon ł hueðer
est in uobis fiat sicut iunior et qui praecessor est sicut ministrator 27 *Nam * 271. x.

huelc hera is seðe gehlinað ł oðða seðe embehtað ahne seðe ge*h*restað ic uut*edlice* ł ðon*ne* on
quis maior est qui recumbit án qui ministrat nonne qui recumbit ego autem in

middu*m* Iuerra am suæ seðe embehtað ł
medio uestrum sum sicut qui ministrat

---

17. ⁊ on-feng ðæm calice ðoncunge dyde ⁊ cwæð onfoað ⁊ to-dælað bitwih iow 18. ic cweðo *for*ðon iow ðætte ne drinco ic of cneoreswa wingeardes oððæt rice godes cymeð 19. ⁊ onfeng hlafe ðoncunge dyde ⁊ bræc ⁊ salde him cweðende ðis is lichoma min ꝥte *for*e iowih sald bið ðis doað on minum efne-gimynde 20. on-gilic ⁊ ðon*e* calic æfter ðon ða giriordade cwæð ðis is celc niowe cyðnisse in blode minu*m* ðæt *for*e iowih agoten bið 21. soð-hweðre heonu hond ðæs sellende mið mec is on disce 22. ⁊ ec suno monnes æfter ðætte giendad is gæð soð-hweðre wæ ðæm menn ðerh ðon*e* gisald bið 23. ⁊ ða ongunnun soeca bitwih hi*m* hwelc were of him seðe ðis doende were 24. aworden wæs ða giflitt bitwih him hwelc hiora gisegen were mara 25. cwæð ða him cynigas hæðna gionwælded bioðon hiora ⁊ ðaðe on-wæld habbað ofer hiæ welfremende gicegde 26. ge wut*edlice* ne swa ah seðe mara is in iow sie swa mara (*sic*) ⁊ seðe *for*elatow is swa embeht-mon 27. *for*ðon hwelc mara is seðe gihlionað ł seðe embihtas ah ne seðe gihlionað ic wutudl*ice* in middum iowrum am swa seðe embihtað

28 Ge synt þe mid me þurh-wunedon on mīnu*m* geswincu*m*

29 ⁊ ic eow dihte swa min fæder me rice dihte.

30 ꝥ ge eton ⁊ drincon ofer mine mȳsan on mīnu*m* rīce ⁊ ge sitton ofer þrym-setl demende twelf mægða israhel;

31 Ða cwæð drihten. Simon Simon. nu satanas gyrnde ꝥ he eow hridrude swa swa hwǣte;

32 Ic gebæd for þe ꝥ ðin geleafa ne geteorige; And þu æt sumu*m* cyrre gewend ⁊tryme þine gebroðru;

33 Ða cwæð he drihten. ic eom gearu to farenne mid þe. ge on cwertern ge on deað;

34 Ða cwæþ he. ic secge þe petrus. ne cræwþ se hāna to-dǣg ær þu me ætsæcst;

35 Ða cwæð he to hi*m* þa ic eow sende butan seode ⁊ codde ⁊ ge-scy wæs eow ænig þing wana; Ða cwædon hig nan þing;

36 Ða cwæð he. ac nū se þe hæfð seod gelīce nime codd. ⁊ se ðe næfð sylle his tunecan ⁊ bicge hi*m* swurd;

37 Soðlice ic eow secge ꝥ gyt scyl beon gefylled ꝥ be me awriten is. ⁊ ꝥ he mid rihtwisu*m* getēald wæs. witudlice þa þing þe be me synt habbað ende;

38 And hig cwædon. drihten. her synt twa swurd ⁊ he cwæð ꝥ ys ge-noh;

28 Ge synden þe mid me þurh-wunedan on minen ge-swinchen.

29 ⁊ ic eow dihte swa min fader me rice dihte.

30 ꝥ ge æten ⁊ drincan ofer mine mysan on minen rice ⁊ ge sitten ofer þrim-settel demende twelf mægðe israel.

31 Ða cwæð drihten. symon symon nu sathanas gyrnde þæt he eow riddrede swa swa hwæte.

32 Ic ge-bæd for þe ꝥ þin ge-leafe ne geteorige. Ænd þu æt sume cyre ge-wend ⁊-tryme þine broðre.

33 Ða cwæð he drihten ic eom gære to farene mid þe ge on cwarterne ge on deað.

34 Þa cwæð he. Ic segge þe petrus; ne cræwð se cōc to-daig ær þu me æt-secst þreowe.

35 Þa cwæð he to heom. Ða ich eow sende buton seode ⁊ codde. ⁊ ge-scy. wæs eow anig þing wane. Ða cwæðen hyo nan þing.

36 Ða cwæð he. ac se þe hæfð seod gelice nyme codd. ⁊ se þe næfð sylle hys tunecan ⁊ begge hym sweord.

37 Soðlice ich segge eow ꝥ gyot scel byon ge-fulled. ꝥ be me awriten ys. ⁊ ꝥ he mid rihtwisan ge-teald wæs. Witodlice þa þing þe be me synd hæbbeð ænde.

38 ⁊ hyo cwæðen. drihten her synde twa sword. ⁊ he cw̄. þæt ys ge-noh.

Various Readings.

28. A. synd. C. þurð-. 30. A. etan. C. .yrm-setl. 31. A. hrydrode. 32. A. ateorie, *alt. to* geteorie; B. geteorie. A. getryme [*for* ⁊tryme]. A. gebroðro. 33. B. C. faranne. A. cweartern. 36. A. he nyme [*for* nime]. A. sweord. 37. A. sceal. A. ryhtwysu*m* (*alt. to* unryhtwysu*m*). A. witodlice. A. synd. 38. A. synd. A. sweord.

Various Readings.

28. synt; minu*m* geswencum. 29. fæder. 30. ten [*sic; for* æten]; minum [*for* minen]; -setl demenda. 31. satanas. 32. ge-teorie. 33. gare; faran; cwærterne. 34. hana [*for* coc]; æt-sacst þriwe. 35. ic; wana. 36. bygge. 37. gyt; rihtwisum; synt; ende. 38. cwaðon; sind; swurd.

gie uut*edlice* aron ðaðe ðorh-wunadon mec mið in suoenccu*m* ł costungu*m* minu*m* ⁊
28 uos autem estis qui permansistis mecum in temtationibu*s* meis 29 et

ic to-sceado iuh suæ to-sceadde me fæder min ꝥ ric ꝥte gie ēta ⁊ drincga
ego dispono uobis sicut disposuit mihi pater meus regnum 30 ut edatis et bibatis

on ł of*er* bead ł disc mīn in rīc ⁊ gie sittað of*er* heh-sedlo dōemendo tuoelf strynd*um*
super mensam mea*m* in regno *Et sedeatis super thronos iudicantes duo-decim trib*us* * 272. u. mt. cxcuii.

israhe*l* cuoeð ða drihten simon simon heono se wiðerworda gesohta ł iuih ꝥte awoxe ł
isr*ael* 31 *Ait autem d*omi*n*us* simon simon ecce satanas expetiuit uos ut cribraret * 273. x.

suæ huæte ic uut*edlice* gebæd *fore* ðec ꝥte ne sceortiga ł geleafo ðin ⁊ ðū
sicut triticum 32 ego autem rogaui pro té ut non deficiat fides tua *Et tú * 274. uiiii. io. ccxxuiiii.

huilu*m* ł oðer huile gecerred bist getrymeg broðro ðino seðe cuoeð him drih*ten* ðec mið gearo
aliquando conuersus confirma fratres tuos 33 *Qui dixit ei d*omi*ne tecum paratus * XC. 275. i. mt.cclxxxuiiii. mr. clxx. io. cxxui.

ic am ⁊ in carc-erne ⁊ æc In deaðe geonga ⁊ he cuoeð ic cuoeðo ðe petr*e* ne
sum et in carcerem et in mortem ire 34 et ille dixit dico tibi petrae non

singes ł todæge se hona oð ꝥte ðria ðu onsæccest ꝥte ðu wistes ł cuðes meh ⁊ cuoeð him ðonn*e* ł ða
cantabit hodie gallus donec tér abneges nosse me 35 *ET dixit eis quando * 276. x.

ic sende Iuih buta seame ⁊ met-bælig ⁊ scoeum huoeðer ł huoðhuoegu woere wona ł iuh soð hia
missi uos sine sacculo et pera et calciamentis num-quid aliquid defuit uobis at illi

cuoedon noht cuoeð *for*ðon ł him ah huoeðre nu seðe hæfeð ꝥ seam nioma gelīc ⁊
dixerunt nihil 36 dixit ergo eis sed nunc qui habet sacculum tollat similiter et

ꝥ metbælig ⁊ seðe ne hæfeð bebycgeð ł cyrtel his ⁊ bygeð ł suord ic cuoeðo uut*edlice*
pera*m* et qui non habet uendat tunicam sua*m* et emat gladium 37 *Dico autem * 277. uiii. mr. ccxui.

iuh ꝥte ł *for*ðon ðaget ł ðis ꝥ awritten is geriseð ł ꝥte se gefylled In mec ⁊ ꝥte mið
uobis quoniam athuc hoc quod scribtum est oportet impleri in me et quod cum

unsoðfæstu*m* ge-teled ł wæs ⁊ *for*ðon ða ðaðe sint ł biðon of mec ende habbað soð hia
iniustis deputatus est etenim ea quae sunt de me finem habent 38 *At illi * 278. x.

cuoedon drih*ten* heono suordas tuoege hēr soð he cuoeð him genoh is
dixerunt d*omi*ne ecce gladii duo hic at ille dixit eis sat est

---

28. iow wutudl*ice* arun ðaðe ðerh-wunadun mec mið on swencum ł costungu*m* minum 29. ⁊ ic to-sceodo iow swa to-sceodo mec fæder min rice 30. ꝥte gieotas ⁊ drincas of*er* ł on beode ł disce minum in rice ⁊ ge sittas ofer heh-sedle doemmende twelfe strynd*um* israhela 31. cwæð ða ðe hæl*end* symon ðas symon heono ðe wiðerworda ⁊ gisohte iowih ꝥte awoxe swa hwæte 32. ic ðonne gibæd *fore* ðec ꝥte . . scortige gileofa ðin ⁊ ðu hwilu*m* ł oðer hwile gicerred bist gitryme broðer ðine ⁊ gibiddas ꝥte ne gae in costunge 33. seðe cwæð drih*ten* ðec mið gearo ic am ⁊ in carc-ern. ⁊ ec in deoð gonga 34. he cwæð ic cweðo ðe petrus ne swigað to dæge ðe hona oððæt ðrige ðu sæces ðæt ðu cuðes mec 35. ⁊ cwæð him ðonne i[c] sende iowih buta seome ⁊ metbælge ⁊ scoum hwæt hwoegnu were wona iow soð hiæ cwedun noht 36. cwæð forðon him ah hweðre seðe hæfeð ðon*ne* seom nimeð gilice ⁊ ðone met-bælig ⁊ seðe ne hæfeð sword gibycge cyrtel his ⁊ bygeð sword 37. ic cweðo forðon iow ꝥte ł *for*ðon ðagett ðis ðætte awriten is giriseð gifylled in mec ðæt miððy unsoðfæstu*m* giteled is ⁊ forðon ða ðaðe sindun of me ende habbað 38. soð hia cwedun drihten heonu twoeg sworde her soð he cwæð him genog is

39 And æft*er* gewunan he ut-eode on
þæne munt oliuarum ꝥ ys ele-bergena. ⁊
his leorning-cnihtas him fyligdon;
40 And þa he com to þære stôwe he
sæde him. ge-bidda'ð ꝥ ge on costnunge
ne gân;
41 And he wæs fra*m* hi*m* alocen swa
mycel swa is anes stanes wyrp. ⁊ gebige-
du*m* cneowu*m* he hyne gebæd
42 ⁊ cwæð; Fæder gif þu wylt. afyr
þysne calic fra*m* me þeah-hwæðere ne ge-
wurðe min willa ac þin;
43 Þa æt-ywde hi*m* godes engel. of heofone ⁊ hyne gestrangode
44 ⁊ he wæs on gewinne ⁊ hine lange
gebæd ⁊ his swat wæs swylce blodes dropan
on eorðan yrnende.
45 ⁊ þa he of gebede aras ⁊ com to his
leorning-cnihtu*m* he hig funde slæpende for
unrotnesse.
46 ⁊ he sǽde hi*m*. hwi slape ge. arisað
⁊ biddað ge on costunge ne gan;
47 Him þa þa gyt sprecendu*m* þa com
ꝥ wered ⁊ hi*m* to-foran eode ân of þa*m*
twelfu*m* se wæs genemned iudas ⁊ he ge-
nealæhte þa*m* hælende ꝥ he hine cyste;
48 Ða cwæð se hælend iudas. mannes
sunu þu mid cosse sylst;
49 Ða gesawon þa ðe hi*m* abutan wǽron
ꝥ þær towerd wæs ⁊ cwǽdon. drihten. slea
we mid swûrde;

39 Ænd æfter ge-wunen he ut-geode on
þanne munt oliuarum. ꝥ ys elebgerena
(*sic*). ⁊ his leorning-cnihtes hym fylgdon.
40 ⁊ þa he com to þare stowe he sæde
heom. ge byddað ꝥ ge on costnenga ne
gan.
41 And he wæs fram heom aloken swa
mycel swa ys anes stanes werp. ⁊ ge-beig-
den cneowen he hine ge-bæð.
42 ⁊ cwæð. Fader gyf þu wilt; afyr
þisne calic fram me þeah-hwæðere ne ge-
wurðe min wille ac þin.
43 Ða tywde (*sic*) him godes ængel of
heofene ⁊ hine ge-strangode.
44 ⁊ he wæs on ge-winne. ⁊ hine lange
ge-bæd. ⁊ his swat wæs swilce* blodes
dropen on eorðe eornende.
45 ⁊ þa he of ge-bede aras; ⁊ com to hys
leorning-cnihten. he hyo funde slæpende
for sarignesse.
46 ⁊ he saide heom; hwi slæpe ge;
arisað ⁊ biddað þæt ge on costnunge ne gan.
47 Hym þa þa gyt swæccenden (*sic*). Þa
com ꝥ wered ⁊ him to-foren eode an of þam
twelfen. se wæs ge-nemned iudas. ⁊ he
ge-neahlahte þam hælende ꝥ he hine keste.
48 Ða cwæð se hælend. judas. mannes
sune þu mid cosse sylst.
49 Ða ge-seagen þa þe hym abuton
wæren. þæt þær toward wæs ⁊ cwæðen.
drihten sla we mid sweorde.

* MS. swilc corr. to swi

Various Readings.

39. A. gewuna. A. þone. 40. A. þa sæde [*for* sǽde]. 42. A. geweorðe. 43. A. heofene. 45. A. *inserts* he *after* com, *above the line.* A. unrotnysse. 46. A. hwig. A. costnunge. 47. B. specendu*m*. 49. C. habutan. B. þar. A. toweard. B. sleawe [*for* slea we]. A. sweorde.

Various Readings.

39. -eode; þæne; eleberena (*altered to* elebgerena, *instead of to* elebergena); -cnihtas; fyligdon. 40. þara; costnunge. 41. Ænd; alocen; wyrp; ge-bygdu*m* cneowu*m*; gebæed. 43. ætywde; engel; heofone. 44. swylces (*sic*); yrnende. 45. -cnihtu*m*; heo; unrotnysse [*for* sarignesse]. 46. sæde eom. 47. speccendu*m*; to-foran; twelfu*m*; ge-neahlæcte; cyste. 48. halend. 49. gesawen; abutan wæron; toweard; cwæðon; slawe [*for* sla we]; swurde.

⁊ miððy wæs færende eade ða æft*er* gewuna ł on more olebearua fylgendo woeron
39 *ET egressus ibat secundum consuetudinem in montem oliuarum secuti sunt * 279. i. mt. ccxci. mr. clxxii. io. clui.

ða ł uut*edlice* hine æc ða ðegnas ⁊ miððy ðerh-cuome to stoue cuoeð him gebiddas
autem illu*m* et discipuli 40 *ET cum peruenisset ad locum dixit illis orate * 280. ii. mt. ccxcui. mr. clxxuii.

þte gie ne in*n*gae in costunge ⁊ he gefearrad ł wæs fro*m* him sua micle woerp ł wyrp is stanes
ne intretis in temtationem 41 *ET ipse áuulsus est ab eis quantum iactus est lapidis * 281. i. mt. ccxciiii. mr. clxxu. io. clxi.

⁊ mið gesetnu*m* cneou*m* gebæd cuoeð fader gif ðu welle ł of*er*-leor calic ðiosne fro*m* mec
et positis genib*us* orabat 42 dicens *Pater si uís trans-fer calicem istum á me * 282. i. mt. ccxc[u]. mr. clxxui. io. luii.

soð-huoeðre ł ne min willo ah ðin sie æd-eaude ða him se encgel ofro*m* (*sic*)
uerumtamen non mea uoluntas sed tua fiat 43 *Apparuit autem illi angelus de caelo * 283. x.

getry*m*mede him ⁊ aworden wæs in gecomp ⁊ suiðe longe gebæd ⁊ aworden wæs suat his
con-fortans eum 44 et factus est in agonia et prolixius orabat et factus est sudor eius

suæ ł droppo blodes iornendes ł on eorðu ⁊ miððy arisen wæs ł aras fro*m* ðæm gebed ⁊
sicut guttae sanguinis decurrentis in terram 45 *Et cum surrexisset ab oratione et * 284. ii. mt. ccxcui. mr. clxxuii.

ge-cuome to ðegnu*m* his gemitte hia slepende f*or*e unrotnisse ⁊ cuoeð him huæd
uenisset ad discipulos suos inuenit eos dormientes prae tristitiam 46 et ait illis quid

slepes gie arisað gebiddað þte gie ne Inngeonga In costun*cge* ł in gesuoen*cge* f*or*ðor ðaget hine spreccende
dormitis surgite orate ne intretis in temtatione*m* 47 *Athuc eo loquente * 285. i. mt. ccc. mr. clxxxi. io. cluiii.

heono þ here ł ða menigo ⁊ seðe geceiged wæs iud*as* an of ðæm tuoelfu*m* f*ore*-foerde ł hia ⁊ ge-neo-
ecce turba et qui uocabatur iudas unus de duo-decim ante-cedebat eos et appro-

lecde se hæl*end* þte gecyste hine se hæl*end* ða cuoeð him la iud*as* mið cosse sunu
pinquauit *iesu* ut oscularetur eu*m* 48 *I*esu*s autem dixit ei iuda osculo filium * 286. ii. mt. ccci. mr. clxxxii.

monnes ðu selles ge-segon uut*edlice* ða ðaðe ymb hine woeron þte towoeard wæs
hominis tradis 49 *Uidentes autem hí qui circum ipsum erant quod futurum erat * 287. i. mt. cccii. mr. clxxxiii. io. clx.

cuoedon him drih*ten* gif woe geslâs ł huoeðer mote we geslaa in suorde
dixerunt ei d*omi*n*e* si percutimus in gladio

---

39. ⁊ mið-ðy wæs gongende æfter giwuna his on mor oele-bearwes fylgende werun wutudl*ice* ða him ⁊ ðegnas his 40. ⁊ miððy ðerh-comon to stowe cwæð him gibiddað þ ge ne gæ in costunge 41. ⁊ he gifearrad wæs fro*m* him swa micel wyrp stanes is ⁊ miððy gisetnun comun gibæd 42. cwæð fæder gif ðu welle of*er*liora ðon*e* calic ðiosne fro*m* me soð-hweðre ne min willa ah ðin sie 43. æt-eowde ðá him engel of heofne gitrymede hine 44. ⁊ awordes (*sic*) wæs in geco[*m*]p ⁊ swiðe longe gibæd ⁊ aworden wæs swat his swa dropo blodes iornende on eorðo 45. ⁊ miððy arisen wæs from ðæm gibede ⁊ gicom to ðegnum his gimitte hiæ slepende f*ore* un-rotnisse 46. ⁊ cwæð ðæm arisað ⁊ gibiddað ðæt ge ne gæ in costunge 47. to him sprecende heono ðe here ⁊ seðe giceged wæs iudas ana of ðæm twelfu*m* fore-foerde hiæ ⁊ to-gineolicadun ðæm hæl*ende* þ he gicyste hine 48. ðe hæl*end* ðon*ne* cwæð him la iudas mið cosse suno monnes ðu seles 49. gisegun wutudl*ice* ða ðaðe ymb hine werun ðætte toword wæs cwedun him drih*ten* gif ðe sellað gi-sla mið sworde

50 Ða sloh hyra án þara sacerda ealdres þeow ⁊ hys swyðre eare of-acerf;

51 Þa ⁊swarude se hælend lætað þus; ⁊ þa he æt-hran hys eare he hyt gehǽlde;

52 Ða cwæð se hælend to þa*m* ealdormannu*m* ⁊ to þa*m* witu*m* ⁊ þæs temples ealdru*m*; Ge ferdon swa swa to* anu*m* sceaðan mid swurdu*m* ⁊ mid sahlu*m* ꝥ ge me gefengon;

* MS. *repeats* to.

53 Ðá ic wæs dæg-hwa*m*lice on temple mid eow. ne aþenedon ge eower handa on me. ac þis is eower tíd ⁊ þystra anweald;

54 Ða namon hig hine ⁊ læddon to þæra sacerda ealdres huse. ⁊ petrus fyligde feorran;

55 And petrus wæs mid hi*m* on middan þa*m* cafertune. þar hig æt þa*m* fyre sæton;

56 Ða hine geseah su*m* þinen æt leohte sittende ⁊ hine beheold. þa cwæð heo. ⁊ þes wæs mid hi*m*;

57 Ða æt-soc he ⁊ cwæð. eala wíf ne can ic hyne;

58 And þa embe lytel hine ge-seah oðer. ⁊ cwæð. þu eart of hi*m*; Ða cwæð petrus eala mann ic ne eom;

59 ⁊ þa æfter lytlu*m* fæce swylce ánre tíde. sum oðer seðde ⁊ cwæð; Soðlice þes wæs mid hi*m*. witodlice he is galileisc;

50 Þa sloh heore an þare sacerda ealdres þeow ⁊ his swiðre eare of-akarf.

51 Ða andswerede se hælend læted þus. ⁊ þa he æt-ran his eare he hit ge-hælde.

52 Þa cwæð se hælend to þam ealdormannen ⁊ to þa*m* witon ⁊ to þas temples ealdren. Ge ferden to me swa swa to anen sceaðen. mid sweorden. ⁊ mid sæglen. ꝥ ge me ge-fengen.

53 Ða ich wæs daighwam-lice mid eow on þam temple. ne aþeneden ge eower handa on me. ac þis ys eower tid ⁊ þeostre anweald.

54 Ða namen hyo hine ⁊ lædden hyne to þare sacerde ealdres huse. ⁊ petrus felygede feorran.

55 And petrus wæs mid heom on middan þam cafertune þær hyo æt þa*m* fyre sæton.

56 Ða hine ge-seah sum þinen æt leohte sittende ⁊ hine be-heold. þa cwæð hye. ⁊ þes wæs mid hym.

57 Ða æt-soch he. ⁊ cw̄. eale wif ne can ich hine.

58 ⁊ þa embe litel hine ge-seah oðer. ⁊ cwæð. þu ert of heom. Ða cwæð petrus. eale man ic ne eom.

59 ⁊ þa æfter litlen faece swilce anre tide sum oðer saigde ⁊ cwæð. Soðlice þes wæs mid eom. witodlice he ys galileisc.

Various Readings.

50. A. heora. A. þæra. A. of-acearf. 51. A. ⁊swarode. 52. C. *repeats* to (*as does the* Corpus MS.). A. sweordu*m*. 53. B. anwald. 54. B. þara. 58. A. ymbe. A. C. man. 59. A. seðde (*as in text*). B. s . . de (*two letters erased; altered to* seðde *in pencil*).

Various Readings.

50. hyora; þara; swyðere; -acearf. 51. læteð. 52. halend; -mannu*m*; R. *om.* to *before* þas temples; ealdru*m*; ferdon; anu*m* sceaðum; sweordu*m*; saglum. 53. ic; dæghwa*m*lice; aþenedon; þeastra. 54. naman; þara sacerda; fyligde. 55. Ænd. 56. hyo; eom. 57. et-soc; eala; ic. 58. eala mann. 59. litlum fæce; sæde; galileis (*sic*).

⁊ geslog enne ł an of ðæm esne aldormonnes *sacerda* ⁊ to-cearf ear-lipprıcco
50 et percussit unus ex illis seruum principis sacerdotum et amputauit auricula*m*

his ðio suiðro geondsuarade ða se hæl*end* cuoeð *for*letas ł blinnað wið hider ł ⁊ miððy
eius dextram 51 *Respondens *autem* ie*sus* ait sinite usq*ue* huc et cum * 288. x.

gehran ear-liprico his gehælde hine cuoeð ða se hæl*end* to him ł ðæm ðaðe cuomon
tetegisset auriculam eius sanauit eum 52 *Dixit autem ie*sus* ad eos qui uenerant * 289. i. mt. ccciiii. mr. clxxxiiii.

to him aldormenn *sacerda* ⁊ laruas temples ⁊ ða ældesto suæ ł to hreafere gie cuomon
ad sé principes sacerdotu*m* et magistratus templi et seniores quasi ad latronem existis io. clxx.

mið suordum ⁊ stencgum miððy dæghuæmlice iuih mið Ic woere ł in temple ⁊ ne rahton gie ł
cum gladiis et fustib*us* 53 cum cotidie uobiscum fueram in templo non extendistis

hondo In mēc ah ðios is tíd iuera ⁊ mæht ðiostrana efne-gelahton ł
manus in me sed haec est hora uestra et potestas tenebrarum 54 *Com-prehendentes * 290. i. mt. cccui. mr. clxxxuii.

ðon*ne* hine læddon to huse aldormonnes *sacerda* petr*us* uut*edlice* ł æc gefylgde fearra
autem eum duxerun*t* ad domum principis sacerdotum *Petrus uero sequebatur á longe io. clxxiiii. * 291. i. mt. cccxiiii. mr. cxcu.

to-geboetad wæs uut*edlice* ł ða fyr on middu*m* cæfer-tune ⁊ ymb-sittendu*m* ðæm wæs petr*us* on
55 accenso autem igni in medio átrio et circum-sedentib*us* illis erat petrus in io. clxuiii.

middu*m* hiora ðone miððy gesæh ł gesege ðiua ł ðignen summ sittende to leht ⁊
medio eoru*m* 56 quem cum uidisset ancilla quaedam sedentem ad lumen et

miððy woere hio sceaunde hine cuoeð ⁊ ðes mið hine wæs soð he onsóc hine cuoeð
cum fuisset intuita dixit et hic cum illò erat 57 at ille negauit eum dicens

wif ne conn ic hine ⁊ æft*er* lytlu*m* ł ymb lytle huile oðer gesæh hine cuoeð ⁊ ðu
mulier non noui illum 58 *ET post pussillu*m* alius uidens eum dixit et tú * 292. i. mt. cccxu. mr. cxcui.

of him ł ðæm arð petr*us* æc ł uut*edlice* cuoeð la monn ne am ic ⁊ ymb huile was aworden ł
de illis és petrus uero ait ó homo non sum 59 et interuallo facto io. clxxu.

suelce anes tides oðer sum getrymede cuoeð soðlice ⁊ ðes mið hine wæs *for*ðon ⁊
quasi horæ unius alius quidam affirmabat dicens uere et hic cum illo erat nam et

galilesc is
galilaeus est

---

50. ⁊ slog enne of ðæm esne aldormonnes sacerda ⁊ to-ceorf ear-liprica his ðæt swiðra 51. giondsworade wut*udlice* ðe hæl*end* cwæð for-letað wið hider ⁊ mið gihran ear-liprica his gihælde hine 52. cwæð ða ðe hæl*end* to him ðaðe comun to him aldor sacerda ⁊ larwas temples ⁊ ða ældesto swa swa to reofere ge comun mið swordum ⁊ stenggum 53. miððy dæghwæmlice iowih mið wæs in temple ne rahtun ge honda on mec ah ðios is tid iower ⁊ mæht ðiostrana 54. efne-girahtun ðonne hine læddun to huse aldor-monnes sacerda petrus wutudl*ice* fyligde fearra 55. giboeted wæs ða fyr on middu*m* cæfertune ⁊ ymb-sitendum ðæm wæs .... in middu*m* hiora 56. ðon*e* miððy gisæh ðiowa sum sittende to lehte ⁊ hio wæs scomende hine cwæð ⁊ ðes mið hine wæs 57. soð he onsoc hine cweðende wif ne con ic hine 58. æfter lytlum hwile oðer gisæh hine cwæð ⁊ ðu of ðæm arð petr*us* ec wutudl*ice* cwæð la mon ne an (*sic*) ic 59. ⁊ efter-sona aworden wæs swelce tide an oðero sum gi-trymide cwæð soðlice ⁊ ðes mið hine wæs forðon ⁊ galilesc is

60 Ða cwæð petrus. eala man nat ic hwæt þu segst; And þa hig ꝥ spræcon samninga sé hána creow.

61 þa drihten bewende híne ⁊ beseah to petre. Ða gemunde petrus drihtnes wordes þe he cwæð. ꝥ ðu mín æt-sæcst. þriwa to-dæg ær se hana cráwe;

62 Ða eode petrus út ⁊ biterlice weop.

63 ⁊ þa ðe þæne hælend heoldon hine bysmrodon ⁊ beoton.

64 ⁊ ofer-wrugon hys ansyne ⁊ þurhsun his nebb. ⁊ ahsodon hyne. arǽd. hwylc ys. se ðe þe sloh;

65 And manega oðre þing hig him to cwǽdon dysigende;

66 And þa ða dǽg wæs þa to-gædere comun þæs folces yldran ⁊ þara sacerda ealder-menn ⁊ boceras ⁊ læddon hine to hyra gemote ⁊ cwǽdon;

67 Sege us gif þu sy crist; Ða cwæþ he þeah ic eow secge. ge me ne* gelyfaþ.

68 þeh ic eow ahsige ge ne ⁊swariað mé ne ne forlætað;

69 Heonun-forð bið mannes sunu sittende on godes mægnes swyþran healfe;

70 Ða cwǽdon hig ealle. eart þu godes sunu; Ða cwæð he ge secgað ꝥ ic eom;

71 And hig cwædon. hwi gyrne wé gyt gewitnesse. sylfe we gehyrdon of hys muðe;

* MS. gemne, *with part of an e erased after* m.

Various Readings.

60. A. B. samnunga. 61. B. C. crewe. 63. A. þone. A. bysmredon. 64. A. þurcson. A. acsedon. 65. A. dysgiende. 66. A. comon. A. þæra. A. ealdor-men. A. heora. 67. A. sig. A. B. C. ge me ne (*plainly*). 68. A. þeah. A. acsige; B. ahsie. 69. A. heonen-. A. mægenes. 71. A. hwig.

60 þa cwæð petrus. eala mann nat ich hwæt þu sægest. And þa hyo þæt spræken samnunga se coc creow.

61 þa drihten be-wende hine ⁊ be-seah to petre. Ða ge-munede petrus drihtnes wordes þe he cwæð. þæt þu min æt-sæcst þrewa to-daig ær se coc crawe.

62 Ða eode petrus ut ⁊ biterlice weop.

63 ⁊ þa þe þane hælend heolden hine bismeredon ⁊ beoton.

64 ⁊ ofer-wrugen hys ansiene. ⁊ þurscen his nebb. ⁊ axoden hine ared wlych (*sic*) ys se þe þe smat.

65 And manega oðre þing hyo hym to cwæðen. desigende.

66 And þa þa daig wæs. þa to-gædere comen þas folces aldren ⁊ þare sacerda ealdor-menn. ⁊ bokeras. ⁊ lædden hine to heore ge-mote ⁊ cwæðen.

67 Sege us gyf þu syo crist. Ða cwæð he. þeah ich eow segge; ge me ne lyfað.

68 þeah ich eow axsie ge ne andsweriað me. ne ne for-læteð.

69 Heonen-forð byoð mannes sune sittende on godes mægnes swiðre healfe.

70 Ða cwæðen hyo ealle ert þu godes sune; Ða cwæð he. ge seggeð þæt ich eom.

71 And hyo cwæðen. hwi georne we geot ge-witnysse. we sylfe ge-herden of his muðe.

Various Readings.

60. ic; secgst; spræcon; hana [*for* coc]. 61. æt-sacst þriwa; hana cræwe. 63. þæne; heoldon; bysmeroden. 64. þurhson; axodon; æræd; hwylc; slog [*for* smat]. 65. cwæðon. dysigende. 66. dæg; to-gadere coman; yldran; sacerde-ealder-; boceras; heora. 67. ic; secge. 68. þeh ic; axsige. 69. heonon-; bið. 70. cwæðon; eart; ic. 71. Ænd; cwæðon; gyrne; gyt; sylfe we ge-hyrdon.

⁊ cuoeð pet*rus* la monn nat ic huæd ðu cuoeðes ⁊ sona for*ð*or ða get hine sprecende gesang
60 et ait petrus homo nescio quid dicis et continuo athuc illo loquente cantauit

se hona ⁊ efne-gecerred wæs se drih*ten* eft-besæh pet*rum* ⁊ eft-gemyndig wæs pet*rus* wordes
gallus 61 *Et conuersus do*minus* respexit petrum et recordatus est petrus uerbi * 293. ii. mt. cccxui. mr. cxcuii.

drihtnes suæ cuoeð ꝥte ær ðon se hona gesinga ðriga mec ðu onsæccest ⁊ foerde uta
do*mi*ni sicut dixit prius-quam gallus cantet tér me negabis 62 et egressus foras

pet*rus* geweap bitt*er*lice ⁊ ða waras ðaðe gehealdon hine bismeredon him aslogon ł ðurscon
petrus fleuit ámare 63 *Et uiri qui tenebant eu*m* inludebant ei caedentes * 294. i. mt. cccxiii. mr. cxciiii. io. clxxii.

⁊ awrigon ł hine ⁊ slogon ondwlitto his ⁊ frugnon hine cuoeðendo gewitga
64 et uelauerunt eum et percutiebant faciem eius et interrogabant eum dicentes prophetiza

huælc is seðe ðec slóg ⁊ oðero menigo ebalsadon ł ebolsande cuoedon in hine ⁊
quis est qui té percussit 65 et alia multa blasphemantes dicebant in eum 66 *Et * 295. ii. mt. cccxuii. mr. cxcuiii.

ꝥte aworden wæs dæge efne-cuomon ða ældesto ðæs folces ⁊ aldormenn sac*erda* ⁊ uðwutto ⁊
ut factus est dies con-uenerunt seniores plebis et principes sacerdotum et scribae et

læddon hine in somnung hiora cuoeðendo gif ðu arð crist sæge ús ⁊ cuoeð
duxerunt illum in concilium suum dicentes 67 si tú és *christus* dic nobis *Et ait * 296. x.

ðæm gif iuh ic cuoeðo ne gelefeð gée mē gif ðon*ne* ⁊ gif ic frægno ne gie ondsuariges
illis si uobis dixero non creditis mihi 68 si autem et interrogauero non respondebitis

me ne for*l*etes gie of ðis uut*edlice* bið sunu monnes sittende to suið*rum* mægnes
mihi neq*ue* dimittetis 69 *Ex hoc autem erit filius hominis sedens á dextris uirtutis * 297. i. mt. cccx. mr. cxci. io. lxuiiii.

goddes cuoedon ða alle ðu *for*ðon arð sunu godes seðe cuoeð gie cuoeðas ꝥte ic
d*e*i 70 *Dixerunt autem omnes tú ergo és filius d*e*i qui ait uos dicitis quia ego * 298. x.

am soð hia cuoedon huæd ł ðaget *for*ðor woe willnigas cyðnisse ł wittnessa woe seolf*o* *for*ðon
sum 71 *At illi dixerunt quid athuc desideramus testimonium ipsi enim * 299. ii. mt. cccxii. mr. cxciii.

geherdon of mūðe his
audiuimus de ore eius

---

60. ⁊ cwæð petr*us* la mon nat ic hwæt ðu cweðes ⁊ sona forðor ða-gett hine sprecende ðe hona gisang 61. ⁊ efne-gicerred wæs drih*ten* eft-gisæh petr*um* ⁊ gimyndig wæs petr*us* word drih*tnes* swa cwæð ðæt ærðon ðe hona sunge ðrige ðū ne (*sic*) onsæces 62. ⁊ foerde utt petr*us* weop biterlice 63. ⁊ ða wearas ðaðe giheoldun hine bismeradun hine slogun ł ðurscun 64. ł wrigun hine ⁊ spitun ł slogun on ondwlita his ⁊ frugnun hine cweðende witga hwelc is ðe ðec slog 65. ⁊ oðre monige eofol-sadon cwedun in hine 66. ⁊ ꝥ dæg giworden wæs efne-comun ða ældestu ðæs folches ⁊ aldormen sacerda ⁊ uð-wuta ⁊ læddun hine in somnunge hiora ⁊ gi-frugnun hine cweðende 67. gif ðu arð crist sæge us ⁊ cwæð ðæm gif iow ic cweðo ne gi-lefas ge me 68. gif ðon*ne* ⁊ gif ic fregno ne gi-ondsworiað me ne forletas ge 69. of ðisse wutudl*ice* bið suno monnes sites to ðær swiðra mægnes godes 70. cwedun ða alle ðu forðon arð sunu godes se ðe cwæð gie cweoðas forðon ic am 71. soð hia cwedun hwæt ðagett forðor we wilnigas cyðnisse we solfa for*ð*on giherdun of muðe his

CHAPTER XXIII.

1 Ða aras eall hyra menegeo ⁊ lǽddon hine to pilate

2 ⁊ agunnon hyne wregan ⁊ cwǽdon; Ðisne we gemétton for-hwyrfende ure þeode. ⁊ for-beodende ꝥ man þa*m* casere gafol ne sealde. ⁊ segð ꝥ he sí crist cyning;

3 Ða ahsode pilatus hine eart þu iudea cining; Ða ⁊swarude he þu hit segst;

4 þa cwæþ pilatus to þa*m* ealdru*m* ⁊ þa*m* werede ne finde íc nanne intingan on þysu*m* men;

5 Ða hlyddon hig ⁊ cwǽdon. he astyrað þis folc lærende þurh ealle iudeam agynnende of [galilea oð hyder.

6 Ða pilatus gehyrde] galilea*m*. he ahsude hwæðer he wǽre galileisc man;

7 ⁊ þa he gecneow ꝥ he wæs of herodes anwalde. he hine ágen-sende to herode. he wæs on þa*m* dagu*m* on hierusale*m*;

8 Soðlice herodes fagnude þa he þæne hælend geseah. mycelre tíde he wilnode hine geseon* forþa*m* ðe he ge-hyrde mycel be hi*m*; ⁊ he hopode ꝥ he ge-sáwe sum tacen þe fra*m* hi*m* gewurde;

9 þa ahsode he hine manegu*m* wordu*m* ⁊ he naht ne ⁊swarude;

10 Ða stódon þara sacerda ealdras hine an-rædlice wregende.

* MS. geseah, *alt. to* geseon.

CHAPTER XXIII.

1 Ða aras eall heora manigeo ⁊ lædden hine to pilate.

2 ⁊ agunnen hine wreigen ⁊ cwæðen. Ðisne we ge-metton for-hwerfende ure þeode. ⁊ for-beodende ꝥ man þam caysere gafol ne sealde. ⁊ sægð þæt he syo crist kyning;

3 Ða axode pilat*us* hi*m* ert þu iudea cyng; þa andswerede he. þu hyt sægst.

4 þa cw̄ pilat*us* to þam ealdren ⁊ þam werede. ne finde ich nænne intinge on þisen men.

5 þa hlydden hyo ⁊ cwæðen. He astyred þis folc lærende þurh ealle iudean aginnende of galileam oð hider.

6 Ða pilatus ge-hyrde galileam. he axode hwader he wære galileisc man.

7 ⁊ þa he ge-cneow ꝥ he wæs of herodes anwealde. he hine agen-sende to herode. he wæs on þam dagen on ierusalem.

8 Soðlice herodes fagenede þa he þanne hælend ge-seah. langere tide he wilnode hine ge-seon. for-þan þe he ge-herde mychel be him. ⁊ he hopede ꝥ he ge-seage sum taken þe fram him ge-wurðe.

9 þa axode he hine manege worden. ⁊ he naht ne andswerede.

10 Ða stoden þare sacerda aldres hine anrædlice wreigende.

Various Readings.

Cap. xxiii. 1. A. heora. A. mænigeo; B. menego. 2. A. ongunnon. A. cweðan. A. for-hwyrfedne (*sic*). A. sig. 3. A. acsode. A. ⁊sworode (*sic*). 4. A. nænne. A. þyssu*m*. 5, 6. *The omitted passage is found in* A. B. C. A. acsode. A. mann. 7. A. anwealde. A. ongean-. 8. A. fahnode. A. þone. A. B. C. geseon. 9. A. acsode. A. ⁊swarode. 10. A. þæra.

Various Readings.

Cap. xxiii. 1. hyra mænega; ladden. 2. agunnon; cwæðon; caisere; segð; sy; cyning. 3. hine [*for* hi*m*]; eart; iuda cyning; ⁊swarude. 4. ealdru*m*; ic nanne intingan; þissum. 5. hlyddon; cwædon; astyreð; galilea. 6. axsode hweðer; ware. 7. dagu*m*. 8. fagenode; þo*n*ne; mycelere [*for* lange]; ge-hyrde micel; opede (*sic*); ge-sæwe; tacen. 9. wordon. 10. þara sacerde aldras.

CAP. XXIII.

⁊ arás all ðio menigo hiara brohton ł læddon hine to pilat*e* ongunnon
1 *Et surgens omnis multitudo eorum duxerunt illum ad pilatum 2 †Coeperunt * 300. i. mt. cccxiiii. mr. cxcuiiii. io. clxxui. † 301. x.

ða hine ge-hena cuoeðendo ðiosne woe gemitton under-cerrende ł cynn userne ⁊
autem illum accusare dicentes hunc inuenimus sub-uertentem gentem nostram et

*for*beadende ł woerdende gæfelo ł to seallanne ł ꝥte se gesald ðæm caseri ⁊ cuoeðende hine crist*um* cyni*ng*
prohibentem tributa dari caesari et dicentem sé *christum* regem

ꝥte woere ł ꝥte sē ða gefraign hine cuoeð ðu arð cyni*ng* iudeana soð he
esse 3 *Pilatus autem interrogauit eum dicens tú és rex iudaeorum at ille * 302. i. mt. cccxx. mr. cc. io. clxxuiii.

ondsuarede cuoeð ðu cuoeðes cuoeð ða se geroefa to aldormonnu*m* sac*erda* ⁊ to ðæm menigu*m*
respondens ait tú dicis 4 *Ait autem pilatus ad principes sacerdotu*m* et turbas * 303. uiiii. io. cxc.

noht ic gemitto Inðinges in ðissu*m* menn soð hia ł ða ontry*m*medon ł cuoeðendo gecerreð
nihil inuenio causae in hoc hominem (*sic*) 5 *At illi inualiscebant dicentes commouet * 304. x.

ꝥ folc lærd ł ðerh allne iudea ⁊ agann ł fro*m* gal*ilea* oðð hider se geroefa
populu*m* docens per uniuersam iudaeam et incipiens a galilaea usq*ue* huc 6 pilatus

ða geherde gali*leam* gefraign huoeðer ł gif *monn* galilesca woere ⁊ ꝥte ł miððy ongætt ꝥte
autem audiens galilaeam interrogauit si homo galilaeus esset 7 et ut cognouit quod

of hero*des* onwæld woere eft-sende hine to hero*de* seðe ⁊ seilca hieru*salem* wæs ðæm dagum
de herodis potestate esset remisit eum ad herode*m* qui et ipse hierosolimis erat illis dieb*us*

hero*des* ðon*ne* gesene ł ðone hæl*end* glæd wæs suiðe wæs *for*ðon willnande of menigo tíd
8 herodes autem uiso i*es*u gauisus est ualde erat enim cupiens ex multo tempore

to geseanne hine *for*eðon geherde feolo of him ⁊ hyhtade ł becon huoelc-huoene to gesean*ne* fro*m*
uidere eum eo quod audiret multa de illo et sperabat signum aliquod uidere ab

him ꝥte woere aworden gefraignde ðon*ne* hine monigu*m* wordu*m* soð he noht him
eo fieri 9 interrogabat autem illum multis sermonib*us* at ipse nihil illi

geondsuarede stodon æc soðlic*e* aldormen sac*erda* ⁊ uðutto fæstlice gehendon hine
respondebat 10 *Stabant etiam principes sacerdotum et scribæ constanter accusantes eum * 305. ii. mt. cccuiii. mr. clxxxuiiii.

Cap. XXIII. 1. ⁊ aras all ðio mengo hiora læddun hine to pylate 2. ongunnun gehene hine cweðenðe ðiosne we gemitton under-cerrende cynn usera ⁊ *for*beodende ææ ⁊ wigga (*sic*) ⁊ for-beodende gæfel to sellanna ðæm casera ·⁊ cweðende hine crist cynig ꝥte were 3. pylatus ða gifrægn hine cwæð ðu arð cynig iudana hiora soð he ondswarade cwæð ðu cweðes 4. cwæð ða ðe groefa to aldormonnum sacerda ⁊ to ðæm mengum noht ic mitto intincga in ðissum menn 5. soð hia ða on-trymedun cweðende gecerrað ꝥ folc læreð ðerh alla iudea ⁊ on-gann from galileum oððe hiðer 6. ðe groefa ða giherde galileam in-frægn ⁊ gif monn galilesc were 7. ⁊ ꝥte ongæt ðætte of herode onwald were eft-sende hine to herode seðe ⁊ seilca hierusolimesc wæs ðæm dagum 8. her*odes* ðone gesene ðone hæl*end* glæd wæs swiðe wæs forðon wilnende of mongum tidum to geseanne hine *for*ðon ꝥte ge-herde feolu ⁊ hyhtade becon hwelc-hweogne from him gesegen were 9. gefrægn ðonne hine monigum wordum soð he noht geondswarade 10. stodon æc soðlice aldor*men* sacerda ⁊ uðw*uto* fæst-lice geherdun (*sic*) hine

11 þa ofer-hogode herodes hine mid [hys] hyrede ⁊ bysmrode hine gescrydne hwitu*m* reafe. ⁊ hyne agen-sende to pilate;

12 And on þa*m* dæge wurdun herodes ⁊ pilatus gefrynd. Soðlice hig wæron ǽr gefynd hi*m* betwynan;

13 Ða cwæð pilatus to þara sacerda ealdru*m* ⁊ duguðe ealdru*m* ⁊ to þa*m* folce.

14 ge brohton me þi̅sne man swylce he þis folc forhwyrfde. ⁊ nu ic beforan eow ahsiende. ic nanne intingan findan ne mǽg on þisu*m* men of þa*m* þe ge hine wregað

15 ne furðun herodes; Ic hine sende agen to hi*m* ⁊ hi*m* naht þæs-lices deaðe gedon wæs.

16 Ic hine gebetne forlǽte;

17 Niede he sceolde hi*m* forgyfan anne to hyra freols-dæge.

18 þa hrymde eall ꝥ folc æt-gædere ⁊ cwæþ; Nim þisne ⁊ forgyf us barrabban

19 se wæs for sumere twyrædnesse ⁊ man-slyhte on cwertern asend;

20 Eft spæc pilatus to hi*m* ⁊ wolde forlætan þæne hælend;

21 Ða hrymdon hig ⁊ cwǽdon ahoð hine ahoð hine;

22 Ða cwæð he to hi*m* þriddan siðe. hwæt dyde þes yfeles. ne mette ic nan þing yfeles on þissu*m* men ꝥ he si deaþes scyldig. ic hine þreage ⁊ forlæte;

11 Ða ofer-hugede herodes hine mid hys hyrde ⁊ bisemerede hine ge-scridne mid hwiten reafe. ⁊ hine agen-sente to pilaten.

12 And on þam daige wurðen herodes ⁊ pilatus ge-freond. Soðlice hyo wæren ær ge-feond heom be-tweonen.

13 Ða cwæð pilatus to þare sacerda ealdren. ⁊ ðugeðe (*sic*) ealdren ⁊ to þa*m* folke.

14 Ge brohten me þisne man swilce he þis folc for-hwyrfde. ⁊ nu ich be-foren eow axiende. ich nænne intinge finden ne maig on þisen men. of þan þe ge hine wreigeð.

15 Ne for-þan herodes. ich hine asende agen to him. ⁊ him naht þæs lices deade ge-don wæs.

16 ich hine ge-betne for-læte.

17 Niede he scolde heom for-gefen ænne to heore freols-daige.

18 Þa grette eall þæt folc to-gadere. ⁊ cwæð. Nym þisne ⁊ for-gyf us barraban.

19 se wæs for sumere twirednysse ⁊ manslehte of cwarterne asend.

20 Eft spræc pilatus to heom ⁊ wolde for-læten þane hælend.

21 Ða gretten hyo ⁊ cwæðen. á-hó hine á-ho hine.

22 Ða cwæð he to heom ðridde syðe. Hwæt dyde þes yfeles. ne afunde ic nan þing yfeles on þise men. þæt he syo deaðes scyldig. ic hine þreage ⁊ for-læte.

Various Readings.

11. A. hys; B. his; *omitted in* Corpus MS. A. here [*for* hyrede]. A. ongean-: 12. A. wurdon. A. betweonan. 13. A. þæra. 14. A. *om.* ic *after* nu. A. acsiende. 15. A. furðon. A. agean. 16. A. gebendne, *alt. to* gebetne *in late hand.* 17. B. C. Niede (*as in text*); A. Nede, *alt. to* Nyde. A. ænne. A. heora. 19. A. twyrædnysse. A. cweartern. 20. A. pilatus spræc. A. þone. 21. B. aho (*followed by an erasure; twice*). 22. A. B. gemette. B. C. þincg. A. *om.* yfeles *after* þing. A. þysu*m*; B. C. þisu*m*. A. sig.

Various Readings.

11. hyrede; bismerode; pilate. 12. dæge wurdon; gefrnd (*sic*); gefynd; be-tweonon. 13. þara; ealdru*m*; dugeðe caldru*m*; folce. 14. brohton; swylc; ic beforan; axsiende. ic nanne intingan; mæg; þisum; þa*m*; wregað. 15. Ic; sende; deaðe; waes. 17. him forgyfan. 18. rymde (*for* grette); æt-gædere. 19. manslyhte. 20. him (*alt. to* heom); for-læton þo*n*ne halend. 21. hrymden [*for* gretten]. 22. ge-mette [*for* afunde]; for-late.

telde ł ða hine hero*des* mið here his ⁊ bissmerede ł bisuac ge-gearuad huite
11 *Spreuit autem illum erodes cum exercitu suo et inlusit indutum ueste * 306. x.

gegerela ⁊ eft-sende to pila*te* ⁊ aworden woeron friondas hero*des* ⁊ py*latus* on ðæm dæge
alba et remisit ad pilatum 12 et facti sunt amici herodes et pilatus in ipsa die

for*ð*on ær fiondas woeron him bituih py*latus* ða efne-geceigdu*m* aldor*monnu*m sac*erda*
nam antea inimici erant adinuicem 13 *Pilatus autem conuocatis principib*us* sacerdotum * 307. iiiii. io. clxxxiii.

⁊ laruu*m* ⁊ ꝥ folc cuoeð to him ł to ðæm gio brohton me ðiosne monno suelce
et magistratib*us* et plebem 14 dixit ad illos optulistis mihi hunc hominem quasi

woere fro*m*-cerrende ꝥ folc ⁊ heono ic *fora* iuih gefregno næniht Inðing ic ge-moete on
áuertentem populum et ecce ego coram uobis interrogans nullam causam inueni in

ðissu*m* menn of ðæm ilc*um* in ðæm hine gie ahenas ł ah ne hero*des* for*ð*on eft ic sende
homine isto ex his in quib*us* eum accusatis 15 *Sed neq*ue* herodes nam remissi * 308. x.

iuih to him ⁊ *h*eono noht wyrðe to deaðe gedoen ł wæs him geböetad ł for*ð*on hine
uos ad illum et ecce nihil dignum morte actum est ei 16 *Emendatum ergo illu*m* * 309. ii. mt. cccxxii. mr. ccii.

ic f*or*gefo ned-ðarf ðon*ne* hæfeð ł hæfde to *for*geafanne him ðerh ðone symbel-dæg enne ł an
dimittam 17 necesse autem habebat dimittere eis per diem festum unum

ofe*r*-cliopp*ade* ða ætgædre all-efne ꝥ folc cuoeðende nim ðiosne ⁊ *for*gef us bar*abban*
18 *Exclamauit autem simul uniuersa turba dicens tolle hunc et dimitte nobis barabban * 310. i. mt. cccxxu.

seðe wæs *fore* setnung ł huilu*m* ł *for* longe awordeno in ðær ceastra ⁊ morðor wæs gesended mr. cciiii.
19 qui erat propter siditionem (*sic*) quondam facta (*sic*) in ciuitate et homicidium missus io. clxxxiiii.

in carc-erne eft*er*-sona ða py*latus* sprecend wæs to him willnade *for*leta ðone hæl*end*
in carcerem 20 *Iterum autem pilatus locutus est ad illos uolens dimittere i*esum* * 311. i. mt. cccxxui.

soð hia suiðe cliop*pado* cuoeðendo ahoh ahoh hine he ða ðirddan siða cuoeð mr. ccu.
21 at illi succlamabant dicentes crucifige crucifige illum 22 *Ille autem tertio dixit io. clxxxuiii. * 312. uiiii. io. cxc.

to him huæd for*ð*on yfles dyde ðes næneht ł ne oht inðing deadæs ic gemitte in him ic ðrea ł
ad illos quid enim mali fecit iste nullam causam mortis inueni in eo corripiam

for*ð*on hine ⁊ ic *for*lēto
ergo illum et dimittam

---

11. telde ða hine hero*des* mið herge his ⁊ bismerede gegeorwade hwite gegerla ⁊ eft-sende to py*late*
12. ⁊ aworden weron friondas hero*des* ⁊ pyl*atus* on ðæm dæge forðon ær fiondas weron him bitwih
13. ⁊ pyl*atus* ða efne-gecegde aldormonnum ðara . . . . ⁊ ꝥ folc 14. cwæð to him g . . . . ðiosne monne hwelc were f*or*cerrende . . . . [he]ono ic bifora iowh ic fregno . . . . ic gimoette in menn ðassum of ðæm ilcum in ðæm hine ge ahenas 15. ah ne hero*des* f*or*ðon sende iowh to him ⁊ noht wyrðe to deoðe gidoen wæs him
16. geboetað forðon hine ic f*or*gefe 17. ned-ðærfe ðonne hæfeð to forgeofunne him ðerh ðon*e* symbeldæg enne 18. ⁊ ofer-cliopade ða æt-geddre alefne ꝥ folc cweðende nim ðiosne ⁊ forgef us baraban 19. seðe wæs fore setnunge hwilum ł forlonge aworden in ðær cæstre ⁊ morðor wæs gesended in carc-ern 20. efter-sona ða pyl*atus* sprecende wæs to him wilnade forlete ðone hæl*end* 21. soð hia cliopade cweðende ahoh ahoh hine 22. he ða ðirda siðe cwæð to him hwæt forðon yfel dyde ðæs næniht ł noht inðinga deoðes ic gemitte in him ic ðria f*or*ðon hine ⁊ ic forleta

23 And hig astodon ⁊ mycelre stēfne bǣdon ꝥ he wære ahangen; ⁊ hyra stēfna swiðredon.

24

25 ⁊ he for-gef him þæne þe wæs for man-slyhte ⁊ sumere sace on cwerterne. þone hi bædon ⁊ þæne hælend he sealde to hyra willan;

26 And þa hig hine læddon hi gefengon sumne cyreniscne simonem. se com of þan tune ⁊ þa rode him on-setton ꝥ he hi bǣre æfter þam hælende.

27 him fylide mycel wered folces ⁊ wifa þa hine heofun ⁊ weopun;

28 þa cwæþ se hælend bewend eala dohtra hierusalem. nelle ge ofer me wepan. ac wepað ofer eow sylfe. ⁊ ofer eower bearn.

29 forðam þa dagas cumað on þam hig cweþað. eadige synt þa untymyndan ⁊ innoþas þe ne cendun ⁊ þa breost þe ne sictun.

30 þonne agynnað hig cweðan to þam muntum feallað ofer ús. ⁊ to beorgum ofer-wreoð ús.

31 forþam gif hig on grēnum treowe þas þing doð hwæt doð hig on þam drigean;

32 And mid him wæron gelædde twegen manfulle ꝥ hig wǣron ofslegene;

23 And hyo stoden ⁊ mycelere stefne bæden ꝥ he wære á-hangen. ⁊ hire stefne sweðeredon.

24

25 ⁊ he for-gef heom þane þe wæs for manslihte ⁊ sumere sake on cwarterne þane hyo bæden. ⁊ þane hælend he sealde to hire willan.

26 And þa hyo hine lædden hyo gefengen sumne cyreniscan symonem se com of þam tune. ⁊ þa rode him onsetten. ꝥ he hyo bære æfter þam hælende.

27 hym felgede mycel wered folces ⁊ wife. þa hine heofen ⁊ weopen.

28 þa cwæð se hælend be-wend. Eala dohter ierusalem; nelle ge ofer me wepen. ac wepeð ofer eow sylfe. ⁊ ofer eower bearn.

29 for-þan þa dages cumeð on þam hyo cweðeð. eadige synden þa un-temenden ⁊ in-noðes þe ne akenden. ⁊ þa breost þe ne sucen.

30 þanne aginneð hyo cweðen to þam munten falled ofer us. ⁊ to bergen ofer-wreod us.

31 for-þan gyf hyo on grenen treowe þas þing doð. hwæt doð hyo on þam dreigen.

32 And mid hym wæren ge-lædde twege oðre manfulle ꝥ hyo wæren of-slegene.

Various Readings.

23. A. stemne. A. heora stefna. 24. A. B. C. *omit.* 25. A. for-geaf. A. þone. A. sumre. A. cwearterne. A. hig. A. þone. A. heora. 26. hig [*for* hi; *twice*]. B. C. þan (*as in text*); A. þam *or* þan. 27. A. fyligde. A. heofedan. A. weopon. 28. A. eowre. 29. A. forþam þe ða. A. synd. A. untymendan. A. cendon. A. sycton. 30. A. ongynnað. 31. A. drigum. 32. A. B. C. *insert* oðre *after* twegen.

Various Readings.

23. stodon; bædon; ware; hyra; swiðredon. 25. forgeaf; þonne; sace; cwærterne. þenne (*sic*); bædon. þonne halend. 26. Ænd; læddon; halende. 27. fylgyde; wifa; heofon; weopon. 28. halend; dohtra; eowre. 29. dagas; eadig sind; untymendon (*sic*); cendon; syctun (*with* y *nearly erased*). 30. aginnað; cweðan; muntum falleð; byrgum; -wreoð. 31. grenum; drigen. 32. Ænd; wæron (*twice*); twegen.

soð hia on-stodon stefnum miclum gebedon ꝥte ahoen woere ⁊ on-trymmedon ꝉ stefno
23 *At illi instabant uocib*us* magnis postulantes ut crucifigeretur et inuallescebant uoces * 313. i. mt. cccxxui. mr. ccu. io. cxciiii.

hiora ⁊ py*latus* to-doemde ꝥte woere gebed hiora forgeæf ða him
eorum 24 *Et pilatus adiudicauit fieri petitionem eoru*m* 25 dimisit autem illis * 314. i. mt. cccxxuiii. mr. ccui. io. cxcui.

hine seðe *fore* morðor ⁊ setnung gesendad wæs in carc-erne ðone bedon
eum qui propter homicidium et seditionem missus fuerat in carcerem quem petebant

ðone hæl*end* ẽc salde to willo hiora ⁊ miððy gelæddon hine ge-grippedon ꝉ
i*esu*m uero tradidit uoluntati eorum 26 *Et cum ducerent eum appraehenderunt * 315. i. mt. cccxxxi. mr. ccuiiii.

sumne simon cyrinisce cymmende of londe ⁊ geseton him ꝥ rod to bearanne æft*er* io. cxcuii.
simonem quendam cyrinensem uenient*em* de uilla et imposuerunt illi crucem portare post [MS. cxxuii.]

ðone hæl*end* fylgde ða hine menigo hergas ðæs folces ⁊ ðara wifana ðaðe gemæn-
i*esu*m 27 *Sequebatur autem illum multa turba populi et mulierum quae plange- * 316. x.

don ꝉ ⁊ hond-bæftadon hine efne-gecerred wæs ða to him ꝉ ðæm se hæl*end* cuoeð dohtero
bant et lamantabantur (*sic*) eum 28 conuersus autem ad illas i*esu*s dixit filiae

hieru*salem* nallað gie woepa of*er* mec ah of*er* iuh seol*fo* woepað [⁊] of*er* suno iuero
hierusalem nolite flere super me sed super uos ipsas flete [et] super filios uestros

for*ð*on heono cymað dagas in ðæm hia cuoaðas eadgo biðon ða unberendo ⁊ ða wombo ðaðe ne
29 quoniam ecce uenient dies in quib*us* dicent beatae steriles et uentres qui non

acendon ꝉ ⁊ ða breosto ðaðe ne gemilcadon ꝉ ne gefoedon ðon*ne* ꝉ ða hia onginnað cuoeða
genuerunt et ubera quae non lactauerunt 30 tunc incipient dicere

ðæ*m* mōrum fallað of*er* ūsih ⁊ hyllum aw*u*riað usic for*ð*on ꝉ gif In groene ꝉ tree ðas
montib*us* cadete (*sic*) super nos et collib*us* operite nos 31 quia si in uiridi ligno haec

doað in drygi ꝉ in alde huæd bið ꝉ worðes woeron gelædet ða ⁊ oðoro tuoege woh-fullo ꝉ
faciunt in arido quid fiet 32 *Ducebantur autem et alii duo ne- * 317. i. mt. cccxxxui. mr. ccxu. io. cxcuiii.

unrehto mið hine ꝥte hia woere gedeðed ꝉ gecuelledo
quam cum eo ut inter-ficerentur

---

23. soð hia on-stodun stefnum miclum ge-beodon ꝥte he ahongen were ⁊ in-trymedun stefnum hiora 24. ⁊ pyl*atus* todoemde ðæt were gibed hiora 25. for*g*æf ða ðæm hine seðe fore morðre ⁊ set-nunge gisended wæs in carc-ern ðon*e* bedon ð...... willum hiora 26. miððy.... [hi]ne gigriopun simon... cymende of londe ⁊ giseto[n].... rode to bearanne æft*er* ðæm hæl*end* 27. fyligdun ða him monige hergas ðæs folches ⁊ wif ðaðe gimændun ⁊ hondum beoftun hine 28. efne-gicerred wæs ða to him ðæ hæl*end* cwæð dohter.... nallað giwoepa ofer mec ah fore iowih solfe woepað ⁊ ofer suno iowre 29. forðon heono cymeð dagas in ðæm hiæ cweoðas eadge eadge (*sic*) bioðon ⁊ ða wombe ðaðe ne acendun ⁊ ða breost ðaðe gi-milcadun 30. ða hiæ onginneð cweoða ðæm morum falleð ofer usih ⁊ hyll biwriað usih 31. ðæt in groenu*m* treoum ðas doað on dryge ðæt bið 32. werun gilæded ða ⁊ oðre twoege wohfulle mið him ꝥ hiæ werun gideðed

33 And syððan hig comon on þa stowe
þe is genemned caluarie ꝥ is heafod-pannan
stów. þar hig hine hengon ⁊ anne sceaþan
on his swiðran healfe ⁊ oðerne on his wynstran;

34 Ða cwæð se hælend. fæder. forgyf
him forþam hig nyton hwæt hig doð; Soðlice hig dældon hys reaf ⁊ wurpun hlótu.

35 ⁊ ꝥ folc stod geanbidiende. ⁊ þa ealdras hine tældon mid him ⁊ cwædon; Oþre
he ge-hælde gehæle hine sylfne gif he síg
godes gecorena;

36 And þa cempan hine by[s]mredon ⁊
him eced brohton

37 ⁊ þus cwædon; Gif þu si iudea cining
gedo þe halne;

38 Ða wæs his ofer-gewrit ofer hine a-
wríten. greciscum stafum ⁊ ebreiscum. þis
is iudea cining;

39 Án of þam sceaþum þe mid him hangode hine gremede ⁊ cwæþ; Gif þu crist
eart gehæl þe sylfne ⁊ unc;

40 Ða ⁊swarude se oþer ⁊ hine þreade ⁊
cwæþ; Ne þu god ne ondrætst ꝥ ðu eart on
þære ylcan genyðerunge.

41 ⁊ wyt witodlice be uncer ǽrdædum
on-foð; Soðlice þes naht yfeles ne dyde

42 ⁊ he cwæþ to þam hælende; Drihten.
gemun þu me þonne þu cymst on þin
ríce;

33 ⁊ syððen hyo comen on þare stowe.
þe ys ge-nemned caluarie þæt ys heafed-
panne stow. þær hyo hine hengen. ⁊ ænne
scaþan on hys swydren healfe ⁊ oðer on hys
wenstran.

34 Þa cwæð se hælend fader for-gef heom
for-þan hy nyten hwæt hyo doð. Soðlice
hyo dælden his reaf ⁊ wurpen hloten.

35 ⁊ ꝥ folc stod ge-ambadiende. ⁊ þa
ealdres hine tælden mid heom ⁊ cwæðen.
Oðre he ge-hælde. hine sylfne he ge-hæle
gyf he syo godes ge-corene.

36 And þa cempen hine bysmereden. ænd
hym æched brohten.

37 ⁊ þus cwæðen. Gyf þu syo iudea
kyning ge-do þe sylfne halne.

38 Ða wæs his ofer-ge-writ ofer hine
awriten. grekiscen stafen ⁊ hebreiscen.
þis is judea kyning.

39 And (*sic*) of þam scaðen þe mid hym
hangede. hine gremede. ⁊ cw̄. Gyf þu
crist ært ge-hæl þe sylfne ⁊ unc.

40 Ða andswerede se oðer ⁊ hine þreadde
⁊ cwæð. Ne þu god ne on-drædst. þæt
þu ert on þare ylcan ge-nyðerunge.

41 ⁊ we her* witodlice be uncer ær-dæden
on-foð. Soðlice þes naht yfeles ne dyde.

42 ⁊ he cwæð to þam hælende. Drihten
ge-mune þu me. þanne þu kymst on þin
rice.

* we her *on an erasure.*

Various Readings.

33. A. þær. A. ænne. A. þa wynstran [*for* his wynstran]. 34. A. B. wurpon. 35. A. ge-anbydigende. B. sý; C. sy [*for* síg]. 36. A. B. bysmredon. 37. A. sig. 38. A. cyningc. 39. A. gremode. C. *om.* eart. 40. A. ⁊swarode. C. ondræst. 41. C. *om.* be.

Various Readings.

33. siððan; comon; heafod-; hengon; swyðran; winstran. 34. fæder for-geaf; hyo niten; wurpan hloton. 35. ge-ambodiende; ealdras; tældon; cwæðon; R. *om.* he *after* sylfne; gecorena. 36. Ǽnd; cempan; bysmoroden; eced brohton. 37. cwæðon; sy; cyning. 38. greciscum stafum ⁊ ebreiscum; iudea cyning. 39. Ǽnd; scaðum; hangode; eart. 40. ondrætst; eart; ylca. 41. wyt [*for* we her]; ærdædum. 42. gemun; þonne; cymst.

⁊ æft*er* ðon cuomon in stow*u* seðe geceiged bið heafod-ponna stoue ðer ahengon hine
33 *ET postquam uenerun*t* in locum qui uocatur caluariae ibi crucifixerunt eum * 318. i. mt. cccxxxii. mr. ccx.

⁊ ða mórsceaðo an ł enne to suiðru*m* ⁊ oðerne of ðæm winstr*um* se hæl*end* ða gecuoeðað io. cxcuii.
*ET latrones unum á dextris et alterum á sinistris 34 †*Iesus* autem dicebat * 319. i. mt. cccxxxui. mr. ccxu.

fader *for*gef him ne *for*ðon wuton huæd hia doas to-dældon uut*edlice* ge-wóedo ł his sendon io. cxcuiiii.
pater dimitte illis non enim sciunt quid faciunt *Diuidentes uero uestimenta eius miserunt † XCI. 320. x. * 321. i.

tanas ⁊ gestód ꝥ folc basnende ⁊ bismeredon ł hlogon hine ða aldormenn mið him mt. cccxxxiiii. mr. ccxii.
sortes 35 et stabat populus spectans *ET deridebant illum principes cum eis * 322. ii. mt. cccxxxuiii. mr. ccxuiii.

cuoeðendo oðoro halo dyde hine hal*o* gedoe gif ðis is crist godes gecoren teldon ł
dicentes alios saluos fecit sé saluum faciat si hic est *christus* d*e*i electus 36 *INlude- * 323. ii. mt. cccxlii. mr. ccxxii.

bisme*redon* ða him ⁊ ða cemp geneolecdon ⁊ æcced brohton him cuoeðendo gif ðu
bant autem ei et milites accedentes et accetum (*sic*) afferentes illi 37 dicentes si tú

arð cynig iudeana hal ðéc dóo wæs ðon*ne* ⁊ æc of*er*-awritt inawritten of*er* hine
és rex iudaeorum saluum té fac 38 *ERat autem et super-scribtio inscribta super illum * 324. i. mt. cccxxxu. mr. ccxiiii.

stafum mið creciscu*m* ⁊ latinu*m* ⁊ ebriscu*m* ðis is cynig iudeana ân ðon*ne* of io. cxcuiiii.
litteris graecis et latinis et haebraicis hic est rex iudaeorum 39 *Unus autem de * 325. ii. mt. cccxxxuiiii.

ðæm ðaðe ahongadon mórsceaðu*m* gebolsade hine cuoeð gif ðu arð crist hal dóo ðec mr. ccxuiiii.
his qui pendebant latronib*us* blasphemabat eum dicens si tú és *christus* saluum fac témet-

seolfne ⁊ usih ondsuarede ða se oðer *for*cuoæð ł geðreade hine cuoeð ne ⁊ ðu
ipsum et nos 40 *Respondens autem alter increpabat illum dicens neque tú * 326. x.

ondredes ðe god ꝥte ł *for*ðon on ða ilco eu*u*erdlu ł niðrung arð ⁊ ǽc wóe æcsoð rehtlice *for*ðon
times d*eu*m quod in eadem damnatione és 41 et nos quidem iuste nam

wyrðo mið woerc*um* woe onfengon ðes uut*edlice* noht yfles dyde ⁊ cuoeð to ðæm hæl*ende*
digna factis recepimus hic uero nihil mali gessit 42 et dicebat ad i*esum*

drihten gemyne mín ł mec miððy ðu cymes in ríc ðin
d*omi*ne memento mei cum ueneris in regnum tuum

---

33. ⁊ æfter ðon comun in stowwe seðe giceged bið heofodponna stow ðer ahengun hine ⁊ ða morscæðo enne to ðær swiðra ⁊ oðerne on ða wynstra 34. ðe hæl*end* ða cwæð fæder forgef him ne *for*ðon wutun ꝥ hwæt hie doað todæleð wutudl*ice* giwede his sendun hlott 35. ⁊ stod ðæt folc basnade ⁊ bismeradun ł hlogun hine ða aldor-menn mið him cweðende oðre hale dyde hine ne halne doeð gif ðis is crist godes gicoren 36. teldun ł bismeradun ða hine ⁊ ða cempu gineolicadun ⁊ æceð brohtun him 37. cweðende gif ðu arð cynig iudea halne doa ðec 38. wæs ðon*ne* ⁊ ofer-wriotum awriten ofer hine stafum creciscum ⁊ lædenum ⁊ ebriscum ðis is cynig iudeana 39. an ðonne of ðæm ðaðe ahengon morsceoðo gi-eofulsadan hine cwæð gif ðu arð crist halne gidoa ðec solfne ⁊ usih 40. ondsworade ða ðe oðer *for*cwæð ł ðreade hine cwæð ne ðu ðe ondredes god ðætte *for*ðon on ða awerdlo ł niðrung is 41. ec we ecsoð rehtlice *for*ðon wyrðe mið wercum we on-fengun ðer wutudlice noht yfles dyde 42. ⁊ cwæð to ðæm hæl*ende* drihten gimyne min miððy cymes in rice ðin

43 Ða cwæþ se hælend to him; To-dæg þu bist mid me on paradiso;

44 Þa wæs nean seo syxte tíd. ⁊ þystro wæron ofer ealle eorþan oð þa nigoþan tíde.

45 ⁊ sunne wæs aþystrod ⁊ þæs temples wahryft wearð toslyten on middan;

46 Ða cwæð se hǽlend clypiende mycelre stéfne; Fǽder ic bebeode minne gast on þinre handa. ⁊ þus cweþende he forþferde;

47 Þa se hundred-man geseah ꝥ þar geworden wæs. he god wuldrode ⁊ cwæð; Soþlice þes man wæs riht-wis.

48 ⁊ eall wered þe æt þisse wæfer-synne wæron ⁊ gesawon þa þing þe ge-wurdon. wæron agen gewende hyra breost beoton;

49 Ða stodon ealle hys cuþan feorran. ⁊ þa wíf þe him fyligdon fra*m* galilea þas þing geseonde.

50 ⁊ þa an man on náman iosep. se wæs gerefa gód wer ⁊ rihtwis.

51 þes ne ge-þwærode hyra geþeahte ⁊ hyra dædu*m* fra*m* arimathia iudea ceastre se sylfa ge-anbidude godes ríce.

52 þes genealæhte to pilate ⁊ bæd þæs hælendes lichaman

53 ⁊ nyðer-alede hyne ⁊ on scytan befeold ⁊ lede hine on aheawene byrgene on þære næs þa gyt nænig aléd;

43 Þa cwæð se hælend to hym. to-daig þu byst mid me on paradise.

44 Ða wæs neoh syo sixte tid. ⁊ þeostre wæren ofer ealle eorðan. oððan nigeþen tide.

45 ⁊ sunne wæs astyred ⁊ þas temples wahrift wærð to-sliten on midden.

46 Ða cw̄. se hælend clepiende mycele stefne. Fader ich be-beode minne gast on þinre hande. ⁊ þus cweðende he forðferde.

47 Ða se hundred-man ge-seah ꝥ þær geworðen wæs. he god wuldrede. ⁊ cwæð. Soðlice þes man wæs rihtwis.

48 ⁊ eall wered þe æt þisse wæfernyssen wæren ⁊ ge-seagen þa þing þe ge-worðen wæren. agen ge-wende heore breost beoten.

49 Ða stoden ealle his cuðan feorren. ⁊ þa wif þe hym felgden fram galilea þas þing ge-seonde.

50 ⁊ þa an man on namen ioseph se wæs ge-refe. ⁊ god wer ⁊ rihtwis.

51 þes ne ge-ðwærede hyore ge-þohte ⁊ hyra dæden fram arimathia iudéé cestre. se sylfe ge-ambadede godes riche.

52 þes ge-neahlahte to pilate ⁊ bæd þas hælendes lichamen.

53 and niðer-aleigde hine. ⁊ on scetan be-feold. ⁊ leigde hine on aheawene byregene on þare næs na ġeot on ánig aleigð.

Various Readings.

44. A. neah. 46. A. clypigende. A. stemne. A. þyne. 48. A. werod. B. wæfersynne (*with the letters* ne *nearly erased*). A. ongean. A. heora. 50. A. ioseph. 51. A. ge-þwærede heora. A. heora. A. ge-anbydode.

Various Readings.

43. halend. 44. neah; þystre wæron; eall; nigoþan. 45. aþystrod; wearð; middan. 46. halend; mycelere; Fæder ic; þinra handa. 47. geworden; wuldrodede (*sic*). 48. wæfer-syn; ge-sawan; ge-wurdon wæron; hiora; beoton. 49. feorran; heom fylgdon. 50. naman; ge-reafe. 51. hyora ge-þeahte; dædu*m*; iudea ceastre; ge-anbydode; rice. 52. ge-neah-lachte; lichaman. 53. alegde; scyetan be-feald; legde; a-hewenne byrigenne; gyt anyg aled (*omitting* on).

⁊ cuoeð him se hæl*end* soð is ꝥ ic cuoeðo ðe todæg mec mið ðu bist in nercsna-wong
43 et dixit illi ie*sus* amen dico tibi hodie mecum eris in paradiso

wæs uut*edlice* ł ða ꝥ ic leto ł suoelce tíd ðio seista ⁊ ðiostro aworden woeron on alle eorðo wið
44 *Erat autem fere hora sexta et tenebrae factae sunt in uniuersa terra usq*ue* * 327. ii. mt. ccexl. mr. ccxx.

on non tíd ⁊ fo*re*-awrigen ł wæs sunna ⁊ waghræl tempeles toslitten wæs on middu*m*
in nonam horam 45 et obscuratus est sol *Et uelum templi scissum est medium * 328. ii. mt. cccxliiii. mr. ccxx[iiii].

⁊ clioppade stefne micle ł mið miclu*m* stefnu*m* se hæl*end* la fader In hondu*m* ðinu*m* ic bebiodo ł ic fæsto
46 *Et clamans magna uoce ie*sus* pater in manus tuas commendo , * 329. i. mt. cccxliii. mr. ccxxiii. io. cciiii.

gast min*ne* ⁊ miððy ðas cuoeð gást of-gæf ł gesæh ða ðe aldorm*onn* ꝥte aworden
sp*iritu*m meu*m* et haec dicens expirau*it* 47 *Uidens autem centurio quod factum * 330. ii. mt. cccxlui. mr. ccxxu.

wæs gewuldrade god cuoeð soðlice ðes monn soðfæst is ⁊ all ꝥ here ðara
fuerat glorificauit d*eu*m dicens uere hic homo iustus est 48 *Et omnis turba eorum * 331. x.

ðaðe æd-geædre to-cuom*on* ł to-weron to sceawanne ł ꝥ ł ⁊ gesegon ł ðaðe woeron aworden slægendo woeron
qui simul aderant ad specta[cul]um istud et uidebant quæ fiebant percutientes

hiora breosto eft-cerrdon ł gestodon ðon*ne* ł ða alle megas ł his farra to ⁊ ða wifo
pectora sua reuertebantur 49 stabant autem omnes noti eius á lo*n*ge et mulieres

ðaðe fylgende woeron hine fro*m* galilea ðas gesegon ⁊ heono wer ðæs noma wæs
quae secutæ erant eum á galilaea haec uidentes 50 *Et ecce uir nomine * 332. i. mt. cccxluiii. mr. ccxxuii. io. ccui.

ios*eph* seðe wæs of ł ðær byrig wer gód ⁊ soðfæst ðes ne efne-genehuade ł to somnung ⁊
ioseph qui erat decurio uir bonus et iustus 51 hic non consenserat concilio et

dēdu*m* hiora fro*m* arimathia byrig ł ceastre iudeæ seðe gebasnade ł ⁊ æc he ríc godes
actib*us* eorum ab arimathia ciuitate iudeae qui expectabat et ipse regnum d*e*i

ðes geneolecde to pyl*ate* ⁊ giude ł bæd lic-homa ðæs hæl*endes* ⁊ miððy ofasette ł i*n*nbewand mið
52 hic accessit ad pilatum et petiit corpus ie*s*u 53 *Et depositum inuoluit * 333. i. mt. cccxluiiii. mr. ccxxuiii. io. ccuiii.

linen*e* hrægle ⁊ gesette hine In byrgenne ł aheawu*n* ł in ðæm ne ða get ænig *monn* gesettet wæs
sindone et posuit eum in monumento excisso in quo nondum quis-quam positus fuerat

---

43. ⁊ cwæð him ðe hæl*end* soð ic cweðo ðe todæge mec mið ðu bist on [n]erexnawonga 44. wæs wutudl*ice* swelce tid ðio sexta ⁊ ðiostro giwordne werun on alre eorðo oððe on non tide 45. ⁊ for-wrigen wæs sunne ⁊ wag-hrægl temples tosliten wæs on middum 46. ⁊ cliopade stefne micelre ðe hæl*end* cwæð fæder in honda ðine ic bifæsto gast minne ⁊ miððy ðus cwæð of-gæf gast 47. gisæh ða ðe aldormon ðæt aworden wæs giwuldrade god cwæð soðlice ðes mon soð-fæst wæs 48. ⁊ al ðe here hiora ðaðe ætsceowunga togedre comu*n* to sceawunga ðæt ⁊ gisegun ðaðe aworden werun slænde on breost hiora eft-cerdun 49. gistodon ða alle megas his fearra to ⁊ ða wif ðaðe fylgende werun him from galilea ðas gisegun 50. ⁊ heono wer ðæs noma wæs, . . . seðe wæs of ðær byrig wer gōd ⁊ soð-fæst 51. ðes ne efne-ginehwada to gisomnunge ⁊ dedum hiora from arimat*hia* ðær cæstre iudea seðe gibasnade ⁊ ec he rice godes 52. ðes ginoelicade to pylato ⁊ bæd lichoma ðæs hæl*endes* 53. ⁊ of-asette biwand in line ⁊ gisette hine in byrgenne aheowne in ðæm ne ða gett ænig mon giseted wæs

54 And þa wæs se dæg parasceue ꝥ is gegearwunge. ⁊ sæter-dæg onlyhte;

55 Ða wīf þe hi*m* fyligdon þe comon mid hi*m* of galilea hig gesawon þa byrgene. ⁊ hu his lichama aled wæs

56 ⁊ hig cyrdon. ⁊ gea[r]wodun wyrtgemang ⁊ sealfa ⁊ on sætern-dæg hig gestildon æfter bebode;

CHAPTER XXIV.

1 On anu*m* reste-dæge swyþe ǽr on dægered hig comun to þære byrgene ⁊ bǽron mid hi*m* þa wyrt-gemang þe hi gegearwodon.

2 ⁊ hig gemetton þæne stān awyltne of þære byrgene;

3 And þa hi in to þære byrgene eodon. hig ne gemetton nā þæs hælendes lichaman;

4 And þa wæs geworden þa hig on mōde āfǽryde wǽron be þyson þa stodon twegen weras wiđ hīg on hwītu*m* reafe.

5 ⁊ þa hig adredon ⁊ hyra andwlitan on eorþan hyldun hig cwǽdon to hi*m*; Hwi sece gē lybbendne mid deadu*m*.

6 nis he hēr ac he arās. geþencađ hu he spæc wiđ eow þa gȳt þa he wæs on galilea

54 And þa wæs se daig parasceue ꝥ is gegarewunge ⁊ sæter-daig onlihte.

55 Ða wif þe hym felgden. þe comen mid hym of galilea hyo ge-seagen þa byrigenne ⁊ hu his lichame aligd wæs.

56 ⁊ hyo chyrden ⁊ gerewedon wyrt-gemang ⁊ sealfe. ⁊ on sætern-daig hyo gestylden æfter be-bode.

CHAPTER XXIV.

1 On anan reste-daige swiđe ær on daigrede hyo comen to þare byregene ⁊ bæren mid heo*m* þa wertege-mang þe hyo gærewedon

2 ⁊ hyo funden þane stan awyltne of þare byregene.

3 And þa hyo in-to þare byrigene eoden hyo ne gefunden na þæs hælendes lichamen.

4 Ǣnd þa wæs ge-worđen þa hyo on mode afereden wæren be þysen. þa stoden twegen weres wiđ hyo on hwiten reafe.

5 ⁊ þa hyo adredden ⁊ heore andhwliten on eorđan heoldan hyo cwæđen to heom. Hwi sece ge libbendne mid deaden.

6 nis he her ac he aras. Be-þencheđ (*sic*) hu he spæc wiđ eow. þa geot þe he wæs on galilea.

Various Readings.

54. A. ge-earwunge. A. *om.* ⁊. A. sæternes dæg. 55. A byrgyne; B. byrgenæ. 56. A. gearwedon; B. gearwodun; C. gearwo... A. sæterdæg.

Cap. xxiv. 1. A. dægred. A comon. A. hig ge-earwedon. 2. A. hi. A. þone. A. awyledne. 3. A. hig. A. byrgenne. 4. A. wæron afærede be þyssu*m*. 5. A. on-dredon. A. heora ⁊wlytan. A. hyldon. A. hwig. 6. A. spræc. A. þe [*for* 2*nd* þa].

Various Readings.

54. End (*with red capital* E); sater-dæg. 55. fyligdon; comon; ge-sæwon; byrgenne; lic-hama alegd. 56. hy cyrdon; gareweden; sealfa; gestildon.

Cap. xxiv. 1. dægered; byrigenne; wyrtge-mang; gegarewoden. 2. ge-metton [*for* fundon]; þæne; byrigenne. 3. Ǣnd; birigenne eodon; ge-metton [*for* gefunden]; þas halendes lichaman. 4. And; gewordon; afærede wæron; þyson; tweigen weras; wytu*m*. 5. adredon; hyora andwlytan; hyldon; cwæđon; mideaden (*sic*). 6. Ge-þencеđ hwu; gyt þa [*for* geot þe].

7 dæge wæs.i.*for*egearuung 7 sunnad*æg* in-lixade under-fylgdon ða ł ða wifo
54 *Et dies erat parasceue et sabbatum inlucescebat 55 sub-secutæ *autem* mulieres * 334. x.

ðaðe mið hine cuomon fro*m* galilea gesegon þ byrgenn 7 huu gesetted wæs
quae cum ipso uenerant de galilaea uiderunt monumentu*m* et quem-admodum positum erat

lic-homa his 7 eft-cerdon ge-gearuadon wyrta gemong ł su*u*eti stēnc 7 smiriniso 7 sun*na-dæg*
corpus eius 56 *ET reuertentes parauerunt áromata et ungenta et sabbato * 335. uiii. mr. ccxxx.

æcsoð suigadon ł æft*er* be-bod
quidem siluerunt secundum mandatum

CAP. XXIV.

ān uut*edlice* ðara dagana.i.sun*na-dæg* suiðe arlice ł cuomon to þæm byrgenne beron ł ða ðe
1 *Una autem sabbati ualde diliculo uenerunt ad monumentum portantes quae * XCII. 336. i. mt. ccclii.

ge-gearuadon ða su*u*eti stēnco 7 gemōeton ðæt stan eft fro*m*-awælted of ðæm byrgenne 7
parauerunt áromata 2 et inuenerunt lapide*m* reuolutum á monumento 3 et mr. ccxxxi. io. ccxi.

Inn-foerdon ne gemoeton þ lic-homa drihtnes hæl*endes* 7 aworden wæs mіððy ðohte gelegeno ł
ingressae non inuenerunt corpus d*omi*ni i*es*u 4 et factum est dum mente conster-

f*or*cumeno woeron of ðisu*m* heono tuoege wæras gestodon æt ł neh ðæm In gegerelo lixende mіððy
natae essent de isto ecce duo uiri steterunt secus illas in ueste fulgenti 5 *Cum * 337. ii. mt. cccliii. mr. ccxxxii.

ondreardon ða ł uut*edlice* 7 ahældon þ onsion on eorðo cuoedon to ðæm huæd soecað gie
timerent autem et declinarent uultu*m* in terram dixerunt ad illas quid quaeritis

ðone lifiende mið deadu*m* ne is hēr ah hueðre æft-aras eft-ðencgað ł hū sprecend
uiuentem cum mortuis 6 non est hic sed resurrexit recordamini qualiter locutus

wæs iuh mіððy ðaget In gali*lea* were ł wæs
est uobis cum athuc in galilaea esset

---

54. 7 dæg wæs fore-georwunge 7 sunna-dæg in-lixende 55. under-fyligdon ða wif ðaðe mið hine werun of galilea gisegun ða byrgenne giseted wæs 7 hu to-gisetted wæs licho[ma] his 56. 7 eft-cerdun gegeorwadun wyrtgimong 7 smirnisse 7 synna-dæg ec-soð swigadun æfter bibode

Cap. XXIV. 1. an wutudl*ice* swiðe comun arlice ł fegre to ðær byrgenne .... ðio magðalenisca 7 oðoro maria 7 oðre mið him beron ðaðe georwadon ða smirnisse 2. 7 gimoettun ðone stan awæltedne from ðær byrgenne 3. 7 in-foerdun ne gi-mittun lichoma drih*tnes* hælendes 4. 7 aworden wæs mіððy *for*cumne ł gelegne werun of ðissum 7 heono twoege wearas gistodun neh ðæm gigerlan lix-ende 5. mіððy ondreordun ða 7 ahældun ðæt on-sion on eorðo cwedon to ðæm hwæt soecað ge ðone lifgende mið deadum 6. ne is her ah he aras eft-giðencað hu sprecende wæs iow mіððy gett in gali*lea* were ł wæs

7 ⁊ cwæð; Ðæt mannes sunu bið geseald on handa synfulra manna ⁊ beon ahangen ⁊ þy þriddan dæge arisan.

8 ⁊ hig gemundon his worda

9 ⁊ hig gewendon fram þære byrgene ⁊ cyddon eall þis þam endlufenum ⁊ eallum oðrum

10 Soþlice wæs maria magdalene. ⁊ iohanna. ⁊ maria iacobi. ⁊ oðre þe mid him wæron þa sædon þas þing þam apostolum

11 ⁊ þas word wæron geþuhte beforan him swa woffunng ⁊ hig ne ge-lyfdon him;

12 Þa aras petrus ⁊ arn to þære byrgyne. ⁊ alutende he geseah þa lin-wæda sylfe alede. ⁊ he ferde wundrigende þæs þar geworden wæs.

Ðys gebyrað on oðerne easter-dæg. Exierunt duo ex discipulis iesu. A.

13 ⁊ þa ferdon twegen of him on ꝥ castel ꝥ wæs on fæce syxtig furlanga fram hierusalem on naman emaus.

14 ⁊ hig spæcon him betwynan be eallum þam þe þar ge-wordene wæron;

15 And þa hig spelledon ⁊ mid him smeadon. se hælend genealæchte ⁊ ferde mid him;

16 Soðlice hyra eagan wærun forhæfde ꝥ hig hine ne ge-cneowun.

17 ⁊ he cwæð to him hwæt synt þa spæca þe gyt recceað inc betwynan gangende. ⁊ synt unrote;

7 ⁊ cwæð. Ðæt mannes sune beoð geseald on hande synfulle manne. ⁊ beon ahangen. ⁊ þa þridden daige arisan.

8 ⁊ hyo gemunda his worda.

9 ⁊ hyo ge-wenten fram þare byregene ⁊ kydden eall þis ðam endlefenen ⁊ eallen oðren.

10 Soðlice wæs maria magdalene. ⁊ Iohanna ⁊ maria Iacobi. ⁊ oðre þe mid heom wæren. ⁊ þa saigdon þas þing þam apostlen

11 ⁊ þas word wæren ge-þuhte be-foren heom swa woffung ⁊ hyo ne ge-lefden heom.

12 Ða aras petrus. ⁊ arn to þare byregene ⁊ alutede. he ge-seah þa linwæde sylfe aleigde. ⁊ he ferde wundriende. þas þær ge-worðen wæs.

13 And þa ferden twegen of heom on ꝥ castel þæt wæs on fæce sixtig furlenga fram ierusalem. on naman emaus.

14 ⁊ hyo spæcen heom be-tweonen be eallen þan þe þær ge-worðene wæren.

15 And þa hyo spelleden ⁊ mid heom smeagden. se hælend ge-nehlahte. ⁊ ferde mid heom.

16 Soðlice heore eagen wæren for-hæfde. ꝥ hyo hine ne cneowen.

17 ⁊ he cwæð to heom. Hwæt syndon þa spæce þe gyt recceð me be-tweonen gangende ⁊ synden un-rote.

Various Readings.

7. *After* þriddan, C. *has lost a leaf; it begins again with* dæg wæs ahyld *in v.* 29. 9. A. his [*for* þære]. A. endleofenum. 11. A. B. woffung. 12. A. B. byrgene. 14. A. spræcon. A. be-tweonan. 15. A. B. ge-nealæhte. 16. A. heora. A. wæron. 17. A. synd. A. spræca. A. reccað. A. be-tweonan. A. synd.

Various Readings.

7. byð; handæ synfulre manna; ðriddan daig. 8. gemunda [*as in* H.]. 9. ge-wendon; byrienne; cyddon; endleofenum; allum oðrum. 10. wæron; R. *om.* ⁊ *before* þa; sægdon; apostlum. 11. wæron; be-foran; ge-lyfdom (*sic*) hym. 12. byrienne; alutende; linwæda; alegde; wundrigende; ge-worden. 13. End; ferdon; furlunga. 14. spæcon; be-tweonon; allum þam; þar gewordenne wæron. 15. Ǽnd; hi (*for* hyo, *over erasure*); smeahdon; halend ge-neahlahte. 16. heora; hwæron (*sic*). 17. inc [*for* me] be-twenon gangonde; sint.

cuoeðende ł ꝥte ł *for*ðon gedæfned is sunu monnes ꝥte sē gesāld in hōnd monno synnfulra
7 dicens quia oportet filium hominis tradi in manus hominum peccatorum

⁊ to ł ꝥte were ahoeñ ⁊ ðirddan doege arisa ⁊ eft-gemyndigo weron wordana his ⁊
et crucifigi et die tertia resurgere 8 et recordati sunt uerborum eius 9 *ET * 338. ii. mt. ccclìiii. mr. ccxxxiii. [MS. cccxxxiii.]

eft-færendo woeron fro*m* ðæm byrgenne sægdon ðas alle ðæm ællefnu*m* ⁊ oðoro*m* allu*m*
regressae a monumento nuntiauerunt haec omnia illis undecim et ceteris omnib*us*

wæs ða maria ðio mag*dalena* ⁊ ⁊ ia*cobi* ⁊ ða oðoro ðaðe mið hi*m* woeron
10 *Erat autem maria magdalenæ et iohanna et maria iacobi et ceteræ quae cum eis erant * 339. x.

ða cuoedon ⁊ ða apostolas ðas ⁊ gesene woeron *fora* ł ær hia ł sua fro*m* doen ł wordo ðas
quae dicebant et apostolos haec 11 et uisa sunt ante illos sicut deleramentum uerba ista

⁊ ne gelefdon him ðon*ne* arās gearn to ðæm byrgenne ⁊ gebegde ł
et non credebant illis 12 petrus autem surgens cucurrit ad monumentum et procumbens

gesæh ða linen hrægla gesettedo ⁊ ðona eoda mið hi*m* wundrade ꝥte aworden wæs ⁊ heono
uidit linteamina posita et abiit secum mirans quod factum fuerat 13 *ET ecce * XCIII. [340. uiii. mr. ccxxxiiii.]

tuoege of ðæm ł fro*m* hi*m* eado ðe ilca dæge in ꝥ woerc ꝥ wæs in huarf ðara spyrda hund-teañ
duo ex illis ibant ipsa die in castellum quod erat in spatio stadiorum centum

sexdeih fro*m* hie*rusalem* ðæs wæs em*maus* ⁊ ðailco gesprecon him bituih of ðæm
sexaginta ab hierusale*m* nomine emmaus 14 et ipsi loquebantur adinuicem de hís

allu*m* ðaðe geneolecdon ⁊ aworden wæs miððy woeron spellendo ł gespelledon ⁊ mið him soh-
omnib*us* quae acciderant 15 et factum est dum fabularentur et secum quae-

ton ⁊ he se hæl*end* geneolecde eade mið ðæm ł hi*m* ego uut*edlice* hiora
rerent et ipse i*esus* appropinquans ibat cum illis 16 oculi autem eorum

gehalden weron ꝥte hine ne ongetōn ł ongeatta mæhton ⁊ cuoeð to hi*m* huæd aron ł ðas word
tenebantur ne agnoscerent 17 et ait ad illos quid sunt hii sermones

ða ðe gie sæcgað ł bituih geongende ⁊ gie aron unrōt ł
quos confertis adinuicem ambulantes et estis tristes

---

7. cweðende forðon gidæfnað sunu monnes ðæt gisald were in hond monna synnfulra ⁊ ðætte were ahongen ⁊ ðy ðirda dæge ariseð 8. ⁊ eft-gemyndge werun worda his 9. ⁊ eft-færende werun from ðær byrgenne sægdun ðas alle ðæm ællefnu*m* ⁊ oðrum allum 10. wæs ða ðio magðalenisca ⁊.... ⁊....⁊ ða oðre ðaðe mið him werun ðaðe cwedun ðas to ðæm postolum 11. ⁊ gisene werun *fore* ł ær hiæ swa from-doe word ðas ⁊ ne gi-lefdun him 12. ....ðonne aras gi-arn to ðær byrgenne ⁊ gibegde gisæh ða lineno hrægl hwite asetedo ⁊ eode ðona mið him wundrade ꝥte aworden wæs 13. ⁊ heono twoege of ðæm eodun ðe ilca dæge to ðæm werche ꝥte wæs on hweorfe ðara spyrda sextig from.... ðæs noma wæs amaus 14. ⁊ ðailco gisprecun him bitwion of ðæm allum ðaðe gineolicadun 15. ⁊ aworden wæs miððy werun spellende ⁊ mið him sohtun ⁊ he ðe hæl*end* to-gineolicade eode mið him 16. ego wutudl*ice* hiora gihaldne werun ne ongetun hine 17. ⁊ cwæð to him hwæt arun ðas word ðaðe ge gisæcgað bitwih iow gongende ⁊ ge arun unrote

18 Ða ⁊swarude him ân. þæs nama wæs cleofas ⁊ cwæð; Eart þu âna forwrecen on hierusalem. ⁊ nystest þu þa þing þe on hyre gewordene synt on ðysum dagum;

19 He sǽde þa. hwæt synt þa þing; And hig sǽdon be þam nazareniscean hælende. se wæs wer ⁊ witega mihtig. on spæce ⁊ on weorce be-foran góde ⁊ eallum folce.

20 ⁊ hu hine sealdun þa heah-sacerdas ⁊ ure ealdras on deaðes genyþerunge ⁊ ahengon hine.

21 we hopedon ꝥ he to alysenne wære israhel; ⁊ nu is se ðridda dæg to-dæg ꝥ þis wæs geworden.

22 ⁊ eac sume wíf óf úrum us brégdon. þa wǽron ær leohte æt þære byrgene.

23 ⁊ na his lichaman gemettun. hig comon ⁊ sædun ꝥ hig gesawun engĺa ge-sihðe. þa secgað hine lybban.

24 ⁊ þa ferdun sume of úrum to þǽre byrgyne ⁊ swa gemetton swa þa wíf sǽdon hine hig ne gesawon;

25 Ða cwæð se hælend to him eala dy-segan ⁊ on heortan lǽte to gelyfenne eallum þam þe witegan spæcon.

26 hu ne gebyrede criste þas þing þoli-gean. ⁊ swa on his wuldor gân;

27 And he rehte him of moyse ⁊ of eallum haligum gewritum þe be him awri-tene wæron;

18 Ða andswerede hym an þas name wæs cleophas. ⁊ cw̄. eart þu ane for-wrecen on ierusalem. ⁊ nystest þu þa þing þe on hire ge-worðen synde on þissen dagen.

19 He saide þa. hwæt synde þa þing. Ænd hyo saiden þa be þam nazarenisce hælende. se wæs wer ⁊ witege mihtig. on spræce ⁊ on weorce. be-foren gode ⁊ eallen folce.

20 ⁊ hu hine sealden þa heah-sacerdas. ⁊ ure ealdres on deaðes nyðerunge ⁊ ahengen hine.

21 We hopeden ꝥ he to alysende wære israel. ⁊ nu is se þridde daig to-daig. ꝥ þis wæs ge-worðen.

22 ⁊ eac sume wif of ure us bregden. þa wæren ær leohte æt þare byregene.

23 ⁊ na his lichame ne ge-seagen. hyo comen ⁊ saiden þæt hyo ge-seagen engle ge-sihðe. þa seggeð hine libban.

24 ⁊ þa ferden sume of uren to þare by-regene. ⁊ swa ge-metton swa þa wif saiden. hine hyo ne seagen.

25 Þa cweð se hælend to heom. Eale desige on heortan. late to ge-lefene eallen þam þe þa witegan spræcen.

26 hu ne byregede criste þas þing þolien ⁊ swa on his wuldor gan.

27 Ænd he rehte heom of moyse ⁊ of eallen haligen ge-writen þe be him awritene wæren.

Various Readings.

18. A. ⁊swarode. A. B. cleophas. A. synd. 19. A. synd. A. nazarenyscan. A. spræce. 20. A. hu hig hine sealdon (*sic*). 21. A. *om.* to. A. alysende. 22. A. hus [*for* us]. A. bregdan. 23. A. gemettan (*sic*). A. sædon. A. gesawon. 24. A. *om.* þa. A. ferdon. A. B. byrgene. A. gemettan (*as in v.* 23). 25. A. ge-lyfanne. A. spræcon. 26. A. þolian. 27. A. halgum.

Various Readings.

18. þa [*for* þas] nama; ana for-wrecon; ge-worden synt; þissum dagum. 19. sægde; synt; sægdon; R. *om.* þa *before* be; nazarescan (*sic*); witega; sprace; worce; allvm. 20. selden. 21. opeden (*sic*); alysenne ware; ge-worden. 22. urum; bregdon; wæron; byrigene. 23. lichama; ge-metton [*for* 1*st* ge-seagen]; sægdon; ge-sawen engla; seggað. 24. urum; byrigenne; sægdon; sawen. 25. cwæð; halend; Eala dysigan; ge-lyfenne eallum. 26. byrigede; þoligen. 27. allum haligum; wæron.

⁊ ge-ondsuarede ān ðæm wæs noma ꝉ ðæs noma cleophas cuoeð hi*m* ðu āna fremðe ꝉ ellðiodig
18 et respondens unus cui nomen cleopas dixit ei tú solus peregrinus

arð in hie*rusalem* ⁊ ne ongete ðu ꝉ ða ðe awordeno sint in ðær ðissu*m* dagu*m* ðæm
és in hierusalem et non cognouisti quae facta sunt in illa hiis diebus 19 quib*us*

he cwæð huælco ⁊ cuoedon fr*om* ꝉ of ðæm nazarenisco hælend seðe wæs wer witge mæhtih in woerc
ille dixit quæ et dixerunt de i*e*su nazareno qui fuit uir propheta potens in opere

⁊ *in* worde fo*r*e gode ⁊ allu*m* folce ⁊ huu hine saldon ða heisto
et sermone coram d*e*o et omni populo 20 et quomodo eum tradiderunt summi

sac*erda* ⁊ aldorm*en* usra in niðrung ꝉ *in* suoenc deaðes ⁊ ahengon hine woe
sacerdotum et principes nostri in damnatione*m* mortis et crucifixerunt eum 21 nos

uut*edlice* gehyhton ꝉ ꝥte he were eft-lēsing ꝉ isr*ae*les ⁊ nu of*er* ðas alle is ðirddan
autem sperabamus quia ipse esset redemturus israhel et nunc super hæc omnia tertia

doege to dæge of ðon ꝉ ðas awordeno weron ah ⁊ wifo sume of usra gefyrhtadon ꝉ
dies hodie quo hæc facta sunt 22 sed et mulieres quædam ex nostris terruerunt

usig ða ær leht weron to ðæ*m* byrgenne ⁊ ne wæs gemoetad ꝉ lichoma his
nos quae ante lucem fuerunt ad monumentum 23 et non inuento corpore eius

cuomon cuoeðendo hia uut*edlice* ꝥ gesihðō ðara engla gesega ðaðe cuoedon hine lifiga ꝉ ꝥte lifde
uenerunt dicentes se etiam uisionem angelorum uidisse qui dicunt eum uiuere

⁊ foerdon ꝉ eadon sume fr*om* usra to ðæm byrgenne ⁊ suæ gemoeton suæ ða wifo
24 et abierunt quidam ex nostris ad monumentum et ita inuenerunt sicut mulieres

cuoedon hine uut*edlice* nege moeton ꝉ ⁊ he cuoeð to hi*m* la ūnwiso ⁊ *h*lætto
dixerunt ipsum uero non inuenerunt 25 et ipse dixit ad eos ó stulti et tardi

of*er* hearta to ge-lefanne in allu*m* ðaðe gespreccendo woeron ða witgo ahne ðas
corde ad credendum in omnib*us* quae locuti sunt prophetae 26 nonne haec

gerās geðrouia crist ⁊ on ða wisa ingeonga in wuldre his ⁊ Ingann fr*om* moise ⁊
oportuit pati *christu*m et ita intrare in gloriam suam 27 et incipiens á mose et

allu*m* witgom tosceadade ꝉ him In allu*m* gewuriotu*m* ðaðe of hi*m* woeron
omnib*us* prophetis interpraetabatur illis in omnib*us* scribturis quae de ipso erant

---

18. ⁊ ondsworade an ðæs noma wæs cleo*pas* cwæð hi*m* ðu ana færende ꝉ elðiodig arð in .... ⁊ ne ongete ðu ðaðe awordne sindun under ðissu*m* dagum 19. ðæm he cwæð hwelce ⁊ cwedon him of ðæm h*ælende* nazarenisco seðe wæs witga mæhtig on werche ⁊ on worde fore gode ⁊ allum folche 20. ⁊ hu hine saldun him ða hesta sacerdas ⁊ aldormen usera in swenche ꝉ costunge deoðes ⁊ ahengon hine 21. we wutudl*ice* gihyhton ðætte he were eft-lesing isr*aeles* ⁊ nu ofer ðas alle is ðirda dæg to dæge of ðon ðas awordne werun 22. ah ⁊ wif sume of usera giforhtadun usih ðaðe ær lehte werun to ðær byrgenne 23. ⁊ ne wæs gimoeted lic-homa his comun cweðende him wutudl*ice* ða gisihðe ðara engla gesege ðaðe cwedun hine lifga 24. ⁊ foerdon ꝉ eodon sume from usra to ðær byrgenne ⁊ swa gimoetun swa ða wif cwedun hine wutudl*ice* ne gi-segun 25. ⁊ he cwæð to him la unwiso ⁊ læte of heorte to gilefanne in allum ðaðe sprecende werun ða witgo 26. ah ne ðas giras giðrowiga crist ⁊ on ða wise ingonga in wuldor his 27. ⁊ wæs in-gunnen from moyse ⁊ allum witgum to-gisceode him in allum giwriotum ðaðe of him werun

28 ⁊ hig genea[læ]hton þam castele þe hig to ferdun ⁊ he dyde swylce he fyr faran wolde

29 ⁊ hig nyddon hyne ⁊ cwǽdon. wúna mid unc forþam þe hit æfen-læcð ⁊ se dæg wæs áhyld. ⁊ he in-eode ꝥ he mid him wunude;

30 ⁊ þa he mid him sæt he onfeng hláf ⁊ hine bletsude ⁊ bræc ⁊ him ræhte;

31 Þa wurdon hyra eagan geopenude ⁊ hig gecneowon hine ⁊ he gewat fram him.

32 And hig cwǽdon him betwynan næs uncer heorte byrnende þa he on wege wið unc spæc. ⁊ unc halige gewritu ontýnde;

33 And hig arison on þære ylcan tíde ⁊ wendon to hierusalem ⁊ gemetton endlufan gegaderude ⁊ þa ðe mid him wǽron.

34 ⁊ cwædun ꝥ drihten soðlice aras ⁊ simone æt-ywde;

35 And hig rehton þa þing þa ðe on wége gewordene wǽron. ⁊ hu hig hine oncneowun on hlafes bríce;

Đys ge-byrađ on þryddan caster-dæg. Stetit *iesus* in medio discipulor*um* suor*um*. A.

36 Soðlice þa hig þis spræcon se hælend stód on hyra midlene. ⁊ sæde him. sib sy eow ic hit eom ne on-dræde ge eow;

37 Đa wǽron hig gedrefede ⁊ afærede ⁊ hig wéndon ꝥ hig gast gesawon;

38 And he sǽde him hwi synt ge gedrefede ⁊ geþancas on eowre heortan ástigađ;

28 ⁊ hyo ge-nehlacte þam castele þe hyo to ferden. ⁊ he dyde swilce he ferrer faren wolde.

29 ⁊ hyo nedden hine ⁊ cwæðen. þene (*sic*) mid úncc for-þan hit æfenlecð ⁊ se daig wæs á-helt. ⁊ he in eode ꝥ he mid heom wunede.

30 ⁊ þa he mid heom sett he on-feng hlaf ⁊ hine bletsede. ⁊ bræc ⁊ heom rahte.

31 Đa wurðan heore eagen ge-openede. ⁊ hyo ge-cneowen hine ⁊ he ge-wat fram heom.

32 Ǽnd hyo cwæðen heom be-tweonen. Næs unker heorte beornende þa he on weige wið únc spæc. ⁊ unc halige write untynde.

33 ⁊ hyo arisen on þare ylcan tide ⁊ wenten to ierusalem ⁊ ge-metten endlefene gegaderede. ⁊ þa þe mid heom wæren.

34 ⁊ cwæðen ꝥ drihten soðlice aras ⁊ symone atewede.

35 ⁊ hyo rehton þa þing. þa þe on weige ge-worðene wæren. ⁊ hu hyo hine on-cneowen on hlafes breche.

36 Soðlice þa hyo þis spræcen. se hælend stod heom on midden. ⁊ saide heom sib syo eow. ich hit em*. ne on-dræde ge eow.

* *al*

37 Đa wæren hyo ge-drefede. ⁊ aferede ⁊ hyo wenden ꝥ hyo gast ge-seagen.

38 And he saide heom hwi sinde ge gedrefede. ⁊ ge-þances on eowre heorten ástiged.

Various Readings.

28. A. B. ge-nealæhton; *Corpus MS.* geneahton. A. ferdon. A. fyrr. 29. C. *begins again at* dæg; *see note to v.* 7. A. wunode. 30. B. C. on-fencg. A. bletsode. 31. A. heora. A. ge-openode. 32. A. spræc. 33. A. *om.* on. A. endleofen gegaderode. 34. A. cwædon. 35. A. C. oncneowon. 36. B. C. spæcon. A. heora. A. sig. 37. A. hwig synd.

Various Readings.

28. ge-neahton (*sic*); ferdon; fyrrer faran. 29. Wune; unc for-þan for-þam þe hit æfen-lacð (*sic*); dæg; ahelt; eom. 30. eom sætt; bletsode. 31. wurdon heora eagan; ge-cneowon. 32. eom betweonan; uncer; byrnende; spræc; ge-write. 33. ylcen; wenden; gemetton; wæron. 34. ætywde. 35. gewordene wæron; brice. 36. hy; hale*n*d stod on hyora midlene; sægde; ic; em [*as in* H.]. 37. afyrede; wendon; ge-seawen. 38. sægde eom; synt; gedrefde; ge-ðancas; heorte astigađ.

⁊ geneolecdon ðæm woerce ðidder eadon ⁊ he gedyde ł gebinde hine lengre ł firr gāa
28 et appropinquauerunt castello quo ibant et ipse finxit sé longius ire

⁊ nedon ł hine cuoeðendo wuna usig mið forðon ꝥ efternlocað ⁊ ofgebeged wæs ł is
29 et coegerunt illum dicentes mane nobis-cum* quoniam aduesperascit et declinata est

soðlice dæge ⁊ in-eode mið him ⁊ aworden wæs miððy eft-geræste ł mið him onfeng
iam dies et intrauit cum illis 30 et factum est dum recumberet cum illis accipit

ꝥ laf ⁊ gebloedsade ⁊ gebræcg ⁊ gerahte him ⁊ untyndo woeron ego hiora ⁊
panem et benedixit et fregit et porrigebat illis 31 et áperti sunt oculi eorum et

ongeton hine ⁊ he gedrysnade from egum hiora ⁊ cuoedon bituih him ahne
cognouerunt eum et ipse euanuit ex oculis eorum 32 et dixerunt adinuicem nonne

heorta usra bernende wæs in usic miððy gespræcc In woege ⁊ miððy untynde us ða gewriotto
cór nostrum ardens erat in nobis dum loqueretur in uia et aperiret nobis scripturas

⁊ arisson ðio ilco tíd eft-færende woeron in hierusalem ⁊ gemoeton ða gesomnado ællefno
33 et surgentes eadem hora regressi sunt in hierusalem et inuenerunt congregatos undecim

⁊ ða ðaðe mið him ł ðæm ilcum woeron cuoedon ł ꝥte arās drihten soðlice ⁊ æd-eawade
et eos qui cum ipsis erant 34 dicentes quod surrexit dominus uere et apparuit

simone ⁊ hia ł sægdon ðaðe gedoen ł wundra weron on woege ⁊ huu ongeton ł
simoni 35 et ipsi narrabant quae gesta erant in uia et quomodo cognouerunt

hine in breting ł hlafes miððy ðas uutedlice gesprecon se hælend astōd In middum hiora ⁊
eum in fractione panis 36 *Dum haec autem locuntur iesus stetit in medio eorum et

cuoeð him sibb iuh ic am nallað ondrede efne-gestyredo woeron uutedlice ⁊ gefyrhtedo weron
dicit eis pax uobis ego sum nolite timere 37 conturbati uero et conterriti

wōendon ł hine gāst ꝥte hia gesego ⁊ cuoeð him huæd gestyredo arogie ⁊ smeaungas ł
existimabant sé spiritum uidere 38 et dixit eis quid turbati estis et cogitationes

astigað In hearta iuera
áscendunt in corda uestra

* MS. uobis cum, corrected to nobis cum.

* XCIIII. 341. uiiii. io. ccxxi. [MS. cccxl. uiiii. io. cccxiii.]

---

28. ⁊ gineolicade werun ðæm werche ðider eodun ⁊ he gidyde ł gibinde hine lengre ł firme 29. ⁊ neddun hine cweðende wuna usih mið forðon efern longeð ðu wast ⁊ ofgi-beged wæs soðlice dæges ⁊ in-eode to wunanne mið him 30. ⁊ aworden wæs miððy eftgireste mið him onfeng hlafe ⁊ bletsade ⁊ bræc ⁊ girahte him 31. ⁊ ontynde werun ego hiora ⁊ ongetun hine ⁊ he gi-drysnade from egum hiora 32. ⁊ cwedun bitwih him ah ne heorte userra biornende wæs in us miððy we gisprecun on woege ⁊ miððy ontynde us ða giwriotu 33. ⁊ arisende ðailco tide eft-færende werun in hierusalem ⁊ gimoettun ða gisomnade ællefne ⁊ ða ðaðe mið him werun 34. cweðende ꝥte soðlice aras drihten ⁊ æt-eowde symone 35. ⁊ hie sægdun ðaðe gidoen werun on woege ⁊ hu on-getun hine on bretinge breodes 36. miððy ðas wutudlice gisprecun ðe hælend stod on middum hiora ⁊ cwæð him sib iowih mið ic am nallað geondreda 37. efne-gistyrede werun wutudlice ⁊ fyrhtede werun woendun hine gast ꝥ gisege 38. ⁊ cwæð him hwæt gi-styred aron ge ⁊ smeaunge astigeð in heorte iowre

39 Geseoð mine handa ⁊ mine fet ꝥ ic
sylf hit eom. grápiað. ⁊ geseoð ꝥ gást
næfþ flǽsc ⁊ ban. swa ge ge-seoð me
habban;
40 And þa he þis sæde he æt-eowde
him fet ⁊ handa;
41 Ða cwæð he to him þa hig þa gyt ne
gelyfdon ⁊ for geféan wundredon; Hæbbe
ge her ænig þing to etenne
42 ⁊ hig brohton him dæl gebræddes
fisces ⁊ beo-bréad
43 And þa he æt beforan him he nam
þa lafa ⁊ him sealde
44 ⁊ cwæð to him; Þis synt þa word þe
ic spæc to eow þa ic wæs þa gyt mid eow
forþam þe hit is neod ꝥ beon ealle þing ge-
fyllede þe be me awritene synt on moyses
ǽ. ⁊ on witegum ⁊ on sealmum be mé;
45 Ða atynde he him andgyt ꝥ hig
ongeton hálige gewrítu.
46 ⁊ he cwæð to him ꝥ ðus is awriten ⁊
þus gebyrede crist þolian. ⁊ þy ðriddan
dæge of deaðum arísan
47 ⁊ beon bodud on his naman dædbote
⁊ synna forgyfenesse on ealle þeóda. agyn-
nendum fram hierusalem;
48 Soðlice ge synt þinga gewitan
49 ⁊ ic sende on eow mines fæder behát;
Sitte ge on ceastre oð ge syn ufene ge-
scrydde;

39 Ge seoð mine handa ⁊ mine fet. ꝥ ic
self hyt em. ⁊ grapieð ⁊ ge-seoð ꝥ gast
næfð flæsc ne ban swa ge ge-seoð me
hæbben.
40 And þa he þis saide he atewede heom
fet ⁊ handa.
41 Ða cwæð he to heom. þa hyo þa
gyt ne lefden ⁊ for blisse wundredon. Hæbbe
ge her anig þing to ætene
42 ⁊ hyo brohten him dæl ge-bræddes
fisces ⁊ bei-brad
43 ⁊ he braecc. ⁊ þa æt beforen heom.
he nam þa lafa ⁊ heom sealde.
44 ⁊ cwæð to heom. Þis synde þa word
þe ich spæc to eow. þa ic wæs þa geot mid
eow. for-þan þe hit ys neod ꝥ beon ealle
þing ge-felde. þe be me awritene synde. on
moyses lage. ⁊ on witegan ⁊ on salmen be me.
45 Ða atynde he heom andgyt þæt hyo
on-géten halige ge-writen.
46 ⁊ he cw̄ to heom ꝥ þus is awriten ⁊
þus ge-byrede crist þolian. ⁊ þe þridden
daige of deaðe arisen.
47 ⁊ beon bodeð on his naman deadbote
⁊ synne for-gefenesse. on ealle þeode aginnende fram ierusalem.
48 Soðlice ge synde þinge ge-witen.
49 ⁊ ic sende on eow mines fader be-hat.
Sitte ge on ceastre oððe ge seon ufene ge-
scredde.

Various Readings.

40. A. *om.* þa. A. æt-ywde. 41. A. *om.* her. A. etanne. 44. A. synd. A. spræc. A. *om.* be me (1*st time*); *but* B. C. *repeat it, as in text.* A. synd. 45. A. ontynde. A. ongeaton. 46. A. criste. B. þoligean. A. deaðe. 47. A. bodod. A. Ongynnendum (*with green capital letter*). 48. A. synd. 49. A. oððe [*for* oð ge].

Various Readings.

39. hand; fett; silf hit æm; grapiað; nafð; habben. 40. Ænd; sægde; ætywede. 41. lefdon; fean [*for* blisse]; ænig; etene. 42. ge-breddes; beo-breadd. 43. R. *om.* ⁊ he braecc; he æt [*for* æt]; beforan. 44. cwaeð; sint; ic spec; gyt; ge-fyllede; sint; ǽ. [*for* lage]; salmum. 45. on-geaton; gewritv. 46. þoligan; ðryddan dæige; deaðum arisan. 47. bodad; næmon dædbote; forgyfenysse; þeoda agynendvm. 48. synt. 49. gescrudde.

geseas honda mino ⁊ fǒet ꝥte ic seolf am grāpað ⁊ geseað *for*ðon se gaast
39 uidete manus meas et pedes quia ipse ego sum palpate et uidete quia sp*iritus*

lichoma ⁊ bāno ne hæfeð suæ mec gie seas habba ⁊ mið-ðy gecuoeð æd-eawade hi*m*
carnem et ossa non habet sicut me uidetis habere 40 et cum dixisset ostendit eis

hondo ⁊ fǒet ðaget ðon*ne* ðæm ungelefendu*m* ł ⁊ wundrandu*m* *fore* gefea cuoeð
manus et pedes 41 *Athuc autem illis non credentib*us* et mirantibus prae gaudio dixit * 342. uiiii. io. ccxxu. [MS. cccxli. uiiii. io. ccxxi.]

habbað gie her huoet-huoego ꝥte ētlic sē soð hia gebrohton hi*m* ðæt dæl fisces gebrededes
habetis hic aliquid quod manducetur 42 at illi optulerunt ei partem piscis assi

⁊ biobread huniges ⁊ miððy gebrēc fo*ra* hi*m* geno*m* ða screadungo ł salde hi*m*
et fauum mellis 43 et cum manducasset coram eis sumens reliquias dedit eis

⁊ cuoeð to hi*m* ðas aron wordo ða sprecend ic am miððy ðaget ic wæs iuih mið *for*ðon
44 *ET dixit ad eos haec sunt uerba quæ locutus sum cum athuc essem uobis-cum quoniam * 343. x. [MS. cccxlii. x.]

ned-ðarf is ꝥte se gefylledo alle ða awritteno sindon in æ mo*ses* ⁊ witgo ⁊ salmas of
necesse est impleri omnia quæ scribta sunt in lege mosi et prophetis et psalmis de

mec ða untynde him ꝥ ondget ꝥte on-gēton ða wrioto ⁊ cuoeð him
me 45 tunc áperuit illis sensum ut intellegeren*t* scribturas 46 et dixit eis

*for*ðon suæ awritten is ł wæs ⁊ suæ were rehtlic ꝥte crist geðrowade ⁊ eft-arisa fro*m* deadu*m* ðirdda
quoniam sic scribtu*m* *est* et sic oportebat *christu*m pati et resurgere á mortuis die

dæge ⁊ ꝥte were abodenn in noma his hreonise ⁊ eft-*for*gefnise ðara syn*na* in
tertio 47 et praedicari in nomine eius paenitentiam et remissionem peccator*um* in

allu*m* cynnu*m* onginnendu*m* fro*m* hie*rusalem* gie uut*edlice* aron witneso ðisra ł ðara ⁊
omnes gentes incipientib*us* ab hierosolyma 48 uos autem estis testes horum 49 et

ic sendo hāt ł fadores mines in iuih gie ðon*ne* sittas in ða ceastra wið-ðy
ego mitto promissum patris mei in uobis uos autem sedete in ciuitate quo-adusq*ue*

gie sie gegearuad ł mið mægne ufa ł
induamini uirtutem ex alto

---

39. giseas honda mine ⁊ fo[et] mine ꝥte solfa ic am grapiað ⁊ giseað *for*ðon ðe gast lichoma ⁊ ban ne hæfeð swa mec giseað habba 40. ⁊ miððy ðis gicwæð æt-eowde him honda ⁊ foett 41. ðaget ðonne ðæm ne gilefendum ⁊ wundrade werun *fore* gifeo cwæð habbað ge her hwæthwoegno ꝥte ettlic sie 42. soð hiæ gibrohtun him ꝥ dæl fisces gibreddes ⁊ bio-breod hunges (*sic*) 43. ⁊ miððy gibrec fora him ginom ða screadungæ salde him 44. ⁊ cwæð to him ðas sint word mine ðaðe sprecende ic am to iow miððy get ic wæs ł were iowih mið *for*ðon nedðarf is ðæt we ge-fylle alle ðaðe awritne sindun in æ .... ⁊ witgana ⁊ salmes of mec 45. ða ontynde ongett hiora ꝥte on-getun ða giwriotu 46. ⁊ cwæð him forðon swa awriten is ⁊ swa were rehtlic ꝥ crist ðrowade ⁊ eft arise from deoðe dæg ðirda 47. ⁊ were bodad on noma his hreownisse ⁊ eft-forgefnisse ðara synnfulra in allum cynnum onginnendu*m* fro*m* hierusalem 48. ge wutudl*ice* aron witnisse ðisra 49. ⁊ ic sendo gihat fædres mines in iowih ge ðonne sittað in ðær cæstre wið-ðy ge gi-gerwed se mið mægne on ufa

50 Soðlice he gelædde hig út on bethaniam ⁊ he bletsode hig his handum úpahafenum.

51 ⁊ hit wæs geworden þa he bletsude híg. he ferde fram him ⁊ wæs féred on heofen.

52 ⁊ hig gebiddende hig gehwurfon on hierusalem mid mycelum gefean.

53 ⁊ hig wǽron symle on þam temple god hergende ⁊ hyne eac bletsigende. Amen.

Various Readings.

50. A. bletsade. 51. B. *repeats* geworden. A. bletsode. 52. A. *om.* mid. 53. A. herigende ; C. heregende.

Note. From þa he (*in v.* 51) *to the end is omitted in* B. *owing to the loss of a leaf, though supplied afterwards on an inserted leaf, in a later hand.*

50 Soðlice he ge-lædde hyo ut on* betha- * MS. uton.
niam ⁊ he bletsode hyo his hand upp-á-hafen.

51 Ænd hit wæs ge-worðen þæt he hyo ge-bletsode. he wente fram heom ⁊ he smat (*sic*) in-to heofene.

52 Ænd hyo þa hyo ge-biddende ge-cyrden into ierusalem mid muchelere blisse.

53 ⁊ wæren efre in þare temple heriende ⁊ bletsiende god. Amen.

Various Readings.

50. bethanian ; handa up ahafenum. 51. ge-worden.

Note. From þæt he (*in v.* 51) *to the end is omitted in* R. *by the original scribe, but inserted by the scribe of* MS. H. *without any variation of spelling.*

of-lædde ða hia úta in ðær byrig ⁊ ahefenum ł hondum his gebloedsade him
50 eduxit autem eos foras in bethania et eleuatis manibus suis benedixit eis

⁊ aworden wæs miððy gebloedsade him eft-foerde from him ⁊ wæs gefered in heofnum ⁊
51 et factum est dum benediceret illis recessit ab eis et ferebatur in caelum 52 et

ða ł hia geworðadon eft-færendo woeron in hierusalem mið glædnisse miclo ⁊ woeron symble
ipsi adorantes regressi sunt in hierusalem cum gaudio magno 53 et erant semper

in tempel lofando ⁊ gebloedsando gód soðlice
in templo laudantes et benedicentes deum amen

asægd is bóc god-spelles æfter lucas
EXPLICIT LIBER EUANGELII SECUNDUM LUCANUM

---

50. of-lædde ða hia utt in ðær byrig ⁊ a-hæfnum hondum his bletsade hiæ 51. ⁊ aworden wæs miððy gibletsade hiæ eftfoerde from him ⁊ wæs gi-fered on heofnas 52. ⁊ ða gi-gi-worðadun (*sic*) hine eft-færende werun in .... mið glædnisse micler 53. ⁊ werun symle on temple herende ⁊ bletsadun god

EXPLICIT EUANGELIUM SECUNDUM LUCAM

APPENDIX.

The following is a list of all the readings of the Latin text in the Rushworth MS. *which differ from the text in the* Lindisfarne MS. *as printed in this volume. Note that most of the corrections mentioned as being added "above the line" are in a later hand.*

CAP. I. 1. conpletae; rerum *comes after* narrationem. 3. adsecuto; omnibus; obtime theofile. 5. iudiae; di fice [*for* de uice]; di filiabus áarón; ei [*for* eius]; elizabeth. 6. d*ominum* [*for* deum]. 7. elizabeth sterelis; processiss*et*. 8. fugeretur zacharias; ficis. 9. ingresus. 12. inruit. 13. angelus ad illum; zacharias quia; elizabeth; eius [*for* suum]. 15. enim [*for* autem]; sic eram [*for* sicera]; adhuc. 16. israhel. 17. praecedit; *om.* spiritu et; incredibilis. 19. ad-esto. 21. pleps. 22. uissionem; eis [*for* illis]. 23. inpleti. 24. elizabeth. 25. obproprium. 26. misus; galiliae. 27. disponsatam uiro; domu; maria. 28. inter [*for* in]. 31. concipies. 32. d*ominus* d*eus*. 35. obumbrabit; ideo-que quod [*omitting* et]. 36. elizabeth; ille [*for* illi]; sterelis. 38. *om.* ecce; ancella. 39. exsurgens; abit. 40. zalutauit elizabeth. 41. elizabeth exsultauit; elizabeth. 42. mulieris. 44. enim ut facta; & exsultauit in utero meo infans in gaudio. 45. credidisti. 47. exsultauit. 48. ancellae. 51. dispersit supersit superbos. 52. depossuit. 54. suscipit; suæ *added above the line.* 55. abracham; eius usque in saeculum. 56. quassi. 57. elizabeth; inpletum. 58. missericordiam. 59. octabo ut uenirent & circumciderent; uocabant. 60. iohannis. 61. illum; *om.* quia.' 62. & innuebant patris eius. 63. postulans accipit pugillarum & scripsit; iohannis; omnes [*for* uniuersi]. 64. *om.* est; illico; lingua ei*us* tua loquebatur (ei*us added after* lingua, *which word ended a line*). 65. factum; iudae & deuulgabantur. 66. possuerunt; audierunt; enim [*for 2nd* erit]; cum [*for* erat coram]. 67. inpletum; sp*iritus* s*anctus*; profetauit. 68. uissitauit; redemptionem plebis. 69. cornu; domu. 70, 71. s*anct*orum profetarum suoru*m* qui ab euo sunt & liberauit nos ab inimicis; nos *comes before* oderunt. 72. missericordiam. 73. iurabit; abracham. 74. manibus. 75. iustitiam. 76. profeta; uocaueris; preribís (*the 1st* r *added above the line*). 77. & [*for* ad]; meorum [*for* eorum]. 78. missericordia; uissitauit; exalta. 79. & dirigandos; nostras; uiam. 80. confortabatur in sp*iritu*; desertis; ad diem [*for* in diem] ostentionis; & [*for* ad].

CAP. II. 1. illis diebus; accessare [*for* a cesare]. 2. professio [*for* describtio]; cirino nomine. 3. profeterentur. 4. *om.* 1*st* et; galilia; iudeam. 5. profeterentur; sponsa [*altered to* dissponsata]; prigante. 6. inpleti; parir*et*. 7. reclinauit; deuersorio. 8. uigilantes [*for* uigilias]. 11. uobis [*for* nobis]. 12. possitum. 13. *om.* cum angelo; exercitus [*for* militiae]. 15. uero *added above the line after* pastores; betlem; uidiamus; *om.* fecit; *om.* et *before* ostendit. 16. *om.* festinantes et inuenerunt; possitum. 17. est [*for* erat]. 19. conseruat; conuerens [*for* conferent]. 20. audierunt & uiderunt. 21. puer uocatum; concoepit [*for* conciperetur]. 22. inpleti; purificationis [*for* purgationis]; moysi tullerunt; *after* hierusalem R. *adds* ut adsisterent illum d*omi*no. 23. scriptum; masculum; s*anct*am. 24. hostias; lege d*omi*ni; turtorum. 25. nomen erat semeon; consulationes; ipso [*for* eo]. 26. acciperat; uisuram. 27. introducerent parentes eius puerum i*esum*. 28. accipit; ullas. 29. dimitte. 31. praeparasti. 33. mater eius; dicebatur. 34. illos symeon; possitus; *om.* in *before* signum; contradicet. 35. pertransi & gladius. 36. profetiza; fanuel. 37. usque ad annos. lxxxiii, *glossed* hund-æhtetig; discendebat a templo ieiunis & obseruationib*us* seruiens d*eo*. 38. confitebantur; exspectabant redemptionem hirusalem. 39. galileam. 41. sollempni. 42. ess*et* [*for* fuisset]. 42. ierusolima; fecisti [*for* festi]. 43. quae [*for* que]; *om.* non. 44. cognatos & notos in (*ending the line; sic*). 45. regressi [*for* reuersi]. 46. eum [*for* illum]; R. *adds* illos *after* interrogantem. 47. prudentiam. 48. admirati; mater eius; R. *inserts* síc *before* ecce; querebamus. 49. querebatis; quoniam [*for* quia]; patris; ess*et*. 50. ipse (*sic*). 51. discendit. 52. proficiat; & aetate; omnes (*for* homines), *glossed* alle.

Cap. III. 1. imperi tiberis cessaris procurrante; pylato iudea*m* tetracha; galiliae; pilipo (*sic*); tetracha iturae; traconitidis; lisania abilianae tetracha. 2. caifa; iohannem; & filium. 3. babtismum poenitentiae. 4. sicut scut (*sic*), *the latter word is glossed* swa; scriptum; sermonem essaiae profetae. 5. replebitur; colles. 7. Dicebant; exiebat; babtizarentur; fugere a futura ira. 8. dignos penitentiae; coeperitis; abracham; abrachae. 9. radices; possita; fructum bonum; *om.* in *before* ignem; mittetur. 11. tonicas; det nonbenti, *glossed* seleð ðæm næbbende. 12. puplicani; babtizarentur. 13. *om.* quam. 14. autem *comes before* interrogabant; eum *added above the line;* stipentis. 15. existimantis; cogitationibus. 16. iohannis; babtizo uos in poenitentia uenit autem (in poenitentia *not glossed*); calcimentorum (*with a tag below* i); babtizauit. 17. congregabit triticum suum in orreum suu*m* (*the 2nd* suu*m added, at the end of the line*); conbur*et*. 19. Herodis; tetracha; hrodiade (*sic*); herodis. 20. super; carcerem. 21. babtizaretur; babtizati; opertum. 22. discendit; conplacuit. 23. quassi; putabatur; eli. 24. mathae [*for* mattat]; fui (*sic*) leui. 25. mathathiae; nauum; essau [*for* ésli]; nagae. 26. math, *altered to* maáh; ioseph [*for* iosec]; iuda [*for* ioda]. 27. rassa [*for* resa]; hiorababel [*for* sorobabel]. 28. elmadam; er, *altered to* her. 29. iessu [*for* ihesu]; elizer; sorim [*for* iorim]; mathathiel [*for* matthad]. 30. semeon. 31. melcha [*for* melea]; mathathiae [*for* matthata]. 32. obeth; bos; nason. /33. aram; esram. 34. isác; abrachā. 35. seruc; raugau; falac. 36. cainan; noae. 37. mathusale; iareth; malelel. 38. qui fuít d*ei*, *glossed* seðe wæs goding.

Cap. IV. 1. regresus; a [*for* ab]. 2. temptabatur; diabulo; essurit. 3. illís [*for* illi]; sabulus [*for* diabolus], *glossed* ðe diawul. 4. scriptum; enim quia, *glossed* forðon ðætte; uiuit; 5. eum (*above the line*) zabulus [*for* illum diabolus]. 6. uoluero [*for* uolo], *glossed* ic wyllo. 7. ero [*for* ergo], *glossed* forðon; *om.* procidens; R. *inserts* & *before* erunt (*an addition*). 8. scriptum. 9. dixit *altered to* duxit; eum [*for* illum]; pinnaculum. 10. scriptum; mandauit; de te *added in later hand.* 11. *om.* et; manibus tuis. 12. temptabis. 13. omni temptatione diabulus; eo [*for* illo]. 14. *om.* est; galileam. 15. sinagogís; magnificabantur. 16. consuitudinem; sinagogam. 17. profetae essaiae; *om.* ut; locum [*for* loco]; scriptum est. 18. uncxit; missit; diuisum [*for* uisum], *glossed* gisihðe; demittere. 19. retribuitionis (*sic*). 20. omnia in sinagoga. 21. inpleta; scriptura. 22. que [*for* quae]. 23. dicitis; curati, *altered to* curatute (*sic*); cafarnauum. 24. profeta. 25. israhel quanto; cu*m* *added above the line after* cum; famis. 26. sirepta sidoniae; & [*for 2nd* ad]. 27. helesio profeta; nemán; sinagoga. 29. iecerunt; *om.* ad; supercilicium (*sic*).

After ciuitas *there are* 8 *leaves wanting in the Rushworth MS. to* uiri *in verse* 38 *of Chapter VIII.*

* * * * * * * *

Cap. VIII. 38. uiri; demonia exirent. 39. reddi; d*ominus* [*for* d*eus*]; habiit; praedicas; quantat (*sic*); fecit d*ominus* [*for* fecisset i*esus*]. 40. autem [*for* enim]. 41. uiri eamus [*for* uir cui nomen iairus]; sinagoga; cicidit & pedes ipsum rogans eum. 42. uere [*for* fere]; *om. 1st* et; moriabatur; contegit; turbis conprimebatur. 43. que in medicis; curare. 44. *om. 1st* ei*us*. 45. erat [*for* erant]; tante [*for* te]; conpraemuit & adfliguit. 46. nam & ego; exipse, *altered to* exisse. 47. uidentes; procedit; eius [*for* illius]; tetigerat; iudicauit [*for* indicauit]; quem-admodum confestum. 48. & [*for* at]; flia [*for* filia]. 49. Adhuc eo; princeps [*for* a principe]; mea [*for* tua], *glossed* min; nolii. 50. nolii; *om.* et; saluar*et* [*for* salua erit]. 51. ad *inserted before* domum, *in later*
ingonga hine mið ænigne
hand; permissit; intrase eum quem-quam, *so glossed;* & iohannem & iacobum; puelle. 52. il illam (*sic*). 53. diridebant. 54. R. *inserts* eos *after* tenens; & clamauit; R. *inserts* sunt *after* puella. 55. iusi dari illum [*for* iussit illi dari]. 56. R. *inserts* eius *after* parentes.

Cap. IX. 1. demonia; langores. 2. missit. 3. tolleretis; peccuniam; duos; abetis [*for* habeatis]. 4. & qua-cum-que domui; ubi [*for* ibi]; *om.* ne. 5. reciperit; super [*for* supra]. 6. Egresi; euangelizantur. 7. herodis tetracha; essitauit de eo; *om.* á quibusdam quia iohannes surrexit á mortuis. 8. elias aparuit; alís; profeta. 9. herodis iohannis; decolaui; estis te de, *so divided, but glossed* is ðes of; *om.* audio; *after* talia R. *inserts* iudo (*for* audio), *glossed* doema; uidere *comes after* eum. 10. qui-cum-que; adsumtis eis secesit; que [*for* qui]. 11. quod cum que cognouisent; secute; excoepit ilos (*sic*). 12. Die; caeperat; ascendentes; demitte; diuertuntur; ut [*for 2nd* et]; *om.* in *before* loco. 13. eos [*for* illos]; eis [*for* illis]; manducate; eamus [*for* emamus], *the word being repeated;* escas. 14. *om.* 2*nd* autem; discumbere *to 2nd* et *in verse* 15 *omitted.* 17. eis [*for* illis]; cofini. 18. R. *inserts* et *before* orans; et [*for* erant]; discipuli eius [*for* et discipuli; eius *added above the line*]; beati [*for* esse turbae], *glossed* ead-ge. 19. *om.* at; babtistam; eliam; profeta. 20. *om.* me; esset sed dicitis; R. *inserts* illis *after 2nd* dixit; spiritum [*for christum*]. 21. *om.* hoc. 22. oborportet; occidet. 23. adnegat; cotedie. 24. saluum; eam [*for* illam]; & [*for* nam]; saluum; eam [*for* illam]. 25. profecit homini; rentum [*for* detrimentum]; *om.* sui. 26. filium homonis erubescet con uenerunt. 27. alii qui [*for* aliqui]; *om.* hic; uidiant. 28. *om.* et *after* .uiii., *which is put for* octo; adsumsit; & iohannem & iacobum. 30. loquebatur (*sic*); *om.* autem; moyses. 31. nisi, *glossed* werun gisene; exquesum; *om.* quem; conpleturus; hirusalem. 32. sommo; euigilantes; maiestatis; qustabant [*for* qui stabant]. 33. disceserunt; eo [*for* illo]; ut petrum [*for* ait petrus]; nobis [*for* nos]; *om.* et *after* esse; trea; moysi; dicerit. 34. eo [*for* illo]; nubs (*sic*); umbrauit. 35. electus [*for* dilectus]; in spiritu [*for* ipsum], *glossed* in gaste. 36. fuerit [*for* fieret]; nimini; que [*for* quae]. 37. discentibus (*sic*) [*for* descendentibus]; R. *inserts* & *before* occurrit; & [*for* illi]. 38. uiri; in mé domine [*for* in filium meum], *glossed* on mec drihten. 39. adpraehendit eum; eledit; disipat; discendit delanians. 40. suos [*for* tuos]; ut [*for 2nd* et]; iecerent. 41. *om.* iesus; adhuc; flium (*sic*) [*for* filium]. 42. accideret eledit eum demonium; incrauit [*for* increpauit]. 43. que [*for* quae; *twice*]. 44. filium meum [*for* filius enim]; homonis futurum; traderetur. 45. ad [*for* at]; R. *adds* est *after* uelatum; et *for* ut; *om.* et *before* timebant; interrogarent, *alt. to* interrogaret. 46. Interrogauit [*for* Intrauit]; R. *omits the words from* maior *to* illorum *in verse* 47. 47. adpraechendens; *om.* eum. 48. susciperunt; istud, *corr. to* istum; suscipit [*for* recipit]; reciperint reciperit; R. *adds, after* misit, reciperit eum; maior [*for* minor]. 49. iohannis; *om.* dixit; quendam; meo [*for* tuo] iecentem demonia; proibimus. 50. aduersum. 51. conplerentur; adsumtionis. 52. missit; ut [*for 2nd* et]. 53. reciperunt; quod [*for* quia]; euntes in hierusalem. 54. R. *inserts* autem *before* discipuli; iocob (*sic*) & iohannis; ignem discendit; eos [*for* illos]. 55. R. *inserts* (*above the line*) iesus *before* increpauit; eos [*for* illos], *after which* R. *adds* —& dixit nescitis cui spiritus estis [56] filius hominis non uenit animas hominum perdere sed saluare. 56. habieruit (*sic*); aliut. 57. ierimus. [*for* ieris]. 58. ei [*for* illi]; filios [*for* filius]; homines; R. *inserts* suum *after* caput (*above the line*); reclinat. 59. irae. 60. dixit quae eí iesus; *om.* ut; *om.* autem; adnuntia. 61. sed per primum ire nuntiare hís qui in domu sunt. 62. atrum [*for* aratrum].

Cap. X. 1. disignauit; missit eos. 2. quidam; ero [*for* ergo]; operios [*for* operarios]; suam *added above the line.* 4. nemini. 5. R. *omits the words from* In *to* intraueritis; dicete; 6. filiís; requiescet; uestras sin [*the* s *in* sin *has been added above the line*]. 7. *om.* autem; domum; aput; est *comes before* enim; operios cibo suo; domu. 8. qua [*for* quam]; susciperint; *om.* quae; adponentur. 9. *om. 2nd* et; eís adpropinquauit ad uos. 10. qua [*for* quam]; reciperunt; platias & dicite. 11. R. *omits the words from* puluerem *to* scitote; adpropinquauit enim. 12. remisius. 13. corozam; betsaida; tiro; R. *omits from 1st* et *to* fuissent; uirtutis que; facite [*for* facte]; ollim; peneterent. 14. tiro; remisius; nobís [*for* uobis]. 15. cafarnauum (ca *added above the line*); exalta; in [*for* ad]; demergis. 16. R. *inserts* & *before the 3rd* qui. 17. demonia sibiciuntur (*sic*); nomini. 18. eís [*for* illis]. 19. super (*twice*); nos [*for* 2*nd* uobis], *but glossed* iow.

Verses 20—38, *to the word* mulier, *are wanting in the* MS.

38. quedam [*for* quaedam]; excoepit; domu sua. 39. huc [*for* huic]; que quam [*for* quae etiam], *glossed* ðio ðe; audierbat (*sic*) uerba. 40. satagagabat (*sic*); frecens (*sic*); que stit; cura tibi [*for* tibi curae]; sola; ei [*for* illi]; me *comes before* adiuuet. 41. *om.* 1*st* et; eí [*for* illi]; *iesus* [*for dominus*]; *om.* 2*nd* martha; solicita. 42. Maria autem obtimam partem; que [*for* quae].

Cap. XI. 1. ei*us* [*above the line, for* suis]; R. *inserts* mé *after* doce, *glossed* mec ł; *om.* et *after* sicut; iohannis. 2. eis [*for* illis]; orates; *after* Pater R. *inserts* noster qui és in caelis; *after* regnum tuum R. *inserts* fiat uoluntas tua sicut in caelo & in terra. 3. hodie [*for* cotidie], *glossed* to dæge. 4. demitte; pecata; sicut [*for* si]; debitoribus nostris [*for* omni—nobis]; temptationem, *after which* R. *adds* sed libera nos a malo. 5. hab*et*. 6. quaniam; meus *follows* uenit. 7. inde [*for* de]; R. *inserts* respondens *before* dicat; puer meus. 8. R. *inserts before* dico, *at the beginning*, & ille si perseuerauerit pulsans; ei [*for* illi] (*twice*); inprobrietatem; *om.* tamen, *though* hweðre *is in the gloss; amici eius* surg*et*; R. *inserts* quot *after* 2*nd* quod. 9. Et ecce ego dico uobis; querite. 10. Omnes; querit. 11. enim [*for* autem]; R. *inserts* filius *after* uobis; lapidem dabitur; *om.* 1*st* illi; ille [*for* 2*nd* illi], *added above the line*. 12. peterit óuam; porrig*et* ei. 13. *om.* data. 14. demonium; iecisset demonium; admirati. 15. omnes quidam; phariseis [*for* eis]; belzebul (*sic*) principe demoniorum iecit demonia. 16. temptans; querebant *precedes* de caelo. 17. cogitationis; ipsum [*for* ipso]; desolabitur. 18. *After* satanas R. *adds* satanam iecit; belzebub; iecise [*for* eicere]; demonia. 19. R. *omits the words from* si *to* daemonia; iecipunt. 20. iecio demonio. 21. armatis (*sic*); custodiat; que posset. 22. illa; uincerit. 23. quia [*for* qui] (*twice*); dispargit. 24. inmundus; exierat de ab (*sic*) homine perambulabat; ininaquosa (*sic*) queriens. 25. mandatam (R. *then adds* & ornatam). 26. adsum*et*; spiritus nequitior esse (*so divided, but glossed* woh-fulra him); ingresi; fiunt [*for* sunt]; homini eius. 27. quedam; que sunt existi [*for* quae suxisti]. 28. ad eos immo [*for* quippini]. 29. querit; eí [*for* illi]; ione profetae. 30. in signum fuit [*for* fuit signum]; ninuetis. 31. austri; contempnabit; salamonis; ecee (*sic*); salamone. 32. ninuete; contemnabunt; quia quia (*sic*); penetentiam; plus ionae hic (*sic*). 33. lucernam; absconso; uidiant. 34. occulus (*twice*); semplex; nequa-quam; etiam &; *om.* tuum. 35. *om.* est. 36. erit *comes after* 2*nd* lucidum. 37. pariseus (*sic*); prandir*et* aput; ingresus. 38. phariseus; *om.* autem; primum babtizatus. 39. pharisei prius quod; cateni. 40. *om.* 1*st* quod; *om.* id; *om.* 2*nd* de. 41. elimosinam. 42. pharisei; quid [*for* quia]; praeteris. 43. pharissei quia diligistis proximas cadedras in sinagoga; salutationis. 44. qui [*for* quia]; mumenta que (*sic*); homones (*corrected*); ambulentes super illa. 45. *om.* quidam; ei [*for* illi]; dicis [*for* dicens]. 46. Uae uobis quia honoratis homones honoribus que; una [*for* uno]; R. *adds* ipsius *after* sarcinas. 47. qui [*for* quia]; monumenta profetarum; eos [*for* illos]. 48. *om.* quod; consentire; *om.* eos; *om.* eorum; sepultura. 49. & praeteria [*for* propterea]; profetas; apostolos; occidentur. 50. inquinatur sanguinis; profetarum; effussus; constitione (*sic*); generatione. 51. R. *inserts* & *before* qui; eadem. 52. qui [*for* quia]; abstullistis; R. *inserts* & *before* ipsi; introibat, *alt. to* introibant. 53. pharissei; obprimere. 54. insidientes ei querentes; accussarent; eum *written above the line*.

Cap. XII. 1. primum Adtendite ad fermento phariseorum que est hipocrisis. 3. que [*for* quae]; audistis [*for* dixistis]; *after* aurem R. *adds* audistis &; cubilis praedicatur; *after* tectis R. *adds* & in plateis. 4. terremini; eís [*for* his]; quae faciunt [*for* quod faciant]. 5. timiatis timite eam; ad gegenam. 6. nonne passeri*bus* .u. uenerunt duo pondio; eís [*for* illis]. 7. multi. 10. omnis; spiritu sancto; *after* 2*nd* remittetur R. *adds* & omnis qui dixerit uerbum in filium hominis remittur ei. 11. inducant; *om.* ad; magistratibus; soliciti estis; respondetis (R. *then adds* aut quid dicatis). 12. que obportat. 13. ei *comes before* quidam, *after which* R. *adds* uir; dico [*for* dic]. 14. comé [*for* me], (*a mis-*

take of the scribe, who had missed me *and begun to write the next word*). 15. abaritia; *om.* in; habundantia quis-quam; que [*for* quae]; possedet. 16. eos [*for* illos]; homonis; uberis; adtullit. 17. congregam. 18. distruam; que [*for* quae]. 19. anima [*for* meae anima], *glossed* mine; possita; come [*for* comede], *glossed* riording (requiesce *is glossed* ræst bryce). 20. ei [*for* illi]; que [*for* quae]. 21. quis ibi tessaurizat. 23. corpus plus quam. 24. curuos [*for* corbos]; seminat; pascit; pluri estis eís. 25. enim [*for* autem]; adiecire. 27. neunt (*sic*); salamon; uestiabatur. 28. fenum; agros; *om.* est; mittetur; pussilli. 29. querere; bibetis; extolle [*for* tolli]. 30. querunt; quis [*for* quoniam]. 31. querite ergo primum regnum. 32. pussillus; conplacuit. 33. que [*for* quae]; habetis [*for* possidetis]; elimoysinam; saculos; tensaurum; dificientem; adpropiat; tenea. 34. nam ubi thensaurus; ubi [*for* ibi]; *om.* uestrum. 35. Sunt autem lumbi; lucerna uestrae (*sic*). 36. homnibus (*sic*); uenerint (*sic*); conuestim. 37. inuelantes [*for* inuenerit uigilantes], *glossed* wæcende; praecinget; eos [*for* illos]; ministrabat eis. 38. *om. 2nd* uigilia; R. *adds* sunt *after* beati. 39. haec [*for* Hoc]; quia [*for* quoniam]; ueneret; perfoderi. 40. *om.* qua; potatis; homonis; uenturus est [*for* ueniet]. 41. *om.* ei; hác [*for* hanc]; parabulam; *om.* án; ad nós omnes. 42. putans. 43. con [*for* cum]; inueniet. 44. uero; super; que possedet; eum [*for* illum]. 45. R. *inserts* dicens *after* suo; ueniret; percuterit; ancellas. 46. & partem-q*ue* (& *added above the line*). 47. uapulauit multas. 48. *om. 2nd* non; a paucis; queritur; commendauerit; petent. 49. sic [*for* si]; acendatur. 50. coartor; perficiantur. 52. domu. 53. murum [*for* nurum]. 54. ab oriente [*for* orientem]; occassu. 55. aestus [*for* uentus]. 56. hippocritae. 57. quod [*for 2nd* quid]. 58. tradat [*for* trahat], *glossed* he ge-nime; R. *omits* apud iudicem et iudex tradat té. 59. raddas.

CAP. XIII. 1. ipsò *follows* tempore; nuntians; galilia; sacrificís. 2. in galilia [*for* hi galilaei], *glossed* ðes galilesco; galilia [*for* galilaeis]. 4. R. *inserts* & *before* illi; siloiam. 5. aegeritis; *om.* omnes. 6. uinia. 7. uiniae; querens; succide. 8. ille [*for* illi]; dimittam. 9. *om.* et; si [*for* sin]. 10. autem erat; sinagogis. 11. spiritus; decim; retrorsum [*for* sursum]. 12. uideret; dimisa. 13. inpossuit, *glossed* gesette; creata [*for* erecta]; glorificata est deum. 14. archisinagogus; sabbatis; *after* turbae R. *inserts* quia; *om.* sunt; *om.* in *before* die. 15. respondit; hyppochritae; soluet. 16. filiam abraechae. 17. gaudebit; R. *then omits the remainder of the verse.* 18. *om.* Dicebat. 19. sinapis; missit; ortum; requierunt. 20. simile existimabo; R. *omits* et cui, *and begins verse* 21 *with* simile est. 21. mulier mulier (*sic*); firmentaretur. 22. & toibat (*sic*), *glossed* ⁊ foerde; ciuiuitatem (ciuì *ends a line*). 24. querent; potuerunt. 25. clauserit hostium; scitis. R. *omits verse* 26, *and part of* 27 *to the word* sitis. 27. discidete; omnes qui operamini iniquitatem. 28. sibi [*for* ibi], *glossed* ðer; fletos; abracham; isác; profetas; *om.* introire. 30. erant [*for* erunt], *twice.* 31. illa [*for* ipsa]; ille exi & uadet, *glossed* him gaa ⁊ gong; herodis; uulte [*for* uult té]. 32. R. *inserts* & *before* dicite; ece [*for* ecce]; demonia; tertia die. 33. *om.* me; qui [*for* quia]; capet profetem, *alt. to* profetam. 34. prophetae (*sic*); quem-admodum; *after* pinnis R. *inserts* congregat. 35. relinquetur; *after* uestra R. *inserts* deserta.

CAP. XIV. 1. principis; ipsum [*for* ipsi].
aldor' hiæ cwedun
2. illūd [*for* illum]. 3. pharissa eos dicens
gif gilefed is on symbel dæge
si licet sabbatis, *so glossed; after* curare R. *adds* aut non. 4. adpraehensum hominum sanauit eum. 5. *om.* ad illos; ait [*for* dixit]; assinus; extrachet. 6. ille [*for* illi]. 7. *om.* et; uitatos parabulam; accupitos (*altered from* accipitos); elegerunt. 8. inuitatos; te té (*sic*). 9. dicet; *the 2nd* locum *comes before* nouissimum. 10. sùperitis (*sic*). 11. huiliat (*sic*) [*for* humiliat]. 12. *om. 1st* et; R. *inserts* quae *after* diuites; ipse té inuitent & faciat tibi retribuitio. 13. conuium (*sic*); debelis. 14. abent [*for* habent] ('bent' *joined to the previous word* 'non' *with* a *inserted above the line*); tribuetur; resurrectione. 15. fecit [*for* de simul], *glossed* of ðæm dyde; illi [*for* ei]. 16. & [*for* at]; illi [*for* ei]; caenam. 17. cenae. 18. excussare; uillam enim [*for* uillam emi], *glossed* lond ih bohte forðon; rogate [*for* rogo té], *glossed* ic byddo ðec; excussatam. 19. bouum; roga te (*as in v.* 18);

excussatum. 21. Exíi; dibeles; cludos introduc húc. 22. adhuc locutus est (*sic*). 23. *om.* 1*st* et; ait *follows dominus*; exii; conpelle; *after* intrare R. *adds* quos cum-que inueneris. 24. uirorum; quia [*for* qui]; uoti [*for* uocati]; gustabit caenam. 25. eos [*for* illos]. 26. folios [*for* filios]; adhuc; *om.* et *before* anima*m*. 27. baiolat; crucrem (*sic*); esse *comes after* meus. 28. non [*for* nonne]; conputat sumptus. 29. possuerit; potuerit; incipiat. 30. *om.* et. 31. qui [*for* quis]; aduersus; regi [*for* ei], *glossed* ðæm cynige, him *being over the previous word.* 32. adhuc longe illo; paci. 33. renuntiatiat (*sic*). 35. sterculinum; fofas (*sic*); mittitur.

CAP. XV. 1. adpropinquantes. 2. pharissei; *om.* illis. 3. illis [*for* ad illos]; parabulam. 4. demittit nonagenta. 5. eam [*for* illam]; inponit sup*er* humeros; gaudens. 7. agente [*for* habentem]; digent [*for* indigent]. 8. acendit. 9. uocat [*for* conuocans]. 10. penitentiam agente. 12. adoliscentior; conting*et*; diuissit. 13. adoliscentior; *om.* filius.

After regionem, *there are* 2 *leaves wanting in the MS., to* autem *in verse* 25 *of Chapter XVI.*

* * * * * * * *

CAP. XVI. 25. consulatur. 26. chaus; hii; lunt [*sic; for* uolunt]; in die [*for* inde], *glossed* on dæge ⁊ ona; transmare. 27. rogate ergo [*for* rogo ergo té]; dimittas; domo. 28. testatur. 29. abracham; moysen. 30. abracham; erit [*for* ierit]. 31. moysen; resurrexerit.

CAP. XVII. 1. ueniant. 2. utilius; lapes; scanlizat (*sic*); pussillis. 3. Attendite *autem;* aegerit. 4. dimitt*et*. 5. auge [*for* adauge]. 6. habueritis; arbore morere. 7. aut oues pascentem cui; dicit. 8. *om.* ei; R. *inserts* mihi *after* para; cenam. 11. hirusalem; galileam. 12. ingrediretur quodam. 15. regresus. 16. cicidit. 17. *om.* dixit; .uiiii. [*for* nouem]. 19. & uade; uides [*for* fides]. 20. farisaeis. 22. discipulos suos. 23. uobis ecce uobis híc & ec (*sic*) illic; exire [*for* ire]. 24. erat. 26. dibus (*sic*); ad uentus [*for* in die]. 27. aedebant; & uxores. 28. aemebant; & aedificabant. 29. exiuit; de [*for* á]; pluuit; sulphor; omnis. 31. fuerit; uassa; domu; discendit; redeat. 33. Quicumque *autem; om.* 2*nd* illam. 34. Dico autem; in illa; lecto [*for* tecto], *glossed* hrofe; adsumetur. 35. adsumetur; alter. 36. adsumetur. 37. respondit [*for* dixit].

CAP. XVIII. 1. Dicebant; parabulam; qm [*for* quomodo]. 2. iudex oport*et*; in quam ciuitatem. 3. ueniebant; illum [*for* eum]; tuo [*for* meo]. 4. uereor [*for* reuereor]. 5. ueni-eniens (*sic*); sugill*et*. 6. dicit [*for* dixit]. 7. d*eus* [*for* domin*us*]. 8. dico autem. 9. conficiebant; aspernebant caeteros parabulam. 10. pharisa (*sic*). 11. pharisaei (*sic*); d*eus* [*for* deo]; uelud. 12. dicimas deo; possedeo. 13. occulos. 14. discendit. 15. Adferebant; imfantes (*sic*); tangerent; uidissent. 16. paruulos [*for* pueros.] 17. R. *omits from* Amen *to* dei. 18. *om.* Et. 19. *om.* ei. 20. R. *repeats* d*eus before* mandata. 22. adhuc; omnia q*uae* cum q*ue*; tehsaurum (*sic*). 24. dificile; peccunias; ibunt [*for* intrabunt]. 25. camellum. 26. audierunt. 27. aput hominis (*sic*), R. *then omits from* possibilia *to* d*eum*. 29. reliquerit; *after* filios R. *adds* aut agros. 30. in uita*m* aetena*m* (*sic*) possedebit. 31. Adsumpsit; hierusolima & consummabuntur; scripta. 32. cum [*for* enim]. 33. flagillabit*ur* occident; tertia die resurgat. 34. absconsum; que [*for* quae]. 35. adpropinquar*et*. 36. praterreuntem (*sic*). 38. i*esus* filii. 39. praeteribant; ei [*for* eum]; clamabant filii; misserere. 40. iusit (*sic*); duci ad sé; adpropinquass*et*. 42. ille [*for* illi]. 43. eum [*for* illum].

CAP. XIX. 1. ingresus; hiericcho. 2. ecec (*sic*); *after* uir R. *adds in the margin* erat quidem; iacheus (*altered in pencil to* sacheus, *with like alteration in verses* 5 *and* 8); pulicanorum (*sic*). 4. sycimorum. 5. iache; discende; domu. 6. discendit; excipit; gaudens. 7. deuertiss*et*. 8. iacheus; dn̄m, *altered apparently to* ihm̄; dimedium. 9. domin*us* [*for* i*esus*]; factae; est filius [*for* filius sit]; abrachae. 10. fiius (*sic*); saluum facere [*for* saluare]. 11. parabulam. 12. abít. 13. seruis .x.; *om.* suis; minas; dixit eis [*for* ait ad illos]. 14. oderunt. 15. rego *altered to* regno; iusit (*sic*); quis [*for* quisq*ue*]. 16. mina; minas; adquessiuit. 18. mina; minas. 20. mina; repossita*m*. 21. enim té quia; austeris; possuisti; ubi [*for* 2*nd* quod]. 22. homo austeris. 23. peccuniam; cu*m* ussuris *comes at the end of verse;* illam [*for* illud]. 24. minam; hab*et comes after* qui; minas. 25. minas. 26.

ahbet [*for* 1*st* habet]. 28. in hierusalem. 29. *om.* Et; cum adpropinquass*et*; bethphage; bethaniam. 30. contra uos; sededit [*for* sedit]. 31. operam. 32. misi. 33. eís [*for* illis]. 35. dixerunt; inpossuerunt. 37. adpropinquar*et*; *om.* iam; discensum; oleueti; uirtubus (*sic*). 38. gloriam; R. *adds* deo *after* excelsis. 39. pharissaeorum; suos (*altered to* tuos). 40. quasi hii [*for* quia si hi]; tacuerunt. 41. at [*for* ut], *the* a *marked for erasure, not glossed;* adpropinquauit; eam [*for* illa]. 42. *om.* 1*st* et. 43. in té dies; & con-angustabunt té *comes after the* 1*st* circumdabunt té. 44. & ad; prosternenté (*sic*); filios tuos; supra; cognueris; uissitationis. 45. *after* ingressus, R. *adds* iesus, *above the line;* uententes; templo [*for* illo]. 46. scriptum. 47. principes; *twice.* 48. quid [*for* quod].

CAP. XX. 2. *om.* et aiunt; & [*for* aut]. 3. *om.* unum; respondite. 5. R. *inserts* nobis *after* dic*et*; credidisti illi. 6. sí [*for* sin]. 8. & iesus *repeated.* 9. Caepit; parabulam. 10. uiniae; caessum dimisserunt. 11. *verse omitted.* 12. addedit; eicerunt. 13. dixerunt; uiniae. 14. intra sé; & [*for* ut]; fiat *comes after* hereditas. 15. iectum; *om.* illis; uiniae. 16. uiniam alís. 17. ait [*for* dixit]; scriptum. 18. cicidit; conquassauitur; super [*for* 2*nd* supra]. 19. in illa hora; cognuerunt; dixit [*for* dixerit]. 20. obseruatione; similarent; ut *repeated.* 21. doces & dicis; personas. 22. cessari aut non. 23. illos [*for* eos]; temptatis. 24. inscriptionem; caessaris. 25. cessaris; caessari. 26. plebe; responso; R. *inserts* & *before* tacuerunt, *above the line.* 27. sadduce orum, *glossed* ðara hiora. 28. *om.* magister; moyses scripsit; accipiat; *om.* eius *before* uxorem; & suscit*et*. 29. R. *inserts* eius *after* fratres; accipit. 30. accipit; *after* illam R. *omits to the end of verse, and to* illam *in the next verse.* 31. reliquerunt. 32. R. *inserts* '*autem*' *after* nouissima. 33. *om.* uxorem. 35. uero [*for* autem]. 36. R. *inserts* iam *after* ultra; poterunt equales; flii [*for* 1*st* filii]; resurrectiones. 37. uere resurgent; *om.* 1*st* et; moyses; secus [*for* secum], *which follows* rubum; abracham. 38. uiunt [*for* uiuunt]. 39. responden (*sic*); *om.* autem; *om.* magister. 40. quicquam *follows* interrogare. 41. esse dauid. 42. salmorum. 43. scapillum. 46. sinagogis; conuiuus (*sic*). 47. domus; híi accipiat (*sic*); dampnationem.

CAP. XXI. 1. *After* mittebant R. *inserts* mane, *glossed* ar; gazophilacio. 2. *om.* et; quandam. 3. uiduā; paupercula; missit. 4. híi omnes. 6. lapes supra. 7. *om.* autem. 8. seduducamini; *after* sum R. *inserts* '*christus*'; adpropinquauit. 11. R. *inserts* & *before* terrae. 12. incipient [*for* inicient]; *om.* suas; sinagogis; custodientes; ad reges [*for* et reges]; *om.* ad *before* praesides. 14. Ponite me; quem-admodum. 15. poterunt; respondere [*for* resistere]; aduersari. 16. adficiant. 17. odie. 19. *om.* et; possedebetis. 20. adpropinquauit. 21. inudia [*for* in iudæa]. 21. discendant. 22. híi; quiae [*for* quae], *glossed* ðaðe; scripta. 23. praegantibus (*sic*); super. 24. inpleantur. 25. *om.* in *before* stellis; terrís praesura; & maris & fluctum. 26. timore; exspectatione; superuenient; uirtutis; commouebuntur. 27. *om.* Et. 28. hiis; *om.* fieri; adpropinquat redemptio. 31. erat [*for* est]. 34. superueniat. 35. superueniat. 36. staræ (*sic*). 38. mane-cadebat; *instead of* audire eum R. *has* dixit deus (*written over* templo; *the first two words in* Ch. xxii *being also above the line*).

CAP. XXII. 1. adpropinquabat; azemorum. 2. summi [*for* principes]; saecerdotum; timebant *repeated.* 3. cognominatur [*for* uocatur]; unus. 4. abít; locutum; quæm-admodum; illis [*for* eis]. 6. querebat. 7. dies festus azemorum. 8. iohannem. 10. eos & ecce; ciuitatibus occurr*et*; anphoram aquam; sequemini. 11. patri-familias; dt [*for* dicet]. 12. uobis *follows* ostend*et*; caenaculum. 14. fuiss*et* [*for* esset]. 15. manducaui. 16. inpleatur. 17. calicae; diuidete. 20. quid [*for* quod]. 21. *om.* me. 22. difinitum. 24. *om.* et; ess*et* [*for* esse]. 26. es [*for* 2*nd* est]. 28. temptationibus. 29. dispossuit. 30. aedatis; israhel. 31. iesus [*for* dominus]; symon haec symon; satanan; cribar*et*. 32. *After* tuos R. *adds* & rogate né intretis in temptationem. 33. *om.* ei. 34. *om.* et; petre; cantauit. 35. misi. 36. R. *inserts* gladium *after* 2*nd* habet; tonicam. 37. enim [*for* autem]; dhuc (*sic*) [*for* athuc]; scriptum; inplere; *om.* et *before* quod. 38. dicebat [*for* dixerunt]; duo gladii hiic; satis [*for* sat]. 39. R. *inserts* suam *after* consuetudinem; discipuli (*altered to* discipulis suis, *in later hand*).

40. temptationem. 41. auuls (*sic*); lapidis est; possitis. 43. confirmans (*with* t *written above* a). 44. prolixus; discurrentis; terra. 45. ob oriente [*for* ab oratione]; illos [*for* eos]; tristitia. 46. *om.* quid dormitis; temptationem. 47. Ad illo [*for* Athuc eo]; adpropinquauit; *iesus*. 49. hii; circa eum; percutiebat. 50. dexteram. 51. dixit [*for* ait]; sinete; adhuc [*for* huc]; tetigisse*t*. 52. tam-quam [*for* quasi]; gladis. 53. cotidiae; fuerim. 54. Conpraehendentes. 55. igne. 56. eum [*for* 2*nd* cum], *glossed* hio. 57. eum [*for* illum]. 58. *om.* ó. 59. quassi; adfirmauit; galileus. 60. quod [*for* quid]; adhuc. 61. R. *inserts* quia *after* dixit; ter megabis, *with* ne *written over the* 'eg.' 63. tenebat illum. 64. *om.* 1*st* et; *om.* 3*rd* et. 66. dies *comes before* factus; *after* suum R. *inserts* & interrogabant eum. 68. respondetis; demittetis. 69. filium. 71. adhuc dessideram*us*.

CAP. XXIII. 1. pylatum. 2. *om.* autem; accussare illum; *after* nostram R. *inserts* & soluente*m* legem & prophetas; cessari. 3. Pylatus; illi respondit ait (*sic;* ait *in later hand*). 4. pylatus; sacerdotes; homine. 5. inuallescebant; cummouit; iudeam; gallia [*for* galilaea]. 6. pylatus; galilea*m*; galileus. 7. cognuit; remissit; quia [*for* qui]; hierusolimis. 8. herodis; autem [*for* enim]; *om.* de illo; R. *puts* ab eo *before* uidere. 9. eum [*for* illum]; *om.* illi. 10. Stabat; accussantes. 11. spraeuit; herodis; remissit. 12. amice herodis; ante. 13, 14. *a piece torn out of the MS. here.* 13. plebe. 14. ob[tulistis]; quassi; inuenio; hiis; accussatis. 15. herodis; remisi; *om.* ecce. 18. decens. 19. seditionem quandam factam; ciuitatem; humicidium misus; carcere. 20. pylatus. 21. eum [*for* illum]. 22. inuenio. 23. magis [*for* magnis]; inualescebant. 24. pylatus. 25. dimissit; humicidium; petebat (?); *a hole in the MS. here.* 26. adpraehenderunt; [cyrin]ensam; inpossue[runt]. 27. lamentabant. 28. propter uos [*for* super uos]; R. *inserts* & *after* flete. 29. beate sterelis. 30. cadite. 35. exspectans; diridebant; saddoces [*for* eis], *glossed* him; sé non saluum facit. 36. offerentes. 38. superscriptio inscripta; literis grecis; hebraeicis. 39. hiis. 40. eum [*for* illum]; damnationem (*corrected to* damnatione). 41. recipimus; gesse*t* (*with an alteration of the last two letters to* it ?). 43. paradisso. 45. tem [*for* templi]; scisum. 46. uoce magna; R. *inserts* ait *after iesus*. 47. centorio; erat [*for* est]. 48. adherant; spectaculum; pectura. 49. galilia. 50. erant (*corrected to* erat). 51. consilio; iudae; exspectabat. 52. petit. 53. depossitum; in sindone; possuit; possitus. 54. parasceuen. 55. *om.* autem; mulier eris (*with a letter erased between the words*); galilea; monumentum possitum & quem-admodum possitum. 56. unguenta.

CAP. XXIV. 1. *om.* ualde; uenerunt deluculo; *after* monumentum R. *inserts* maria magdalena & altera maria & quaedam cum eis. 4. & ecce. 5. eas [*for* illas]. 6. surrexit; adhuc; galilea. 7. tertia die. 8. recordatae. 9. caeteris. 10. ioseph [*for* iacobi]; haec ad apostolos [*for* et apostolos haec]. 11. deleramenta. 12. procum [*for* procumbens], *ends a line;* linteamina sola possita; abít. 13. *om.* centum; ammaus. 14. hiis; accederant. 15. famularen [*for* fabularentur] (*sic*), *ends a line;* adpropinquans. 16. illorum [*for* eorum]; R. *adds* eum *after* agnoscerent. 17. qui [*for* quid]; conuertis. 18. R. *inserts* erat *after* nomen; cognuisti; *om.* in *before* illa; hís. 19. R. *inserts* ei *after* dixerunt, *above the line; om.* uir. 20. eum *follows* tradiderunt; sacerdotes; dampnationem. 21. redempturus; ex quo. 24. uiderunt [*for* 2*nd* inuenerunt]. 25. tradi [*for* tardi]. 27. et erat incipiens a moyse; scripturis. 28. 1*st* et *above the line;* adpropinquauerunt; fincxit; longuis (*sic*). 29. cogerunt; aduesperescit; inclinata [*for* declinata]; R. *inserts* manere *after* intrauit. 30. ac fregit [*for* et fregit]. 31. occuli; cognuerunt; eum *repeated.* 33. reuersi [*for* regressi]. 34. uere *comes before* surrexit. 35. narra (*sic*), *ends a line;* cognuerunt; fratione (*sic*). 36. dixit; uobis-cum. 38. illis [*for* eis]; ascenderunt; corde. 39. R. *inserts* meos *after* pedes; habentem [*for* habere]. 40. cum hoc. 41. Adhuc. 42. obtullerunt. 43. reliquas. 44. uerba mea quae; *after* sum R. *inserts* ad uos; adhuc; inplene *or* inplere [*for* impleri]; scripta; moysi; & in psalmis. 45. sensus eorum [*for* illis sensum]; scripturas. 46. scriptum; tertia. 47. remisionem; hierusolima. 49. promisum; uos [*for* uobis]. 50. bethania*m*. 52. R. *inserts* eum *after* adorantes; hirusalem. 53. *om.* amen.

CRITICAL NOTES.

N.B. In the notes to the Chapters of the Gospel, the letter L. means the Lindisfarne MS.; H. the Hatton MS. and R. the Rushworth MS.

Page 1. This imperfect Table of Lessons is printed as it is in the MS., without correction of errors. I am not aware that it has been printed before.

Page 2. PRAEFATIO LUCAE. Printed in Bouterwek's Screadunga, p. 5. A few corrections are here noted. See the Codex Amiatinus, ed. Tischendorf, p. 90.

L. 1. MS. anthiocensiae; *read* natione anthiocensis.

L. 4. MS. hundseofentig, *altered to* hundseofontig. MS. bithiniā (*sic*); *read* bithinia.

L. 5. MS. scribata; *read* scripta *or* scribta; *Cod. Amiat.* descripta. MS. iudeam; *read* iudea.

L. 9. prophetatione; *Cod. Amiat.* perfectione.

L. 10. MS. manifesta humanitas; *read* manifestata humanitate. (*Gloss to* adtendi); MS. behealdenne, *altered to* behaldanne. *Also, for* adtendi, *read* adtenti *or* attenti.

L. 11. MS. sollicitudinibus; *read* sollicitationibus.

L. 12. MS. excederent; *read* exciderent (?)

L. 13. (*Gloss to* cui); MS. to ðæm, *altered to* to hwæm. (*Gloss to* et indicaret); MS. ⁊ ge-tahte, *altered to* ꝥte tahte.

L. 14. (*Gloss to* esse); MS. were, *altered to* weron.

L. 15. (*Gloss to* babtismum); MS. fulwihte, *with* e *expuncted. After* impletæ *supply* et.

Last line. *Read* apprehendens erat per nathan filium dauid introitu recurrentis in, &c.

Page 3; line 1. *Before* hominis *insert* hominibus Christum suum perfecti opus.

L. 2. MS. interpretabat; *read* iter praebebat. *In the gloss*, MS. *has* tosceade, *altered to* tosceada.

L. 4. MS. proditionis; *read* perditionis. *Insert* ab *before* apostolis.

L. 5. *After* numerus *insert* compleretur.

L. 6. (*Gloss to* elegisset); MS. gesease, *altered to* gecease.

L. 7. MS. expediari; *read* expediri. (*Gloss to* utile); MS. darflice, *with* e *expuncted.* MS. sciens; *read* scientes.

L. 9. (*Gloss to* curiositatem); MS. forwitgiornis, *altered to* feruitgiornis. *Insert* demonstrasse *before* uideremur; *for* prodissæ *read* prodidisse.

L. 13. (*Gloss to* memoratur); MS. gemyndiged, *with* i *expuncted.*

Page 4; line 2. (*Gloss to* repprerunt); MS. gemoetedn (*sic*); *with last* e *expuncted.*

L. 3. MS. prophetiae; *read* prophetia.

L. 4. *The gloss to* suis *is written* his fost, *with a curl over the* o; *the gloss to* templo *is* tempele, *altered to* temple.

L. 9. (*Gloss to* septuaginta); *the mark* ⁊ (*though in the* MS.) *is superfluous.*

L. 11. MS. diabolis; *probably an error for* diabolus.

L. 18. (*Gloss to* completis); MS. were gefylde, *altered to* wero gefylde. *For* quae (*as in* MS.) *read* que; *the gloss is wrong.*

Page 5; line 6. (*Gloss to* tangentes); *Here and elsewhere the italic* h *represents the old symbol which is written* ꜧ; *see note in* Wanley's Catalogue, p. 156; *cf.* Critical Note *to* St Mark, xii. 4.

L. 9. MS. parabola; *read* parabolas.

L. 18. (*Gloss to* In); MS. on, *alt. to* in.

L. 20. MS. profluio; *read* profluuio.

Page 6; line 2. MS. praedicaturus; *read* praedicaturos.

L. 3. MS. herodis; *read* herodes.

L. 4. MS. *christi* (xpī); read christum.

L. 8. (*Gloss to* filium); MS. sune, *alt. to* sunu.

L. 10. MS. primato; *read* primatu.

L. 13. MS. iuuenis; *read* iuueni. (*Gloss to* tenentem); MS. haldonde, *alt. to* haldond.

L. 20. (*Gloss to* misericordiam); *miswritten* mildheortnisnise.

Page 7; line 3. MS. petiti; *read* petentis.

L. 4. MS. persuadit; *read* persuadet. MS. daemonia; *read* daemonium (?)

L. 7. (*Gloss to 2nd* beatum); MS. eadíge, *alt. to* eadig.

L. 9. MS. poni; *read* ponendam.

L. 13. MS. Petenti; *read* Petente.

L. 15. *Supply* qua *or* quibus *before* carent. MS. euitandum; *read* euitandam. (*Gloss to* Pusillo); MS. lytle, *alt. to* lytlo.

L. 19. MS. necessitudinem, *alt. to* necessitudinum; it means *relationships;* see p. 8, l. 13. In both places the glossator is at fault.

Page 8; line 3. (*Gloss to* sterili); MS. unberende, *alt. to* unberendum. MS. arbori; *read* arbore; *the gloss is written* trees, *with an accent over the first* e, *and a flourish over the second.*

L. 7. (*Gloss to 1st* nouissimi); hlætmesto, *alt. to* hlætmest.

L. 8. *The glossator has mistaken* alis *for* aliis.

L. 13. (*Gloss to* studentes); *printed* gearnende *by* Bouterwek; *but* gearuende (i. e. preparing) *in* MS.

L. 14. MS. secuturi; *read* secuturis.

L. 18. MS. reuersionem; *read* reuersione.

Page 9; line 4. (*Gloss to* dicit); cuæ (*sic*); *for* cuæð.

L. 10. MS. eumque; *read* seque.

L. 16. MS. abscidit; *read* abscedit. *Observe the odd mistake in the gloss.*

Page 10; line 1. MS. decemnas; *for* decem mnas.

L. 3. (*Gloss to* tacent); sægdon, *clearly miswritten for* suigdon.

L. 10. MS. dño; *read* dñus, *for* dominus.

L. 12. MS. praedicito cuius; *read* praedicit cito id.

Page 11. Above the title is drawn a winged bull, the symbol of St Luke.

L. 2. Bouterwek *prints* pascisciturus, *and suggests the reading* paciscitur. *This seems to be a mistake, as the* MS. *has* paciscitur. MS. mysterium; *read* mysteria.

L. 6. MS. auricula; *read* auriculam.

L. 8. *The gloss to* crucifixum *is as printed; that to* confitentem *is miswritten for* ondetende.

L. 14. MS. pisces; *read* piscis.

On the reverse side of Leaf 136 is a coloured picture of St Luke writing, with the name—"O agios Iucas;" above him is a winged bull, with the words—"imago uituli." One side of Leaf 137 is blank; on the reverse side is a beautifully coloured geometrical pattern, without any inscription. The Gospel begins on Leaf 138.

CHAP. I. 1. R. cymende; *for* cunnendo. 6. H. *has* ba twa wrohte, *as printed; read* buton wrohte. 16. L. (*gloss to* israel); isræles, *alt. to* isræle. 17. L. ingredibiles, *alt. to* incredibiles. L. R. perfectum (*sic*). 27. L. uirgo, *an evident error for* uiro; *the correction in the margin is quite a modern one.* 31. L. concipiens; *hence the gloss* ge-ecnande. *It should rather be* concipies. 36. R. hælo; *but* L. hældo. 59. L. þone, *not* ðone. *This use of initial* þ *is very rare in* L. 63. L. arat, *as gloss to* scribsit; *put for* awrat. 80. L. (*gloss to* ostensionis); ædeaudnise, *alt. to* ædeaunise.

CHAP. II. 1. L. ymb-hyrft; *a mistake for* ymb-hwyrft. 4. H. nazareht (*sic*). 5. L. praegnate; *for* praegnante. 15. L. hiorde, *alt. to* hiorda. 19. L. conferent (*sic*); *for* conferens. 37. L. (*gloss to* quatuor); feoure, *altered to* feouer. 38. L. ge-onditteð; *for* ge-ondetteð. 39. R. woemde; *for* woende. 44. H. ge-ferrede; *for* ge-fere. 52. L. *omits the* et *in brackets.*

CHAP. III. 1. *Sub-section* 6 *not marked in margin of* L. 12. L. (*gloss to* baptizarentur); were, *altered to* weron. 20. R. untynde; *for* intynde. 38. *In* R., *the words* qui fuit dei *are glossed* seðe wæs goding.

CHAP. IV. 5. Corp. byrhm (*sic*). 16. L. (*gloss to* sabbati); sun, *with a curl above, which the reader may expand as he pleases; it is* not sim, *though it is remarkable that* R. *has* symbles. 29. L. (*gloss to* praecipitarent); geglendredon, *altered to* geglendradon. 35. L. (*gloss to* proiecisset); foerde awarp; *but there is a line drawn above* foerde, *to signify that it is to be expunged.*

CHAP. V. 5. H. andswerede; *for* answerende. *Also*, swikende, for swinkende. 17. L. (*gloss to* pharisaei); alde, *alt. to* aldo. 21. L. (*gloss to* coeperunt); onginnun, *alt. to* ongunnun. 26. L. (*gloss to* stupor); feer-stylt, *with a curl through the* l. 28. L. for-leort; *with a curl above the* t. 32. L. *has* seiganne soðfæst, *altered to* ceiganne soðfæst (*with a curl above the* t). 34. *The form* cwystuþu *in the* Corpus MS. *is wrong; read* cwyst þu. 36. L. (*gloss to* conuenit); *the italic* h *in* gehriseð *means that the symbol* ⊢ *is employed instead of* h; *so elsewhere.*

CHAP. VI. 1. L. (*gloss to* spicas); hehras, *alt. to* ehras. 8. L. (*gloss to* eorum); hiara, *alt. to* hiora. *The gloss to* sta *should have been* stond; *the glossator was thinking of* statim. 17. L. (*gloss to* sanarentur); gehældon, *alt. to* gehældo. 19. L. (*gloss to* uirtus); mæht *vel* mægn, *with curls above the ends of the words.* The glossator may have been puzzled by the false concord in *uirtus exiebant.* 22. *Observe the gloss to* malum; i.e. evil or apple-tree. 28. L. (*gloss to* calumniantibus); *there is a curl over* oe *in* cuoedum; *perhaps it means* cuoedendum. 31. L. (*gloss to* faciant); hia doað ł gedoe; *but a stroke is drawn over* hia doað, *to mark it for expunction.* 34. L. mutum; *but* mutuum *in v.* 35. 42. L. (*gloss to* educas); osgebrenge, *an obvious error for* ofgebrenge. 48. L. (*gloss to* flumen); se stream; *but in v.* 49 ꝥ stream.

CHAP. VII. 2. L. (*gloss to* habens); hæbbende, *alt. to* hæbbend. 25. L. (*gloss to* domibus); husum, *alt. to* huso. *The verse ends with* estum *in the other* MSS.; *supply* synd on cyninga husum. 28. L. (*gloss to* natos); suno, *alt. to* sunvm. 36. L. (*gloss to* Rogabat); gebeaed, *alt. to* gebaed. 42. L. (*gloss to* donauit); for-geaef, *alt. to* for-gaef. L. (*gloss to* utrisque); beaem, *alt. to* baem.

CHAP. VIII. 7. L. (*gloss to* exortae); ariseon, *alt. to* arison. 9. L. (*gloss to* quae); huæt ðio, *with* ðio *underlined for expunction.* 14. L. *has* ðorNū, *with a capital* N. *The gloss to* suffocantur *suggests that the glossator was thinking of* suffodiantur. 16. L. monn (*denoted by the usual rune*). L. (*gloss to* ponit, *1st time only*); setteð, *alt. to* sette. 33. L. ðamenn (*sic*). 43. L. (*gloss to* medicos); legum, *alt. to* lecum.

CHAP. IX. 11. L. (*gloss to* secutae); gefylgedon, *alt. to* gefylgendo. 32. L. (*gloss to* grauati); gehefigade, *alt. to* gehefigad.

CHAP. XI. 19. L. (*gloss to* filii); sunu, *alt. to* suno. 22. L. ofercummend, *alt. to* ofercymmend. 28. L. (*gloss to* custodiunt); gehaldes, *alt. to* gehaldas. 49. L. (*gloss to* prophetas) iwtgo, *for* witgo.

CHAP. XII. 25. L. (*gloss to* potest); meæge, *alt. to* mæge. 39. L. (*gloss to* si); gife, *alt. to* gif. 42. L. monn (*denoted by the usual rune*). 50. H. *The gloss to* habeo *shews that it was read as* ab eo. L. (*gloss to* dum); hwile, *alt. to* hwil.

CHAP. XIII. 1. L. galilaeis, *which the glossator has read as* galila eis; *whence his gloss.* 2. L. (*gloss to* peccatores); synfullum, *alt. to* synfullo. L. (*gloss to* talia); ðusloco, *alt. to* ðuslico. 6. L. monn (*denoted by the usual rune*). 14. *The use of the capital* H *in* He (*in* L.) *is remarkable.* 23. L. monn (*denoted by the rune*). 26. L. (*gloss* to bibimus); druncgon, *alt. to* drunccon. 31. L. (*gloss to* quidam); summe, *alt. to* summo. 34. L. ðu stanað (*sic*); *cf.* ðu gedoeð, xiv. 12.

CHAP. XIV. 7. L. (*gloss to* eligerent); hia gesceason, *alt. to* hia geceason; *this has given rise to* gefeasan *in* R., *the* f *being due to the* s. 22. L. R. *both have* locutus est; *but the real reading is, of course,* locus est. 35. L. (*gloss to 2nd* in); on, *alt. to* in.

CHAP. XV. 11. L. monn (*denoted by the rune*). 13. L. (*gloss to* uiuendo); mid hlife, *alt. to* mid life. 16. L. monn (*denoted by the rune*). 26. L. (*gloss to* interrogauit); gefraigende, *alt. to* gefraignde. 27. L. frater, *alt. to* pater (*as printed*); *glossed by* fader broðer (*the latter being underlined*).

CHAP. XVI. 8. L. (*gloss to* filii); sunu, *alt. to* suno. 14. *Here a leaf has been lost in* B. *from a very early period; see* Pref. p. vii. 14. L. hlogun, *alt. to* hlogon. 22. L. were, *alt. to* wero.

CHAP. XVII. 20. R. aldrumonnum, *alt. to* aldormonnum.

CHAP. XVIII. 11. L. oðero, *alt. to* oðoro. 13. L. gesloge, *alt. to* geslog.

CHAP. XIX. 26. L. (*gloss to* dabitur); *merely the letter* g, *followed by a blank;* R. *has* gisald bið. 33. (*last word*) L. fola, *alt. to* folo.

CHAP. XX. *The omission of v.* 11 *in* R. *is clearly due to the repetition of* inanem. 13. L. (*Latin text*) uerebantur, *alt. to* uerebuntur. 30, 31. *Omission in* R. *due to repetition of* accepit illam.

CHAP. XXI. 34. *Here the rune for* dæg *occurs in* L.; *its form is identical with that for* monn.

CHAP. XXII. 21. L. (*gloss to* ecce); heoeðre, *alt. to* hoeðre. 24. L. awoerden, *alt. to* aworden. 28. L. (*gloss to* disposuit); to sceadade, *alt. to* to sceadde. 30. L. dóemende, *alt. to* dóemendo. 41. R. gesettun, *alt. to* gisetnun. 42. L. (*Latin text*) iustum, *corrected to* istum; *glossed* ðiosne. 47. L. (*gloss to* iesu); ðe hælend, *alt. from* se hælend; *but indistinct.* 58. *In* R., an ic *is an obvious error for* am ic. 61. *In* R., ne onsæces *is an obvious error for* me onsæces.

CHAP. XXIII. 2. R. wigga; *read* witga. 4. L. hominem, *an error for* homine. 5. L. (*gloss to* docens), lærd, *apparently miswritten for* lærend. 10. R. geherdun; *an error for* gehendun. 13. L. plebem; *an error for* plebe. 35. L. (*gloss to* faciat) gedoeð, *corrected to* gedoe. 38. L. ofer-awritteno inawritten; *but the last three letters in* awritteno *have a line drawn above them, signifying expunction.* 43. *The last word in* R. *is indistinct; it is either* erexnawonga *or* erecanawonga, *the doubtful letter being written as* c *with a tag; both forms are wrong.* 50. L. (*gloss to* uir); woer, *alt. to* wer. 53. *In* R., *at the end of the verse, is written* hic finit; *it marks the end of a lesson.* 55. R. to-g-gisetted, *for* to-gisetted. 56. L. dæg, *denoted by the rune.*

CHAP. XXIV. 1. L. sun, *with a flourish over* u, *followed by the rune for* dæg. 6. *The* Hatton MS. *has* Be-þencheð, *by error; as the* Royal MS. *has* Ge-þenceð, *the scribe possibly mistook* G *for* B. 7. L. (*gloss to* hominum) monna, *alt. to* monno. 8. R. ⁊ eftfærend gemyndge, *but* færend *has a line drawn above it for expunction; the scribe was beginning to write v.* 9 *by mistake.* 9. L. eftfærende, *alt. to* eft-færendo. 11. L. deleramentum (*sic*). L. (*gloss to* uerba) worda, *alt. to* wordo. 13. *In* L., *the subsection is not marked, and the three remaining subsections are therefore misnumbered; see vv.* 36, 41, 44. 17. L. (*gloss to* sermones), wordo, *alt. to* word. 21. L. (*gloss to* nunc) nu niwæ; *but* niwæ *has a line drawn above it, for expunction.* 29. *The scribe of* H., *in writing* Þene *for* Wune, *was misled by the similarity of the sign for* W *to the sign* Þ. *In* R. *the singular gloss* efern longeð ðu wast *is written over* aduespere-scit, *as it is written;* ðu wast (thou knowest) *was suggested by the syllable* scit. 43. L. screadunga, *alt. to* screadungo. 51. Observe that the passage omitted in the Royal MS. is the same as that omitted in the Bodley MS., shewing that a leaf had been lost from the latter at this place at an early period, before the former was copied from it. 53. L. lofande, *alt. to* lofando.

*** This seems to be the most convenient place for remarking that in the Rushworth MS., in the last three chapters of the Gospel, frequent large crosses appear above certain words in the Latin text, which seem to have been added before the gloss was written. These are given in Mr Waring's edition, with a few exceptions. The object of them is clear, viz. to *mark the expressions used by Christ himself.* This will be evident from the following list of the places where they occur, though in one or two places they have been wrongly inserted, as will be pointed out. The Latin words thus marked are the following:

CHAP. XXII. 8. euntes. 15. desiderio. 17. accipite. 19. hoc. 20. hic. 25. reges (*unnoticed by* Mr Waring). 32. ego (*the marked word should have been* simon *in v.* 31). 34. dico. 38. satis est. 40. orate. 42. pater. 46. surgite (quid dormitis *being omitted in* R). 47. illo loquente (*marked by mistake*). 51. sinete (*unnoticed by* Mr Waring). 52. tanquam (L. *has* quasi). 55. igne (*unnoticed by* Mr Waring, *and marked by mistake*). 67. si uobis. 70. uos dicitis.

CHAP. XXIII. 3. tu dicis. 28. filiae. 34. pater. 43. amen. 46. pater. 50. ecce (*marked by mistake*).

CAMBRIDGE: PRINTED BY C. J. CLAY, M.A. AT THE UNIVERSITY PRESS.

www.ingramcontent.com/pod-product-compliance
Lightning Source LLC
LaVergne TN
LVHW010243110826
845151LV00004B/1376

* 9 7 8 1 4 2 5 5 2 3 3 7 4 *